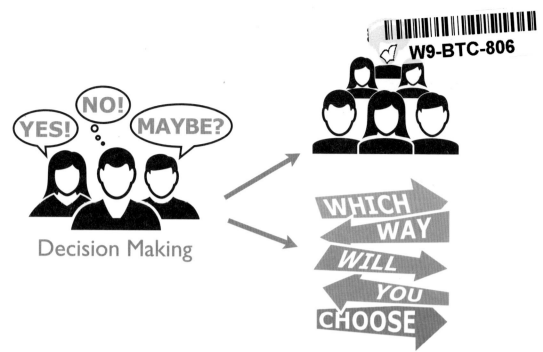

- **Decision making simulations** – place your students in the role of a key decision-maker where they are asked to make a series of decisions. The simulation will change and branch based on the decisions students make, providing a variation of scenario paths. Upon completion of each simulation, students receive a grade, as well as a detailed report of the choices they made during the simulation and the associated consequences of those decisions.

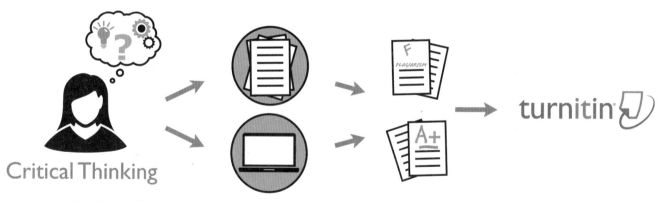

- **Writing Space** – better writers make great learners—who perform better in their courses. Providing a single location to develop and assess concept mastery and critical thinking, the Writing Space offers automatic graded, assisted graded and create your own writing assignments; allowing you to exchange personalized feedback with students quickly and easily.

  Writing Space can also check students' work for improper citation or plagiarism by comparing it against the world's most accurate text comparison database available from **Turnitin**.

http://www.pearsonmylabandmastering.com

PEARSON

STRATEGIC COMPENSATION

A Human Resource Management Approach

EIGHTH EDITION

STRATEGIC COMPENSATION
A Human Resource Management Approach

Joseph J. Martocchio
University of Illinois at Urbana-Champaign

PEARSON

Boston   Columbus   Indianapolis   New York   San Francisco   Upper Saddle River
Amsterdam   Cape Town   Dubai   London   Madrid   Milan   Munich   Paris   Montréal   Toronto
Delhi   Mexico City   São Paulo   Sydney   Hong Kong   Seoul   Singapore   Taipei   Tokyo

In Loving Memory of Orlando "Lundy" Martocchio

Editor in Chief: Stephanie Wall
Senior Acquisitions Editor: Kris Ellis-Levy
Program Management Lead: Ashley Santora
Program Manager: Sarah Holle
Editorial Assistant: Bernard Ollila
Director of Marketing: Maggie Moylan
Senior Marketing Manager: Erin Gardner
Marketing Assistant: Gianna Sandri
Project Management Lead: Judy Leale
Project Manager: Karalyn Holland
Procurement Specialist: Michelle Klein
Creative Director: Blair Brown
Senior Art Director: Kenny Beck
Interior Designer: LCI Design

Cover Designer: Suzanne Behnke
Cover Photo: Damian Palus/Shutterstock
VP, Director of Digital Strategy & Assessment: Paul Gentile
Digital Editor: Brian Surette
Digital Development Manager: Robin Lazrus
MyLab Project Manager: Joan Waxman
Digital Project Manager: Alana Coles
Media Project Manager: Lisa Rinaldi
Full-Service Project Management: Integra
Composition: Integra
Printer/Binder: Courier/Kendallville
Cover Printer: Lehigh-Phoenix Color/Hagarstown
Text Font: 10/12, Times Roman

Credits and acknowledgments borrowed from other sources and reproduced, with permission, in this textbook appear on the appropriate page within text.

Library of Congress Cataloging-in-Publication Data

Martocchio, Joseph J.
   Strategic compensation: a human resource management approach/Joseph J. Martocchio,
University of Illinois at Urbana-Champaign. — Eighth edition.
      pages cm
   ISBN-13: 978-0-13-345710-0
   ISBN-10: 0-13-345710-9
   1. Compensation management.   I. Title.
   HF5549.5.C67M284 2015
   658.3'22—dc23

                                                      2013034104

10 9 8 7 6 5 4 3 2 1

ISBN 10:   0-13-345710-9
ISBN 13: 978-0-13-345710-0

Contents

Preface

The measure of a company's success is as much a function of the way it manages its employees as it is a function of its structures and financial resources. Compensating employees represents a critical human resource management practice: Without strategic compensation systems, companies cannot attract and retain the best-qualified employees. Spending more than is necessary to attract and retain top talent adds costs unnecessarily to companies in search of competitive advantage.

The purpose of this book is to provide knowledge of the art and science of compensation practice and its role in promoting companies' competitive advantage. Students will be best prepared to assume the roles of competent compensation professionals if they possess a grounded understanding of compensation practices and the environments in which business professionals plan, implement, and evaluate compensation systems. Thus, we examine the context of compensation practice, the criteria used to compensate employees, compensation system design issues, employee benefits, challenges of compensating key strategic employee groups, pay and benefits around the world, and challenges facing compensation professionals.

New to the Eighth Edition

1. Chapter 16, titled "Challenges Facing Compensation Professionals," covers more pertinent issues than included in the seventh edition. This chapter informs students that there is much more to consider besides the fundamentals of compensation design that are detailed in Chapters 1 through 15. Chapter 16 also addresses seven key issues among many that will shape the work of compensation and benefits professionals in the future:
   - Fallout from the "Great Recession"
   - Underemployment: Implications for compensation
   - Executive compensation
   - Rising wages in China
   - Challenges in health care reform
   - Workforce demographic shifts
   - Marriage between same-sex individuals and the U.S. Supreme Court ruling on the Defense of Marriage Act
2. Chapter 7 adds a section on pay policy mix, which is a key element that compensation professionals must consider when designing market competitive pay systems.
3. Chapter 2 describes the main provisions of the Patient Protection and Affordable Care Act of 2010.
4. All chapters have been thoroughly revised to describe current statistics and issues of importance for compensation professionals.
5. The *Building Strategic Compensation Systems* case is now available online in MyManagementLab and includes the CompAnalysis Software necessary to complete sections of the project. The software is compatible with Windows and Mac platforms.

About This Book

This book contains 16 chapters, lending itself well to courses offered as 10-week quarters or 15-week semesters. The chapters are organized in six parts and an epilogue (containing Chapter 16):

- Part I: Setting the Stage for Strategic Compensation
- Part II: Bases for Pay
- Part III: Designing Compensation Systems

- Part IV: Employee Benefits
- Part V: Contemporary Strategic Compensation Challenges
- Part VI: Compensation Issues around the World
- Epilogue: Challenges Facing Compensation Professionals

Course instructors on a 10-week schedule might consider spending about 2 weeks on each part. Instructors on a 15-week schedule might consider spending about 1 week on each chapter. Compressed 8-week schedules can accommodate 2 chapters per week.

This textbook is well suited to a variety of students, including undergraduate and master's degree students. In addition, the book was prepared for use by all business students, regardless of their majors. Both human resource management majors and other majors (e.g., accounting, finance, general management, international management, marketing, and organizational behavior) will benefit equally well from *Strategic Compensation*. After all, virtually every manager, regardless of functional area, will be involved in making compensation decisions. Both practitioners beginning work in compensation and current professionals will find *Strategic Compensation* a useful reference. The "Compensation in Action" feature will clarify the connections between compensation and other functions.

Available Teaching and Learning Aids

The teaching and learning accessories are designed to promote a positive experience for both instructors and students.

A feature titled "Compensation in Action" appears at the end of every chapter in the text. This feature provides clear operational points to illustrate how line managers, employees, and compensation professionals interact to put compensation concepts into practice. It was prepared by Mr. Gentz Franz, Director of Development at the University of Illinois.

Short end-of-chapter cases have been included in the text. These cases were written by Professor Lori Long of Baldwin-Wallace College about real-world compensation issues, with questions to facilitate class discussion or to be used as homework assignments. Recommended answers are available to instructors in the Instructor's Manunal, which can be accessed by logging onto the Instructor's Resource Center's website (*www.pearsonhighered.com/irc*).

MyManagementLab®

MyManagementLab is an online homework, tutorial, and assessment program that truly engages students in learning. It helps students better prepare for class, quizzes, and exams—resulting in better performance in the course—and provides educators a dynamic set of tools for gauging individual and class progress. In addition to quizzes and pre- and post-tests, MyManagementLab to accompany this text includes:

Building Strategic Compensation Systems Project

This accompanying experiential case available online only in MyManagement Lab will allow students to work in small compensation consulting teams charged with the responsibility for developing a compensation plan for a company named e-sonic. The project is divided into four sections. The first section, *Strategic Analysis*, is described fully in the casebook for faculty and students who choose to complete this analysis of the business environment prior to the remaining three sections that directly address compensation system design.

Section 1: Chapter 6

Section 2: Chapter 7

Section 3: Chapters 2 through 5, 8 through 11

The development of a strategic analysis guides all decisions made regarding students' compensation systems throughout the project. The strategic analysis reveals firm-specific challenges, objectives, and initiatives that allow students to align the goals of a compensation system effectively with that of their company strategy.

Section 1 introduces students to the specification of internally consistent job structures. Through writing job descriptions, the development of job structures, and both the development and implementation of a point evaluation method to quantify job differences objectively, students build the framework for internal equity.

Section 2 shifts students' focus outside of their firm to understand its relationship with the external marketplace. Students will use market survey data to compare pay rates of positions inside the firm with those in the marketplace to establish the foundations of market-competitive pay. The analysis of market data also leads students to the determination of appropriate pay-policy mixes for each of their job structures. In this section, students are asked to use CompAnalysis software developed by Howard Weiss at Temple University, which is also available in MyManagementLab.

Finally, in Section 3, students will recognize the contributions of individual employees through the creation of a merit-pay system and put their plan into action by paying employees within their firm. Hypothetical pay discrepancies are introduced to each student group for resolution within the parameters of their designed compensation system. They are tasked with many of the difficult decisions that compensation professionals face on a daily basis.

The Strategic Analysis section and Sections 1 through 3 may each be completed in 2 to 3 weeks, which fits well with semester-long courses. Instructors whose courses include a variety of additional activities or span only 7 to 10 weeks may have students complete only three of the four sections in either configuration (Strategic Analysis and Sections 1 and 2 or Sections 1 through 3). The instructor may have student groups prepare written reports or oral presentations to the class. Report outlines are included in the instructor's and student's casebook versions.

Two Assisted-Graded Writing Prompts

Two assisted-graded writing prompts per chapter are provided in MyManagementLab via the Writing Space tool that allows for the online submission and grading of essay questions. The writing prompts also appear at the end of each chapter.

Supplemental Short Cases

Short cases, also written by Professor Lori Long of Baldwin-Wallace College, correspond to each chapter. Suggested answers are available to instructors under the Instructor's Manual on MyManagementLab and on Pearson's Instructor's Resource Center.

Instructor Supplements

All of the following supplements can be downloaded from our Instructor's Resource Center. Request your user name and password from your Pearson Sales Representative. *www.pearsonhighered.com/irc*

Instructor's Manual: The Instructor's Manual has been completely revised. For each chapter, the Instructor's Manual provides a comprehensive lecture outline as well as additional Teaching Resources.

Test Item File: The Test Item File consists of multiple-choice questions, true/false, and essay questions. Each question will have a difficulty rating of easy, moderate, or difficult and a classification of either application or recall to help you build a well-balanced test.

PowerPoints: The PowerPoint package is a fully revised, comprehensive package that outlines each chapter and includes figures from the text. It is designed to aid the educator and supplement in-class lectures.

TestGen Software: Containing all of the questions in the printed Test Item File, TestGen is a comprehensive suite of tools for testing and assessment.

Acknowledgments

Many individuals made valuable contributions to the previous editions. I am indebted to the reviewers who provided thoughtful remarks on chapter drafts during the development of this edition:

Dennis J. Nirtaut, Loyola University Chicago, Quinlan School of Business

Tim Brown, San Jose State University

Dana M. Cosby, Ph.D., Western Kentucky University, Bowling Green, KY

Carol A. Decker, Ph.D., PHR Professor, Tennessee Wesleyan College

Dow Scott, Loyola University

Debbie L. Mackey, Ph.D., PHR University of Tennessee, Director of HRM Master's Program

Victor L. Lipe, Trident Technical College

Paul W. Mulvey, Ph.D., Associate Professor, Department of Management, Innovation, and Entrepreneurship, Poole College of Management, North Carolina State University

From Pearson Education I would like to thank Kris Ellis-Levy and Sarah Holle for their guidance and expertise as well as for the many other professionals who worked behind the scenes in the design, marketing, and production of this edition. I thank each and every one of those individuals for their contributions.

Joseph J. Martocchio

SETTING THE STAGE FOR STRATEGIC COMPENSATION

MyManagementLab®

⭐ You can access the CompAnalysis Software to complete the online Building Strategic Compensation Systems Project by logging into **www.mymanagementlab.com**.

1

STRATEGIC COMPENSATION
A Component of Human Resource Systems

MyManagementLab®

⭐ **Improve Your Grade!**

When you see this icon, visit **www.mymanagementlab.com** for activities that are applied, personalized, and offer immediate feedback.

LEARNING OBJECTIVES

When you finish studying this chapter, you should be able to:

1. Describe what compensation is and give at least three examples of core compensation practices and at least three examples of employee benefits practices.
2. Summarize at least two historical events in the evolution of compensation practice leading to the current strategic compensation era.
3. Discuss at least two differences between strategic and tactical compensation.
4. Name and summarize the goals of compensation professionals.
5. Identify the stakeholders of the compensation and summarize their stake in the work compensation professionals perform.

For most of the twentieth century, the predecessor to contemporary human resource (HR) management practices was initially referred to as manpower planning or personnel management. In the earlier part of that century, manpower planning often focused on the effective deployment of employees in factories to achieve the highest manufacturing output per employee per unit of time. For instance, management sought to increase the number of handmade garments per hour.

Extensive government regulation involving payroll taxes, minimum wage laws, and antidiscrimination laws later gave rise to the personnel management function. Legal compliance necessitated that personnel management take on the role of an administrative, support function to maintain compliance with the myriad details of the laws (e.g., determining what equal work is and the prevailing wage in specific localities). Since the 1970s, there has been widespread recognition that managing employees or human resources can contribute to company success. Administrative efficiency of the personnel functions (e.g., recruiting, performance appraisal, and compensating employees) certainly contributes indirectly to company success through cost control.

In recent years, researchers and HR practitioners have worked steadily to quantify the impact of managing human resources on business success in terms of such outcomes as innovation, higher sales, product quality, exemplary customer service, and so forth. Some have described the HR professional's role as evolving from compliance (policing) to consultation, with a carpenter's eye toward quality HR system design. Designing HR practices with business outcomes in mind is a necessary first step, and compensation plays an important role in contributing to successful business outcomes.

EXPLORING AND DEFINING THE COMPENSATION CONTEXT

The compensation function does not operate in isolation. To the contrary, it is just one component of a company's human resource system. In addition, compensation professionals interact with members of various constituencies, including union representatives and top executives. We will explore these ideas in more detail after we have introduced some fundamental compensation concepts.

What Is Compensation?

Compensation represents both the intrinsic and extrinsic rewards employees receive for performing their jobs. Together, both intrinsic and extrinsic compensation describe a company's total compensation system. This system of practices is depicted in Figure 1-1.

Intrinsic compensation reflects employees' psychological mind-sets that result from performing their jobs. **Extrinsic compensation** includes both monetary and nonmonetary rewards. Organizational development professionals promote intrinsic compensation through effective job design. Compensation professionals are responsible for extrinsic compensation, which will be the focus of this textbook.

Extrinsic compensation includes both monetary and nonmonetary rewards. Compensation professionals establish monetary compensation programs to reward employees according to their job performance levels or for learning job-related knowledge or skills. As we will discuss shortly, monetary compensation represents **core compensation**. Nonmonetary rewards include protection programs (e.g., medical insurance), paid time off (e.g., vacations), and services (e.g., day care assistance). Most compensation professionals refer to nonmonetary rewards as **employee benefits**.

Core Compensation

There are seven types of monetary, or core, compensation (two types of which are listed as base pay). The elements of base pay adjustments are listed in Table 1-1.

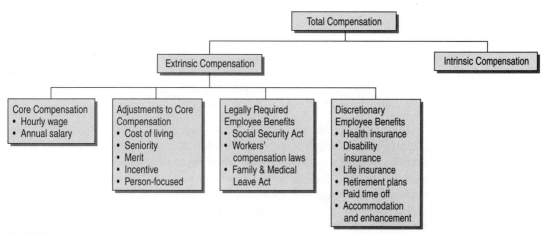

FIGURE 1-1 Total Compensation System

TABLE 1-1 **Elements of Core Compensation**

Base Pay

- Hourly pay
- Annual salary

How Base Pay Is Adjusted over Time

- Cost-of-living adjustments
- Seniority pay
- Merit pay
- Incentive pay
- Person-focused pay: pay-for-knowledge and skill-based pay

BASE PAY Employees receive **base pay**, or money, for performing their jobs (Chapter 7). Base pay is recurring; that is, employees continue to receive base pay as long as they remain in their jobs. Companies disburse base pay to employees in one of two forms: **hourly pay** or **wage**, or as **salary**. Employees earn hourly pay for each hour worked. They earn salaries for performing their jobs, regardless of the actual number of hours worked. Companies measure salary on an annual basis. The Fair Labor Standards Act (Chapter 2) established criteria for determining whether employees should be paid hourly or by salary. In 2012, the average weekly rate for workers was $818.[1] On an annual basis, this figure translates to $42,536 (based on a 40-hour work week over 52 calendar weeks).

Companies typically set base pay amounts for jobs according to the level of skill, effort, and responsibility required to perform the jobs and the severity of the working conditions. Compensation professionals refer to skill, effort, responsibility, and working condition factors as **compensable factors** because they influence pay level (Chapters 2 and 6). Courts of law use these four compensable factors to determine whether jobs are equal per the Equal Pay Act of 1963. According to the Equal Pay Act, it is against the law to pay women less than men for performing equal work. Compensation professionals use these compensable factors to help meet three pressing challenges, which we will introduce later in this chapter: internal consistency (Chapter 6), market competitiveness (Chapter 7), and recognition of individual contributions (Chapter 8).

Over time, employers adjust employees' base pay to recognize increases in the cost of living, differences in employees' performance, or differences in employees' acquisition of job-related knowledge and skills. We will discuss these core compensation elements next.

COST-OF-LIVING ADJUSTMENTS (COLAS) **Cost-of-living adjustments (COLAs)** represent periodic base pay increases that are founded on changes in prices as recorded by the consumer price index (CPI). In recent years, the typical COLA equaled approximately 2–3 percent annually. COLAs enable workers to maintain their purchasing power and standard of living by adjusting base pay for inflation. COLAs are most common among workers represented by unions. Union leaders fought hard for these improvements to maintain their members' loyalty and support. Many employers use the CPI to adjust base pay levels for newly hired employees.

SENIORITY PAY **Seniority pay** systems reward employees with periodic additions to base pay according to employees' length of service in performing their jobs (Chapter 3). These pay plans assume that employees become more valuable to companies with time and that valued employees will leave if they do not have a clear idea that their wages will progress over time. This rationale comes from **human capital theory**,[2] which states that employees' knowledge and skills generate productive capital known as **human capital**. Employees can develop such knowledge and skills from formal education and training, including on-the-job experience. Over time, employees presumably refine existing skills or acquire new ones that enable them to work more productively. Seniority pay rewards employees for acquiring and refining their skills as indexed by length (years) of employment.

MERIT PAY **Merit pay** programs assume that employees' compensation over time should be determined, at least in part, by differences in job performance (Chapter 3). Employees earn permanent increases to base pay according to their performance. Merit pay rewards excellent effort or results, motivates future performance, and helps employers retain valued employees.

INCENTIVE PAY **Incentive pay** or **variable pay** rewards employees for partially or completely attaining a predetermined work objective. Incentive pay is defined as compensation (other than base wages or salaries) that fluctuates according to employees' attainment of some standard based on a preestablished formula, individual or group goals, or company earnings (Chapter 4).

PAY-FOR-KNOWLEDGE PLANS AND SKILL-BASED PAY **Pay-for-knowledge** plans reward managerial, service, or professional workers for successfully learning specific curricula (Chapter 5). **Skill-based pay**, used mostly for employees who perform physical work, increases these workers' pay as they master new skills (Chapter 5). Both skill- and knowledge-based pay programs reward employees for the range, depth, and types of skills or knowledge they are capable of applying productively to their jobs. This feature distinguishes pay-for-knowledge plans from merit pay, which rewards employees' job performance. Said another way, pay-for-knowledge programs reward employees for their potential to make meaningful contributions on the job.

Employee Benefits

Earlier, we noted that employee benefits represent nonmonetary rewards. Employee benefits include any variety of programs that provide paid time off, employee services, and protection programs. Companies offer many benefits on a discretionary basis. We refer to these as **discretionary benefits** (Chapters 9 and 10). In addition, the U.S. government requires most employers to provide particular sets of benefits to employees. We refer to these as **legally required benefits** (Chapter 11). Different forces led to the rise of legally required and discretionary employee benefits, which we discuss shortly.

DISCRETIONARY BENEFITS The first signs of contemporary discretionary employee benefits were evident in the late 1800s when large companies such as American Express offered pension plans to employees. Most of the development in employee benefits practice for the next few decades resulted from government legislation, as previously noted. Discretionary benefits offerings became more prominent in the 1940s and 1950s due in large part to federal government restrictions placed on increasing wage levels. Employee benefits were not subject to those restrictions.

Discretionary benefits fall into three broad categories: protection programs, paid time off, and services (Chapter 10). Protection programs provide family benefits, promote health, and guard against income loss caused by such catastrophic factors as unemployment, disability, or serious illness. Not surprisingly, **paid time off** provides employees with pay for time when they are not working (e.g., vacation). **Services** provide such enhancements as tuition reimbursement and day care assistance to employees and their families.

LEGALLY REQUIRED BENEFITS Legally required benefits historically provided a form of social insurance. Prompted largely by the rapid growth of industrialization in the United States during the late nineteenth and early twentieth centuries as well as the Great Depression of the 1930s, initial social insurance programs were designed to minimize the possibility of destitution for individuals who were unemployed or became severely injured while working. In addition, social insurance programs aimed to stabilize the well-being of dependent family members of injured or unemployed individuals. Further, early social insurance programs were designed to enable retirees to maintain subsistence income levels. These intents of legally

TABLE 1-2 Employer Costs per Hour Worked for Employee Compensation, Civilian Workers[a]

	Total Compensation	Wages and Salaries	All Benefits	Paid Leave	Supplemental Pay	Insurance	Retirement and Savings	Legally Required Benefits
			Cost per hour worked (in dollars)					
Civilian Workers	30.84	21.35	9.49	2.15	0.74	2.76	1.44	2.40
Occupational Group								
Management, professional, and related	51.03	35.46	15.56	4.10	1.22	4.16	2.74	3.35
Sales and office	23.11	16.24	6.88	1.48	0.47	2.30	0.79	1.83
Natural resources, construction, and maintenance	32.36	21.68	10.68	1.85	0.90	2.96	1.88	3.08
Production, transportation, and material moving	24.97	16.54	8.43	1.48	0.86	2.74	0.94	2.41
Industry Group								
Goods-producing	34.18	22.84	11.34	2.25	1.34	3.23	1.54	2.98
Service	30.28	21.10	9.17	2.13	0.64	2.68	1.42	2.30

[a] Includes workers in the private nonfarm economy excluding households and the public sector excluding the federal government.

Source: U.S. Department of Labor (March 12, 2013). Employer costs for employee compensation, December 2012 (USDL: 13-0421). Available: www.bls.gov/ect/htm, accessed March 31, 2013.

required benefits remain intact today. The U.S. government has established programs to protect individuals from such catastrophic events as disability and unemployment. Legally required benefits are **protection programs** that attempt to promote worker safety and health, maintain the influx of family income, and assist families in crisis. The key legally required benefits are mandated by the Social Security Act of 1935, various state workers' compensation laws, and the Family and Medical Leave Act of 1993. All provide protection programs to employees and their dependents (Chapter 11).

Employers typically spend substantial amounts to pay employees and provide benefits. Table 1-2 lists the major legally required and discretionary benefits and the typical expenses incurred by employers to offer these benefits as of December 2012.[3] This table also includes the cost of wages and salaries based on a sample of occupations and industry types. The costs are expressed on an hourly basis per employee. For example, in December 2012, employers characteristically spent $30.84 per employee per hour worked, incuding wages and salaries as well as benefits. Of this figure, $21.35 was spent on wages and salaries and $9.49 was spent on benefits ($2.40 for legally required benefits and $7.09 for discretionary benefits).

A HISTORICAL PERSPECTIVE ON COMPENSATION: THE ROAD TOWARD STRATEGIC COMPENSATION

Agriculture and small family craft businesses were the bases for the U.S. economy before the 1900s. The turn of the twentieth century marked the beginning of the Industrial Revolution in the United States. During the Industrial Revolution, the economy's transition from agrarian and craft businesses to large-scale manufacturing began. Individuals were increasingly becoming employees of large factories instead of self-employed farmers or small-business owners. This shift from the agricultural sector to the industrial sector promoted the beginnings of the field of human resource management.[4]

The factory system gave rise to divisions of labor based on differences in worker skill, effort, and responsibilities. The growth in the size of the workplace necessitated practices to guide such activities as hiring, training, setting wages, handling grievances, and terminating employment. At the time, practitioners referred to these activities as personnel administration, which is the predecessor of modern human resource management.

The early personnel (and compensation) function emphasized labor cost control and management control over labor. Many employers instituted so-called **scientific management practices** to control labor costs, as well as welfare practices to maintain control over labor. Scientific management practices gave rise to individual incentive pay systems. Welfare practices represent the forerunner of modern discretionary employee benefits practices.

Scientific management practices promoted labor cost control by replacing inefficient production methods with efficient ones. Factory owners used time-and-motion studies and job analysis to meet that objective. **Time-and-motion studies** analyzed the time it took employees to complete their jobs. These studies literally focused on employees' movements and the identification of the most efficient steps to complete jobs in the least amount of time.[5] Job analysis is a systematic process for gathering, documenting, and analyzing information in order to describe jobs. At the time, employers used job analysis to classify the most efficient ways to perform jobs.

How did scientific management methods influence compensation practices? Scientific management methods gave rise to the use of piecework plans (Chapter 4). Under piecework plans, an employee's compensation depends on the number of units she or he produces over a given period. Specifically, these plans reward employees on the basis of their individual hourly production against an objective output standard, determined by the pace at which manufacturing equipment operates. For each hour, workers receive piecework incentives for every item produced over the designated production standard.

There were also developments in the area of employee benefits during World War II. **Welfare practices** were generous endeavors undertaken by some employers, motivated in part to minimize employees' desire for union representation, to promote good management, and to enhance worker productivity. Welfare practices were "anything for the comfort and improvement, intellectual or social, of the employees, over and above wages paid, which is not a necessity of the industry nor required by law."[6] Companies' welfare practices varied. For example, some employers offered such facilities as libraries and recreational areas; others offered financial assistance for education, home purchases, and home improvements. In addition, employer sponsorship of medical insurance coverage became common. The use of welfare practices created the need to administer them. Welfare secretaries served as an intermediary between the company and its employees, and they were essentially predecessors of human resource professionals.[7]

In the 1960s, the U.S. government instituted major legislation aimed at protecting individual rights to fair treatment in the workplace. Most often, fair treatment means making employment-related decisions according to job performance—for example, awarding higher merit pay increases to better performers.

Federal laws led to the bureaucratization of compensation practice. Personnel and compensation administrators took the lead in developing and implementing employment practices that upheld the myriad federal employment laws. These professionals also maintained records, creating documentation in the event of legal challenges to employment practices. In short, compensation professionals were largely administrators who reacted to government regulation.

Personnel administration was transformed from a purely administrative function to a competitive resource in many companies during the 1980s as technology transformed the workplace and pressures from global competitors intensified. Since the early 1980s, compensation professionals have designed and implemented compensation programs that contribute to companies' competitive advantage by motivating employees to excel, learn new knowledge and skills, and take on a sense of ownership in the company.[8]

Competitive advantage describes a company's success. **Competitive advantage** refers specifically to a company's ability to maintain market share and profitability over a sustained period of several years. Employers began to recognize that employees are key resources necessary for a company's success, particularly in changing business environments characterized by rapid technological change and intense business competition from foreign countries. Employers' recognition that employees represent an important resource led to the view of employees as human resources. In line with this view, companies design human resource management practices to promote competitive advantage.

As technology leads to the automation of more tasks, employers combine jobs and confer broader responsibilities on workers. For example, the technology of advanced automated manufacturing, such as that used in the automobile industry, began doing the jobs of people, including the laborer, the materials handler, the operator-assembler, and the maintenance person. A single employee now performs all of these tasks in a position called "manufacturing technician." The expanding range of tasks and responsibilities in this job demands higher levels of reading, writing, and computation skills than did the jobs that it replaced, which required strong eye–hand coordination. Most employees must possess higher levels of reading skills than before because they must be able to read the operating and troubleshooting manuals (when problems arise) of automated manufacturing equipment that is based on computer technology. Manufacturing equipment previously had a relatively simple design, based on such easily understood mechanical principles as pulleys, and it was easy to operate.

Increased global competition has forced companies in the United States to become more productive. More than ever, companies must now provide their employees with leading-edge skills and encourage them to apply their skills proficiently to sustain a competitive advantage. Evidence suggests that workers in other countries are more skilled and able to work more productively than U.S. employees.[9] In addition, companies, particularly in Japan, adopted lean manufacturing and process development techniques that enabled workers to contribute to products of outstanding quality.

Compensation practices contribute to competitive advantage by developing more productive and highly skilled workforces. Well-designed merit pay programs reinforce excellent performance by awarding pay raises commensurate with performance attainments. The use of incentive pay practices is instrumental in changing the prevalent entitlement mentality U.S. workers have toward pay and in containing compensation costs by awarding one-time increases to base pay once work objectives have been attained. Pay-for-knowledge and skill-based pay programs are key to giving employees the necessary knowledge and skills to use new workplace technology effectively. Management can use discretionary benefit offerings to promote particular employee behaviors that have strategic value. For example, employees who take advantage of tuition reimbursement programs are more likely to contribute to the strategic imperatives of product or service differentiation and cost-reduction objectives.

Moving to the realm of executive compensation (Chapter 12) becomes quite interesting because the rules for establishing compensation and benefits for employees are cast aside for a set of unique rules that creates tremendous wealth for executives. In addition, the pay-for-performance ethic that we stress for nonexecutive employees is debated among shareholders of companies, employees, labor unions, and the government.

Compensation professionals face additional challenges, as defining who is an employee becomes complex and, as a result, who is responsible for compensating and providing benefits for nonemployees. These nonemployees are members of the growing contingent workforce in the United States. As we will learn in Chapter 13, there are multiple types of contingent workers, and the compensation and benefits issues vary with these various contingent worker classifications.

It is not surprising that the globalization of business often requires that employees be sent from their home countries (e.g., a U.S. citizen working for Microsoft) as expatriates to manage business activities throughout the world. As we will see in Chapter 14, compensation professionals must learn about the techniques for compensating expatriate employees. In addition, as U.S. companies expand their operations to the far reaches of the world, it is essential that they become familiar with the laws and norms that define compensation and benefits practices in those countries. We will review the compensation and benefits issues around the globe in Chapter 15.

STRATEGIC VERSUS TACTICAL DECISIONS

Business professionals make two kinds of decisions—strategic decisions and tactical decisions. **Strategic decisions** guide the activities of companies in the market; **tactical decisions** support the fulfillment of strategic decisions. Business professionals apply these decisions to companies' functions, including manufacturing, engineering, research and development, management information systems, HR, and marketing. For example, HR professionals make strategic compensation decisions and tactical compensation decisions. Figure 1-2 shows the relationship between strategic decisions and tactical decisions.

Strategic management entails a series of judgments, under uncertainty, that companies direct toward achieving specific goals.[10] Companies base strategy formulation on environmental scanning activities (as described later in this chapter). Discerning threats and opportunities is the main focus of environmental scanning. Strategic management is an inexact process because companies distinguish between threats and opportunities based on interpretation. A threat suggests a negative situation in which loss is likely and over which an individual has relatively little control. An opportunity implies a positive situation in which gain is likely and over which an individual has a fair amount of control.[11]

For instance, Mercedes-Benz, a manufacturer of luxury automobiles, stepped outside its typical product offerings by introducing the C230, a well-equipped hatchback model in the $25,000–$30,000 price range. Most new well-equipped Mercedes vehicles retail well above the $50,000 level and are bought by affluent individuals who are into their forties and beyond. Mercedes's offering was geared toward extending its market base to car buyers in their twenties and thirties who typically cannot afford the Mercedes price tag. Given so many fine car

FIGURE 1-2 Relationship between Strategic and Tactical Decisions

alternatives, Mercedes hoped to build loyalty among a younger following of car buyers with the idea that loyal Mercedes owners will continue to buy Mercedes in the future. Unfortunately, the company was unsuccessful in attracting the younger market segment and ultimately discontinued the C230 model after a few short years.

Tactical decisions support the fulfillment of strategic decisions, which we discuss shortly. We will look at Eli Lilly's Web site to illustrate these practices in the following paragraphs.

Strategic planning supports business objectives. Companies' executives communicate business objectives in competitive strategy statements. **Competitive strategy** refers to the planned use of company resources—technology, capital, and human—to promote and sustain competitive advantage. The time horizon for strategic decisions may span 2 or more years. Lilly's competitive strategy focuses on creating innovative medicines that improve patient health outcomes.[12]

Human resource executives collaborate with other company executives to develop human resource strategies. **Human resource strategies** specify the use of multiple HR practices. These statements are consistent with a company's competitive strategy. At Lilly:

Lilly, a leading innovation driven corporation, is developing a growing portfolio of pharmaceutical products by applying the latest research from its own worldwide laboratories and from collaborations with eminent scientific organizations. Headquartered in Indianapolis, Ind., Lilly provides answers through medicines and information for some of the world's most urgent medical needs. This drive is what we are looking for in our people. We have created an open environment designed to stimulate the flow of information. And we will achieve our goals by placing teams of intellectually-driven people in this environment. People like you. Join the Lilly team and find yourself among the approximate 40,000 people devoted to improving the lives of others. And we'll give you the opportunities you want to make the most of your career and life.[13]

Compensation and benefits executives work with the lead HR executive and the company's chief budget officer to prepare total compensation strategies. Total compensation strategies describe the use of compensation and benefits practices that support both human resource strategies and competitive strategies.

At Lilly, we're all about helping people live healthy, happy lives. And we want the same for our employees. To that end, we believe in rewards and balance. The benefits we provide are designed to give you exactly that.

We believe in compensation that truly expresses appreciation for your contributions. It's the most effective morale booster we know. As for our benefits packages, we believe they should answer your needs and wishes for the way you want to lead your life at work—and outside of it. You'll find benefits that advance your career. Strengthen your financial well-being. Aid you in health matters. And encourage time away from work for self-enrichment.

Take a look at what we have to offer. The list is comprehensive, covering everything from traditional benefits to unique perks. We think you'll find our collection will help you make the most of what's important to you: A healthy, balanced life.[14]

Competitive Strategy Choices

LOWEST-COST STRATEGY The **cost leadership** or **lowest-cost strategy** focuses on gaining competitive advantage by being the lowest-cost producer of a product or service within the marketplace, while selling the product or service at a price advantage relative to the industry average. Lowest-cost strategies require aggressive construction of efficient-scale facilities and vigorous pursuit of cost minimization in such areas as operations, marketing, and HR.

Ryanair, a low-cost commercial airline based in Ireland, is an excellent illustration of an organization that pursues a lowest-cost strategy because its management successfully reduced operations costs. At least two noteworthy decisions have contributed to Ryanair's goals. First, Ryanair's training and aircraft maintenance costs are lower than similar competitors' costs because the airline uses only Boeing 737 aircraft. Ryanair enjoys substantial cost savings because it does not need to buy different curricula for training flight attendants, mechanics, and pilots to learn about procedures specific to different aircraft makes (e.g., Boeing) and models (e.g., Boeing 747). Second, newer aircraft sport spartan seats that do not recline, have seat-back pockets, or have life jackets stowed under the seat (life jackets are stowed elsewhere on Ryanair planes). Not only does such seating cost less, but it also allows service personnel to clean aircraft more quickly, saving on labor costs. Third, Ryanair airplanes have one toilet to make room for additional passenger seats. Fourth, Ryanair passengers are required to carry their luggage to the plane, reducing the costs of baggage handling.

DIFFERENTIATION STRATEGY Companies adopt **differentiation strategies** to develop products or services that are unique from those of their competitors. Differentiation strategy can take many forms, including design or brand image, technology, features, customer service, and price. Differentiation strategies lead to competitive advantage through building brand loyalty among devoted consumers. Brand-loyal consumers are less sensitive to price increases, which enables companies to invest in research and development initiatives to further differentiate themselves from competing companies.

Proctor & Gamble (P&G) Corporation manufactures, markets, and distributes a variety of consumer goods products, including dog food. This company successfully pursues a differentiation strategy based on brand image and price premiums. The company offers two separate dog food lines—Iams, a superpremium line that is nutritionally well balanced for dogs and that uses high-quality ingredients, and Eukanuba, an ultrapremium line that contains more chicken and vital nutrients than the Iams line, as well as OmegaCOAT Nutritional Science (fatty acids), which promotes shiny and healthy coats. Together, the Iams and Eukanuba brands appeal to a substantial set of dog owners. The Iams Company distinguishes Eukanuba from Iams by claiming that Eukanuba delivers "Extraordinary Nutrition." The Eukanuba slogan is the company's basis for brand image.

In addition to brand image, P&G also differentiates its Eukanuba line by charging a price premium. This price premium has enabled the Iams Company to be an innovator in canine nutrition by investing heavily in product research and development. Eukanuba was one of the first brands to offer several formulas to meet the needs of small, medium, and large breeds of dogs according to life stage, activity level, and particular health conditions.

Tactical Decisions that Support the Firm's Strategy

Human resource tactics and practices in other functional areas support a company's competitive strategy. Functional area capabilities include manufacturing, engineering, research and development, management information systems, HR, and marketing. Compensation and HR professionals can orchestrate human resource and other functional tactics to promote competitive strategy. In addition, HR practices support competitive advantage through energizing employees to perform the jobs for which they were hired.

TACTICS IN OTHER FUNCTIONAL AREAS Companies must determine which functional capabilities are most crucial to maintaining a competitive advantage. For example, rapid advances in medical science are moving it toward less-invasive surgical procedures that require special surgical instruments. One noteworthy example is arthroscopic surgery. Arthroscopes enable surgeons to perform knee and shoulder surgeries without invasive surgical openings. A competitive advantage in this industry depends largely on researching, developing, and manufacturing leading-edge surgical instruments for these new, less-invasive surgical procedures.

EMPLOYEE ROLES ASSOCIATED WITH COMPETITIVE STRATEGIES Common wisdom and experience tell us that HR professionals must decide which employee roles are instrumental to the attainment of competitive strategies. Knowledge of these required roles should enable HR professionals to implement HR tactics that encourage their enactment of these roles. Of course, compensation professionals are responsible for designing and implementing compensation tactics that elicit strategy-consistent employee roles.

For the lowest-cost strategy, the imperative is to reduce output costs per employee. The desired employee roles for attaining a lowest-cost strategy include repetitive and predictable behaviors, a relatively short-term focus, primarily autonomous or individual activity, high concern for quantity of output, and a primary concern for results.

The key employees' roles for differentiation strategies include highly creative behavior, a relatively long-term focus, cooperative and interdependent behavior, and a greater degree of risk taking. Compared with lowest-cost strategies, successful attainment of differentiation strategies depends on employee creativity, openness to novel work approaches, and willingness to take risks. In addition, differentiation strategies require longer time frames to provide sufficient opportunity to yield the benefits of these behaviors.

COMPENSATION PROFESSIONALS' GOALS

Understanding compensation professionals' goals requires knowing the role of HR within companies and specific HR practices, particularly how HR professionals fit into the corporate hierarchy and how the compensation function fits into HR departments.

How HR Professionals Fit into the Corporate Hierarchy

Line function and staff function broadly describe all employee functions. **Line employees** are directly involved in producing companies' goods or delivering their services. Assembler, production worker, and salesperson are examples of line jobs. **Staff employees'** functions support the line functions. Human resource professionals and accountants are examples of staff employees. Human resource professionals are staff employees because they offer a wide variety of support services for line employees. In a nutshell, HR professionals promote the effective use of all employees in companies. Effective use means attaining work objectives that fit with the overall mission of the company. According to Jay Hannah, BancFirst Corp. executive vice president of financial services, "The HR department is the source and keeper of critical information, which is key in today's workplace. With the information they provide, we in turn can build and design strategies to hire and retain the best workforce possible. And this may sound clichéd, but it's very true—the real competitive advantage is our company's human resources."[15]

Human resource professionals design and implement a variety of HR practices that advance this objective. In addition to compensation, HR practices include:

- Recruitment
- Selection
- Performance appraisal
- Training
- Career development
- Labor–management relations
- Employment termination
- Managing HR within the context of legislation

Most company structures include an HR department. Traditionally, HR departments were thought of as an administrative or support function for the company because the financial or market value of HR was not as readily apparent as sales, manufacturing, or marketing functions. Some practitioners and researchers are suspect about the future of internal HR functions.

How the Compensation Function Fits into HR Departments

Human resource practices do not operate in isolation. Every HR practice is related to others in different ways. For example, as an employer, U.S. federal government agencies publicly acknowledge the relationships between incentive compensation and other HR practices, including recruitment, relocation, and retention:

Recruitment: An agency may pay a recruitment incentive to a newly appointed career executive if the agency has determined that the position is likely to be difficult to fill in the absence of an incentive. A recruitment incentive may not exceed 25 percent of the executive's annual rate of basic pay in effect at the beginning of the service period multiplied by the number of years (including fractions of a year) in the service period (not to exceed 4 years).

Relocation: An agency may pay a relocation incentive to a current career executive who must relocate to accept a position in a different geographic area if the agency determines that the position is likely to be difficult to fill in the absence of an incentive. A relocation incentive may be paid only when the executive's rating of record under an official performance appraisal or evaluation system is at least "Fully Successful" or equivalent. A relocation incentive may not exceed 25 percent of the executive's annual rate of basic pay in effect at the beginning of the service period multiplied by the number of years (including fractions of a year) in the service period (not to exceed 4 years).

Retention: An agency may pay a retention incentive to a current career executive if (1) the agency determines that the unusually high or unique qualifications of the executive or a special need of the agency for the executive's services makes it essential to retain the executive, and that the executive would be likely to leave the Federal service in the absence of a retention incentive, or (2) the agency has a special need for the employee's services that makes it essential to retain the employee in his or her current position during a period of time before the closure or relocation of the employee's office, facility, activity, or organization and the employee would be likely to leave for a different position in the Federal service in the absence of a retention incentive. A retention incentive may be paid only when the executive's rating of record under an official performance appraisal or evaluation system is at least "Fully Successful" or equivalent. A retention incentive rate, expressed as a percentage of the executive's rate of basic pay, may not exceed 25 percent.[16]

Let's consider additional relationships between compensation and each of the HR practices.

COMPENSATION, RECRUITMENT, AND SELECTION Job candidates choose to work for particular companies for a number of reasons, including career advancement opportunities, training, the company's reputation for being a "good" place to work, location, and compensation. Companies try to spark job candidates' interest by communicating the positive features of the core compensation and employee benefits programs. As we will discuss in Chapter 7, companies use compensation to compete for the very best candidates. In addition, companies may offer such inducements as one-time signing bonuses to entice high-quality applicants. It is not uncommon for signing bonuses to amount to as much as 20 percent of starting annual salaries. Signing bonuses are useful when the supply of qualified candidates falls short of companies' needs for these candidates.

The next three sections will address performance appraisal, training, and career development. Before discussing these issues, however, let's look at how the U.S. federal government explicitly acknowledges the relationship between compensation and these HR practices:

Chapter 43 of title 5, United States Code, provides for performance management for the Senior Executive Service (SES), the establishment of SES performance appraisal systems, and appraisal of senior executive performance. Agencies establish performance management systems that hold senior executives accountable for their individual and organizational performance in order to improve the overall performance of Government by:

1. Expecting excellence in senior executive performance;
2. Linking performance management with the results-oriented goals of the Government Performance and Results Act of 1993;
3. Setting and communicating individual and organizational goals and expectations;
4. Systematically appraising senior executive performance using measures that balance organizational results with customer, employee, or other perspectives; and
5. Using performance results as a basis for pay, awards, development, retention, removal and other personnel decisions.

Agencies develop performance management systems subject to OPM (Office of Personnel Management) regulations and approval.

The supervisor establishes performance elements and requirements in consultation with the executive and consistent with the goals and performance expectations in the agency's strategic planning initiatives. The supervisor proposes the initial summary rating, based on both individual and organizational performance, and taking into account customer satisfaction and employee perspective.[17]

COMPENSATION AND PERFORMANCE APPRAISAL Accurate performance appraisals are integral to effective merit pay programs. For merit pay programs to succeed, employees must know that their efforts toward meeting production quotas or quality standards will lead to pay raises. Job requirements must be realistic, and employees must be prepared to meet job goals with respect to their skills and abilities. Moreover, employees must perceive a strong relationship between attaining performance standards and receiving pay increases. Merit pay systems require specific performance appraisal approaches. Administering successful merit pay programs depends as much on sound performance appraisal practices as it does on the compensation professional's skill in designing and implementing such plans.

COMPENSATION AND TRAINING Successful pay-for-knowledge plans depend on a company's ability to develop and implement systematic training programs. When training is well designed, employees should be able to learn the skills needed to increase their pay, as well as the skills necessary to teach and coach other employees at lower skill levels. Companies implementing pay-for-knowledge plans typically increase the amount of classroom and on-the-job training. Pay-for-knowledge systems make training necessary rather than optional. Companies that adopt pay-for-knowledge systems must accordingly ensure that all employees have equal access to the training needed to acquire higher-level skills.

COMPENSATION AND CAREER DEVELOPMENT Most employees expect to experience career development within their present companies. Employees' careers develop in two different ways. First, some employees change the focus of their work—for example, from supervisor of payroll clerks to supervisor of inventory clerks. This change represents a lateral move across the company's hierarchy. Second, others maintain their focus and assume greater responsibilities. This change illustrates advancement upward through the company's hierarchy. Advancing from payroll clerk to manager of payroll administration is an example of moving upward through a company's hierarchy. Employees' compensation changes to reflect career development.

COMPENSATION AND LABOR–MANAGEMENT RELATIONS Collective bargaining agreements describe the terms of employment (e.g., pay and work hours) reached between management and the union. Compensation is a key topic. Unions have fought hard for general pay increases and regular COLAs to promote their members' standard of living. In Chapter 2, we will review the role of unions in compensation, and in Chapter 3, we indicate that unions have traditionally bargained for seniority pay systems in negotiations with management. More recently, unions have been willing to incorporate particular incentive pay systems. For example, unions appear to be receptive to behavioral encouragement plans because improving worker safety and minimizing absenteeism serve the best interests of both employees and employers.

COMPENSATION AND EMPLOYMENT TERMINATION Employment termination takes place when an employee's agreement to perform work is terminated. Employment terminations are either involuntary or voluntary. The HR department plays a central role in managing involuntary employment terminations. Companies initiate involuntary terminations for a variety of reasons, including poor job performance, insubordination, violation of work rules, reduced business activity due to sluggish economic conditions, and plant closings. Discharge represents involuntary termination for poor job performance, insubordination, or gross violation of work rules. Involuntary layoff describes termination under sluggish economic conditions or because of plant closings. In the case of involuntary layoffs, HR professionals typically provide outplacement counseling to help employees find work elsewhere. Companies may choose to award **severance pay**, which usually amounts to several months' pay following involuntary termination and, in some cases, continued coverage under the employer's medical insurance plan. Employees often rely on severance pay to meet financial obligations while they search for employment. In the past, companies commonly offered a year or more of severance pay. Severance benefits today tend to be less generous. For example, as part of Delta Airlines's 2005 closure of its Boston reservation center, the company offered only 6 weeks of severance pay regardless of seniority with the company.

Employees initiate voluntary terminations, most often to work for other companies or to retire. In the case of retirement, companies sponsor pension programs. **Pension programs** provide income to individuals throughout their retirement. Companies sometimes use **early retirement programs** to reduce workforce size and trim compensation expenditures. Early retirement programs contain incentives designed to encourage highly paid employees with substantial seniority to retire earlier than they had planned. These incentives expedite senior employees' retirement eligibility and increase their retirement income. In addition, some companies continue retirees' medical benefits.

COMPENSATION AND LEGISLATION Employment laws establish bounds of both acceptable employment practices and employee rights. Federal laws that apply to compensation practices are grouped according to four themes:

- Income continuity, safety, and work hours
- Pay discrimination
- Accommodating of disabilities and family needs
- Prevailing wage laws

Table 1-3 lists for each theme some of the major laws that influence compensation practice.

The federal government enacted income continuity, safety, and work hours laws (e.g., the Fair Labor Standards Act of 1938) to stabilize individuals' incomes when the individuals became unemployed because of poor business conditions or workplace injuries, as well as to set pay minimums and work-hour limits for children. The civil rights movement of the 1960s led to the passage of key legislation (e.g., the Equal Pay Act of 1963 and the Civil Rights Act of 1964) designed to protect designated classes of employees and to uphold their individual rights against discriminatory employment decisions, including matters of pay. Congress enacted legislation (e.g., the Pregnancy Discrimination Act of 1978, the Americans with Disabilities Act of 1990, and the Family and Medical Leave Act of 1993) to accommodate employees with disabilities

TABLE 1-3 Laws that Influence Compensation

Income Continuity, Safety, and Work Hours
Minimum wage laws—Fair Labor Standards Act of 1938
   Minimum wage
   Overtime provisions
     Portal-to-Portal Act of 1947
     Equal Pay Act of 1963
   Child labor provisions
Work Hours and Safety Standards Act of 1962
McNamara–O'Hara Service Contract Act of 1965

Pay Discrimination
Equal Pay Act of 1963
Lilly Ledbetter Fair Pay Act (2009)
Civil Rights Act of 1964, Title VII
Bennett Amendment (1964)
Executive Order 11246 (1965)
Age Discrimination in Employment Act of 1967 (amended in 1978, 1986, and 1990)
Executive Order 11141 (1964)
Civil Rights Act of 1991

Accommodating Disabilities and Family Needs
Pregnancy Discrimination Act of 1978
Americans with Disabilities Act of 1990 (amended in 2008)
Family and Medical Leave Act of 1993

Prevailing Wage Laws
Davis–Bacon Act of 1931
Walsh–Healey Public Contracts Act of 1936

and pressing family needs. Prevailing wage laws (e.g., the Davis–Bacon Act of 1931) set minimum wage rates for companies that provide paid services—such as building maintenance—to the U.S. government.

The Compensation Department's Main Goals

Compensation professionals promote effective compensation systems by meeting three important goals: internal consistency, market competitiveness, and recognition of individual contributions.

INTERNAL CONSISTENCY **Internally consistent compensation systems** clearly define the relative value of each job among all jobs within a company. This ordered set of jobs represents the job structure or hierarchy. Companies rely on a simple, yet fundamental, principle for building internally consistent compensation systems: Employees in jobs that require greater qualifications, more responsibilities, and more complex job duties should be paid more than employees whose jobs require lesser qualifications, fewer responsibilities, and less-complex job duties. Internally consistent job structures formally recognize differences in job characteristics, which therefore enable compensation managers to set pay accordingly.

Compensation professionals use job analysis and job evaluation to achieve internal consistency. **Job analysis** is a systematic process for gathering, documenting, and analyzing information in order to describe jobs. Job analyses describe content or job duties, worker requirements, and sometimes the job context or working conditions.

Compensation professionals use **job evaluation** systematically to recognize differences in the relative worth among a set of jobs and to establish pay differentials accordingly. Whereas job analysis is almost purely descriptive, job evaluation partly reflects the values and priorities that management places on various positions. Based on job content differences (e.g., job analysis results) and the firm's priorities, managers establish pay differentials for virtually all positions within the company.

MARKET COMPETITIVENESS **Market-competitive pay systems** play a significant role in attracting and retaining the most qualified employees. Compensation professionals build market-competitive compensation systems based on the results of market surveys (Chapter 7) and compensation surveys.

A **strategic analysis** entails an examination of a company's external market context and internal factors. Examples of external market context are the industry profile, information about competitors, and long-term growth prospects. Internal factors encompass the company's financial condition and functional capabilities—for example, marketing and human resources. Strategic analyses permit business professionals to see where they stand in the market based on external and internal factors.

Compensation surveys collect and then analyze competitors' compensation data. Compensation surveys traditionally focused on competitors' wage and salary practices. Now, employee benefits are also a target of surveys because benefits are a key element of market-competitive pay systems. Compensation surveys are important because they enable compensation professionals to obtain realistic views of competitors' pay practices. In the absence of compensation survey data, compensation professionals would have to use guesswork to build market-competitive compensation systems.

RECOGNIZING INDIVIDUAL CONTRIBUTIONS **Pay structures** represent pay rate differences for jobs of unequal worth and the framework for recognizing differences in employee contributions. No two employees possess identical credentials or perform the same jobs equally well. Companies recognize these differences by paying individuals according to their credentials, knowledge, or job performance. When completed, pay structures should define the boundaries for recognizing employee contributions. Well-designed structures should promote the retention of valued employees.

Pay grades and pay ranges are structural features of pay structures. **Pay grades** group jobs for pay policy application. Human resource professionals typically group jobs into pay grades based on similar compensable factors and value. These criteria are not precise. In fact, no single formula determines what is sufficiently similar in terms of content and value to warrant grouping into a pay grade. **Pay ranges** build upon pay grades. Pay ranges include minimum, maximum, and midpoint pay rates. The minimum and maximum values denote the acceptable lower and upper bounds of pay for the jobs in particular pay grades. The midpoint pay value is the halfway mark between the minimum and maximum pay rates.

STAKEHOLDERS OF THE COMPENSATION SYSTEM

The HR department provides services to stakeholders within and outside the company. These include:

- Employees
- Line managers
- Executives
- Unions
- U.S. government

The success of HR departments depends on how well they serve various stakeholders. "Each constituency [stakeholder] has its own set of expectations regarding the personnel department's activities; each holds its own standards for effective performance; each applies its own standards for assessing the extent to which the department's activities meets its expectations; and each attempts to prescribe preferred goals for the subunit or presents constraints to its sphere of discretion. Multiple stakeholders often compete directly or indirectly for the attention and priority of the personnel department."[18] Our focus is on some of the ways compensation professionals serve these stakeholders.

Employees

As we discussed earlier, successful pay-for-knowledge programs depend on a company's ability to develop and implement systematic training programs. Compensation professionals must educate employees about their training options and how successful training will lead to increased pay and advancement opportunities within the company. These professionals should not assume that employees will necessarily recognize these opportunities unless they are clearly communicated. Written memos and informational meetings conducted by compensation professionals and HR representatives are effective communication media.

Discretionary benefits provide protection programs, paid time off, and services. As compensation professionals plan and manage employee benefits programs, they should keep these functions in mind. There is probably no single company that expects its employee benefits program to meet all these objectives. Compensation professionals as representatives of company management, along with union representatives, must therefore determine which objectives are the most important for their particular workforce.

Line Managers

Compensation professionals use their expert knowledge of the laws that influence pay and benefits practices to help line managers make sound compensation judgments. For example, the Equal Pay Act of 1963 (discussed in Chapter 2) prohibits sex discrimination in pay for employees performing equal work, so compensation professionals should advise line managers to pay the same hourly pay rate or annual salary for men and women hired to perform the same job.

Line managers turn to compensation professionals for advice about appropriate pay rates for jobs. Compensation professionals oversee the use of job evaluation to establish pay differentials among jobs within a company. In addition, they train line managers in how to evaluate jobs properly.

Consistent, innovative, and fair compensation practices are central to ensuring the success of both human resource strategies and overall company competitive strategies. While it is HR's role to decide what kind of people are critical to fill roles that will lead to successful execution of competitive strategies, compensation professionals must align practices that will enable attraction, appropriate job placement, and development of these individuals. Many companies have moved from the personnel management model to the HR as business partner model; however, some still look to HR to guarantee that policies are being enforced and the company mitigates legal risk. Depending on the company where you are employed—and whether you are a line manager or HR professional—you may find yourself in a position to understand the competitive strategy of the business and align compensation practices with the strategic thrust of the business.

Action checklist for line managers and HR—aligning compensation with strategy

HR takes the lead
- Work with line managers to fully understand which roles and types of employees will best support the execution of company strategy.
- Collaborate with compensation specialists to run analysis of market factors (competitors, industry standards, local labor market) to get indicators of compensation norms and standards in order to keep your company's compensation practices competitive.
- Create, together with line managers, pay structures wherein roles are placed into appropriate pay grades. Each grade will have a corresponding range that will serve as the basis for assigning pay rates for roles.

Line managers take the lead
- Educate staff positions, along with other business leaders, in order for all to understand what strategy is being employed to achieve specific company objectives.
- Educate HR on certain aspects of roles (e.g., autonomy, skill variety, task significance, etc.) that, when enhanced, could improve intrinsic motivation, thus leading to benefits for employees and employers. HR works on ways to couple the intrinsic compensation with the identified plan for the core compensation plan.
- Work together with HR to implement a plan that ties the compensation plan to a successful recruitment, training, and development plan, ensuring that the company is retaining the talent that is critical to the implementation and delivery of the strategic objectives.

Executives

Compensation professionals serve company executives by developing and managing sound compensation systems. Executives look to them to ensure that the design and implementation of pay and benefits practices comply with pertinent legislation. Violation of these laws can lead to substantial monetary penalties to companies. Executives also depend on compensation professionals' expertise to design pay and benefits systems that will attract and retain the best-qualified employees.

Unions

As noted earlier, collective bargaining agreements describe the terms of employment reached between management and the union. Compensation professionals are responsible for administering the pay and benefits policies specified in collective bargaining agreements. They mainly ensure that employees receive COLAs and seniority pay increases on a timely basis.

U.S. Government

The U.S. government requires that companies comply with all employment legislation. Compensation professionals apply their expertise regarding pertinent legislation to design legally sound pay and benefits practices. In addition, since the passage of the Civil Rights Act of 1991, compensation professionals have applied their expertise to demonstrate that alleged discriminatory pay practices are a business necessity. As we will discuss in Chapter 2, the burden of proof to demonstrate that alleged discriminatory pay practices are not discriminatory rests with compensation professionals.

END OF CHAPTER

MyManagementLab

Go to **mymanagementlab.com** to complete the problems marked with this icon .

Summary

This chapter introduced basic compensation concepts and the context of compensation practice. We distinguished between intrinsic and extrinsic compensation, noting that our focus is on extrinsic compensation. Next, we reviewed the evolution of compensation from an administrative function to a strategic function, as well as the strategic role of compensation in attaining competitive advantage. We then looked at how HR professionals fit in the corporate hierarchy and how compensation professionals fit into HR departments. Specifically, we learned that compensation professionals focus on internal and external pay differentials among jobs, as well as on creating pay structures that recognize employees for their particular contributions. Finally, we concluded with how compensation professionals relate to a company's various stakeholders.

Students of compensation should keep the following in mind: Compensation systems are changing. Change creates many exciting challenges for those who wish to work as compensation professionals. This book highlights those challenges.

Key Terms

intrinsic compensation   3
extrinsic compensation   3
core compensation   3
employee benefits   3
base pay   4
hourly pay   4
wage   4
salary   4
compensable factors   4
cost-of-living adjustments
    (COLAs)   4
seniority pay   4
human capital theory   4
human capital   4
merit pay   5
incentive pay   5
variable pay   5
pay-for-knowledge   5
skill-based pay   5
discretionary benefits   5
legally required benefits   5
paid time off   5
services   5
protection programs   7
scientific management practices   7
time-and-motion studies   7
welfare practices   8
competitive advantage   8
strategic decisions   9
tactical decisions   9
strategic management   9
competitive strategy   10
human resource strategies   10
cost leadership   11
lowest-cost strategy   11
differentiation strategies   11
line employees   12
staff employees   12
severance pay   15
pension programs   15
early retirement programs   15
internally consistent compensation
    systems   17
job analysis   17
job evaluation   17
market-competitive pay systems   17
strategic analysis   17
compensation surveys   17
pay structures   17
pay grades   18
pay ranges   18

✪ Discussion Questions

1-1. Define compensation.
1-2. Identify two companies—one that you believe pursues a lowest-cost strategy and another that pursues a differentiation strategy. Relying on personal knowledge, company annual reports, or articles in newspapers and business periodicals, discuss these companies' competitive strategies.

1-3. Describe your reaction to the following statement: Compensation has no bearing on a company's performance.
1-4. Are the three main goals of compensation departments equally important, or do you believe that they differ in importance? Give your rationale.

CASE
Competitive Strategy at Sportsman Shoes

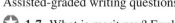 *An additional Supplemental Case can be found on MyManagementLab.*

Sportsman Shoes has been a leader in the shoe industry for more than 30 years. Sportsman manufactures and sells athletic shoes for all types of sports. The company has pursued a low-cost strategy in order to sustain its success. It sells a limited number of shoe designs and has held costs low through manufacturing efficiency and standardized operations. However, the past years have been a struggle at Sportsman. The shoe market has seen a rise in the availability of low-cost imported shoes that has threatened Sportsman's competitive position. As a result, company executives have decided it is time for a strategy shift.

Sportsman executives have done extensive market research and determined that many niche athletic shoe markets exist where athletes are willing to pay more for shoes designed to meet the unique needs of their sport. There are very few competitors in these niche athletic shoe markets, and most do not have Sportsman's past experience in keeping control of manufacturing costs. Sportsman has determined that with talented shoe designers in place, they can manufacture athletic shoes to meet the needs of the niche markets using their current manufacturing facilities and employees. By designing shoes that have features that differ from competitors and meet the specific needs of a new group of customers, Sportsman believes the company can create a competitive advantage. Further, while their shoes will not be as low cost as they were in the past, they will likely be able to sell their shoes for less than market competitors and still make a healthy profit.

Therefore, Sportsman has decided to shift from its current low-cost strategy to a differentiation strategy and will begin production to make specialty athletic shoes. Sportsman must now make many tactical decisions in various functional areas of the company to support its decision to shift its overall business strategy. Its first priority is to restructure the product development function. As it will need to understand the needs of the niche markets and design shoes to meet those needs, it will need to hire and retain talented shoe designers. The company will also need to hire operations specialists to transition its manufacturing operations to produce the new shoe designs. Beyond hiring new staff, Sportsman also must consider the implications for current employees to help them successfully transition to their new work requirements. Therefore, there are several considerations the company must address in the area of human resource management.

Questions:
1-5. Following Sportsman's shift in competitive strategy, what are some considerations for the company's human resource management practices?
1-6. What kind of challenges will Sportsman face specifically in the area of compensation?

MyManagementLab

Go to **mymanagementlab.com** for Auto-graded writing questions as well as the following Assisted-graded writing questions:

⭐ **1-7.** What is merit pay? Explain the role of performance appraisals in merit pay programs.
⭐ **1-8.** What is a pay-for-knowledge plan? Explain the role of training in pay-for-knowledge plans.

Endnotes

1. U.S. Bureau of Labor Statistics. (2013). *The Employment Situation—January 2013* (USDL 13-0144). Available: *www.bls.gov*, accessed March 3, 2013.
2. Becker, G. (1976). *Human Capital*. New York: National Bureau of Economic Research.
3. U.S. Department of Labor. (2013, March 12). Employer costs for employee compensation, December 2012 (USDL: 13-0421). Available: *www.bls.gov*, accessed March 31, 2013.
4. Baron, J. N., Dobbin, F., & Jennings, P. D. (1986). War and peace: The evolution of modern personnel administration

in U.S. industry. *American Journal of Sociology, 92*, pp. 350–383.

5. Person, H. S. (1929). The new attitude toward management. In H. S. Person (Ed.), *Scientific Management in American Industry*. New York: Harper & Brothers.

6. U.S. Bureau of Labor Statistics. (1919). Welfare work for employees in industrial establishments in the United States. *Bulletin #250*, pp. 119–123.

7. Eilbirt, H. (1959). The development of personnel management in the United States. *Business History Review, 33*, pp. 345–364.

8. Pfeffer, J. (1995). Producing sustainable competitive advantage through the effective management of people. *Academy of Management Executives, 9*, pp. 55–69.

9. Carnevale, A. P., & Johnston, J. W. (1989). *Training in America: Strategies for the Nation*. Alexandria, VA: National Center on Education and the Economy and the American Society for Training and Development.

10. Lengnick-Hall, C. A., & Lengnick-Hall, M. L. (1990). *Interactive Human Resource Management and Strategic Planning*. New York: Quorum Books.

11. Dutton, J. E., & Jackson, S. E. (1987). The categorization of strategic issues by decision makers and its links to organizational action. *Academy of Management Review, 12*, pp. 76–90.

12. *Eli Lilly's Annual Report*. (2009). Available: *http://investor .lilly.com/annuals.cfm*, accessed January 28, 2011.

13. *Why Lilly?* Available: *http://www.lilly.com/careers/why _choose/*, accessed January 28, 2011.

14. *The Benefits of Working at Lilly*. Available: *http://www.lilly .com/careers/benefits/*, accessed January 28, 2011.

15. Quotation excerpted from Leonard, B. (2002). Straight talk: Executives sound off on why they think HR professionals lost strategic ground, and what they can do to earn a place "at the table." *HRMagazine*, January, Vol. 47, No. 1., p. 48. Available: *www.shrm.org*, accessed March 10, 2013.

16. U.S. Federal Government. (2011). Performance & compensation: Incentive payments. Available: *http://www .opm.gov/ses/performance/incentive.asp*, accessed July 13, 2011.

17. U.S. Federal Government. (2011). Performance management. Available: *http://www.opm.gov/ses/performance /index.asp*, accessed July 13, 2011.

18. Tsui, A. S. (1984). Personnel department effectiveness: A tripartite approach. *Industrial Relations, 23*, p. 187.

2 CONTEXTUAL INFLUENCES ON COMPENSATION PRACTICE

MyManagementLab®

⭐ **Improve Your Grade!**

When you see this icon, visit **www.mymanagementlab.com** for activities that are applied, personalized, and offer immediate feedback.

LEARNING OBJECTIVES

When you finish studying this chapter, you should be able to:

1. List four groups of federal laws that apply to compensation tactics.
2. Identify and describe at least one law in each of the four groups of federal laws that apply to compensation practice.
3. Define at least two federal laws that shape discretionary benefits practices and identify the relevant employee benefits practices to which they apply.
4. Summarize at least three laws that apply exclusively to federal employers' compensation practices.
5. Explain how labor unions influence compensation practices.

The era of the Great Depression of the 1930s created extreme desperation among the masses of individuals who became unemployed as a multitude of companies went out of business. The majority of the unemployed were unable to find jobs, which left them without income to provide the basic necessities for their families. Many of the companies that remained in business recognized the desperation of the unemployed. From an economic perspective, employers also realized that the extremely large supply of available workers relative to business demand to employ them was unprecedented. As a result, employers often chose to compensate workers a pittance, which still made it difficult for families to fulfill basic necessities, including food and rent payments. Unfortunately, it became common for adolescent children to drop out of school to find odd jobs so that they could help their families meet basic those necessities. Similarly, many companies took advantage of child labor by employing them in hazardous jobs for excessive hours, at low pay rates.

> *Anne Brown, the claims department manager of a small insurance company, said to Bill Smith, the human resource (HR) manager, "I'm sick and tired of having clerks who just don't work out. The quality of their work is not very good, nor are they reliable—they are frequently absent or late. They are limiting my ability to maintain timely and accurate claims processing." Bill replied, "You get no argument from me. It's been nearly impossible to recruit top quality clerks ever since ABC Automobile Parts Company established a manufacturing facility across town. After all, ABC's clerks earn nearly 40 percent more than our clerks."*

The previous quotations illustrate three major contextual influences on companies' compensation practices. The first quotation captures the inherent conflict between employers and employees—employers' profit maximization objectives and employees' desire for equitable and fair treatment. This conflict gave rise to the first two contextual influences that we will review in this chapter—federal protective legislation and labor unions.

The second quotation represents a third contextual influence—market forces. In particular, this quotation illustrates a potential consequence of interindustry compensation differentials—the inability to recruit top-quality employees. We will address these differentials later in the chapter.

EMPLOYMENT LAWS THAT INFLUENCE COMPENSATION TACTICS

Employment laws are essential to maintain a balance of power between employers and employees; in the case of compensation practice, helping to ensure that pursuit of goals by any one group does not undermine others' goals, particularly those with the least amount of power—employees. In a nutshell:

> The freedom to contract is crucial to freedom of the market; an employee may choose to work or not to work for a given employer, and an employer may choose to hire or not to hire a given applicant. As a result, the employment relationship is regulated in some important ways. Congress tries to avoid telling employers how to manage their employees.... However, Congress has passed employment-related laws when it believes that the employee is not on equal footing with the employer. For example, Congress has passed laws that require employers to pay minimum wages and to refrain from using certain criteria, such as race or gender, in arriving at specific employment decisions. These laws reflect the reality that employers stand in a position of power in the employment relationship. Legal protections granted to employees seek to make the power relationship between employer and employee one that is fair and equitable.[1]

The **federal constitution** forms the basis for employment laws. The following four amendments of the Constitution are most applicable:

Article I, Section 8. "The Congress shall have Power...to regulate Commerce with foreign Nations, and among the several States, and with the Indian Tribes...."
First Amendment. "Congress shall make no law respecting an establishment of religion, or prohibiting the free exercise thereof; or abridging the freedom of speech, or of the press; or the right of the people peaceably to assemble, and to petition the Government for a redress of grievances."

Fifth Amendment. "No person shall…be deprived of life, liberty, or property, without due process of law…."

Fourteenth Amendment, Section 1. "…No State shall make or enforce any law which shall abridge the privileges or immunities of citizens of the United States, nor shall any State deprive any person of life, liberty, or property without due process of law; nor deny any person within its jurisdiction the equal protection of the laws."

Government in the United States is organized at three levels roughly defined by geographic scope:

- Federal
- State
- Local

A single **federal government** oversees the entire United States and its territories. The vast majority of laws that influence compensation were established at the federal level. Next, individual **state governments** enact and enforce laws that pertain exclusively to their respective regions (e.g., Illinois and Michigan). Most noteworthy are differences in state minimum wage laws, which we will discuss shortly. Finally, **local governments** enact and enforce laws that are most pertinent to smaller geographic regions (e.g., Champaign County in Illinois and the city of Los Angeles). Many of the federal laws have counterparts in state and local legislation. State and local legislation may be concurrent with federal law or may exist in the absence of similar federal legislation. Federal law prevails wherever state or local laws are inconsistent with federal legislation.

The federal government has three branches:

- Legislative branch
- Executive branch
- Judicial branch

Congress creates and passes laws within the **legislative branch**. The **executive branch** enforces the laws of various quasi-legislative and judicial agencies. The president of the United States possesses the authority to establish **executive orders** that influence the operation of the federal government and companies that are engaged in business relationships with the federal government. The **judicial branch** is responsible for interpreting the laws. The U.S. Supreme Court, which consists of nine life-appointed justices, is the forum for these interpretations.

Federal laws that apply to compensation practices are grouped according to key themes:

- Income continuity, safety, and work hours
- Pay discrimination
- Accommodating disabilities and family needs
- Prevailing wage laws

Income Continuity, Safety, and Work Hours

Three factors led to the passage of income continuity, safety, and work hours legislation. The first factor was the **Great Depression**, the move from family businesses to large factories, and divisions of labor within factories. During the Great Depression, which took place in the 1930s, scores of businesses failed, and many workers became chronically unemployed. Government enacted key legislation designed to stabilize the income of an individual who became unemployed because of poor business conditions or workplace injuries. The **Social Security Act of 1935 (Title IX)** provided temporary income to workers who became unemployed through no fault of their own. **Workers' compensation** programs granted income to workers who were unable to work because of injuries sustained on the job. Supporting workers during these misfortunes promoted the well-being of the economy: These income provisions enabled the unemployed to participate in the economy as consumers of essential goods and services. We will defer a more detailed discussion of the Social Security Act of 1935 and workers' compensation laws until Chapter 11 because these laws represent legally required employee benefits.

Second, the main U.S. economic activities prior to the twentieth century were agriculture and small family businesses that were organized along craft lines. Workers began to move from their farms and small family businesses to capitalists' factories for employment. The character of work changed dramatically with the move of workers to factories. An individual's status changed from owner to employee. This status change meant that individuals lost control over their earnings and working conditions.

Third, the factory system also created divisions of labor characterized by differences in skills and responsibilities. Some workers received training, whereas others did not. This contributed greatly to differences in skills and responsibilities. Workers with higher skills and responsibilities did not necessarily earn higher wages than workers with fewer skills and responsibilities. Paying some workers more than others only increased costs, which is something factory owners avoided whenever possible.

In sum, factory workers received very low wages and worked in unsafe conditions because factory owners sought to maximize profits. Offering workers high wages and providing safe working conditions would have cut into factory owners' profits. These conditions led to the passage of the **Fair Labor Standards Act of 1938 (FLSA)**. The FLSA addresses major abuses that intensified during the Great Depression and the transition from agricultural to industrial enterprises. These include substandard pay, excessive work hours, and the employment of children in oppressive working conditions.

FAIR LABOR STANDARDS ACT OF 1938   The FLSA addresses three broad issues:

- Minimum wage
- Overtime pay
- Child labor provisions

The U.S. Department of Labor enforces the FLSA.

Minimum Wage   The purpose of the minimum wage provision is to ensure a minimally acceptable standard of living for workers. The original minimum wage was 25 cents per hour. Since the act's passage in 1938, the federal government has raised the minimum wage several times. The previous minimum wage increase, to $5.15 per hour, was signed into law in August of 1996. In 2007, Congress passed an increase in the federal minimum wage from $5.15 in increments to $7.25 in 2009.

Twenty-one states have minimum wage laws that currently specify higher minimum wage rates than the federal level specified in the FLSA. This number of states represent a substantial decrease from approximately 30 states when the minimum wage rate was $5.15. There would likely be more states that offer higher minimum wage rates, but for pressure from businesses that insist higher minimum wage rates would cut into profits. Business owners are concerned that workers with pay above the minimum wage will expect pay increases to maintain the spread between their earnings and the recently implemented federal minimum rate. Nine states either possess no minimum wage law (5 states) or offer minimum wage rates below the federal level (4 states).

Specific FLSA exemptions permit employers to pay some workers less than the minimum wage. Students employed in retail or service businesses, on farms, or in institutions of higher education may be paid less than the minimum wage with the consent of the Department of Labor. With explicit permission from the Department of Labor, employers can pay less than the minimum wage for trainee positions or to prevent a reduction in the employment of mentally or physically disabled individuals. Table 2-1 lists the six factors that define trainees.

Overtime Provisions   The FLSA requires employers to pay workers at a rate equal to time and one-half for all hours worked in excess of 40 hours within a period of 7 consecutive days.

TABLE 2-1 Six Defining Factors of a Trainee for the FLSA

- The training, even though it includes actual operation of the employers' facilities, is similar to that which would be provided in a vocational school.
- The training is for the benefit of the trainee.
- The trainee works under closer supervision and does not displace regular employees.
- The employer providing the training gains no immediate advantage from the trainees' activities; on occasion, the employer's operation may in fact be hindered.
- The trainee is not guaranteed a job at the completion of the training.
- The employer and the trainee understand that the employer is not obligated to pay wages during the training period.

Source: J. E. Kalet, *Primer on Wage and Hour Laws* (Washington, DC: Bureau of National Affairs, 1987).

For example, a worker's regular hourly rate is $10 for working 40 hours or less within a 7-day period. The FLSA requires the employer to pay this employee $15 per hour for each additional hour worked beyond the regular 40 hours within this 7-day period.

The overtime provision does not apply to all jobs. Executive, administrative, learned professional, creative professional, computer workers, and outside sales employees are generally **exempt** from the FLSA overtime and minimum wage provisions. Table 2-2 describes the definition of these job categories. Most other jobs are **nonexempt**. Nonexempt jobs are subject to the FLSA overtime pay provision.

Classifying jobs as either exempt or nonexempt is not always clear-cut. In *Aaron v. City of Wichita, Kansas*,[2] the city contended that its fire chiefs were exempt as executives under the FLSA because they spent more than 80 percent of their work hours managing the fire department. The fire chiefs maintained that they should not be exempt from the FLSA because they did not possess the authority to hire, fire, authorize shift trades, give pay raises, or make policy decisions. Determining whether jobs are exempt from the FLSA overtime pay provision has become even more complex since the U.S. Department of Labor

TABLE 2-2 FLSA Exemption Criteria

Executive	Management of the enterprise or a recognized department or subdivision.
Administrative	Performing office or nonmanual work directly related to the management or general business operations of the employer or employer's customers.
Learned Professional	Performing office or nonmanual work requiring knowledge of an advanced type in a field of science or learning, customarily acquired by a prolonged course of specialized intellectual instruction, but which also may be acquired by such alternative means as an equivalent combination of intellectual instruction and work experience.
Creative Professional	Performing work requiring invention, imagination, originality, or talent in a recognized field of artistic or creative endeavor.
Computer	Employed as a computer systems analyst, computer programmer, software engineer, or other similarly skilled worker in the computer field.
Outside Sales	Making sales or obtaining orders or contracts for services or for future use of facilities for which a consideration will be paid by the client or customer. Customarily and regularly engaged away from the employer's place or places of business.

Note: No minimum salary requirement.
Source: U.S. Department of Labor (2007). Wage and Hour Division Web site. Available: *www.dol.gov/esa/whd*, accessed February 11, 2011.

introduced revised guidelines known as the **FairPay Rules** in August 2004. An employee was previously considered exempt under the FLSA overtime pay provisions if an employee earned more than the minimum wage and exercised independent judgment when working (see Table 2-2). Under the new FairPay Rules, workers earning less than $23,660 per year— or $455 per week—are guaranteed overtime protection. The U.S. Department of Labor provides extensive information regarding the new FairPay Rules, including instructional videos and a "frequently asked questions" section *(www.dol.gov)*.

The federal government broadened the scope of the FLSA twice since 1938 through the passage of two acts:

- Portal-to-Portal Act of 1947
- Equal Pay Act of 1963

The **Portal-to-Portal Act of 1947** defines the term *hours worked* that appears in the FLSA. Table 2-3 lists the compensable work activities. For example, time spent by state correctional officers caring for police dogs at home is compensable under the FLSA *(Andres v. DuBois)*.[3] The care of dogs, including feeding, grooming, and walking, is indispensable to maintaining dogs as a critical law enforcement tool, it is part of officers' principal activities, and it benefits the corrections department; however, this court ruled that time spent by state correction canine handlers transporting dogs between home and correctional facilities is not compensable under FLSA.

TABLE 2-3 Compensable Work Activities

Waiting Time: Whether waiting time is hours worked under the act depends upon the particular circumstances. Generally, the facts may show that the employee was engaged to wait (which is work time), or the facts may show that the employee was waiting to be engaged (which is not work time). For example, a secretary who reads a book while waiting for dictation or a fireman who plays checkers while waiting for an alarm is working during such periods of inactivity. These employees have been "engaged to wait."

On-Call Time: An employee who is required to remain on call on the employer's premises is working while "on call." An employee who is required to remain on call at home, or who is allowed to leave a message where he/she can be reached, is not working (in most cases) while on call. Additional constraints on the employee's freedom could require this time to be compensated.

Rest and Meal Periods: Rest periods of short duration, usually 20 minutes or less, are common in industry (and promote the efficiency of the employee) and are customarily paid for as working time. These short periods must be counted as hours worked. Unauthorized extensions of authorized work breaks need not be counted as hours worked when the employer has expressly and unambiguously communicated to the employee that the authorized break may only last for a specific length of time, that any extension of the break is contrary to the employer's rules, and that any extension of the break will be punished. Bona fide meal periods (typically 30 minutes or more) generally need not be compensated as work time. The employee must be completely relieved from duty for the purpose of eating regular meals. The employee is not relieved if he or she is required to perform any duties, whether active or inactive, while eating.

Sleeping Time and Certain Other Activities: An employee who is required to be on duty for less than 24 hours is working even though he or she is permitted to sleep or engage in other personal activities when not busy. An employee required to be on duty for 24 hours or more may agree with the employer to exclude from hours worked bona fide regularly scheduled sleeping periods of not more than 8 hours, provided adequate sleeping facilities are furnished by the employer and the employee can usually enjoy an uninterrupted night's sleep. No reduction is permitted unless at least 5 hours of sleep is taken.

Lectures, Meetings, and Training Programs: Attendance at lectures, meetings, training programs, and similar activities need not be counted as working time only if four criteria are met, namely: It is outside normal hours, voluntary, not job related, and no other work is concurrently performed. In other words, the time spent in employer-mandated training counts as compensable time.

TABLE 2-3 (Continued)

Travel time: The principles that apply in determining whether time spent in travel is compensable time depends upon the kind of travel involved.

- **Home-to-work travel:** An employee who travels from home before the regular workday and returns to his or her home at the end of the workday is engaged in ordinary home-to-work travel, which is not work time.
- **Home-to-work travel on a special one-day assignment, including employer-mandated training, in another city:** An employee who regularly works at a fixed location in one city is given a special one-day assignment, including employer-mandated training, in another city and returns home the same day. The time spent in traveling to and returning from the other city is work time, except that the employer may deduct/not count that time the employee would normally spend commuting to the regular work site.
- **Travel that is all in a day's work:** Time spent by an employee in travel as part of his or her principal activity, such as travel from job site to job site during the workday, is work time and must be counted as hours worked.
- **Travel away from home community:** Travel that keeps an employee away from home overnight is travel away from home. Travel away from home is clearly work time when it cuts across the employee's workday. The time is not only hours worked on regular working days during normal working hours but also during corresponding hours on nonworking days. As an enforcement policy, the U.S. Department of Labor will not consider as work time that time spent in travel away from home outside of regular working hours as a passenger on an airplane, train, boat, bus, or automobile.

Source: Adapted from U.S. Department of Labor. (2011). Compliance Assistance—Fair Labor Standards Act (FLSA). Available: *http://www.dol.gov*, accessed February 19, 2013.

The **Equal Pay Act of 1963** prohibits sex discrimination in pay for employees performing equal work. We will discuss the Equal Pay Act of 1963 later in this chapter.

Child Labor Provisions The FLSA child labor provisions protect children from being overworked, working in potentially hazardous settings, and having their education jeopardized due to excessive work hours. The restrictions vary by age:

- Children under age 14 usually cannot be employed.
- Children ages 14 and 15 may work in safe occupations outside school hours if their work does not exceed 3 hours on a school day (18 hours per week while school is in session). When school is not in session, as in the summer, children cannot work more than 40 hours per week.
- Children ages 16 and 17 do not have hourly restrictions; however, they cannot work in hazardous jobs (e.g., the use of heavy industrial equipment or exposure to harmful substances).

Pay Discrimination

The civil rights movement of the 1960s led to the passage of key legislation designed to protect designated classes of employees and to uphold their rights individually against discriminatory employment decisions. Some of these laws, such as the **Civil Rights Act of 1964**, apply to all employment-related decisions (e.g., recruitment, selection, performance appraisal, compensation, and termination). Other laws, such as the Equal Pay Act of 1963, apply specifically to compensation practices. These laws limit employers' authority over employment decisions.

EQUAL PAY ACT OF 1963 Congress enacted the Equal Pay Act of 1963 to remedy a serious problem of employment discrimination in private industry: "Many segments of American industry [have] been based on an ancient but outmoded belief that a man, because of his role in society, should be paid more than a woman even though his duties are the same."[4] The Equal Pay Act of 1963 is based on a simple principle: Men and women should receive equal pay for performing equal work.

The Equal Employment Opportunity Commission (EEOC) enforces the Equal Pay Act of 1963. The EEOC possesses the authority to investigate and reconcile charges of illegal discrimination. The act applies to all employers and labor organizations. In particular,

No employer...shall discriminate within any establishment in which such employees are employed, between employees on the basis of sex by paying wages to employees in such establishment at a rate less than the rate at which he pays wages to employees of the opposite sex...for equal work on jobs the performance of which requires equal skill, effort, and responsibility, and which are performed under similar working conditions....[29 USC 206, Section 6, paragraph (d)]

The Equal Pay Act of 1963 pertains explicitly to jobs of equal worth. Companies assign pay rates to jobs according to the skill, effort, responsibility, and working conditions required. Skill, effort, responsibility, and working conditions represent **compensable factors**. The U.S. Department of Labor's definitions of these compensable factors are listed in Table 2-4.

How do we judge whether jobs are equal? The case ***EEOC v. Madison Community Unit School District No. 12***[5] sheds light on this important issue. The school district paid female athletic coaches of girls' sports teams less than it paid male athletic coaches of boys' teams. The judge concluded:

The jobs that are compared must be in some sense the same to count as "equal work" under the Equal Pay Act of 1963; and here we come to the main difficulty in applying the Act; whether two jobs are the same depends on how fine a system of job classification the courts will accept. If coaching an athletic team in the Madison, Illinois, school system is considered a single job rather than a [collection] of jobs, the school district violated the Equal Pay Act prima facie by paying female holders of this job less than male holders....If on the other hand coaching the girls' tennis team is considered a different job from coaching the boys' tennis team, and if coaching the girls' volleyball or basketball team is considered a different job (or jobs) from coaching the boys' soccer team, there is no prima facie violation. So the question is how narrow a definition of job the courts should be using in deciding whether the Equal Pay Act is applicable. We can get some guidance from the language of the Act. The act requires that the jobs compared have "similar working conditions," not the same working conditions. This implies that some comparison of different jobs is possible...since the working conditions need not be "equal," the jobs need not be completely identical....Above the lowest rank of employee, every employee has a somewhat different job from every other one, even if the two employees being compared are in the same department. So, if "equal work" and "equal skill, effort, and responsibility" were taken literally, the Act would have a minute domain....

TABLE 2-4 **U.S. Department of Labor Definitions of Compensable Factors**

Factor	Definition
Skill	Experience, training, education, and ability as measured by the performance requirements of a job.
Effort	The amount of mental or physical effort expended in the performance of a job.
Responsibility	The degree of accountability required in the performance of a job.
Working conditions	The physical surroundings and hazards of a job, including dimensions such as inside versus outside work, heat, cold, and poor ventilation.

Source: U.S. Department of Labor, *Equal pay for equal work under the Fair Labor Standards Act* (Washington, DC: U.S. Government Printing Office, December 31, 1971).

The courts have thus had to steer a narrow course. The cases do not require an absolute identity between the jobs, but do require substantial identity.

Pay differentials for equal work are not always illegal. Pay differentials between men and women who are performing equal work are acceptable where

> …such payment is made pursuant to (i) a seniority system; (ii) a merit system; (iii) a system which measures earnings by quantity or quality of production; or (iv) a differential based on any other factor other than sex: Provided, that an employer who is paying a wage rate differential…shall not…reduce the wage rate of any employee. [29 USC 206, Section 6, paragraph (d)]

Civil Rights Act of 1964

The Civil Rights Act of 1964 is a comprehensive piece of legislation. **Title VII** of the Civil Rights Act is the most pertinent to compensation. Legislators designed Title VII to promote equal employment opportunities for underrepresented minorities. According to Title VII:

> It shall be an unlawful employment practice for an employer—(1) to fail or refuse to hire or to discharge any individual, or otherwise to discriminate against any individual with respect to his compensation, terms, conditions, or privileges of employment, because of such individual's race, color, religion, sex, or national origin; or (2) to limit, segregate, or classify his employees or applicants for employment in any way which would deprive or tend to deprive any individual of employment opportunities or otherwise adversely affect his status as an employee, because of such individual's race, color, religion, sex, or national origin. (42 USC 2000e-2, Section 703)

The courts have distinguished between two types of discrimination covered by Title VII: disparate treatment and disparate impact. **Disparate treatment** represents intentional discrimination, occurring whenever employers intentionally treat some workers less favorably than others because of their race, color, sex, national origin, or religion. Applying different standards to determine pay increases for blacks and whites may result in disparate treatment. For example, choosing to award a high-performing African American employee a smaller pay raise than a lower-performing Caucasian employee could be considered disparate treatment.

Disparate impact represents unintentional discrimination. It occurs whenever an employer applies an employment practice to all employees, but the practice leads to unequal treatment of protected employee groups. Awarding pay increases to male and female production workers according to seniority could lead to disparate impact if females had less seniority, on average, than males.

Title VII protects employees who work for all private sector employers; local, state, and federal governments; and educational institutions that employ 15 or more individuals. Title VII also applies to private and public employment agencies, labor organizations, and joint labor management committees controlling apprenticeship and training.

It had become more difficult to sue employers for pay discrimination under Title VII. Title VII imposes a statute of limitation period, typically 180 days, after which employees may file claims of illegal discrimination against employers. In 2007, the U.S. Supreme Court rendered a very strict interpretation as to when the statute of limitations period begins for women to sue their employers for discrimination in pay. In *Ledbetter v. Goodyear Tire & Rubber Co.*,[6] a female employee named Ledbetter sued Goodyear Tire & Rubber Co. after she learned that some male employees with the same job had been paid substantially more than her over a period of several years. Ledbetter claimed that the statute of limitation period began when each discriminatory pay decision was made and communicated to her. She argued that multiple pay decisions were made over the years each time Goodyear endorsed each paycheck, making each paycheck a separate act of illegal pay discrimination. The Supreme Court rejected Ledbetter's allegation that each paycheck (following the initial paycheck when the pay disparity first existed) represented an intentionally discriminatory act by the employer. Instead, any act of discrimination occurred each time pay raise decisions were made. In Ledbetter's case, the court argued that any discriminatory decisions literally occurred years prior to raising her concerns with the EEOC. The later effects of past discrimination do not restart the clock for filing an EEOC charge, making Ledbetter's claim an untimely one. Not all of the judges agreed with this ruling, noting that given pay secrecy policies in most companies many employees would have no idea within 180 days that they had received a lower raise than others. In addition, an initial disparity in pay may be small, leading a woman or minority group member not to make waves in order to try to succeed.

In 2009, the *Ledbetter* court decision was overturned with the passage of the **Lilly Ledbetter Fair Pay Act**, a key initiative in closing the pay gap between men and women. This act restores the law as it was prior to the narrowly decided (5–4) Supreme Court *Ledbetter* decision in 2007. That decision tossed aside long-standing prior law and made it much harder for women and other workers to pursue pay discrimination claims—stating a pay discrimination charge must be filed within 180 days of the employer's initial decision to pay an employee less. The bill restores prior law—providing that a pay discrimination charge must simply be filed within 180 days of a discriminatory paycheck. The **Paycheck Fairness Act** is a second key initiative in closing the pay gap between men and women. This bill strengthens the Equal Pay Act of 1963 by strengthening the remedies available to put sex-based pay discrimination on par with race-based pay discrimination. That is, employers are now required to justify unequal pay by showing that the pay disparity is not sex based, but, rather, job related. This act also prohibits employers from retaliating against employees who share salary information with their coworkers.

BENNETT AMENDMENT   This provision is an amendment to Title VII. The **Bennett Amendment** allows female employees to charge employers with Title VII violations regarding pay only when the employer has violated the Equal Pay Act of 1963. The Bennett Amendment is necessary because lawmakers could not agree on the answers to the following questions:

- Does Title VII incorporate both the Equal Pay Act of 1963's equal pay standard and the four defenses for unequal work [(i) a seniority system; (ii) merit system; (iii) a system which measures earnings by quantity or quality of production; or (iv) a differential based on any other factor other than sex]?
- Does Title VII include only the four exceptions to the Equal Pay Act of 1963 standard?

Some lawmakers believed that Title VII incorporates the equal pay standard (i.e., answering *yes* to the first question and *no* to the second question); however, other lawmakers believed that Title VII does not incorporate the equal pay standard (i.e., answering *no* to the first question and *yes* to the second question). If Title VII did not incorporate the equal pay standard, then employees could raise charges of illegal pay discrimination (on the basis of race, religion, color, sex, or national origin) for unequal jobs. Pay differentials based on different or unequal jobs fit with the foundation for effective compensation systems—internal consistency and market competitiveness, which we will address in Chapters 6 and 7, respectively.

EXECUTIVE ORDER 11246   This executive order extends Title VII standards to companies holding government contracts worth more than $10,000 per year. In addition, **Executive Order 11246** imposes additional requirements on contractors with government contracts worth more than $50,000 per year and 50 or more employees. These companies must develop written plans each year (i.e., **affirmative action** plans). In affirmative action plans, companies specify goals and practices that they will use to avoid or reduce Title VII discrimination over time.

AGE DISCRIMINATION IN EMPLOYMENT ACT OF 1967 (AS AMENDED IN 1978, 1986, AND 1990) Congress passed the **Age Discrimination in Employment Act of 1967 (ADEA)** to protect workers age 40 and older from illegal discrimination. This act provides protection to a large segment of the U.S. population known as the **baby boom generation** or "baby boomers." The baby boom generation was born roughly between 1946 and 1964 and represented a swell in the American population. Some members of the baby boom generation reached age 40 in 1986, and all baby boomers are now over age 40.

A large segment of the population will probably continue to work beyond age 67, which is the retirement age, because many fear that Social Security retirement income (Chapter 11) will not provide adequate support. The U.S. Census Bureau predicts that individuals age 65 and older will increase from about 25 million in 2001 (12.4 percent of the population) to about 77 million (20.3 percent of the population) by 2050.[7] Thus, the ADEA should be extremely relevant for some time to come.

The ADEA established guidelines prohibiting age-related discrimination in employment. Its purpose is "to promote the employment of older persons based on their ability rather than age, to prohibit arbitrary age discrimination in employment, and to help employers and workers find ways of meeting problems arising from the impact of age on employment." The ADEA specifies that it is unlawful for an employer:

(1) to fail or refuse to hire or to discharge any individual or otherwise discriminate against any individual with respect to his compensation, terms, conditions, or privileges of employment, because of such individual's age; (2) to limit, segregate or classify his employees in any way which would deprive or tend to deprive any individual of employment opportunities or otherwise adversely affect his status as an employee, because of such individual's age; or (3) to reduce the wage rate of any employee in order to comply with this act. (29 USC 623, Section 4)

The ADEA applies to employee benefits practices as well:

[A]ny employer must provide that any employee aged 65 or older, and any employee's spouse aged 65 or older, shall be entitled to coverage under any group health plan offered to such employees under the same conditions as any employee, and the spouse of such employee, under age 65. [29 USC 623, Section 4, paragraph (g)(1)]

The ADEA also sets limits on the development and implementation of employers' "early retirement" practices, which many companies use to reduce workforce sizes. Most early retirement programs are offered to employees who are at least 55 years of age. These early retirement programs are permissible when companies offer them to employees on a voluntary basis. Forcing early retirement upon older workers represents age discrimination (*EEOC v. Chrysler*).[8]

The **Older Workers Benefit Protection Act (OWBPA)**[9]—the 1990 amendment to the ADEA—placed additional restrictions on employer benefits practices. When employers require employee contributions toward their benefits, under particular circumstances, employers can require older employees to pay more for health care, disability, or life insurance than younger employees because these benefits generally become more costly with age (e.g., older workers may be more likely to incur serious illnesses, thus, insurance companies may charge employers higher rates to provide coverage to older workers than younger ones).

- An older employee may not be required to pay more for the benefit *as a condition of employment*. Where the premium has increased for an older employee, the employer must offer the employee the option of withdrawing from the benefit plan altogether. The employer can alternatively offer the employee the option of reducing his or her benefit coverage in order to keep his or her premium cost the same.

- An older employee may be offered the *option* of paying—or paying more—for the benefit in order to avoid otherwise justified reductions in coverage. Where the employee does choose to pay more, he or she can be charged no more than the amount that is necessary to maintain full coverage.
- An older employee who chooses to participate in a voluntary plan *can* be required to pay more for the benefit, but only if the employee does not pay a greater percentage of his or her premium cost than younger employees do.

To illustrate the previous point, let's assume that Company A has 3,000 employees, and 25 percent (750 employees) are age 40 or older while 75 percent (2,250 employees) are age 39 or younger. Let's also assume that the annual employee contributions total $120,000 for Company A's workforce. Finally, an analysis of these contributions reveals that the older workers paid $84,000, accounting for 70 percent of these contributions (70% × $120,000). The younger workers paid $36,000, accounting for only 30 percent (30% × $120,000). The older workers paid disproportionately more than the younger workers.

- Older workers: 25 percent of the workforce paid 70 percent of the total contributions.
- Younger workers: 75 percent of the workforce paid 30 percent of the total contributions.

In addition, employers can legally reduce the coverage of older workers for benefits that may become more costly as they further age. Benefits that may meet this criterion include disability insurance, health insurance, and life insurance. The employer may reduce the coverage of these benefits *only if* the costs for providing insurance to them are significantly greater than the cost for younger workers and not simply assumed to be more expensive. When costs differ significantly, the employer may reduce the benefit for older workers only to the point where it is paying just as much per older worker (with lower coverage) as it is for younger workers (with higher coverage). This practice is referred to as the **equal benefit or equal cost principle**.

The ADEA covers private employers with 20 or more employees, labor unions with 25 or more members, and employment agencies. The EEOC enforces this act.

EXECUTIVE ORDER 11141 This executive order extends ADEA coverage to federal contractors.

CIVIL RIGHTS ACT OF 1991 Congress enacted the **Civil Rights Act of 1991** to overturn several Supreme Court rulings. The reversal of the ***Atonio v. Wards Cove Packing Co***. court decision is perhaps the most noteworthy.[10] The Supreme Court ruled that plaintiffs (employees) must indicate which employment practice created disparate impact and demonstrate how the employment practice created disparate impact. Since the passage of the Civil Rights Act of 1991, employers must show that the challenged employment practice is a business necessity. Thus, the Civil Rights Act of 1991 shifted the burden of proof from employees to employers.

Two additional sections of the Civil Rights Act of 1991 apply to compensation practice. The first feature pertains to seniority systems. As we will discuss in Chapter 3, public sector employers make employment decisions based on employees' seniority. For example, public sector employers award more vacation days to employees with higher seniority than to employees with lower seniority. The Civil Rights Act of 1991 overturned the Supreme Court's decision in ***Lorance v. AT&T Technologies***,[11] which allowed employees to challenge the use of seniority systems only within 180 days from the system's implementation date. Employees may now file suits claiming discrimination either when the system is implemented or whenever the system negatively affects them.

A second development addresses the geographic scope of federal job discrimination. Prior to the Civil Rights Act of 1991, the U.S. Supreme Court (***Boureslan v. Aramco***)[12] ruled that federal job discrimination laws do not apply to U.S. citizens working for U.S. companies in foreign countries. Since the act's passage, U.S. citizens working overseas may file suit against U.S. businesses for discriminatory employment practices.

The Civil Rights Act of 1991 provides coverage to the same groups protected under the Civil Rights Act of 1964. The 1991 act also extends coverage to Senate employees and political appointees of the federal government's executive branch. The EEOC enforces the Civil Rights Act of 1991. Since the passage of the 1991 act, the EEOC helps employers avoid discriminatory employment practices through the Technical Assistance Training Institute.

Accommodating Disabilities and Family Needs

Congress enacted the Pregnancy Discrimination Act of 1978, the Americans with Disabilities Act of 1990, and the Family and Medical Leave Act of 1993 to accommodate employees with disabilities and pressing family needs. These laws protect a significant number of employees: In 2000, approximately 68 percent of employed women were responsible for children under the age of 18. The preamble to the Americans with Disabilities Act states that it covers 43 million Americans. Many employees will benefit from the Family and Medical Leave Act if they need substantial time away from work to care for newborns or elderly family members. Two trends explain this need. First, many elderly and seriously ill parents of the employed baby boom generation depend on their children. Second, both husbands and wives work full-time jobs now more than ever before, necessitating extended leave to care for newborns or for children who become ill.

PREGNANCY DISCRIMINATION ACT OF 1978 The **Pregnancy Discrimination Act of 1978 (PDA)** is an amendment to Title VII of the Civil Rights Act of 1964. The PDA prohibits disparate impact discrimination against pregnant women for all employment practices. Employers must not treat pregnancy less favorably than other medical conditions covered under employee benefits plans. In addition, employers must treat pregnancy and childbirth the same way they treat other causes of disability. Furthermore, the PDA protects the rights of women who take leave for pregnancy-related reasons. The protected rights include:

- Credit for previous service
- Accrued retirement benefits
- Accumulated seniority

AMERICANS WITH DISABILITIES ACT OF 1990 The **Americans with Disabilities Act of 1990 (ADA)** prohibits discrimination against individuals with mental or physical disabilities within and outside employment settings, including public services and transportation, public accommodations, and employment. It applies to all employers with 15 or more employees, and the EEOC is the enforcement agency. In employment contexts, the ADA:

> [P]rohibits covered employers from discriminating against a "qualified individual with a disability" in regard to job applications, hiring, advancement, discharge, compensation, training or other terms, conditions, or privileges of employment. Employers are required to make "reasonable accommodations" to the known physical or mental limitations of an otherwise qualified individual with a disability unless to do so would impose an "undue hardship."[13]

Title I of the ADA requires that employers provide "reasonable accommodation" to disabled employees. Reasonable accommodation may include such efforts as making existing facilities readily accessible, restructuring job, and modifying work schedules. Every "qualified individual with a disability" is entitled to reasonable accommodation. A qualified individual with a disability, however, must be able to perform the "essential functions" of the job in question. Essential functions are those job duties that are critical to the job.

Let's apply these principles to an example. Producing printed memoranda is a key activity of a clerical worker's job. Most employees manually keyboard the information by using a word processing program to generate written text. In this case, the essential function is producing memoranda using word processing software; however, manual input represents only one method to enter information. Information input based on a voice recognition input device is an alternative method for entering information. If a clerk develops crippling arthritis, the ADA may require that the employer make reasonable accommodation by providing him or her with a voice-recognition input device.

On September 25, 2008, former president George W. Bush signed the Americans with Disabilities Act Amendments Act of 2008, making important changes to the definition of the term *disability*. These changes make it easier for an individual seeking protection under the ADA to establish that he or she has a disability within the meaning of the ADA.

The act retains the ADA's basic definition of *disability* as an impairment that substantially limits one or more major life activities, a record of such an impairment, or being regarded as having such an impairment. However, it changes the way that these statutory terms should be interpreted:

- Expands the definition of "major life activities" by including two non-exhaustive lists:
- The first list includes many activities that the EEOC has recognized (e.g., walking) as well as activities that EEOC has not specifically recognized (e.g., reading, bending, and communicating);
- The second list includes major bodily functions (e.g., "functions of the immune system, normal cell growth, digestive, bowel, bladder, neurological, brain, respiratory, circulatory, endocrine, and reproductive functions");
- States that mitigating measures other than "ordinary eyeglasses or contact lenses" shall not be considered in assessing whether an individual has a disability;
- Clarifies that an impairment that is episodic or in remission is a disability if it would substantially limit a major life activity when active.

FAMILY AND MEDICAL LEAVE ACT OF 1993   The **Family and Medical Leave Act of 1993 (FMLA)** aimed to provide employees with job protection in cases of family or medical emergency. The basic thrust of the act is guaranteed leave, and a key element of that guarantee is the right of the employee to return to either the position he or she left when the leave began or to an equivalent position with the same benefits, pay, and other terms and conditions of employment. We will discuss this act in greater detail in Chapter 11 because compensation professionals treat such leave as a legally required benefit.

Prevailing Wage Laws

DAVIS–BACON ACT OF 1931   The **Davis–Bacon Act of 1931** establishes employment standards for construction contractors holding federal government contracts valued at more than $2,000. Covered contracts include highway building, dredging, demolition, and cleaning, as well as painting and decorating public buildings. This act applies to laborers and mechanics who are employed on site. Contractors must pay wages at least equal to the prevailing wage in the local area. The U.S. secretary of labor determines prevailing wage rates based on compensation surveys of different areas. In this context, "local" area refers to the general location where work is performed. Cities and counties represent local areas. The "prevailing wage" is the typical hourly wage paid to more than 50 percent of all laborers and mechanics employed in the local area. The act also requires that contractors offer fringe benefits that are equal in scope and value to fringe compensation that prevails in the local area.

WALSH–HEALEY PUBLIC CONTRACTS ACT OF 1936   This act covers contractors and manufacturers who sell supplies, materials, and equipment to the federal government. Its coverage is more extensive than is the Davis–Bacon Act. The **Walsh–Healey Public Contracts Act of 1936** applies to both construction and nonconstruction activities. In addition, this act covers all of the contractors' employees except office, supervisory, custodial, and maintenance workers who do any work in preparation for the performance of the contract. The minimum contract amount that qualifies for coverage is $10,000 rather than the $2,000 amount under the Davis–Bacon Act of 1931.

The Walsh–Healey Act of 1936 mandates that contractors with federal contracts meet guidelines regarding wages and hours, child labor, convict labor, and hazardous working conditions. Contractors must observe the minimum wage and overtime provisions of the FLSA. In addition, this act prohibits the employment of individuals younger than 16 as well as convicted criminals. Furthermore, this act prohibits contractors from exposing workers to any conditions that violate the **Occupational Safety and Health Act of 1970**. This act was passed to ensure safe and healthful working conditions for working men and women by authorizing enforcement of the standards under the act.

LAWS THAT GUIDE DISCRETIONARY EMPLOYEE BENEFITS

Many laws guide discretionary employee benefits practices. Here we review only the major laws on this topic: the Internal Revenue Code (IRC), the Employee Retirement Income Security Act of 1974 (ERISA), the Consolidated Omnibus Budget Reconciliation Act of 1985 (COBRA), the Health Insurance Portability and Accountability Act of 1996, the Pension Protection Act of 2006, key antidiscrimination laws, and the Fair Labor Standards Act.

Internal Revenue Code

The **Internal Revenue Code (IRC)** is the set of regulations pertaining to taxation in the United States (e.g., sales tax, company [employer] income tax, individual [employee] income tax, and property tax). Taxes represent the main source of revenue to fund federal, state, and local government programs. The Internal Revenue Service (IRS) is the government agency that develops and implements the IRC and levies penalties against companies and individuals who violate the IRC. Since 1916, the federal government has encouraged employers to provide retirement benefits to employees with tax breaks or deductions. In other words, the government allowed employers to exclude retirement plan payments from their income subject to taxation. This "break" reduced the amount of a company's required tax payments. In general, the larger the contributions to retirement plans, the greater the reduction in the amount of taxes owed to the government.

The IRC contains multiple regulations for legally required and discretionary benefits. For example, the **Federal Insurance Contributions Act (FICA)** taxes employees and employers to finance the Social Security Old-Age, Survivor and Disability Insurance program (OASDI). Unemployment insurance benefits are financed by federal and, sometimes, state taxes levied on employers. Federal tax is levied on employers under the **Federal Unemployment Tax Act (FUTA)**.

Since the inception of the IRC, the federal government also contains incentives for employers who offer discretionary benefits and for employees as recipients of these benefits. An employee may deduct the cost of benefits from annual income, thereby reducing tax liability. Employers may also deduct the cost of benefits from their annual income as a business or trade expense when the cost is an ordinary and necessary expense of the company's trade or business. For example, the costs of electricity for a factory and the purchase of raw materials to manufacture products are ordinary and necessary expenses. Payroll costs and benefits costs also qualify as ordinary and necessary business expenses. Without pay and benefits, companies would not be able to recruit and retain competent employees who are crucial for business operations. In addition, companies can deduct these costs only during the current tax period, so the benefits costs incurred during 2014 may be deducted only for the 2014 tax year.

The tax deductibility of benefits costs also requires that employers meet additional requirements set forth by the Employee Retirement Income Security Act of 1974. Benefits qualify for tax deductibility when they meet nondiscrimination rules. **Nondiscrimination rules** prohibit employers from giving preferential treatment to key employees and highly compensated employees, for example, by contributing 10 percent of annual salary to their retirement accounts, but only 5 percent to other employees. The IRS defines the meanings of these employee groups. The term **key employee** means any employee who at any time during the year is:

- A 5 percent owner of the employer,
- A 1 percent owner of the employer having an annual compensation from the employer of more than $165,000, or
- An officer of the employer having an annual compensation greater than $165,000 in 2013 (indexed for inflation in increments of $5,000 beginning in 2003).

U.S. Treasury Regulations define the term *officer* used in this definition of key employees:[14]

Generally, the term officer means an administrative executive who is in regular and continued service. The term officer implies continuity of service and excludes those employed for a special and single transaction. An employee who merely has the title of an officer but not the authority of an officer is not considered an officer for purposes of the key employee test. Similarly, an employee who does not have the title of an officer but has the authority of an officer is an officer for purposes of the key employee test. In the case of one or more employers treated as a single employer under sections 414(b), (c), or (m), whether or not an individual is an officer shall be determined based upon his responsibilities with respect to the employer or employers for which he is directly employed, and not with respect to the controlled group of corporations, employers under common control or affiliated service group.

A partner of a partnership will not be treated as an officer for purposes of the key employee test merely because he or she owns a capital or profits interest in the partnership, exercises voting rights as a partner, and may, for limited purposes, be authorized and does in fact act as an agent of the partnership.

The IRS defines a **highly compensated employee** as one of the following during the current or preceding year:

- A 5 percent owner at any time during the year or the preceding year.
- For the preceding year had compensation from the employer in excess of $115,000 in 2013.
- If the employer elects the application of this clause for a plan year, was in the top-paid group of employees for the preceding year.

Employee Retirement Income Security Act of 1974 (ERISA)

ERISA was established to regulate the implementation of various employee benefits programs, including medical, life, and disability programs, as well as pension programs. The essence of ERISA is protection of employee benefits rights.

ERISA addresses matters of employers' reporting and disclosure duties, funding of benefits, the fiduciary responsibilities for these plans, and vesting rights. Companies must provide their employees with straightforward descriptions of their employee benefit plans, updates when substantive changes to the plan are implemented, annual synopses on the financing and operation of the plans, and advance notification if the company intends to terminate the benefits plan. The funding requirement mandates that companies meet strict guidelines to ensure having sufficient funds when employees reach retirement. Similarly, the fiduciary responsibilities require that companies not engage in transactions with parties having interests adverse to those of the recipients of the plan and not deal with the income or assets of the employee benefits plan in the company's own interests.

Vesting refers to an employee's acquisition of nonforfeitable rights to an employer's contributions to fund pension benefits. Employees often must be 100 percent vested between 3 and 6 years of service, depending on the vesting schedule. One hundred percent vested means that an employee cannot lose the pension benefits even if the employee leaves the job before retirement; employees are entitled to every dollar contributed on their behalf by the employer.

There are two minimum criteria for eligibility under ERISA. First, employees must be allowed to participate in a pension plan after they reach age 21. Second, employees must have completed 1 year of service based on at least 1,000 hours of work. There is no maximum age limit for eligibility.

Since the passage of ERISA, there have been a number of amendments to this act. The impetus for these amendments has been the ever-changing laws relating to the tax treatment of employees' contributions to pension plans. For example, the tax laws offer employees the opportunity to deduct a limited amount of their gross income (i.e., income before any federal, state, or local taxes are assessed) for investment in a pension plan. Such deductions reduce the taxable gross pay amount on which taxes are assessed, thereby clearly lowering employees' tax burdens. The amendments are quite complex and technical, requiring familiarity with the IRC. The key amendments include the Tax Equity and Fiscal Responsibility Act of 1982, Deficit Reduction Act of 1984, the Tax Reform Act of 1986, and the **Economic Growth and Tax Relief Reconciliation Act of 2001**.

Consolidated Omnibus Budget Reconciliation Act of 1985 (COBRA)

The **Consolidated Omnibus Budget Reconciliation Act of 1985 (COBRA)** was enacted to provide employees with the opportunity to continue receiving their employer-sponsored medical care insurance temporarily under their employer's plan if their coverage otherwise would cease because of termination, layoff, or other change in employment status. COBRA applies to a wide variety of employers, with exemptions available only for companies that normally employ fewer than 20 workers, church plans, and plans maintained by the U.S. government.

Under COBRA, individuals may continue their coverage, as well as coverage for their spouses and dependents, for up to 18 months. Coverage may extend for up to 36 months for spouses and dependents facing a loss of employer-provided coverage because of an employee's death, a divorce or legal separation, or certain other qualifying events, which include employee termination, retirement, and layoff. Table 2-5 displays the maximum continuation period for particular qualifying events.

Companies are permitted to charge COBRA beneficiaries a premium for continuation coverage of up to 102 percent of the cost of the coverage to the plan. The 2 percent markup reflects a charge for administering COBRA. Employers that violate the COBRA requirements are subject

TABLE 2-5 COBRA Continuation Requirements

Qualifying Events	Maximum Continuation Period
Employee	
a. Termination of employment for any reason, including termination of disability benefits and layoff, except for gross misconduct.	18 months[a]
b. Loss of eligibility due to reduction in work hours.	18 months
c. Determination by the Social Security Administration (SSA) of disability that existed at time of qualifying event.	18 months
Dependent	
a. Loss of dependent child status.	36 months
b. Employee's death, divorce, or legal separation.	36 months
Spouse (entitled to Medicare)	36 months

[a]This 18-month period may be extended for all qualified beneficiaries if certain conditions are met in cases where a qualified beneficiary is determined to be disabled for purposes of COBRA.

to an excise tax per affected employee for each day that the violation continues. In addition, plan administrators who fail to provide required COBRA notices to employees may be personally liable for a civil penalty for each day the notice is not provided.

Continuation of Coverage under COBRA

The following information applies to health, vision, and dental coverage only. For information on life insurance when employment terminates, refer to Chapter 9 for other areas that describe life coverage.

COBRA was signed into law on April 7, 1986. Under COBRA, the employer must provide covered members and their dependents who would lose coverage under the plan the option to continue coverage. The mandate is restricted to certain conditions under which coverage is lost, and the election to continue must be made within a specified election period. COBRA went into effect for members and their dependents on July 1, 1986.

Health Insurance Portability and Accountability Act of 1996 (HIPAA)

This act contains four main provisions. The first provision is intended to guarantee that employees and their dependents that leave their employer's group health plan will have ready access to coverage under a subsequent employer's health plan, regardless of their health or claims experience. The second provision sets limits on the length of time that health plans and health insurance issuers may impose preexisting health conditions and identify conditions to which no preexisting condition may apply. A preexisting health condition generally refers to a medical condition for which a diagnosis was made or treatment given prior to enrolling in a health insurance plan. The third provision counts periods of continuous coverage under another form of comprehensive health coverage toward a preexisting condition limit. In other words, time covered under a previous health insurance plan reduces the preexisting condition requirement imposed by a new health insurance company. The fourth provision protects the transfer, disclosure, and use of health care information.

Pension Protection Act of 2006

The Pension Protection Act is designed to strengthen protections for employees' company-sponsored retirement plans in at least two ways. The first consideration refers to **defined benefit plans** and the second refers to **defined contribution plans**. Defined benefit plans guarantee monthly income for the duration of a retiree's life, which employers typically fund in full. Defined contribution plans are savings plans that employees may contribute to for use during their retirement. First, this law should strengthen the financial condition of the Pension Benefit Guaranty Corporation (PBGC) by requiring that private sector companies that underfund their defined benefit plans pay substantially higher premiums (i.e., cost to provide insurance protection) to insure retirement benefits. After all, experience tells us there is a greater likelihood that the PBGC has had to take over highly underfunded defined benefit plans. The increase in underfunded plans poses a greater risk to the financial solvency of the PBGC. In other words, think of the PBGC as an automobile insurance company and young drivers with automobile insurance as companies with underfunded defined benefit plans. An automobile insurance company charges higher premiums to drivers under age 25 because years of data show that young drivers are more likely to get into multiple serious accidents than older drivers. After getting into a car accident, a person files a claim to the insurance company to pay for the costs of repairs. Of course, repair costs for serious accidents will be much more expensive than for minor accidents. So, insurance companies charge higher premiums to these drivers because they are more likely to file claims. Higher premiums will make it easier for insurance companies to stay financially solvent because they anticipated such claims. The Pension Protection Act law also aims to strengthen the PBGC financial condition by making it more difficult for companies to skip making premium payments. Finally, this new law raises the amount that employers can contribute to pension funding with tax advantages, creating an additional incentive to adequately fund pension plans.

Second, the Pension Protection Act makes it easier for employees to participate in such employer-sponsored defined contribution plans as 401(k) plans. Millions of workers who are eligible to participate in their employers' defined contribution plans do not contribute to them. There are a variety of reasons why employees choose not to participate; however, a prominent reason is that most individuals feel they do not have sufficient knowledge about how to choose investment options (e.g., a high-risk mutual fund versus a fixed-rate annuity) that will help them earn sufficient money for retirement. In addition, once employees make the decision to participate in these plans and have been making regular contributions, they are not likely to stop. With these issues in mind, the Pension Protection Act enables companies to enroll their employees automatically in defined contribution plans and provides greater access to professional advice about investing for retirement. In addition, this act requires that companies give multiple investment options to allow employees to select how much risk they are willing to bear. As an aside, risky investments usually have the potential for substantial gains or losses in value. Less risky investments usually have the potential for lower gains or losses. Some companies previously limited investment opportunities to company stock, which exposes employees to substantial investment risk.

Patient Protection and Affordable Care Act of 2010 (PPACA)

The Patient Protection and Affordable Care Act (PPACA), enacted on March 23, 2010, is a comprehensive law that has been in the implementation phase since its passage. The implementation of all provisions will be complete by 2018. This act applies to a multitude of issues surrounding health care in the United States. The federal government documents these features on a dedicated Web site (*www.healthcare.gov*).

PPACA is expected to extend coverage to more people by providing incentives to businesses to offer health insurance or by imposing penalties on businesses that do not provide coverage. This law will also require that individuals without health insurance purchase reasonably priced policies through health insurance exchanges.

Many provisions of the law will have a broad impact on employment-sponsored health insurance plans that do not have grandfathered status. PPACA distinguishes between health plans that existed prior to the March 23, 2010, enactment date and those that come into existence afterward. Individual and group health plans already in existence prior to enactment are referred to as "grandfathered" plans, and new health plans (or plans that have been substantially modified after March 23, 2010) are referred to as "non-grandfathered" plans.

Grandfathered plans could lose this status if at least one of the following modifications were made:

- Changing insurance carriers for individuals (for example, the employer no longer offers insurance coverage through Blue Cross and Blue Shield, which it had offered prior to March 23, 2010, and now offers coverage through Humana Health Care).
- Changing coinsurance amounts. Coinsurance refers to the percentage of covered expenses paid by the insured.
- Increase since March 23, 2010, to fixed-amount copayment where the increase is more than $5 plus the rate of medical inflation or is 15 percentage points higher than medical inflation (whichever is greater). Copayments represent nominal payments an individual makes as a condition of receiving services. Medical inflation is defined in this regulation as the medical care component of the Consumer Price Index for All Urban Consumers.
- Increases since March 23, 2010, to fixed-amount cost-sharing other than copayment (i.e., raising a deductible) that exceed the rate of medical inflation by 15 percentage points. Over a designated period, employees must pay for services (i.e., meet a deductible) that they have to pay before insurance benefits become active.

- Decrease in the overall percentage of costs paid by the employer (i.e., the employer's share of premium costs) by more than 5 percent.
- Elimination of benefits specific to certain health conditions. (Additionally, elimination of a benefit for any necessary element to diagnose or treat a condition is considered for this purpose to be an elimination of benefits, resulting in loss of the plan grandfather status.)
- For plans with no annual or lifetime dollar limits, the addition of an annual or lifetime dollar limit.
- For plans with lifetime dollar limits, but no annual dollar limits, the addition of an annual dollar limit that is lower than the existing lifetime dollar limit.
- For plans with annual dollar limits, a reduction in annual dollar limits.

Reducing or eliminating coverage for one or more "essential benefits" will cause a grandfathered plan to lose this status. Essential health benefits must include items and services within at least the following 10 categories:

1. Ambulatory patient services
2. Emergency services
3. Hospitalization
4. Maternity and newborn care
5. Mental health and substance use disorder services, including behavioral health treatment
6. Prescription drugs
7. Rehabilitative services and devices
8. Laboratory services
9. Preventive and wellness services and chronic disease management
10. Pediatric services, including oral and vision care

In 2015, PPACA began requiring that health plans remove annual dollar limits on essential health benefits as well as eliminate preexisting condition clauses. As we will see in Chapter 10, a preexisting condition is a condition for which medical advice, diagnosis, care, or treatment was received or recommended during a designated period preceding the beginning of health insurance coverage. Previously, health insurance plans could disqualify preexisting conditions for coverage; however, that is no longer legally permissible. Another provision is limits to waiting periods. Earlier, health plans could require that new employees be excluded from participation in health care coverage until reaching a minimum service requirement. Oftentimes, the waiting periods could span several months. PPACA limits waiting periods to no more than 90 days.

A key provision in the act, referred to as the individual mandate, became effective in 2014. According to this mandate, individuals who can afford to purchase health insurance must do so either by participating in an employer-sponsored plan or purchasing health insurance coverage independently; otherwise, they will pay a penalty of $695 or 2½ percent of their income. Without this mandate, many individuals would likely put off purchasing health insurance until they need it, that is, at the onset of serious medical conditions, when premium rates are highest (as compared to purchasing health insurance when healthy). This practice would also cause insurance premiums to rise for those who maintain coverage, including the cost of health insurance premiums to employers: Insurance companies may spread rate increases to protect profits.

CONTEXTUAL INFLUENCES ON THE FEDERAL GOVERNMENT AS AN EMPLOYER

As we discussed previously, federal government employees do not receive protection under Title VII, ADEA, and the Equal Pay Act of 1963. Shortly after the passage of these acts during the 1960s, the president of the United States and Congress enacted executive orders and laws

TABLE 2-6 Executive Orders and Laws Enacted to Protect Federal Government Employees

- **Executive Order 11478** prohibits employment discrimination on the basis of race, color, religion, sex, national origin, handicap, and age (401 *FEP Manual* 4061).
- **Executive Order 11935** prohibits employment of nonresidents in U.S. civil service jobs (401 *FEP Manual* 4121).
- The **Rehabilitation Act** mandates that federal government agencies take affirmative action in providing jobs for individuals with disabilities (401 *FEP Manual* 325).
- The **Vietnam Era Veterans Readjustment Assistance Act** applies the principles of the Rehabilitation Act to veterans with disabilities and veterans of the Vietnam War (401 *FEP Manual* 379).
- The **Government Employee Rights Act of 1991** protects U.S. Senate employees from employment discrimination on the basis of race, color, religion, sex, national origin, age, and disability (401 *FEP Manual* 851).
- The **Family and Medical Leave Act of 1993** grants civil service employees, U.S. Senate employees, and U.S. House of Representatives employees a maximum of 12 weeks unpaid leave in any 12-month period to care for a newborn or a seriously ill family member (401 *FEP Manual* 891).

to prohibit job discrimination and promote equal opportunity in the federal government. These executive orders and laws apply to employees who work within:

- Military service (civilian employees only)
- Executive agencies
- Postal service
- Library of Congress
- Judicial and legislative branches

Table 2-6 contains a summary of these key executive orders and laws. We already discussed the FMLA because it also applies to private sector employers.

LABOR UNIONS AS CONTEXTUAL INFLUENCES

Since the passage of the **National Labor Relations Act of 1935 (NLRA)**, the federal government requires employers to enter into good-faith negotiations with workers over the terms of employment. Workers join unions to influence employment-related decisions, especially when they are dissatisfied with job security, wages, benefits, and supervisory practices.

Since 1954 when union representation was at its highest (28.3 percent of the U.S. labor force), the percentage of U.S. civilian workers in both the public and private sectors represented by unions has declined steadily. In 2012, the percentage of U.S. civilian workers in both the public and private sectors represented by unions declined steadily to a 11.3 percent representation since 1983 when the representation rate was 20.1 percent.[15] The unionization rate of government workers was 35.9 percent, compared with 6.6 percent among private sector employees in 2012. As we will discuss shortly, union representation will probably continue to decline in the future. This decline may be attributed to the reduced influence of unions. We will present reasons for this conclusion later in this section. Nevertheless, 11.3 percent of the U.S. civilian workforce stands for a large number of workers—more than14 million.

NATIONAL LABOR RELATIONS ACT OF 1935 The purpose of this act was to remove barriers to free commerce and to restore equality of bargaining power between employees and employers. Employers denied workers the rights to bargain collectively with them on such issues as wages, work hours, and working conditions. Employees consequently experienced poor working conditions, substandard wage rates, and excessive work hours. Section 1 of the NLRA declares the policy of the United States to protect commerce:

> …by encouraging the practice and procedure of collective bargaining and by protecting the exercise by workers of full freedom of association, self-organization, and designation of representatives of their own choosing for the purpose of negotiating the terms and conditions of employment….

Sections 8(a)(5), 8(d), and 9(a) are key provisions of this act. Section 8(a)(5) provides that it is an unfair labor practice for an employer "…to refuse to bargain collectively with the representatives of his employees subject to the provisions of Section 9(a)."

Section 8(d) defines the phrase "to bargain collectively" as the "performance of the mutual obligation of the employer and the representative of the employees to meet at reasonable times and confer in good faith with respect to wages, hours, and other terms and conditions of employment…."

Section 9(a) declares:

> Representatives designated or selected for the purposes of collective bargaining by the majority of employees in a unit appropriate for such purposes shall be the exclusive representatives of all the employees in such unit for the purposes of collective bargaining in respect to rates of pay, wages, hours of employment, or other conditions of employment….

The National Labor Relations Board (NLRB) oversees the enforcement of the NLRA. The president of the United States appoints members to the NLRB for 5-year terms.

COMPENSATION ISSUES IN COLLECTIVE BARGAINING Union and management negotiations usually center on pay raises and fringe benefits. Unions fought hard for general pay increases and regular COLAs. COLAs, or cost-of-living adjustments, represent automatic pay increases that are based on changes in prices, as recorded by the consumer price index (CPI). COLAs enable workers to maintain their standards of living by adjusting wages for inflation. Union leaders fought hard for these improvements to maintain the memberships' loyalty and support.

Unions generally secured high wages for their members through the early 1980s. In fact, it was not uncommon for union members to earn as much as 30 percent more than their nonunion counterparts. Unions also improved members' employee benefits. The establishment of sound retirement income programs was most noteworthy.

Unions' gains also influenced nonunion companies' compensation practices. Many nonunion companies offered similar compensation to their employees. This phenomenon is known as a **spillover effect** because management of nonunion firms generally offered somewhat higher wages and benefits to reduce the chance that employees would seek union representation.[16]

Unions' influence has declined since the 1980s for three key reasons. First, union companies demonstrated consistently lower profits than nonunion companies.[17] As a result, management has been more reluctant to agree on large pay increases, which represent costs that lead to lower profits. Second, drastic employment cuts have taken place in various industries, including the highly unionized commercial airline, automobile, and steel industries.[18] In the case of automobiles and steel, technological advances and foreign competition have contributed to declines in those industries. Automated work processes in both the automobile and steel industries made many workers' skills obsolete. Moreover, Japanese automobile manufacturers produced higher-quality vehicles than did U.S. automobile manufacturers. Although these vehicles were more expensive, U.S. consumers were willing to pay higher prices in exchange for better quality. Workforces in Japanese automakers are not unionized, which allows them to devote more resources to quality improvement. As a result of the changing business landscape, unions tempered their stance in negotiations with management. Many unions focused more heavily on promoting job security than securing large pay increases. This is known as **concessionary bargaining**. Available data indicate that annual negotiated pay raises declined steadily after 1980. During the 1980s, concessions were most prevalent in small companies, in high-wage companies, and in companies with a small percentage of employees covered by unions. We've more recently begun witnessing some employee groups giving substantially larger concessions to management than ever before. For instance, the union that represents the pilots of Delta Air Lines agreed to substantial cuts in base pay and in future retirement income to help the company avoid dissolution. Substantial cuts like these were not prevalent during the 1980s and would not have been tolerated previously by the unions; however, the dire financial conditions of companies have led unions to give in to such demands in order to keep their members employed with the hope of regaining some of the lost pay and benefits in the future when companies' financial condition improves.

Companies with labor unions often try to avoid instituting mass layoffs whenever possible because of recall features in collective bargaining agreements. In other words, management is expected to rehire most of its laid-off workers when business conditions rebound. However, with the deep recessionary period that began in December 2007 and ended in June 2009, companies are still trying to make permanent cuts to their workforces for substantial labor force savings. For example, the auto sales declines in the United States are said to be the worst since the early 1980s during a deep recessionary period.

In early 2009, in response to this dire situation, Ford Motor Company announced to local union leaders that it will make buyout or early retirement offers to all of its 42,000 U.S. hourly workers. These cuts are part of a series of contract concessions in a tentative agreement reached between the United Auto Workers union and Ford Motor Company's management. In addition, the union agreed to a suspension of cost-of-living pay raises and lump-sum performance bonuses in the remaining 3 years of the recently negotiated collective bargaining agreement.

In 2011, the management of General Motors Corporation argued the need to adopt pay-for-performance programs for its union workforce. Pay-for-performance systems apply to nonunion salaried workers; thus, the union workforce is not being singled out within the company. If the United Auto Workers were to agree to the use of a pay-for-performance program, this change would represent yet another noteworthy concession.

Even more recently, the Teamsters' union pension plan has become critically underfunded. Critical underfunding raises concerns that the plan will not be able to meet all of its future obligations to pay retirees the pension benefits they have earned. As a result, many of the 1,900 companies that employ Teamsters' workers are considering whether to withdraw participation in the plan. Withdrawing from participation in the plan means that lower contributions will be made to fund the plan, which increases the risk of failure. This example adds to many recent instances in which unions' ability to represent the interests of their members is being diminished. Pension plans represent one of the attractive features of joining a labor union, particularly because the prevalence of pension plans (compared to defined contribution plans such as less generous 401(k) savings plans) is much lower in nonunion settings than union settings. As a result, it may be more difficult for the Teamsters' union to increase its membership because it has less to offer.

MARKET INFLUENCES

In competitive labor markets, companies attempt to attract and retain the best individuals for employment partly by offering lucrative wage and benefits packages. Some companies unfortunately are unable to compete on the basis of wage and benefits, as illustrated in the second opening quotation. Indeed, there are differences in wages across industries. These differences are known as **interindustry wage or compensation differentials**. Table 2-7 displays the average weekly earnings in various industries for selected years between 2005

TABLE 2-7 **Average Weekly Earnings by Industry Group, Selected Years 2005–2013**

Industry	2005 ($)	2007 ($)	2011 ($)	2013 ($)[a]
Mining	800	946	1276	1276
Construction	750	794	988	1010
Manufacturing	673	707	969	976
Retail trade	377	380	506	516

[a]2013 figures for January.

Source: U.S. Bureau of Labor Statistics. *Employment Situation, January 2013.* USDL 13-0144. Available: *www.bls.gov*, accessed February 19, 2013.

and 2013. Construction and mining establishments paid the highest wages throughout this period; retail trade and service companies paid the lowest wages.

Interindustry differentials can be attributed to a number of factors, including the industry's product market, the degree of capital intensity, the profitability of the industry, unionization, and gender mix of the workforce.[19] Companies that operate in product markets where there is relatively little competition from other companies tend to pay higher wages because these companies exhibit substantial profits. This phenomenon can be attributed to such factors as higher barriers to entry into the product market and an insignificant influence of foreign competition. Government regulation and extremely expensive equipment represent entry barriers. The U.S. defense industry and the public utilities industry have high entry barriers and no threats from foreign competitors.

Capital intensity (i.e., the extent to which companies' operations are based on the use of large-scale equipment) also explains pay differentials between industries. The amount of average pay varies with the degree of capital intensity. On average, capital-intensive industries (e.g., manufacturing) pay more than industries that are less capital intensive (e.g., retail). Capital-intensive businesses require highly capable employees who have the aptitude to learn how to use complex technology. Service such as retail industries are not capital intensive, and most have the reputation of paying low wages. The operation of service industries depends almost exclusively on employees with relatively common skills rather than on employees with specialized skills to operate such physical equipment as casting machines or robotics.

Furthermore, companies in profitable industries tend to pay higher compensation, on average, than companies in less profitable industries. Employees in profitable industries presumably receive higher pay because their skills and abilities contribute to companies' success and are more productive; however, as more companies have failed to meet financial goals over the past few years, they have struggled with how best to pay for performance.

Following our recent discussion of unionization, highly unionized industries tend to pay higher wages, on average, than do nonunion industries. At the same time, most highly unionized industries (e.g., manufacturing, construction, and mining) are capital intensive, requiring employees with the aptitude to learn and use complex production technology.

Most recently, U.S. companies' practices of outsourcing jobs to people from other countries have had a significant impact on compensation in the United States. Companies typically establish operations in other countries where labor costs are substantially lower than they are in the United States and fewer laws restrict companies' wage setting. Companies traditionally outsourced factory (blue-collar) jobs to Mexico and Southeast Asian countries. U.S. companies are increasingly outsourcing professional (white-collar) jobs to India because the wage levels in India are only about one-fifth as much as in the United States for information technology and financial services workers. U.S. companies often may have the best of both worlds because they pay much less to hire (often) individuals in India who were trained in prestigious U.S. universities.

COMPENSATION IN ACTION

It is critical for HR and compensation professionals to have a working knowledge of legislative imperatives and organizational policies designed to oversee certain aspects of compensation and benefits. Together with the legal department, HR has the responsibility to educate line managers and other decision makers in the organization as to what should and should not be done in working with employees on compensation and benefits issues. While ultimately the administration of compensation and benefits will be the responsibility of HR, line managers must have enough awareness to make informed decisions which will both protect the company from certain liabilities as well as ensure the retention and engagement of employees critical to the success of the organization. The most successful line managers are often quite adept at explaining these nuances and are respected by their employees for their concern with the factors that influence the employee experience.

Action checklist for line managers and HR—understanding and applying the legal landscape

HR takes the lead
- Work with the legal department to conduct training sessions designed to educate line managers on some of the most important legislation that will govern employee-related actions (e.g., FLSA, Civil Rights Acts, ADEA, ADA, and FMLA).

- Conduct an audit to identify certain potential for disparate impact; disparate impact training is conducted to ensure that line managers and other decision makers are aware of some of the pitfalls.
- Give careful consideration to private sector companies that hold government contracts to understand what additional standards may be placed on them because of their relationship with the federal government.
- Provide legal updates to line managers, with legislation changing fairly quickly (particularly in these times). Many law firms provide this type of service via pro bono teleconferences. In-house employment lawyers could also provide these updates.
- Make sure that the legislative necessities create a starting point for establishing company policy and not merely the justification for doing the bare minimum.

Line managers take the lead
- Identify employees who fall into a group addressed specifically by law or company policy (e.g., ADA) which may be a new experience for you to work with as a manager (e.g., in most jobs, you will have more experience working with minority employees than disabled employees).

END OF CHAPTER

MyManagementLab

Go to **mymanagementlab.com** to complete the problems marked with this icon ⭐.

Summary

This chapter provided a discussion of the various contextual influences on compensation practice. These include laws, labor unions, and market forces. These contextual influences pose significant challenges for compensation professionals.

Aspiring compensation professionals must be familiar with the current contextual influences and anticipate impending ones. For example, most companies must adjust in order to accommodate workers with disabilities.

Key Terms

federal constitution   24
federal government   25
state governments   25

local governments   25
legislative branch   25
executive branch   25

executive orders   25
judicial branch   25
Great Depression   25

✪ Discussion Questions

2-1. Identify the contextual influence that you believe will pose the greatest challenge to companies' competitiveness, and identify the contextual influence that will pose the least challenge to companies' competitiveness. Explain your rationale.

2-2. Should the government raise the minimum wage? Explain your answer.

2-3. Do unions make it difficult for companies to attain competitive advantage? Explain your answer.

2-4. Select one of the contextual influences presented in this chapter. Identify a company that has dealt with this influence, and conduct some research on the company's experience. Be prepared to present a summary of the company's experience in class.

2-5. Some people argue that there is too much government intervention, while others say there is not enough. Based on the presentation of laws in this chapter, do you think there is too little or too much government intervention? Explain your answer.

CASE
Exempt or Nonexempt?

✪ *An additional Supplemental Case can be found on MyManagementLab.*

Jane Swift is becoming frustrated with her job as a shift leader at Jones Department Store. She's worked there for 6 months, and the full-time job has turned into more than full time. Several associates have left the store, and as a result, the past several weeks she has worked 45–50 hours each week. She doesn't mind working the extra hours; she is just frustrated because she is not getting paid overtime pay.

She asked the store manager, Amy Kostner, about the overtime pay she was due. Amy informed Jane that shift leaders are part of the management team and are classified as exempt under the Fair Labor Standards Act. The store is not required to pay exempt workers overtime pay.

Jane agrees that she is part of the management team. As a shift leader, Jane runs the floor when she is on duty. One of the assistant managers sets the daily schedule of associates each week, but Jane and other shift leaders assign the associates to various work areas as needed. Depending on store traffic, associates need to be moved from stocking shelves and cleaning to cashiering or assisting customers. When not working on such management responsibilities, the shift leaders generally assume the duties of associates by assisting customers and cashiering. Jane reports that she typically spends only a little more than half of her time performing associate duties.

Shift leaders are also involved in managerial decisions. For example, they often sit in on employment interviews and typically are aware of employee terminations before the employee is fired. They also give feedback about the associates to the assistant managers who write the annual performance appraisals.

Just like a manager, Jane makes a lot of decisions during the course of her shift each day. If there is a dispute on a sale price, Jane searches the weekly sales flyer to determine the correct price. If a customer has a return, Jane reviews the transaction and initials it before the cashier can give a refund. However, she does not have complete autonomy in making decisions. For example, if a return is greater than $50.00, an assistant manager or the store manager needs to approve the refund.

But even though she agrees that she is part of the management team, Jane isn't satisfied with Amy's answer on her question about pay. If she isn't eligible for overtime pay, she thinks that she should be paid more. While she is paid at a higher rate than most of the associates, she is not paid nearly as much as the assistant managers. A pay increase or overtime pay would at least make it worthwhile for her to put in the extra hours.

Questions:

2-6. Why did Amy classify the shift leaders as exempt? Are there any advantages to Jones Department Store to having the shift leaders classified as exempt?

2-7. Do you think that the shift leaders are properly classified as exempt? Why or why not?

2-8. What are some factors that Amy should consider when determining whether shift leaders are exempt or nonexempt?

MyManagementLab

Go to **mymanagementlab.com** for Auto-graded writing questions as well as the following Assisted-graded writing questions:

⭐ **2-9.** How would the compensation system change if the minimum wage provision of the Fair Labor Standards Act of 1938 were repealed?

⭐ **2-10.** Distinguish between disparate treatment and disparate impact in a compensation context.

Endnotes

1. Bennett-Alexander, D. D., & Hartman, L. P. (2007). *Employment Law for Business* (5th ed.). Burr Ridge, IL: McGraw-Hill/Irwin, p. 3.
2. *Aaron v. City of Wichita, Kansas*, 54 F. 3d 652 (10th Cir. 1995), 2 WH Cases 2d 1159 (1995).
3. *Andres v. DuBois*, 888 F. Supp. 213 (D.C. Mass 1995), 2 WH Cases 2d 1297 (1995).
4. S. Rep. No. 176, 88th Congress, 1st Session, 1 (1963).
5. *EEOC v. Madison Community Unit School District No. 12*, 818 F. 2d 577 (7th Cir., 1987).
6. *Ledbetter v. Goodyear Tire & Rubber Co.*, No. 05–1074 (U.S. Supreme Court, May 29, 2007).
7. U.S. Department of Commerce. (2004–2005). *Statistical Abstracts of the United States* (124th ed.), U.S. Department of Census (May 2001). Profile of general demographic statistics, Table DP–1. Available: *www.census.gov*, accessed February 12, 2011.
8. *EEOC v. Chrysler Corp.*, 652 F. Supp. 1523 (D.C. Ohio 1987), 45 FEP Cases 513.

9. Older Workers Benefit Protection Act of 1990, Pub. L. No.PL 101-433.

10. *Atonio v. Wards Cove Packing Co.*, 490 U.S. 642, 49 FEP Cases 1519 (1989).

11. *Lorance v. AT&T Technologies*, 49 FEP Cases 1656 (1989).

12. *Boureslan v. Aramco*, 499 U.S. 244, 55 FEP Cases 449 (1991).

13. Bureau of National Affairs. (1990). Americans with Disabilities Act of 1990: Text and analysis. *Labor Relations Reporter*, Vol. 134, No. 3. Washington, DC: Author.

14. I.R.C. §3121(d); Treas. Reg. §§31.3121(d)-2; 31.3121(d)-1.

15. U.S. Bureau of Labor Statistics. (2013). *Union Members—2012*. USDL 13-0105. Available: *http://www.bls.gov*, accessed February 19, 2013.

16. Solnick, L. (1985). The effect of the blue collar unions on white collar wages and benefits. *Industrial and Labor Relations Review, 38*, pp. 23–35.

17. Blanchflower, D. G., & Freeman, R. B. (1992). Unionism in the United States and other advanced OFCD countries. *Industrial Relations, 31*, pp. 56–79.

18. Kochan, T. R., Katz, H. C., & McKersie, R. B. (1994). *The Transformation of American Industrial Relations*. Ithaca, NY: ILR Press.

19. Osburn, J. (2000). Interindustry wage differentials: Patterns and possible sources. *Monthly Labor Review*, February, pp. 34–46; Krueger, A. B., & Summers, L. H. (1987). Reflections on inter-industry wage structure. In K. Lang & J. S. Leonard (Eds.), *Unemployment and the Structure of the Labor Market*. New York: Basil Blackwell, pp. 14–17.

Where We Are Now:

PART I, SETTING THE STAGE FOR STRATEGIC COMPENSATION explained what compensation is, strategic compensation concepts, compensation professionals' goals, employment laws that influence compensation tactics, and the roles of unions and market forces in influencing compensation practices. Now, we turn to the methods for determining employee pay.

In **PART II, BASES FOR PAY, WE WILL THEREFORE STUDY**

Chapter **3** TRADITIONAL BASES FOR PAY

Chapter **4** INCENTIVE PAY

Chapter **5** PERSON-FOCUSED PAY

3

TRADITIONAL BASES FOR PAY
Seniority and Merit

LEARNING OBJECTIVES

When you finish studying this chapter, you should be able to:

1. Describe seniority and longevity pay practices.
2. List at least three elements of merit pay.
3. Give examples and definitions of performance appraisal methods.
4. Explain at least three ways compensation professionals can strengthen the pay-for-performance link and summarize each one.
5. Discuss three possible limitations of merit pay programs.

For decades, companies have awarded raises to base pay according to employees' seniority or job performance. Many companies, such as IBM, tended to pay employees according to performance, but the system became one of entitlements (i.e., employees expected pay raises regardless of performance). Changes in the global marketplace forced many companies to reconsider their approach to employee compensation. Fierce global competition requires that employees perform their jobs better than ever before to enable companies to offer the best possible products and services at the lowest cost. As a solution, many companies use compensation programs that emphasize rewards according to performance attainment.

In this chapter, we will consider the traditional seniority and longevity approaches to compensating employees. We will then turn our attention to merit pay, which is a widely used form of performance-based pay in U.S. companies. In Chapter 4, we will take up a variety of incentive programs that also reward pay for performance.

SENIORITY AND LONGEVITY PAY

Seniority pay and **longevity pay** systems reward employees with periodic additions to base pay according to employees' length of service in performing their jobs. These pay plans assume that employees become more valuable to companies with time and that valued employees will leave if they do not have a clear idea that their salaries will progress over time.[1] This rationale comes from **human capital theory**,[2] which states that employees' knowledge and skills generate productive capital known as **human capital**. Employees can develop such knowledge and skills from formal education and training, including on-the-job experience. Over time, employees presumably refine existing skills or acquire new ones that enable them to work more productively. Thus, seniority pay rewards employees for acquiring and refining their skills as indexed by seniority.

Historical Overview

A quick look back into U.S. labor relations history can shed light on the adoption of seniority pay in many companies. President Franklin D. Roosevelt advocated policies designed to improve workers' economic status in response to the severely depressed economic conditions that had started in 1929. Congress instituted the National Labor Relations Act (NLRA) in 1935 to protect workers' rights, predicated on a fundamental, but limited, conflict of interest between workers and employers. President Roosevelt and other leaders felt that companies needed to be regulated to establish an appropriate balance of power between the parties. The NLRA established a collective bargaining system nationwide to accommodate employers' and employees' partially conflicting and partially shared goals.

Collective bargaining led to **job control unionism**,[3] in which collective bargaining units negotiate formal contracts with employees and provide quasi-judicial grievance procedures to adjudicate disputes between union members and employers. Union shops establish workers' rights and obligations and participate in describing and delineating jobs. In unionized workplaces, terms of collective bargaining agreements may determine the specific type of seniority system used, and seniority tends to be the deciding factor in nearly all job scheduling, transfer, layoff, compensation, and promotion decisions. Moreover, seniority may become a principal criterion for selecting one employee over another for transfer or promotion. Table 3-1 illustrates the rules for a seniority pay program contained in a collective bargaining agreement between the Board of Trustees of the University of Illinois and Local 698 of the American Federation of State, County, and Municipal Employees. It shows the actual rates for job classification and seniority level.

Employees shall be paid a starting rate equal to 80 percent of the full base rate of the job classification and shall advance to the full base rate as follows:

Number of months worked	Percentage of full base rate
9	85
18	90
27	95
36	100

TABLE 3-1 **Hourly Wage Rates by Seniority Level**

Classification Title	Start ($)	13 Months ($)	25 Months ($)	37 Months ($)	49 Months ($)
Staff Nurse I	19.07	20.19	21.31	22.40	23.49
Nursing Assistant	9.94	10.17	10.53	10.83	11.01
Medical Assistant	14.65	15.40	16.13	16.92	17.83
Medical Technologist	17.66	18.90	20.13	21.38	22.60

Source: Agreement between the Board of Trustees of the University of Illinois and Local 698 of The American Federation of State, County, and Municipal Employees, AFL-CIO.

Political pressures probably drive the prevalence of public sector seniority pay. Seniority-based pay systems essentially provide automatic pay increases. Performance assessments tend to be subjective rather than objective (e.g., production data including dollar volume of sales and units produced and human resource data including accidents and absenteeism) because accurate job performance measurements are very difficult to obtain. In contrast, employees' seniority is easily indexed (because time on the job is a relatively straightforward and concrete concept). Implementing such a system that specifies the amount of pay raise an employee will receive according to his or her seniority is automatic. Politically, "automatic" pay adjustments protect public sector employees from the quirks of election-year politics.[4] In addition, the federal, state, and local governments can avoid direct responsibility for pay raises so employees can receive fair pay without political objections.

Who Participates?

Today, most unionized private sector and public sector organizations continue to base salary on seniority or length of employee service, though the number of these workplaces is steadily declining as described in Chapter 2. The total number of unionized employees in both sectors is quite large. Members of union-bargaining units whose contracts include seniority provisions, usually rank-and-file as well as clerical workers, receive automatic raises based on the number of years they have been with the company. In the public sector (i.e., municipal, state, and federal government organizations), most administrative, professional, and even managerial employees receive such automatic pay raises.

Effectiveness of Seniority Pay Systems

Virtually no systematic research has demonstrated these pay plans' effectiveness nor is there any documentation regarding their prevalence in the private sector. Seniority or longevity pay plans are likely to disappear from for-profit companies in increasingly competitive markets. Such external influences as increased global competition, rapid technological advancement, and skill deficits of new and current members of the workforce necessitate a strategic orientation toward compensation. These influences will probably force companies to establish compensation tactics that reward their employees for learning job-relevant knowledge and skills and for making tangible contributions toward companies' quests for competitive advantage. Seniority pay meets neither goal.

Public sector organizations had until the 1990s faced less pressure to change these systems because they exist to serve the public rather than make profits. For example, the Internal Revenue Service (IRS) is responsible for collecting taxes from U.S. citizens. Paying taxes to the federal government is an obligation of virtually all U.S. citizens. The amount of taxes each citizen pays is based on established tax codes. The IRS is not in the business of finding new customers to pay taxes. It does not compete against any other businesses for taxpayers.

The federal government, however, has now raised questions about the effectiveness of its seniority pay system for white-collar workers—the General Schedule—because most employees receive raises regardless of how well they perform. Questions about the effectiveness of its seniority pay system are based on how the world of work has dramatically changed since the system's inception in 1949. The federal government has extensively considered the strategic importance of moving beyond seniority-based pay by studying the experience of private sector companies, though it has not made noteworthy modifications to its current pay system.[5]

Design of Seniority Pay and Longevity Pay Plans

Although seniority pay and longevity pay are similar, there are some important distinctions between them. The object of seniority pay is to reward job tenure or employees' time as members of a company explicitly through permanent increases to base salary. Employees begin their employment at the starting pay rate established for the particular jobs. At specified time intervals, which can be as short as 3 months and as long as 3 years, employees receive designated pay increases. These

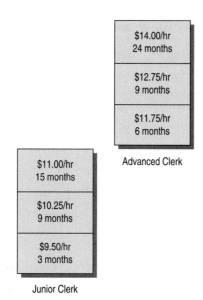

FIGURE 3-1 A Sample Seniority Policy for Junior and Advanced Clerk Jobs

pay increases are permanent additions to current pay levels. Over time, employees will reach the maximum pay rate for their jobs. Companies expect that most employees will earn promotions into higher-paying jobs that have seniority pay schedules. Figure 3-1 illustrates a seniority pay policy for a junior clerk job and an advanced clerk job. Pay rates are associated with seniority. When employees reach the top pay rate for the junior clerk position, they are presumably qualified to assume the duties of the advanced clerk position.

Longevity pay rewards employees who have reached pay grade maximums and who are not likely to move into higher grades. State and local governments often use longevity pay as an incentive to reduce employee turnover and to reward employees for continuous years of service. Longevity pay may take the form of a percentage of base pay, a flat dollar amount, or a special step increase based on the number of years the employee has spent with the organization.[6]

Federal employees are subject to longevity pay via the **General Schedule (GS)**, which is shown in Table 3-2. The General Schedule classifies federal government jobs into 15 classifications (GS-1 through GS-15) based on such factors as skill, education, and experience levels. In addition, jobs that require high levels of specialized education (e.g., a physicist), influence public policy significantly (e.g., law judges), or require executive decision making are classified in separate categories: Senior Level (SL), Scientific and Professional (SP) positions, and the Senior Executive Service (SES). The government typically increases all pay amounts annually to adjust for inflation; however, President Barack Obama instituted a pay freeze for most federal employees since 2010 because of poor economic conditions. The 2013 rates displayed in Table 3-2 were instituted in 2010.

Employees are eligible for 10 within-grade step pay increases. At present, it takes employees 18 years to progress from Step 1 to Step 10. The waiting periods within steps are:

- Steps 1–3: 1 year
- Steps 4–6: 2 years
- Steps 7–9: 3 years

The aging of the baby boom generation may make companies' use of seniority or longevity pay infeasible. Most individuals in the baby boom generation are currently in the workforce, and only a small segment of them are presently approaching retirement age. Companies that use seniority plans are likely to find the costs burdensome, particularly because many baby boom employees are delaying the start of retirement out of financial necessity.

TABLE 3-2 **Salary Table 2013-GS (Annual Rates by Grade and Step)**

Grade	Step 1	Step 2	Step 3	Step 4	Step 5	Step 6	Step 7	Step 8	Step 9	Step 10
1	17,803	18,398	18,990	19,579	20,171	20,519	21,104	21,694	21,717	22,269
2	20,017	20,493	21,155	21,717	21,961	22,607	23,253	23,899	24,545	25,191
3	21,840	22,568	23,296	24,024	24,752	25,480	26,208	26,936	27,664	28,392
4	24,518	25,335	26,152	26,969	27,786	28,603	29,420	30,237	31,054	31,871
5	27,431	28,345	29,259	30,173	31,087	32,001	32,915	33,829	34,743	35,657
6	30,577	31,596	32,615	33,634	34,653	35,672	36,691	37,710	38,729	39,748
7	33,979	35,112	36,245	37,378	38,511	39,644	40,777	41,910	43,043	44,176
8	37,631	38,885	40,139	41,393	42,647	43,901	45,155	46,409	47,663	48,917
9	41,563	42,948	44,333	45,718	47,103	48,488	49,873	51,258	52,643	54,028
10	45,771	47,297	48,823	50,349	51,875	53,401	54,927	56,453	57,979	59,505
11	50,287	51,963	53,639	55,315	56,991	58,667	60,343	62,019	63,695	65,371
12	60,274	62,283	64,292	66,301	68,310	70,319	72,328	74,337	76,346	78,355
13	71,674	74,063	76,452	78,841	81,230	83,619	86,008	88,397	90,786	93,175
14	84,697	87,520	90,343	93,166	95,989	98,812	101,635	104,458	107,281	110,104
15	99,628	102,949	106,270	109,591	112,912	116,233	119,554	122,875	126,196	129,517

Source: U.S. Office of Personnel Management. Available: *www.opm.gov*, accessed August 13, 2013.

Advantages of Seniority Pay

Seniority pay offers a number of advantages to both employees and employers. Employees are likely to perceive they are treated fairly because they earn pay increases according to seniority, which is an objective standard. Seniority stands in contrast to subjective standards based on supervisory judgment. The inherent objectivity of seniority pay systems should lead to greater cooperation among coworkers.

Seniority pay offers two key advantages to employers. First, seniority pay facilitates the administration of pay programs. Pay increase amounts are set in advance, and employers award raises according to a pay schedule, much like the federal government's GS. A second advantage is that employers are less likely to offend some employees by showing favoritism to others because seniority is an objective basis for making awards. The absence of favoritism should enable supervisors and managers effectively to motivate employees to perform their jobs.

Fitting Seniority Pay with Competitive Strategies

Seniority pay does not fit well with the imperatives of competitive strategies because employees can count on receiving the same pay raises for average and exemplary performance, and this fact represents the greatest disadvantage of seniority pay systems. Employees who make significant contributions in the workplace receive the same pay increases as coworkers who make modest contributions. In addition, employees receive pay raises without regard to whether companies are meeting their competitive objectives. Employees clearly do not have any incentives to actively improve their skills or to take risks on the job because they receive pay raises regardless of any initiative they show.

So, in light of increased external pressures on companies to promote productivity and product quality, will seniority or longevity pay be gradually phased out? With the exception of companies that are shielded from competitive pressures (e.g., public utilities), it is likely that companies that intend to remain competitive will set aside seniority pay practices. Although seniority pay plans reflect employees' increased worth, they measure such contributions indirectly rather than based on tangible contributions or the successful acquisition of job-related knowledge or skills. Now more than ever, companies need to be accountable to shareholders, which will require direct measurement of employee job performance.

To illustrate the incompatibility of seniority pay structures with the attainment of competitive strategy further, Toyota, a manufacturer of automobiles, abandoned its seniority-based wage system for a performance-based pay system. Traditional Japanese companies defined *seniority* as employee age. Despite Toyota's worldwide reputation as a manufacturer of high-quality automobiles, company management continually adopts employment practices that encourage even better-quality products. Performance-based pay fits with Toyota's mission.

MERIT PAY

Merit pay programs assume that employees' compensation over time should be determined, at least in part, by differences in job performance.[7] Employees earn permanent merit increases based on their performance. The increases reward excellent effort or results, motivate future performance, and help employers retain valued employees. Merit increases are usually expressed as a percentage of hourly wages for nonexempt employees and as a percentage of annual salaries for exempt employees. In 2013, employees earned average merit increases of 2.8 percent. The rate varied according to the level of employee performance. The highest performers earned 4.6 percent to base pay, average performers earned 2.6 percent, and the lowest performers earned 0.2 percent.[8]

Who Participates?

Merit pay is one of the most commonly used compensation methods in the United States. Various small-scale surveys of no more than a few thousand companies, conducted by compensation consulting firms and professional associations, demonstrate that merit pay plans are firmly entrenched within U.S. business. Its popularity may result from the fact that merit pay fits well with U.S. cultural ideals that reward individual achievement.[9] Merit pay programs occur most often in the private "for-profit" sector of the economy rather than in such public sector organizations as local and state governments.[10]

Exploring the Elements of Merit Pay

Managers rely on objective as well as subjective performance indicators to determine whether an employee will receive a merit increase and the amount of increase warranted. As a rule, supervisors give merit increases to employees based on subjective appraisal of employees' performance.[11] Supervisors periodically review individual employee performance to evaluate how well each worker is accomplishing assigned duties relative to established standards and goals. Thus, as we will discuss later in this chapter, accurate performance appraisals are key to effective merit pay programs.

For merit pay programs to succeed, employees must know that their efforts in meeting production quotas or quality standards will lead to pay raises. Job requirements must be realistic, and employees must have the skills and abilities to meet job goals. Moreover, employees must perceive a strong relationship between attaining performance standards and receiving pay increases.

Furthermore, companies that use merit programs must ensure that the funds needed to fulfill these promises to compensate employees are available. For now, we assume that adequate funding for merit pay programs is in place. We will address the ramifications of insufficient budgets for funding merit pay programs in Chapter 8.

Finally, companies should make adjustments to base pay according to changes in the cost of living or inflation before awarding merit pay raises. Merit pay raises should always reward employee performance rather than represent adjustments for inflation. Inflation represents rises in the cost of consumer goods and services (e.g., food and health care) that boost the overall cost of living. Over time, inflation erodes the purchasing power of the dollar. You've no doubt heard the comment, "It's harder to stretch a dollar these days." Employees are concerned about how well merit increases raise purchasing power. Compensation professionals attempt to minimize negative inflationary effects by making permanent increases to base pay known as cost-of-living adjustments. For now, let's assume that inflation is not an issue. (As an aside, this principle also applies to seniority pay. Pay increases should reflect additional seniority after making specific adjustments for inflation.)

Although fairly common, merit pay systems are not appropriate for all companies. Compensation professionals should consider two factors—commitment from top management and the design of jobs—before endorsing the use of merit pay systems. Top management must be willing to reward employees' job performances with meaningful pay differentials that match employee performance differentials. Companies ideally should grant sufficiently large pay increases to reward employees for exemplary job performance and to encourage similar expectations about future good work.

The amount of a merit pay increase should reflect prior job performance levels and motivate employees toward striving for exemplary performance. The pay raise amount should be meaningful to employees. The concept of **just-meaningful pay increase** refers to the minimum pay increase that employees will see as making a meaningful change in compensation.[12] The basic premise of this concept is that a trivial pay increase for average or better employees is not likely to reinforce their performance or to motivate enhanced future performance. In addition to top management's commitment to merit pay programs, HR professionals must design jobs explicitly enough that employees' performance can be measured accurately. Merit programs are most appropriate when employees have control over their performances and when conditions outside employees' control do not substantially affect their performance. Conditions beyond employees' control that are likely to limit job performance vary by the type of job. For sales professionals, recessionary economic spells generally lead consumers to limit spending on new purchases because they anticipate the possibility of layoffs. Sales professionals certainly do not create recessionary periods nor can they allay consumers' fears about the future. For production workers, regular equipment breakdowns will lead to lower output.

Furthermore, there must be explicit performance standards that specify the procedures or outcomes against which employees' job performance can be clearly evaluated. At Pratt & Whitney, HR professionals and employees worked together to rewrite job descriptions. The purpose was to define and put into writing the major duties of a job and to specify written performance standards for each duty to ensure that the job requirements provided a useful measurement standard for evaluation. The main performance standards included such factors as quality, quantity, and timeliness of work.

Table 3-3 displays a job description for a Human Resources Assistant in the Department of the Army. The description lists the activities the jobholder performs and qualifications necessary to perform the job at an acceptable level. For instance, a successful candidate must demonstrate knowledge of health care benefits offered in the Department of the Army.

TABLE 3-3 **Human Resources Assistant**

Job: Human Resources Assistant
Department: Department of the Army
Agency: Army National Guard Units

JOB SUMMARY:

This position is located in Army Aviation, San Antonio Army Aviation Support Facility (SAAASF), San Antonio, TX. The purpose of this position is to provide services and basic information regarding human resources issues to technicians and Active Guard Reserves (AGRs) who are remote from the Human Resource Office (HRO). The primary function of this position is to provide support and clerical assistance on human resource matters to commanders, line supervisors, managers, and technicians at the base or unit organizational level and to coordinate such matters with the HRO.

TABLE 3-3 (Continued)

KEY REQUIREMENTS DUTIES:

As a **Human Resources Assistant** with the **Texas Army National Guard (ARNG)**, your duties will include, but will not be limited to:

- Processes human resources transactions related to recruitment, placement, classification, employee and labor relations, benefits, entitlements, training, and incentive awards. These duties require technical understanding and knowledge of numerous human resources guidelines, instructions, directives, procedures, policies and precedent situations which involve considering the interrelationship and impact that various human resources actions in different functional areas may have on non-dual and dual status technicians or Active Guard Reserve (AGR) personnel. Participates in the annual federal wage grade survey, when requested.

- Conducts initial in processing and orientation of new employees. Explains eligibility for leave, health benefits, life insurance as well as local organizational/base policies. Conducts exit interviews and explains entitlements such as retirement plans and refunds, continuation of insurance benefits, etc. Makes arrangements for eligible separating employees to receive retirement counseling, explanation of severance pay entitlements and other appropriate benefits or services.

- Obtains vacancy requirements from functional area supervisors, prepares drafts and requests for vacancy announcements. Forwards request to the HRO for final approval. Upon receipt of the announcement, incumbent makes distribution to units/sections. Furnishes information to employees or job applicants regarding vacancies and mandatory requirements for competitive/excepted status positions. Forwards applications to HRO for rating, and distributes certificates of eligibility to selecting supervisors, coordinating selections/non-selections with HRO as appropriate.

- Assists managers and supervisors in resolving AGR problems relative exclusively to AGR tours in day-to-day operations. Serves as primary point-of-contact regarding AGR matters between the ARNG/ANG organization/unit and the HRO. Processes all military human resources actions associated with a military assignment of an AGR member. Conducts orientation program to outline military requirements, benefits, and entitlements. Implements and interprets AGR policies and programs. Advises and counsels AGR members and dependents on support agencies and benefits programs. Explains the TRICARE program and how to file claims and locations of servicing Health Benefits Advisors. Schedules retirement counseling of AGR members and coordinates retirement actions with the ARNG/ANG organization/unit and HRO. Coordinates with the local medical facility on physical examinations for current, potential AGR members, and AGR members projected for separation/retirement. Analyzes, interprets, and clarifies policies, directives, and other issues regarding military human resources matters. Monitors AGR controlled grade program and requirements at unit/wing/base level. Monitors promotions, reassignments, performance appraisals, tour renewals, orders, and transfers of all assigned AGR personnel.

- Performs other duties as assigned.

QUALIFICATIONS REQUIRED:

General Experience Required

Administrative or clerical experience, education, or training which demonstrates the candidate's ability to perform the duties of the position. Experience using computer and automation systems.

Specialized Experience Required

In addition to the General Experience required, you must:

- Possess at least 9 months experience, education, or training that provided knowledge of general office work which may include but is not limited to: answering telephones, receiving and distributing mail and maintaining records. Experience following oral or written instructions to accomplish work. Experience establishing and retrieving files and information. Experience using common computer software designed for word processing.

Source: *www.opm.gov*.

PERFORMANCE APPRAISAL

Effective performance appraisals drive effective merit pay programs. Merit pay systems require specific performance appraisal approaches, as noted previously. Administering successful merit pay programs depends as much on supervisors' appraisal approaches as it does on the professionals' skills in designing and implementing such plans.

Types of Performance Appraisal Plans

Performance appraisal methods fall into four broad categories:

- Trait systems
- Comparison systems
- Behavioral systems
- Goal-oriented systems

The four kinds of performance appraisal methods are next described in order.

TRAIT SYSTEMS **Trait systems** ask raters to evaluate each employee's traits or characteristics (e.g., quality of work, quantity of work, appearance, dependability, cooperation, initiative, judgment, leadership responsibility, decision-making ability, or creativity). Appraisals are typically scored using descriptors ranging from unsatisfactory to outstanding. Table 3-4 contains an illustration of a trait method of performance appraisal.

Trait systems are easy to construct, use, and apply to a wide range of jobs. They are also easy to quantify for merit pay purposes. Trait systems are increasingly becoming common in companies that focus on the quality of interactions with customers. For example, Leon Leonwood Bean, founder of L. L. Bean, made customer service the foundation of his business from its beginning in 1912. Bean referred to the necessity of positive customer service as one of the business's golden rules: Sell good merchandise at a reasonable profit, treat your customers like human beings, and they will always come back for more.[13]

The trait approach does have limitations. First, trait systems are highly subjective[14] because they are based on the assumption that every supervisor's perception of a given trait is the same. For example, the trait "quality of work" may be defined by one supervisor as "the extent to which an employee's performance is free of errors." To another supervisor, quality of work might mean "the

TABLE 3-4 **A Trait-Oriented Performance Appraisal Rating Form**

Employee's Name:		Employee's Position:		
Supervisor's Name:		Review Period:		

Instructions: For each trait below, circle the phrase that best represents the employee.

1. Diligence

a. outstanding	b. above average	c. average	d. below average	e. poor

2. Cooperation with others

a. outstanding	b. above average	c. average	d. below average	e. poor

3. Communication skills

a. outstanding	b. above average	c. average	d. below average	e. poor

4. Leadership

a. outstanding	b. above average	c. average	d. below average	e. poor

5. Decisiveness

a. outstanding	b. above average	c. average	d. below average	e. poor

extent to which an employee's performance is thorough." Human resource professionals and supervisors can avoid this problem by working together in advance to specify the definition of traits clearly.

Another drawback is that systems rate individuals on subjective personality factors rather than on objective job performance data. Essentially, trait assessment focuses attention on employees rather than on job performance. Employees may simply become defensive rather than trying to understand the role that the particular trait plays in shaping their job performance and then taking corrective actions.

COMPARISON SYSTEMS **Comparison systems** evaluate a given employee's performance against that of other employees. Employees are ranked from the best performer to the poorest performer. In simplest form, supervisors rank each employee and establish a performance hierarchy such that the employee with the best performance receives the highest ranking. Employees may be ranked on overall performance or on various traits.

An alternative approach, called a **forced distribution** performance appraisal, assigns employees to groups that represent the entire range of performance. For example, three categories that might be used are best performers, moderate performers, and poor performers. A forced distribution approach, in which the rater must place a specific number of employees into each of the performance groups, can be used with this method. Table 3-5 displays a forced distribution rating form for an animal keeper job with five performance categories.

Many companies use forced distribution approaches to minimize the tendency for supervisors to rate most employees as excellent performers. This tendency usually arises out of supervisors' self-promotion motives. Supervisors often provide positive performance ratings to most of their employees because they do not want to alienate them. After all, their performance as supervisors depends largely on how well their employees perform their jobs.

Forced distribution approaches have drawbacks. The forced distribution approach can distort ratings because employee performance may not fall into these predetermined distributions. Let's assume that a supervisor must use the following forced distribution to rate her employees' performance:

- 15 percent well below average
- 25 percent below average
- 40 percent average
- 15 percent above average
- 5 percent well above average

TABLE 3-5 A Forced Distribution Performance Appraisal Rating Form

Instructions: You are required to rate the performance for the previous 3 months of the 15 workers employed as animal keepers to conform with the following performance distribution:

- *15 percent* of the animal keepers will be rated as having exhibited poor performance.
- *20 percent* of the animal keepers will be rated as having exhibited below-average performance.
- *35 percent* of the animal keepers will be rated as having exhibited average performance.
- *20 percent* of the animal keepers will be rated as having exhibited above-average performance.
- *10 percent* of the animal keepers will be rated as having exhibited superior performance.

Use the following guidelines for rating performance. On the basis of the five duties listed in the job description for animal keeper, the employee's performance is characterized as:

- *Poor* if the incumbent performs only one of the duties well.
- *Below average* if the incumbent performs only two of the duties well.
- *Average* if the incumbent performs only three of the duties well.
- *Above average* if the incumbent performs only four of the duties well.
- *Superior* if the incumbent performs all five of the duties well.

TABLE 3-6 A Paired Comparison Performance Appraisal Rating Form

Instructions: Please indicate by placing an X next to which employee of each pair has performed most effectively during the past year.

X	Bob Brown		X	Mary Green
	Mary Green			Jim Smith
X	Bob Brown			Mary Green
	Jim Smith		X	Allen Jones
	Bob Brown			Jim Smith
X	Allen Jones		X	Allen Jones

This distribution is problematic to the extent that the actual distribution of employee performance is substantially different from this forced distribution. If 35 percent of the employees' performance were either above average or well above average, then the supervisor would be required to underrate the performance of 15 percent of the employees. Based on this forced distribution, the supervisor can rate only 20 percent of the employees as having demonstrated above-average or well-above-average job performance. Management–employee relationships ultimately suffer because workers feel that ratings are dictated by unreal models rather than by individual performance.

A third comparative technique for ranking employees establishes **paired comparisons.** Supervisors compare each employee to every other employee, identifying the better performer in each pair. Table 3-6 displays a paired comparison form. Following the comparison, the employees are ranked according to the number of times they were identified as being the better performer. In this example, Allen Jones is the best performer because he was identified most often as the better performer, followed by Bob Brown (identified twice as the better performer) and Mary Green (identified once as the better performer).

Comparative methods are best suited for small groups of employees who perform the same or similar jobs. They are cumbersome for large groups of employees or for employees who perform different jobs. For example, it would be difficult to judge whether a production worker's performance is better than a secretary's performance because the jobs are substantively different. The assessment of a production worker's performance is based on the number of units he or she produces during each work shift; a secretary's performance is based on the accuracy with which he or she types memos and letters.

As do trait systems, comparison approaches have limitations. They tend to encourage subjective judgments, which increase the chance for rater errors and biases. In addition, small differences in performance between employees may become exaggerated by using such a method if supervisors feel compelled to distinguish among levels of employee performance.

BEHAVIORAL SYSTEMS **Behavioral systems** rate employees on the extent to which they display successful job performance behaviors. In contrast to trait and comparison methods, behavioral methods rate objective job behaviors. When correctly developed and applied, behavioral models provide results that are relatively free of rater errors and biases. The three main types of behavioral systems are the critical incident technique (CIT), behaviorally anchored rating scales (BARS), and behavioral observation scales (BOS).

The **critical incident technique (CIT)**[15] requires job incumbents and their supervisors to identify performance incidents (e.g., on-the-job behaviors and behavioral outcomes) that distinguish successful performances from unsuccessful ones. The supervisor then observes the employees and records their performance on these critical job aspects. Supervisors usually rate employees on how often they display the behaviors described in each critical incident. Table 3-7

TABLE 3-7 A Critical Incidents Performance Appraisal Rating Form

Instructions: For each description of work behavior below, circle the number that best describes how frequently the employee engages in that behavior.

1. The incumbent removes manure and unconsumed food from the animal enclosures.

1	2	3	4	5
Never	Almost never	Sometimes	Fairly often	Very often

2. The incumbent haphazardly measures the feed items when placing them in the animal enclosures.

1	2	3	4	5
Never	Almost never	Sometimes	Fairly often	Very often

3. The incumbent leaves refuse dropped by visitors on and around the public walkways.

1	2	3	4	5
Never	Almost never	Sometimes	Fairly often	Very often

4. The incumbent skillfully identifies instances of abnormal behavior among the animals, which represent signs of illness.

1	2	3	4	5
Never	Almost never	Sometimes	Fairly often	Very often

illustrates a CIT form for an animal keeper job. Two statements represent examples of ineffective job performance (numbers 2 and 3), and two statements represent examples of effective job performance (numbers 1 and 4).

The CIT tends to be useful because this procedure requires extensive documentation that identifies successful and unsuccessful job performance behaviors by both the employee and the supervisor. The CIT's strength, however, is also its weakness: Implementation of the CIT demands continuous and close observation of the employee. Supervisors may find the record keeping to be overly burdensome.

Behaviorally anchored rating scales (BARS)[16] are based on the CIT, and these scales are developed in the same fashion with one exception. For the CIT, a critical incident would be written as "the incumbent completed the task in a timely fashion." For the BARS format, this incident would be written as "the incumbent is expected to complete the task in a timely fashion." The designers of BARS write the incidents as expectations to emphasize the fact that the employee does not have to demonstrate the exact behavior that is used as an anchor in order to be rated at that level. Because a complete array of behaviors that characterize a particular job would take many pages of description, it is not feasible to place examples of all job behaviors on the scale. Experts therefore list only those behaviors that they believe are most representative of the job the employee must perform. A typical job might have 8–10 dimensions under BARS, each with a separate rating scale. Table 3-8 contains an illustration of a BARS for one dimension of an animal keeper job (i.e., cleaning animal enclosures and removing refuse from the public walkways). The scale reflects the range of performance on the job dimension from ineffective performance (1) to effective performance (7).

As with all performance appraisal techniques, BARS has its advantages and disadvantages.[17] Among the various performance appraisal techniques, BARS is the most defensible in court because it is based on actual observable job behaviors. In addition, BARS encourages all raters to make evaluations in the same way. Perhaps the main disadvantage of BARS is the difficulty of developing and maintaining the volume of data necessary to make it effective. The BARS method requires companies to maintain distinct appraisal documents for each job. As jobs change over time, the documentation must be updated for each job.

Another kind of behavior system, a **behavioral observation scale (BOS)**,[18] displays illustrations of positive incidents (or behaviors) of job performance for various job dimensions.

TABLE 3-8 A Behaviorally Anchored Rating Scale

Instructions: On the scale below, from 7 to 1, circle the number that best describes how frequently the employee engages in that behavior.

7   The incumbent could be expected to clean the animal enclosures thoroughly and remove refuse from the public walkways as often as needed.

|

6

|

5   The incumbent could be expected to clean the animal enclosures thoroughly and remove refuse from the public walkways twice daily.

|

4

|

3   The incumbent could be expected to clean the animal enclosures and remove refuse from the public walkways in a haphazard fashion twice daily.

|

2

|

1   The incumbent could be expected rarely to clean the animal enclosures or remove refuse from the public walkways.

The evaluator rates the employee on each behavior according to the extent to which the employee performs in a manner consistent with each behavioral description. Scores from each job dimension are averaged to provide an overall rating of performance. BOS is developed in the same way as a BARS instrument, except that it incorporates only positive performance behaviors. The BOS method tends to be difficult and time-consuming to develop and maintain. Moreover, to ensure accurate appraisal, raters must be able to observe employees closely and regularly. However, observing employees on a regular basis may not be feasible where supervisors are responsible for several people.

GOAL-ORIENTED SYSTEMS **Management by objectives (MBO)**[19] could be the most effective performance appraisal technique because supervisors and employees determine objectives for employees to meet during the rating period and employees appraise how well they have achieved their objectives. Management by objectives is used mainly for managerial and professional employees and typically evaluates employees' progress toward strategic planning objectives.

Employees and supervisors together determine particular objectives tied to corporate strategies. Employees are expected to attain these objectives during the rating period. At the end of the rating period, the employee writes a report explaining his or her progress toward accomplishing the objectives, and the employee's supervisor appraises the employee's performance based on accomplishment of the objectives. Despite the importance of managerial employees to company success, it is often difficult to establish appropriate performance goals because many companies simply do not fully describe the scope of these positions. Management by objectives can promote effective communication between employees and their supervisors. On the downside, management by objectives is time-consuming and requires a constant flow of information between employees and employers. Moreover, its focus is only on the attainment of particular goals, often to the exclusion of other important outcomes. This drawback is known as a "results at any cost" mentality.[20] The role of automobile sales professionals historically was literally limited to making sales. Once these professionals and customers agreed on the price of a car, the sales professionals' work with customers was completed. Automobile salespeople today remain in contact with clients for as long as several months following the completion of the sale. The purpose is to ensure customer satisfaction and build loyalty to the product and dealership by addressing questions about the vehicle's features and reminding clients about scheduled service checks.

Goal-oriented systems are often a component of broader development programs that help employees achieve career goals. ExxonMobil blends goal-oriented systems with performance discussions between managers and employees in the HR function:

> When you join ExxonMobil, your career path in Human Resources is marked by assignments of increasing responsibility. You may progress from analyst to supervisory and management positions. You will be offered exposure and high visibility with senior management through a variety of experiences which will provide developmental skills to prepare you to handle complex assignments. You will have the opportunity to achieve your professional goals in both technical and managerial areas through a multitude of job assignments, mentoring and world class training over your career.

Exploring the Performance Appraisal Process

Performance appraisals represent a company's way of telling employees what is expected of them in their jobs and how well they are meeting those expectations. Performance appraisals typically require supervisors to monitor employees' performance, complete performance appraisal forms about the employees, and hold discussions with employees about their performance. Companies that use merit pay plans must assess employee job performance, which serves as a basis for awarding merit pay raises. Awarding merit pay increases on factors other than job performance, except for four exceptions (i.e., a seniority system, merit system, quality or quantity of production, and any factor besides sex), could lead some employees to level charges of illegal pay discrimination against the employer based on the Equal Pay Act of 1963.

One such violation of the Equal Pay Act involved two female employees of Cascade Wood Components Company, which remanufactures lumber products.[21] The job in question was the sawyer job; a sawyer is responsible for cutting the best-grade wood segments that will be manufactured into the highest-grade lumber. Cascade awarded pay increases to male sawyers before awarding pay increases to more experienced female sawyers. The court found Cascade in violation of the Equal Pay Act because the higher pay raises awarded to the male sawyers could not be accounted for by commensurate differences in job performance, seniority, a merit system that measures earnings by quantity or quality of production, or any factor other than sex.

Chapter 2 emphasized how U.S. civil rights laws protect employees from illegal discrimination based on age, race, color, religion, sex, national origin, or qualified disability. Because negative performance appraisals can affect an individual's employment status and such related decisions as pay levels and increases, promotions, and discharges, appraisals must be based on job-related factors and not on any discriminatory factors.

Legislation and court decisions have subjected performance appraisals to close scrutiny. In *Brito v. Zia Company*, the court found that the Zia Company violated Title VII when a disproportionate number of protected class individuals were laid off on the basis of low performance appraisal scores. Zia's action was a violation of Title VII because the use of the performance appraisal system in determining layoffs was indeed an employment test. In addition, the court ruled that the Zia Company had not demonstrated that its performance appraisal instrument was valid. In other words, the appraisal did not assess any job-related criteria based on quality or quantity of work.[22]

FOUR ACTIVITIES TO PROMOTE NONDISCRIMINATORY PERFORMANCE APPRAISAL PRACTICES Since the *Brito v. Zia Company* decision, court opinions and compensation experts suggest the following four points to ensure nondiscriminatory performance appraisal practices and to protect firms using merit pay systems if legal issues arise.[23] Nondiscriminatory performance appraisal systems are key to effective merit pay systems because they accurately measure job performance.

1. **Conduct job analyses to ascertain characteristics necessary for successful job performance.**

   Companies must first establish definitions of the jobs and then discover what employee behaviors are necessary to perform the jobs. Job analysis is essential for the development of content-valid performance appraisal systems. Content validity displays connections between the measurable factors upon which the employee is being appraised and the job itself. For example, customer service associates' performance might be judged on the basis of courtesy and knowledge of the company's products or services, and these measures would be content-valid dimensions. Both measures are representative of and relative to the job. On the other hand, knowledge of the company's financial accounting practices would not be a content-valid criterion of customer service associates' performance.

   Human resource and compensation experts must review performance appraisal tools regularly to ensure that the tools adequately reflect the key behaviors necessary for effective job performance. Jobholders, supervisors, and clients can often give the most relevant input to determine whether a performance appraisal system contains dimensions that relate to a particular job.

2. **Incorporate these characteristics into a rating instrument.**

   Although the professional literature recommends rating instruments that are tied to specific job behaviors (e.g., behaviorally anchored rating scales), the courts routinely accept such less-sophisticated approaches as simple graphic rating scales and trait ranges. Regardless of the method, HR departments should provide all supervisors and raters with written definitive standards.

   The examples given earlier about the animal keeper job indicate that effective performance appraisal instruments are based on explicitly written job duties conveyed in the job description.

3. **Train supervisors to use the rating instrument properly.**

   Raters need to know how to apply performance appraisal standards when they make judgments. The uniform application of standards is extremely important. In addition, evaluators should be aware of common rater errors, which will be discussed later in this chapter.

4. **Several cases demonstrate that formal appeal mechanisms and review of ratings by upper-level personnel help make performance appraisal processes more accurate and effective.**

   Allowing employees to voice their concerns over ratings they believe to be inaccurate or unjust opens a dialogue between employees and their supervisors that may shed light on the performance appraisal outcomes. Employees may be able to point out instances of their performances that may have been overlooked in the appraisal process or explain particular extreme instances as the result of extraordinary circumstances. For example, an ill parent in need of regular attention is the reason for an employee's absence rather than an employee's deliberate breach of work responsibilities because the employee chose to relax at the beach.

SOURCES OF PERFORMANCE APPRAISAL INFORMATION Information for performance appraisal can be ascertained from five sources:

- Employee (i.e., the individual whose job performance is being appraised)
- Employee's supervisor
- Employee's coworkers
- Employee's supervisees
- Employee's customers or clients

More than one source can provide performance appraisal information. Although supervisory input is the most common source of performance appraisal information, companies are increasingly calling on as many sources of information as possible to gain a more complete picture of employee job performance. Performance appraisal systems that rely on many appropriate sources of information are known as **360-degree performance appraisals.**

Companies are increasingly relying on the 360-degree performance appraisal methods to reduce the costs of recruiting and hiring new employees. This method helps companies develop a more complete understanding of current employee performance by formulating a judgment on input from multiple sources. Companies often feel more confident about promoting employees from within when multiple sources of information support positive performance judgments.

Three criteria should be used to judge the appropriateness of the information source.[24] First, the evaluators should be aware of the objectives of the employee's job. Second, the evaluators should frequently have occasion to observe the employee on the job. Third, the evaluators should be capable of determining whether the employee's performance is satisfactory.

The use of 360-degree performance appraisals is on the rise in U.S. businesses. Three main factors account for this trend. First, as companies downsize, the organizational structures are becoming less hierarchical. As a result, managers and supervisors are increasingly responsible for more workers. With responsibility for more employees, it has become difficult for managers and supervisors to provide sufficient attention to each employee throughout the appraisal period.

Second, the use of 360-degree performance appraisal methods is consistent with the increased prevalence of work teams in companies. At Whirlpool Corporation, members of semiautonomous work teams communicate their work goals to the entire team. At the end of the designated appraisal period, team members judge others' performances based on the prior statement of work goals.

Third, companies are placing greater emphasis on customer satisfaction as competition for a limited set of customers increases. Companies presently turn to customers as a source of performance appraisal information. For example, it is common for restaurants, furniture stores, moving companies, and automobile manufacturers to ask customers to complete short surveys designed to measure how well they were satisfied with various aspects of their interactions. Volkswagen (VW) of America uses the services of a professional survey company to call VW car owners to rate their experiences with VW dealer service departments. Table 3-9 illustrates a major moving company's customer satisfaction survey, which it mails to customers after a move.

TABLE 3-9 Sample Customer Satisfaction Survey

Before and During Your Move:	Yes	No
1. Did our moving consultant help with packing and moving-day suggestions?	☐	☐
2. Were we on time?	☐	☐
3. Was our packing service satisfactory?	☐	☐
4. Were our moving personnel courteous?	☐	☐
5. Did your possessions arrive in good condition?	☐	☐
6. Would you recommend us to your friends?	☐	☐

Why did you choose us?

☐ Reputation   ☐ Contacted by salesperson
☐ Have used before   ☐ Recommended by friends
☐ Selected by employer   ☐ Recommended by employer
☐ Contacted by telemarketer   ☐ Other: _____

How can we better serve you?

_____
_____
_____
_____

ERRORS IN THE PERFORMANCE APPRAISAL PROCESS Almost all raters make **rating errors**. Rating errors reflect differences between human judgment processes versus objective, accurate assessments uncolored by bias, prejudice, or other subjective, extraneous influences.[25] Rating errors occur because raters must always make subjective judgments. Human resource departments can help raters to minimize errors by carefully choosing rating systems and to recognize and avoid common errors. Major types of rating errors include:[26]

- Bias errors
- Contrast errors
- Errors of central tendency
- Errors of leniency or strictness

Bias Errors **Bias errors** happen when the rater evaluates the employee based on a personal negative or positive opinion of the employee rather than on the employee's actual performance. Four ways supervisors may bias evaluation results are first-impression effects, positive and negative halo effects, similar-to-me effects, and illegal discriminatory biases.

A manager biased by a **first-impression effect** might make an initial favorable or unfavorable judgment about an employee and then ignore or distort the employee's actual performance based on this impression. For instance, a manager expects that a newly hired graduate of a prestigious Ivy League university will be an exemplary performer. After 1 year on the job, this employee fails to meet many of the work objectives; nevertheless, the manager rates the job performance more highly because of the initial impression.

A **positive halo effect** or **negative halo effect** occurs when a rater generalizes an employee's good or bad behavior on one aspect of the job to all aspects of the job. A secretary with offensive interpersonal skills is a proficient user of various computer software programs and an outstanding typist. The secretary's supervisor receives frequent complaints from other employees and customers. At performance appraisal time, the supervisor gives this employee an overall negative performance rating.

A **similar-to-me effect** refers to the tendency on the part of raters to judge favorably employees whom they perceive as similar to themselves. Supervisors biased by this effect rate more favorably employees who have attitudes, values, backgrounds, or interests similar to theirs. For example, employees whose children attend the same elementary school as their manager's children receive higher performance appraisal ratings than do employees who do not have children. "Similar-to-me" errors or biases easily can lead to charges of **illegal discriminatory bias,** wherein a supervisor rates members of his or her race, gender, nationality, or religion more favorably than members of other classes.

Contrast Errors Supervisors make **contrast errors** when they compare an employee with other employees rather than to specific, explicit performance standards. Such comparisons qualify as errors because other employees are required to perform only at minimum acceptable standards. Employees performing at minimally acceptable levels should receive satisfactory ratings, even if every other employee doing the job is performing at outstanding or above-average levels.

Errors of Central Tendency When supervisors rate all employees as average or close to average, they commit **errors of central tendency.** Such errors are most often committed when raters are forced to justify only extreme behavior (i.e., high or low ratings) with written explanations; therefore, HR professionals should require justification for ratings at every level of the scale and not just at the extremes.

Errors of Leniency or Strictness Raters sometimes place every employee at the high or low end of the scale, regardless of actual performance. With a **leniency error,** managers tend to appraise employees' performance more highly than they really rate compared with objective criteria. Over time, if supervisors commit positive errors, their employees will expect higher-than-deserved pay rates.

On the other hand, **strictness errors** occur when a supervisor rates an employee's performance lower than it would be if compared against objective criteria. If supervisors make this error over time, employees may receive smaller pay raises than deserved, lower their effort, and perform poorly. In effect, this error erodes employees' beliefs that effort varies positively with performance and that performance influences the amount of pay raises.

STRENGTHENING THE PAY-FOR-PERFORMANCE LINK

Companies who don't consider these possible limitations ultimately weaken the relationship between pay and performance. Human resource managers can employ a number of approaches to strengthen the link between pay and job performance.

Link Performance Appraisals to Business Goals

The standards by which employee performance is judged should be linked to a company's competitive strategy or strategies. For example, each member of a product development team that is charged with the responsibility of marketing a new product might be given merit increases if certain sales goals are reached.

Analyze Jobs

Job analysis (Chapter 6) is vital to companies that wish to establish **internally consistent compensation systems.** As discussed earlier, job descriptions (Chapter 6)—a product of job analyses—can be used by supervisors to create objective performance measures. Job descriptions note the duties, requirements, and relative importance of a job within the company. Supervisors appraising performances can match employees' performance to these criteria. This approach may help reduce supervisors' arbitrary decisions about merit increases by clarifying the standards against which employees' performance is judged.

Communicate

For merit pay programs to succeed, employees must clearly understand what they need to do to receive merit increases and what the rewards for their performance will be. Open communication helps an employee develop reasonable expectations and encourages him or her to trust the system and those who operate it. Figure 3-2 illustrates worksheets both supervisors and employers may use to establish performance expectations.

Establish Effective Appraisals

During performance appraisal meetings with employees, supervisors should discuss goals for future performance and employee career plans. When performance deficiencies are evident, the supervisor and employee should work together to identify possible causes and develop an action plan to remedy these deficiencies. The performance standards listed within job descriptions should serve as the guides for establishing performance targets. For example, a company's job description for a secretary specifies that the job incumbent must be able to use one word processing software package proficiently. The supervisor should clearly explain what software usage proficiency means. Proficiency may refer to the ability to operate certain features of the software well, including the mail merge utility, the table generator, and the various outlining utilities, or proficiency may refer to the ability to operate all features of the software well.

Empower Employees

Because formal performance appraisals are conducted periodically—maybe only once per year—supervisors must empower their employees to make performance self-appraisals

---

Supervisor's Performance Planning Worksheet

To be filled out by supervisor

Name of Employee: **Date:**

Employee Title: **Department:**

1. List what you consider to be the primary job duties or assignments at this time (list in order of priority):
2. Describe contributions, achievements, or improvements made by the employee during the past appraisal period:
3. Describe any specific change, improvements, or goals desired for the employee's performance in the next appraisal period:
4. Describe the coaching, training, or development activities you would support in pursuit of improved performance, employee growth, learning, and/or career development:

_____   _____   _____   _____
Employee   Date   Supervisor   Date

Employee's Performance Planning Worksheet

To be filled out by employee

Name of Employee: **Date:**

Employee Title: **Department:**

1. List what you consider to be your primary job duties or assignments at this time (list in order of priority):
2. Describe contributions or achievements that indicate your success at improving your performance or exceeding job requirements during the past appraisal period:
3. Describe any specific changes or improvements you want to make in your performance in the next appraisal period. Describe obstacles to getting your job done and suggest possible solutions:
4. Describe the coaching, training, or development activities that would help you pursue improved performance, job growth, learning, and/or career development:

_____   _____
Employee Signature   Date

_____(Initial) I have been given the opportunity to fill this out and choose not to do so.

FIGURE 3-2 Supervisor's and Employee's Performance Planning Worksheets

between formal sessions.[27] Moreover, supervisors need to take on a coach's role to empower their workers.[28] As coaches, supervisors must ensure that employees have access to the resources necessary to perform their jobs. Supervisors-as-coaches should also help employees interpret and respond to work problems as they develop. Empowering employees in this fashion should lead to more self-corrective actions rather than reactive courses of action to supervisory feedback and only to the criticisms addressed in performance appraisal meetings.

Differentiate among Performers

Merit increases should consist of meaningful increments. If employees do not see significant distinctions between top performers and poor performers, top performers may become frustrated and reduce their levels of performance. When companies' merit increases don't clearly reflect differences in actual job performance, they may need to provide alternative rewards (e.g., employee benefits—additional vacation days or higher discounts on the company's product or service—can complement merit pay increases).

POSSIBLE LIMITATIONS OF MERIT PAY PROGRAMS

Despite the popularity of merit pay systems, these programs are not without potential limitations, which may lessen their credibility with employees. If employees do not believe in a merit pay program, the pay system will not bring about the expected motivational impacts. Supervisors, HR managers, and compensation professionals must address the following eight potential problems with merit pay programs.

Failure to Differentiate among Performers

Employees may receive merit increases even if their performance does not warrant them because supervisors want to avoid creating animosity among employees. Poor performers, therefore, may receive the same pay increase as exemplary performers, and poor performers may come to view merit pay increases as entitlements. Superior performers consequently may question the value of striving for excellent performance.

Poor Performance Measures

Accurate and comprehensive performance measures that capture the entire scope of an employee's job are essential to successful merit pay programs. In most companies, employees' job performance tends to be assessed subjectively, based on their supervisors' judgments. As discussed, merit pay programs rely on supervisors' subjective assessments of employees' prior job performances. Developing performance measures for every single job unfortunately is both difficult and expensive.

Supervisors' Biased Ratings of Employee Job Performance

As we discussed earlier, supervisors are subject to a number of errors when they make subjective assessments of employees' job performances. These errors often undermine the credibility of the performance evaluation process. Performance evaluation processes that lack credibility do little to create the perception among employees that pay reflects performance.

Lack of Open Communication between Management and Employees

If managers cannot communicate effectively with employees, employees will not trust the performance appraisal processes. Trust is difficult to build when decisions are kept secret and employees have no influence on pay decisions. Thus, merit pay decision systems can cause conflict between management and employees. If mistrust characterizes the relationship, then performance appraisals will mean little to employees and could even lead to accusations of bias. In an environment of secrecy, employees lack the information necessary to determine if pay actually is linked to job performance.

Undesirable Social Structures

We acknowledged that relative pay grades can reflect status differentials within a company: Employees with lucrative salaries are usually granted higher status than lower-paid employees. Permanent merit increases may rigidify the relative pay status of employees over

TABLE 3-10 The Impact of Equal Pay Raise Percentage Amounts for Distinct Salaries

At the end of 2013, Anne Brown earned $50,000 per year as a systems analyst and John Williams earned $35,000 per year as an administrative assistant. Each received a 5 percent pay increase every year until the year 2018.

	Anne Brown ($)	John Williams ($)
2014	52,500	36,750
2015	55,125	38,587
2016	57,881	40,516
2017	60,775	42,542
2018	63,814	44,669

time.[29] Table 3-10 shows the permanence of the relative pay difference between two distinct jobs that each receives a 5 percent merit increase each year. Even though both employees performed well and received "equal" merit increases in percentage terms, the actual salary differentials prevail each year. Thus, where pay level is an indicator of status, permanent merit increases may reinforce an undesirable social structure. Lower-paid employees may resent never being able to catch up.

Factors Other than Merit

Merit increases may be based on factors other than merit, which will clearly reduce the emphasis on job performance. For example, supervisors may subconsciously use their employees' ages or seniority as bases for awarding merit increases. Studies show that the extent to which supervisors like the employees for whom they are responsible determines the size of pay raises in a merit pay program.[30] In addition, company politics assumes that the value of an employee's contributions depends on the agenda, or goals, of the supervisor[31] rather than on the objective impact of an employee's contributions to a rationally determined work goal. For instance, an accounting manager wishes to employ accounting methods other than top management's accounting methods. She believes that she can gain top management support by demonstrating that the accounting staff agrees with her position. The accounting manager may give generally positive performance evaluations, regardless of demonstrated performance, to those who endorse her accounting methods.

Undesirable Competition

Because merit pay programs focus fundamentally on individual employees, these programs do little to integrate workforce members.[32] With limited budgets for merit increases, employees must compete for a larger share of this limited amount. Competition among employees is counterproductive if teamwork is essential for successfully completing projects. Thus, merit increases are best suited for jobs where the employee works independently (e.g., clerical positions) and many professional positions from job families (e.g., accounting).

Little Motivational Value

Notwithstanding their intended purpose, merit pay programs may not positively influence employee motivation. Employers and employees may differ in what they see as "large enough" merit increases really to motivate positive worker behavior. For example, increases diminish after deducting income taxes and contributions to Social Security, and differences in employees' monthly paychecks may be negligible.

COMPENSATION IN ACTION

Employee compensation will ultimately be a managerial decision. As a line manager, your focus will be on the broader issues of production, revenue, and competition; however, the rate at which employees are paid—and why—will be an important factor in sustaining high levels of production, revenue, and competitive advantage. In making these decisions, line managers and HR (and in many cases the compensation specialist within the HR department) must work together in order to reward employees on measurable accomplishments and effectively communicate how the measured performance led to the resulting compensation decision.

Action checklist for line managers and HR—accurately tying performance to compensation

HR takes the lead
- Work with line managers to design the performance appraisal plan that best fits the specific duties and responsibilities of particular roles.
- Consider implementing a training program wherein line managers are trained in two areas: (1) accurately assessing performance and (2) recording the assessment in a way that is lawful and easily understood by both the employer and employee.

- Review the final distribution allocation made by the managers and, after approving the complete plan, set in motion the discussions between managers and employees where performance will be discussed and compensation increases will be communicated.

Line managers take the lead
- Determine performance criteria and accurate measurements to ensure that a specific output is the expectation of both the employee and employer.
- Work with HR to become educated on the subjective limitations of performance reviews. While certain roles may have very objective standards (e.g., sales numbers) by which employees are measured, supervisor judgment is subject to error.
- Use appraisals to accurately compensate employees. Working with HR, use the total annual increase to make compensation increases accordingly (e.g., if you are allotted a 5 percent increase to distribute among your employees, top performers may get an 8–10 percent increase, steady performers 5–6 percent, and underperformers 0–2 percent).

END OF CHAPTER

MyManagementLab

Go to **mymanagementlab.com** to complete the problems marked with this icon ⭐.

Summary

This chapter provided a discussion of the seniority pay and merit pay concepts. Companies should move away from rewarding employees solely on the basis of seniority and toward rewarding employees for measurable accomplishments. To be successful, merit pay programs must be founded on well-designed performance appraisal systems that accurately measure performance. In addition, rewards should be commensurate with past performance. Perhaps the greatest challenge for companies is to ensure that employees are given the opportunity to perform at exemplary levels.

Key Terms

seniority pay   52
longevity pay   52
human capital theory   52
human capital   52
job control unionism   53

General Schedule (GS)   55
merit pay programs   57
just-meaningful pay increase   58
trait systems   60
comparison systems   61

forced distribution   61
paired comparisons   62
behavioral systems   62
critical incident technique
  (CIT)   62

✪ Discussion Questions

3-1. Human capital theory has been advanced as a rationale underlying seniority pay. Identify two individuals you know who have performed the same job for at least 2 years. Ask them to describe the changes in knowledge and skills they experienced from the time they assumed their jobs to the present. Discuss your findings with the class.

3-2. Subjective performance evaluations are subject to several rater errors, which makes objective measures seem a better alternative. Discuss when subjective performance evaluations might be better (or more feasible) than objective ratings.

3-3. Consider a summer job that you have held. Write a detailed job description for that job. Then develop a behaviorally anchored rating scale (BARS) that can be used to evaluate an individual who performs that job in the future.

3-4. This chapter indicates that merit pay plans appear to be the most common form of compensation in the United States. Although widely used, these systems are not suitable for all kinds of jobs. Based on your knowledge of merit pay systems, identify at least three jobs for which merit pay is inappropriate. Be sure to provide your rationale given the information in this chapter.

3-5. Select three distinct jobs of your choice (e.g., a clerical job, a technical job, and a professional job). For each job, identify what you believe is the most appropriate performance appraisal method. Based on your choices, sketch a performance appraisal instrument. Discuss the rationale for your choice of performance appraisal methods.

CASE
Appraising Performance at Precision

✪ *An additional Supplemental Case can be found on MyManagementLab.*

Precision Manufacturing produces machine parts and has nearly 200 production employees and 50 employees in its front office with responsibilities ranging from data entry to marketing. Jackson Smith is the new compensation manager at Precision, and his first task is to implement a merit pay program that would tie to the company's performance appraisal process. For the last 10 years, all employees have received an annual pay increase, but it has been an across-the-board increase, with all employees receiving the same percentage increase in base pay. Jackson and the company president have agreed that implementing a merit pay program to provide pay increases based on performance would support the company's competitive strategy by rewarding employee productivity.

The first step in developing the merit pay program is to ensure that the performance appraisal process aligns with the proposed program. The purpose in implementing the merit pay program is to provide employees with pay increases as a reward for performance, and, therefore, effective measurement of performance is essential. Jackson must now review the current appraisal process to ensure it will tie to the proposed merit pay program.

The current appraisal process is fairly simple. Once each year, the supervisors at Precision provide their employees a written performance appraisal. The supervisors use a generic form to conduct their appraisals, and the same form is used for all employees. The form asks the supervisor to rate the employee on a scale of 1 to 5 in four areas: quantity of work, quality of work, attendance, and attitude. Once the form is completed, the supervisor meets with the employee to share the results. Both the supervisor and the employee sign the form, and then it is placed in the employee's personnel file.

Jackson's initial research on the appraisals has brought several concerns to his attention. First, employees do not have written job descriptions that clearly state their performance expectations. Further, his review of past appraisals suggests that the supervisors tend to rate all of the employees about the same. Very rarely is an employee rated exceptionally high or low; most are rated as average. Finally, it seems that employees and supervisors communicate very little about performance. Aside from the one meeting a year to deliver the performance appraisal, the supervisors tend to talk to employees about their performances only if the employee is having a problem.

Jackson knows he has a lot of work ahead of him to create a performance appraisal process that will provide a reliable assessment to support a merit pay program. First, he must clearly identify the problems with the current performance appraisal process, and then he must lay out a plan to correct any deficiencies.

Questions:

3-6. What are some problems with Precision's performance appraisal process that might cause challenges for Jackson to implement a merit pay program?

3-7. What changes do you recommend Precision make to the performance appraisal process to align it with a merit pay program?

MyManagementLab

Go to **mymanagementlab.com** for auto-graded writing questions as well as the following assisted-graded writing questions:

⭐ **3-8.** Discuss the concept of "just-meaningful pay increase." How can it strengthen the pay-for-performance link?

⭐ **3-9.** A company of 15 employees has recently decided to overhaul its performance appraisal system. Which plan would be most appropriate for the company to adopt? Why?

Endnotes

1. Cayer, N. J. (1975). *Public Personnel Administration in the United States*. New York: St. Martin Press.
2. Becker, G. (1975). *Human Capital*. New York: St. Martin Press.
3. Kochan, T. R., Katz, H. C., & McKersie, R. B. (1994). *The Transformation of American Industrial Relations*. Ithaca, NY: ILR Press.
4. Cayer, *Public Personnel Administration*.
5. James, K. C. (April 2002). *A Fresh Start for Federal Pay: The Case for Modernization*. Washington, DC: U.S. Government Printing Office.
6. Kernel, R. C., & Moorage, K. S. (1990). Longevity pay in the States: Echo from the past or sound of the future? *Public Personnel Management, 19*, pp. 191–200.
7. Peck, C. (1984). *Pay and Performance: The Interaction of Compensation and Performance Appraisal* (Research Bulletin No. 155). New York: The Conference Board.
8. WorldatWork. (2013). *Pay Increases for U.S. Employees Illustrate the 'New Normal' by staying the course*. Available: *http://www.worldatwork.org*, accessed August 13, 2013.
9. Heneman, R. L., & Werner, J. M. (2005). *Merit Pay: Linking Pay to Performance in a Changing World*. Greenwich, CT: Information Age Publishers.
10. Ibid.
11. Latham, G. P., & Wexley, K. N. (1982). *Increasing Productivity through Performance Appraisal*. Reading, MA: Addison-Wesley.
12. Krefting, L. A., & Mahoney, T. A. (1977). Determining the size of a meaningful pay increase. *Industrial Relations, 16*, pp. 83–93.
13. Bean, L. L. *Today's Commitment to Customer Values: L. L. Bean's Golden Rule*. Available: *www.llbean.com*, accessed April 13, 2011.
14. Bernardin, H. J., & Beatty, R. W. (1984). *Performance Appraisal: Assessing Human Behavior at Work*. Boston, MA: Kent.
15. Fivars, G. (1975). The critical incident technique: A bibliography. *JSAS Catalog of Selected Documents in Psychology, 5*, p. 210.

16. Smith, P., & Kendall, L. M. (1963). Retranslation of expectation: An approach to the construction of unambiguous anchors for rating scales. *Journal of Applied Psychology*, *47*, pp. 149–155.

17. Latham & Wexley, *Increasing Productivity*.

18. Latham, G. P., & Wexley, K. N. (1977). Behavioral observation scales for performance appraisal purposes. *Personnel Psychology*, *30*, pp. 255–268.

19. Bernardin & Beatty, *Performance Appraisal*.

20. Ibid.

21. *Coe v. Cascade Wood Components*, 48 FEP Cases 664 (W.D. OR. 1988).

22. *Brito v. Zia Company*, 478 F2d 1200, CA 10 (1973).

23. Barrett, G. V., & Kernan, M. C. (1987). Performance appraisal and terminations: A review of court decisions since *Brito v. Zia Company* with implication for personnel practices. *Personnel Psychology*, *40*, pp. 489–503.

24. Latham & Wexley, *Increasing Productivity*.

25. Blum, M. L., & Naylor, J. C. (1968). *Industrial Psychology: Its Theoretical and Social Foundations*. New York: Harper & Row.

26. Bernardin & Beatty, *Performance Appraisal*.

27. Noe, R. A. (2005). *Employee Training* (3rd ed.). Burr Ridge, IL: McGraw-Hill.

28. Evered, R. D., & Selman, J. C. (1989). Coaching and the art of management. *Organizational Dynamics*, *18*, pp. 16–33.

29. Haire, M., Ghiselli, E. E., & Gordon, M. E. (1967). A psychological study of pay. *Journal of Applied Psychology Monograph*, *51* (Whole No. 636), pp. 1–24.

30. Cardy, R. L., & Dobbins, G. H. (1986). Affect and appraisal: Liking as an integral dimension in evaluating performance. *Journal of Applied Psychology*, *71*, pp. 672–678.

31. Murphy, K. R., & Cleveland, J. N. (1991). *Performance Appraisal: An Organizational Perspective*. Boston, MA: Allyn & Bacon.

32. Lawler, E. E., III, & Cohen, S. G. (1992). Designing a pay system for teams. *American Compensation Association Journal*, *1*, pp. 6–19.

4 INCENTIVE PAY

LEARNING OBJECTIVES

When you finish studying this chapter, you should be able to:

1. Explain two reasons why companies use incentive pay.
2. Concisely provide a contrast between incentive pay methods and traditional pay methods.
3. List three categories of incentive pay plans.
4. Define individual incentive plans and give one example.
5. Provide the definition group incentives and summarize two examples of group incentive plans.
6. Discuss the advantages and disadvantages of group incentive plans.
7. Offer a definition of company-wide incentive plans with an example.
8. List and summarize five factors in the design of incentive pay programs.

As we will discuss momentarily, incentive pay places some portion of employee compensation at risk. When employees, groups of employees, or entire companies fail to meet preestablished performance standards (e.g., annual sales), they forfeit some or all of their compensation. Expert incentive pay consultants argue that a critical element of successful incentive pay plans is the provision of regular, honest communication to employees. We will explore this issue and several others related to effective incentive pay design.

EXPLORING INCENTIVE PAY

Incentive pay or **variable pay** rewards employees for partially or completely attaining a predetermined work objective. Incentive or variable pay is defined as compensation, other than base wages or salaries, that fluctuates according to employees' attainment of some standard, such as a preestablished formula, individual or group goals, or company earnings.[1]

Effective incentive pay systems are based on three assumptions:[2]

- Individual employees and work teams differ in how much they contribute to the company, both in what they do as well as in how well they do it.
- The company's overall performance depends to a large degree on the performance of individuals and groups within the company.
- To attract, retain, and motivate high performers and to be fair to all employees, a company needs to reward employees on the basis of their relative performance.

Much like seniority and merit pay approaches, incentive pay augments employees' base pay, but incentive pay appears as one-time payments. Employees usually receive a combination of recurring base pay and incentive pay, with base pay representing the greater portion of core compensation. More employees are presently eligible for incentive pay than ever before, as companies seek to control costs and motivate personnel continually to strive for exemplary performance. Companies increasingly recognize the importance of applying incentive pay programs to various kinds of employees as well, including production workers, technical employees, and service workers.

Some companies use incentive pay extensively. Lincoln Electric Company, a manufacturer of welding machines and motors, is renowned for its use of incentive pay plans. At Lincoln Electric, production employees receive recurring base pay as well as incentive pay. The company determines incentive pay awards according to five performance criteria: quality, output, dependability, cooperation, and ideas. The company has awarded incentive payments every year since 1934 through prosperous and poor economic times. The average annual incentive payment (profit sharing) per employee amounts to approximately 40 percent of annual salary.[3]

Companies generally institute incentive pay programs to control payroll costs or to motivate employee productivity. Companies can control costs by replacing annual merit or seniority increases or fixed salaries with incentive plans that award pay raises only when the company enjoys an offsetting rise in productivity, profits, or some other measure of business success. Well-developed incentive programs base pay on performance, so employees control their own compensation levels. Companies can choose incentives to further business objectives. For example, the management of H. Lee Moffitt Cancer Center and Research Institute at the University of South Florida continually strives to improve patient care as well as control costs. Moffitt's incentives are usually tied to net income or operating surplus, quality of care measures, patient satisfaction scores, and operating efficiencies. Princess Cruise Lines is another company that relies heavily on incentive pay to remain competitive. One goal of Princess Cruise Lines is to provide passengers with excellent service (e.g., food, entertainment, and shore excursions) in the hope that they will select Princess Cruise Lines for their next vacation instead of a competing cruise line (e.g., Carnival Cruises). Princess Cruise Lines offers regular incentives to the crews of each ship based on the overall level of customer satisfaction.

CONTRASTING INCENTIVE PAY WITH TRADITIONAL PAY

In traditional pay plans, employees receive compensation based on a fixed hourly pay rate or annual salary. Annual raises are linked to such factors as seniority and past performance. Some companies use incentive pay programs that replace all or a portion of base pay in order to control payroll expenditures and to link pay to performance. Companies use incentive pay programs in varying degrees for different kinds of positions. Some compensation programs consist of both traditional base pay and incentive pay, whereas other programs, usually for sales jobs, offer only incentive pay, in which case all pay is at risk.[4]

Traditional core compensation generally includes an annual salary or hourly wage that is increased periodically on a seniority or merit basis. Companies usually base pay rates on the importance they place on each job within their corporate structure and on the "going rate" that each job commands in similar companies. For example, Lincoln Electric determines the importance of the jobs within its job structure based on job evaluation techniques. The five criteria on which Lincoln evaluates jobs are skill, responsibility, mental aptitude, physical application, and working conditions. Lincoln Electric next surveys the pay rates of competitors, and it uses these data to set base pay rates.

As we discussed in Chapter 3, employees under traditional pay structures earn raises according to their length of service in the organization and to supervisors' subjective appraisals of employees' job performance. Again, both merit pay raises and seniority pay raises are permanent increases to base pay. Annual merit pay increase amounts usually total no more than a small percentage of base pay (i.e., 2–6 percent is presently not uncommon), but the dollar impact represents a significant cost to employers over time. Table 4-1 shows the contrast in rate of compensation increase between a traditional merit compensation plan and an incentive plan.

Companies use incentive pay to reward individual employees, teams of employees, or whole companies based on their performance. Incentive pay plans are not limited solely to production or nonsupervisory workers. Many incentive plans apply to such categories of employees as sales professionals, managers, and executives. Management typically relies on business objectives to determine incentive pay levels. At Taco Bell, restaurant managers receive biannual bonuses based on the attainment of three objectives:

- Target profit levels
- Quality of customer service based on an independent assessment by a market research company
- Store sales

Management then communicates these planned incentive levels and performance goals to restaurant managers. Although merit pay performance standards aim to be measurable and objective, incentive levels tend to be based on even more objective criteria, such as quantity of items an employee produces per production period or market indicators of a company's performance (e.g., an increase in market share for the fiscal year). Moreover, supervisors communicate the incentive award amounts in advance that correspond to objective performance levels. On the other hand, supervisors generally do not communicate the merit award amounts until after they offer subjective assessments of employees' performance.

TABLE 4-1 Permanent Annual Merit Increases versus Incentive Awards: A Comparison

(At the end of 2012, John Smith earned an annual salary of $35,000.)

Year	Increase Amount (%)	Permanent Merit Increase ($)	Incentive Award ($)	Permanent Merit Increase (Percent Increase × Previous Annual Salary) ($)	Incentive Award Annual (Percent Increase × 2012 Salary) ($)
2013	3	1,050	1,050	36,050	36,050
2014	5	2,853	1,750	37,853	36,750
2015	4	4,367	1,400	39,367	36,400
2016	7	7,122	2,450	42,122	37,450
2017	6	9,649	2,100	44,649	37,100
2018	5	11,881	1,750	46,881	36,750
2019	3	13,287	1,050	48,287	36,050
2020	6	16,185	2,100	51,185	37,100
2021	8	20,279	2,800	55,279	37,800
2022	7	24,148	2,450	59,148	37,450

TABLE 4-2 **Typical Performance Measures for Individual, Group, and Companywide Incentive Plans**

Individual Incentive Plans
Quantity of work output
Quality of work output
Monthly sales
Work safety record
Work attendance

Group Incentive Plans
Customer satisfaction
Labor cost savings (base pay, overtime pay, benefits)
Materials cost savings
Reduction in accidents
Services cost savings (e.g., utilities)

Companywide Incentive Plans
Company profits
Cost containment
Market share
Sales revenue

Incentive pay plans can be broadly classified into three categories:

- *Individual incentive plans.* These plans reward employees whose work is performed independently. Some companies have piecework plans, typically for their production employees. Under piecework plans, an employee's compensation depends on the number of units she or he produces over a given period.
- *Group incentive plans.* These plans promote supportive, collaborative behavior among employees. Group incentives work well in manufacturing and service delivery environments that rely on interdependent teams. In gain sharing programs, group improvements in productivity, cost savings, or product quality are shared by employees within the group.
- *Companywide incentive plans.* These plans tie employee compensation to a company's performance over a short time frame, usually from a 3-month period to a 5-year period.

Table 4-2 lists common performance measures used in individual, group, and companywide incentive plans.

INDIVIDUAL INCENTIVES

Individual incentive pay plans are most appropriate under three conditions. First, employees' performance can be measured objectively. Examples of objective performance measures include:

- Number of units produced—an automobile parts production worker's completion of a turn signal lighting assembly
- Sales amount—a Mary Kay Cosmetics sales professional's monthly sales revenue
- Reduction in error rate—a word processor's reduction in typing errors

Second, individual incentive plans are appropriate when employees have sufficient control over work outcomes. Factors such as frequent equipment breakdowns and delays in receipt of raw materials limit employees' ability to control their performance levels. Employees are not likely to be diligent when they encounter interference: Chances are good that employees who previously experienced interference will expect to encounter interference in the future. Employees' resistance threatens profits because companies will find it difficult to motivate people to work hard when problem factors are not present.

Third, individual incentive plans are appropriate when they do not create a level of unhealthy competition among workers that ultimately leads to poor quality. For example, a company may create unhealthy competition when it limits the number of incentive awards to only 10 percent of the employees who have demonstrated the highest levels of performance. If the company judges performance according to volume, then employees may sacrifice quality as they compete against each other to outmatch quantity. In addition, under an incentive plan that rewards quantity of output, those employees who meet or exceed the highest standard established by their employer may be subject to intimidation by workers whose work falls below the standard.[5] Unions may use these intimidation tactics to prevent plan standards from being raised.

Defining Individual Incentives

Individual incentive plans reward employees for meeting such work-related performance standards as quality, productivity, customer satisfaction, safety, or attendance. Any one of these standards by itself or in combination may be used. A company ultimately should employ the standards that represent work that an employee actually performs. For instance, take the case of telemarketers. Customer satisfaction and sales volume measures indicate telemarketers' performance. Tardiness would not be as relevant unless absenteeism was a general management problem.

Managers should also choose factors that are within the individual employee's control when they create individual performance standards. Furthermore, employees must know about standards and potential awards before the performance period starts. When designed and implemented well, individual incentive plans reward employees based on results for which they are directly responsible. The end result should be that excellent performers receive higher incentive awards than poor performers.

Types of Individual Incentive Plans

There are four common types of individual incentive plans:

- Piecework plans
- Management incentive plans
- Behavioral encouragement plans
- Referral plans

PIECEWORK PLANS Companies generally use one of two **piecework plans.**[6] The first, which is typically found in manufacturing settings, rewards employees based on their individual hourly production against an objective output standard and is determined by the pace at which manufacturing equipment operates. For each hour, workers receive piecework incentives for every item produced over the designated production standard. Workers also receive a guaranteed hourly pay rate regardless of whether they meet the designated production standard. Table 4-3 illustrates the calculation of a piecework incentive.

Companies use piecework plans when the time to produce a unit is relatively short, usually less than 15 minutes, and the cycle repeats continuously. Piecework plans are usually found in such manufacturing industries as textiles and apparel.

Quality is also an important consideration. Companies do not reward employees for producing defective products. In the apparel industry, manufacturers attempt to minimize defect rates because they cannot sell defective clothing for the same price as nondefective clothing. Selling defective clothing at a lower price reduces company profits.

TABLE 4-3 **Calculation of a Piecework Award for a Garment Worker**

Piecework standard: 15 stitched garments per hour

Hourly base pay rate awarded to employees when the standard is not met: $4.50 per hour

That is, workers receive $4.50 per hour worked regardless of whether they meet the piecework standard of 15 stitched garments per hour.

Piecework incentive award: $0.75 per garment stitched per hour above the piecework standard

	Guaranteed Hourly Base Pay ($)	Piecework Award (No. of Garments Stitched above the Piecework Standard × Piecework Incentive Award)	Total Hourly Earnings ($)
First hour	4.50	10 garments × $0.75/garment = $7.50	12.00
Second hour	4.50	Fewer than 15 stitched garments, thus piecework award equals $0	4.50

The second type of piecework incentive plan establishes individual performance standards that include both objective and subjective criteria. Units produced represent an objective standard. Overall work quality is a subjective criterion that is based on supervisors' interpretations and judgments. For example, supervisors may judge customer service representatives' performances to be higher when sales professionals emphasize the benefits of purchasing extended product warranties than when sales professionals merely mention the availability and price of extended product warranties.

Economists argue that there are two advantages to companies of using piecework plans in manufacturing settings known as the **incentive effect** and **sorting effect**.[7] The incentive effect refers to a worker's willingness to work diligently to produce more quality output than simply attending work without putting in the effort. To put this simply, employees earn much less under the piecework system than they would under a standard hourly pay system. Whereas employees are certainly expected to perform without an incentive (piece rate), research shows that incentives often are associated with higher employee performance. The sorting effect addresses an employee's choice to stay versus leave his or her employer for another job, presumably one without an incentive pay contingency. Specifically, a hardworking, highly skilled employee is likely to choose to remain employed under an incentive system because both diligence and skill presumably contribute to higher quantity and quality of output—thus, higher pay.

MANAGEMENT INCENTIVE PLANS **Management incentive plans** award bonuses to managers when they meet or exceed objectives based on sales, profit, production, or other measures for their division, department, or unit. Management incentive plans differ from piecework plans in that piecework plans base rewards on the attainment of one specific objective and management incentive plans often require multiple complex objectives. For example, management incentive plans reward managers for increasing market share or reducing their budgets without compromising the quality and quantity of output. The best-known management incentive plan is management by objectives (MBO).[8] In Chapter 3, MBO was presented as an outcome-oriented performance appraisal technique for merit pay systems. When MBO is used as part of merit pay systems, superiors make subjective assessments of managers' performances, and they use these assessments to determine permanent merit pay increases. When used as part of incentive programs, superiors communicate the amount of incentive pay managers will receive based on the attainment of specific goals.

BEHAVIORAL ENCOURAGEMENT PLANS Under **behavioral encouragement plans,** employees receive payments for specific behavioral accomplishments (e.g., good attendance or safety records). For example, companies usually award monetary bonuses to employees who have exemplary attendance records for a specified period. When behavioral encouragement plans

TABLE 4-4 **A Sample Behavioral Encouragement Plan that Rewards Employee Attendance**

At the end of each 3-month period, employees with exemplary attendance records will receive monetary incentive awards according to the following schedule. Note that the number of days absent does not refer to such company-approved absences as vacation, personal illness, jury duty, bereavement leave, military duty, scheduled holidays, and educational leave.

Number of Days Absent	Monetary Incentive Award ($)
0 (perfect attendance)	250
1	200
2	100
3	50
4	25

are applied to safety records, workers earn awards for lower personal injury or accident rates associated with the improper use of heavy equipment or hazardous chemicals. Table 4-4 contains an illustration of a sample behavioral encouragement plan that rewards employees for excellent attendance. Employees can earn $250 for perfect attendance during a 3-month period. With perfect attendance for an entire year, employees can earn $1,000. Behavioral encouragement plans have the potential to save companies substantially more money than the cost of these awards. For example, frequent absenteeism in a company's workforce could disrupt production goals and quality. Customers may respond by choosing to make purchases for better quality products from other companies. Loss of customer bases will have a negative impact on profitability and reputation that prompts prospective customers to choose alternate sources to purchase products.

REFERRAL PLANS Companies commonly rely on referral bonuses to enhance recruitment of highly qualified employees. Employees may receive monetary bonuses under **referral plans** for referring new customers or recruiting successful job applicants. In the case of recruitment, employees can earn bonuses for making successful referrals for job openings. For example, there has been a tremendous shortage of nurses for the past several years. Because of the shortage, hospitals offer sign-on bonuses of up to $15,000 to recruit nurses and referral bonuses of up to $5,000. A successful referral usually means that companies award bonuses only if hired referrals remain employed with the company in good standing beyond a designated period, often at least 30 days. Referral plans rely on the idea that current employees' familiarity with company culture should enable them to identify viable candidates for job openings more efficiently than employment agencies could because agents are probably less familiar with client companies' cultures. Employees are likely to make only those referrals they truly believe are worthwhile because their personal reputations are at stake.

Advantages of Individual Incentive Pay Programs

There are three key advantages of individual incentive pay plans. First, individual incentive plans can promote the relationship between pay and performance. As discussed in Chapter 1, employees in the United States are motivated primarily by earning money. Employees strive for excellence when they expect to earn incentive awards commensurate with their job performance.

Second, individual incentive plans promote an equitable distribution of compensation within companies (i.e., the amount employees earn depends on their job performance). The better they perform, the more they earn. Equitable pay ultimately enables companies to retain the best performers. Paying better performers more money sends a signal that the company appropriately values positive job performance.

A third advantage of individual incentive plans is their compatibility with such individualistic cultures as the United States. Because U.S. employees are socialized to make individual contributions and be recognized for them, the national culture of the United States probably enhances the motivational value of individual incentive programs.

Disadvantages of Individual Incentive Pay Programs

Although individual incentive plans can prove effective in certain settings, these programs also have serious limitations. Supervisors, human resource (HR) managers, and compensation professionals should know about three potential problems with individual incentive plans.

Individual incentive plans possess the potential to promote inflexibility. Because supervisors determine employee performance levels, workers under individual incentive plans become dependent on supervisors for setting work goals. If employees become highly proficient performers, they are not likely to increase their performance beyond their reward compensation. For example, let's assume that management defines the maximum incentive award as $500 per month, which is awarded to employees whose productivity rates 15 percent above the performance standard. Employees who produce more than 15 percent above the production standard will not receive additional incentive pay beyond the $500. With this design, employees would not be motivated to improve their performance.

With merit pay systems, supervisors must develop and maintain comprehensive performance measures to properly grant incentive awards. Individual incentive programs pose measurement problems when management implements improved work methods or equipment. When such changes occur, it will take some time for employees to become proficient performers. Thus, it will be difficult for companies to determine equitable incentive awards, which may lead to employees' resistance to the new methods.

A third limitation of individual incentive plans is that they may encourage undesirable workplace behavior when these plans reward only one or a subset of dimensions that constitute employees' total job performance. Let's assume that an incentive plan rewards employees for quantity of output. If employees' jobs address such various dimensions as quantity of output, quality, and customer satisfaction, employees may focus on the one dimension—in this case, quantity of output—that leads to incentive pay and thereby neglect the other dimensions.

GROUP INCENTIVES

U.S. employers are increasingly using teams to get work done. Two main changes in the business environment have led to an increased use of teams in the workplace.[9] First, in the 1980s, many Japanese companies began conducting business in the United States, particularly in the automobile industry. A common feature of Japanese companies was the use of teams, which contributed to superior product quality. Second, team-based job design promotes innovation in the workplace.[10] At Rubbermaid, a manufacturer of such plastic household products as snap-together furniture and storage boxes, product innovation has become the rule since the implementation of project teams. Team members represent various cross-functional areas, including research and development (R&D), marketing, finance, and manufacturing. Rubbermaid attributes the rush on innovation to the cross-fertilization of ideas that has resulted from the work of these diverse teams.

Companies that use work teams need to change individualistic compensation practices so that groups are rewarded for their behavior together.[11] Team-based pay plans should accordingly emphasize cooperation between and within teams, compensate employees for additional responsibilities they often must assume in their roles as members of a team, and encourage team members to attain predetermined objectives for the team.[12] Merit, seniority, or individual incentives do not encourage team behaviors and may potentially limit team effectiveness. Experts suggest that traditional pay programs will undermine the ability of teams to function effectively.[13] Both merit- and seniority-based pay emphasize hierarchy among employees, which is incompatible with the very concept of a team.

Team-based organizational structures encourage team members to learn new skills and assume broader responsibility than is expected of them under traditional pay structures that are geared toward individuals. Rather than following specific orders from a supervisor, employees who work in teams must initiate plans for achieving their team's production. A pay plan for teams usually emphasizes cooperation and rewards its members for the additional responsibilities they must take on, as well as the skills a nd knowledge they must acquire. Chapter 5 will show how skill- and knowledge-based pay plans can address these additional responsibilities.

Defining Group Incentives

Group incentive programs reward employees for their collective performance, rather than for each employee's individual performance. Group incentive programs are most effective when all group members have some impact on achieving the goal, even though individual contributions might not be equal. Boeing utilizes a team-based approach to manufacture its model 777 jumbo jet. More than 200 cross-functional teams contribute to the construction of each jet, and the contribution of each individual is clearly not equal. Installing such interior trim features as upholstery is not nearly as essential to the airworthiness of each jet as are the jobs of ensuring the aerodynamic integrity of each aircraft.

Well-designed group incentive plans ultimately reinforce teamwork, cultivate loyalty to the company, and increase productivity. For instance, at Volvo's Uddevalla manufacturing facility in Sweden, each team is responsible for managing itself. As a result, each team manages its own budget and determines whom to hire. The renowned quality of Volvo automobiles has been attributed to the effective utilization of teams.

Types of Group Incentive Plans

Companies use two major types of group incentive plans:

- *Team-based or small-group incentive plans.* A small group of employees shares a financial reward when a specific objective is met.
- *Gain sharing plans.* A group of employees, generally a department or work unit, is rewarded for productivity gains.

TEAM-BASED OR SMALL-GROUP INCENTIVE PLANS **Team-based incentives** are similar to individual incentives with one exception. Each group member receives a financial reward for the attainment of a group goal. The timely completion of a market survey report depends on the collaborative efforts of several individual employees. For example, some group members design the survey; another set collects the survey data; and a third set analyzes the data and writes the report. It is the timely completion of the market survey report, not the completion of any one of the jobs that are required to produce it, which determines whether group members will receive incentive pay.

There are many kinds of team incentive programs. Most companies define these programs based on the type of team:[14]

Work (process) teams refer to organizational units that perform the work of the organization on an ongoing basis. Membership is relatively permanent, and members work full time in the team. Customer service teams and assembly teams on production lines represent excellent examples of work teams. Work teams are effective when individuals are cross-trained to perform team members' work when they are absent. The goal is to maintain consistency in performance quality (e.g., addressing customer concerns promptly even when one or more team members are absent) and output (e.g., in the case of assembly teams). Team members ultimately engage in performance sharing rather than focusing exclusively on one set of tasks. The knowledge and skill sets required to contribute effectively to the work of a process team can be acquired with the assistance of person-focused pay, which we discuss in Chapter 5.

Project teams consist of a group of people assigned to complete a one-time project. Members usually have well-defined roles and may work on specific phases of the project, either full time or in addition to other work responsibilities of the team. Project teams usually work across such functions as engineering, product development, and marketing to ensure that the final product meets company specifications in terms of cost, quality, and responsiveness to market demands (e.g., Toyota's hybrid vehicles). Many individuals collaborated to ensure the production of cars that rely less on fossil fuels, demonstrate excellent gas mileage, and offer the same driving experience that people have come to expect of gasoline-powered automobiles.

Parallel teams, or task forces, include employees assigned to work on a specific task in addition to normal work duties. The modifier *parallel* indicates that an employee works on the team task while continuing to work on normal duties. Also, parallel teams or task forces operate on a temporary basis until their work culminates in a recommendation to top management. Task forces are used to evaluate existing systems and processes, to select new technology, and to improve existing products. People often serve on a voluntary basis or are appointed; in many cases, they are not compensated specifically for extra work or outcome of extra work.

Teams or groups may ultimately receive incentive pay based on such criteria as customer satisfaction (i.e., customer service quality), safety records, quality, and production records. Although these criteria apply to other categories of incentive programs as well (individual, companywide, and group plans), companies allocate awards to each worker based on the group's attainment of predetermined performance standards.

Human resource managers must devise methods for allocating incentives to team members. Although the team-based reward is generated by the performance of the team, the incentive payments are typically distributed to members of the team individually. Human resource experts allocate rewards in one of three ways:

- Equal incentive payments to all team members.
- Differential incentive payments to team members based on their contribution to the team's performance.
- Differential payments determined by a ratio of each team member's base pay to the total base pay of the group.

The first method—the equal incentives payment approach—reinforces cooperation among team members except when team members perceive differences in members' contributions or performance. The second method—the differential incentive payments approach—distributes rewards based to some extent on individual performance. Differential approaches obviously can hinder cooperative behavior. Some employees may focus on their own performance rather than on the group's performance because they wish to maximize their income. As a compromise, companies may base part of the incentive on individual performance, with the remainder based on the team's performance. The third disbursement method—differential payments by ratio of base pay—rewards each group member in proportion to her or his base pay. This approach assumes that employees with higher base pay contribute more to the company and so should be rewarded in accord with that worth.

GAIN SHARING PLANS **Gain sharing** describes group incentive systems that provide participating employees with an incentive payment based on improved company performance for increased productivity, increased customer satisfaction, lower costs, or better safety records.[15] Gain sharing was developed so that all employees could benefit financially from productivity improvements resulting from the suggestion system. In addition to serving as a compensation tool, most gain sharing reflects a management philosophy that emphasizes employee involvement. The use of gain sharing is most appropriate where workplace technology does not constrain productivity improvements. For example, assembly line workers' abilities to improve productivity may be limited. Increasing the speed of the conveyor belts may compromise workers' safety.

Most gain sharing programs have three components:[16]

- Leadership philosophy
- Employee involvement systems
- Bonus

The first component—leadership philosophy—refers to a cooperative organizational climate that promotes high levels of trust, open communication, and participation. The second component—employee involvement systems—drives organizational productivity improvements. Employee involvement systems use broadly based suggestion systems. Anyone can make suggestions to a committee made up of both hourly and management employees who oversee the suggestion implementation. This involvement system also may include other innovative employee involvement practices (e.g., problem-solving task forces).

The bonus is the third component of a gain sharing plan. A company awards gain sharing bonuses when its actual productivity exceeds its targeted productivity level. The gain sharing bonuses are usually based on a formula that measures productivity that employees perceive as fair and the employer believes will result in improvements in company performance. Employees typically receive gain sharing bonuses on a monthly basis. Most bonuses range between 5 and 10 percent of an employee's base annual pay. A noteworthy exception to this norm is AmeriSteel. On average, AmeriSteel's gain sharing plan pays out between 35 and 45 percent of base pay.

Although many accounts of gain sharing use can be found in the practitioner and scholarly literature, no one has completed a comprehensive, soundly designed investigation of the effectiveness of gain sharing programs.[17] Meanwhile, gain sharing programs' success has been attributed to company cultures that support cooperation among employees.[18] Some gain sharing attempts have failed. Such organizational, external environment, and financial information factors as poor communications within and across departments, highly competitive product markets, and variable corporate profits over time can inhibit effective gain sharing programs.[19] Poor communications will stifle the creativity needed to improve the efficiency of work processes when employees focus exclusively on their own work. Highly competitive product markets often require companies to make frequent changes to their production methods, as in the automobile industry, where such changes occur each year with the introduction of new models. When companies make frequent or sudden changes, employees must have time to learn the new processes well before they can offer productive suggestions. Companies that experience variable profits from year to year most likely do not use gain sharing because management sets aside as much excess cash as possible in reserve for periods when profits are down and excess cash is scarce.

The Scanlon, Rucker, and Improshare gain sharing plans are the most common forms used in companies, and they were also the first types of gain sharing plans developed and used by employers. These plans were adopted wholesale in the early days of gain sharing. Employers today generally modify one of these traditional plans to meet their needs or adopt hybrid plans.

THE SCANLON PLAN Joseph Scanlon first developed the gain sharing concept in 1935 as an employee involvement system without a pay element. The hallmark of the **Scanlon plan** is its emphasis on employee involvement. Scanlon believed that employees will exercise self-direction and self-control if they are committed to company objectives and that employees will accept and seek out responsibility if given the opportunity.[20] Current Scanlon plans include monetary rewards to employees for productivity improvements. Scanlon plans assume that companies will be able to offer higher pay to workers, generate increased profits for stockholders, and lower prices for consumers. The *Scanlon plan* is a generic term referring to any gain sharing plan that has characteristics common to the original gain sharing plan devised by Scanlon. Scanlon plans have the following three components:[21]

- An emphasis on teamwork to reduce costs, assisted by management-supplied information on production concerns.
- Suggestion systems that route cost-saving ideas from the workforce through a labor–management committee that evaluates and acts on accepted suggestions.
- A monetary reward based on productivity improvements to encourage employee involvement.

Scanlon plan employee involvement systems include a formal suggestion program structured at two levels. Production-level committees, usually including a department foreman or supervisor and at least one elected worker, communicate the suggestion program and its reward features to workers. Production committee members encourage and assist workers in making suggestions and formally record suggestions for consideration. Production committees may also reject suggestions that are not feasible, but they must provide a written explanation of the reasons for the rejection to the worker who made the suggestion. Providing the written rationale under this circumstance is key to helping employees understand why the suggestions are not feasible and, thus, workers are not discouraged from making suggestions in the future. After employees' suggestions have been fully implemented, they typically receive bonuses on a monthly basis.

The production committee forwards appropriate suggestions to a companywide screening committee, which also includes worker representatives. This committee reviews suggestions referred by the production committees, serves as a communications link between management and employees, and reviews the company's performance each month.

Actual gain sharing formulas are designed to suit the individual needs of the company.[22] Formulas are usually based on the ratio between labor costs and **sales value of production (SVOP).**[23] The SVOP is the sum of sales revenue plus the value of goods in inventory.

Smaller Scanlon ratios indicate that labor costs are lower relative to SVOP. Companies definitely strive for lower ratios, as Table 4-5 illustrates. In addition, Table 4-5 shows the calculation for a bonus distribution under a Scanlon plan.

THE RUCKER PLAN Similar to Scanlon's plan, the **Rucker plan** was developed by Allan W. Rucker in 1933. Both the Scanlon and Rucker plans emphasize employee involvement and provide monetary incentives to encourage employee participation. The main difference lies in the formula

TABLE 4-5 Illustration of a Scanlon Plan

For the period 2000–2003, the labor costs of XYZ Manufacturing Company have averaged $44,000,000 per year. During the same 3-year period, the sales value of XYZ's production (SVOP) averaged $83,000,000 per year. (As an aside, of the $83,000,000, $65,000,000 represents sales revenue and $18,000,000 represents the value of goods held in inventory.) The Scanlon ratio for XYZ Manufacturing Company is:

$$\$44,000,000/\$83,000,000 = 0.53$$

The ratio of 0.53 is the base line. Any benefits that result from an improvement (e.g., an improvement in production methods that results in a reduction in labor costs) are shared with workers. In other words, when improvements lead to a Scanlon ratio that is lower than the standard of 0.53, employees will receive gain sharing bonuses.

The operating information for XYZ Manufacturing Company for March 2003 was as follows:

Total labor costs	$3,100,000
SVOP	$7,200,000

The Scanlon ratio, based on March 2003 information was

$$\frac{\$3,100,000}{\$7,200,000} = 0.43$$

The Scanlon ratio for March 2003 was less than the standard of 0.53, which was based on historical data. In order for there to be a payout, labor costs for March 2003 must be less than $3,816,000 (i.e., 0.53 × $7,200,000); $3,816,000 represents allowable labor costs for March 2003 based on the Scanlon standard established for XYZ Manufacturing.

In summary, the allowable labor costs for March 2003 were $3,816,000. The actual labor costs were $3,100,000. Thus, the savings $716,000 ($3,816,000–$3,100,000) is available for distribution as a bonus.

used to measure productivity. Rucker plans use a **value-added formula** to measure productivity. Value added is the difference between the value of the sales price of a product and the value of materials purchased to make the product. The following example illustrates the concept of value added based on the sequence of events that eventually lead to selling bread to consumers. These events include growing the wheat, milling the wheat, adding the wheat to other ingredients to make bread, and selling the bread to consumers.

A farmer grows the wheat and sells it to a miller; the added value is the difference in the income the farmer receives for the wheat and the costs incurred for purchasing seed, fertilizer, fuel, and other supplies. The miller, in turn, buys the wheat from the farmer, mills it, and then sells it to a bakery. The difference in the cost of buying the wheat and the price it is sold for to the baker is the amount of "value" the miller "adds" in the milling processes. The same process is repeated by the baker, as the flour that was milled by the miller is mixed with other ingredients, baked, and sold as bread either to the consumer or to a retailer who in turn sells it to the consumer. The baker "adds value" by blending in the other ingredients to the flour and baking the bread. If the bread is sold to the consumer through a retailer, then the retailer also "adds value" by buying the bread from the bakery, transporting it to a store convenient for the consumer, displaying the bread, and selling it. The total of all the added values from each step along the way equals the total contribution to the overall economy from the chain of events.[24]

The following ratio is used to determine whether bonuses will be awarded under a Rucker plan:

$$\frac{\text{Value added}}{\text{Total employment costs}}$$

In contrast to the Scanlon ratio, companies prefer a larger Rucker ratio. A larger Rucker ratio indicates that the value added is greater than total employment costs. Table 4-6 illustrates the calculation for bonus distribution under the Rucker plan.

TABLE 4-6 Illustration of a Rucker Plan

In 2002, ABC Manufacturing Company generated net sales of $7,500,000. The company paid $3,200,000 for materials, $250,000 for sundry supplies, and $225,000 for such services as liability insurance, basic maintenance, and utilities. On the basis of these data, value added was $3,825,000 (i.e., net sales − costs of materials, supplies, and services rendered), that is, $7,500,000 − ($3,200,000 + $250,000 + $225,000).

For the same year, total employment costs were $2,400,000, which includes hourly wages for nonexempt workers, annual salaries for exempt employees, payroll taxes, and all benefit costs. Based on the Rucker formula, the ratio of value added to total employment costs was 1.59. This ratio means that if there are to be bonuses, each dollar attributed to employment costs must be accompanied by creating at least $1.59 of value added.

The operating information for ABC Manufacturing Company for the month July 2000 was as follows:

Value added	$670,000
Total employment costs	$625,000

The Rucker ratio, based on July 2002 information, was:

$$\frac{\$670,000}{\$625,000} = 1.07$$

The Rucker ratio for July 2003 is less than the standard of 1.59, which was based on historical data. In order for there to be a payout, value added for July 2003 must be more than the standard, which would be $1,065,300 (1.59 × $670,000). However, based on the Rucker ratio obtained for July 2003 (1.07), value added was only $716,900. Employees of ABC Manufacturing, therefore, will not receive any gain sharing bonuses for July 2003 performance.

Invented by Mitchell Fein in 1973, **Improshare**—Improved Productivity through Sharing—measures productivity physically rather than in terms of dollar savings like those used in the Scanlon and Rucker plans. These programs aim to produce more products with fewer labor hours. Under Improshare, the emphasis is on providing employees with an incentive to finish products.

The Improshare bonus is based on a **labor hour ratio formula.** A standard is determined by analyzing historical accounting data to find the number of labor hours needed to complete a product. Productivity is then measured as a ratio of standard labor hours and actual labor hours. Unlike the Rucker and Scanlon plans, employee participation is not a feature, and workers receive bonuses on a weekly basis.

Improshare plans feature a **buy-back provision**. Under this provision, a maximum productivity improvement payout level is placed on productivity gains. Any bonus money that is generated because of improvements above the maximum is placed in a reserve. If productivity improves to the point where the maximum is repeatedly exceeded, the firm buys back the amount of the productivity improvement over the maximum with a one-time payment to employees. This payment usually is equal to the amount in the reserve. The company then is permitted to adjust the standards so that a new ceiling can be set at a higher level of productivity. In unionized settings, management's discretion may be challenged by unions when union leadership believes that management is simply trying to exploit workers by making it more difficult for them to receive bonuses.

In summary, the Scanlon, Rucker, and Improshare plans are among the best-known kinds of gain sharing programs that are used by companies. Although the principle underlying these different plans is the same (i.e., a group incentive system that provides all or most employees a bonus payment based on improved company performance), they each rest on slightly different assumptions. Table 4-7 details a comparison of these three plans.

One final point about gain sharing plans warrants attention. We reviewed the most common types of gain sharing plans used in the United States. Companies are increasingly combining typical gain sharing plans with other approaches to boost productivity and cost savings to an even greater degree than ever before.

Advantages of Group Incentives

The use of group incentive plans has two advantages for companies. First, companies can more easily develop performance measures for group incentive plans than they can for individual

TABLE 4-7 Scanlon, Rucker, and Improshare Plans: A Comparison of Key Features

Feature	Scanlon	Rucker	Improshare
Program goal	Productivity improvement	Productivity improvement	Productivity improvement
Basis for savings	Labor costs	Labor costs plus raw materials costs plus services costs (e.g., utilities)	Completing work at or sooner than production standard
Employee involvement	Required	Required	NA
Type of employee involvement	Screening and production committees	Screening and production committees	NA
Bonus payout frequency	Monthly	Monthly	Weekly

incentive plans. There are obviously fewer groups in a company than individuals. Thus, companies generally use fewer resources (e.g., staff time) to develop performance measures. In addition, judging the quality of the final product makes the most sense because companies must deliver high-quality products to maintain competitiveness. During the late 1970s and early 1980s, U.S. automobile manufacturers (especially Chrysler Corporation) lost substantial market share to foreign automobile manufacturers (e.g., Honda and Toyota) because foreign automakers marketed automobiles of substantially higher quality than U.S. automakers. The trend did not change until U.S. automakers manufactured high-quality vehicles, which they began to market in the late 1980s.

Greater group cohesion is the second advantage associated with group incentive plans.[25] Cohesive groups usually work more effectively toward achieving common goals than do individual group members focusing on the specific tasks for which they are responsible. Working collaboratively is undoubtedly in group members' best interests in order to maximize their incentive awards.

Disadvantages of Group Incentives

The main disadvantage of group incentive compensation is employee turnover. Companies' implementation of group incentive programs may lead to turnover because of the **free-rider effect.** Some employees may make fewer contributions to the group goals because they possess lower ability, skills, or experience than other group members. In some groups, members may deliberately choose to put forth less effort, particularly when each group member receives the same incentive compensation regardless of individual contributions to the group goals. In any case, the free-rider effect initially leads to feelings of inequity among those who make the greatest contributions to the attainment of the group goal. Over time, members who make the greatest contributions are likely to leave.

Group members may feel uncomfortable with the fact that other members' performance influences their compensation level. Exemplary performers are more likely to feel this way when other group members are not contributing equally to the attainment of group goals. The lower performance of a few group members may lead to lower earnings for all members of the group. Discomfort with group incentive plans is likely to be heightened where incentive compensation represents the lion's share of core compensation.

COMPANYWIDE INCENTIVES

The use of companywide incentive plans can be traced to the nineteenth century. Companies instituted profit sharing programs to ease workers' dissatisfaction with low pay and to change their beliefs that company management paid workers substandard wages while earning substantial profits. Quite simply, management believed that workers would be less likely to challenge managerial practices if they received a share of company profits.

Defining Companywide Incentives

Companywide incentive plans reward employees when the company exceeds minimum acceptable performance standards (e.g., profits or the overall value of the company based on its stock price). As competitive pressures on companies increased, management sought methods to improve employee productivity. Companies presently use companywide incentive programs to motivate employees to work harder for increased profits or increased company value to owners. Advocates of companywide incentive plans believe that well-designed programs make workers' and owners' goals more compatible as workers strive toward increasing company profits or value.

Types of Companywide Incentive Plans

Companies use two major types of companywide incentive plans:

- *Profit sharing plans.* Employees earn a financial reward when their company's profit objective is met.
- *Employee stock option plans.* Companies grant employees the right to purchase shares of company stock.

PROFIT SHARING PLANS **Profit sharing plans** pay a portion of company profits to employees, separate from base pay, cost-of-living adjustments, or permanent merit pay increases. Two basic kinds of profit sharing plans are used widely today. First, **current profit sharing** plans award cash to employees, typically on a quarterly or annual basis. Second, **deferred profit sharing** plans place cash awards in trust accounts for employees. These trusts are set aside on employees' behalf as a source of retirement income. Apart from the time horizon, these plans differ with regard to taxation. Current profit sharing plans provide cash to employees as part of their regular core compensation; thus, these payments are subject to IRS taxation when they are earned. Deferred profit sharing plans are not taxed until the employee begins to make withdrawals during retirement. Premature withdrawal of funds that were secured under a deferred compensation plan is subject to stiff tax penalties. The IRS established this penalty to discourage employees from making premature withdrawals. Some companies offer deferred compensation as one kind of retirement program. We will discuss deferred profit sharing plans in Chapter 10. The focus here will be on current profit sharing plans because employees receive cash compensation as a reward for on-the-job performance.

Calculating Profit Sharing Awards HR professionals determine the pool of profit sharing money with any of three possible formulas. A fixed first-dollar-of-profits formula uses a specific percentage of either pretax or posttax annual profits, contingent upon the successful attainment of a company goal. For instance, a company might establish that the profit sharing fund will equal 7 percent of corporate profits; however, payment is contingent on a specified reduction in scrap rates.

Second, companies may use a graduated first-dollar-of-profits formula instead of a fixed percentage. For example, a company may choose to share 3 percent of the first $8 million of profits and 6 percent of the profits in excess of that level. Graduated formulas motivate employees to strive for extraordinary profit targets by sharing even more of the incremental gain.

Third, profitability threshold formulas fund profit sharing pools only if profits exceed a predetermined minimum level but fall below some established maximum level. Companies establish minimums to guarantee a return to shareholders before they distribute profits to employees. They establish maximums because they attribute any profits beyond this level to factors other than employee productivity or creativity (e.g., technological innovation).

After management selects a funding formula for the profit sharing pool, they must consider how to distribute pool money among employees. Companies usually make distributions in one of three ways: equal payments to all employees, proportional payments to employees based on annual salary, and proportional payments to employees based on their contribution to profits. Equal payments to all employees reflect a belief that all employees should share equally in the company's gain in order to promote cooperation among employees; however, employee contributions to profits probably vary. Most employers accordingly divide the profit sharing pool among employees based on a differential basis.

Companies may disburse profits based on proportional payments to employees based on their annual salaries. As we will detail in Chapters 6 and 7, salary levels vary based on both internal and external factors; in general, the higher the salary, the more work the company assigns to a job. Higher-paying jobs presumably indicate more potential to influence a company's competitive position. For any given job, pay will differ according to performance or seniority. Chapter 3 notes that higher performance levels and seniority result in greater worth.

Still another approach is to disburse profits as proportional payments to employees based on their contribution to profits. Some companies measure employee contributions to profit based on job performance; however, this approach is not very feasible because it is difficult to isolate each employee's contributions to profits. For example, how does a secretary's performance (based on answering telephones, greeting visitors, and typing memos) directly contribute to company performance?

Companies can treat profit sharing distributions either as compensation awarded in addition to an employee's base pay or as "pay at risk." In the former case, base pay is set at externally competitive levels, which makes any profit sharing tantamount to a bonus. In the latter case, base pay is set below the average for competing employers, which creates a sense of risk. Employees' earnings for a given period may thus be relatively meager or relatively sizable, compared with what they could earn elsewhere.

Advantages of Profit Sharing Plans The use of a profit sharing plan has two main advantages, one for employees and the other for companies. When properly designed, profit sharing plans enable employees to share in companies' fortunes. As employees benefit from profit sharing plans, they will be more likely to work productively to promote profits. The upshot of enhanced employee productivity obviously is greater profits for companies that use profit sharing plans.

Companies that use profit sharing programs gain greater financial flexibility. As we discussed, monetary payouts to employees vary with profit levels. During economic downturns, payout levels are significantly lower than they are during economic boom periods. This feature of profit sharing plans enables companies to use limited cash reserves where needed (e.g., for R&D activities).

Disadvantages of Profit Sharing Plans There are two main disadvantages associated with profit sharing plans. The first one directly affects employees; the second affects companies. Profit sharing plans may undermine the economic security of employees, particularly if profit sharing represents a sizable portion of direct compensation. Because company profits vary from year to year, so do employees' earnings. Thus, employees will find it difficult to predict their earnings, which will affect their saving and buying behavior. If there is significant variability in earnings, a company's excellent performers are likely to leave for employment with competitors. The turnover of excellent performers certainly represents a significant disadvantage to companies.

Employers also find profit sharing programs to be problematic under certain conditions. Profit sharing plans may fail to motivate employees because they do not see a direct link between their efforts and corporate profits. Hourly employees in particular may have trouble seeing this connection because their efforts appear to be several steps removed from the company's performance. For instance, an assembly line worker who installs interior trim (e.g., carpeting and seats) to automobiles may not find any connection between his or her efforts and the level of company profits because interior trim represents just one of many steps in the production of automobiles.

EMPLOYEE STOCK OPTION PLANS Under **employee stock option plans,** companies grant employees the right to purchase shares of company stock. **Company stock** represents total equity of a company. **Company stock shares** represent equity segments of equal value. Equity interest increases positively with the number of stock shares. **Stock options** describe an employee's right to purchase company stock. Employees do not actually own stock until they exercise the stock option rights. This is done by purchasing stock at a designated price after a company-chosen time period lapses, usually no more than 5 years. Employee stock options provide an incentive to work productively, with the expectation that collective employee productivity will increase the value of company stock over time. Employees earn monetary compensation when they sell the stock at a higher price than they originally paid for it.

Employee stock option plans represent just one type of general stock compensation plan. Two other basic kinds of stock plans are widely used today. First, **employee stock ownership** plans (ESOPs) place company stock in trust accounts for employees. The purpose of ESOPs is similar to deferred profit sharing because these trusts are set aside on employees' behalf as a source of retirement income and these awards provide favorable treatment to employees. Discussion of ESOPs is deferred to Chapter 10. Second, **stock compensation plans** represent an important type of deferred compensation for executives. **Deferred compensation** is supposed to create a sense of ownership, aligning the interests of the executive with those of the owners or shareholders of the company over the long term. There are several kinds of stock compensation plans for executives. Discussion of these types of plans is set aside for Chapter 12.

DESIGNING INCENTIVE PAY PROGRAMS

When designing an incentive pay plan, HR professionals and line managers should consider five key factors:

- Whether the plan should be based on group or individual employee performance.
- The level of risk employees will be willing to accept in their overall compensation package.
- Whether incentive pay should replace or complement traditional pay.
- The criteria by which performance should be judged.
- The time horizon for goals—long term, short term, or a combination of both.

Group versus Individual Incentives

Companies considering various design alternatives should choose a design that fits the structure of the company. Group incentive programs are most suitable where the nature of the work is interdependent and the contributions of individual employees are difficult to measure. In such situations, companies require cooperative behavior among their employees. Companies may be able to encourage team behavior by linking compensation to the achievement of department or division goals and eliminating from the pay determination process such factors that are outside the group's control as the late delivery of raw materials by an independent vendor.

On the other hand, individual incentive plans reward employees for meeting or surpassing such predetermined individual goals as production or sales quotas. The attainment of individual goals should be well within employees' grasp as is the case for group incentives. Moreover, goals for individual incentive programs should be based on independent work rather than interdependent work. For example, it would be appropriate to base an employee's incentive on typing accuracy because the work can be performed independently and there are few external constraints on an employee's ability to complete such work. At the group level, it would be reasonable to provide incentives to the individual members of a sales team. In the case of computer hardware and networks, the sale and implementation of these products involve a team of marketing professionals and technical experts who depend on the others' expertise to identify the appropriate configuration of hardware and networking equipment (i.e., meeting the client's needs) and to install the equipment in the client's company successfully.

Level of Risk

Careful consideration should be given to the level of risk employees are willing to accept. As mentioned previously, incentive pay may complement base salary or may be used in place of all or a portion of base salary. The level of risk clearly increases as incentive pay represents a greater proportion of total core compensation. The level of risk tends to be greater among higher-level employees than among those who are at the lower levels of a company's job structure. It is reasonable to infer that the attainment of a first-line supervisor's goal of maintaining a packing department's level of productivity above a predetermined level is less risky than the achievement of a sales manager's goal of increasing market share by 10 percent in a market where the competition is already quite stiff. Apart from an employee's rank, the level of risk chosen should depend on the extent to which employees control the attainment of the desired goal. The adoption of incentive pay programs makes the most sense when participants have a reasonable degree of control over the attainment of the plan's goals. Incentive programs logically are bound to fail when the goals are simply out of reach because they are too difficult or because extraneous factors are hampering employees' efforts to meet goals.

Complementing or Replacing Base Pay

When complementing base pay, a company awards incentive pay in addition to an employee's base pay and benefits. On the other hand, companies may reduce base pay by placing the reduced portion at risk in an incentive plan. For instance, if a company grants its employees 10 percent raises each year, the company could, instead, grant its employees a 4 percent cost-of-living increase and use the remaining 6 percent as incentive by awarding none of it to below-average performers, only half of it to employees whose performance is average, and the entire 6 percent to employees whose performance is above average. In this scenario, the 6 percent that was expected by the employees to become part of their base pay is no longer a guarantee because that potential salary has been placed at risk. By introducing risk into the pay program, employees have the potential to earn more than the 6 percent because poor performers will receive less, leaving more to be distributed to exemplary performers.

Companies in such cyclical industries as retail sales could benefit by including an incentive component in the core compensation programs they offer to employees. During slow business periods, the use of regular merit pay programs that add permanent increments to base pay can create budget problems. If incentive pay were used instead of permanent merit raises, then the level of expenditure on compensation would vary with levels of business activity. In effect, the use of incentive pay can lower payroll costs during lean periods and enhance the level of rewards when business activity picks up.

Performance Criteria

As seen in the discussion of performance appraisal in Chapter 3, the measures used to appraise employee performance obviously should be quantifiable and accessible. For incentive pay programs, common measures of employee performance are company profits, sales revenue, and number of units produced by a business unit. The measures chosen preferably should relate to the company's competitive strategy. For instance, if a company is attempting to enhance quality, its incentive plan would probably reward employees on the basis of customer satisfaction with quality.

In reality, more than one performance measure may be relevant. In such instances, a company is likely to employ all of the measures as a basis for awarding incentives. The weighting scheme would reflect the relative importance of each performance criterion to the company's competitive strategy [e.g., company performance (10 percent), unit performance (40 percent), and individual performance (50 percent), incorporating all of the organizational levels]. An employee clearly would receive an incentive even if company or departmental performance was poor. In effect, the relative weights are indicative of the degree of risk to an employee that is inherent in these plans. Compared with the previous example, the following plan would be quite risky: 50 percent company performance, 35 percent departmental performance, and 15 percent individual performance. Employees' earnings would depend mainly on company and departmental performance over which they possess less control than they do over their own performance.

Time Horizon: Short Term versus Long Term

A key feature of incentive pay plans is the time orientation. There are no definitive standards to distinguish between short term and long term. A general rule of thumb is that short-term goals generally can be achieved in 5 years or less and that long-term goals may require even longer.

In general, incentives for lower-level employees tend to be based on short-term goals that are within the control of such employees. For example, production workers' performance is judged on periods as short as 1 hour. On the other hand, incentive programs for professionals and executives have a long-term orientation. For instance, rewarding an engineer's innovation in product design requires a long-term orientation because it takes an extended amount of time to move through the series of steps required to bring the innovation to the marketplace (e.g., patent approval, manufacturing, and market distribution). The incentives that executives receive are based on a long-term horizon because their success is matched against the endurance of a company over time.

COMPENSATION IN ACTION

The use of incentive pay by an employer can be an effective way to tie individual or team performance to compensation. Many of the items in the *Action Checklist* for Chapter 4 are critical to the proper formation and administration of an incentive pay program (i.e., accurate criteria and measurement along with ongoing and honest performance discussions). Once this critical foundation is established, line managers and HR and compensation specialists must ensure that the plan is understood by employees and they can see the link between their performance and the portion of pay at risk.

Action checklist for line managers and HR—establishing an incentive pay program

HR takes the lead

- Work with compensation specialists on your team to benchmark industry competitors to identify whether individual, group, or companywide programs are being used (to stay current with trends and ensure that the best people are retained).

- Work with line managers, based on the chosen program (individual, group, or companywide), to choose which types of plan are utilized.
- Hold roundtable discussions with employees to gather feedback on proposed program and to identify potential areas where additional buy-in may be necessary.

Line managers take the lead

- Work with HR to identify the desired behavior(s) you want to tie to incentives—ensuring that the focus on these behaviors does not come at the expense of other desired outcomes.
- Seek the education of HR to understand limitations of the chosen plan and how to overcome some of the potential pitfalls; plan should be monitored and/or tailored if these obstacles lead to the wrong behaviors being rewarded.
- Provide proper information to HR so that a communication plan is created for rollout and implementation of the program—HR will form frequently asked questions (FAQs) and talking points that detail rationale for the change.

END OF CHAPTER

MyManagementLab

Go to **mymanagementlab.com** to complete the problems marked with this icon ⭐.

Summary

This chapter provided a discussion of the incentive pay concept—how incentive pay differs from traditional bases for pay such as seniority pay and merit pay; varieties of individual, group, and companywide incentives; issues about designing incentive pay programs; and its fit with competitive strategy. Companies should seriously consider adopting incentive pay programs when the conditions for using them are appropriate.

Perhaps one of the greatest challenges for companies is to ensure that employees perceive a connection between job performance and the rewards they receive. Another challenge is for companies to balance the level of risk employees will bear, particularly given the fact that U.S. employees are accustomed to receiving base pay and regular permanent increases according to seniority or merit pay systems.

Key Terms

incentive pay 77
variable pay 77
piecework plans 81
incentive effect 82
sorting effect 82
management incentive plans 82
behavioral encouragement plans 82
referral plans 83
group incentive programs 85
team-based incentives 85

gain sharing 86
Scanlon plan 87
sales value of production (SVOP) 88
Rucker plan 88
value-added formula 89
Improshare 90
labor hour ratio formula 90
buy-back provision 90
free-rider effect 91
profit sharing plans 92

current profit sharing 92
deferred profit sharing 92
employee stock option plans 93
company stock 93
company stock shares 93
stock options 93
employee stock ownership plans (ESOPs) 93
stock compensation plans 94
deferred compensation 94

⭐ Discussion Questions

4-1. Indicate whether you agree or disagree with the following statement: "Individual incentive plans are less preferable than group incentives and companywide incentives." Explain your answer.

4-2. There is currently a tendency among business professionals to endorse the use of incentive pay plans. Identify two jobs for which individual incentive pay is appropriate and two jobs for which individual incentive pay is inappropriate. Be sure to include your justification.

4-3. Critics of profit sharing plans maintain that these plans do not motivate employees to perform at higher levels. Under what conditions are profit sharing plans not likely to motivate employees?

4-4. Unlike individual incentive programs, group and companywide incentive programs reward individuals based on group (e.g., cost savings in a department) and companywide (e.g., profits) performance standards, respectively. Under group and companywide incentive programs, it is possible for poor performers to benefit without making substantial contributions to group or company goals. What can companies do to ensure that poor performers do not benefit?

4-5. Opponents of incentive pay programs argue that these programs manipulate employees more than seniority and merit pay programs. Discuss your views of this statement.

CASE
Individual or Team Reward?

⭐ *An additional Supplemental Case can be found on MyManagementLab.*

Jack Hopson has been making wood furniture for more than 10 years. He recently joined Metropolitan Furniture and has some ideas for Sally Boston, the company's CEO. Jack likes working for Sally because she is very open to employee suggestions and is serious about making the company a success. Metropolitan is currently paying Jack a competitive hourly pay rate for him to build various designs of tables and chairs. However, Jack thinks that an incentive pay plan might convince him and his coworkers to put forth more effort.

At Jack's previous employer, a competing furniture maker, Jack was paid on a piece-rate pay plan. The company paid Jack a designated payment for every chair or table that he completed. Jack felt this plan provided him an incentive to work harder to build the furniture pieces. Sally likes Jack's idea; however, Sally is concerned about how such a plan would affect the employees' need to work together as a team.

While the workers at Metropolitan build most furniture pieces individually, they often need to pitch in and work as a team. Each worker receives individual assignments, but as a delivery date approaches for a preordered furniture set due to a customer, the workers must help each other complete certain pieces of the set to ensure on-time delivery. A reputation for on-time delivery differentiates Metropolitan from its competitors. Several companies that compete against Metropolitan have a reputation of late deliveries, which gives Metropolitan a competitive edge. Because their promise of on-time delivery is such a high priority, Sally is concerned that a piece-rate pay plan may prevent employees from working together to complete furniture sets.

Sally agrees with Jack that an incentive pay plan would help boost productivity, but she thinks that a team-based incentive pay plan may be a better approach. She has considered offering a team-based plan that provides a bonus payment when each set of furniture is completed in time for scheduled delivery. However, after hearing from Jack about the success of the piece-rate pay plan at his previous employer, she is unsure of which path to take.

Questions:
4-6. What are some advantages of offering a piece-rate pay plan to the furniture builders at Metropolitan Furniture?

4-7. What are some advantages of offering a team-based incentive pay plan?

4-8. What do you think Sally should do?

MyManagementLab

Go to **mymanagementlab.com** for Auto-graded writing questions as well as the following Assisted-graded writing questions:

⭐ **4-9.** How can incentive pay systems, when properly applied, contribute to companies meeting the goals of lowest cost and differentiation strategies?

⭐ **4-10.** Compare and contrast individual and group incentive plans.

Endnotes

1. Peck, C. (1993). *Variable Pay: Nontraditional Programs for Motivation and Reward.* New York: The Conference Board.
2. Gómez-Mejía, L. R., & Balkin, D. R. (1992). *Compensation, Organizational Strategy and Firm Performance.* Cincinnati, OH: South-Western.
3. Lincoln Electric. (2013). *I Choose Lincoln....* Available: *www.lincolnelectric.com*, accessed August 13, 2013.
4. Schuster, J. R., & Zingheim, P. K. (1992). *The New Pay: Linking Employee and Organizational Performance.* New York: Lexington Books.
5. Dulles, F. R., & Dubofsky, M. (1984). *Labor in America: A History* (4th ed.). Arlington Heights, IL: Harlan Davidson.
6. Peck, *Variable Pay.*
7. Lazear, E. P. (1998). *Personnel Economics for Managers.* New York: John Wiley & Sons.
8. Drucker, P. (1954). *The Practice of Management.* New York: Harper.
9. Jackson, S. E. (1992). Team composition in organizational settings: Issues in managing an increasingly diverse workforce. In S. Worchel, W. Wood & J. A. Simpson (Eds.),

Group Process and Productivity (pp. 138–173). Newbury Park, CA: Sage.

10. Kanter, R. M. (1988). When a thousand flowers bloom: Structural, collective, and social conditions for innovation in organizations. In B. M. Staw & L. L. Cummings (Eds.), *Research in Organizational Behavior* (Vol. 10, pp. 169–211). Greenwich, CT: JAI.

11. Worchel, S., Wood, W., & Simpson, J. A. (Eds.). (1992). *Group Process and Productivity*. Newbury Park, CA: Sage.

12. Kanin-Lovers, J., & Cameron, M. (1993). Team-based reward systems. *Journal of Compensation and Benefits*, January–February, pp. 55–60.

13. Schuster, J. R., & Zingheim, P. K. (1993). Building pay environments to facilitate high-performance teams. *ACA Journal*, 2, pp. 40–51.

14. Greene, R. J. (2007). Team incentives. In D. Scott (Ed.), *Incentive Pay: Creating a Competitive Advantage*. Phoenix, AZ: WorldatWork Press.

15. Belcher, J. G., Jr. (1994). Gain sharing and variable pay: The state of the art. *Compensation & Benefits Review*, May–June, pp. 50–60.

16. Doyle, R. J. (1983). *Gain Sharing and Productivity*. New York: American Management Association.

17. Peck, *Variable Pay*.

18. Milkovich, G. T., & Newman, J. M. (1993). *Compensation* (4th ed.). Homewood, IL: Irwin.

19. Ross, T. (1990). Why gain sharing sometimes fails. In B. Graham-Moore & T. Ross (Eds.), *Gain Sharing: Plans for Improving Performance* (pp. 100–115). Washington, DC: Bureau of National Affairs.

20. Lesiur, F. G. (Ed.). (1958). *The Scanlon Plan: A Frontier in Labor–Management Cooperation*. Cambridge, MA: MIT Press.

21. Bullock, R. J., & Lawler, E. E., III. (1984). Gain sharing: A few questions and fewer answers. *Human Resource Management*, 23, pp. 18–20.

22. Smith, B. T. (1986). The Scanlon Plan revisited: A way to a competitive tomorrow. *Production Engineering*, 33, pp. 28–31.

23. Geare, A. J. (1976). Productivity from Scanlon type plans. *Academy of Management Review*, 1, pp. 99–108.

24. Myers, D. W. (1989). *Compensation Management*. Chicago, IL: Commerce Clearing House.

25. Lawler, E. E., III, & Cohen, S. G. (1992). Designing a pay system for teams. *American Compensation Association Journal*, 1, pp. 6–19.

5

PERSON-FOCUSED PAY

LEARNING OBJECTIVES

When you finish studying this chapter, you should be able to:

1. Explain the concept and practice of person-focused pay.
2. Describe the type of setting in which person-focused pay is most likely to be used.
3. Name and explain the reasons companies adopt person-focused pay programs.
4. Summarize the varieties of person-focused pay programs.
5. Contrast person-focused pay with job-based pay.
6. Provide an explanation of the advantages and disadvantages of person-focused pay plans.

In Chapters 3 and 4, we discussed compensation systems that reward employees for performance. Since the 1980s, strong competitive pressures and technological changes often have swiftly left employees with obsolete knowledge and skills. In the health care industry, for example, patient financial specialists have faced many challenges. Patient financial specialists, typically employed in hospitals, clinics, and doctors' offices, ensure that insurance providers pay claims on behalf of insured patients. The increasing variety of different types of "insurance" (e.g., high deductible health insurance plans, HMOs, PPOs, all of which we discuss in Chapter 10) rendered many patient financial services employees outdated in their knowledge and skills. In addition, the ongoing developments in diagnostic testing and treatments have added volumes to what these specialists must know. Since the 1990s, person-focused pay has been adopted in a variety of work settings in a variety of company departments such as back-office operations, call centers, retail, and managerial and professional settings.[1] This chapter will review person-focused pay practices and the many challenges companies face when considering person-focused pay approaches.

DEFINING PERSON-FOCUSED PAY: COMPETENCY-BASED, PAY-FOR-KNOWLEDGE, AND SKILL-BASED PAY

Person-focused pay plans, or **competency-based pay**, generally reward employees for acquiring job-related competencies, knowledge, or skills rather than for demonstrating successful job performance. This approach to compensating employees often refers to two basic types of person-focused pay programs: pay-for-knowledge and skill-based pay. These competency-based pay programs sometimes incorporate a combination of both types of person-focused pay systems, which reward employees for successfully acquiring new job-related knowledge or skills. There are other times when companies combine competency-based pay programs with traditional merit pay programs by awarding pay raises to employees according to how well they demonstrate competencies.

Pay-for-knowledge plans reward managerial, service, or professional workers for successfully learning specific curricula. **Skill-based pay,** a term used mostly for employees who do physical work, increases these workers' pay as they master new skills. For example, both unions and contractors who employ carpenters use skill-based pay plans. Carpenters earn additional pay as they master more advanced woodworking skills (e.g., cabinet making).

Both skill- and knowledge-based pay programs reward employees for the range, depth, and types of skills or knowledge they are capable of applying productively to their jobs. This feature distinguishes pay-for-knowledge plans from merit pay, which rewards employees' job performance. Said another way, pay-for-knowledge programs reward employees for their potential to make meaningful contributions on the job.

In this chapter, we use the term *person-focused pay* to refer to both pay-for-knowledge and skill-based pay programs. Although we noted differences between the two earlier, the basic principles underlying these programs are similar.

Human resource (HR) professionals can design person-focused pay plans to reward employees for acquiring new horizontal skills, vertical skills, or a greater depth of knowledge or skills. Employees can earn rewards for developing skills in one or more of these dimensions based on the kind of skills the company wants to foster. **Horizontal skills** (or **horizontal knowledge**) refer to similar skills or knowledge. For example, clerical employees of a retail store might be trained to perform several kinds of record-keeping tasks. They may maintain employee attendance records, schedule salespeople's work shifts, and monitor the use of office supplies (e.g., paper clips and toner cartridges for laser printers) for reordering. Although focused on different aspects of a store's operations, all three of these tasks are based on employees' fundamental knowledge of record keeping.

Vertical skills (or **vertical knowledge**) are those skills traditionally considered supervisory (e.g., scheduling, coordinating, training, and leading others). These types of supervisory skills are often emphasized in person-focused pay plans designed for self-managed work teams because team members often need to learn how to manage one another.[2] Such work teams, which can be referred to as self-regulating work groups, autonomous work groups, or semiautonomous work groups, typically bring employees together from various functional areas to plan, design, and complete one product or service. For example:

A manager of a food processing plant [who] wanted employees who were "a combination of self-reliant and resourceful." In this plant, good hiring systems and excellent training systems were critical, including systems for training operators in maintenance skills. Several plants had adopted interesting innovations to promote good training and certification. These innovations included:

- Several plants put all training on their intranet, so employees could access it at any time.
- One plant used hundreds of "One-Point Lessons" (OPLs—one-page sheets including a digital photograph of the appropriate equipment). Because each OPL focused on only one problem and its solution, OPLs were easy to search and use on the job.
- Several plants invested heavily in documentation of training and required practical skills demonstration.[3]

Depth of skills (or **depth of knowledge**) refer to the level of specialization or expertise an employee brings to a particular job. Some person-focused pay plans reward employees for increasing their depth of skills or knowledge. Human resource professionals may choose to specialize in managing a particular aspect of the HR function (e.g., compensation, benefits administration, training evaluation, or new employee orientation). To be considered a compensation specialist, HR professionals must develop depth of knowledge by taking courses offered by WorldatWork on job evaluation, salary survey analysis, principles of person-focused pay system design, merit pay system design, and incentive pay system design, among others. The more compensation topics HR professionals master, the greater will be their depth of knowledge about compensation.

What Is a "Competency"?

Many HR professionals and other functional managers (e.g., marketing) comment on the importance of paying employees based on competencies. There unfortunately seem to be almost as many definitions of competencies as there are professionals' calls for competency-based pay. Many HR professionals typically refer to competencies as uniquely combined characteristics of the person, including personality, attitudes, knowledge, skills, and behaviors that enable an employee to fulfill job requirements well. Others simply use the terms *knowledge* and *skills* as synonyms for competencies. Competency-based pay programs apply to technical, managerial, service, or professional employees (e.g., HR manager, marketing director) for whom it is difficult to define job performance according to observable or concrete behaviors. For instance, an animal keeper can be observed removing debris from enclosed animal habitats. On the other hand, a compensation director may be responsible for overseeing the ongoing development and implementation of an effective compensation system.

Core competencies are often derived from the overall strategic statements of companies. For example, General Electric (GE) emphasizes three strategic goals for corporate growth: Globalization, Product Services, and Six Sigma (quality improvement). GE's top management relies on four core competencies to drive business success, which they call the four "Es": high Energy, the ability to Energize others, Edge (i.e., the ability to make tough calls), and Execute (i.e., the ability to turn vision into results).

Core competencies are very general, as you can see from the previous example. Companies often offer training to help employees develop particular competency sets (e.g., technical skills, knowledge of the business) or to become more aware of competencies they already possess (e.g., leadership).

USAGE OF PERSON-FOCUSED PAY PROGRAMS

A wide variety of employers have established person-focused pay programs;[4] however, no systematic survey research documents the actual number. Nevertheless, anecdotal information suggests that companies of various sizes use person-focused pay programs. More than half of the companies known to be using this kind of pay system employ between 150 and 2,000 employees. The absence of detailed evaluative data makes it impossible to conclude whether size is related to the success of these programs. The lack of data is due, in part, to the fact that person-focused pay systems did not become popular until the 1990s, giving little opportunity to determine the long-term effectiveness.[5] However, one study found that a skill-based pay plan in a manufacturing setting increased plant productivity by 58 percent.[6]

These programs are most commonly found in continuous process settings (e.g., manufacturing companies that use assembly lines where one employee's job depends on the work of at least one other employee).[7] At Bell Sports, a manufacturer of motorcycle safety helmets, the assembly process includes applying enamel and attaching visors to the helmets. Both tasks clearly require different sets of skills. Applying enamel requires the ability to use automated sprayers. This skill specifically demands that workers possess strong literacy skills so they can interpret readouts from the sprayers that suggest possible problems. Attaching visors to the helmets requires proficient motor skills that involve eye–hand coordination. When employees learn how to perform different jobs, they can cover for absent coworkers. In the event of absenteeism or turnover, Bell

Sports benefits from having cross-trained employees because they are more capable of meeting its production schedules.

Person-focused pay programs that emphasize vertical skills work well at manufacturing companies that organize work flow around high-performance work teams in which employees are expected to learn both functional and managerial tasks (e.g., work scheduling, budgeting, and quality control). This means that groups of employees work together to assemble entire products such as cellular telephones (Motorola) and furniture (Steelcase, a manufacturer of office furniture), and each team member learns how to perform the jobs of other team members.

Companies increasingly recognize the importance of using person-focused pay. Person-focused pay programs have been adopted most widely in service and manufacturing industries. Companies have more recently been striving to adopt person-focused pay programs for professional employees. Person-focused pay programs also represent a prevalent basis for pay among clerical and skilled trade employees (e.g., carpenters and electricians).

REASONS TO ADOPT PERSON-FOCUSED PAY PROGRAMS

Person-focused pay programs represent important innovations in the compensation field. Person-focused pay systems imply that employees must move away from viewing pay as an entitlement. Instead, these systems treat compensation as a reward earned for acquiring and implementing job-relevant knowledge and skills. Advocates of person-focused pay programs offer two key reasons that firms seeking competitive advantage should adopt this form of compensation: technological innovation and increased global competition.[8]

Technological Innovation

In an age of technological innovation in which robots, telecommunications, artificial intelligence, software, and lasers perform routine tasks, some skills have become obsolete.[9] Jobs therefore require new and different worker skills. The skills needed by automobile mechanics, for instance, have changed dramatically. Competent automobile mechanics previously were adept at manually assembling and disassembling carburetors. Since then, electronic fuel injection systems, which are regulated by onboard computers, have replaced carburetors, necessitating that auto mechanics possess different kinds of skills. Auto mechanics specifically must now be able to use computerized diagnostic systems to assess the functioning of fuel injectors.

As technology leads to the automation of more tasks, employers combine jobs and confer broader responsibilities on workers. For example, the technology of advanced automated manufacturing (e.g., in the automobile industry) has required some employees to begin doing the jobs of other employees, including the laborer, the materials handler, the operator-assembler, and the maintenance person. A single employee now performs all of these tasks in a position called "manufacturing technician." The expanding range of tasks and responsibilities in this job demands higher levels of reading, writing, and computation skills than did its predecessor, which required strong eye–hand coordination. Most employees must possess better reading skills than before because they must be able to read the operating manuals and, when problems arise, the troubleshooting manuals of automated manufacturing equipment based on computer technology. The design of manufacturing equipment previously was relatively simple and easy to operate, based on such simple mechanical principles as pulleys.

These technological changes have fostered increased autonomy and team-oriented workplaces, which also demand different job-related skills than employees needed previously.[10] The manufacturing technician's job is generally more autonomous than was his or her predecessor's. Thus, technicians must be able to manage themselves and their time.

Employers now rely on working teams' technical and interpersonal skills to drive efficiency and improve quality. Today's consumers often expect customized products and applications, and employees must have sufficient technical skill to tailor products and services to customers' needs, as well as the interpersonal skills necessary to determine client needs and handle customer service.[11] Telephone service providers such as AT&T and Verizon seek competitive advantage by serving clients' present needs as well as by anticipating possible changes in customers' service needs. Lower costs of cellular phone service, with the inclusion of domestic long-distance service, create an even stronger imperative for landline service providers to be as responsive as possible to market needs and preferences. As a result, these companies offer programs to provide clients the most favorable long-distance telephone rates based on their particular calling patterns. To be successful, these companies must have customer service associates who maintain current knowledge of these programs as well as the skills needed to match service plans to clients' long-distance service requirements.

Increased Global Competition

Increased global competition has forced companies in the United States to become more productive. Now more than ever, to sustain competitive advantage, companies must provide their employees with leading-edge skills and encourage employees to apply their skills proficiently. Evidence clearly shows that the foreign workers are better skilled and able to work more productively than U.S. employees in at least two ways.

First, employers in both the European Common Market and some Pacific Rim economies emphasize learning. In both cases, employers use classes and instruction as proactive tools for responding to strategic change. In Ireland, the private sector offers graduate employment programs to employees in such skill areas as science, marketing, and technology.[12] An example of a marketing skill is the application of inferential statistics to a market analysis. Marketing professionals use inferential statistics to draw conclusions about whether the level of satisfaction with Brand A athletic shoes among a small sample of Brand A athletic shoe owners represents the level of satisfaction among every person who has purchased Brand A athletic shoes.

Second, both Western European and some Pacific Rim cultures provide better academic preparation and continuing workplace instruction for the non-college-bound portions of their workforces. Although the United States is well regarded for the quality of education its colleges and universities provide to such skilled professionals as engineers, the Europeans are much better at educating the "vocational" segment of their workforces. Western European workplaces emphasize applied rather than theoretical instruction for vocational employees. The European apprenticeship structure mixes academic and applied learning both in "high schools" and in continuing education for employees.

Companies strive to market the highest quality of products and services in the face of increased global competition and the availability of new technology. To establish and maintain competitive advantage, companies should carefully consider person-focused pay systems. As discussed earlier, many companies already compensate employees on this basis because they have discovered the advantages of such plans. Of course, as companies consider adopting these pay systems, they must tailor compensation programs to the particular kinds of skills they wish to foster. Human resource professionals can guide employee development through a variety of person-focused pay systems.

Training lies at the heart of person-focused pay programs. Indeed, as technological advances occur at a breakneck pace and as competition among companies intensifies, companies must make a number of decisions, including whether to develop talent internally or to hire talent away from competitors.

In manufacturing settings within the United States, many employers struggle to find sufficiently higher-skilled workers, notwithstanding the persistently high unemployment rate. According to GE CEO Jeffrey Immelt, he believes that manufacturing workers should possess the following:

Computing ability: Everyone needs to be able to interact with digital equipment and link that ability to a classic trade like welding that's increasingly tied to computing. "It's going to be more multi-faceted," he said. Emerging areas such as 3-D printing are "game-changing technology. It's going to be done in a manufacturing setting, but it's going to have to be by people that are facile in both ends of that. But it can be done."

Trained up: Even with those classic skills and computing skills together, workers still need hands-on training to meet manufacturers' needs. Community colleges can help through apprenticeship programs. "In every GE town we have a direct linkage to the community college in town," Immelt said.

Team skills: Factory workers today must operate as a group more than ever. "A lot of our facilities are lean manufacturing plus teaming," Immelt said. One GE location in Durham, NC, has 400 hourly workers but just one manager. "It's a completely teaming facility and they're quite productive."[13]

VARIETIES OF PERSON-FOCUSED PAY PROGRAMS

A **stair-step model** actually resembles a flight of stairs, much like the arrangement illustrated in Figure 5-1 for an assembly technician. The steps represent jobs from a particular job family that differ in terms of complexity. Jobs that require more skills are more complex than jobs with fewer skills. For example, an Assembly Technician 1 job requires employees to possess two skills: line restocking and pallet breakdown. An Assembly Technician 3 job requires employees to possess six skills: line restocking, pallet breakdown, burr removal, line jockey, major assembly, and soldering. In terms of the stairs, higher steps represent jobs that require more skills than lower steps. Compensation specialists develop separate stair-step models for individual job families (e.g., clerks or accountants). Thus, a company may have more than one stair-step model, each corresponding to a particular job family such as accounting, finance, or clerical. No stair-step model should include both clerical workers and skilled trade workers (e.g., carpenters, electricians, and plumbers).

How do employees earn increases in hourly pay based on a stair-step model? Using the model in Figure 5-1, Howard Jones wants to become an assembly technician. ABC Manufacturing Company hires Howard as an assembly technician trainee at $8 per hour. Howard starts by completing three core workshops designed for Assembly Technician 1: a company orientation, a safety workshop, and a quality workshop. After successfully completing all three courses, based on earning greater than the minimum scores on tests for each subject, he receives a $0.50 per hour pay increase, making his total hourly pay $8.50. In addition, Howard completes the core electives designated for his Assembly Technician 1 job: He learns how to restock lines and break down pallets.

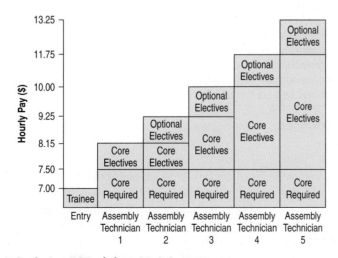

FIGURE 5-1 A Stair-Step Model at ABC Company

Core Required

Employees must complete all three workshops.

1. Orientation Workshop: The goal of this workshop is to familiarize employees with ABC's pay schedule, offerings of employee benefits, work hours, holiday and vacation policies, and grievance procedures.
2. Safety Workshop: The goal of this workshop is to educate employees about the procedures for ensuring the health and safety of themselves and coworkers while using and being around the machinery.
3. Quality Workshop: The goal of this workshop is to acquaint employees with ABC's procedures for maintaining quality standards for parts assembly.

Core Electives

Employees must complete all core elective courses for the designated job before they assume the commensurate duties and responsibilities.

Assembly Technician 1:	a. Line restocking
	b. Pallet breakdown
Assembly Technician 2:	a. Core electives for Assembly Technician 1
	b. Burr removal
	c. Line jockey
Assembly Technician 3:	a. Core electives for Assembly Technician 2
	b. Major assembly
	c. Soldering
Assembly Technician 4:	a. Core electives for Assembly Technician 3
	b. Acid bath
	c. Final inspection
Assembly Technician 5:	a. Core electives for Assembly Technician 4
	b. Equipment calibration
	c. Training

Optional Electives

Employees may choose to complete up to two optional electives at each step.
Administrative procedures
Public relations
Group facilitation
Grievance resolution
Training
Marketing fundamentals (basic)
Marketing fundamentals (intermediate)
Finance fundamentals (basic)
Finance fundamentals (intermediate)
Accounting fundamentals (basic)
Accounting fundamentals (intermediate)
Human resource management fundamentals (basic)
Human resource management fundamentals (intermediate)

FIGURE 5-1 Continued

Upon successfully completing both courses, he receives a $0.65 per hour pay raise, making his total hourly pay $9.15 and earning him the Assembly Technician 1 title. Howard may continue to learn more skills for an assembly technician by completing the curriculum for the Assembly 2 level. If he chooses so thereafter, Howard can complete the curricula to move to Level 3.

Training courses may be offered in-house by the company, at a local vocational school, or at a local community college or 4-year university. Companies usually offer specialized courses in-house for skills that pertain to highly specialized work or to work that bears on a company's competitive advantage. Federal Express sponsors customer service training internally because the skills and knowledge required to be an effective Federal Express customer service employee distinguish its service from other express mail companies, including United Parcel Service (UPS). For more common skills or skills that do not have an effect on competitive advantage, companies typically arrange to have their employees take training courses offered by such external agents as community colleges. Most companies require clerical employees to be able to use word processing programs effectively. Thus, companies commonly sponsor their employees' training in word processing at local community colleges.

The **skill blocks model** also applies to jobs from within the same job family. Just as in the stair-step model, employees progress to increasingly complex jobs; however, in a skill blocks program, skills do not necessarily build on each other. Thus, an employee may progress two or more steps, earning the pay that corresponds with each step. Although similar, the stair-step model and the skill blocks model differ in an important way. The stair-step model addresses the development of knowledge or skills depth. In particular, Howard Jones could develop his skills depth as an assembly technician by taking the five separate curricula. With the successful completion of each curriculum, Howard will enhance the depth of his skills as an assembly technician. As we will see shortly, the skill blocks model emphasizes both horizontal and vertical skills.

As shown in Figure 5-2, Pro Company hired Bobby Smith as a Clerk 1 because her employment tests demonstrated her proficiency in the skills and knowledge that she needs for this level job. These required skills correspond to Clerk 1 core requirements (i.e., filing, typing, and possessing a working knowledge of one word processing program). Moreover, Bobby knows transcription and shorthand, which are Level 1 core electives. During employee orientation for new clerical hires, an HR representative explained the pay-for-knowledge pay program available to this employee group. In particular, Bobby knows that she can advance to any level in the clerical pay structure by successfully completing the corresponding curriculum. To make her goal of becoming a Clerk 4, Bobby simply needs to complete the Level 4 curriculum. She need not take the curricula for the Clerk 2 and Clerk 3 jobs. Taking the Clerk 2, 3, or 4 curricula will enhance Bobby's horizontal skills. The Clerk 3 curriculum provides the knowledge required to successfully manage different types of ledgers. Taking the Clerk 5 curriculum will increase Bobby's vertical skills, including project scheduling and assigning personnel to projects.

A **job-point accrual model** encourages employees to develop skills and learn to perform jobs from different job families. A company would benefit if its employees were proficient in a small subset of jobs. Employees are generally not free to learn as many jobs as they would like. Companies limit the number of jobs employees are allowed to learn in order to avoid having them become "jacks of all trades." Job-point accrual methods create organizational flexibility and promote company goals by assigning a relatively greater number of points to skills that address key company concerns (e.g., customer relations). The more points employees accrue, the higher their core compensation level will be.

For example, let's assume that ZIP-MAIL is a new company that competes in express mail delivery service against established firms in the business (e.g., Federal Express and UPS). ZIP-MAIL couriers must meet their delivery promise of 7:30 A.M., which is at least a half-hour earlier than some of the competitors. They must also convey a professional image and establish rapport with corporate clients to encourage individuals and representatives from client companies to choose ZIP-MAIL over other competitors. In other words, customer relations skills are essential to ZIP-MAIL's success. ZIP-MAIL stands to benefit from a person-focused pay program, particularly one that follows the job-point accrual model. Under this system, employees who successfully complete customer relations training courses would earn more points than they would earn by taking other kinds of training offered by ZIP-MAIL, creating an incentive for employees to learn customer relations skills over other kinds of skills.

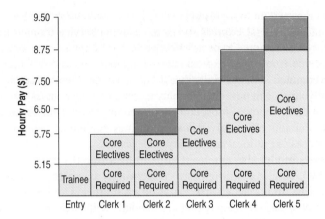

Core Required

All employees must be proficient in all of the following skills or take the necessary courses that are offered by Pro Company in order to become proficient.

Principles of filing

Typing skill, 40 words per minute minimum speed

Working knowledge of one word processing program such as Word or WordPerfect

Core Electives

Employees must complete all core elective courses for the designated job before they assume the commensurate duties and responsibilities.

Clerk 1:	a. Transcription
	b. Shorthand
Clerk 2:	a. Maintaining office supplies inventory
	b. Ordering office supplies from local vendor
Clerk 3:	a. Accounts receivable ledgers
	b. Accounts payable ledgers
	c. Working knowledge of one spreadsheet program, for example, Lotus 1-2-3 or Excel
Clerk 4:	a. Payroll records
	b. Maintaining records of sick pay usage, vacation usage, and performance bonus awards based on company policy
Clerk 5:	a. Project scheduling
	b. Assigning personnel to projects

Optional Electives

Employees may choose to complete up to two optional electives at each step.

Public relations (basic, intermediate, advanced)

Supervisory skills

Resolving minor employee conflicts

Effective written communication skills (basic, intermediate, advanced)

Effective oral communication skills (basic, intermediate, advanced)

FIGURE 5-2 A Skill Blocks Model at Pro Company

Although the job-point accrual model and the cross-departmental model are similar, the intended purposes of these programs differ. The job-point accrual model encourages employees to learn skills and acquire knowledge that bear directly on companies' attainment of competitive advantage, as in the case of ZIP-MAIL. **Cross-departmental models** promote staffing flexibility by training employees in one department with critical skills they would need to perform effectively in other departments. If the shipping department experienced a temporary staffing shortage, a production department supervisor who has been trained in distribution methods can be "lent" to the shipping department. The cross-departmental model can help production environments manage sporadic, short-term staffing shortages. Such cross-training can also help companies meet seasonal fluctuations in demand for their products or services.

The holiday shopping rush represents an excellent context in which a company can benefit from cross-departmental training systems. Retail business activity varies widely, with enhanced volume during the holiday shopping season during the fall months. Business activity tends to subside dramatically. Let's consider a company that manufactures and distributes custom-made shoes. For weeks prior to the holidays, employees in the production department are working rapidly to complete all the telephone gift orders that must be shipped before Chanukah and Christmas Day. Within a few days of the holidays, the company is likely to receive fewer orders because purchasers of custom-made shoes recognize that they need to place orders well in advance of the date they expect to receive their shoes. As orders drop off, many workers in both sales and production will be less busy than workers in the distribution department. Under the cross-departmental person-focused pay system, sales and production department workers will be rewarded for learning how to package shoes properly and how to complete express mail invoices so they can assist the shipping department during its peak activity periods.

CONTRASTING PERSON-FOCUSED PAY WITH JOB-BASED PAY

Companies institute job-based pay plans or person-focused pay plans based on very different fundamental principles and goals. Table 5-1 lists the key differences between these two pay programs. **Job-based pay** compensates employees for jobs they currently perform. Human resource professionals establish a minimum and maximum acceptable amount of pay for each job. In the case of merit pay, managers evaluate employees based on how well they fulfilled their designated roles as specified by their job descriptions and periodic objectives. Managers then award a permanent merit addition to base pay, based on employee performance.

With incentive pay, managers award one-time additions to base pay. Pay raise amounts are based on the attainment of work goals, which managers communicate to employees in advance.

TABLE 5-1 Person-Focused and Job-Based Pay: A Comparison

Feature	Person-Focused	Job-Based
Pay level determination	Market basis for skill valuation	Market basis for job valuation
Base pay	Awarded on how much an employee knows or on skill level	Awarded on the value of compensable factors
Base pay increases	Awarded on an employee's gain in knowledge or skills	Awarded on attaining a job-defined goal
Job promotion	Awarded on an employee's skills base and proficiency on past work	Awarded on exceeding job performance standards
Key advantage to employees	Job variety and enrichment	Perform work and receive pay for a defined job
Key advantage to employers	Work scheduling flexibility	Easy pay system administration

TABLE 5-2 Acme's Incentive Plan for Reductions in Monthly Defect Rates

Acme's goal is to achieve a monthly defect rate of 3,000 disk drives per employee to match Do-Rite's (the competition's) per employee defect rate. Employees whose monthly defect rates falls below 3,000 disk drives will receive an incentive award that is commensurate with the following schedule.

Reduction in Error Rate (%)	Monthly Incentive Award ($)
91–100	500
81–90	450
71–80	400
61–70	350
51–60	300
41–50	250
31–40	200
21–30	150
11–20	100
1–10	50

Consider the executives of Acme Manufacturing Company, who are dissatisfied with their level of defective disk drives for computers, which is significantly higher than that of their competitor, Do-Rite Manufacturing Company. Acme's monthly defect rate is 6,500 disk drives per employee, whereas Do-Rite's monthly defect rate is significantly less at 3,000 disk drives per employee. Acme executives decide to implement an incentive system to encourage employees to make fewer defective disk drives, with the ultimate goal of having a lower defect rate than Do-Rite. At the end of every month, Acme employees receive a monetary award based on their defect rate for that month. Table 5-2 displays the incentive plan for Acme. As you can see, employees earn a larger incentive award as the defect rate decreases.

Person-focused pay compensates employees for developing the flexibility and skills to perform a number of jobs effectively. Moreover, these programs reward employees on their potential to make positive contributions to the workplace based on their successful acquisition of work-related skills or knowledge. Job-based pay plans reward employees for the work they have done as specified in their job descriptions or periodic goals (i.e., how well they have fulfilled their potential to make positive contributions in the workplace).

Finally, job-based pay programs apply to an organization-wide context because employees earn base pay rates for the jobs they perform. (We will address how management establishes these pay rates in Chapter 7.) Person-focused pay plans apply in more limited contexts because not all jobs can be assessed based on skill or knowledge. Table 5-3 describes the duties that toll booth operators perform. This position would clearly not be appropriate in a person-focused pay

TABLE 5-3 Job Description for a Toll Collector

Collects toll charged for use of bridges, highways, or tunnels by motor vehicles, or fare for vehicle and passengers on ferryboats. Collects money and gives customer change. Accepts toll and fare tickets previously purchased. At end of shift balances cash and records money and tickets received. May sell round-trip booklets. May be designated according to place of employment as toll-bridge attendant (government service), or type of fare as vehicle-fare collector (motor trans.; water trans.). May admit passengers through turnstile and be designated turnstile collector (water trans.).

Source: Reprinted from *Dictionary of Occupational Titles*, Vol. 1, 4th ed. (Washington, DC: U.S. Government Printing Office, 1991).

system because the job is narrowly defined and the skills are very basic. Toll booth operators probably master the required skills and knowledge soon after assuming their responsibilities.

ADVANTAGES OF PERSON-FOCUSED PAY PROGRAMS

Although no large-scale studies have clearly demonstrated these benefits, case studies suggest that employees and companies enjoy advantages from person-focused pay programs. Well-designed person-focused pay systems, which will be discussed in Chapter 9, can provide employees and employers with distinct advantages over traditional pay systems.

Advantages to Employees

Employees usually like person-focused pay systems for the following two reasons. First, they can provide employees with both job enrichment and job security. Job enrichment refers to a job design approach that creates more intrinsically motivating and interesting work environments. Companies can enrich jobs by combining narrowly designed tasks so an employee is responsible for producing an entire product or service.[14]

According to job characteristics theory, employees are more motivated to perform jobs that contain a high degree of core characteristics, such as:[15]

1. *Skill variety.* The degree to which the job requires the person to do different tasks and involves the use of different skills, abilities, and talents.
2. *Task identity.* The degree to which a job enables a person to complete an entire job from start to finish.
3. *Autonomy.* The amount of freedom, independence, and discretion the employee enjoys in determining how to do the job.
4. *Feedback.* The degree to which the job or employer provides the employee with clear and direct information about job outcomes and performance.

At Volvo's Uddevalla manufacturing facility in Sweden, teams of 7–10 hourly workers produce entire vehicles rather than focusing solely on certain aspects such as installing a drive-train assembly or attaching upholstery to a car's interior.[16] Contributing to all aspects of manufacturing automobiles expands the horizontal dimensions (skill variety) of workers' jobs. In some cases, an employer empowers teams to manage themselves and the work they do. These managing duties, including controlling schedules, dividing up tasks, learning multiple jobs, and training one another, represent the vertical dimensions (autonomy) of work. Person-focused pay programs can help companies design such intrinsically motivating jobs, especially with regard to skill variety and autonomy. Both person-focused pay programs and job enrichment programs expand both horizontal and vertical work dimensions.

So far, evidence does suggest that person-focused pay plans lead to increased employee commitment, enhanced work motivation, and improved employee satisfaction.[17] These results are probably due to the fact that well-designed person-focused pay plans promote skill variety and autonomy. Some experts attribute these positive outcomes of person-focused pay programs to the fact that employees can increase their skills and be paid for it.[18]

The second advantage for employees is that, because person-focused pay programs create more flexible workers, these programs can actually represent better job security for employees. Rather than being laid off during periods of low product demand, employees can perform a variety of jobs that draw on the skills they have attained through person-focused pay programs. During periods of slow sales, many companies conduct inventories of their products. Customer service employees who have learned inventory accounting techniques are less likely to be laid off during periods of low sales than those who have not. Furthermore, employees who update their skills will also be more attractive applicants to other employers. Clerical employees who become proficient in the use of Windows-based computer software will definitely have more employment opportunities available to them than clerical employees who have resisted learning these programs. Likewise, HR professionals who become familiar with the constraints placed on compensation practice by many laws (for example, Civil Rights Act of 1991 and the Americans with Disabilities Act) will probably have more employment opportunities available to them than will HR professionals who choose not to become familiar with these pertinent laws.

Advantages to Employers

Employers like person-focused pay systems because, when properly designed and implemented, these programs can lead to enhanced job performance, reduced staffing, and greater flexibility. First, person-focused pay programs can influence both the quantity and the quality of an employee's work. Employees who participate in a person-focused pay program often exhibit higher productivity levels because employees who know more about an entire process may also be able to identify production shortcuts that result in increased productivity. For example, electrical wiring in an automobile runs along the vehicle's interior beneath the seats and carpeting. Members of auto assembly teams familiar with all aspects of the automobile manufacturing process could potentially identify and fix problems with the wiring before the seats and carpeting are installed. If such problems were identified after the seats and carpeting were installed, completion of the vehicle would be delayed, and fewer automobiles could be counted as finished.

Product or service quality should also gain from these programs. As employees learn more about the entire production process, the quality of both the product and its delivery often improve. Schott Transformers, a supplier of magnetic components and power systems to the computer and telecommunications industries, instituted a person-focused pay program and experienced a significant increase in the quality of its service as measured by customer satisfaction surveys.[19] Such customer satisfaction increases usually follow a company's implementation of self-directed work teams in which employees develop both horizontal and vertical skills. If employees feel responsible for entire products, they take more care to ensure that customers are satisfied.

Second, companies that use person-focused pay systems can usually rely on leaner staffing because multiskilled employees are better able to cover for unexpected absenteeism, family or medical leave, and training sessions that take individual employees away from their work. The successful operation of a restaurant depends on coordinated efforts from buspersons, waitstaff, chefs, and other food preparers. When one or two buspeople are absent, the restaurant will not be able to serve its reservations customers on time. If employees are cross-trained in a number of jobs, fewer employees will have to be on hand to provide backup for absent buspeople.

Third, person-focused pay systems provide companies with greater flexibility in meeting staffing demands at any particular time. Quite simply, because participants in person-focused pay plans have acquired a variety of skills, they can perform a wider range of tasks. This kind of staffing flexibility helps companies when unexpected changes in demand occur. After a tornado devastated a densely populated area in Illinois, the municipal water supply was not fit for drinking because areawide power outages disabled the pumps that purify the water. As a result, residents living in the affected areas rushed to grocery stores to purchase bottled water. Because this sudden demand exceeded the normal inventories of bottled water in grocery stores, such wholesale distributors as SuperValu had to respond quickly by moving bottled water inventories from their warehouses to the retail grocery stores.

DISADVANTAGES OF PERSON-FOCUSED PAY PROGRAMS

Although person-focused pay programs present many advantages, they have the following four limitations. First, employers feel that the main drawback of person-focused pay systems is that hourly labor costs, training costs, and overhead costs can all increase. Hourly labor costs often increase because greater skills should translate into higher pay levels for the majority of workers.

Because training is an integral component of person-focused pay systems, training costs are generally higher than they are at companies with job-based pay programs. These costs can be especially high during initial start-up periods as HR professionals attempt to standardize employee backgrounds. This process begins with assessing the skill levels of employees. Federal Express tests its employees twice per year.[20] The company pays for 4 hours of study time and 2 hours of actual test time, which are bound to be quite expensive.

Second, person-focused pay systems may not mesh well with existing incentive pay systems.[21] When both person-focused and incentive pay systems are in operation, employees may not want to learn new skills when the pay increase associated with learning a new skill is less than an incentive award employees could earn based on skills they already possess. Employees often place greater emphasis on maximizing rewards in the short term rather than preparing themselves to maximize the level of rewards over time, which can be facilitated through person-focused pay programs.

An assembly-line worker chooses to focus on his or her work because he or she receives monetary incentives for meeting weekly production goals set by management rather than taking skills training in inventory control for which he or she will earn additional pay upon successful completion of the training. In the short term, this worker is earning a relatively large sum of money; in the long term, however, he or she may be jeopardizing earnings potential and

COMPENSATION IN ACTION

Whether your company is considering the transition into a person-focused pay program or already has such a program in place, as a line manager or HR professional you will have responsibilities to guide the process and keep critical features at the forefront. By clearly outlining the expectations and metrics of the program, you will be able to provide a program that equips the company with tools to deliver its strategy and employees who possess valuable skills that will help them internally as they perform and externally should they choose to test their marketability in other companies or organizations.

Action checklist for line managers and HR—keeping the focus in person-focused pay

HR takes the lead
- Work with line managers to ensure that the benefit of the program is measurable and can be easily explained to employees and members of senior management.

- Communicate with employees and line managers so they understand the long-term benefits of the approach and how it will allow both parties to achieve individual and shared objectives.
- Explore potential partnerships with local community colleges or universities that could provide the necessary training to enhance the identified competencies at a fraction of the cost, but with added benefit to the employees (e.g., college credit and degree completion).

Line managers take the lead
- Educate HR on the competencies that are critical to company strategy.
- Inform HR of jobs that have obvious potential for cross-training. Some jobs will lend themselves to cross-training, while others may require too much training with relatively little return.

job security. In the future, the company may experience reduced demand for its product, which would eliminate the incentive program. During such times, the company may also place production workers in other jobs (e.g., in the warehouse) until the demand for the product returns to normal. Without the skills required to work in the warehouse, this employee may be targeted for a layoff or a reduced work schedule, clearly leading to lower personal earnings.

Third, effective person-focused pay programs depend, in large part, on well-designed training programs. There is a lot at stake: Person-focused pay systems include costly training programs, and these systems award pay raises to employees who successfully complete training. These programs also require that employers bear the price of base pay and benefits while employees attend training during regular work hours. Finally, companies must wait patiently before realizing a return on investment for training. Several months may pass before employees apply newly learned knowledge and skills to their jobs. After all, practice makes perfect, and training programs cannot anticipate all the circumstances employees face when performing their jobs.

Fourth, companies struggle with determining the monetary value of skill and knowledge sets. As we will discuss in Chapter 7, compensation surveys report the monetary value of entire jobs rather than individual skill sets. This fact is not surprising because most companies subscribe to job-based pay approaches that we described in Chapters 3 and 4, so it makes sense that surveys will focus on whole job value. In addition, knowledge and skill sets are usually company specific, which would make comparability difficult if surveys were common.

END OF CHAPTER

MyManagementLab

Go to **mymanagementlab.com** to complete the problems marked with this icon ⭐.

Summary

This chapter discussed person-focused pay, reasons companies should adopt person-focused pay programs, varieties of person-focused pay programs, how person-focused pay relates to merit pay and incentive pay programs, advantages as well as disadvantages of person-focused pay programs, and the fit of these programs with competitive strategy. Companies should seriously consider adopting person-focused pay programs in order to keep up with technological innovation and to compete internationally. Perhaps the greatest challenge for companies is to ensure that employees are given the opportunity to apply newly learned skills in productive ways.

Key Terms

person-focused pay plans   100
competency-based pay   100
pay-for-knowledge   101
skill-based pay   101
horizontal skills   101

horizontal knowledge   101
vertical skills   101
vertical knowledge   101
depth of skills   101
depth of knowledge   101

stair-step model   105
skill blocks model   107
job-point accrual model   107
cross-departmental models   109
job-based pay   109

✪ Discussion Questions

5-1. "Person-focused pay plans are least preferable compared with individual incentive pay programs" (Chapter 4). Indicate whether you agree or disagree with this statement. Detail your arguments to support your position.

5-2. Person-focused pay is becoming more prevalent in companies; however, person-focused pay programs are not always an appropriate basis for compensation. Discuss the conditions under which incentive pay (Chapter 4) is more appropriate than person-focused pay programs. Be sure to include your justification.

5-3. Name at least three jobs that have been influenced by such technological advances as robotics, word processing software, fax machines, and electronic mail. Describe the jobs prior to the technological advances, and explain how these jobs have changed or will change because of the technological advances. For each job, list the new skills that you feel are relevant for person-focused pay programs.

5-4. Discuss your reaction to the following statement: "Companies should not provide training to employees because it is the responsibility of individuals to possess the necessary knowledge and skills prior to becoming employed."

5-5. As discussed in the chapter, person-focused pay programs are not suitable for all kinds of jobs. Based on your understanding of person-focused pay concepts, identify at least three jobs for which this basis for pay is inappropriate. Be sure to provide your rationale, given the information in this chapter.

CASE
Person-Focused Pay at Mitron Computers

✪ *An additional Supplemental Case can be found on MyManagementLab.*

The technicians at Mitron Computers are integral to the company's success. Mitron builds custom personal computers for several office supply chains. The company's ability to build a quality product to specifications in an efficient manner allows Mitron to hold an advantage over competitors. However, recently the company has experienced some delays in shipments, and the plant manager is growing concerned.

Mitron works directly with the retail locations of the office supply chains to meet the needs of customers ordering computers with specific capabilities. A customer at a retail store orders a computer with certain components, and the order is sent to Mitron to be fulfilled within a specified time frame. The technicians work in teams to build the computers to the desired specifications. It is a complex process, and the technician's ability to build the computers efficiently has helped build Mitron's reputation as a quality producer of personal computers.

Depending on the specifications, building each computer can involve between 10 and 18 different steps. Most technicians have the knowledge and skills to complete one or two of the steps, but some technicians can complete multiple steps. The technicians that can complete multiple steps provide the company greater flexibility in scheduling and ensuring the computers are built on time. Each step in the building process involves intricate procedures, and a technician must take the initiative to attend training to learn each new step. However, there is little incentive for the technicians to attend the training.

The technicians work in teams to build the computers, and they are paid an hourly pay rate plus a team-based bonus payment for each computer that is built on time with no defects. The teams are composed of technicians that have complementary skills, but the company has had some delays when a team member with the skills to complete a certain step is absent or already working on another computer. This problem occurs often as few technicians have the skills to complete the higher-level steps in the building process. Most technicians do not want to take time away from their work to attend the training as they will likely lose some of their team-based bonuses.

Holly Turner, Mitron's human resource director, has been asked by the plant manager to examine the technician's pay structure to determine if a change in the structure could affect the technician's efficiency. Holly is confident that the more steps each technician can complete, the more efficient Mitron will be in building computers. Therefore, Holly is considering implementing a person-focused program that would tie the technician's pay to the steps in the building process that he or she is trained to complete. By doing so, Holly believes the technicians will be more likely to attend training and learn the new skills. With more technicians trained to complete the higher-level steps in the building process, the teams will be better prepared to meet shipping deadlines.

Questions:

5-6. What are some advantages of a person-focused pay system at Mitron?

5-7. What are some disadvantages?

5-8. What approach would you recommend for Holly to take in designing a person-focused pay system?

MyManagementLab

Go to **mymanagementlab.com** for Auto-graded writing questions as well as the following Assisted-graded writing questions:

⭐ 5-9. Compare and contrast the stair-step model and the skill blocks model. What kinds of skills are applicable in each model?

⭐ 5-10. Compare and contrast person-focused pay and job-based pay. Discuss the advantages of person-focused pay to employers.

Endnotes

1. Ledford, G. E. (2008). Factors affecting the long-term success of skill-based pay. *WorldatWork Journal*, First Quarter, pp. 6–17.

2. Bureau of National Affairs. (2002). Skill-based pay. *BNA's Library on Compensation & Benefits CD* [CD-ROM]. Washington, DC: Author.

3. Ledford, Factors affecting the long term.

4. Jenkins, G. D., Jr., Ledford, G. E., Jr., Gupta, N., & Doty, D. H. (1992). *Skill-Based Pay: Practices, Payoffs, Pitfalls, and Prescriptions*. Scottsdale, AZ: American Compensation Association.

5. Giancola, F. (2008). Why people-based pay is struggling. *Workspan*, April, pp. 35–37.

6. Murray, B., & Gerhart, B. (1998). An empirical analysis of a skill-based pay program and plant performance outcomes. *Academy of Management Journal, 41*, pp. 68–78.

7. Canavan, J. (2008). Overcoming the challenge of aligning skill-based pay levels to the external market. *WorldatWork Journal*, First Quarter, pp. 18–25.

8. Schuster, J. R., & Zingheim, P. K. (1992). *The New Pay: Linking Employee and Organizational Performance*. New York: Lexington Books.

9. American Society for Training and Development. (1989). *Training America: Learning to Work for the 21st Century*. Alexandria, VA: Author.

10. Doeringer, P. B. (1991). *Turbulence in the American Workplace*. New York: Oxford University Press.

11. Manz, C. C., & Sims H. P., Jr. (1993). *Business without Bosses: How Self-Managing Work Teams Are Building High Performance Companies*. New York: John Wiley & Sons.

12. Carnevale, A. P., & Johnston, J. W. (1989). *Training in America: Strategies for the Nation*. Alexandria, VA: National Center on Education and the Economy and the American Society for Training and Development.

13. Reddy, S. GE's wishlist for American workers. Available: *http://blogs.wsj.com/corporate-intelligence/2013/02/08/general-electrics-wishlist-for-american-workers/tab/print/*, Accessed February 16, 2013.

14. Lawler, E. E. (1986). *High Involvement Management*. San Francisco, CA: Jossey-Bass.

15. Nadler, D. A., Hackman, J. R., & Lawler, E. E. (1979). *Managing Organizational Behavior*. Boston, MA: Little, Brown.

16. Carrell, M. R., Elbert, N. F., & Hatfield, R. D. (1995). *Human Resource Management: Global Strategies for Managing a Diverse Workforce* (5th ed.). Upper Saddle River, NJ: Prentice Hall.

17. Gupta, N., Schweizer, T. P., & Jenkins, G. D., Jr. (1987). Pay-for-knowledge compensation plans: Hypotheses and survey results. *Monthly Labor Review, 110*, pp. 40–43.

18. Caudron, S. (1993). Master the compensation maze. *Personnel Journal, 72*, pp. 64a–64o.

19. Schilder, J. (1992). Work teams boost productivity. *Personnel Journal, 72*, pp. 64–71.

20. Filipowski, D. (1992). How Federal Express makes your package its most important. *Personnel Journal, 71*, pp. 40–46.

21. Jenkins, G. D., Jr., & Gupta, N. (1985). The payoffs of paying for knowledge. *National Productivity Review, 4*, pp. 121–130.

PART III
DESIGNING COMPENSATION SYSTEMS

Where We Are Now:

PART II, BASES FOR PAY, explained the concepts and practices available to compensation professionals for setting base pay as well as for determining pay increases over time. After gaining an understanding of these basics, compensation professionals turn to using tools to determine the relative worth of jobs, set base pay, and award pay increases according to the chosen basis for pay. We therefore turn to methods for building internally cosistent job structures, establishing market-competitive pay rates, and creating pay structures that recognize employee contributions according to the bases for pay concepts.

In **PART III, WE WILL COVER**

MyManagementLab®
⭐ You can access the CompAnalysis Software to complete the online Building Strategic Compensation Systems Project by logging into **www.mymanagementlab.com**.

6

BUILDING INTERNALLY CONSISTENT COMPENSATION SYSTEMS

MyManagementLab®

⭐ **Improve Your Grade!**

When you see this icon, visit **www.mymanagementlab.com** for activities that are applied, personalized, and offer immediate feedback.

LEARNING OBJECTIVES

When you finish studying this chapter, you should be able to:

1. Explain the concept of internally consistent compensation systems.
2. Summarize the practice of job analysis.
3. Describe the practice of job evaluation.
4. Give two examples of job evaluation techniques and briefly summarize each one.
5. Explain how internally consistent compensation systems and competitive strategy relate to each other.

Job descriptions serve as a cornerstone in the development of internally consistent compensation systems as well as performance standards in performance evaluation systems; however, human resource (HR) professionals have debated over the usefulness of job descriptions. For example, opponents often say that job descriptions simply are not realistic depictions of what many employees actually do each day. Nevertheless, as we will see shortly, job descriptions serve as the cornerstone for determining the relative worth of jobs.

INTERNAL CONSISTENCY

Internally consistent compensation systems clearly define the relative value of each job among all jobs within a company. This ordered set of jobs represents the job structure or hierarchy. Companies rely on a simple yet fundamental principle for building internally consistent compensation systems: Jobs that require higher qualifications, more responsibilities, and more complex job duties should be paid more than jobs that require lower qualifications, fewer responsibilities, and less-complex job duties. Internally consistent job structures formally recognize differences in job characteristics that enable compensation managers to set pay accordingly. Figure 6-1 illustrates an internally consistent job structure for employee benefits professionals. As Figure 6-1 indicates, a benefits manager should earn substantially more than a benefits counselor I. Benefits managers have far greater responsibility for ensuring effective benefits practices than does the entry-level counselor. The difference in average pay rates between benefits counselor II and benefits counselor I jobs should be far less than that between benefits manager and benefits counselor I jobs because the differences in responsibility between benefits counselor II and benefits counselor I are far less than the differences between benefits manager and benefits counselor I.

Compensation experts and HR professionals create internally consistent job structures through two processes—job analysis followed by job evaluation. **Job analysis** is almost purely a descriptive procedure; job evaluation reflects value judgments. Effective job analysis identifies and defines **job content.** Job content describes job duties and tasks as well as such pertinent factors as the skill and effort (i.e., compensable factors) needed to perform the job adequately.

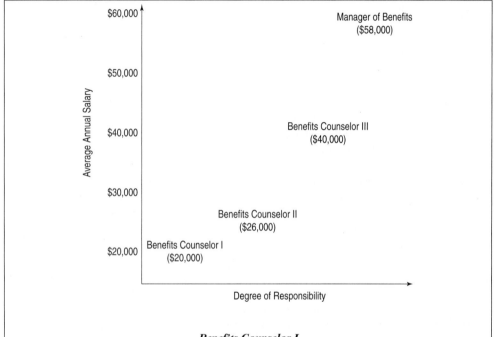

Benefits Counselor I

Provides basic counseling services to employees and assistance to higher-level personnel in more complex benefits activities. Works under general supervision of higher-level counselors or other personnel.

Benefits Counselor II

Provides skilled counseling services to employees concerning specialized benefits programs or complex areas of other programs. Also completes special projects or carries out assigned phases of the benefits counseling service operations. Works under general supervision from Benefits Counselor III or other personnel.

Benefits Counselor III

Coordinates the daily activities of an employee benefits counseling service and supervises its staff. Works under direction from higher-level personnel.

Manager of Benefits

Responsible for managing the entire benefits function from evaluating benefits programs to ensuring that Benefits Counselors are adequately trained. Reports to the Director of Compensation and Benefits.

FIGURE 6-1 Internally Consistent Compensation Structure

Human resource specialists lead the job analysis process. As we will discuss shortly, they solicit the involvement of employees and supervisors, who offer their perspectives on the nature of the jobs being analyzed. Based on this information, HR specialists write job descriptions that describe the job duties and minimum qualifications required of individuals to perform their jobs effectively.

Job evaluation is key for casting internally consistent compensation systems as strategic tools. Compensation professionals use job evaluation to establish pay differentials among employees within a company. The descriptive job analysis results directly aid compensation professionals in their pay-setting decisions by quantifying the key similarities and differences between jobs based on job content identified in the job analysis process.

JOB ANALYSIS

Competent compensation professionals are familiar with job analysis concepts, the process of conducting job analysis, and fundamental job analysis techniques. Job analysis is a systematic process for gathering, documenting, and analyzing information in order to describe jobs. Job analyses describe content or job duties, worker requirements or job specifications, and, sometimes, the job context or working conditions.

Job content refers to the actual activities that employees must perform on the job. Job-content descriptions may be broad, general statements of job activities or detailed descriptions of duties and tasks performed on the job. Greeting clients is common to receptionist jobs. The job activity of greeting clients represents a broad statement. Describing the particular activities associated with greeting clients (e.g., saying "hello," asking the clients' names, using the telephone to notify the employees of their clients' arrivals, and offering beverages) represents a detailed statement.

Worker requirements represent the minimum qualifications and the knowledge, skills, and abilities (KSAs) that people must have to perform a particular job. Such requirements usually include education; experience; licenses; permits; and specific abilities and skills such as typing, drafting, or editing. For example, HR managers must have knowledge of principles and procedures for recruitment, selection, training, compensation and benefits, labor relations and negotiations, and HR information systems. Active listening and critical thinking are two examples of many necessary skills for effective HR managers. Human resource managers must possess abilities such as oral comprehension and written comprehension.

Working conditions are the social context or physical environment where work will be performed. For instance, social context is a key factor for jobs in the hospitality industry. Hospitality industry managers emphasize the importance of employees' interactions with guests. Hotel registration desk clerks should convey an air of enthusiasm toward guests and be willing to accommodate each guest's specific requests for a nonsmoking room or an early check-in time.

Physical environments vary along several dimensions, based on the level of noise and possible exposure to hazardous factors, including hazardous chemicals. Work equipment also defines the character of the physical environment. Nuclear power plant employees work in rather hazardous physical environments because of possible exposure to dangerous radiation levels. Accountants perform their jobs in relatively safe working environments because office buildings must meet local building safety standards.

Steps in the Job Analysis Process

The job analysis process has five main activities:

- Determine a job analysis program.
- Select and train analysts.
- Direct job analyst orientation.
- Conduct the study: data collection methods and sources of data.
- Summarize the results: writing job descriptions.

DETERMINE A JOB ANALYSIS PROGRAM A company must decide between using an established system or developing its own system tailored to specific requirements. Both established and custom job analysis programs vary in the method of gathering data. The most typical methods for collecting job analysis information are questionnaires, interviews, observation, and participation. Administrative costs often represent a major consideration in selecting a job analysis method.

SELECT AND TRAIN ANALYSTS Job analysts generally must be able to collect job-related information through various methods, relate to a wide variety of employees, analyze the information, and write clearly and succinctly. A task force of representatives from throughout the company ideally conducts the analysis, and HR staff members coordinate it. Although some companies rely on HR professionals to coordinate and conduct job analysis, many use teams to represent varying perspectives on work because virtually all employees interact with coworkers and supervisors.

Before the task force embarks on a job analysis, members need to be taught about the basic assumptions of the model and the procedures they must follow. The training should include discussions of the study's objectives, how the information will be used, methodology overviews, and discussions and demonstrations of the information-gathering techniques. Analysts also should be trained to minimize the chance that they will conduct ineffective job analyses. For example, analysts should involve as many job incumbents as possible within the constraints of staff time to have representative samples of job incumbents' perceptions.

Finally, job analysts must be familiar with the structure of pertinent job data. Job analysis data are configured in levels, hierarchically from specific bits of information to progressively broader categories that include the prior specific pieces. Table 6-1 defines representative analysis levels and lists examples of each one. The most specific information is a job element, and the broadest element is an occupation.

TABLE 6-1 Units of Analysis in the Job Analysis Process

1. An element is the smallest step into which it is practical to subdivide any work activity without analyzing separate motions, movements, and mental processes involved. Connecting a flash drive into a USB port is an example of a job element.

2. A task is one or more elements and is one of the distinct activities that constitute logical and necessary steps in the performance of work by the worker. A task is created whenever human effort, physical or mental, is exerted to accomplish a specific purpose. Keyboarding text into memo format represents a job task.

3. A position is a collection of tasks constituting the total work assignment of a single worker. There are as many positions as there are workers. John Smith's position in the company is clerk typist. His tasks, which include keyboarding text into memo format, running a spell check on the text, and printing the text on company letterhead, combine to represent John Smith's position.

4. A job is a group of positions within a company that are identical with respect to their major or significant tasks and sufficiently alike to justify their being covered by a single analysis. There may be one or many persons employed in the same job. For example, Bob Arnold, John Smith, and Jason Colbert are clerk typists. With minor variations, they essentially perform the same tasks.

5. A job family is a group of two or more jobs that call for either similar worker characteristics or similar work tasks. File clerk, clerk typist, and administrative clerk represent a clerical job family because each job mainly requires employees to perform clerical tasks.

6. An occupation is a group of jobs, found at more than one establishment, in which a common set of tasks are performed or are related in terms of similar objectives, methodologies, materials, products, worker actions, or worker characteristics. File clerk, clerk typist, administrative clerk, staff secretary, and administrative secretary represent an office support occupation. Compensation analyst, training and development specialist, recruiter, and benefits counselor represent jobs from the human resources management occupation.

Source: U.S. Department of Labor (1991). *The Revised Handbook for Analyzing Jobs.* Washington, DC: U.S. Government Printing Office.

The U.S. Office of Management and Budget published *The Standard Occupational Classification System* (*SOC*), which identifies 23 **major occupational groups.** The SOC system replaces the government's longstanding *The Dictionary of Occupational Titles* (published in 1938 and subsequently revised in 1949, 1964, 1977, and 1991). Table 6-2 lists the 23 major occupational groups based on the 2010 edition. It is available on the U.S. Bureau of Labor Statistics Web site (*www.bls.gov/soc/*).

These occupational group concepts are relevant for making compensation decisions, but the current version of the SOC has limited use because of its focus on broad occupations. Considering the units of analysis may ultimately influence compensation professionals' judgments about whether work is dissimilar or similar. Human resource manager, purchasing manager, and payroll clerk are dissimilar jobs because employees in these jobs perform different duties; however, HR manager and purchasing manager are similar at the occupational level because they fall under the management occupation. In addition, HR manager and payroll clerk are quite different at the occupational level because HR manager is classified as a management occupation, whereas payroll clerk falls under the office and administrative support occupation. The revised SOC is expected to include detailed information about jobs, allowing compensation professionals to make more precise comparisons for pay-setting purposes.

DIRECT JOB ANALYST ORIENTATION Before analysts start specific job analysis techniques, they must analyze the context in which employees perform their work to better understand influencing factors. In addition, analysts should obtain and review such internal information as organizational

TABLE 6-2 **Major Occupational Groups of the Standard Occupational Classification**

- Management occupations
- Business and financial operations occupations
- Computer and mathematical occupations
- Architecture and engineering occupations
- Life, physical, and social science occupations
- Community and social service occupations
- Legal occupations
- Education, training, and library occupations
- Arts, design, entertainment, sports, and media occupations
- Health care practitioners and technical occupations
- Health care support occupations
- Protective service occupations
- Food preparation and serving-related occupations
- Building and grounds cleaning and maintenance occupations
- Personal care and service occupations
- Sales and related occupations
- Office and administrative support occupations
- Farming, fishing, and forestry occupations
- Construction and extraction occupations
- Installation, maintenance, and repair occupations
- Production occupations
- Transportation and material-moving occupations
- Military-specific occupations

Source: U.S. Bureau of Labor Statistics (2010). *2010 SOC User Guide.* Available: *www.bls.gov/soc/*, accessed August 25, 2013.

charts, listings of job titles, classifications of each position to be analyzed, job incumbent names and pay rates, and any instructional booklets or handbooks for operating equipment. Job analysts may also find pertinent job information in such external sources as *The Standard Occupational Classification System*, trade associations, professional societies, and trade unions.

CONDUCT THE STUDY: DATA COLLECTION METHODS AND SOURCES OF DATA Once analysts have gathered and made sense of these preliminary data, they can begin gathering and recording information for each job in the company. Analysts should carefully choose the method of data collection and the sources of data. The most common methods are questionnaires and observation. Questionnaires direct job incumbents' and supervisors' descriptions of the incumbents' work through a series of questions and statements, for example:

- Describe the task you perform most frequently.
- How often do you perform this task?
- List any licenses, permits, or certifications required to perform duties assigned to your position.
- List any equipment, machines, or tools you normally operate as part of your position's duties.
- Does your job require any contacts with other department personnel, other departments, outside companies, or agencies? If yes, please describe.
- Does your job require supervisory responsibilities? If yes, for which jobs and for how many employees?

Observation requires job analysts to record perceptions they form while watching employees perform their jobs.

The most common sources of job analysis data are job incumbents, supervisors, and the job analysts. Job incumbents should provide the most extensive and detailed information about how they perform job duties. Experienced job incumbents will probably offer the most details and insights. Supervisors also should provide extensive and detailed information, but with a different focus. Supervisors specifically are most familiar with the interrelationships among jobs within their departments. They are probably in the best position to describe how employees performing different jobs interact. Job analysts also should involve as many job incumbents and supervisors as possible because employees with the same job titles may have different experiences.

For example, parts assembler John Smith reports that a higher level of manual dexterity is required than parts assembler Barbara Bleen reports. Parts assembler supervisor Jan Johnson indicates that assemblers interact several times a day to help each other solve unexpected problems, and supervisor Bill Black reports no interaction among parts assemblers. Including as many job incumbents and supervisors as possible will provide a truer assessment of the parts assembler job duties.

Of course, job analysts represent a source of information. In the case of observation, job analysts write descriptions. Job analysts, when using questionnaires, often ask follow-up questions to clarify job incumbents' and supervisors' answers. In either case, job analysts' HR expertise should guide the selection of pertinent follow-up questions.

Companies ultimately strive to conduct job analyses that lead to reliable and valid job evaluation results. A **reliable job analysis** yields consistent results under similar conditions. For example, let's assume that two job analysts independently observe John Smith perform his job as a retail store manager. The method is reliable if the two analysts reach similar conclusions about the duties that constitute the retail store manager job. Although important, reliable job analysis methods are not enough. Job analyses also must be valid.

A valid job analysis method accurately assesses each job's duties. Neither researchers nor practitioners unfortunately can demonstrate whether job analysis results are definitively accurate. At present, the "best" approach to producing valid job descriptions requires that results among multiple sources of job data (e.g., job incumbents, analysts, supervisors, and customers) and multiple methods (e.g., interview, questionnaire, and observation) converge.[1]

Reliable and valid job analysis methods are essential to building internally consistent compensation systems. The factors that describe a particular job should indeed reflect the actual work. Failure to match accurately compensable factors with the work employees perform may result in either inadequate or excessive pay rates. Both cases are detrimental to the company. Inadequate pay may lead to dysfunctional turnover (i.e., the departure of high-quality employees). Excessive pay represents a cost burden to the company that can ultimately undermine its competitive position. Moreover, basing pay on factors that do not relate to job duties leaves a company vulnerable to allegations of illegal discrimination.

What can compensation professionals do to increase the likelihood that they will use reliable and valid job analysis methods? Whenever time and budgetary constraints permit, job analysts should use more than one data collection method, and they should collect data from more than one source. Including multiple data collection methods and sources minimizes the inherent biases associated with any particular one. For example, job incumbents may view their work as having greater impact on the effectiveness of the company than does the incumbents' supervisor. Observation techniques do not readily indicate why an employee performs a task in a specific way, but the interview method provides analysts with an opportunity to make probing inquiries.

SUMMARIZE THE RESULTS: WRITING JOB DESCRIPTIONS   **Job descriptions** summarize a job's purpose and list its tasks, duties, and responsibilities, as well as the skills, knowledge, and abilities necessary to perform the job at a minimum level. Effective job descriptions generally explain:

- What the employee must do to perform the job
- How the employee performs the job
- Why the employee performs the job in terms of its contribution to the functioning of the company
- Supervisory responsibilities, if any
- Contacts (and purpose of these contacts) with other employees inside or outside the company
- The skills, knowledge, and abilities the employee should have or must have to perform the job duties
- The physical and social conditions under which the employee must perform the job

Job descriptions usually contain four sections:

- Job title
- Job summary
- Job duties
- Worker specifications

Table 6-3 contains a job description for a training and development specialist.

Job titles indicate the name of each job within a company's job structure. In Table 6-3, the job title is training and development specialist. The **job summary** statement concisely summarizes the job with two to four descriptive statements. This section usually indicates whether the job incumbent receives supervision and by whom. The training and development specialist works under general supervision from higher-level training and development professionals or other designated administrators.

The **job duties** section describes the major work activities and, if pertinent, supervisory responsibilities. For instance, the training and development specialist evaluates training needs of employees and departments by conducting personal interviews, questionnaires, and statistical studies.

The **worker specifications** section lists the education, skills, abilities, knowledge, and other qualifications individuals must possess to perform the job adequately. **Education** refers to formal training. Minimum educational levels can be a high school diploma or a general equivalency diploma (GED) through such advanced levels as masters' or doctoral degrees.

TABLE 6-3 Job Description: Training and Development Specialist

Job Summary

Training and development specialists perform training and development activities for supervisors, managers, and staff to improve efficiency, effectiveness, and productivity. They work under general supervision from higher-level training and development professionals.

Job Duties

A training and development specialist typically:

1. Recommends, plans, and implements training seminars and workshops for administrators and supervisors, and evaluates program effectiveness.
2. Evaluates training needs of employees and departments by conducting personal interviews, questionnaires, and statistical studies.
3. Researches, writes, and develops instructional materials for career, staff, and supervisor workshops and seminars.
4. Counsels supervisors and employees on policies and rules.
5. Performs related duties as assigned.

Worker Specifications

1. Any one or any combination of the following types of preparation:
   a. credit for college training leading to a major or concentration in education or other fields closely related to training and development (such as human resource management or vocational education).

   —or—

   b. two years of work experience as a professional staff member in a human resource management department.
2. Two years of professional work experience in the training and development area in addition to the training and experience required in item 1, above.

The **Equal Employment Opportunity Commission (EEOC)** guidelines distinguish among the terms *knowledge*, *skill*, and *ability*. **Skill** refers to an observable competence to perform a learned psychomotor act. Typing 50 words per minute is an example of a psychomotor act. Typing requires knowledge of the keyboard layout and manual dexterity. According to the EEOC, **ability** refers to a present competence to perform an observable behavior or a behavior that results in an observable product. For example, possessing the competence to mediate a dispute between labor and management successfully reflects ability. **Knowledge** refers to a body of information applied directly to the performance of a function. Companies measure knowledge with tests, or they infer that employees have knowledge based on formal education completed. For instance, compensation professionals should know about the Fair Labor Standards Act's overtime pay requirements.

Legal Considerations for Job Analysis

The government does not require companies to conduct job analysis; however, conducting job analyses increases the chance that employment decisions are based solely on pertinent job requirements. Under the Equal Pay Act (Chapter 2), companies must justify pay differences between men and women who perform equal work. Different job titles do not suffice as justification. Instead, companies must demonstrate substantive differences in job functions. Job analysis helps HR professionals discern whether substantive differences between job functions exist. Job analysis is also useful for determining whether a job is exempt or nonexempt under the Fair Labor Standards Act (FLSA). As we discussed in Chapter 2, failure to pay nonexempt employees an overtime hourly pay rate violates the FLSA.

Companies may perform job analysis to see if they comply with the Americans with Disabilities Act (ADA) and the American with Disabilities Act (ADA) Amendments Act of 2008, also discussed in Chapter 2. The amendments emphasize that the definition of disability should be construed in favor of broad coverage of individuals to the maximum extent permitted by the terms of the ADA.

As long as disabled applicants can perform the essential functions of a job with reasonable accommodation, companies must not discriminate against these applicants by paying them less than other employees performing the same job. Human resource professionals use job analysis to define essential job functions systematically. Companies may consult the EEOC's interpretive guidelines to determine whether a job function is essential. Table 6-4 lists these guidelines.

TABLE 6-4 EEOC Interpretive Guidelines for Essential Job Functions under the Americans with Disabilities Act

Based on the Original Act Passed in 1990

- The reason the position exists is to perform the function.
- The function is essential or possibly essential. If other employees are available to perform the function, the function probably is not essential.
- A high degree of expertise or skill is required to perform the function.
- The function is probably essential; and
- Whether a particular job function is essential is a determination that must be made on a case-by-case basis and should be addressed during job analysis. Any job functions that are not essential are determined to be marginal. Marginal job functions could be traded to another position or not done at all.

Based on Revisions to the Original Act Passed in 2008

The Act makes important changes to the definition of the term *disability* by rejecting the holdings in several Supreme Court decisions and portions of EEOC's ADA regulations. The effect of these changes is to make it easier for an individual seeking protection under the ADA to establish that he or she has a disability within the meaning of the ADA.

The Act retains the ADA's basic definition of "disability" as an impairment that substantially limits one or more major life activities, a record of such an impairment, or being regarded as having such an impairment. However, it changes the way that these statutory terms should be interpreted in several ways. Most significantly, the Act:

directs EEOC to revise that portion of its regulations defining the term *substantially limits*;

expands the definition of "major life activities" by including two non-exhaustive lists:

the first list includes many activities that the EEOC has recognized (e.g., walking) as well as activities that EEOC has not specifically recognized (e.g., reading, bending, and communicating);

the second list includes major bodily functions (e.g., functions of the immune system; normal cell growth; and digestive, bowel, bladder, neurological, brain, respiratory, circulatory, endocrine, and reproductive functions);

states that mitigating measures other than "ordinary eyeglasses or contact lenses" shall not be considered in assessing whether an individual has a disability;

clarifies that an impairment that is episodic or in remission is a disability if it would substantially limit a major life activity when active;

changes the definition of "regarded as" so that it no longer requires a showing that the employer perceived the individual to be substantially limited in a major life activity, and instead says that an applicant or employee is "regarded as" disabled if he or she is subject to an action prohibited by the ADA (e.g., failure to hire or termination) based on an impairment that is not transitory and minor;

provides that individuals covered only under the "regarded as" prong are not entitled to reasonable accommodation.

Source: U.S. Equal Employment Opportunity Commission (2008). *Notice Concerning the Americans with Disabilities Act (ADA) Amendments Act of 2008.* Available: *http://www.eeoc.gov/laws/statutes/adaaa _notice.cfm.*

Job Analysis Techniques

Human resource professionals can either choose from a variety of established job analysis techniques or custom-design them. Most companies generally choose to use established job analysis techniques because the costs of custom-made job analysis techniques often outweigh the benefits. Besides, many of the established job analysis techniques apply to a wide variety of jobs and both researchers and practitioners have already tested and refined them.

Choosing one established plan over another depends on two considerations: applicability and cost. Some job analysis techniques apply only to particular job families (e.g., managerial jobs), but others can be applied more broadly. In addition, some methods are proprietary, yet others are available to the public at no charge. Private consultants or consulting firms charge substantial fees to companies that use their methods, but the U.S. Department of Labor does not charge fees to use its job analysis method. Next, we will review the U.S. Department of Labor's **Occupational Information Network (O*NET)**.

U.S. Department of Labor's Occupational Information Network (O*NET)

The U.S. Department of Labor's Employment and Training Administration spearheaded the development of O*NET during the 1990s to replace its previous methods of analyzing and describing jobs (*Revised Handbook for Analyzing Jobs*[2] and *The Dictionary of Occupational Titles*[3]). O*NET is a database, and it was created for two reasons. First, it is designed to describe jobs in the relatively new service sector of the economy (e.g., wireless telecommunications). Second, O*NET more accurately describes jobs that evolved as the result of technological advances (e.g., software and hardware engineering).

O*NET is comprehensive because it incorporates information about both jobs and workers. The O*NET **Content Model** lists six categories of job and worker information. Job information contains the components that relate to the actual work activities of a job (i.e., information that HR professionals should include in the summary and duties sections of job descriptions). Worker information represents characteristics of employees that contribute to successful job performance. Figure 6-2 shows the six categories of the O*NET Content Model. According to the creators of O*NET, the Content Model was developed using research on job and organizational analysis. It embodies a view that reflects the character of occupations (via job-oriented descriptors) and people (via worker-oriented descriptors). The Content Model also allows occupational information to be applied across jobs, sectors, or industries (cross-occupational descriptors) and within occupations (occupational-specific descriptors). A description of each content area follows.

EXPERIENCE REQUIREMENTS Experience requirements include:

- Experience and training
- Licensing

Experience and training information describes specific preparation required for entry into a job plus past work experience contributing to qualifications for an occupation. **Licensing** information describes licenses, certificates, or registrations that are used to identify levels of skill and that are required for entry and advancement in an occupation, preferred education or training, and required apprenticeships will be documented by this part of the model. Table 6-5 lists the specific experience requirements.

OCCUPATIONAL REQUIREMENTS **Occupational requirements** include:

- Generalized work activities
- Organizational context
- Work context

The occupational requirements domain includes information about typical activities required across occupations. Identifying generalized work activities and detailed work activities summarizes the broad and more specific types of job behaviors and tasks that may be performed within

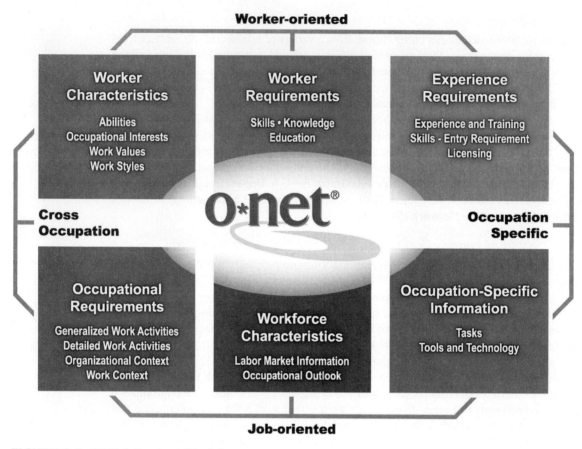

FIGURE 6-2 O*Net Content Model

TABLE 6-5 O*NET Content Model: Experience Requirements (sample of full list)

Experience Requirements

- Experience and training
  1. Related work experience
  2. On-site or in-plant training
  3. On-the-job training
- Licensing
- License, certificate, or registration required
- Education, training, examination or other requirements for license, certificate, or registration
  1. Post-secondary degree
  2. Graduate degree
  3. On-the-job training
- Additional education and training
- Organization and agency requirements
  1. Legal requirement
  2. Employer requirement
  3. Union, guild, or professional association requirement

Source: Occupational Information Network Consortium. Content model. Available: *www.onetcenter.org/content.html*, accessed May 23, 2013.

multiple occupations. Using this framework makes it possible to use a single set of descriptors to describe many occupations. Contextual variables such as the physical, social, or structural context of work that may impose specific demands on the worker or activities are also included in this section.

Generalized work activities information describes general types of job behaviors occurring on multiple jobs. **Organizational context** information indicates the characteristics of the organization that influence how people do their work. **Work context** information describes physical and social factors that influence the nature of work. Table 6-6 lists examples of particular occupational requirements.

TABLE 6-6 **O*NET Content Model: Occupational Requirements (sample of full list)**

- Generalized work activities
- Information input
  - Looking for and receiving job-related information
  - Identifying/evaluating job-relevant information
- Mental processes
  - Information/data processing
  - Reasoning/decision making
- Work output
  - Performing physical and manual work activities
  - Performing complex/technical activities
- Interacting with others
  - Communicating/interacting
  - Coordinating/developing/managing/advising others
- Organizational context
  - Structural characteristics
    - Organizational structure
      - Decision-making system
        - Decentralization and employee empowerment
        - Individual versus team structure
    - Job characteristics
      - Skill variety
      - Task significance
      - Task identity
      - Autonomy
      - Feedback
- Human resources systems and practices
  - Recruitment and selection
    - Recruitment operations
    - Reward system
      - Basis of compensation
        - Which of the following is part of your compensation package?
        1. Profit sharing
        2. Gain sharing
        3. Knowledge/skill-based pay
        4. Pay based on your individual performance
        5. Pay based on the performance of your team
        6. Pay based on customer satisfaction
        7. Pay based on job tenure/seniority
        8. Pay based on job attributes
        9. None of the above

(continued)

TABLE 6-6 Continued

- Benefits
  - Which of the following is part of your benefits?
  1. Stock ownership in the organization
  2. Retirement plan
  3. Major medical insurance
  4. Life insurance
  5. Disability insurance
  6. Flexible working hours
  7. Daycare
  8. Paid leave
  9. None of the above

Source: Occupational Information Network Consortium. Content model. Available: *www.onetcenter.org/content.html*, accessed May 23, 2013.

OCCUPATION-SPECIFIC INFORMATION REQUIREMENTS **Occupation-specific information requirements** detail a comprehensive set of elements that apply to a single occupation or a narrowly defined job family. These particular requirements are occupational skills, knowledge, tasks, duties, machines, tools, and equipment. This domain parallels other Content Model domains because it includes requirements such as work-related knowledge, skills, and tasks in addition to the machines, equipment, tools, software, and information technology workers may use in their workplace.

WORKFORCE CHARACTERISTICS **Workforce characteristics** refer to variables that define and describe the general characteristics of occupations that may influence occupational requirements. Organizations do not exist in isolation. They must operate within a broader social and economic structure. To be useful, an occupational classification system must incorporate global contextual characteristics. O*NET provides this information by linking descriptive occupational information to statistical labor market information. This includes compensation and wage data, employment outlook, and industry size information. Much of this information is collected outside of the O*NET program's immediate scope. Collaborative efforts with such organizations as the Bureau of Labor Statistics, the Department of Commerce, the Department of Defense, Career One Stop, the U.S. Bureau of the Census, and the Employment and Training Administration facilitate these labor market information linkages. These characteristics include:

- Labor market information
- Occupational outlook

Labor market information describes current labor force characteristics of occupations. Occupational outlook describes future labor force characteristics of occupations.

WORKER CHARACTERISTICS **Worker characteristics** information includes:

- Abilities
- Interests
- Work styles

Abilities are enduring attributes of the individual that influence performance. **Interests** describe preferences for work environments and outcomes. **Work styles** are personal characteristics that describe important interpersonal and work style requirements in jobs and occupations. Table 6-7 lists the particular abilities, interests, and work styles.

TABLE 6-7 O*NET Content Model: Worker Characteristics (sample of full list)

- Abilities
- Cognitive abilities
    - Verbal abilities
        1. Oral comprehension
        2. Written comprehension
        3. Oral expression
        4. Written expression
    - Idea generation and reasoning abilities
        1. Fluency of ideas
        2. Originality
        3. Problem sensitivity
    - Quantitative abilities
        1. Mathematical reasoning
        2. Number facility
    - Memory
        1. Memorization
    - Perceptual abilities
        1. Speed of closure
        2. Flexibility of closure
        3. Perceptual speed

Source: Occupational Information Network Consortium. Content model. Available: *www.onetcenter.org/content.html*, accessed May 23, 2013.

WORKER REQUIREMENTS Worker requirements include:

- Basic skills
- Cross-functional skills
- Knowledge
- Education

Worker requirements represent developed or acquired attributes of an individual that may be related to work performance such as work-related knowledge and skill. Knowledge represents the acquisition of facts and principles about a domain of information. Experience lays the foundation for establishing procedures to work with given knowledge. These procedures are more commonly known as skills. Skills may be divided further into basic skills and cross-functional skills. Basic skills (e.g., reading) facilitate the acquisition of new knowledge. Cross-functional skills (e.g., problem solving) extend across several domains of activities.

Basic skills information describes developed capacities that facilitate learning or the more rapid acquisition of knowledge. **Cross-functional skills** information indicates developed capacities that facilitate performance of activities that occur across jobs. Knowledge information describes organized sets of principles and facts applying in general domains. Education information details prior educational experience required to perform in a job. Table 6-8 lists the particular basic skills, cross-functional skills, knowledge, and educational requirements.

USING O*NET Human resource professionals use O*NET by consulting the **O*NET User's Guide** as well as the most current **O*NET database.**[4] They may find the latest O*NET information on the U.S. Department of Labor Employment and Training Administration's Web site (*http://online.onetcenter.org*).

TABLE 6-8 O*NET Content Model: Worker Requirements (sample of full list)

- Basic Skills
  - Content
    1. Reading comprehension
    2. Active listening
    3. Writing
  - Process
    1. Critical thinking
    2. Active learning
    3. Learning strategies
- Cross-functional skills
  - Social skills
    1. Social perceptiveness
    2. Coordination
    3. Persuasion
- Complex problem-solving skills
    1. Problem identification
    2. Information gathering
    3. Information organization

Source: Occupational Information Network Consortium. Content model. Available: *www.onetcenter.org/content.html*, accessed May 23, 2013.

JOB EVALUATION

Compensation professionals use job evaluation to systematically recognize differences in the relative worth among a set of jobs and establish pay differentials accordingly. Whereas job analysis is almost purely descriptive, job evaluation partly reflects the values and priorities that management places on various positions. Based on job content and the firm's priorities, managers establish pay differentials for virtually all positions within the company.

Compensable Factors

Compensation professionals generally base job evaluations on **compensable factors**, which are the salient job characteristics by which companies establish relative pay rates. Most companies consider skill, effort, responsibility, and working conditions, which were derived from the Equal Pay Act. These four dimensions help managers determine whether dissimilar jobs are "equal."

Skill, effort, responsibility, and working conditions are **universal compensable factors** because virtually every job contains these four factors. How, then, can meaningful distinctions regarding the value of jobs be made with such broad factors? Many companies break these general factors into more specific factors. For example, responsibility required could be further classified as responsibility for financial matters and responsibility for personnel matters.

Most jobs today can be described broadly in terms of knowledge, skills, and abilities given the evolution of jobs that require greater cognitive skills and mental (versus physical) effort. A working conditions compensable factor is most helpful when a company expects a substantial difference in working conditions for similar jobs. For example, a company may employ geologists, but while some of them are required to work in the field where possible dangers are greater, other geologists are required to work within the safe confines of a laboratory.

In any event, compensation professionals should choose compensable factors based on two considerations. First, factors must be job related. The factors that describe a particular job should indeed reflect the actual work that is performed.

Second, compensation professionals should select compensable factors that further a company's strategies. For example, companies that value product differentiation probably consider innovation to be an important compensable factor for research scientist and marketing manager jobs. Companies that distinguish themselves through high-quality customer relations are likely to place great value on such compensable factors as product knowledge and interpersonal skills. Lowest-cost strategies may emphasize different kinds of compensable factors (e.g., efficiency and timeliness).

The Job Evaluation Process

The job evaluation process entails six steps:

- Determining single versus multiple job evaluation techniques
- Choosing the job evaluation committee
- Training employees to conduct job evaluations
- Documenting the job evaluation plan
- Communicating with employees
- Setting up the appeals process

DETERMINING SINGLE VERSUS MULTIPLE JOB EVALUATION TECHNIQUES Compensation professionals must determine whether a single job evaluation technique is sufficiently broad to assess a diverse set of jobs. In particular, the decision is prompted by such questions as, "Can we use the same compensable factors to evaluate a forklift operator's job and the plant manager's job?" If the answer is *yes*, then a single job evaluation technique is appropriate. If not, then more than one job evaluation approach should be employed. It is not reasonable to expect that a single job evaluation technique, based on one set of compensable factors, can adequately assess diverse sets of jobs (i.e., operative, clerical, administrative, managerial, professional, technical, and executive). A carpenter's job is clearly distinct from a certified public accountant's position because manual dexterity is an important compensable factor that describes carpentry work and is not nearly as central to an accounting position.

CHOOSING THE JOB EVALUATION COMMITTEE Human resource professionals help put together a committee of rank-and-file employees, supervisors, managers, and, if relevant, union representatives to design, oversee, and evaluate job evaluation results. The functions, duties, responsibilities, and authority of job evaluation committees vary considerably from company to company. In general, committees simply review job descriptions and analyses and then evaluate jobs. Larger companies with a multitude of jobs often establish separate committees to evaluate particular job classifications such as nonexempt, exempt, managerial, and executive jobs. The immense number of jobs in large companies would otherwise preclude committee members from performing their regular duties.

Job evaluation is an important determinant of a job's worth within many companies. All employees, regardless of their functions, wish to be compensated and valued for their efforts. All employees strive for a reasonable pay-effort bargain (i.e., a compensation level consistent with their contributions). Managers strive to balance employee motivation with cost control because they have limited resources for operating their departments. Union representatives strive to ensure that members enjoy a good standard of living. Therefore, unions try to prevent the undervaluation of jobs.

Job evaluation committees help ensure commitment from employees throughout companies. They also provide a checks-and-balances system. Job evaluation procedures are not scientifically accurate because these evaluation decisions are based on ordinary human judgment. Therefore, a consensus of several employees helps to minimize the biases of individual job evaluators.

TRAINING EMPLOYEES TO CONDUCT JOB EVALUATIONS Individuals should understand the process objectives. In addition to knowing company objectives, evaluators also should practice using the chosen job evaluation criteria before applying them to actual jobs. Similar to job analysis procedures, evaluators should base their decisions on sound job- and business-related rationales to ensure legal compliance.

DOCUMENTING THE JOB EVALUATION PLAN   Documenting the job evaluation plan is useful for legal and training purposes. From an employer's perspective, a well-documented evaluation plan clearly specifies job- and business-related criteria against which jobs are evaluated. Well-documented plans can allow employees to understand clearly how their jobs were evaluated and the outcome of the process. In addition, well-documented plans provide guidelines for clarifying ambiguities in the event of employee appeals or legal challenges.

COMMUNICATING WITH EMPLOYEES   Job evaluation results matter personally to all employees. Companies must formally communicate with employees throughout the job analysis and evaluation processes to ensure employees' understanding and acceptance of the job evaluation process and results. Information sessions and memoranda are useful media. Employers should share basic information, and employees should be given the opportunity to respond to what they believe are either unsatisfactory procedures or inaccurate outcomes of the job evaluation process.

SETTING UP THE APPEALS PROCESS   Companies should set up appeals procedures that permit reviews on a case-by-case basis to provide a check on the process through reexamination. Such appeals reduce charges of illegal discrimination that would be more likely to occur if employees were not given a voice. Compensation professionals usually review employees' appeals. Companies increasingly process appeals through committees made up of compensation professionals and a representative sample of employees and supervisors. Grievants are more likely to judge appeals decisions as fair if committees are involved: Committee decisions should reflect the varied perspectives of participants rather than the judgment of one individual.

JOB EVALUATION TECHNIQUES

Compensation professionals categorize job evaluation methods as either market-based evaluation or job-content evaluation techniques. **Market-based evaluation** plans use market data to determine differences in job worth. Many companies choose market-based evaluation methods because they wish to assign job pay rates that are neither too low nor too high relative to the market. Setting pay rates too low will make it difficult to recruit talented candidates, whereas setting pay rates too high will result in an excessive cost burden for the employer. Compensation professionals rely on compensation surveys to determine prevailing pay rates of jobs in the relevant labor market. We will address that issue in Chapter 7.

Job-content evaluation plans emphasize the company's internal value system by establishing a hierarchy of internal job worth based on each job's role in company strategy. Compensation professionals review preliminary structures for consistency with market pay rates on a representative sample of jobs known as benchmark jobs. Compensation professionals ultimately must balance external market considerations with internal consistency objectives. In practice, compensation professionals judge the adequacy of pay differentials by comparing both market rates and pay differences among jobs within their companies. They consult with the top HR official and chief financial officer when discrepancies arise, particularly if company pay rates are generally lower than the market rates. Upon careful consideration of the company's financial resources and the strategic value of the jobs in question, these executives decide whether to adjust internal pay rates for jobs with below-market pay rates.

Neither market-based nor job-content evaluation approaches alone enable compensation professionals to balance internal and external considerations. Most companies therefore rely on both approaches. The point method is the most popular job-content method because it gives compensation professionals better control over balancing internal and market considerations. Chapter 7 fully addresses how compensation professionals combine point method results with market approaches; however, a brief overview will follow our discussion of the point method in this chapter.

The Point Method

The **point method** is a job-content valuation technique that uses quantitative methodology. Quantitative methods assign numerical values to compensable factors that describe jobs, and these values are summed as an indicator of the overall value for the job. The relative worth of jobs is established by the magnitude of the overall numerical value for the jobs.

The point method evaluates jobs by comparing compensable factors. Each factor is defined and assigned a range of points based on the factor's relative value to the company. Compensable factors are weighted to represent the relative importance of each factor to the job. Job evaluation committees follow seven steps to complete the point method.

STEP 1: SELECT BENCHMARK JOBS Point method job evaluations use **benchmark jobs** to develop factors and their definitions to select jobs to represent the entire range of jobs in the company. Benchmark jobs, found outside the company, provide reference points against which jobs within the company are judged.

STEP 2: CHOOSE COMPENSABLE FACTORS BASED ON BENCHMARK JOBS Managers must define compensable factors that adequately represent the scope of jobs slated for evaluation. Each benchmark job should be described by those factors that help distinguish it from the value of all other jobs. In addition to the "universal" factors (e.g., skill, effort, responsibility, and working conditions), additional factors may be developed to the extent that they are job- and business-related.

Compensable factor categories may be broken down further into specific related factors or subfactors. For example, skill may include job knowledge, education, mental ability, physical ability, accuracy, and dexterity. Effort may include factors relating to both physical and mental exertion. Responsibility may include considerations related to fiscal, material, or personnel responsibilities. Working conditions may be unpleasant because of extreme temperatures or possible exposure to hazardous chemicals.

The number of compensable factors companies should use varies. Compensation professionals should select as many compensable factors as are needed to describe the range of benchmark jobs adequately.

STEP 3: DEFINE FACTOR DEGREES Although compensable factors describe the range of benchmark jobs, individual jobs vary in scope and content. Evaluators must therefore divide each factor into a sufficient number of degrees to identify the level of a factor present in each job. To clarify this idea of factor degrees, it is helpful to think about a paint sample that can be found in any home improvement store. Specifying a color such as gray is not straightforward because there are various shades of gray. Likewise, a compensable factor is similar to a color. For example, the compensable factor *writing ability* can be described in degrees (shades of color) ranging from the ability to write simple sentences to the ability to write paragraphs of complex information.

Table 6-9 illustrates a factor definition for writing ability and its degree statements. Degree definitions should set forth and limit the meaning of each degree so evaluators can uniformly interpret job descriptions. It is generally helpful to include a few actual work examples as anchors.

The number of degrees will vary based on the comprehensiveness of the plan. For example, if the plan covers only a limited segment of jobs (e.g., clerical employees), fewer degrees will be required than if the plan covered every group of employees. Take education as an example. Only two degrees may be necessary to describe the educational requirements for clerical jobs (i.e., high school diploma or equivalent and an associate's degree). More than two degrees would be required to describe adequately the educational requirements for administrative, production, managerial, and professional jobs (i.e., high school diploma or equivalent, associate's degree, bachelor's degree, master's degree, and doctorate). Most analyses anchor minimum and maximum degrees, with specific jobs representing these points.

STEP 4: DETERMINE THE WEIGHT OF EACH FACTOR Weighting compensable factors represents the importance of the factor to the overall value of the job. The weights of compensable factors are

TABLE 6-9 **Writing Ability: Factor Definition and Degree Statements**

Definition	Capacity to communicate with others in written form.
First Degree	Print simple phrases and sentences, using normal work order and present and past tenses.
Sample Anchor	Prints shipping labels for packages, indicating the destination and the contents of the packages.
Second Degree	Write compound and complex sentences, using proper end punctuation and adjectives and adverbs.
Sample Anchor	Fills requisitions, work orders, or requests for materials, tools, or other stock items.
Third Degree	Write reports and essays with proper format, punctuation, spelling, and grammar, using all parts of speech.
Sample Anchor	Types letters, reports, or straight-copy materials from rough draft or corrected copy.
Fourth Degree	Prepare business letters, expositions, summaries, and reports using prescribed format and conforming to all rules of punctuation, grammar, diction, and style.
Sample Anchor	Composes letters in reply to correspondence concerning such items as request for merchandise, damage claims, credit information, or delinquent accounts or to request information.
Fifth Degree	Write manuals or speeches.
Sample Anchor	Writes service manuals and related technical publications concerned with installation, operation, and maintenance of electronic, electrical, mechanical, and other equipment.

usually expressed as percentages. Weighting is often done by management or by a job evaluation committee's decision. All of the factors are ranked according to their relative importance, and final weights are assigned after discussion and consensus. For example, let's assume the relative importance of skill, effort, responsibility, and working conditions to ABC Manufacturing Corporation:

- Skill is the most highly valued compensable factor, weighted at 60 percent.
- Responsibility is the next most important factor, weighted at 25 percent.
- Effort is weighted at 10 percent.
- The working conditions factor is least important, weighted at 5 percent.

STEP 5: DETERMINE POINT VALUES FOR EACH COMPENSABLE FACTOR Compensation professionals set point values for each compensable factor in three stages. First, they must establish the maximum possible point values for the complete set of compensable factors. This total number is arbitrary, but it represents the possible maximum value jobs can possess. As a rule of thumb, the total point value for a set of compensable factors should be determined by a simple formula (e.g., the number of compensable factors times 250). ABC Manufacturing sets 1,000 (4 compensable factors * 250) as the possible maximum number of points.

Second, the maximum possible point value for each compensable factor is based on total weight as described in Step 4. Again, for ABC Manufacturing, skill equals 60 percent, responsibility 25 percent, effort 10 percent, and working conditions 5 percent:

- The maximum possible total points for skills equal 600 points (60 percent × 1,000 points).
- The maximum possible total points for responsibility equal 250 points (25 percent × 1,000 points).
- The maximum possible total points for effort equal 100 points (10 percent × 1,000 points).
- The maximum possible total points for working conditions equal 50 points (5 percent × 1,000 points).

Third, compensation professionals distribute these points across degree statements within each compensable factor. The point progression by degrees from the lowest to the highest point value advances arithmetically (i.e., a scale of even incremental values). This characteristic is essential for conducting regression analysis (i.e., a statistical analysis method that we will address in Chapter 7 in the discussion of integrating internal job structures—based on job evaluation points—with external pay rates for benchmark jobs).

How do compensation professionals assign point values to each degree? Let's illustrate this procedure by example, using the skill compensable factor. Let's also assume that the skill factor has five degree statements. Degree 1 represents the most basic skill level, and degree 5 represents the most advanced skill level. The increment from one degree to the next highest is 120 points (600 point maximum divided by 5 degree statements).

- Degree 1 = 120 points (120 points × 1)
- Degree 2 = 240 points (120 points × 2)
- Degree 3 = 360 points (120 points × 3)
- Degree 4 = 480 points (120 points × 4)
- Degree 5 = 600 points (120 points × 5)

STEP 6: VERIFY FACTOR DEGREES AND POINT VALUES Committee members should independently calculate the point values for a random sample of jobs. Table 6-10 shows a sample job evaluation worksheet. After calculating the point values for this sample, committee members should review the point totals for each job. Committee members give careful consideration to whether the hierarchy of jobs makes sense in the context of the company's strategic plan, as well as to the inherent content of the jobs. For instance, sales jobs should rank relatively high on the job hierarchy within a sales-oriented company such as the pharmaceuticals industry. Research scientist jobs ought to rank relatively high for a company that pursues a differentiation strategy. Messenger jobs should not rank more highly than claims analyst jobs in an insurance company. In short, where peculiarities are apparent, committee members reconsider compensable factor definitions, weights, and actual ratings of the benchmark jobs.

TABLE 6-10 Sample Job Evaluation Worksheet

Job Title: _____

Evaluation Date: _____

Name of Evaluator: _____

Compensable Factor	Degree					Total
	1	2	3	4	5	
Skill						
Mental skill	60	120	180	240	(300)	300
Manual skill	60	(120)	180	240	300	120
Effort						
Mental effort	10	20	30	40	(50)	50
Physical effort	10	20	(30)	40	50	30
Responsibility						
Supervisory	25	50	(75)	100	125	75
Department budgeting	(25)	50	75	100	125	25
Working conditions						
Hazards	10	20	30	(40)	50	40
Total job value						640

STEP 7: EVALUATE ALL JOBS Committee members evaluate all jobs in the company once the evaluation system has been tested and refined. Each job then is evaluated by determining which degree definition best fits the job and by assigning the corresponding point factors. All points are totaled for each job, and all jobs are ranked according to their point values.

BALANCING INTERNAL AND MARKET CONSIDERATIONS USING THE POINT METHOD How do compensation professionals balance internal and market considerations with point method results? They convert point values into the market value of jobs through regression analysis, a statistical technique. As we will discuss in Chapter 7, regression analysis enables compensation professionals to set base pay rates in line with market rates for benchmark or representative jobs. Companies identify market pay rates through compensation surveys. Of course, a company's value structure for jobs based on the point method will probably differ somewhat from the market pay rates for similar jobs. Regression analysis indicates base pay rates that minimize the differences between the company's point method results and the market pay rates.

Alternative Job-Content Evaluation Approaches

Most other job-content approaches use qualitative methods. Qualitative methods evaluate entire jobs and typically compare jobs with each other or some general criteria. These criteria are usually vague (e.g., importance of jobs to departmental effectiveness). The prevalent kinds of qualitative job evaluation techniques include:

- Simple ranking plans
- Paired comparisons
- Alternation ranking
- Classification plans

SIMPLE RANKING PLANS **Simple ranking plans** order all jobs from lowest to highest according to a single criterion (e.g., job complexity or the centrality of the job to the company's competitive strategy). This approach considers each job in its entirety, usually used in small companies that have relatively few employees. In large companies that classify many jobs, members of job evaluation committees independently rank jobs on a departmental basis. Different rankings will likely result. When this occurs, job evaluation committees discuss the differences in rankings and choose one set of rankings by consensus.

PAIRED COMPARISON AND ALTERNATION RANKING Two common variations of the ranking plan are paired comparison and alternation ranking. The **paired comparison** technique is useful if there are many jobs to rate, usually more than 20. Job evaluation committees generate every possible pair of jobs. For each pair, committee members assign a point to the job with the highest value, whereas the lowest-value job does not receive a point. After evaluating each pair, the evaluator sums the points for each job. Jobs with higher points are more valuable than are jobs with fewer points. The job with the most points is ranked the highest; the job with the fewest points is ranked the lowest.

The **alternation ranking** method orders jobs by extremes. Yet again, committee members judge the relative value of jobs according to a single criterion (e.g., job complexity or the centrality of the job to the company's competitive strategy). This ranking process begins by determining which job is the most valuable, followed by determining which job is the least valuable. Committee members then judge the next most valuable job and the next least valuable job. This process continues until all jobs have been evaluated.

Despite the simplicity of ranking plans, they exhibit three limitations. First, ranking results rely on purely subjective data; the process lacks objective standards, guidelines, and principles that would aid in resolving differences of opinion among committee members. Companies usually do not fully define their ranking criteria. For example, the criterion job complexity can be defined as level of education or as number of distinct tasks that the workers must perform daily.

Second, ranking methods use neither job analyses nor job descriptions, which makes this method difficult to defend legally. Committee members rely on their own impressions of the jobs.

Third, ranking approaches do not incorporate objective scales that indicate how different in value one job is from another. For instance, let's assume that a committee decides on the following ranking for training and development professionals (listed from most valuable to least valuable):

- Director of training and development
- Manager of training and development
- Senior training and development specialist
- Training and development specialist
- Training and development assistant

Rankings do not offer standards for compensation professionals to facilitate answering such questions as, "Is the director of training and development job worth four times as much as the training and development assistant job?" Compensation professionals' inability to answer such questions makes it difficult to establish pay levels according to job-content differences.

CLASSIFICATION PLANS   Companies use **classification plans** to place jobs into categories based on compensable factors. Public sector organizations (e.g., civil service systems) use classification systems most prevalently. The federal government's classification system is a well-known example. As we discussed in Chapter 3, the General Schedule classifies federal government jobs into 15 classifications (GS-1 through GS-15) based on such factors as skill, education, and experience levels. In addition, jobs that require high levels of specialized education (e.g., a physicist), significantly influence public policy (e.g., law judges), or require executive decision making are classified in separate categories: Senior Level (SL) positions, Scientific and Professional (SP) positions, and the Senior Executive Service (SES).

The GS classification system enables the federal government to set pay rates for thousands of unique jobs based on 18 classes. Pay administration is relatively simple because pay rates depend on GS level and the employees' relevant work seniority, as we discussed in Chapter 3. The most noteworthy disadvantage is the absence of regular procedures for rewarding exceptional performance, which, ultimately, discourages employees from working as productively as possible.

Alternatives to Job Evaluation

Compensation professionals assign pay rates to jobs in numerous ways other than through the job evaluation process as previously defined. These alternate methods include reliance on market pay rates, pay incentives, individual rates, and collective bargaining. Many companies determine the value of jobs by paying the average rate in the external labor market. The procedures for assessing market rates are addressed fully in Chapter 7.

In addition to the market pay rate, pay incentives may also be the basis for establishing the core compensation for jobs. As we discussed extensively in Chapter 4, incentives tie part or all of an employee's core compensation to the attainment of a predetermined performance objective. Next, both core and fringe compensation may be determined through negotiations between an individual and an employer. The employer typically uses the market rate as a basis for negotiations, agreeing to higher pay if the supply of talented individuals is scarce and the individual in question has an established track record of performance. Finally, when unions are present, pay rates are established through the collective bargaining process, which we already considered in Chapter 2.

INTERNALLY CONSISTENT COMPENSATION SYSTEMS AND COMPETITIVE STRATEGY

To this point, we have examined the principles of internally consistent compensation systems and the rationale for building them. Moreover, we reviewed the key processes (i.e., job analysis and job evaluation) that lead to internally consistent compensation systems. Although we made the case for building internally consistent pay systems, these systems do have some limitations.

Internally consistent pay systems may reduce a company's flexibility to respond to changes in competitors' pay practices because job analysis leads to structured job descriptions and job structures. In addition, job evaluation establishes the relative worth of jobs within the company. Responding to the competition may require employees to engage in duties that extend beyond what's written in their job descriptions whenever competitive pressures demand. In the process, the definitions of jobs become more fluid, which makes equity assessments more difficult.

Another potential limitation of internally consistent compensation structures is the resultant bureaucracy. Companies that establish job hierarchies tend to create narrowly defined jobs that lead to greater numbers of jobs and staffing levels.[5] Such structures promote heavy compensation burdens. Employees' core compensation depends on the jobs they perform, how well they perform their jobs, or the skills they possess. Employee benefits (Chapters 9, 10, and 11), however, represent fixed costs that typically do not vary with employees' job performance or their skills.

COMPENSATION IN ACTION

Creating a clear expectation of performance and organizing employee roles in a way that aligns strategy, pay, and performance will benefit you as a line manager or HR professional. Line managers and HR should employ the help of those who know roles the best—the employees who fill those roles—in order to arrive at conclusions that are fair, informed, and consistent. Line managers will have insight in many cases to choose the right people to help out in this process. HR will ensure that these individuals receive proper training and are equipped to assess roles and provide appropriate and objective recommendations. As a line manager or HR professional, your main responsibility in creating a system is to ensure that employee compensation is equitable internally and competitive externally.

- Compensation specialists work with HR professionals to identify the compensable factors within each job description; these factors will serve as the basis for pay differentials (the more critical these factors are to company strategy, the more they will be compensated).
- Work with compensation specialists to evaluate differentials across departments in the organization and compare them with similar jobs in other organizations (ideally competitors); consult with line managers and senior finance executives as discrepancies arise and adjustments appear to be necessary.
- Monitor the match of performance expectations and job descriptions to guard against role stagnation in the face of competition that could require jobs to flex and people to take on unexpected responsibilities—monitor equity carefully.

Action checklist for line managers and HR— building an equitable and competitive system

HR takes the lead
- Capture the analysis provided by incumbents and create job descriptions for each role.
- Compare the newly created job descriptions with those found on O*NET to validate the decisions made based on the incumbent information.

Line managers take the lead
- Partner with job incumbents to understand job content of their roles.
- Select workers to sit on committees that will be given the task of assessing the accuracy of the assigned pay differentials.

Accurate identification of job content → Creation of job descriptions → Comparison of job descriptions with those found on O*NET

Pay differentials are compared internally and externally to confirm equity and competitiveness ← Pay differentials are assessed and confirmed ← Pay differentials are established based on compensable factors within each job

HR monitors process to ensure that people adapt to changing requirements as dictated by competitive pressures—also ensure the equity remains constant in these situations. Also, HR will monitor that, as a result of these defined and hierarchical differentials, headcount and inflation do not create barriers to nimble and decisive leadership

END OF CHAPTER

MyManagementLab

Go to **mymanagementlab.com** to complete the problems marked with this icon.

Summary

This chapter discussed internally consistent pay systems and described two important tools HR and compensation professionals use to build them (i.e., job analysis and job evaluation). Job analysis represents a descriptive process that enables HR professionals to systematically describe job duties, worker specifications, and job context. Compensation professionals use job evaluation to assess the relative worth of jobs within companies. Job analysis

and job evaluation are an art because they require the HR and compensation professionals' sound judgments. We discussed the strategic role that job analysis and job evaluation play in companies' quests for competitive advantage; however, we also pointed out some of the shortcomings of these approaches. Compensation professionals must carefully weigh the possible benefits and consequences of these methods in attaining competitive advantage.

Key Terms

internally consistent compensation
   systems 118
job analysis 119
job content 119
job evaluation 120
worker requirements 120
working conditions 120
major occupational groups 122
reliable job analysis 123
job descriptions 124
job titles 124
job summary 124
job duties 124
worker specifications 124
education 124
Equal Employment Opportunity
   Commission (EEOC) 125

skill 125
ability 125
knowledge 125
Occupational Information Network
   (O*NET) 127
Content Model 127
experience and training 127
licensing 127
occupational requirements 127
generalized work activities 129
organizational context 129
work context 129
occupation-specific information
   requirements 130
workforce characteristics 130
worker characteristics 130
abilities 130

interests 130
work styles 130
basic skills 131
cross-functional skills 131
O*NET User's Guide 131
O*NET database 131
compensable factors 132
universal compensable
   factors 132
market-based evaluation 134
job-content evaluation 134
point method 135
benchmark jobs 135
simple ranking plans 138
paired comparison 138
alternation ranking 138
classification plans 139

✪ Discussion Questions

6-1. Discuss the differences between job analysis and job evaluation. How do these practices help establish internally consistent job structures?

6-2. Conduct a job analysis of a person you know, and write a complete job description (no longer than one page) according to the principles described in this chapter. In class, be prepared to discuss the method you used for conducting the job analysis and some of the challenges you encountered.

6-3. This chapter provides rationale for conducting job analysis, and it indicates some of the limitations. Take a stand for or against the use of job analysis, and provide convincing arguments for your position.

6-4. Respond to the statement "Building an internally consistent job structure is burdensome to companies. Instead, it is best to simply define and evaluate the worth of jobs by surveying the market."

6-5. Do you consider job evaluation to be an art or a science? Please explain.

CASE
Internal Consistency at Customers First

⭐ *An additional Supplemental Case can be found on MyManagementLab.*

After 3 months in her new role as Director of Human Resources (HR) at Customers First, Deborah Ketson feels confident she has identified the significant HR issues at the company. She has prioritized the issues and is meeting with company president Joan Bates to make her recommendations. Deborah is prepared to discuss her top priority, which is to conduct an organization-wide job analysis and job evaluation project in order to start building a more internally consistent pay structure.

Customers First is a company that provides customer service for other companies. Small-to-medium-sized companies outsource their customer service function to Customers First, which manages all customer service for their clients through a call center and also via an online customer service center. The company works with a diverse group of clients ranging from small retail stores to larger online retailers. Customers First has grown quickly in the 5 years since Joan started the company and now employs more than 150 customer service representatives (CSRs) and other support staff.

The company's quick growth has led to several problems with its compensation structure. Much of the company's hiring has occurred in response to a new contract, and pay was set based on the current market rate for CSRs in order to attract the right talent. For example, an early client was a small retail store that needed fairly simple customer support. Four CSRs were hired and their pay was set at just slightly above minimum wage. In comparison, a more recent client required hiring 18 CSRs. The labor market was competitive at the time, and the company hired these 18 new employees at a pay rate well above what others at the company were paid. Such variance has occurred often in the hiring process, resulting in groups of CSRs at much different levels of pay for doing substantially similar work.

Deborah has heard many complaints from the supervisors about inequities in the pay of the CSRs. The supervisors are concerned that the inequities may lead to turnover among some of the staff. Deborah has examined the pay rates of the CSRs across the organization and agrees with the supervisors that there are some concerns. One particular concern is that the lowest paid group of CSRs is primarily female, while the highest paid group includes all male employees. By talking with the supervisors, Deborah has learned that there are some CSRs with different levels of responsibilities and skills, but they all hold the same job title. Deborah believes that an organization-wide job analysis and job evaluation is necessary to build an internally consistent compensation structure.

However, when she shared her recommendation with Joan, she did not receive the response she expected. Joan is resistant of the job analysis and job evaluation process as she thinks that having such a structured compensation system will limit the company's ability to be flexible in the marketplace. Often hiring happens quickly in response to a new client contract, and they must hire the right skill set, which might vary based on the current market rates. Further, Joan suggested the entire project would be too time-consuming for Deborah and the other staff that would need to be involved. She felt their time would be better spent on other concerns such as recruiting new staff.

Questions:

6-6. Do you think that job analysis and job evaluation will benefit Customers First?

6-7. What is your opinion on Joan's view on job analysis and job evaluation?

6-8. What do you recommend Customers First do? Why?

MyManagementLab

Go to **mymanagementlab.com** for Auto-graded writing questions as well as the following Assisted-graded writing questions:

⭐ 6-9. Why must a job analysis be reliable and valid? What can a compensation professional do to ensure that a job analysis *is* reliable and valid?

⭐ 6-10. After completing the job analysis, your boss has asked you to conduct a job evaluation of the various positions in the company. Detail the steps you would take in accomplishing this task.

Endnotes

1. Cascio, W. F., & Aguinis, H. (2011). *Applied Psychology in Personnel Management* (7th ed.). Upper Saddle River, NJ: Prentice Hall.
2. U.S. Department of Labor. (1991). *The Revised Handbook for Analyzing Jobs*. Washington, DC: Government Printing Office.
3. U.S. Department of Labor. (1991). *The Dictionary of Occupational Titles*. Washington, DC: Government Printing Office.
4. U.S. Department of Labor, Employment and Training Administration. (2011). *O*NET*. Washington, DC: Government Printing Office. Available: *www.onetcenter. gov*, accessed January 11, 2011.
5. Lawler, E. E., III. (1986). What's wrong with point-factor job evaluation? *Compensation and Benefits Review, 18*, pp. 20–28.

7

BUILDING MARKET-COMPETITIVE COMPENSATION SYSTEMS

LEARNING OBJECTIVES

When you finish studying this chapter, you should be able to:

1. Explain the concept of market-competitive compensation systems and summarize the four activities compensation professionals engage in to create these systems.
2. Discuss how compensation professionals integrate job structures with external market pay rates.
3. Present the basic concepts of two compensation policy types: pay mix and pay level.

Companies rely on compensation surveys as a benchmark for setting pay and benefits to recruit highly qualified applicants and to retain valued employees. The number of salary surveys has risen with the popularity of the Internet. The end-of-chapter appendix contains an excellent example of a salary survey that is administered each year by WorldatWork.

MARKET-COMPETITIVE PAY SYSTEMS: THE BASIC BUILDING BLOCKS

Market-competitive pay systems represent companies' compensation policies that fit the imperatives of competitive advantage. Market-competitive pay systems play a significant role in attracting and retaining the most qualified employees. Well-designed pay systems should promote companies' attainment of competitive strategies. Paying more than necessary can undermine lowest-cost strategies: Excessive pay levels represent an undue burden. In addition, excessive pay restricts companies' abilities to invest in other important strategic activities (e.g., research and development, training) because money is a limited resource. Companies that pursue differentiation strategies must strike a balance between offering sufficiently high salaries to attract and retain talented candidates and providing sufficient resources to enable them to be productively creative.

Compensation professionals create market-competitive pay systems based on four activities:

- Conducting strategic analyses
- Assessing competitors' pay practices with compensation surveys
- Integrating the internal job structure with external market pay rates
- Determining compensation policies

First, a **strategic analysis** entails an examination of a company's external market context and internal factors. Examples of external market factors include industry profile, information about competitors, and long-term growth prospects. Internal factors encompass financial condition and functional capabilities (e.g., marketing and human resources).

Second, **compensation surveys** involve the collection and subsequent analysis of competitors' compensation data. Compensation surveys traditionally focused on competitors' wage and salary practices. Employee benefits have more recently also become a target of surveys because benefits are a key element of market-competitive pay systems. Compensation surveys are important because they enable compensation professionals to obtain realistic views of competitors' pay practices. In the absence of compensation survey data, compensation professionals would have to use guesswork to try to build market-competitive compensation systems, and making too many wrong guesses could lead to noncompetitive compensation systems that undermine competitive advantage.

Third, compensation professionals integrate the internal job structure (Chapter 6) with the external market pay rates identified through compensation surveys. This integration results in pay rates that reflect both the company's and the external market's valuations of jobs. Most often, compensation professionals rely on regression analysis, a statistical method, to achieve this integration.

Finally, compensation professionals recommend pay policies that fit with their companies' standing and competitive strategies. As we discuss later in this chapter, compensation professionals must strike a balance between managing costs and attracting and retaining the best-qualified employees. Top management ultimately makes compensation policy decisions after careful consideration of compensation professionals' interpretation of the data.

COMPENSATION SURVEYS

The second step compensation professionals undertake to ensure external competitiveness is to consult or develop compensation surveys. Compensation surveys contain data about competing companies' compensation practices.

Preliminary Considerations

There are two important preliminary considerations compensation professionals take under advisement before investing time and money into compensation surveys:

- What companies hope to gain from compensation surveys
- Custom development versus use of an existing compensation survey

WHAT COMPANIES HOPE TO GAIN FROM COMPENSATION SURVEYS Clarifying what companies hope to gain from compensation surveys is critical to developing effective compensation systems. Compensation professionals usually want to learn about competitors' compensation practices and something about employees' preferences for alternative forms of compensation due to economic changes. Staying abreast of new developments in market surveys will enable compensation professionals to get the most out of surveys. Information to be learned about competitors' compensation offerings includes base pay levels, incentive award structures, and both the mix and levels of discretionary benefits. Mix can be described as the percentage of employer compensation costs applied to compensation and benefits. For example, health insurance coverage accounts for 40 percent of total dollars spent on employee benefits. Levels refer to amounts actually or potentially paid to employees or beneficiaries. For instance, the average annual pay for day care workers is $16,000, and life insurance benefits are subject to a maximum payout of $250,000.

Compensation professionals wish to make sound decisions about pay levels based on what the competition pays its employees. Sound pay decisions promote companies' efforts to sustain competitive advantage, and poor pay decisions compromise those efforts. Compensation surveys enable compensation professionals to make sound judgments about how much to pay employees. Offering too little will limit a company's ability to recruit and retain high-quality employees. Paying well above the competition represents opportunity costs. Financial resources are limited. Companies therefore cannot afford to spend money on everything they wish. Excessive pay represents an opportunity cost because it is money companies could have spent on other important matters.

CUSTOM DEVELOPMENT VERSUS USE OF AN EXISTING COMPENSATION SURVEY Managers must decide whether to develop their own survey instruments and administer them or rely on the results of surveys conducted by others. In theory, customized surveys are preferable because the survey taker can tailor the questions the survey asks and select respondent companies to provide the most useful and informative data. Custom survey development should enable employers to monitor the quality of the survey developers' methodologies.

In practice, companies choose not to develop and implement their own surveys for three reasons. First, most companies lack employees qualified to undertake this task. Developing and implementing valid surveys require specialized knowledge and expertise in sound questionnaire design, sampling methods, and statistical methods.

Second, rival companies are understandably reluctant to surrender information about their compensation packages to competitors because compensation systems are instrumental to competitive advantage issues. If companies are willing to cooperate, the information may be incomplete or inaccurate. For example, rival companies may choose to report the salaries for their lowest-paid accountants instead of the typical salary levels. Such information may lead the surveying company to set accountants' salaries much lower than if they had accurate, complete information about typical salary levels. Setting accountants' salaries too low may hinder recruitment efforts. Thus, custom development is potentially risky.

Third, custom survey development can be costly. Although cost figures are not readily available, it is reasonable to conclude that most companies use published survey data to minimize such costs as staff salaries and benefits (i.e., for those involved in developing a compensation survey as well as analyzing and interpreting the data), telephone and mail charges (depending on the data collection method), and computers for data analyses.

Using Published Compensation Survey Data

Companies usually rely on existing compensation surveys rather than creating their own. Using published compensation survey data starts with two important considerations:

- Survey focus: core or employee benefits
- Sources of published compensation surveys

SURVEY FOCUS: CORE OR EMPLOYEE BENEFITS Human resource professionals should decide whether to obtain survey information about base pay, employee benefits, or both. Companies historically competed for employees mainly on the basis of base pay. Many companies offered similar, substantial benefits packages to employees without regard to the costs. Companies typically did not use benefits offerings to compete for the best employees.

Times have changed. Benefits costs are now extremely high, which has led to greater variability in benefits offerings among companies. As of December 2012, companies spent an average approaching $20,000 per employee annually to provide discretionary benefits.[1] In 2012, discretionary benefits accounted for as much as 30.8 percent of employers' total payroll costs (i.e., the sum of core compensation and all employee benefits costs). That is a huge cost to employers, but one that cannot be avoided; benefits have become a basis for attracting and retaining the best employees, particularly as noted earlier in this chapter. As a result, employers are likely to use compensation surveys to obtain information about competitors' base pay and benefits practices so they can compete effectively for the best candidates.

SOURCES OF PUBLISHED COMPENSATION SURVEYS Companies can obtain published survey data from various sources (e.g., professional associations, industry associations, consulting firms, and the federal government). Professional and industry associations survey members' salaries, compile the information in summary form, and disseminate the results to members. The survey data tend to be accurate because participants—as well as association members—benefit from the survey results. In addition, membership fees often entitle members to survey information at no additional cost.

For example, the Society for Industrial and Organizational Psychology's (SIOP) primary membership includes college and university faculty members and practitioners who specialize in such HR management-related fields as selection, training, performance appraisal, and career development. SIOP periodically provides members' salary information based on gender, age, employment status (i.e., part time versus full time), years since earning degree, and geographic region according to metropolitan area (e.g., Boston, San Francisco/San Jose, and Washington, DC). Employers use the survey results to judge whether they are paying employees too much or too little relative to the market and to determine how much to pay new hires. Employees use the survey results to judge the adequacy of job offers and to ask their deans for pay raises when their salaries fall below the market rates.

Professional associations that specialize in the field of compensation often conduct surveys that focus on broader types of employees and employers. WorldatWork collects comprehensive data on an annual basis. The end-of-chapter appendix shows WorldatWork's 2009/2010 Total Salary Increase Budget Survey. As you will see, some of the survey topics include salary structures, promotions, and incentive practices designed to attract and retain excellent employees.

Consulting firms are another source of compensation survey information. Some firms specialize in particular occupations (e.g., engineers) or industries (e.g., financial services); other firms do not. Examples of consulting firms that provide compensation services include:

- Buck Consultants (*www.buckconsultants.com*)
- Frederic W. Cook & Company (*www.fwcook.com*)
- The Hay Associates (*www.haygroup.com*)
- Hewitt Associates (*www.hewitt.com*)
- Pearl Meyer & Partners (*www.pearlmeyer.com*)
- Towers Watson (*www.towerswatson.com*)
- William M. Mercer (*www.mercer.com*)

You will find useful updates about compensation and benefits on these firms' Web sites. Clients may have two choices. First, consulting firms may provide survey data from recently completed surveys. Second, these firms may literally conduct surveys from scratch exclusively for a client's use. In most cases, the first option is less expensive to companies than the second option; however, the quality of the second option may be superior because the survey was custom-designed to answer a client's specific compensation questions.

The federal government is an invaluable source of compensation survey information. The U.S. Bureau of Labor Statistics (BLS) provides free salary surveys to the public. Highly qualified survey takers and statisticians are responsible for producing these surveys. Many factors contributed to the implementation of BLS pay and benefits surveys. The government began collecting compensation data in the 1890s to assess the effects of tariff legislation on wages and prices. The government's survey programs have been rooted in competitive concerns ever since.

The BLS presently conducts various surveys that provide the following types of information (the survey names are listed in parentheses):

- Wages (National Compensation Survey)
- Compensation cost trends (Employment Cost Index; Employer Costs for Employee Compensation)
- Benefits (National Compensation Survey)

The following summary of these programs was excerpted from the public domain BLS Web site (*www.bls.gov*). Survey data are available to the public on the Web site. There are no fees associated with accessing information from this Web site.

WAGES The **National Compensation Survey (NCS)** provides comprehensive measures of occupational wages; employment cost trends, benefit incidence, and detailed plan provisions. Detailed occupational earnings are available for metropolitan and non-metropolitan areas, broad geographic regions, and on a national basis. The data available include:

- Average hourly wages for over 800 occupations in approximately 80 metropolitan and selected non-metropolitan localities
- Weekly and annual earnings and hours for full-time workers
- Earnings by work level that permit wage comparisons across occupational groups
- Data at three levels: localities, broad regions, and the nation
- Workers are shown as a total (all workers) and broken out by private industry and state and local government
- Wage data are shown by industry, occupational group, full-time and part-time status, union and nonunion status, establishment size, time and incentive status, and job level

COMPENSATION COST TRENDS Employment cost trends are measured by two quarterly indexes measuring change over time in labor costs (ECI) and quarterly data measuring level of average costs per hour worked.

The Employment Cost Index (ECI) is a quarterly measure of changes in labor costs. It is one of the principal economic indicators used by the Federal Reserve Bank. Some of its main features are that it:

- Shows changes in wages and salaries and benefit costs, as well as changes in total compensation
- Presents data as a total for all workers and separately for private industry and for state and local government workers
- Reports compensation changes by industry, occupational group, union and nonunion status, region, and metropolitan/non-metropolitan status
- Provides seasonally adjusted and unadjusted data
- Presents historical data on changes in labor costs
- Uses fixed weights to control for shifts among occupations and industries

Why was the Employment Cost Index developed?

- The ECI was developed in the mid-1970s in response to the rapid acceleration of both wages and prices at that time.
- Monetary and fiscal policymakers needed a more accurate measure of the actual changes in employers' labor costs.
- The ECI was first published for the third quarter, September through December, of 1975.
- It was initially very limited, covering only wage and salary changes in private industry.
- Benefits and total compensation series were added in 1981.

The Employer Costs for Employee Compensation (ECEC) program is a survey that shows employers' average hourly cost for total compensation and its components. As its key features it:

- Shows compensation costs as a total and broken out by (1) wages and salaries; (2) total benefit costs; (3) separate benefit costs for broad benefit categories such as paid leave, supplemental pay, insurance, retirement and savings, legally required benefits, and other benefits; or (4) separate benefit costs for such detailed benefits as paid holidays, health insurance, defined benefit pension, and workers' compensation
- Provides cost data in dollar amounts and as percentages of compensation

- Breaks out data on civilian workers into estimates for white-collar, blue-collar, and service groups or state and local government workers into estimates for white-collar workers, service occupations, and service industries
- Reports compensation costs by major occupation, industry, region, union and nonunion status, establishment size, and full- or part-time status

EMPLOYEE BENEFITS The National Compensation Survey (NCS) covers the incidence and detailed provisions of selected employee benefit plans in small private establishments, medium and large private establishments, and state and local governments. The data are presented as the percentage of employees who have access to or participate in certain benefits or as average benefit provisions (e.g., the average number of paid holidays provided to employees each year).

Estimates are published by:

- Broad occupational groups
- Full- and part-time status of employees
- Union and nonunion status
- Workers with average wages by selected percentiles
- Selected goods-producing and service-providing industries
- Establishments by selected employment sizes
- Census divisions

The NCS provides incidence and extensive provisions data for two major benefit areas:

- Health insurance
- Retirement (both defined benefit and defined contribution components)

Compensation Surveys: Strategic Considerations

Two essential strategic considerations are:

- Defining the relevant labor market
- Choosing benchmark jobs

DEFINING THE RELEVANT LABOR MARKET **Relevant labor markets** represent the fields of potentially qualified candidates for particular jobs. Companies collect compensation survey data from the appropriate relevant labor markets. Relevant labor markets are defined on the basis of occupational classification, geography, and product or service market competitors.

Occupational classification refers to a group of two or more jobs that are based on similar work characteristics (e.g., blue- versus white-collar work), duties (e.g., work mainly with people or with machines), and responsibilities (e.g., supervision of other employees). The U.S. Bureau of Labor Statistics publishes the *Occupational Classification System Manual*, which helps business professionals and government economists make proper occupational matches for collecting compensation data. In fact, the NCS survey program is based on 12 major occupational groupings described in the manual with detailed information about specific occupations. This manual is available on the BLS Web site (*www.bls.gov/ncs/ocs/ocsm/commain.htm*).

Companies that plan to hire accountants and auditors should consider data about accountants and auditors only, rather than individuals from such other job families as engineers. After all, the worker characteristics and work tasks are clearly different: Accountants and auditors prepare, analyze, and verify financial reports and taxes, as well as monitor information systems that furnish this information to managers in business, industrial, and government organizations. Engineers apply the theories and principles of science and mathematics to the economical solution of practical technical problems. For example, civil engineers design, plan, and supervise the construction of buildings, highways, and rapid transit systems.

Companies search over a wider geographical area for candidates for jobs that require specialized skills or skills that are low in supply relative to the demand. For instance, hospitals are likely to search nationwide for neurosurgeons because their specialized skills are scarce. Companies are likely to limit searches for clerical employees to more confined local areas because clerical employees' skills are relatively common, and their supply tends to be higher relative to companies' demand for them. An insurance company based in Hartford, Connecticut, restricts its search for clerical employees to the Hartford area.

Companies use product or service market competitors to define the relevant labor market when industry-specific knowledge is a key worker qualification and competition for market share is keen. For example, such long-distance telephone companies as AT&T probably prefer to lure marketing managers away from industry competitors rather than from such unrelated industries as snack foods or medical and surgical supplies. Knowledge about customer preferences in snack foods has little to do with customers' preferences for long-distance telephone service.

Occupational classification, geographic scope, and product or service market competitors are not necessarily independent dimensions. For example, a company uses product or service market competitors as the basis for defining the relevant labor market for product managers; however, this dimension overlaps with geographic scope because competitor companies are located throughout the country (e.g., Boston, San Francisco, Dallas, and Miami).

With many professional, technical, and management positions, all three factors (i.e., job family, geographic scope, and companies that compete on the basis of product or service) can be applicable. For more information about relevant labor markets for various occupations, employers can consult professional and industrial associations and consulting firms.

CHOOSING BENCHMARK JOBS As we discussed in Chapter 6, benchmark jobs are key to conducting effective job evaluations. They also play an important role in compensation surveys. Human resource professionals determine the pay levels for jobs based on typical market pay rates for similar jobs. In other words, HR professionals rely on benchmark jobs as reference points for setting pay levels. As we discussed in Chapter 6, benchmark jobs have four characteristics:[2]

- The contents are well known, relatively stable over time, and agreed upon by the employees involved.
- The jobs are common across a number of different employers.
- The jobs represent the entire range of jobs that are being evaluated within a company.
- The jobs are generally accepted in the labor market for the purposes of setting pay levels.

Why are benchmark jobs necessary? Human resource professionals ideally would match each job within their companies to jobs contained in compensation surveys; however, in reality, one-to-one matches are not feasible for two reasons. First, large companies may have hundreds of unique jobs, making one-to-one matches tedious, time-consuming, and expensive because of the salary and benefits paid to staff members responsible for making these matches. Second, it is highly unlikely that HR professionals will find perfect or close matches between each of a company's jobs and jobs contained in the compensation surveys: Companies adapt job duties and scope to fit their particular situations. In other words, jobs with identical titles may differ somewhat in the degrees of compensable factors. Perfect matches are the exception rather than the rule. For example, Company A's Secretary I job may require only a high school education or GED equivalent. Company B's Secretary I job may require an associate's degree in office administration.

Companies can make corrections for differences between their jobs and external benchmark jobs. These corrections are based on subjective judgment rather than on objective criteria. Job incumbents and compensation professionals should independently compare compensable factors for a company's jobs with the compensable factors for the external benchmark jobs. Table 7-1 illustrates a rating scale for this purpose. Both job incumbents and supervisors should complete this questionnaire separately to minimize rater biases (see Chapter 3, performance appraisal section). Differences in ratings can be reconciled through discussion.

The discussion about compensation surveys is focused on U.S. companies' pay rates. Compensation professionals are presently interested in surveying pay rates in other countries because they send U.S. employees to work in foreign outposts (see Chapter 14) or hire foreign

TABLE 7-1 Comparing Companies' Jobs with Benchmark Jobs

Instructions to Job Incumbents: Compare elements of your job with elements of the survey benchmark job.

Instructions to Supervisors: Compare elements of your employee's job with elements of the survey benchmark job.

		Adjust Pay
Skill (Check the statement that most applies.)		(%)
My (employee's) job requires substantially more skill than the benchmark job.	☐	+4
My (employee's) job requires somewhat more skill than the benchmark job.	☐	+2
My (employee's) job and benchmark job require equal skill.	☐	0
My (employee's) job requires somewhat less skill than the benchmark job.	☐	−2
My (employee's) job requires substantially less skill than the benchmark job.	☐	−4
Knowledge (Check the statement that most applies.)		
My (employee's) job requires substantially more knowledge than the benchmark job.	☐	+2
My (employee's) job requires somewhat more knowledge than the benchmark job.	☐	+1
My (employee's) job and benchmark job require equal knowledge.	☐	0
My (employee's) job requires somewhat less knowledge than the benchmark job.	☐	−1
My (employee's) job requires substantially less knowledge than the benchmark job.	☐	−2
Abilities (Check the statement that most applies.)		
My (employee's) job requires substantially more abilities than the benchmark job.	☐	+4
My (employee's) job requires somewhat more abilities than the benchmark job.	☐	+2
My (employee's) job and benchmark job require equal abilities.	☐	0
My (employee's) job requires somewhat less abilities than the benchmark job.	☐	−2
My (employee's) job requires substantially less abilities than the benchmark job.	☐	−4

Pay adjustment calculation: Sum the percentages for the three checked items. Possible range is from +10% to −10%.

Pay adjustment (e.g., a total of 0 percent means no adjustment is required; +3 percent indicates that the job's pay rate be increased by 3 percent, and −3 percent indicates that the job's pay rate be decreased by 3 percent).

nationals to work in their own country for U.S. companies (e.g., IBM hires people from the Indian continent to serve in call centers).

Compensation Survey Data

Compensation professionals should be aware of three compensation survey data characteristics. First, compensation surveys contain immense amounts of information. A perusal of every datum point would be mind-boggling even to the most mathematically inclined individuals. In addition, there is bound to be wide variation in pay rates across companies, making it difficult to build market-competitive pay systems. Thus, compensation professionals should use statistics to describe large sets of data efficiently. Second, compensation survey data are outdated because there is a lag between when the data were collected and when employers implement the compensation plan based on the survey data. Third, compensation professionals must use statistical analyses to integrate their internal job structures (based on job evaluation points; see Chapter 6) with the external market based on the survey data. We will discuss this matter in detail later in this chapter.

Table 7-2 contains sample salary information collected from a salary survey of 35 accounting jobs according to seniority. Accountant I incumbents possess less than 2 years of accounting

TABLE 7-2 Raw Compensation Survey Data for Accountants in Atlanta, Georgia

Company	Job Title	2012 Annual Salary ($)
A	Accountant I	33,000
A	Accountant I	34,500
A	Accountant II	36,000
A	Accountant III	43,500
B	Accountant I	33,000
B	Accountant I	33,000
B	Accountant I	36,000
B	Accountant II	37,500
B	Accountant II	36,000
B	Accountant II	37,500
B	Accountant III	45,000
B	Accountant III	43,500
C	Accountant I	34,500
C	Accountant II	37,500
C	Accountant III	43,500
D	Accountant I	36,000
D	Accountant I	36,000
D	Accountant III	55,000
E	Accountant I	33,000
E	Accountant I	33,000
E	Accountant I	34,500
E	Accountant II	36,000
E	Accountant II	36,000
E	Accountant II	37,500
E	Accountant III	45,000
F	Accountant I	34,500
F	Accountant II	37,500
F	Accountant III	45,000
F	Accountant III	45,000
F	Accountant III	43,500
G	Accountant I	34,500
G	Accountant I	33,000
G	Accountant II	37,500
G	Accountant II	37,500
G	Accountant III	43,500

TABLE 7-3 **Frequency Table for Accountants**

Salary Interval ($)	Number of Salaries from Survey
30,000–35,000	11
35,001–40,000	14
40,000–45,000	9
45,000+	1

work experience. Accountant II incumbents have 2 to less than 4 years of accounting work experience. Accountant III incumbents possess 4 to 6 years of work experience as accountants. Seven companies (A–G) from Atlanta participated in the survey, and most have more than one incumbent at each level. Company B has three accountant I incumbents, three accountant II incumbents, and two accountant III incumbents.

As a starting point, let's begin with basic tabulation of the survey data. Basic tabulation helps organize data, promotes decision makers' familiarization with the data, and reveals possible extreme observations (i.e., outliers). Table 7-3 displays a frequency table, and Figure 7-1 displays a histogram. Both indicate the number of job incumbents whose salaries fall within the specified intervals. For example, 11 accountants' annual salaries range between $30,000 and $35,000. Only one job incumbent falls in the $45,001 and above interval, which suggests the possibility of an outlier. We'll discuss the importance of outliers shortly.

USING THE APPROPRIATE STATISTICS TO SUMMARIZE SURVEY DATA Two properties describe numerical data sets:

• Central tendency
• Variation

Central tendency represents the fact that a set of data clusters or centers around a central point. Central tendency is a number that represents the typical numerical value in the data set. What is

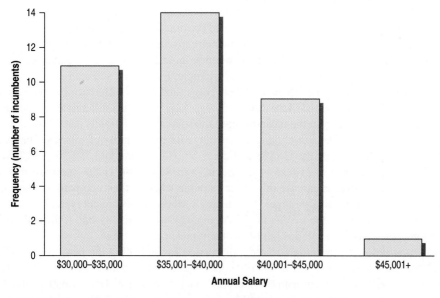

FIGURE 7-1 **Histogram of Survey Data for Accountants**

the typical annual salary for accountants in our data set? Two types of central tendency measures are pertinent to compensation—arithmetic mean (often called mean or average) and median.

We calculate the **mean** annual salary for accountants by adding all the annual salaries in our data set and then dividing the total by the number of annual salaries in the data set. The sum of the salaries in our example is $1,337,500 based on 35 salaries. Thus, the mean equals $38,214.29 (i.e., $1,337,500 divided by 35). In this example, the mean informs compensation professionals about the "typical" salary or going market rate for the group of accountants I, II, and III. Compensation professionals often use the mean as a reference point to judge whether employees' compensation is below or above the market.

We use every data point to calculate the mean. As a result, one or more outliers can lead to a distorted representation of the typical value. The mean understates the "true" typical value when there is one or more extremely small value, and it overstates the "true" typical value when there is one or more extremely large value. The mean's shortcoming has implications for compensation professionals.

Understated mean salaries may cause employers to set starting salaries too low to attract the best-qualified job candidates. Overstated mean salaries probably promote recruitment efforts because employers may set starting salaries higher than necessary, a condition that creates a cost burden to companies.

The **median** is the middle value in an ordered sequence of numerical data. If there is an odd number of data points, the median literally is the middle observation. Our data set contains an odd number of observations. The median is $36,000. Table 7-4 illustrates the calculation of the median.

If there is an even number of data points, the median is the mean of the values corresponding to the two middle numbers. Let's assume that we have four salaries, ordered from the smallest value to the highest value: $25,000, $28,000, $29,500, and $33,000. The median is $28,750. The median does not create distorted representations like the mean because its calculation is independent of the magnitude of each value.

Variation is the second property used to describe data sets. **Variation** represents the amount of spread or dispersion in a set of data. Compensation professionals find three measures of dispersion to be useful (i.e., standard deviation, quartile, and percentile).

Standard deviation refers to the mean distance of each salary figure from the mean (i.e., how larger observations fluctuate above the mean and how smaller observations fluctuate below the mean). Table 7-5 demonstrates the calculation of the standard deviation for our data set.

The standard deviation equals $5,074.86. Compensation professionals find standard deviation to be useful for two reasons. First, as we noted previously, compensation professionals often use the mean as a reference point to judge whether employees' compensations are below or above the market. The standard deviation indicates whether an individual salary's departure below or above the mean is "typical" for the market. For example, Irwin Katz's annual salary is $27,500. His salary falls substantially below the typical average salary: The difference between the mean salary and Katz's salary is $10,714.29 ($38,214.29 − $27,500). This difference is much greater than the typical departure from the mean because the standard deviation is just $5,074.86.

Second, the standard deviation indicates the range for the majority of salaries. The majority of salaries fall between $33,139.43 ($38,214.29 − $5,074.86) and $43,289.15 ($38,214.29 + $5,074.86). Remember, $38,214.29 is the mean, and $5,074.86 is the standard deviation. Compensation professionals can use this range to judge whether their company's salary ranges are similar to the market's salary ranges. A company's salary ranges are not typical of the market if most fall below or above the market range. A company will probably find it difficult to retain good employees when most salaries fall below the typical market range.

Both quartiles and percentiles describe dispersion by indicating the percentage of figures that fall below certain points. Table 7-6 illustrates the use of quartiles and percentiles for our survey data. **Quartiles** allow compensation professionals to describe the distribution of data—in this case, annual base pay amount—based on four groupings. The 1st quartile is $34,500. In other words, 25 percent of the salary figures are less than or equal to $34,500. The 2nd quartile

TABLE 7-4 Calculation of the Median for Accountant Survey Data

The salary data are arranged in ascending order. The median is $(n + 1)/2$, where n equals the number of salaries. The median is item 18 ([35 + 1]/2). Thus, the median value is $36,000.

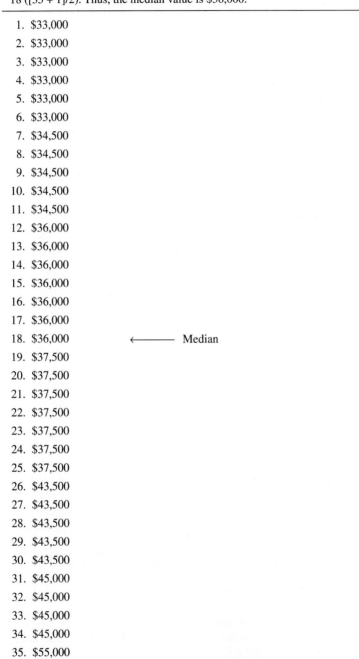

1. $33,000
2. $33,000
3. $33,000
4. $33,000
5. $33,000
6. $33,000
7. $34,500
8. $34,500
9. $34,500
10. $34,500
11. $34,500
12. $36,000
13. $36,000
14. $36,000
15. $36,000
16. $36,000
17. $36,000
18. $36,000   ←——— Median
19. $37,500
20. $37,500
21. $37,500
22. $37,500
23. $37,500
24. $37,500
25. $37,500
26. $43,500
27. $43,500
28. $43,500
29. $43,500
30. $43,500
31. $45,000
32. $45,000
33. $45,000
34. $45,000
35. $55,000

is $36,000. Fifty percent of the salary figures are less than or equal to $36,000. The 3rd quartile is $43,500. Seventy-five percent of the salary figures are less than or equal to $43,500. The 4th quartile is $55,000. One hundred percent of the salary figures are less than or equal to $55,000. There are one hundred **percentiles** ranging from the first percentile to the 100th percentile. For our data, the 10th percentile equals $33,000, and the 90th percentile equals $45,000.

TABLE 7-5 Calculation of the Standard Deviation (S.D.) for Accountant Survey Data

$$S.D. = \sqrt{\frac{\sum_{i=1}^{n} X_i^2 - nM^2}{n-1}}$$

where

$\sum_{i=1}^{n} X_i^2$ = the sum of the squares of the individual salary observations.

nM^2 = the sample size (n; i.e., 35 salaries) multiplied by the square of the mean for the 35 salaries.

$$S.D. = \sqrt{\frac{(\$33,000^2 + \$33,000^2 + \ldots + \$55,000^2) - 35(\$38,214.92)^2}{35-1}}$$

$$S.D. = \sqrt{\frac{51,987,260,000 - 51,111,618,000}{34}}$$

$$S.D. = \$5,074.86$$

Quartiles and percentiles complement standard deviations by indicating the percentage of observations that fall below particular figures. Compensation professionals' reviews of percentiles and quartiles can enhance their insights into the dispersion of salary data. For example, compensation professionals want to know the percentage of accountants earning a particular salary level or less. If $33,000 represents the 10th percentile for accountants' annual salaries, then only 10 percent earn $33,000 or less. Compensation professionals are less likely to recommend similar pay for new accountant hires. Although paying at this level represents a cost savings, companies are likely to experience retention problems because 90 percent of accountants earn more than $33,000.

It is important to keep in mind that statistics of a given type (e.g., central tendency) provide consistent information for a given set of data. As we discussed, the mean and median are measures of central tendency. The mean and median are often different for a given set of data points. When the distribution of data is skewed to the left (i.e., there is a higher frequency of larger values than smaller values), the mean will be less than the median. On the other hand, when the distribution of data is skewed to the right (i.e., there is a lower frequency of larger values than smaller values), the mean will be greater than the median.

Let's look at an example. The mean hourly wage rate for production workers in Company A is $8.72. The union in Company A is demanding that management grant pay raises to production workers because the mean hourly pay rate for production workers in Company B is higher—$9.02. The mean value for Company B is based on the following survey of its production workers:

Hourly Wage Rates of Production Workers						
$8.15	$8.39	$8.51	$8.55	$8.60	$10.25	$10.72

Company A's management is unwilling to raise production workers' pay: Company A's production workers earn a higher mean hourly wage ($8.72) than the median hourly wage rate of Company B's production workers ($8.55).

Updating the Survey Data

Companies establish pay structures for future periods. Let's assume that a compensation professional wants to develop a pay structure for the period January 1, 2010, through December 31, 2010. For this illustration, it is now October 2009 when the compensation professional is establishing this plan. The salary survey data were obtained in October 2009, and these figures

TABLE 7-6 Percentile and Quartile Ranks for Accountant Survey Data

$33,000	
$33,000	
$33,000	←——— 10th percentile
$33,000	
$33,000	
$33,000	
$34,500	
$34,500	
$34,500	←——— 1st quartile
$34,500	
$34,500	
$36,000	
$36,000	
$36,000	
$36,000	
$36,000	
$36,000	
$36,000	←——— 2nd quartile
$37,500	(also 50th percentile)
$37,500	
$37,500	
$37,500	
$37,500	
$37,500	
$37,500	
$43,500	
$43,500	
$43,500	←——— 3rd quartile
$43,500	
$43,500	
$45,000	
$45,000	←——— 90th percentile
$45,000	
$45,000	
$55,000	←——— 4th quartile

represent 2008 annual pay averages. These data will be 12 and 24 months old at the pay plan's implementation (on January 1, 2010) and end (December 31, 2010), respectively. Compensation professionals typically use historical salary data to build market-competitive pay systems because it is impossible to obtain actual salary data for the *future* compensation plan period (January 1, 2010–December 31, 2010) in October 2009 when the plan is being developed. Companies therefore update survey data with simple techniques to correct for such lags (see Table 7-7 as an example). This process updates the salary survey data for the start and end of the plan year (in this

TABLE 7-7 Updating Salary Survey, Using CPI-U, Northeast U.S. Region

October 2009	January 1, 2010	December 31, 2010
Market survey data for 2008 CPI-U, 225.4	Pay plan begins CPI-U, 231.4	Pay plan ends
	Actual increase January 1, 2009–December 31, 2009: 2.8 percent[a]	*Estimated increase* January 1, 2009–December 31, 2009: 2.8[c]
December 2008, Survey mean: $38,000.00	December 2009, Survey mean: 39,064.00[b]	December 31, 2010, Expected survey mean: $40,157.79[d]

[a][(231.4 − 225.4)/225.4] × 100 percent
[b]$38,000.00 + ($38,000.00 × 2.8 percent)
[c]Estimated based on the actual increase for the Northeast region between January and December 2009 [(231.4 − 225.4)/225.4]. Note that 231.4 is the December 2009 CPI-U index reported by the BLS.
[d]$39,064.00 + ($39,064.00 × 2.8 percent)

example, December 1, 2010 and December 31, 2010, respectively). As shown in Table 7-7, footnote c, we estimated the cost-of-living increase based on the previous year's actual increase.

Several factors play an important role in updating. The most influential factors are economic forecasts and changes in the costs of consumer goods and services. Employers generally award small permanent pay increases (e.g., 3–4 percent) when the economic forecast is pessimistic. Pessimistic forecasts suggest the possibility of recession or higher unemployment levels. Thus, employers are less willing to commit substantial amounts to fund pay increases because they may not be able to afford them. Employers typically award higher permanent pay increases when the economic forecast is optimistic. Optimistic forecasts imply enhanced business activity or lower unemployment levels. Management discretion dictates actual pay increase amounts.

Changes in the cost of living tend to make survey data obsolete fairly quickly. Over time, the average cost of goods and services increases. Companies therefore update salary survey data with the **Consumer Price Index (CPI),** the most commonly used method for tracking cost changes throughout the United States. The BLS reports the CPI in the *CPI Detailed Report* every month. Each January issue provides annual averages for the prior year. Current and historical CPI data are also available on the BLS Web site (*www.bls.gov*). Table 7-8 describes some basic facts about the CPI and how to interpret it. Table 7-7 details the procedure for updating salary survey data with the CPI.

INTEGRATING INTERNAL JOB STRUCTURES WITH EXTERNAL MARKET PAY RATES

In Chapter 6, we discussed that compensation professionals use job evaluation methods to establish internally consistent job structures. In other words, companies value jobs that possess higher degrees of compensable factors (e.g., 10 years of relevant work experience) than jobs with fewer degrees of compensable factors (e.g., 1 year of relevant work experience). These valuation differences ultimately should correspond to pay differences based on compensation survey data.

Earlier, we indicated that paying well below or well above the typical market rate for jobs can create a competitive disadvantage for companies. Thus, it is important that companies set pay rates by using market pay rates as reference points. To this end, we use **regression analysis,** which is a statistical analysis technique. Regression analyses enable compensation professionals to establish pay rates for a set of jobs that are consistent with typical pay rates for jobs in the external market.

We'll apply regression analysis to determine pay rates for the accountant I, accountant II, and accountant III jobs listed in Table 7-2. Before presenting the regression analysis technique, we need two sets of information: the job evaluation point totals for each accountant job based on job evaluation and the updated salary survey data. In this sample, the accountant jobs have

TABLE 7-8 The Consumer Price Index: Basic Facts and Interpretation Issues

Basic Facts

The CPI indexes monthly price changes of goods and services that people buy for day-to-day living. The index is based on a representative sample of goods and services, because obtaining information about all goods and services would not be feasible. The BLS gathers price information from thousands of retail and service establishments (e.g., gasoline stations, grocery stores, and department stores). Thousands of landlords provide information about rental costs, and thousands of home owners give cost information pertaining to home ownership.

The CPI represents the average of the price changes for the representative sample of goods and services within each of the following areas:

- Urban United States
- 4 regions
- 4 class sizes based on the number of residents
- 27 local metropolitan statistical areas

The BLS publishes CPI for two population groups: a CPI for All Urban Consumers (CPI-U) and the CPI for Urban Wage Earners and Clerical Workers (CPI-W). The CPI-U represents the spending habits of 80 percent of the population of the United States. The CPI-U covers wage earners; clerical, professional, managerial, and technical workers; short-term and self-employed workers; unemployed persons; retirees; and others not in the labor force. The CPI-W represents the spending habits of 32 percent of the population, and it applies to consumers who earn more than one-half of their income from clerical or wage occupations. The distinction between the CPI-U and CPI-W is important because the CPI-U is most representative of all consumers, whereas unions and management use the CPI-W during negotiations to establish effective cost-of-living adjustments; most unionized jobs are clerical or wage jobs rather than salaried professional, managerial, or executive jobs.

Interpreting the CPI: Percentage Changes versus Point Changes

The span from 1982 to 1984 is the base period for the CPI-U and CPI-W, which is 100. Compensation professionals use the base period to determine the changes in prices over time. How much did consumer prices increase in Atlanta between the base period and December 31, 2001?

The *CPI Detailed Report* indicates that the 2001 CPI-U for Atlanta was 176.2. We know that the base period CPI is 100. Consumer prices in Atlanta increased 76.2 percent between 2001 and the base period. We determine price change with the formula:

$$\frac{(\text{Current CPI} - \text{Previous CPI})}{\text{Previous CPI}} \times 100\%$$

For this example:

$$\frac{(176.2 - 100)}{100} \times 100\% = 76.2\%$$

Compensation professionals are most concerned with annual CPI changes because they are updating recently collected survey data. The same formula yields price changes between periods other than the base period. How much did prices increase in Atlanta between 1999 and 2001? The CPI Detailed Report (January 2002) indicates that the 1999 annual CPI-U for Atlanta was 161.2, and we know that the 2001 annual average is 176.2.

$$\frac{(176.2 - 161.2)}{161.2} \times 100\% = 9.31\%$$

Consumer prices in Atlanta increased 9.31 percent between 1999 and 2001.

Source: U.S. Bureau of Labor Statistics (2002). *CPI Detailed Report.* Washington, DC: U.S. Government Printing Office.

the following job evaluation points: accountant I (100 points), accountant II (500 points), and accountant III (1,000) points.

Regression analysis enables decision makers to predict the values of one variable from another. Compensation professionals' goal are to predict salary levels for each job based on job evaluation points. Why not simply "eyeball" the list of salaries in the survey to identify the market rates? There are two reasons. First, companies pay different rates to employees who are performing the same (or very similar) jobs. Our salary survey indicates that accountant III pay rates vary between $43,500 and $55,000. "Eyeballing" the typical rate from the raw data is difficult when surveys contain large numbers of salaries.

Second, we wish to determine pay rates for a set of jobs in a particular company (i.e., accountant I, accountant II, and accountant III) based on their relative worth to typical market pay rates for the corresponding jobs contained in the salary survey. Our focus is on pricing a job structure in the market pay context, not pricing one job in isolation.

How does regression analysis work? Regression analysis finds the best-fitting line between two variables. Compensation professionals use job evaluation points assigned to benchmark jobs (based on the matching process discussed earlier) and the salary survey data for the benchmark jobs. They refer to the best-fitting line as the **market pay line.** The market pay line is representative of typical market pay rates relative to a company's job structure. Pay levels that correspond with the market pay line are market-competitive pay rates. Figure 7-2 displays the regression results.

The following equation models the prediction.

$$\hat{Y} = a + bX$$

$\hat{Y}$ = predicted salary

X = job evaluation points

a = the Y intercept (This is the Y value at which X = 0.)

b = the slope

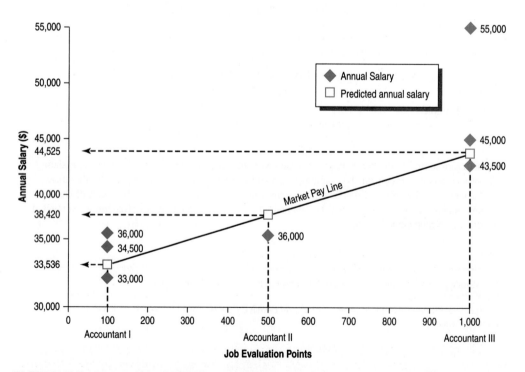

FIGURE 7-2 Regression Analysis Results for the Accountant Survey Data

The slope represents the change in Y for every one unit change in job evaluation points. In other words, the slope represents the dollar value of each job evaluation point. For example, let's assume that the slope is 26. A job consisting of 301 job evaluation points is worth \$26 more than a job consisting of 300 job evaluation points.

For our data, the equation is:

$$\hat{Y} = \$32,315.66 + \$12.21X$$

Thus, this market policy line indicates the following market pay rates:

- Accountant I: \$33,536.66

$\hat{Y} = \$32,315.66 + \$12.21 \times 100$ job evaluation points

- Accountant II: \$38,420.66

$\hat{Y} = \$32,315.66 + \$12.21 \times 500$ job evaluation points

- Accountant III: \$44,525.66

$\hat{Y} = \$32,315.66 + \$12.21 \times 1,000$ job evaluation points

The regression analysis provides an additional important statistic known as R^2. This statistic tells us how well the variation in the company's valuation of jobs based on job evaluation points explains the variation in market pay rates from the compensation survey. The R^2 statistic can range in numerical value between 0 and 1. When R^2 equals 0, none (0 percent, i.e., 0.0×100 percent) of the variation in market pay rates can be explained by the company's job structure. When R^2 equals one, this means that all (100 percent) of the variation in market pay rates can be explained by the company's job structure. Just one more example—when R^2 equals 0.52, 52 percent (i.e., 0.52×100 percent) of the variation in market pay rates can be explained by the company's job structure. As you can see, we interpret R^2 in this context as the percentage variation in y values (market pay rates) that can be explained by x values (job evaluation points).

By now, you may be asking how to describe the difference between an R^2 equal to 1.0 and, for example, an R^2 equal to 0.71 in this situation. The difference (0.29) refers to the percentage of variation in market pay rates that cannot be explained by the company's job structure. In this illustration, 29 percent of the variation is unexplained. Discrepancies often exist between the job duties of the jobs specified in the compensation survey (i.e., the benchmark jobs) and the company's job definitions.

Your HR colleagues are likely to ask you to interpret your conclusion even further because they will want to know whether the obtained R^2 value represents a small, medium, or large amount. As a rule of thumb, R^2 values between 0.0 and 0.30 represent a small amount; between 0.31 and 0.70 represent a medium amount; and between 0.71 and 1.0 represent a large amount.

COMPENSATION POLICIES AND STRATEGIC MANDATES

Compensation policies refer to choices that compensation professionals make to promote competitive advantage. Broadly, choices are made about pay level policies and pay mix policies.

Pay Level Policies

Companies can choose from three pay level policies:

- Market lead
- Market lag
- Market match

The **market lead policy** distinguishes a company from the competition by compensating employees more highly than most competitors. Leading the market denotes pay levels that place in the area above the market pay line (Figure 7-2). The **market lag policy** also distinguishes a company from the competition, but by compensating employees less than most competitors. Lagging the market indicates that pay levels fall below the market pay line (Figure 7-2). The **market match policy** most closely follows the typical market pay rates because companies pay according to the market pay line. Thus, pay rates fall along the market pay line (Figure 7-2). Most often, market lead policies are set to the 3rd quartile (also, 75th percentile) ranking in the salary survey. Similarly, market match policies are set to the 2nd quartile (also, 50th percentile or median) ranking, and market lag policies are set to the 1st quartile (also, 25th percentile) ranking.

The market lead policy is clearly most appropriate for companies that pursue differentiation strategies. A company may choose a market lead pay policy for its accountants because the company needs the very best accountants to promote its competitive strategy of being the top manufacturer of lightest-weight surgical instruments at the lowest possible cost by 2018.

The market lag policy appears to fit well with lowest-cost strategies because companies realize cost savings by paying lower than the market pay line. Paying well below the market will yield short-term cost savings; however, these short-term savings will probably be offset by long-term costs. Companies that use the market lag policy may experience difficulties in recruiting and retaining highly qualified employees. Too much turnover will undercut a company's ability to operate efficiently and to market goods and services on a timely basis. Thus, companies that adopt market lag policies need to balance cost savings with productivity and quality concerns.

The market match policy represents a safe approach for companies because they generally are spending no more or less on compensation (per employee) than competitors. This pay policy does not fit with the lowest-cost strategy for obvious reasons. It does fit better with differentiation strategies. This statement appears to contradict previous ones about differentiation strategies (i.e., pay "high" salaries to attract and retain the best talent). Some companies that pursue differentiation strategies follow a market match policy to fund expensive operating or capital needs that support differentiation (e.g., research equipment and research laboratories).

Pay Mix Policies

Pay mix policies refer to the combination of core compensation and employee benefits components that make up an employee's total compensation package. In Chapter 1 (Figure 1-1), we identified and briefly described the various elements of core compensation and employee benefits; then we discussed core compensation elements fully in Chapters 3, 4, and 5. We will review the main elements of employee benefits in Chapters 9, 10, and 11.

Pay policy mix may be expressed in dollars (or other currency as relevant) or as a percentage of total dollars allocated for an employee's total compensation. The following is an example of a pay policy mix:

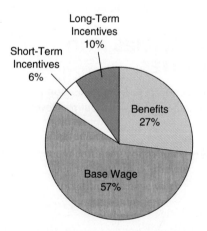

This example indicates that base pay accounts for 57 percent of the money allocated to an employee's total compensation. Let's assume that the company spends $200,000 annually to fund a particular employee's total compensation package. Of the total, an employee receives base pay in the amount of $114,000 (that is, $200,000 × 57 percent).

What is an appropriate pay mix? For policy purposes, it makes sense to consider guidelines for jobs within a particular structure (for example, managerial, administrative, or sales) because of the common job content and worker requirements of jobs within a particular structure. For example, in a technology company, a greater portion of bonus compensation might be allocated to engineers than to administrative staff. Engineers possess crucial skills relating to the company's ability to find innovative applications of technology, and bonus incentives throughout the year may promote innovation initiatives. On the other hand, the administrative staff, though important to the company, may not play as important a role in determining the company's profitability or objectives. Therefore, less of their total compensation would likely be devoted to bonus funds. Also, some job structures, such as sales, employees may receive the majority of their compensation in the form of bonuses. In order to motivate a sales force to continually exceed quarterly targets, quarterly bonuses equal to or exceeding their annual base salaries might be used.

COMPENSATION IN ACTION

What employees are paid internally can have a significant impact on what happens externally. As with any business function, an overemphasis on the activities within the firm can blind decision makers to the activities outside the firm, which could undermine competitive advantage. Paying too little for top talent will ensure that those highly sought-after individuals go elsewhere for employment; paying too much could come at the cost of investing additional capital into resources that are critical to the execution and delivery of company strategy. By measuring the right variables and seeking data that will lead to informed and up-to-date decisions, you as line managers, HR professionals, and compensation specialists will work together in providing a system that is in line with the needs of the organization and the objectives of the individual.

Action checklist for line managers and HR— staying current and attracting the right employees

HR takes the lead
- Work with compensation specialists to access compensation *and* benefits data from other firms to find out what they are offering employees; the means by which this data will be collected—customized survey, professional organization, or compensation consultant—will depend on budget, relationships with competitors, and expertise of staff.
- Together with line managers, compare internal roles with external roles to create job matches that, although subjective, will allow a side-by-side comparison to see how compensation matches up.
- Compensation specialists analyze data using appropriate statistics to identify consistencies with competitors and areas of high discrepancy.

Line managers take the lead
- Identify the types of resources necessary to carry out company strategy; if talent is the top priority, HR will seek to establish a compensation system that will lead competitors; if other resources are deemed a higher priority (e.g., infrastructure and research), the sought-after compensation system will be lower than the industry standard (this will be the context within which the data are assessed).
- Lead the identification of the internal employee market (e.g., marketing professionals, accountants, and finance managers in China) that needs to be assessed.
- Partnering with HR, recommendations are made to members of senior management based on the data that are revealed and the assessment of these data in relation to the strategy of the firm.

In summary, a "one size fits all" approach to pay policy selection is inappropriate. Most companies use more than one pay policy simultaneously. For example, companies generally use market match or market lead policies for professional and managerial talent because these employees contribute most directly to a company's competitive advantages. Companies typically apply market match or market lag policies to clerical, administrative, and unskilled employees (e.g., janitorial). Companies' demands for these employees relative to supply in the relevant labor markets are low, and these employees' contributions to attainment of competitive advantage are less direct. Companies are likely to apply different pay policy mixes to jobs in different structures given differences in the level of strategic importance placed on jobs as well as to promote desired behaviors as previously discussed.

END OF CHAPTER

MyManagementLab

Go to **mymanagementlab.com** to complete the problems marked with this icon ⭐.

Summary

This chapter discussed market-competitive pay systems and described compensation surveys. Compensation surveys provide "snapshots" of competitors' pay practices. Survey information provides the reference points for establishing pay level policies. Conducting compensation surveys requires art,

not science: These practices require compensation professionals' sound judgments for making recommendations that fit well with competitive strategies. Careful thought about the meaning underlying the facts and statistics is the key to successfully building market-competitive pay systems.

Key Terms

market-competitive pay
   systems   144
strategic analysis   145
compensation surveys   145
National Compensation Survey
   (NCS)   148
relevant labor markets   149

central tendency   153
mean   154
median   154
variation   154
standard deviation   154
quartiles   154
percentiles   155

Consumer Price Index
   (CPI)   158
regression analysis   158
market pay line   160
market lead policy   161
market lag policy   161
market match policy   162

⭐ Discussion Questions

7-1. You are a compensation analyst for Worry-Not Insurance Company, which is located in Hartford, Connecticut. Define the relevant labor market for insurance claims adjusters and for data entry clerks. Describe the rationale for your definitions.

7-2. Can companies easily develop compensations that are both internally consistent and market competitive? What are some of the challenges to this goal?

7-3. Which do you believe is most important for a company's competitive advantage: internal consistency or market competitiveness? Explain your answer.

7-4. Refer to the regression equation presented earlier in this chapter. When $b = 0$, the market pay line is parallel to the x-axis (i.e., job evaluation points). Provide your interpretation.

7-5. Refer to Table 7-2. Cross out salaries 26–35. Calculate the mean and median for this reduced data set.

CASE
Nutriment's New Hires

⭐ *An additional Supplemental Case can be found on MyManagementLab.*

With the demand for more nutritional food options growing, Nutriment Biotech is positioned to become a leader in agricultural biotechnology. Nutriment is a start-up biotech company that is working to develop genetically engineered food crops that offer enhanced nutrition along with easier production for farmers. Emily Hart and Harold James established Nutriment as a research organization through national grant funding 5 years ago. Nutriment is one of only a few agricultural biotechnology companies focused on enhancing nutrition in food crops. The company currently has an edge over competitors as its research has led to some scientific discoveries that now position them to grow their company significantly. As a result, Nutriment is ready to start hiring staff to get operations started.

Emily and Harold have hired Jack Stewart, an HR management consultant, to help them determine how to hire the most talented staff to grow their business. Jack works mostly with start-up technology-based companies and plans to help Nutriment implement a recruiting and hiring plan and establish its preliminary HR management practices such as its pay structure.

Nutriment has secured additional funding to allow it to ramp up full operations quickly. An analysis of its projected workload suggests it will need to hire approximately 15 new employees to get started. It will need to hire not only 10 new scientists but also administrative staff members including a receptionist, an office manager, a lab manager, a marketing professional, and an accountant.

As an experienced recruiter, Jack is confident that he will be able to quickly identify strong candidates for the administrative staff positions. The current labor market works in Nutriment's favor, and, therefore, Jack will be able to easily generate a pool of qualified applicants. The scientists, on the other hand, will be challenging to find as they need specific expertise related to agricultural biotechnology and genetic engineering. The number of scientists with this combination of skills is limited, and the scientists are in demand by competitors. However, Nutriment is located in a geographic area rich with research universities and other biotech firms, so Jack is confident that it can attract a good pool of talent if it is able to offer an opportunity that is attractive to the scientists.

To start the recruiting process, Jack must first establish a pay structure. Before he starts researching market rates, Jack plans to meet with Emily and Harold to establish pay level policies and discuss other strategic aspects of determining the compensation structure for the new employees. Nutriment must offer a pay package that will allow it to attract and retain both the administrative staff members and the scientists. Establishing the right pay practices will help ensure that the recruitment process allows it to put talent in place to position Nutriment for success.

Questions:

7-6. What are some strategic considerations in establishing a pay structure at Nutriment?

7-7. Should Jack suggest a pay policy to lead, lag, or match the market? Explain your recommendation.

MyManagementLab

Go to **mymanagementlab.com** for Auto-graded writing questions as well as the following Assisted-graded writing questions:

⭐ **7-8.** Explain the role of compensation surveys. Why is it important to update survey data?

⭐ **7-9.** Explain market pay line. How is it used in the context of pay level policies such as market lead, market lag, and market match?

Endnotes

1. U.S. Bureau of Labor Statistics. (2013). *Employer Costs for Employee Compensation—December 2012*. Available: *www.bls.gov*, accessed May 23, 2013.

2. Milkovich, G. T., & Newman, J. M. (1996). *Compensation* (5th ed.). Homewood, IL: Irwin.

APPENDIX

WorldatWork.
The Total Rewards Association

2009-10 Salary Budget Survey
United States

The deadline to submit the survey is May 4, 2009
Fax or mail your completed survey to:
WorldatWork Survey Team
Fax 480-483-8352 • Toll-free fax 866-816-2962
14040 N. Northsight Blvd. • Scottsdale, AZ 85260

If your organization is multi-industry or if pay practices differ across divisions, regions, business units or subsidiaries, please complete a separate questionnaire for each.

Demographic Profile

1*. How should your company be listed on the participant list in the report?
   Company name: _____

2*. The organizational unit you are reporting data for is:
   ❑ Headquarters (skip to 3)
   ❑ Subsidiary/group/division
   ❑ Regional headquarters
   ❑ Plant/branch
   ❑ Independent consultant
   ❑ Consulting firm
   ❑ Public sector
   ❑ Educational

2a*. Please describe the division, subsidiary, region, etc., that you are reporting data for in this questionnaire
   (i.e., Southern region, manufacturing division, etc.): _____

3*. Please indicate the industry that best describes your organization using the three-digit North American Industry Classification System (NAICS) code.

* Mandatory section/question

4*. What region(s) and state(s) are you reporting data for in this questionnaire? (You must check at least one region; state selections are optional.)

☐ **Eastern U.S.**
Optional: Please indicate the states you are reporting data for in this questionnaire.
☐ All States in this Region

☐ Connecticut	☐ Massachusetts	☐ Rhode Island
☐ Washington D.C.	☐ New Hampshire	☐ Virginia
☐ Delaware	☐ New Jersey	☐ Vermont
☐ Maine	☐ New York	☐ West Virginia
☐ Maryland	☐ Pennsylvania	

☐ **Central U.S.**
Optional: Please indicate the states you are reporting data for in this questionnaire.
☐ All States in this Region

☐ Iowa	☐ Michigan	☐ Ohio
☐ Illinois	☐ Minnesota	☐ South Dakota
☐ Indiana	☐ Missouri	☐ Wisconsin
☐ Kansas	☐ Nebraska	
☐ Kentucky	☐ North Dakota	

☐ **Southern U.S.**
Optional: Please indicate the states you are reporting data for in this questionnaire.
☐ All States in this Region

☐ Alabama	☐ Louisiana	☐ Tennessee
☐ Arkansas	☐ Mississippi	☐ Texas
☐ Florida	☐ North Carolina	☐ Oklahoma
☐ Georgia	☐ South Carolina	

☐ **Western U.S.**
Optional: Please indicate the states you are reporting data for in this questionnaire.
☐ All States in this Region

☐ Alaska	☐ Idaho	☐ Utah
☐ Arizona	☐ Montana	☐ Washington
☐ California	☐ New Mexico	☐ Wyoming
☐ Colorado	☐ Nevada	
☐ Hawaii	☐ Oregon	

5. For which major metropolitan areas are you reporting data in this questionnaire? (Check all that apply.)

Arizona
☐ Phoenix
California
☐ Los Angeles
☐ San Diego
☐ San Francisco
☐ San Jose
Colorado
☐ Denver
Florida
☐ Miami
☐ Tampa
Georgia
☐ Atlanta
Illinois
☐ Chicago

Maryland
☐ Baltimore
Massachusetts
☐ Boston
Michigan
☐ Detroit
Minnesota
☐ Minneapolis
Missouri
☐ St. Louis
New York
☐ New York
Ohio
☐ Cleveland
☐ Cincinnati

Oregon
☐ Portland
Pennsylvania
☐ Philadelphia
☐ Pittsburgh
Texas
☐ Houston
☐ Dallas
Washington
☐ Seattle
☐ Washington D.C.

* Mandatory section/question

6*. How many full-time equivalent (FTE) employees does your company employ worldwide? (Please report your worldwide headcount, even though you will be reporting only your U.S. budget data.)

- ❑ 1 – 499
- ❑ 500 – 2,499
- ❑ 2,500 – 9,999
- ❑ 10,000 – 19,999
- ❑ 20,000+

7. What was the total revenue (the money generated by your company from sales of goods or services on a worldwide basis) for your organization at the end of 2008? (Report in U.S. Dollars)

- ❑ Up to $30 million
- ❑ More than $30 million to $100 million
- ❑ More than $100 million to $300 million
- ❑ More than $300 million to $600 million
- ❑ More than $600 million to $1 billion
- ❑ More than $1 billion to $3 billion
- ❑ More than $3 billion to $5 billion
- ❑ More than $5 billion to $8 billion
- ❑ More than $8 billion to $10 billion
- ❑ More than $10 billion

Base Salary Increase

8. What is your organization's current base pay compensation philosophy for each employee category?

Employee group	To pay below the market	To pay at the market	To pay above the market	No formal compensation philosophy
Nonexempt Hourly Nonunion	☐	☐	☐	☐
Nonexempt Salaried	☐	☐	☐	☐
Exempt Salaried	☐	☐	☐	☐
Officers/Executives	☐	☐	☐	☐

9*. What is your organization's actual base salary budget program for 2009?
*Note: Fill in "0" (zero) **only** if there is no increase budgeted where one is typically budgeted. If a particular program (i.e., general increase, COLA, merit, other) is not used/applicable in your organization, please leave the field blank.*

Number of covered employees	Employee group	Number of months between increases	General increase /COLA	Merit increase	Other increase (not promotional)	Total increase
	Nonexempt Hourly Nonunion		%	%	%	%
	Nonexempt Salaried		%	%	%	%
	Exempt Salaried		%	%	%	%
	Officers/Executives		%	%	%	%
	← TOTAL					

* Mandatory section/question

9a. If you have included an increase in the "Other increase" column, what is the nature of this increase?
(Check all that apply.)
- ❑ Accelerated increase cycle to move employee closer to midpoint (salary progression)
- ❑ Compression
- ❑ Internal equity
- ❑ Market adjustment/competitive adjustment
- ❑ Retention/critical skill adjustment
- ❑ Salary range adjustment
- ❑ Skill-based pay increase
- ❑ Step rate
- ❑ Other increase not listed above

10. Does your organization give lump-sum awards? If so, what percentage of employees received an award in 2008?

Employee group	Do you give lump-sum awards?		If so, what percentage of employees received an award in 2008
	Yes	No	
Nonexempt Hourly Nonunion	❑	❑	%
Nonexempt Salaried	❑	❑	%
Exempt Salaried	❑	❑	%
Officers/Executives	❑	❑	%

11. What percentage of your organization's employees, by category, will be receiving a base salary increase (general, COLA, merit or other) in 2009? Does this represent a larger, similar or smaller percentage of employees than in 2008?

Employee group	Percent receiving increase in 2009	Percentage is larger than 2008	Percentage is similar to 2008	Percentage is smaller than 2008
Nonexempt Hourly Nonunion	%	❑	❑	❑
Nonexempt Salaried	%	❑	❑	❑
Exempt Salaried	%	❑	❑	❑
Officers/Executives	%	❑	❑	❑

12. What is the projection/estimate for the organization's base salary budget program for 2010?
*Note: Fill in "0" (zero) **only** if there is no increase budgeted where one is typically budgeted. If a particular program (i.e., general increase, COLA, merit, other) is not used/applicable in your organization, please leave the field blank.*

Employee group	Number of months between increases	General increase/ COLA	Merit increase	Other increase (not promotional)	Total increase
Nonexempt Hourly Nonunion		%	%	%	%
Nonexempt Salaried		%	%	%	%
Exempt Salaried		%	%	%	%
Officers/Executives		%	%	%	%

* Mandatory section/question

12a. If you have included an increase in the "Other increase" column, what is the nature of this increase? (Check all that apply.)
- ❑ Accelerated increase cycle to move employee closer to midpoint (salary progression)
- ❑ Compression
- ❑ Internal equity
- ❑ Market adjustment/competitive adjustment
- ❑ Retention/critical skill adjustment
- ❑ Salary range adjustment
- ❑ Skill-based pay increase
- ❑ Step rate
- ❑ Other increase not listed above

13. Please complete the following table based only on those employees eligible for a merit increase:

	2008		2009	
	What percentage of your workforce was rated in this performance category for 2008?	What was the average merit increase awarded for this 2008 performance category?	What percentage of your workforce is estimated to be rated in this performance category for 2009?	What is the average merit increase award estimate for this 2009 performance category?
High Performance				
Middle Performance				
Low performance but received a merit increase >0%				
Low performance with a 0% merit increase		0%		0%
Total*	100%		100%	

Salary Structures

14. If your organization uses a formal salary range structure, by what percentage did you increase the structure in 2009?
*Note: Fill in "0" (zero) **only** if there is no increase planned where one is typically given.*

Employee group	2009 salary range structure change
Nonexempt Hourly Nonunion	%
Nonexempt Salaried	%
Exempt Salaried	%
Officers/Executives	%

14a. If no increase was reported (e.g., responded with a zero or blank for any of the employee categories in question 14 above), did the structure remain the same or did you make a negative adjustment?

Employee group	Number of months since last structure increase	Structure remained the same in 2009	Made a negative structure adjustment in 2009
Nonexempt Hourly Nonunion		☐	☐
Nonexempt Salaried		☐	☐
Exempt Salaried		☐	☐
Officers/Executives		☐	☐

* Mandatory section/question

15. By what percentage does your organization plan to increase the salary range structure for 2010?

Employee group	2010 salary range structure change
Nonexempt Hourly Nonunion	%
Nonexempt Salaried	%
Exempt Salaried	%
Officers/Executives	%

Promotions

16. Are promotional increases a separate budget item in your organization?
   - ❑ Yes
   - ❑ No (skip to question 17)

16a. What is your organization's 2009 promotional increase budget as a percent of total base salaries?

[%   ]

17. In 2008, what percentage of the total employee population received a promotional increase?

[%   ]

18. In 2008, what was the average promotional increase as a percent of the promoted employee's base salary (prior to promotion)?

[%   ]

Variable Pay

For purposes of this survey, variable pay is defined as short-term cash awards that are contingent upon performance, discretion or results achieved. Variable pay types include:
- Profit sharing
- Performance sharing (i.e. gain sharing or goal sharing)
- Individual incentives
- Bonuses

The following pay types **should not** be included:
- Sales commission plans
- Long-term incentives, such as stock plans or multi-year cash performance plans
- Non-cash based awards such as merchandise, trips, plaques or trophies
- Plans that require cash awards to be placed in accounts that are not readily accessible to employees (i.e. 401k accounts, pension plans, deferred compensation plans)
- Cash awards for recognition

19. Does your organization currently use variable pay as defined above?
   - ❑ Yes
   - ❑ No (skip to question 25)

20. Which of the following formal plan award types does your organization use? (Check all that apply.)
   - ❑ Organization-wide awards based solely on the success of the entire organization (i.e. cash profit sharing)
   - ❑ Unit/strategic business unit awards based solely on the success of the unit/strategic business unit (i.e., department incentive programs, manufacturing goal sharing, call-center incentives)
   - ❑ Individual incentive awards based on employees' performance in designated jobs (other than sales)
   - ❑ Combination awards based on **both** organization-wide/unit/strategic business unit success and individual performance

* Mandatory section/question

21. For 2008, please indicate the percentage of employees eligible to receive variable pay and the percentage of those employees who actually received an award.

Employee Group	a. Was employee category eligible for variable pay in 2008?	b. Percent of employees eligible in 2008 for variable pay	c. Percent of eligible employees actually paid variable pay for 2008
Nonexempt Hourly Nonunion	o Yes o No		
Nonexempt Salaried	o Yes o No		
Exempt Salaried	o Yes o No		
Officers/Executives	o Yes o No		

22. Does your organization have a formal process for determining the budget for variable pay plans? If so, please indicate the average percentage of base pay budgeted for variable pay in each employee category.

   *NOTE: If variable pay for an employee category is not typically budgeted, or an employee category is not eligible for variable pay, please select "No" in question 22a and leave the remainder of the row blank. Fill in "0" (zero) **only** if your organization typically budgets for variable pay for that employee group, but has/will not budget for the program in the respective year.*

Employee Group	a. Does your organization budget for variable pay?	b.2008 average % budgeted for variable pay	c.2009 average % budgeted for variable pay	d.2010 projected average % budgeted for variable pay
Nonexempt Hourly Nonunion	o Yes o No			
Nonexempt Salaried	o Yes o No			
Exempt Salaried	o Yes o No			
Officers/Executives	o Yes o No			

23. Please provide the average percentage of base pay your variable pay plans actually paid for 2008 and the average percentage projected to be paid for 2009.

Employee Group	a. Average % paid for variable pay for 2008	b. Projected % paid for variable pay for 2009
Nonexempt Hourly Nonunion		
Nonexempt Salaried		
Exempt Salaried		
Officers/Executives		

24. What impact does your variable pay program have on **base salary** budget recommendations?

Employee Group	No Impact	Some Impact	Significant Impact
Nonexempt Hourly Nonunion	o	o	o
Nonexempt Salaried	o	o	o
Exempt Salaried	o	o	o
Officers/Executives	o	o	o

Health Care Cost Impact

25. Does the size of health care cost increases impact your base salary budget recommendations?
   - ❑ Yes
   - ❑ No

* Mandatory section/question

Cost Containment
26. Which of the following cost containment and/or reduction strategies has your organization used in the past 12 months? (Check all that apply.)

	Nonexempt Hourly Nonunion	Nonexempt Salaried	Exempt Salaried	Officers/Executives
Hiring freeze	☐	☐	☐	☐
Wage freeze/no pay increases	☐	☐	☐	☐
Reduction in pay/pay cuts	☐	☐	☐	☐
Limit/eliminate overtime	☐	☐	☐	☐
Voluntary unpaid time off (e.g. employees volunteer in lieu of other cuts, unpaid sabbaticals, etc.)	☐	☐	☐	☐
Furloughs (e.g. temporary layoffs, mandatory unpaid time off)	☐	☐	☐	☐
Voluntary reduction-in-force (RIF)	☐	☐	☐	☐
Mandatory reduction-in-force (RIF)	☐	☐	☐	☐
Increase employee share of health care premiums	☐	☐	☐	☐
Reduce/suspend 401(k) or 403(b) matches	☐	☐	☐	☐
Freeze or close pension plans	☐	☐	☐	☐

Attraction & Retention Practices

27. Which of the following has your organization used in the past 12 months to attract and retain employees? (Check all that apply.)
- ☐ Employee referral bonus
- ☐ Exempt overtime pay or time off
- ☐ Flexible work schedules
  - ☐ Flextime
  - ☐ Compressed work week
  - ☐ Telecommuting/telework
  - ☐ Job sharing
- ☐ Larger merit increase budgets
- ☐ Market adjustments/increase to base salary
- ☐ Paid sabbaticals
- ☐ Paying above market
- ☐ Part-time employment with benefits
- ☐ Phased retirement
- ☐ Project milestone/completion bonus
- ☐ Retention/stay bonus
- ☐ Separate salary structures
- ☐ Sign-on/hiring bonus
- ☐ Special cash bonus/group incentives (not organization wide)
- ☐ Spot bonus (individual)
- ☐ Stock grant programs
- ☐ Stock option program

* Mandatory section/question

28*. Please provide the name of the person completing this survey and that person's contact information. You must be a WorldatWork member to participate in the *2009-10 Salary Budget Survey*. (If you are filling this survey out on behalf of a member, please note that the survey results will be sent directly to the member's address on file.)

WorldatWork Member Number: ☐☐☐☐☐☐☐☐

Name: _____

Title: _____

Company: _____

Phone: _____

E-mail: _____

29*. By submitting this survey form, I understand that if mandatory (*) sections of the survey are not completed correctly, I will not be eligible as a participant to receive a complimentary copy of the survey report.
    o I understand and agree to the statement above.

If you have a question about how to complete the survey, please call WorldatWork Customer Relationship Services at 877-951-9191.

The deadline to submit the survey is May 4, 2009
Fax or mail your completed survey to:
WorldatWork Survey Team • Fax 480-483-8352 • Toll-free fax 866-816-2962
14040 N. Northsight Blvd. • Scottsdale, AZ 85260

---

* Mandatory section/question

8

BUILDING PAY STRUCTURES THAT RECOGNIZE EMPLOYEE CONTRIBUTIONS

MyManagementLab®

✪ Improve Your Grade!

When you see this icon, visit **www.mymanagementlab.com** for activities that are applied, personalized, and offer immediate feedback.

LEARNING OBJECTIVES

When you finish studying this chapter, you should be able to:

1. Explain the concept of pay structures.
2. Specify and explain the five steps necessary to construct a pay structure.
3. Discuss at least two considerations in designing merit pay systems.
4. Explain at least two sales compensation plan design considerations.
5. Describe three main considerations of person-focused pay program design.
6. Present a summary of two pay structure variation practices.

Pay structures assign different pay rates for jobs of unequal worth and provide the framework for recognizing differences in individual employee contributions. No two employees possess identical credentials, nor do they perform the same jobs equally well. Companies recognize these differences by paying individuals according to their credentials, knowledge, or job performance. When completed, pay structures should define the boundaries for recognizing employee contributions. Employee contributions in this context correspond to the pay bases that we addressed in previous chapters (i.e., seniority, merit, incentive pay, and person-based pay). Pay structures also have strategic value. Well-designed structures should promote the retention of valued employees. Most companies support pay-for-performance systems.

In this chapter, we will address how companies structure these pay bases, with the exception of seniority, which is typically not the main basis for pay in companies. We will start out by considering the fundamental process of constructing pay structures. We will then examine the design elements of merit pay structures. Then we will move on to specific pay structures, including merit pay, sales incentive pay, and person-focused pay.

CONSTRUCTING A PAY STRUCTURE

Compensation specialists develop pay structures based on five steps:

- Deciding on the number of pay structures
- Determining a market pay line

- Defining pay grades
- Calculating pay ranges for each pay grade
- Evaluating the results

Step 1: Deciding on the Number of Pay Structures

Companies often establish more than one pay structure, depending on market rates and the company's job structure. Common pay structures include exempt and nonexempt structures, pay structures based on job families, and pay structures based on geography.

EXEMPT AND NONEXEMPT PAY STRUCTURES As you will recall, these categories reflect a distinction in the Fair Labor Standards Act. Exempt jobs are not subject to the overtime pay provisions of the act. Core compensation terms for these jobs are usually expressed as an annual salary. Nonexempt jobs are subject to the overtime pay provision of the act. The core compensation for these jobs is therefore expressed as an hourly pay rate. Companies establish these pay structures for administrative ease. Some broadly consistent features distinguish exempt from nonexempt jobs: Exempt jobs, by the definition of the Fair Labor Standards Act, are generally supervisory, professional, managerial, or executive jobs that contain a wide variety of duties. Nonexempt jobs are generally nonsupervisory in nature, and the duties tend to be narrowly defined.

PAY STRUCTURES BASED ON JOB FAMILY Executive, managerial, professional, technical, clerical, and craft jobs represent distinct job families. Pay structures are also defined on the basis of job family, each of which shows a distinct salary pattern in the market. For example, the Davis–Bacon Act requires contractors and subcontractors to pay wages at least equal to those prevailing in the area where work is performed. This act applies only to employers with federal or federally financed contracts worth more than $2,000 for the construction, alteration, or repair of public works or buildings. Moreover, the Davis–Bacon Act also applies only to laborers and mechanics, excluding clerical, professional, and managerial employees. Thus, companies holding federal contracts meeting these criteria have limited latitude for setting pay for certain jobs; however, the latitude for setting pay rates for other jobs is greater.

PAY STRUCTURES BASED ON GEOGRAPHY Companies with multiple, geographically dispersed locations such as sales offices, manufacturing plants, service centers, and corporate offices may establish pay structures based on going rates in different geographic regions because local conditions may influence pay levels. The cost of living is substantially higher in the northeast region than in the south and southeast regions of the United States. For example, in 2011, a person earning $50,000 annually in Huntsville, Alabama, would have to earn about $97,155 in San Francisco, California, to maintain a comparable standard of living.

Step 2: Determining a Market Pay Line

We discussed how to determine the market pay line in Chapter 7. Again, the market pay line is representative of typical market pay rates relative to a company's job structure. Pay levels that correspond with the market pay line are market-competitive pay rates. Figure 8-1 illustrates a market pay line for a series of clerical jobs. Pay rates that fall along the market pay line represent competitive pay rates based on the company's selection of a relevant labor market, and these rates promote internal consistency because they increase with the value of jobs. The clerk I job has the least complex and demanding duties, and it has fewer worker requirements than do the remaining clerk jobs (clerk II, clerk III, and chief clerk).

Step 3: Defining Pay Grades

Pay grades group jobs for pay policy application. Human resource (HR) professionals typically group jobs into pay grades based on similar compensable factors and value. These criteria are not precise. In fact, no one formula determines what is sufficiently similar in terms of content and value to warrant grouping jobs into a pay grade.

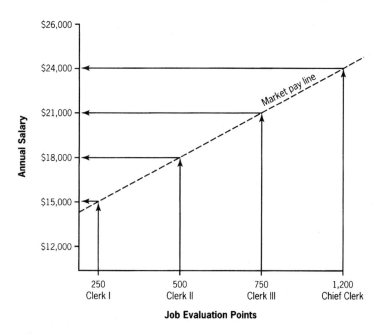

Clerk I

Employees receive training in basic office support procedures, the operation of office equipment, and the specific activities of the unit. Tasks assigned are simple and repetitive in nature and are performed in accordance with explicit instructions and clearly established guidelines. Sample duties include: files materials in established alphabetical order and prepares new file folders and affixes labels. Clerk Is must possess a high school diploma or equivalent.

Clerk II

Employees work under general supervision in support of an office. They perform routine office support tasks that require a knowledge of standard office procedures and the ability to operate a variety of office equipment. Sample duties include: prepares simple factual statements or reports involving computations such as totals or subtotals and composes memos requesting or transmitting factual information. Clerk IIs must possess a high school diploma or equivalent and 1 year work experience performing simple clerical tasks.

Clerk III

Employees work under general supervision in support of an office. They perform office support tasks requiring knowledge of general office and departmental procedures and methods and ability to operate a variety of office equipment. Sample duties include: reconciles discrepancies between unit records and those of other departments and assigns and reviews work performed by Clerks I and II. Clerk IIIs must possess a high school diploma or equivalent, 2 years work experience performing moderately complex clerical tasks, and completed coursework (five in all) in such related topics as word processing and basic accounting principles.

Chief Clerk

Employees work under direction in support of an office. They perform a wide variety of office support tasks that require the use of judgment and initiative. A knowledge of the organization, programs, practices, and procedures of the unit is central to the performance of the duties. Chief clerks must possess a high school diploma or equivalent, 4 years work experience performing moderately difficult clerical tasks, and an associate's degree in office management.

FIGURE 8-1 Pay Structure for Clerk Jobs

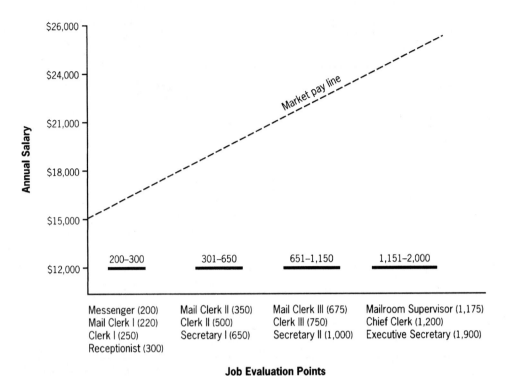

FIGURE 8-2 Pay Grade Definitions

Job groupings are ultimately influenced by such other factors as management's philosophy, as discussed earlier. Wider pay grades (i.e., grades that include a relatively large number of jobs) minimize hierarchy and social distance between employees. Narrower pay grades tend to promote hierarchy and social distance. Figure 8-2 illustrates pay grade definitions, based on the jobs used in Figure 8-1.

Human resource professionals can develop pay grade widths as either "absolute" job evaluation point spreads or as percentage-based job evaluation point spreads. When absolute point spreads are used, grades are based on a set number of job evaluation points for each grade. For example, a compensation professional establishes pay grades equal to 200 points each. Grade 1 includes jobs that range from 1 to 200 job evaluation points, Grade 2 contains jobs that range from 201 to 400 points, and so on.

Companies may choose to vary the "absolute" point spread by increasing the point spread as they move up the pay structure, in recognition of the broader range of skills that higher pay grades represent. For example, certified public accounting jobs require a broader range of skills (e.g., knowledge of financial accounting principles and both state and federal tax codes) than do mailroom clerk jobs. Companies often assign trainee positions to the lower, narrower pay grades because trainees generally have limited job-relevant skills. For instance, Grade 1 may contain trainee positions with job evaluation scores that range from 1 to 150, Grade 2 may contain basic jobs beyond traineeships with scores of 151–400, and Grade 3 may include advanced jobs with scores of 401–1,000.

Step 4: Calculating Pay Ranges for Each Pay Grade

Pay ranges build upon pay grades. Pay grades represent the horizontal dimension of pay structures (i.e., job evaluation points). **Pay ranges** represent the vertical dimension (pay rates). Pay ranges include midpoint, minimum, and maximum pay rates. The minimum and maximum values denote the acceptable lower and upper bounds of pay for the jobs within particular pay grades. Figure 8-3 illustrates pay ranges.

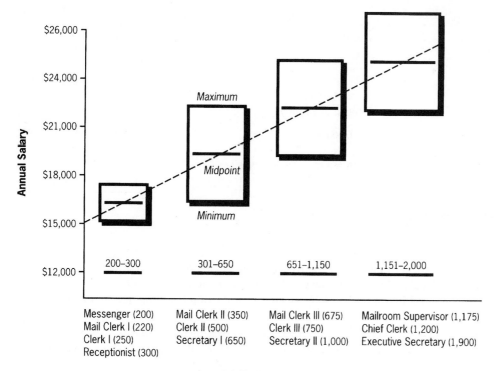

FIGURE 8-3 Pay Range Definitions

Human resource professionals establish midpoints first, followed by minimum and maximum values. The **midpoint pay value** is the halfway mark between the range minimum and maximum rates. Midpoints generally match values along the market pay line, representing the competitive market rate determined by the analysis of compensation survey data. Thus, the midpoint may reflect the market average or median (Chapter 7).

A company sets the midpoints for its pay ranges according to its competitive pay policy, as discussed in Chapter 7. If the company wants to lead the market with respect to pay offerings (market lead policy), it sets the midpoint of the ranges higher than the average for similar jobs at other companies. Companies wanting to pay according to the market norm (market match policy) should set midpoints equal to the market average. Companies wanting to lag the market (market lag policy) would set the midpoints below the market average. A company's base-pay policy line graphically connects the midpoints of each pay grade.

How do compensation professionals calculate pay grade minimums and maximums? They may fashion pay grade minimums and maximums after the minimums and maximums for pay grades that their competitors have established. An alternate approach is to set the pay grade minimums and maximums on the basis of range spread. A **range spread** is the difference between the maximum and minimum pay rates of a given pay grade. It is expressed as a percentage of the difference between the minimum and maximum divided by the minimum.

Companies generally apply different range spreads across pay grades. They most commonly use progressively higher range spreads for pay grades that contain more valuable jobs in terms of the companies' criteria. Smaller range spreads characterize pay grades that contain relatively narrowly defined jobs that require simple skills with generally low responsibility. Entry-level clerical employees perform limited duties ranging from filing folders alphabetically to preparing file folders and affixing labels. These jobs presumably represent bottom-floor opportunities for employees who will probably advance to higher-level jobs as they acquire the skills needed

	Steps	
1. Identify the midpoint:	$20,000	
2. Determine the range spread:	40%	
3. Calculate the minimum:		

$$\frac{midpoint}{100\% + (range\ spread/2)} = \frac{\$20,000}{100\% + (40\%/2)}$$

$$= \$16,666.67$$

4. Calculate the maximum:
   minimum + (range spread × minimum)   = $16,666.67 + (40% × $16,666.67)
   = $23,333.33

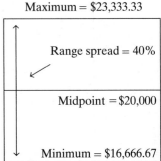

Maximum = $23,333.33

Range spread = 40%

Midpoint = $20,000

Minimum = $16,666.67

FIGURE 8-4 Calculation of Range Spread

to perform these jobs proficiently. Advanced clerical employees review and analyze forms and documents to determine the adequacy and acceptability of information.

Higher-level jobs afford employees greater promotion opportunities than entry-level jobs. Employees also tend to remain in higher pay grades longer, and the specialized skills associated with higher pay grade jobs are considered valuable. It therefore makes sense to apply larger range spreads to these pay grades. The following are typical range spreads for different kinds of positions:[1]

- 20–25 percent: lower-level service, production, and maintenance
- 30–40 percent: clerical, technical, and paraprofessional
- 40–50 percent: high-level professional, administrative, and middle management
- 50 percent and above: high-level managerial and executive

After deciding on range spread, compensation professionals calculate minimum and maximum rates. Figure 8-4 illustrates the calculation of minimum and maximum rates based on knowledge of the pay grade midpoint (as discussed earlier in Step 1) and the chosen range spread. Table 8-1 illustrates the impact of alternative range spread values on minimum and maximum values. This approach is typically applied when a company chooses to base the minimum and maximum rates on budgetary constraints. We will discuss budgeting issues later in this chapter.

Adjacent pay ranges usually overlap with other pay ranges so that the highest rate paid in one range is above the lowest rate of the successive pay grade. Figure 8-5 illustrates how to calculate pay range overlap. Overlapping pay ranges allow companies to promote employees to the next level without adding to their pay. Nonoverlapping pay ranges require pay increases for

TABLE 8-1 The Impact of Alternative Range Spreads on Pay Range Minimum and Maximum Values, with Midpoint of $25,000

	Range Spread ($)			
	20%	50%	80%	120%
Minimum: $\dfrac{midpoint}{100\% + (range\ spread/2)}$	$22,727	$20,000	$17,857	$15,625
Maximum:				
minimum + (range spread × minimum)	$27,272	$30,000	$32,143	$34,375
Difference between maximum and minimum values	$4,545	$10,000	$14,286	$18,750

job promotions. Compensation professionals express overlap as a percentage. For example, the degree of overlap between pay range A and pay range B is about 33 percent.

PAY COMPRESSION The minimum pay rate for a range usually is the lowest pay rate that the company will pay for jobs that fall within that particular pay grade. In theory, newly hired employees receive pay that is at or near the minimum. In practice, new employees often receive well above minimum pay rates, sometimes only slightly below or even higher than the pay moderately tenured employees receive. **Pay compression** occurs whenever a company's pay spread between newly hired or less qualified employees, and more qualified job incumbents is small.[2]

Two situations result in pay compression. The first is a company's failure to raise pay range minimums and maximums. Companies that retain set range maximums over time limit increase amounts. For example, let's assume that the entry-level starting salaries for newly minted certified public accountants have increased 7 percent annually for the past 5 years. Tax-It, a small accounting firm, did not increase its pay range minimums and maximums for entry-level accountants during the same period because of lackluster profits. Nevertheless, Tax-It hired several new accountants at the prevailing market rate. Failure to pay competitive pay rates would hinder Tax-It's ability to recruit talented accountants. As a result, many of the Tax-It accountants with 5 or fewer years' experience have lower salaries (or slightly higher salaries at best) than newly hired accountants without work experience. The second situation that results in pay compression is a scarcity of qualified candidates for particular jobs. When the supply of such candidates falls behind companies' demand, wages for newly hired employees rise, reflecting a bidding process among companies for qualified candidates.

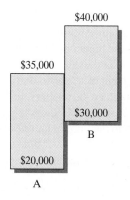

$$100\% \times \frac{(\text{max. rate for A} - \text{min. rate for B})}{(\text{max. rate for A} - \text{min. rate for A})}$$

$$100\% \times \frac{(\$35{,}000 - \$30{,}000)}{(\$35{,}000 - \$20{,}000)}$$

The overlap between range A and range B is 33.33%

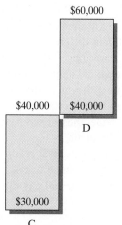

$$100\% \times \frac{(\text{max. rate for C} - \text{min. rate for D})}{(\text{max. rate for C} - \text{min. rate for C})}$$

$$100\% \times \frac{(\$40{,}000 - \$40{,}000)}{(\$40{,}000 - \$30{,}000)}$$

The overlap between range C and range D is 0%

FIGURE 8-5 Calculating Pay Range Overlap

Pay compression can threaten companies' competitive advantage. Dysfunctional employee turnover is a likely consequence of pay compression. Dysfunctional turnover represents high-performing employees' voluntary termination of their employment. High-performing employees will probably perceive their pay as inequitable because they are receiving lower pay relative to their positive contributions (i.e., experience and demonstrated performance) than newly hired employees who are receiving similar pay.

How can companies minimize pay compression? Maximum pay rates represent the most that a company is willing to pay an individual for jobs that fall in that particular range. Maximum pay rates should be set close to the maximum paid by other companies in the labor market for similar jobs. Setting competitive maximum rates enables a company to raise pay rates for high-quality employees who may consider employment opportunities with a competitor; however, maximum rates should not exceed maximum rates offered by competitors for comparable jobs because high maximums represent costs to the company over and above what are needed to be competitive.

GREEN CIRCLE PAY RATES Employees sometimes receive below-minimum pay rates for their pay ranges, especially when they assume jobs for which they do not meet every minimum requirement in the worker specification section of the job description. Below-minimum pay range rates are known as **green circle rates.** The pay rates of employees who are paid at green circle rates should be brought within the normal pay range as quickly as possible, which requires that both employer and employee take the necessary steps to eliminate whatever deficiencies in skill or experience that warranted paying below the pay range minimum. In addition, companies should regularly review current employees' pay relative to the starting pay rates for newly hired employees in comparable jobs to plan for necessary pay adjustments before current employees' pay falls below the minimum rates.[3]

RED CIRCLE PAY RATES On occasion, companies must pay certain employees greater than maximum rates for their pay ranges. Known as **red circle rates**, these higher pay rates help retain valued employees who have lucrative job offers from competitors. On the other hand, exemplary employees may receive red circle rates for exceptional job performance, particularly when a promotion to a higher pay grade is not granted. For these exemplary performers, companies may provide lump sum pay awards that are not added to regular base pay.[4] Red circle rates also apply to employees who receive job demotions to pay grades with lower maximum rates than the employees' current pay. Companies usually reduce demoted employees' pay over time until they receive pay that is consistent with their new jobs. In this case, red circle rates allow employees a chance to adjust to pay decreases.

Step 5: Evaluating the Results

After compensation professionals establish pay structures according to the previous steps, they must evaluate the results. They must specifically analyze significant differences between the company's internal values for jobs and the market's values for the same jobs. If discrepancies are evident, the company must reconsider the internal values they have placed on jobs. If their valuation of particular jobs exceeds the market's valuation of the same jobs, they must decide whether higher-than-market pay rates will undermine attainment of competitive advantage. If a company undervalues jobs relative to the market, managers must consider whether these discrepancies will limit the company's ability to recruit and retain highly qualified individuals.

Compensation professionals must also consider each employee's pay level relative to the midpoint of the pay grade. Again, the midpoint represents a company's competitive stance relative to the market. **Compa-ratios** index the relative competitiveness of internal pay rates based on pay range midpoints. Compa-ratios are calculated as follows:

$$\frac{\text{Employee's pay rate}}{\text{Pay range midpoint}}$$

Compa-ratios are interpreted as follows: A compa-ratio of 1 means that the employee's pay rate equals the pay range midpoint. A compa-ratio less than 1 means that the employee's pay rate falls below the competitive pay rate for the job. Companies with market lag policies strive for compa-ratios of less than 1. A compa-ratio that is greater than 1 means that an employee's pay rate exceeds the competitive pay rate for the job.

Human resource professionals also can use compa-ratios to index job groups that fall within a particular pay grade. Compa-ratios specifically may be calculated to index the competitive position of a job—by averaging the pay rates for each job incumbent. Moreover, compa-ratios may be calculated for all jobs that comprise a pay grade, departments, or such functional areas as accounting.

Compa-ratios provide invaluable information about the competitiveness of companies' pay rates. Compensation professionals can use compa-ratios as diagnostic tools to judge the competitiveness of their companies' pay rates. Compa-ratios that exceed 1 tell compensation professionals that pay is highly competitive with the market. Compa-ratios that fall below 1 tell them that pay is not competitive with the market and that they should consider another course of action to increase pay over a reasonable period.

We've reviewed the elements of pay structures and the steps compensation professionals follow to construct them. Next, we will consider three popular pay structures that should be familiar to compensation professionals:

- Merit pay structure
- Sales incentive compensation structure
- Person-focused structure

DESIGNING MERIT PAY SYSTEMS

As we noted in Chapter 3, companies that use merit pay systems must ensure that employees see definite links between pay and performance. We also reviewed the rationale for using merit pay systems, as well as the possible limitations of this kind of pay system. Establishing an effective merit pay program that recognizes employee contributions requires avoiding such pitfalls as ineffective performance appraisal methods and poor communication regarding the link between pay and performance. In addition to these considerations, managers interested in establishing a merit pay system must determine merit increase amounts, timing, and the type of merit pay increase (i.e., permanent or recurring increases versus one-time or nonrecurring additions to base pay). They must also settle on base-pay levels relative to the base pay of functionally similar jobs.[5]

Merit Increase Amounts

Merit pay increases should reflect prior job performance levels and motivate employees to perform their best. As managers establish merit increase amounts, they must consider both past performance levels and establish rates that will motivate employees even after the impact of inflation and payroll deductions. Updating compensation survey data should account for increases in consumer prices (Chapter 7). As we noted in Chapter 3, "just-meaningful pay increases" refer to the minimum amounts employees will see as making a meaningful change in their compensation.[6] Trivial pay increases for average or better employees will not reinforce their performance or motivate them.

No precise mathematical formula determines the minimum merit increase that will positively affect performance; managers must consider three research findings.[7] First, boosting the merit increase amount will not necessarily improve productivity because research has shown diminishing marginal returns on each additional dollar allocated to merit increases.[8] In other words, each additional merit increase dollar was associated with smaller increases in production.

Second, employees' perceptions of just-meaningful differences in merit increases depend on their cost of living, their attitudes toward the job, and their expectations of rewards from the job.

For employees who value pay for meeting economic necessity, a just-meaningful difference in pay increase tends to depend on changes in the cost of living. On the other hand, for employees who value pay as a form of recognition, the size of the expected pay raise (versus cost of living) affects a just-meaningful difference.[9]

Third, for the pay increase to be considered meaningful, the employee must see the size of the increase as substantive in a relative sense as well as in an absolute sense.[10] **Equity theory** suggests that an employee must regard his or her own ratio of merit increase pay to performance as similar to the ratio for other comparably performing people in the company. In practical terms, managers should award the largest merit pay increases to employees with the best performance, and they should award the smallest increases to employees with the lowest acceptable performance. The difference between these merit increases should be approximately equal to the differences in performance.

It is also essential that compensation professionals design plans that reinforce employees' motivation to perform well, with just-meaningful pay increases and merit increase percentages that clearly distinguish among employees based on their performance; however, the best-laid plans don't always lead to the desired results. Well-designed merit pay structures (and others that we discuss shortly) will fail without adequate funding.

Compensation budgets are blueprints that describe the allocation of monetary resources to fund pay structures. Compensation professionals index budget increases that fund merit pay programs in percentage terms. For example, a 10 percent increase for next year's budget means that it will be 10 percent greater than the size of the current year's budget. This value is often an indicator of the average pay increase employees will receive. It is obvious that the greater the increase in the compensation budget, the more flexibility compensation professionals will have in developing innovative systems with substantial motivating potential.

The magnitude of the increases in compensation budgets in recent years has unfortunately been just slightly more than the average increases in cost of living. For example, the average earnings for social workers in the United States increased only 3.5 percent in 2008.[11] Although this value varies by occupation, industry, and region of the country, it does reflect a trend in the United States of stagnant growth in compensation budgets. The picture becomes less positive because the increase in cost of living for the same period was 3.8 percent.[12] This means that, on average, annual merit pay raises fell below the increase in cost of living by 0.3 percent, taking the motivational value out of pay increases.

Timing

The vast majority of companies allocate merit increases, as well as cost-of-living and other increases, annually. At present, companies typically take one of two approaches in timing these pay raises. Companies may establish a **common review date** or **common review period** so that all employees' performances are evaluated on the same date or during the same period (e.g., the month of June, which immediately follows a company's peak activity period). Best suited for smaller companies, common review dates reduce the administrative burden of the plan by concentrating staff members' efforts to limited periods.

On the other hand, companies may review employee performance and award merit increases on the **employee's anniversary date** (i.e., the day on which the employee began to work for the company). Most employees will thus have different evaluation dates. Although these staggered review dates may not monopolize supervisors' time, this approach can be administratively burdensome because reviews must be conducted regularly throughout the year.

Recurring versus Nonrecurring Merit Pay Increases

Companies have traditionally awarded merit pay increases permanently, and permanent increases are sometimes associated with some undesirable side effects (e.g., placing excessive cost burdens on the employer). In terms of costs, U.S. companies are increasingly concerned with containing costs as just one initiative in their quest to establish and sustain competitive advantage in the marketplace. Companies may advocate **nonrecurring merit increases** (i.e., lump sum bonuses), which lend themselves well to cost containment and have recently begun to gain some favor among unions, including the International Brotherhood of Electrical Workers.[13] Lump sum bonuses strengthen the pay-for-performance link and minimize costs because these increases are not permanent, and subsequent percentage increases are not based on higher base-pay levels.

Present Level of Base Pay

Pay structures specify acceptable pay ranges for jobs within each pay grade. Thus, each job's base-pay level should fall within the minimum and maximum rates for its respective pay grade. In addition, compensation professionals should encourage managers to offer similar base pay to new employees performing similar jobs unless employees' qualifications (i.e., education and relevant work experience) justify pay differences. This practice is consistent with the mandates of several laws (Chapter 2) (i.e., Title VII of the Civil Rights Act of 1964, the Equal Pay Act of 1963, and the Age Discrimination in Employment Act of 1967). Of course, employees' merit pay increases should vary with their performance.

Rewarding Performance: The Merit Pay Grid

Table 8-2 illustrates a typical merit pay grid that managers use to assign merit increases to employees. Managers determine pay raise amounts by two factors jointly: employees' performance ratings and the position of employees' present base-pay rates within pay ranges. Pay raise amounts are expressed as percentages of base pay. For instance, let's say that two employees will each receive a 5 percent merit pay increase. One employee is paid on an hourly basis, earning $8.50 per hour, and the other is paid on an annual basis, earning $32,000. The employee whose pay is based on an hourly rate (usually nonexempt in accord with the Fair Labor Standards Act; one who must be paid overtime for time worked in excess of 40 hours per week) receives a pay raise of $0.44 per hour, increasing her hourly pay to $8.94. The employee whose pay is based on an annual rate, typically exempt from the Fair Labor Standards Act provisions, receives a pay increase of $1,600, boosting her annual pay to $33,600.

TABLE 8-2 **Merit Pay Increase Grid**

		Performance Rating				
		Excellent (%)	Above Average (%)	Average (%)	Below Average (%)	Poor (%)
Q4 ⇒	$70,000 $65,000 $60,000	5	3	1	0	0
Q3 ⇒	$55,000 $50,000 $45,000	7	5	3	0	0
Q2 ⇒	$40,000 $35,000 $30,000	9	7	6	2	0
Q1 ⇒	$25,000 $20,000 $15,000	12	10	8	4	0

In Table 8-2, employees whose current annual salary falls in the 2nd quartile of the pay range and whose performance rates an average score receive a 6 percent merit pay increase. Employees whose current annual salary falls in the 1st quartile of the pay range and whose job performance is excellent receive a 12 percent merit pay increase. The term *cell* (as in spreadsheet software programs such as *Microsoft Excel*) is used to reference the intersection of quartile ranking and performance rating. Table 8-2 contains 20 cells.

EMPLOYEES' PERFORMANCE RATINGS Merit pay systems use performance appraisals to determine employees' performance. Where merit pay systems are in place, an overall performance rating guides the pay raise decision. In Table 8-2, an employee receives any one of five performance ratings ranging from "Poor" to "Excellent." As you can see when we hold position in pay range constant, pay raise amounts increase with level of performance. This pattern fits well with the logic underlying pay-for-performance principles—it recognizes higher performance with greater rewards.

EMPLOYEES' POSITIONS WITHIN THE PAY RANGE Employees' positions within the pay range are indexed by quartile ranking, which, in Chapter 7, we described as a measure of dispersion. Again, quartiles allow compensation professionals to describe the distribution of data (i.e., in this case, hourly or annual base-pay amount) based on four groupings known as quartiles. In Table 8-2, the 1st quartile is the point below which 25 percent of the salary data lie (and above which 75 percent of the salary data are found), which is $25,000. In this example, 25 percent of the salary figures are less than or equal to $25,000 and 75 percent of these figures are greater than $25,000. The 2nd quartile is the point below which 50 percent of the salary data lie (and above which 50 percent of the salary figures are found), which is $40,000 for this example. The 3rd quartile is the point below which 75 percent of the salary figures lie (and above which 25 percent of the salary figures are found), which is $55,000 for this example. The 4th quartile is the point below which all of the salary data lie, which is $70,000. The lower a person's pay falls within its designated pay grade (e.g., the 1st quartile versus the 3rd quartile), the higher the percentage pay raise, all else being equal. Along those lines, the higher a person's pay within its grade, the lower the percentage pay raise, all else being equal.

Holding performance ratings constant, compensation professionals reduce merit pay increase percentages as quartile ranks increase to control employees' progression through their pay ranges. Pay grade minimums and maximums reflect both corporate criteria about the value of various groups of unlike jobs and may be dictated by budgeting. We'll look at the issue of budgeting shortly. Let's take the case of two employees whose performance ratings are identical but whose base pay places them in different quartiles of the pay grade (i.e., one in the 3rd quartile and the other in the 1st quartile). If these employees were to receive the same pay raise percentage, the base-pay rate for the employee in the 3rd quartile likely would exceed the maximum pay rate for the range more quickly than would the base-pay rate for the employee in the 1st quartile.

Merit Pay Increase Budgets

Now that we've considered the design principles for merit pay grids, we'll take a closer look at budgetary considerations. Budgets limit the merit pay increase percentages in each cell. A **merit pay increase budget** is expressed as a percentage of the sum of employees' current base pay. For instance, let's assume that a company's top financial officers and compensation professionals agree to a 5 percent merit pay increase budget. Let's also assume that the sum of all employees' current base pay is $10 million based on an employee population of 350. A 5 percent merit pay increase budget for this example equals $500,000, that is, 5 percent of the sum of all employees' current base pay totaling $10,000,000 (5 percent × $10,000,000). In other words, the company will distribute $500,000 to increase current base pay of its employees. As described earlier, merit pay increases awarded to individual employees will vary according to performance level and position in the pay range; however, the total of the individual pay increases must not exceed the allotted merit pay increase budget, again, $500,000 in this example. As an aside, the typical merit pay increase budget today ranges between 2 and 3 percent for the small proportion of companies that even have awarded pay increases in the past few years. This range is much lower than the average 4 percent increase in recent past years.

Compensation professionals begin plans for setting the merit increase pay grid within the estimated merit increase pay budget with the following six steps:

1. Compensation professionals ask managers and supervisors to indicate the percentage of employees who they expect will fall in each of the performance categories in the performance appraisal instrument. Managers will often use the actual distribution of employees based on recent past years as an estimate for budget planning. The sample merit pay grid illustrated in Table 8-2 lists five performance categories. For illustrative purposes, let's assume the following performance distribution for employees:

   • Excellent: 10 percent
   • Above average: 20 percent
   • Average: 40 percent
   • Below average: 25 percent
   • Poor: 5 percent

2. Compensation professionals rely on position in the pay range to determine the percentage of employees whose pay falls into each pay quartile. For example, let's assume the following distribution of employees in each pay quartile:

   • Q4: 20 percent
   • Q3: 25 percent
   • Q2: 40 percent
   • Q1: 15 percent

   In other words, 20 percent of employees earn pay that falls in the range from $55,000 to $70,000 (4th quartile) in Table 8-2. Similarly, 25 percent of the employees earn pay that falls in the range from $40,000 to $55,000 (3rd quartile). The same rationale applies to the 1st and 2nd quartiles.

3. Compensation professionals combine both sets of information to determine the percentage of employees who fall into each cell. The percentage of employees whose performance rating is excellent and whose base pay falls in the 4th quartile equals 2.0 percent (10 percent × 20 percent). The sum of the cell percentages totals 100 percent.

	Excellent (%)	Above Average (%)	Average (%)	Below Average (%)	Poor (%)
Q4	10 × 20 = 2	20 × 20 = 4	40 × 20 = 8	25 × 20 = 5	5 × 20 = 1
Q3	10 × 25 = 2.5	20 × 25 = 5	40 × 25 = 10	25 × 25 = 6.25	5 × 25 = 1.25
Q2	10 × 40 = 4	20 × 40 = 8	40 × 40 = 16	25 × 40 = 10	5 × 40 = 2
Q1	10 × 15 = 1.5	20 × 15 = 3	40 × 15 = 6	25 × 15 = 3.75	5 × 15 = 0.75

4. Next, compensation professionals calculate the expected number of employees who fall into each cell. It is important to remember that this is the expected (versus actual) number of employees because managers provide only an estimate of employees' performance distribution. For this example, let's assume that the company employs 350 people. The number of employees whose performance rating is excellent and whose base pay falls in the 4th quartile equals 7 (350 people × 2 percent).

	Excellent	Above Average	Average	Below Average	Poor
Q4	350 × 2% = 7	350 × 4% = 14	350 × 8% = 28	350 × 5% = 17.5	350 × 1% = 3.5
Q3	350 × 2.5% = 8.75	350 × 5% = 17.5	350 × 10% = 35	350 × 6.25% = 21.875	350 × 1.25% = 4.375
Q2	350 × 4% = 14	350 × 8% = 28	350 × 16% = 56	350 × 10% = 35	350 × 2% = 7
Q1	350 × 1.5% = 5.25	350 × 3% = 10.5	350 × 6% = 21	350 × 3.75% = 13.125	350 × 0.75% = 2.625

5. Compensation professionals now distribute the merit increase budget amount ($500,000) to each cell based on the following formula:

Expected number of employees in cell × Desired pay increase for cell (%) × Current median pay level for the current quartile

We calculated the expected number of employees in each cell in the previous step. The desired pay increase amount is an estimate that we made (see Table 8-2). Compensation professionals usually specify these percentage amounts initially on pay-for-performance and equity considerations as described earlier (i.e., holding performance constant, individuals in higher pay quartiles receive smaller percentage increases than employees in lower pay quartiles). We calculate the median values as described in Chapter 7. Let's assume for this example that the medians for each quartile are:

- Q4 $65,000
- Q3 $50,000
- Q2 $35,000
- Q1 $20,000

	Excellent	Above Average	Average	Below Average	Poor
Q4	7 × 5% × $65,000 = $22,750	14 × 3% × $65,000 = $27,300	28 × 1% × $65,000 = $18,200	17.5 × 0% × $65,000 = $0	0.5 × 0% × $65,000 = $0
Q3	8.75 × 7% × $50,000 = $30,625	17.5 × 5% × $50,000 = $43,750	35 × 3% × $50,000 = $52,500	21.875 × 0% × $50,000 = $0	4.375 × 0% × $50,000 = $0
Q2	14 × 9% × $35,000 = $44,100	28 × 7% × $35,000 = $68,600	56 × 6% × $35,000 = $117,600	35 × 2% × $35,000 = $24,500	7 × 0% × $35,000 = $0
Q1	5.25 × 12% × $20,000 = $12,600	10.5 × 10% × $20,000 = $21,000	21 × 7% × $20,000 = $29,400	13.125 × 4% × $20,000 = $10,500	2.625 × 0% × $20,000 = $0

The sum of expected merit pay increases equals $523,425.

6. Compensation professionals check whether the expected merit increase total fits within the actual budgeted amount. In this example, the sum of expected increases exceeds the budgeted amount by $23,425 (i.e., $523,425 – $500,000). When the expected increase amount exceeds the budgeted amount, compensation professionals adjust the percentages in the cells with the following considerations in mind: lowering costs, recognizing performance differences, and considering equity.

Pay structures based on merit differ from sales compensation in at least two key ways. First, whereas sales compensation programs center on incentives that specify rewards an employee will receive for meeting a preestablished—often objective—level of performance, merit pay programs generally base an employee's reward on someone else's (most often the employee's supervisor's) subjective evaluation of the employee's past performance. Second, in most instances, a sales employee's compensation is variable to the extent that it is composed of incentives. Under a merit pay system, an employee earns a base pay appropriate for the job (as discussed earlier in this chapter) that is augmented periodically with permanent pay raises or one-time bonuses.

DESIGNING SALES INCENTIVE COMPENSATION PLANS

Compensation programs for salespeople rely on incentives.[14] Sales compensation programs can help businesses meet their objectives by aligning the financial self-interest of sales professionals with the company's marketing objectives.[15] By extension, sales compensation programs can help companies achieve strategic objectives by linking sales professionals' compensation to fulfilling customer needs or other marketing objectives (e.g., increasing market share). Thus, sales compensation plans derive their objectives more or less directly from strategic marketing objectives, which, in turn, are derived from company competitive strategy. Particular sales objectives include:[16]

- *Improve sales productivity:* More volume and profit from current investment in sales resources.
  - New-customer sales volume
  - New-product sales volume
  - New balanced product-line sales
  - Reduced "churn" among current customers

- *Improve sales coverage of current customers:* Regardless of industry, customers want flexibility, customization, faster response, and personalized service. To meet these requirements, market-leading companies improve the coverage of their current customers. This often means investments in new ways to interact with customers.
  - Overall account volume
  - Greater share of the account's business
  - Achievement of customer objectives
  - More lines of business sold
  - Account profitability

- *Grow sales overall:* Track the percentage of sales realized from the following:
  - New direct customers
  - New distribution channels
  - New products

Alternative Sales Compensation Plans

Companies usually use one of five kinds of sales incentive plans. The type of plan appropriate for any given company will depend on the company's competitive strategy. The order of presentation roughly represents the degree of risk (from lowest to highest) to employees.

- Salary-only plans
- Salary-plus-bonus plans
- Salary-plus-commission plans
- Commission-plus-draw plans
- Commission-only plans

SALARY-ONLY PLANS Under **salary-only plans**, sales professionals receive fixed base compensation, which does not vary with the level of units sold, increase in market share, or any other indicator of sales performance. From the employees' perspective, salary-only plans are relatively risk-free because they can expect a certain amount of income. From a company's perspective, salary-only plans are burdensome because the company must compensate its sales employees regardless of their achievement levels. Thus, salary-only plans do not fit well with the directive to link pay with performance through at-risk pay. Nevertheless, salary-only plans may be appropriate for such particular kinds of selling situations as:

- Sales of high-priced products and services or technical products with long lead times for sales
- Situations in which sales representatives are primarily responsible for generating demand, but other employees actually close the sales
- Situations in which it is impossible to follow sales results for each salesperson (i.e., where sales are accomplished through team efforts)
- Training and other periods when sales representatives are unlikely to make sales on their own

SALARY-PLUS-BONUS PLANS **Salary-plus-bonus plans** offer a set salary coupled with a bonus. Bonuses usually are single payments that reward employees for achievement of specific, exceptional goals. For a real estate agent, generating in excess of $2 million in residential sales for a 1-year period may mean earning a bonus totaling several thousand dollars.

SALARY-PLUS-COMMISSION PLANS **Commission** is a form of incentive compensation based on a percentage of the selling price of a product or service. **Salary-plus-commission plans** spread the risk of selling between the company and the sales professional. The salary component presumably enhances a company's ability to attract good employees and allows a company to direct its employees' efforts to nonselling tasks that do not lead directly to commissions (e.g., participating in further training or servicing accounts). The commission component serves as the employees' share in the gains they generated for the company.

COMMISSION-PLUS-DRAW PLANS **Commission-plus-draw plans** award sales professionals with subsistence pay or draws—money to cover basic living expenses—yet provide them with a strong incentive to excel. This subsistence pay component is known as a **draw.** Unlike salaries, however, companies award draws as advances, which are charged against commissions that sales professionals are expected to earn.

Companies use two types of draws. **Recoverable draws** act as company loans to employees that are carried forward indefinitely until employees sell enough to repay their draws. **Nonrecoverable draws** act as salary because employees are not obligated to repay the loans if they do not sell enough. Nonrecoverable draws clearly represent risks to companies because these expenses are not repaid if employee sales performance is lackluster. Companies that adopt nonrecoverable draws may stipulate that employees cannot continue in the employment of the company if they fail to cover their draw for a specified number of months or sales periods during the year. This arrangement is quite common among car salespeople.

COMMISSION-ONLY PLANS Under **commission-only plans**, salespeople derive their entire income from commissions. Three particular types of commissions warrant mention. **Straight commission** is based on a fixed percentage of the sales price of the product or service. For instance, a 10 percent commission would generate a $10 incentive for a product or service sold that is priced at $100 and $55 for a product or service sold that is priced at $550.

Graduated commissions increase percentage pay rates for progressively higher sales volume. For example, a sales professional may earn a 5 percent commission per unit for sales volume up to 100 units, 8 percent for each unit from 101 to 500 units, and 12 percent for each unit in excess of 500 sold during each sales period.

Finally, **multiple-tiered commissions** are similar to graduated commissions, but with one exception. Employees earn a higher rate of commission for all sales made in a given period if the sales level exceeds a predetermined level. For instance, employees might earn only 8 percent for each item if total sales volume falls short of 1,000 units. If total sales volume exceeds

1,000 units, however, then employees might earn a per-item commission equal to 12 percent for every item sold. Commission-only plans are well suited for situations in which:

- The salesperson has substantial influence over the sales.
- Low-to-moderate training or expertise is required.
- The sales cycle—the time between identifying the prospect and closing the sale—is short.

In contrast to salespeople on salary-only plans, commission-only salespeople shoulder all the risk: Employees earn nothing until they sell. Despite this risk, potential rewards are substantial, particularly with graduated and multiple-tiered commission plans.

Although commissions may fit well with cost-cutting measures, these incentives are not always the best tactic for compensating sales professionals. In fact, commission structures probably suffer from many of the same limitations of individual incentive plans that we discussed in Chapter 4 (e.g., competitive behaviors among employees). Moreover, some sales experts argue that commissions undermine employees' intrinsic motivation to sell (i.e., their genuine interest for the challenge and enjoyment that selling brings). These experts argue that once salespeople have lost that intrinsic motivation, commissions act essentially as controls to maintain sales professionals' performance levels. Said another way, such professionals may simply go through the motions in order to earn money without regard to quality and customer satisfaction.[17]

For any sales compensation plan, it is critical that companies establish realistic total sales targets and individual performance standards. Beyond reasonable limits, it is possible that sales compensation plans will backfire. Consequences of such backfire include lower employee motivation, unprofessional behavior, and compromised profits.

Sales Compensation Plans and Competitive Strategy

Sales plans with salary components are most appropriate for differentiation strategies. Under salary-based sales plans, employees can count on receiving income. By design, salary plans do not require employees to focus on attaining sales volume goals or other volume indicators (e.g., market share). Sales professionals who receive salaries can turn their attention to addressing clients' needs during the presale and servicing phases of the relationship. Salary-based sales compensation applies to the sale and servicing of such technical equipment as computer networks, including the hardware (e.g., the individual computers and network server) and the software (e.g., applications programs such as *Microsoft Excel* or the *Microsoft Windows* operating system).

Commission-oriented sales compensation plans are best suited for lowest-cost strategies because compensation expenditures vary with sales revenue. As a result, only the most productive employees earn the best salaries. Commissions essentially represent rewards for "making the sale." For example, real estate sales agents' earnings depend on two factors: number of houses sold and their selling price. New-car salespersons' earnings similarly depend on the number of cars sold and their selling price. In either situation, customers are likely to have questions and concerns following sales transactions. Many real estate sales companies employ real estate assistants at low salaries—not much more than the minimum wage—who mediate such buyers' queries of the sellers as, "What grade of rock salt is most appropriate for the water softener apparatus?" Real estate assistants are often training to be full-fledged real estate agents, and they view low pay as a necessary trade-off for learning the ropes.

Determining Fixed Pay and the Compensation Mix

Managers must balance fixed and incentive pay elements to directly affect employee motivation. The mix depends mainly on three factors:

- Influence of the salesperson on the buying decision
- Competitive pay standards within the industry
- Amount of nonsales activities required

INFLUENCE OF THE SALESPERSON ON THE BUYING DECISION For the most part, the more influence sales professionals have on "buying" decisions, the more the compensation mix will emphasize incentive pay. Salespeople's influence varies greatly with the specific product or service marketed and the way these are sold. Many sales professionals assume an order-taker role, with little influence over purchase decisions. For example, salespeople in such large department stores as Sears and Best Buy have little influence over the merchandise for sale because these stores send their buyers to manufacturers to purchase lines of products that will be sold in their stores throughout the United States and beyond. Product display and promotional efforts (e.g., television or newspaper ad campaigns) are determined by store management.

On the other end of the spectrum, some employees serve as consultants to the client. For instance, when a company decides to invest in computerizing its entire worldwide operations, it may approach a computer manufacturer such as Dell to purchase the necessary equipment. Given the technical complexity of computerizing a company's worldwide operations, the client would depend on Dell to translate its networking needs into the appropriate configuration of hardware and software. These Dell sales professionals ultimately influence the purchaser's decision to buy.

COMPETITIVE PAY STANDARDS WITHIN THE INDUSTRY A company's compensation mix must be as enticing as that offered by competitors if the company wants to recruit high-quality sales professionals. Industry norms and the selling situation are among the key determinants of compensation mix. For instance, competitive standards may dictate that the company must give greater weight to either incentive or fixed pay, which we addressed earlier. Incentive (commission) pay weighs heavily in highly competitive retail industries, including furniture, home electronics, and auto sales. Salary represents a significant pay component in such high entry-barrier industries as pharmaceuticals. In the case of pharmaceuticals, barriers to entry include the U.S. Food and Drug Administration regulations on testing new products that significantly extend the time from product conception through testing to marketing for general use. Salary is an appropriate compensation choice because pharmaceutical companies face little risk of new competition.

AMOUNT OF NONSALES ACTIVITIES REQUIRED In general, the more nonsales duties salespeople have, the more their compensation package should tend toward fixed pay. Some companies and products, for instance, require extensive technical training or customer servicing activities. An excellent example is again the pharmaceuticals industry. Sales professionals employed by such companies as Bristol-Myers Squibb, Lilly, and Merck must maintain a comprehensive understanding of their products' chemical compositions, clinical uses, and contraindications.

DESIGNING PERSON-FOCUSED PROGRAMS

As indicated in Chapters 3 and 4, merit pay and incentive pay represent job-based approaches to compensating employees. In Chapter 5, we discussed the importance of person-focused pay that many companies recognize. For this discussion, we use the terms *knowledge* and *skills* interchangeably, as the design features for both structures are virtually the same. In their purest form, person-focused programs reward employees for the acquisition of job-related knowledge (or skills, in the case of skill-based pay plans). In practice, companies are concerned with how much employees' performance improves as a result of their newly acquired knowledge. Our focus in this section is on the latter.

A fundamental issue in person-focused programs is whether investments in training provide measurable payoffs to companies. The American Society for Training and Development, a premier professional organization of training and development professionals, offered some insight. Based on a research study involving approximately 2,500 companies, training investments are positively related to future total stockholder return, gross profit margin, and income per employee.[18] Since then, there has been evidence for a positive relationship between offering training and return on investment (ROI).[19] In addition, executives within and outside the training function at IBM maintain that training programs have strategic value for companies.[20]

Establishing Skill Blocks

Skill (knowledge) blocks are sets of skills (knowledge) necessary to perform a specific job (e.g., typing skills versus analytical reasoning) or group of similar jobs (e.g., junior accounting clerk, intermediate accounting clerk, and senior accounting clerk). Table 8-3 contains an example of a knowledge block—building market-competitive compensation systems—discussed in the accompanying companion casebook *Building Strategic Compensation Systems*.

The number of skill blocks included in a person-focused structure can range from two to several. The appropriate number of blocks depends on the variety of jobs within a company. The development of skill blocks should occur with three considerations in mind.

First, the company must develop job descriptions, which we discussed in Chapter 6. Job descriptions should be treated as blueprints for the creation of a person-focused system. Well-crafted job descriptions should facilitate the identification of major skills, the training programs employees need to acquire horizontal and vertical skills, and accurate measures of performance.

Second, individual jobs should be organized into job families, or groups of similar jobs such as clerical, technical, and accounting. The information conveyed within a job description should enable the plan developers to identify skills that are common to all jobs in the family and skills that are unique for individual jobs in the family. Based on these groupings, all tasks necessary to perform the jobs in a job family should be listed to facilitate the identification of the skills necessary to perform the tasks.

TABLE 8-3 Knowledge Block: Building Market-Competitive Compensation Systems

I. Strategic analyses
- A. External market environment
  - 1. Industry profile
  - 2. Foreign demand
  - 3. Competition
  - 4. Long-term prospects
  - 5. Labor-market assessment
- B. Internal capabilities
  - 1. Financial condition
  - 2. Functional capabilities
  - 3. Human resource capabilities

II. Compensation surveys
- A. Using published compensation survey data
  - 1. Survey focus: Core or fringe compensation
  - 2. Sources of published compensation surveys
- B. Compensation surveys: Strategic considerations
  - 1. Defining relevant labor market
  - 2. Choosing benchmark jobs
- C. Compensation survey data: Summary, analysis, and interpretation
  - 1. Using the appropriate statistics to summarize survey data
    - a. Central tendency
    - b. Variation
  - 2. Updating the survey data
  - 3. Statistical analysis

Third, skills should be grouped into blocks. There are no hard-and-fast rules compensation professionals can follow to determine skill blocks. A general guideline is that the blocked knowledge should relate to specific job tasks and duties. Referring again to Table 8-3, knowledge about the external environment and a company's internal capabilities—two distinct sets of knowledge—together form the foundation of strategic analyses.

Transition Matters

A number of initial considerations arise in the transition from using job-based pay exclusively to using person-focused programs as well. These issues include assessment of skills, alignment of pay with the knowledge structure, and access to training.[21]

SKILLS ASSESSMENT The skills assessment issue centers on who should assess whether employees possess skills at levels that justify a pay raise, on what basis assessments should be made, and when assessments should be conducted. Gaining employee trust is critical during the transition period because employees may view new systems as threats to job security. Some combination of peer and self-assessments, as well as input from known "experts" such as supervisors, therefore, might be essential. The important ingredients here are employee input and the expertise of supervisors and managers. In the case of knowledge assessment, paper-and-pencil tests are useful tools.

Having established who should conduct assessments, on what basis should assessments be made? During the transition, companies use conventional performance measures that reflect employees' proficiency in skills use, complemented by employees' self-assessments. The use of both types of data is likely to increase an employee's understanding of the new system as well as build faith in it, particularly when testimony and the more conventional performance measures converge.

A final assessment matter concerns timing. During transition phases, managers should assess employees' performance more frequently to keep employees informed of how well they are doing under the new system. In addition, more frequent assessments should reinforce the key aim of pay for knowledge (i.e., to encourage employees to learn more). Performance feedback is essential for this process.

ALIGNING PAY WITH THE KNOWLEDGE STRUCTURE One of the most difficult tasks that managers face as they guide employees toward a person-focused system is aligning pay with the knowledge structure. Upon implementation of pay for knowledge, employees' core compensation must reflect the knowledge or skills they have that the company incorporates into its person-focused structure. If employees' actual earnings are more than what the person-focused system indicates, managers must develop a reasonable course of action so that employees can acquire skills that are commensurate with their current pay. If employees are underpaid, the company must provide pay adjustments as quickly as possible. The length of time required to make these necessary adjustments will depend on two factors: the number of such employees and the extent to which they are underpaid. With limited budgets, companies will obviously require more extended periods as either the number of underpaid employees or the pay deficit increases.

ACCESS TO TRAINING A final transition matter is access to training. Person-focused systems make training necessary, rather than optional, for those employees who are motivated for self-improvement. Companies that adopt pay for knowledge must therefore ensure that all employees have equal access to the needed training for acquiring higher-level skills. They must do so both to meet the intended aim of person-focused programs (i.e., to reward employees for enhancing their skills) and to address legal imperatives. Restricting access to training can lead to a violation of key laws (i.e., Title VII of the Civil Rights Act of 1964 and the Age Discrimination in Employment Act of 1967; see Chapter 2). Companies must also educate employees about what their training options are and how successful training will lead to increased pay and advancement opportunities within the company. In other words, employers should not assume that employees will necessarily recognize the opportunities that are available to them unless they are clearly communicated. Written memos and informational meetings conducted by HR representatives are effective communication media.

Training and Certification

Successful person-focused programs depend on a company's ability to develop and implement systematic training programs. For many of the reasons cited in Chapter 1 (i.e., intense domestic and global competition, rapid technological advancement, and educational deficits of new workforce entrants), progressive companies in the United States have adopted a continuous learning philosophy, which, like person-focused pay programs, encourages employees to take responsibility for enhancing their skills and knowledge.[22] Training clearly represents a key venue for continuous learning.

Because employees are required to learn new skills constantly, training becomes an ongoing process. Companies implementing pay for knowledge typically increase the amount of classroom and on-the-job training.[23] When training is well designed, employees should be able to learn the skills needed to increase their pay as well as the skills necessary to teach and coach other employees at lower skill levels. Accurate job descriptions are useful in determining training needs and focusing training efforts.

Employers must make necessary training available to employees so they can progress through the person-focused system. A systematic method for ensuring adequate training coverage involves matching training programs with each skill block. Accessibility does not require that employers develop and deliver training themselves. Training that is developed and delivered by an agency not directly affiliated with the company (e.g., community college, vocational training institute, university, or private consultant) can be just as accessible when the employer integrates the offering of these other sources with its person-focused program.

IN-HOUSE OR OUTSOURCING TRAINING The following criteria should be used to determine whether to develop and deliver training within the workplace or to outsource.[24]

Expertise Specialized training topics require greater expertise, and more generic topics require less expertise. Employers generally turn to in-house resources if they can draw on existing expertise. If in-house expertise is lacking, employers often seek an outside provider either to fill the need directly or to train individuals who become instructors. Employers usually rely on in-house expertise for employer- and product-specific training. Such training is governed by employer philosophies and procedures and is, therefore, not readily available in the external market.

Timeliness Employers often seek outside services if the in-house staff does not have adequate time to develop and deliver the program within the time frame requested. For example, PeopleSoft, a business applications software development company, trains its clients (e.g., Exxon-Mobil, Walmart, General Motors, Ford, Citigroup, IBM, AT&T, and Verizon) on how to use the systems it installs. Over time, client companies experience turnover, which often includes the departure of employees who are well trained to use installed PeopleSoft systems. To maintain effective business operations, client companies require training on demand. PeopleSoft offers training on demand to its clients through different forms of media, including the Internet and DVDs.

Size of the Employee Population to Be Trained Employers typically rely on in-house resources for larger groups of employees. The major impetus behind this decision is economics. If there is a large demand for training, the program is more likely to be delivered more than once, resulting in economies of scale.

Sensitivity or Proprietary Nature of the Subject Matter Sensitive or proprietary training is defined as training used to gain a competitive advantage or training that gives access to proprietary, product, or strategic knowledge. Employers rarely issue security clearances to outside resources to provide training of this nature. If the area of the training is sensitive or proprietary, the training is likely to be done in-house regardless of the other factors just discussed.

CERTIFICATION AND RECERTIFICATION **Certification** ensures that employees possess at least a minimally acceptable level of skill proficiency upon completion of a training unit. If employees do not have an acceptable degree of skill, then the company quite simply wastes any skill-based compensation expenditure. Supervisors and coworkers, who are presumably most familiar with the intricacies of their work, usually certify workers. Certification methods can include work samples, oral questioning, and written tests.

Recertification, under which employees periodically must demonstrate mastery of all the jobs they have learned or risk losing their pay rates, is necessary to maintain the workforce flexibility offered by a person-focused plan.[25] The recertification process typically is handled by retesting employees, retraining employees, or requiring employees to occasionally perform jobs that use their previously acquired skills.

For example, the Society for Human Resource Management offers two types of professional certification: the Professional in Human Resources and the Senior Professional in Human Resources. Individuals with at least 2 years of work experience in exempt status jobs (Chapter 2) earn certification when they pass a comprehensive examination of knowledge in the HR domain. Because the field of HR knowledge changes over time, individuals with certification must periodically earn continuing education credits to maintain certification. Credits are earned through a wide variety of activities, including course and/or conference attendance, membership in professional organizations, leadership with the association, teaching, speaking, writing, and projects completed on the job. This updating process is known as recertification.

PAY STRUCTURE VARIATIONS

The principles of pay structure development reviewed previously apply to the majority of established pay structures in companies throughout the United States. Broadbanding and two-tier pay structures represent variations to those pay structure principles.

Broadbanding

THE BROADBANDING CONCEPT AND ITS ADVANTAGES Companies may choose **broadbanding** to consolidate existing pay grades and ranges into fewer, wider pay grades and broader pay ranges.[26] Figure 8-6 illustrates a broadbanding structure and its relationship to traditional pay grades and ranges. Broadbanding represents the organizational trend toward flatter, less hierarchical corporate structures that emphasize teamwork over individual contributions alone.[27] Some federal government agencies, including the Navy, the General Accounting Office, and the Central Intelligence Agency, began experimenting with the broadbanding concept in the 1980s to introduce greater flexibility to their pay structures. Some private sector companies began using broadbanding in the late 1980s for the same reason. General Electric's former plastics business is a noteworthy adopter of broadbanding.

Broadbanding uses only a few large salary ranges to span levels within the organization previously covered by several pay grades. Thus, HR professionals place jobs that were separated by one or more pay grades in old pay structures into the same band under broadbanding systems. For example, condensing three consecutive grades into a single broadband eliminates the hierarchical differences among the jobs evident in the original, narrower pay grade configuration. Employees holding jobs in a single broadband now have equal pay potential, unlike employees in a multiple pay grade configuration. In addition, elimination of narrow bands broadens employees' job duties and responsibilities.

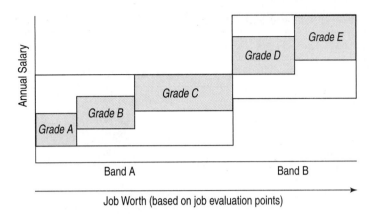

FIGURE 8-6 Broadbanding Structure and Its Relationship to Traditional Pay Grades and Ranges

Some companies establish broadbands for distinct employee groups within the organizational hierarchy (e.g., upper management, middle management, professionals, and staff). This approach reduces management layers dramatically, and it should promote quicker decision-making cycles. Other companies create broadbands on the basis of job families (e.g., clerical, technical, and administrative). Job family–based bands should give employees broader duties within their job classes. Still others may set broadbands according to functional areas, collapsing across job families. For example, a broadband may be established for all HR specialists (i.e., training, compensation, recruitment, and performance appraisal). These bands should encourage employees to expand their knowledge and skills in several HR functions.

Broadbanding shifts greater responsibility to supervisors and managers for administering each employee's compensation within the confines of the broadbands. Because broadbands include a wider range of jobs than narrowly defined pay grades, supervisors have greater latitude in setting employees' pay according to the tasks and duties they perform. Under traditional pay grades, employees receive pay and pay increases based on a limited set of duties stated in their job descriptions.

LIMITATIONS OF BROADBANDING Notwithstanding the benefits of broadbanding, it does possess some limitations. Broadbanding is not a cure-all for all compensation-related dysfunction within companies. For instance, broadbanding changes how compensation dollars are allocated, but not how much is allocated. Managers often think that flatter organizational structures reduce costs. To the contrary, broadbanding may lead to higher compensation expenses because managers have greater latitude in assigning pay to their employees. In fact, the federal government's limited experience showed that broadbanding structures were associated with more rapid increases in compensation costs than traditional pay structures.[28]

Broadbanding also necessitates a trade-off between the flexibility to reward employees for their unique contributions and a perception among employees that fewer promotional opportunities are available. This transition from multiple narrowly defined pay grades to fewer broadbands reduces organizational hierarchies that support job promotions. Employers and employees alike need to rethink the idea of promotions as a positive step through the job hierarchy.

Two-Tier Pay Structures

THE TWO-TIER PAY SYSTEM CONCEPT AND ITS ADVANTAGES **Two-tier pay structures** reward newly hired employees less than established employees. Under the temporary basis, employees

TABLE 8-4 **Two-Tier Wage Structures**

Typical Base Rate		
	Assembler ($)	Tool & Die ($)
BaseRate—Contract End	26.86	31.52
COLA Fold-In	1.19	1.19
New Agreement Base	28.05	32.71
Beginning COLA Float	1.06	1.06
Base Rate Plus COLA	29.11	33.77

Lump Sum Examples		
	Assembler ($)	Tool & Die ($)
October 2014 Settlement Bonus	3,000	3,000
September 2015 Performance Bonus (3%)	2,171	2,534
September 2016 Performance Bonus (4%)	2,894	3,377
September 2017 Performance Bonus (3%)	2,170	2,533

Note: Based on a standard 2,080 year plus 10 percent overtime, with projected COLA adjustments based on inflation averaging 2.44 percent.

have the opportunity to progress from lower entry-level pay rates to the higher rates enjoyed by more senior employees. Permanent two-tier systems reinforce the pay-rate distinction by retaining separate pay scales: Lower-paying scales apply to newly hired employees, and current employees enjoy higher-paying scales. Although pay progresses within each scale, the maximum rates to which newly hired employees can progress are always lower than more senior employees' pay scales. Table 8-4 illustrates a typical two-tier wage structure.

Two-tier wage systems are more prevalent in unionized companies. For example, at Ford Motor Company, a two-tier wage structure will compensate new hires substantially less than other employees, including an hourly base rate that is $10 below the previous one.[29]

Labor representatives have reluctantly agreed to two-tier wage plans as a cost-control measure. In exchange for reduced compensation costs, companies have promised to limit layoffs. These plans represent a departure from unions' traditional stance of single base-pay rates for all employees within job classifications.

Two-tier pay structures also enable companies to reward long-service employees while keeping costs down by paying lower rates to newly hired employees who do not have an established performance record within the company. As senior employees terminate their employment (i.e., taking jobs elsewhere or retiring), they are usually replaced by workers who are compensated according to the lower-paying scale.

LIMITATIONS OF TWO-TIER PAY STRUCTURES A potentially serious limitation of two-tier plans is that the lower pay scale applied to newly hired workers may restrict a company's ability to recruit and retain the most highly qualified individuals. Resentment can build among employees on the lower tier toward their counterparts on the upper tier, which may lead to lower-tier employees' refusal to perform work that extends in any way beyond their job descriptions. Such resentment may lead employees on the upper tier to scale back their willingness to take on additional work to the extent that they perceive pay premiums are not sufficiently large to compensate for extra duties. In addition, opponents of two-tier wage systems contend that pay differentials cause lower employee morale. Finally, conflict between the tiers may lead to excessive turnover. When high performers leave, then the turnover is dysfunctional to the company and can have long-term implications for productivity and quality.

COMPENSATION IN ACTION

As a line manager or HR manager, you will be faced with the challenge of determining which pay structures best suit the employee populations you serve. Regardless of the specifics of the plan (several specific plans are covered in this chapter), there are general guidelines that should be followed to build the link between the pay structure and the successful recognition of employee contributions. As you are educated by compensation specialists, you will provide senior executives with recommendations that appropriately identify correct incentives and produce desired behaviors.

Action checklist for line managers and HR—keeping the focus on employees as structures are built

HR takes the lead

- Assess the organization, and identify factors that will determine the pay structures within the organization (e.g., hourly versus salaried and geographic location). Line managers help in this assessment and provide additional insight to identify the correct factors.
- Partner with compensation specialists to group employees into pay grades that are determined by some similarity in

the work they produce; corresponding ranges will also be established for each grade.
- Compensation specialists conduct market analyses to certify that current employees are being compensated at the right levels and that offers are being made to prospective employees that are comparable to the offers made by competitors (retain and attract top talent).

Line managers take the lead

- Communicate with HR regarding behaviors in employee population—HR and line managers work together to ensure that the compensation and benefits incentives are continuing to target the correct behaviors. HR carefully considers subtle changes to the system in face of market pressures or new leadership and direction within the company.
- Employees will continue to progress within the grade in which they have been placed, receiving pay increases (as determined by line manager in consultation with HR) commensurate with their individual performance—compensation specialists will work with HR to ensure that, with these merit increases, equity still exists in the grade and that the percentage increases in pay correspond with superior levels of performance.

END OF CHAPTER

MyManagementLab

Go to **mymanagementlab.com** to complete the problems marked with this icon ⭐.

Summary

In this chapter, we reviewed the pay structure concept as well as the building blocks needed to establish pay structures. Compensation professionals develop pay structures for the various pay bases. Pay structure development generally entails linking the internal job structure with the

external market's pricing structure for jobs, knowledge, or skills. Once developed, pay structures recognize individual differences in employee contributions, and these structures represent operational plans for implementing and administering pay programs.

Key Terms

✪ Discussion Questions

8-1. Respond to the following statement: "Pay grades limit a company's ability to achieve competitive advantage." Do you agree? Provide a rationale for your position.

8-2. Two employees perform the same job, and each received exemplary performance ratings. Is it fair to give one employee a smaller percentage merit increase because his pay falls within the 3rd quartile but give a larger percentage merit increase to the other because his pay falls within the 1st quartile? Please explain your answer.

8-3. Describe some ethical dilemmas sales professionals may encounter. How can sales compensation programs be modified to minimize ethical dilemmas?

8-4. React to the statement: "Merit pay grids have the potential to undermine employee motivation." Please discuss your views.

8-5. Compression represents a serious dysfunction of pay structures. Discuss some of the major ramifications of compression. Also, discuss how companies can minimize or avoid these ramifications.

CASE
A New Sales Representative

✪ *An additional Supplemental Case can be found on MyManagementLab.*

After 10 years in business, John Shurtman has determined that it is time to hire a sales representative. As the founder and president of United Fleet Service (UFS), John has been the main driver of new business sales for the company. However, as UFS has grown, John has found that he must spend more time on planning and administration, leaving little time to generate new sales leads or call on potential customers.

UFS provides maintenance, mechanical repair services, and body repair services to organizations that maintain fleets of large vehicles. UFS customers include mostly school districts that own bus fleets and municipalities that own fleets of fire and police vehicles. While UFS has a strong hold on these public sector organizations, John sees many opportunities for expansion through targeting other potential customers such as utility companies and commercial trucking companies.

UFS has several competitors in its geographic area, but none provide as comprehensive a service as UFS. For example, several competitors provide mechanical repair services, but do not provide body repair services; on the other hand, several competitors provide body repair services, but do not provide mechanical repair services. UFS also has a reputation for high-quality repairs and fast turnaround times on service. With these strengths in mind, John is convinced that an effective sales representative that can take the time to contact and develop relationships with potential customers can help lead the organization to expansion.

John has experienced steady growth over the past 10 years, acquiring just two or three new customers each year. Leads on potential new customers have come primarily through referrals from current customers. John personally called on the leads to secure sales. Once a target was established as a customer, John handed the customer account over to a service advisor. The service advisor's role is to process incoming vehicles and communicate work progress with customers. Service advisors are also encouraged to generate new sales from current customers by suggesting add-on services or establishing ongoing maintenance schedules. Due to increased volume growth, the service advisors have had little time to develop more significant relationships with customers. Because of this, UFS has missed out on many add-on sales opportunities.

Therefore, John plans to hire a new sales representative to both call on new customers and develop better relationships with current customers. Cultivating new customers will require cold-calling on potential customers as well as following up on referrals from current customers. Because most companies that have vehicle fleets establish contractual relationships with mechanical service providers, some new customers may take a long time to acquire. That is, the sales representative may have to interact with a potential new customer over an extended period of time until the company's contract with another service provider expires.

Working with current customers will require significant interaction with the service advisors to understand each customer's past history of services and identify opportunities to increase the number and frequency of services provided. Growing business from current customers will also require spending time developing relationships with each customer.

Before he begins recruiting for this position, John must determine how to compensate the new sales representative. He's researched market rates for sales representatives in his industry and has a targeted salary range, but he wants to make sure that the compensation plan provides enough incentive to both secure new sales and spend time developing relationships with current customers.

Questions:

8-6. What are the sales objectives for the new sales representative?

8-7. What role will the compensation design play in motivating the new sales representative?

8-8. What kind of sales incentive plan do you recommend? Why?

MyManagementLab

Go to **mymanagementlab.com** for Auto-graded writing questions as well as the following Assisted-graded writing questions:

 8-9. Compare and contrast merit pay systems and sales compensation.

 8-10. Briefly discuss designing job-based pay systems (e.g., merit pay, sales incentive pay) and person-focused programs. What considerations arise when making a transition from using a job-based pay system to using pay-for-knowledge?

Endnotes

1. Bureau of National Affairs. (2005). *Skill-Based Pay*. BNA's Library on Compensation & Benefits on CD [CD-ROM]. Washington, DC: Author.
2. Ulrich, L. (2008). Money talks: Identifying, preventing and alleviating systemic salary compression issues. *Workspan,* November, pp. 43–46.
3. Manoli, R. (2009). Addressing salary compression in any economy. *Workspan,* December, pp. 54–57.
4. Klein, A. L., McMillan, A., & Reiter, G. (2010). The mixed value of using lump sums in lieu of putting merit pay into base pay. *WorldatWork Journal,* First Quarter, pp. 49–57.
5. Heneman, R. L. (1992). *Merit Pay: Linking Pay Increases to Performance*. Reading, MA: Addison-Wesley.
6. Krefting, L. A., & Mahoney, T. A. (1977). Determining the size of a meaningful pay increase. *Industrial Relations, 16,* pp. 83–93.
7. Heneman, *Merit Pay.*
8. Rambo, W. W., & Pinto, J. N. (1989). Employees' perceptions of pay increases. *Journal of Occupational Psychology, 62,* pp. 135–145.
9. Krefting, L. A., Newman, J. M., & Krzystofiak, F. (1987). What is a meaningful pay increase? In D. B. Balkin & L. R. Gómez-Mejía (Eds.), *New Perspectives on Compensation*. Upper Saddle River, NJ: Prentice Hall.
10. Heneman, *Merit Pay.*
11. U.S. Bureau of Labor Statistics. (2011). *Occupational Earning Statistics*. Available: *www.bls.gov*, accessed February 27, 2011.
12. U.S. Bureau of Labor Statistics. (2011). *Consumer Price Index*. Available: *www.bls.gov*, accessed February 27, 2011.
13. Erickson, C. L., & Ichino, A. C. (1994). Lump-sum bonuses in union contracts. *Advances in Industrial and Labor Relations, 6,* pp. 183–218.

14. Carey, J. F. (1992). *Complete Guide to Sales Force Compensation*. Homewood, IL: Irwin.

15. Kuhlman, D. C. (1994). Implementing business strategy through sales compensation. In W. Keenan Jr. (Ed.), *Commissions, Bonuses, & Beyond*. Chicago, IL: Probus Publishing.

16. Colletti-Fiss, J. A., & Colletti-Fiss, M. S. (2007). Designing sales incentive plans for competitive advantage. In D. Scott (Ed.), *Incentive Pay* (pp. 43–56). Scottsdale, AZ: WorldatWork.

17. Keenan, W., Jr. (Ed.). (1994). The case against commissions. In *Commissions, Bonuses, & Beyond*. Chicago, IL: Probus Publishing.

18. American Society for Training and Development. (2000). *Profiting from Learning: Do Firms' Investments in Education and Training Pay Off?* Available: *www.astd.org/virtual—community/research/PFLWhitePaper.pdf*, accessed July 7, 2002.

19. Pulliam Phillips, P. (Ed.). (2010). *ASTD Handbook of Measuring and Evaluating Training*. Alexandria, VA: ASTD Press.

20. American Society for Training and Development. (2006). *C-Level perceptions of the strategic value of learning research report*. January. Available: *www.astd.org/astd/research/research*, accessed June 19, 2007.

21. Dewey, B. J. (1994). Changing to skill-based pay: Disarming the transition landmines. *Compensation & Benefits Review*, 26, pp. 38–43.

22. Rosow, J., & Zager, R. (1988). *Training: The Competitive Edge*. San Francisco, CA: Jossey-Bass.

23. Jenkins, G. D., Jr., & Gupta, N. (1985). The payoffs of paying for knowledge. *National Productivity Review*, 4, pp. 121–130.

24. Noe, R. A. (2010). *Employee Training and Development* (5th ed.). Burr Ridge, IL: McGraw-Hill Higher Education.

25. Jenkins, G. D., Jr., Ledford, G. E., Jr., Gupta, N., & Doty, D. H. (1992). *Skill-Based Pay*. Scottsdale, AZ: American Compensation Association.

26. Dougherty, E. (2010). You want me to talk about *what?* Broadbanding? *Workspan,* March, pp. 69–72.

27. Risher, H. H., & Butler, R. J. (1993–1994). Salary banding: An alternative salary-management concept. *ACA Journal,* 2, pp. 48–57.

28. Schay, B. W., Simons, K. C., Guerra, E., & Caldwell, J. (1992). *Broad-Banding in the Federal Government— Technical Report*. Washington, DC: U.S. Office of Personnel Management.

29. Giancola, F. (2009). Ford Motor Company's 58 years of experience with a cost-of-living allowance plan. *WorldatWork Journal,* Third Quarter, pp. 37–46.

EMPLOYEE BENEFITS

Where We Are Now:

PART III, DESIGNING COMPENSATION SYSTEMS, explained the concepts and methods to build compensation systems that meet important goals of compensation professionals, including internal consistency, market competitiveness, and recognition of employee contributions. Our focus was on base pay. We do know (Chapter 1) that employee benefits represent an important component of total compensation. Now we turn to the myriad employee benefits, including discretionary benefits from which employers may choose to offer, among them retirement and health insurance programs and legally required benefits. We also give attention to designing and planning the benefits program.

In **PART IV, WE WILL COVER**

Chapter **9** DISCRETIONARY BENEFITS

Chapter **10** EMPLOYER-SPONSORED RETIREMENT PLANS AND HEALTH INSURANCE PROGRAMS

Chapter **11** LEGALLY REQUIRED BENEFITS

DISCRETIONARY BENEFITS

MyManagementLab®

⭐ **Improve Your Grade!**

When you see this icon, visit **www.mymanagementlab.com** for activities that are applied, personalized, and offer immediate feedback.

LEARNING OBJECTIVES

When you finish studying this chapter, you should be able to:

1. Give an overview of discretionary benefits.
2. List the three broad components of discretionary benefits.
3. Identify and define one example of income protection programs, paid time off, and services.
4. Explain the benefits and costs of discretionary benefits.

Today, discretionary benefits represent a significant fiscal cost to companies. As of March 2012, companies spent an average exceeding $13,000 per employee annually to provide discretionary benefits.[1] For the same period, discretionary benefits accounted for as much as 21.5 percent of employers' total payroll costs (i.e., the sum of core compensation and all employee benefits costs).

As the term implies, "discretionary benefits" are offered at the will of company management. Unlike in well-designed pay-for-performance systems, employees view such discretionary benefits as paid vacation and holidays as an entitlement much like any of the legally required benefits that we will discuss in Chapter 11. Employers have reinforced an entitlement mentality toward benefits because they usually award discretionary benefits regardless of employee performance.

AN OVERVIEW OF DISCRETIONARY BENEFITS

Discretionary benefits fall into three broad categories: protection programs, paid time off, and services. Protection programs provide family benefits, promote health, and guard against income loss caused by such catastrophic factors as unemployment, disability, or serious illnesses. Paid time off, not surprisingly, provides employees time off with pay for such events as vacation. Services provide such enhancements as tuition reimbursement and day care assistance to employees and their families.

In the past several decades, firms have offered a tremendous number of both legally required and discretionary benefits. In Chapter 11, we will discuss how the growth in legally required benefits from a select body of federal and state legislation developed out of social welfare philosophies. Quite different from these reasons are several factors that have contributed to the rise in discretionary benefits.

Discretionary benefits originated in the 1940s and 1950s. During both World War II and the Korean War, the federal government mandated that companies not increase employees' core compensation, but it did not place restrictions on companies' employee benefits expenditures. Companies invested in expanding their offerings of discretionary benefits as an alternate to pay hikes as a motivational tool. As a result, many companies began to offer **welfare practices.** Welfare practices were "anything for the comfort and improvement, intellectual or social, of the employees, over and above wages paid, which is not a necessity of the industry nor required by law."[2] Moreover, companies offered employees welfare benefits to promote good management and to enhance worker productivity.

The opportunities to employees through welfare practices varied. For example, some employers offered libraries and recreational areas, and others provided financial assistance for education, home purchases, and home improvements. In addition, employers' sponsorships of medical insurance coverage became common.

Quite apart from the benevolence of employers, employee unions also directly contributed to the increase in employee welfare practices through the National Labor Relations Act of 1935 (NLRA), which legitimized bargaining for employee benefits. Union workers tend to participate more in benefits plans than do nonunion employees (92 percent versus 72 percent).[3] Table 9-1 illustrates some of the differences in benefits between major occupational groups, full- and part-time employees, and nonunion and union employees.

Unions also indirectly contributed to the rise in benefits offerings. As we discussed in Chapter 2, nonunion companies often fashion their employment practices after union companies as a tactic to minimize the chance that their employees will seek union representation[4] and may offer their employees benefits that are comparable to the benefits received by employees in union shops.

Employees came to view both legally required benefits and discretionary benefits as entitlements. Anecdotal evidence suggests that most employees still feel this way: From their perspective, company membership entitles them to employee benefits. Until recently, companies have also treated virtually all elements of employee benefits as entitlements. They have not questioned their role as social welfare mediators; however, both rising benefit costs and increased foreign

TABLE 9-1 Percentage of Workers with Access to Selected Employee Benefits in Private Industry: March 2012

Worker Characteristics	Vacation and Holidays	Vacation and Sick Leave	Vacation and Personal Leave	Employee-Assistance Plans	On-site and Off-site Child Care	Wellness Programs	Flexible Workplace
Total	**72**	**59**	**35**	**48**	**9**	**34**	**6**
Management occupations	85	81	52	66	18	51	14
Production, transportation, and material-moving occupations	79	51	28	47	4	33	2
Service occupations	46	37	28	30	8	19	31
Full-time	87	73	43	53	11	39	7
Part-time	26	18	12	34	6	22	1
Union	88	71	44	71	13	44	2
Nonunion	70	57	34	46	9	33	6

Source: U.S. Bureau of Labor Statistics. (2012). *National Compensation Survey: Employee Benefits in the United States, March 2012* (Bulletin 2773). Available: *www.bls.gov*, accessed March 3, 2013.

competition have led companies to question this entitlement ethic. A more recent phenomenon that gives rise to discretionary benefits is the federal government's institution of tax laws that allow companies to lower their tax liability based on the amount of money they allocate to providing employees with particular discretionary benefits. These tax laws permit companies to deduct from their pretaxable income the cost of certain benefits, thereby lowering companies' tax liabilities.

COMPONENTS OF DISCRETIONARY BENEFITS

Several benefits practices fall into the category of discretionary employee benefits. We can explore these practices by recognizing the three broad goals employers hope to achieve when offering discretionary benefits: protection, paid time off, and services to enhance work and life experiences.

Protection Programs

INCOME PROTECTION PROGRAMS

Disability Insurance Disability insurance replaces income for employees who become unable to work because of sicknesses or accidents. Employees unfortunately need this kind of protection. At all working ages, the probability of being disabled for at least 90 consecutive days is much greater than the chance of dying while working; one of every three employees will have a disability that lasts at least 90 days.[5]

Employer-sponsored or group disability insurance typically takes two forms. The first, **short-term disability insurance,** provides benefits for a limited time, usually less than 6 months. The second, **long-term disability insurance,** provides benefits for extended periods between 6 months and life. Disability criteria differ between short- and long-term plans. Short-term plans usually consider disability as an inability to perform any and every duty of the disabled person's occupation. Long-term plans use a more stringent definition, specifying disability as an inability to engage in any occupation for which the individual is qualified by reason of training, education, or experience.

Short-term disability plans classify **short-term disability** as an inability to perform the duties of one's regular job. Manifestations of short-term disability include the following temporary (short-term) conditions:

- Recovery from injuries
- Recovery from surgery
- Treatment of an illness requiring any hospitalization
- Pregnancy—the Pregnancy Discrimination Act of 1978 mandates that employers treat pregnancy and childbirth the same way they treat other causes of disability (Chapter 2)

Most short-term disability plans pay employees 50–66.67 percent of their pretax salary on a monthly or weekly basis; however, some pay as much as 100 percent. Short-term disability plans pay benefits for a limited period, usually no more than 6 months (26 weeks). Many companies set a monthly maximum benefit amount.

Three additional features of short-term disability plans include the preexisting condition clause, two waiting periods, and exclusions of particular health conditions. Similar to health insurance plans, a **preexisting condition** is a mental or physical disability for which medical advice, diagnosis, care, or treatment was received during a designated period preceding the beginning of disability insurance coverage. The designated period is usually any time prior to employment and enrollment in a company's disability insurance plan. Insurance companies impose preexisting conditions to limit their liabilities for disabilities that predate an individual's coverage.

Two waiting periods include the preeligibility period and an elimination period. The **preeligibility period** spans from the initial date of hire to the time of eligibility for coverage in a disability insurance program. Once the preeligibility period has expired, an **elimination period** refers to the minimum amount of time an employee must wait after becoming disabled before disability insurance payments begin. Elimination periods exclude insignificant illnesses or injuries that limit a person's ability to work for just a few days.

Short-term disability plans often contain exclusion provisions. **Exclusion provisions** list the particular health conditions that are ineligible for coverage. Disabilities that result from self-inflicted injuries are almost always excluded. Short-term disability plans often exclude most mental illnesses or disabilities due to chemical dependencies (e.g., addictions to alcohol or illegal drugs). Employers support addicted workers through employee assistance programs, which we will discuss shortly in this chapter.

Long-term disability insurance provides a monthly benefit to employees who, due to illness or injury, are unable to work for an extended period of time. Payments of long-term disability benefits usually begin after 3–6 months of disability and continue until retirement or for a specified number of months. Payments generally equal a fixed percentage of pre-disability earnings.

Long-term disability insurance companies rely on a two-stage definition for long-term disability. **Long-term disability** initially refers to illnesses or accidents that prevent an employee from performing his or her "own occupation" over a designated period. The term *own occupation* applies to employees based on education, training, or experience. After the designated period elapses, the definition becomes more inclusive by adding the phrase "inability to perform any occupation or to engage in any paid employment." The second-stage definition is consistent with the concept of total disability in workers' compensation programs (Chapter 11).

Long-term disability plans traditionally covered only total disabilities. Many long-term disability insurance carriers have more recently also added partial disabilities for the following reason. Including partial disabilities results in cost savings because, in most cases, totally disabled individuals avoid paid employment because they would forfeit future disability benefits. With the **partial disabilities inclusion,** long-term carriers provide supplemental benefits to cover a portion of income loss associated with part-time employment. For example, long-term disability plans become effective when part-time employment falls below a designated level expressed as a percentage of income (adjusted for cost-of-living increases) prior to the qualifying event (e.g., below 75 or 80 percent).

Full benefits usually equal 50–70 percent of monthly pretax salary, subject to a maximum dollar amount. As for short-term plans, the monthly maximum may be as high as $5,000. Long-term benefits are generally subject to a waiting period of anywhere from 6 months to 1 year and usually become active only after an employee's sick leave and short-term disability benefits have been exhausted.

Long-term disability plans also include preexisting condition and exclusion clauses. These are similar to the provisions in short-term disability plans. Long-term plans impose two waiting periods: preeligibility period and elimination period. The preeligibility periods for short- and long-term plans are usually identical. When companies offer both plans, the elimination period expires upon the exhaustion of short-term benefits. As discussed earlier, long-term plans become effective immediately following the end of short-term benefit payments, making the elimination period virtually nonexistent. When companies offer long-term plans only, the elimination period runs between 3 and 6 months following a disability.

Both short- and long-term disability plans may duplicate disability benefits mandated by the Social Security Act and state workers' compensation laws (discussed in Chapter 11). These employer-sponsored plans generally supplement legally required benefits established by the **Employee Retirement Income Security Act of 1974 (ERISA).** Employer-sponsored plans do not replace disability benefits mandated by law.

Life Insurance Employer-provided **life insurance** protects employees' families by paying a specified amount to an employee's beneficiaries upon the employee's death. Most policies pay some multiple of the employee's salary (e.g., twice the employee's annual salary). Employer-sponsored life insurance plans also frequently include accidental death and dismemberment claims, which pay additional benefits if death was the result of an accident or if the insured incurs accidental loss of a limb.

There are three kinds of life insurance: term life insurance, whole life insurance, and universal life insurance. **Term life insurance,** the most common type offered by companies, provides protection to employees' beneficiaries only during a limited period based on a specified number of years (e.g., 5 years) subject to a maximum age (e.g., 65 or 70). After that, the insurance automatically expires. Neither the employee nor his or her beneficiaries receives any benefit upon expiration. In order to continue coverage under a term life plan, an employee must renew the policy and make premium payments as long as he or she is younger than the maximum allowed age for coverage.

Whole life insurance pays an amount to the designated beneficiaries of the deceased employee, but unlike term policies, whole life plans do not terminate until payment is made to beneficiaries. As a result, whole life insurance policies are substantially more expensive than are term life policies, making the whole life insurance approach an uncommon feature of employer-sponsored insurance programs. From the employee's or his or her beneficiary's perspective, whole life insurance policies combine insurance protection with a savings (or cash accumulation plan) because a portion of the money paid to meet the policy's premium will be available in the future with a low fixed annual interest rate of usually no more than 2 or 3 percent. **Universal life insurance** provides protection to employees' beneficiaries based on the insurance feature of term life insurance and a more flexible savings or cash accumulation plan than found in whole life insurance plans.

Individuals can subscribe to life insurance on an individual basis by purchasing policies from independent insurance agents or representatives of insurance companies. On the other hand, they can subscribe to group life insurance through their employers, which has clear benefits. First, group plans allow all participants covered by the policy to benefit from coverage, and employers assume the burden of financing the plan either partly or entirely. Second, group policies permit a larger set of individuals to participate in a plan at a lower cost per person than if each person had to purchase life insurance on an individual basis.

Retirement Programs **Retirement programs,** which are often referred to as **pension plans,** provide income to employees and their beneficiaries during some or all of their retirement. Individuals may participate in more than one pension program simultaneously. It is not uncommon for employees to participate in pension plans sponsored by their companies [e.g., 401(k) plans] as well as in pension plans that they establish themselves [e.g., the individual retirement account (IRA)].

Pension program design and implementation are quite complex, largely because of the many laws that govern their operations, particularly the Employee Retirement Income Security Act of 1974 (ERISA). We will take up a detailed treatment of retirement plan design and current issues at the forefront of a company's decision whether to offer a retirement plan and, if so, in what form in Chapter 10.

HEALTH PROTECTION PROGRAMS Health protection has captured both employees' and employers' attention for several years. From the employees' perspective, health coverage is valuable, particularly as the costs of health care have increased dramatically. Total health care expenditures rose by more than 5,000 percent from $26.9 billion in 1960. From the employers' perspective, providing health care coverage is like a two-edged sword. On one hand, the costs to extend health insurance coverage to employees are rising quickly, thereby representing a substantial cost burden. On the other hand, companies recognize that offering comprehensive health insurance protection helps recruit and retain the best-qualified individuals, and employees stand to be more productive when they can afford to (and actually do) take care of health problems that could interfere with job performance. There have been many innovations in approaches to offering health care coverage to employees. We will discuss these innovations and key issues in Chapter 10.

Paid Time Off

The second type of discretionary benefit is paid time off. This category is relatively straightforward. As the name implies, paid time off policies compensate employees when they are not performing their primary work duties. The major types of paid time off are:

- Holidays
- Vacation
- Sick leave
- Personal leave
- Jury duty
- Funeral leave
- Military leave
- Clean-up, preparation, or travel time
- Rest period "break"
- Lunch period
- Integrated paid time off policies
- Sabbatical leave
- Volunteerism

Companies offer most paid time off as a matter of custom, particularly paid holidays, vacations, and sick leave. In unionized settings, the particulars about paid time off are in the collective bargaining agreement. The paid time off practices that are most typically found in unionized settings are jury duty, funeral leave, military leave, clean-up, preparation, travel time, rest period, and lunch period.

For employees and employers, paid time off benefits are significant. These benefits provide employees the opportunity to balance work and nonwork interests and demands. Companies stand to gain from sponsoring these benefits. Employees may legitimately take time off from scheduled work without incurring loss of pay and benefits, which should help reduce unapproved absenteeism from work. By keeping absenteeism in check, overall productivity and product or service quality should be higher. These benefits also contribute toward positive employee attitudes and commitment to the company, particularly for employees with longer lengths of service. As we will discuss shortly, the length of such paid time off as vacation can increase substantially with length of service.

As previously shown in Table 9-1, the majority of workers received paid time off in 2012. There have been three developments in paid time off offerings: integrated paid time off policies, sabbatical leave, and volunteerism. We will discuss each of these practices in turn, highlighting the benefits of such paid time off practices to employers.

Integrated paid time off policies or **paid time off banks** combine holiday, vacation, sick leave, and personal leave policies into a single paid time off policy. Such policies do not distinguish among reasons for absence as do specific policies. The idea is to provide individuals the freedom to schedule time off without justifying the reasons. This freedom should presumably substantially reduce the incidence of unscheduled absences that can be disruptive to the workplace because these policies require advance notice unless sudden illness is the cause (e.g., you went to sleep one evening feeling fine and then wake up the next morning on a scheduled work day with a stomach virus). Integrated paid time off policies have become an increasingly popular alternative to separate holiday, vacation, sick leave, and personal leave plans because they are more effective in controlling unscheduled absenteeism than other types of absence control policies.[6] Integrated policies also relieve the administrative burden of managing separate plans and the necessity to process medical certifications in the case of sick leave policies.

Paid time off banks do not incorporate all types of time off with pay. Bereavement and funeral leave are stand-alone policies because the death of a friend or relative is typically an unanticipated event beyond an employee's control. Integrating funeral leave into paid time off banks would also likely create dissatisfaction among workers because it would signal that grieving for a deceased friend or relative is equivalent to a casual day off. Jury duty and witness leave, military leave, and nonproduction time are influenced by law, and nonproduction time is negotiated as part of a collective bargaining agreement. Sabbatical leaves are also not included in paid time off banks because these are extended leaves provided as a reward to valued, long-service employees. **Sabbatical leaves** are paid time off for such professional activities as a research project or curriculum development. These practices are common in college and university settings and apply most often to faculty members. Most universities grant sabbatical leaves to faculty members who meet minimum service requirements (e.g., 3 years of full-time service) with partial or full pay for up to an entire academic year. The service requirement is applied each time, which limits the number of leaves taken per faculty member.

Outside academia, sabbatical leaves are usually limited to professional and managerial employees who stand to benefit from intensive training opportunities outside the company's sponsorship. Sabbatical leaves are most suitable for such employees as computer engineers whose standards of knowledge or practice are rapidly evolving. Companies establish guidelines regarding qualification, length of leave, and level of pay. An important guideline pertains to minimum length of employment following completion of a sabbatical. For example, companies require employees to remain employed for a minimum of 1 year following the sabbatical or repay part or all of one's salary received during the sabbatical. This provision is necessary to protect a company's investment and to limit moves to competitors.

Volunteerism refers to giving of one's time to support a meaningful cause. More and more companies are providing employees with paid time off to contribute to causes of their choice. From a company's standpoint, a meaningful cause is associated with the work of not-for-profit organizations such as the United Way to help improve the well-being of people. There are a multitude of meaningful causes throughout the world including improving literacy, providing comfort to terminally ill patients, serving food at shelters for individuals who cannot afford to feed themselves, serving as a mentor to children who do not have one or more parents, and spending time with elderly or disabled residents of nursing homes who may no longer have living friends or family. Companies generally do not dictate the causes for which employees would receive paid time off, except they exclude political campaign and political action groups for eligibility because of possible conflicts of interest with company shareholders and management.

Companies favor providing paid time off for volunteer work for three reasons. First, volunteer opportunities allow employees to balance work and life demands. Second, giving employees the opportunity to contribute to charitable causes on company time represents positive corporate social responsibility, enhancing the company's overall image in the public eye. Third, paid time off to volunteer is believed to help promote retention. Employees are likely to feel that the employer shares similar values, possibly boosting commitment to the company. The amount of time off ultimately varies considerably from company to company, ranging anywhere between 1 hour per week and, in limited cases for long-service employees, several weeks.

Services

EMPLOYEE ASSISTANCE PROGRAMS **Employee assistance programs (EAPs)** help employees cope with such personal problems that may impair their job performance as alcohol or drug abuse, domestic violence, the emotional impact of AIDS and other diseases, clinical depression, and eating disorders. EAPs are widely used.

Companies offer EAPs because many employees are likely to experience difficulties that interfere with job performance. Although EAP costs are substantial, the benefits seem to outweigh the costs. For example, the annual cost per employee of an EAP is approximately $50–$60. Anecdotal evidence, however, indicates that employers' gains outweigh their out-of-pocket expenses for EAPs: savings from reduced employee turnover, absenteeism, medical costs, unemployment insurance rates, workers' compensation rates, accident costs, and disability insurance costs. Most important, the majority of employees who take advantage of EAP resources benefit; unfortunately, large-scale evaluation studies are virtually nonexistent.

Depending on the employer, EAPs provide a range of services and are organized in various ways. In some companies, EAPs are informal programs developed and run on-site by in-house staff. Other employers contract with outside firms to administer their EAPs, or they rely on a combination of their own resources and help from an outside firm.

FAMILY ASSISTANCE PROGRAMS **Family assistance programs** help employees provide elder care and child care. Elder care programs provide physical, emotional, or financial assistance for aging parents, spouses, or other relatives who are not fully self-sufficient because they are too frail or disabled. Child care programs focus on supervising preschool-age dependent children whose parents work outside the home. Many employees now rely on elder care programs because of their parents' increasing longevity and the growing numbers of dual-income families. Child care needs arise from the growing number of single parents and dual-career households with children.

A variety of employer programs and benefits can help employees cope with their family responsibilities. The programs range from making referrals to on-site child care or elder care centers to company-sponsored day care programs, and they vary in the amount of financial and human resources needed to administer them. The least expensive and least labor-intensive programs are generally referral services. Referral services are designed to help workers identify and take advantage of available community resources, conveyed through such media as educational workshops, videos, employee newsletters and magazines, and EAPs.

Flexible scheduling and leave allows employees the leeway to take time off during work hours to care for relatives or react to emergencies. Flexible scheduling, which includes compressed work weeks (e.g., 10-hour days or 12-hour days), flextime, and job sharing, helps employees balance the demands of work and family. In addition to flexible work scheduling, some companies allow employees to extend their legally mandated leave sanctioned by the Family and Medical Leave Act (see Chapter 11). Under extended leave, employers typically continue to provide such employee benefits as insurance and promise to secure individuals comparable jobs upon their return.

Day care is another possible benefit. Some companies subsidize child or elder day care in community-based centers. Elder care programs usually provide self-help, meals, and entertainment activities for the participants. Child care programs typically offer supervision, preschool preparation, and meals. Facilities must usually maintain state or local licenses.

TUITION REIMBURSEMENT Companies offer **tuition reimbursement programs** to promote their employees' education. Under a tuition reimbursement program, an employer fully or partially reimburses an employee for expenses incurred for education or training. There is substantial variability in the percentage of tuition an employer reimburses. Some companies vary the percentage of tuition reimbursed according to the relevance of the course to the companies' goals or the grades employees earn.

Tuition reimbursement programs are not synonymous with pay-for-knowledge programs (Chapter 5). Instead, they fall under the category of employee benefits. Under these programs, employees choose the courses they wish to take when they want to take them. In addition, employees may enroll in courses that are not directly related to their work. As we discussed in Chapter 5, pay-for-knowledge is one kind of core compensation. Companies establish set curricula that employees take, and they generally award pay increases to employees who successfully complete courses within the curricula. Pay increases are not directly associated with tuition reimbursement programs.

TRANSPORTATION SERVICES Some employers sponsor **transportation services** programs that help bring employees to the workplace and back home again by using more energy-efficient forms of transportation. They may sponsor public transportation or vanpools: employer-sponsored vans or buses that transport employees between their homes and the workplace.

Employers provide transit subsidies to employees working in metropolitan and suburban areas served by mass transportation (e.g., buses, subways, and trains). Companies may offer transit passes, tokens, or vouchers. Practices vary from partial subsidy to full subsidy.

Many employers must offer transportation services to comply with the law. Local and state governments increasingly request that companies reduce the number of single-passenger automobiles commuting to their workplace each day because of government mandates for cleaner air. The Clean Air Act Amendments of 1990 require employers in such large metropolitan areas as Los Angeles to comply with state and local commuter-trip reduction laws. Employers may also offer transportation services to recruit individuals who do not care to drive in rush-hour traffic. Furthermore, transportation services enable companies to offset deficits in parking space availability, particularly in congested metropolitan areas.

Employees obviously stand to benefit from these transportation services. For example, using public transportation or joining a vanpool often saves money by eliminating such commuting costs as gas, insurance, car maintenance and repairs, and parking fees. Moreover, commuting time can be quite lengthy for some employees. By leaving the driving to others, employees can use the time more productively by reading, completing paperwork, or "unwinding."

OUTPLACEMENT ASSISTANCE Some companies provide technical and emotional support through **outplacement assistance** to employees who are being laid off or terminated. They do so with a variety of career and personal programs designed to develop employees' job-hunting skills and strategies and to boost employees' self-confidence. A variety of factors leads to employee termination. Those best suited to outplacement assistance programs include:

- Layoffs due to economic hardship
- Mergers and acquisitions
- Company reorganizations
- Changes in management
- Plant closings or relocation
- Elimination of specific positions, often the result of changes in technology

Outplacement assistance provides such services as personal counseling, career assessments and evaluations, training in job search techniques, resume and cover letter preparation, interviewing techniques, and training in the use of such basic workplace technology as computers. Although beneficial to employees, outplacement assistance programs hold possible benefits for companies as well. They can promote a positive image of the company among those being terminated, as well as their families and friends, by helping these employees prepare for employment opportunities.

WELLNESS PROGRAMS In the 1980s, employers began sponsoring **wellness programs** to promote and maintain employees' physical and psychological health. Wellness programs vary in scope. They may emphasize weight loss only, or they may emphasize a range of activities such as weight loss, smoking cessation, and cardiovascular fitness. Programs may be offered on- or off-site. Although some companies invest in staffing professionals for wellness programs, others contract with such external vendors as community health agencies or private health clubs. Although wellness programs are relatively new, some evidence already indicates that these innovations can save companies money and reduce employees' needs for health care.

Smoking cessation, stress reduction, nutrition and weight loss, exercise and fitness activities, and health-screening programs are the most common workplace wellness programs. Smoking cessation plans range from simple campaigns that stress the negative aspects of smoking to intensive programs directed at helping individuals to stop smoking. Many employers offer courses and treatment to help and encourage smokers to quit. Other options include offering nicotine replacement therapy (e.g., nicotine gum and patches) and self-help services. Many companies sponsor such antismoking events as the Great American Smoke-Out, during which companies distribute T-shirts, buttons, and literature that discredit smoking.

Stress management programs can help employees cope with many factors inside and outside work that contribute to stress. For instance, job conditions, health and personal problems, and personal and professional relationships can make employees anxious and therefore less productive. Symptoms of stressful workplaces include low morale, chronic absenteeism, low productivity, and high turnover rates. Employers offer stress management programs to teach workers to cope with conditions and situations that cause stress. Seminars focus on recognizing signs of stress and burnout, as well as on how to handle family- and business-related stress. Stress reduction techniques can improve quality of life inside and outside the workplace. Employers benefit from increased employee productivity, reduced absenteeism, and lower health care costs.

Weight control and nutrition programs are designed to educate employees about proper nutrition and weight loss, both of which are critical to good health. Information from the medical community has clearly indicated that excess weight and poor nutrition are significant risk factors in cardiovascular disease, diabetes, high blood pressure, and cholesterol levels. Over time, these programs should give employees better health, increased morale, and improved appearance. For employers, these programs should result in improved productivity and lower health care costs.

Companies can contribute to employees' weight control and proper nutrition by sponsoring memberships in such weight-loss programs as Weight Watchers. Sponsoring companies may also reinforce weight-loss programs' positive results through support groups, intensive counseling, competitions, and other incentives. Companies sometimes actively attempt to influence employee food choices by stocking vending machines with nutritional food.

FINANCIAL EDUCATION Some companies have added financial education to employee benefit offerings. Financial education programs provide employees with the resource for managing personal budgets and long-term savings (e.g., for retirement). Companies are increasingly including financial education as part of the benefits program. These companies reason that financial education is a relatively low-cost benefit that helps employees plan current and future (retirement) budgets.

THE BENEFITS AND COSTS OF DISCRETIONARY BENEFITS

Discretionary benefits, like core compensation, can contribute to a company's competitive advantage for the reasons discussed earlier (e.g., tax advantages and recruiting the best-qualified candidates). Discretionary benefits can also undermine the imperatives of strategic compensation. Companies that provide discretionary benefits to employees as entitlements are ultimately less likely to promote competitive advantage than companies that design discretionary employee benefits programs to fit the situation.

Management can use discretionary benefit offerings to promote particular employee behaviors that have strategic value. For instance, when employees take advantage of tuition reimbursement programs, they are more likely to contribute to the strategic imperatives of product or service differentiation or cost reduction. Knowledge acquired from job-relevant education may enhance the creative potential of employees, as well as their ability to suggest more cost-effective modes of work. On the other hand, employee stock ownership plans (ESOPs) may contribute to companies' strategic imperatives by instilling a sense of ownership in employees. Having a financial stake in the company should lead employees to behave more strategically.

A company can use discretionary benefits to distinguish itself from the competition. In effect, competitive benefits programs potentially convey the message that the company is a good place to work because it invests in the well-being of its employees. Lucrative benefits programs will presumably attract a large pool of applicants that include high-quality candidates, positioning a company to hire the best possible employees.

Finally, the tax advantage afforded companies from offering particular discretionary benefits has strategic value. In effect, the tax advantage translates into cost savings to companies. These savings can be applied to promote competitive advantage. For example, companies pursuing differentiation strategies may invest these savings into research and development programs. Companies pursuing lowest-cost strategies may be in a better position to compete because these savings may enable companies to lower the prices of their products and services without cutting into profits.

COMPENSATION IN ACTION

Many employees feel entitled to certain benefits that they consider to be the positive consequence of organizational membership. While some benefits are required by law, it will be up to the organization to decide on other benefits that are offered and administered. As a line manager or HR professional, you *might* be in charge of creating a benefits program, but you will *certainly* be called on to interpret policy in order to meet the requests of employees. Whether you are dealing with the creation or interpretation of benefits, you will want to have access to accurate information so your organization's offerings serve as true benefits for employees and not a source of frustration and ambiguity.

Action checklist for line managers and HR—helping employees understand and fully utilize benefits

HR takes the lead
- Ensure that the employee benefits handbook is up to date and accurate. Depending on the employee population, both an online version and a hard copy of the manual should be accessible.
- Create workshops to help employees understand the unique aspects of the benefits offered by the

organization—highlight confusing aspects and aspects that are not well known.
- While many companies now have call centers that answer benefits questions for employees, seek to stay up to date on company policies and legal requirements so that, when more complex benefits issues arise (e.g., long-term disability, sabbaticals, and outplacement services), the questions can be dealt with in a sensitive and timely manner.

Line managers take the lead
- Suggest ways to keep the "explaining your benefits" portion of new employee orientation engaging and interesting. The session should be conducted by HR (or the benefits specialist).
- Keep track of the most common benefits questions that arise. Seek to be educated by HR on the specifics of these specific policies so responses can be given quickly and accurately.
- When changes to benefits are made, call employees together to discuss rationale and what can be done to make full use of the existing benefits.

END OF CHAPTER

MyManagementLab

Go to **mymanagementlab.com** to complete the problems marked with this icon ⭐.

Summary

This chapter reviewed the role of discretionary benefits in strategic compensation and described the major kinds of discretionary benefits. At present, companies offer widely varied kinds of employee benefits practices. Companies are increasingly investing in protection programs and services that are designed to enhance the well-being of employees in a cost-efficient manner. As competition increases, placing greater pressures on cost-containment strategies, companies have already faced hard choices about the benefits they offer their employees. It is likely that this trend will continue in the foreseeable future.

Key Terms

welfare practices   205
short-term disability insurance   206
long-term disability insurance   206
short-term disability   206
preexisting condition   206
preeligibility period   206
elimination period   206
exclusion provisions   207
long-term disability   207
partial disabilities inclusion   207
Employee Retirement Income Security
    Act of 1974 (ERISA)   207
life insurance   207
term life insurance   208
whole life insurance   208
universal life insurance   208
retirement programs   208
pension plans   208
integrated paid time off policies   209
paid time off banks   209
sabbatical leaves   210
volunteerism   210
employee assistance programs
    (EAPs)   210
family assistance programs   211
flexible scheduling and leave   211
day care   211
tuition reimbursement programs   211
transportation services   211
outplacement assistance   212
wellness programs   212
smoking cessation   212
stress management   213
weight control and nutrition
    programs   213

⭐ Discussion Questions

9-1. Many compensation professionals are faced with making choices about which discretionary benefits to drop because funds are limited and the costs of these benefits continually increase. Assume you must make such choices. Rank-order discretionary benefits, starting with the ones you would *most likely drop* to the ones you would *least likely drop*. Explain your rationale. Do such factors as the demographic composition of the workforce of the company matter? Explain.

9-2. Discuss your views about whether discretionary employee benefits should be an entitlement or something earned based on job performance.

9-3. Assume that you are an HRM professional whose responsibility is to develop a brochure for the purpose of conveying the value of your company's benefits program to potential employees. Your company has asked you to showcase the benefits program in a manner that will encourage recruits to join the company. Develop a brochure (of no more than two pages) that meets this objective. Conduct research on companies' benefits practices (in such journals as *Benefits Quarterly*) as a basis for developing your brochure.

9-4. Your instructor will assign you an industry. Conduct some research in order to identify the prevalent employee benefits practices for that industry. Also, what factors (e.g., technology, competition, and government regulation) might influence the present practices? How will these practices change?

CASE
Time Off at Superior Software Services

⭐ *An additional Supplemental Case can be found on MyManagementLab.*

As she hangs up the telephone, Joan Jackson realizes that she needs to consider changing her company's time off policies. She just received a call from an employee reporting off work because he is sick. This is the second employee on the same project team to call off this week, and the unscheduled absence will likely cause a delay in meeting the project deadline.

Joan, the president of Superior Software Services, is proud that her company has earned a reputation for providing high-quality software solutions. Superior recruits and retains top software engineers and also an impressive administrative staff. However, even with a talented staff, Joan is concerned about the company's ongoing ability to meet project deadlines.

Over the past few months, unscheduled absences have caused Superior to delay the delivery of software products to a few clients. When a staff member calls in to take a sick day without prior notice, shifting employees to cover the work in order to meet a deadline is difficult. Joan believes Superior's time off policies may be causing some of the problems.

Superior offers employees 7 vacation days and 5 sick days each year. The company has a policy that employees may use sick days only for illness or emergencies. Employees may not schedule sick days in advance. Vacation days are scheduled at the beginning of the year. Employees receive approval of their requested vacation days on a seniority basis, so most employees designate the days they will take their vacation within the first few weeks of a new year so they are able to effectively plan vacation travel.

Joan believes Superior's current time off policy creates an incentive for employees to call off at the last minute. She has learned from supervisors that many employees use their sick days to take care of personal business such as attending parent–teacher conferences or running personal errands. These are often events that could be prescheduled time off, but employees do not feel they have a time off option to address such needs. Sick days can't be prescheduled, and vacation days are often already committed at the beginning of the year.

Joan believes that changing the time off policies could reduce the number of unscheduled absences, but she is not sure if her idea will address her concerns. She is considering replacing the current vacation/sick day allowance with a paid time off (PTO) bank. Employees would receive 12 PTO days each year. They would be permitted to schedule preferred days off at the beginning of the year so that they can make vacation travel plans, and the remaining days could be saved for days when the employee is ill or could be scheduled ahead of time to take care of personal business. Joan believes this change will encourage employees to schedule their time off in advance when possible. With advance notice of absences, supervisors will be better able to plan projects and meet deadlines.

Questions:
9-5. Do you think changing Superior's time off policies will decrease unscheduled time off?
9-6. Beyond reducing occurrences of unscheduled time off, are there any other benefits to offering PTO?
9-7. Are there any disadvantages to offering PTO?

MyManagementLab

Go to **mymanagementlab.com** for Auto-graded writing questions as well as the following Assisted-graded writing questions:

⭐ 9-8. What are the components of discretionary benefits? Provide two examples for each component of discretionary benefits.

⭐ 9-9. What kind of discretionary benefits would help companies to have better control over absenteeism?

Endnotes

1. U.S. Bureau of Labor Statistics. (2012). *Employer Costs for Employee Compensation—September 2012*. Available: *www.bls.gov*, accessed March 3, 2013.

2. U.S. Bureau of Labor Statistics. (1919). *Welfare Work for Employees in Industrial Establishments in the United States*. Bulletin # 250, pp. 119–123.

3. U.S. Bureau of Labor Statistics. (2012). *National Compensation Survey: Employee Benefits in the United States, March 2012* (USDL 12-1380). Available: *www.bls.gov*, accessed March 3, 2013.

4. Solnick, L. (1985). The effect of the blue collar unions on white collar wages and benefits. *Industrial and Labor Relations Review*, *38*, pp. 23–35.

5. Martocchio, J. J. (2014). *Employee Benefits: A Primer for the Human Resource Professional* (5th ed.). Burr Ridge, IL: Irwin/McGraw-Hill.

6. Markowich, M. M. (2007). *Paid Time-Off Banks*. Phoenix, AZ: WorldatWork Press.

10

EMPLOYER-SPONSORED RETIREMENT PLANS AND HEALTH INSURANCE PROGRAMS

MyManagementLab®

⭐ **Improve Your Grade!**

When you see this icon, visit **www.mymanagementlab.com** for activities that are applied, personalized, and offer immediate feedback.

LEARNING OBJECTIVES

When you finish studying this chapter, you should be able to:

1. State the definitions of qualified plans and nonqualified plans and indicate the main difference between them.
2. List nine minimum standards for qualified plans.
3. Explain what defined benefit plans are.
4. Explain what defined contribution plans are.
5. List and summarize two types of defined contribution plans.
6. Identify and summarize three broad classes of health insurance programs.
7. Briefly state the rationale for consumer-driven health care.

EXPLORING RETIREMENT PLANS

In Chapter 2, we learned that retirement or pension plans function by providing "retirement income to employees, or resulting in a deferral of income by employees for periods extending to the termination of covered employment or beyond, regardless of the method of calculating the contributions made in the plan, the method of calculating benefits under the plan, or the method of distributing benefits from the plan."[1]

The purpose of this chapter is to review the fundamentals of company-sponsored retirement plan and health care insurance design. It is essential to note that individuals may receive retirement benefits from as many as three sources. First, employer-sponsored retirement plans provide employees with income after they have met a minimum retirement age and have left the company. Second, the Social Security Old-Age, Survivor, and Disability Insurance (OASDI) program, to be described in Chapter 11, provides government-mandated retirement income to employees who have made sufficient contributions through payroll taxes. Third, individuals may use their initiative to take advantage of tax regulations that have created such retirement programs as individual retirement accounts (IRAs) and Roth IRAs.

Companies establish retirement or pension plans following one of three design configurations: a defined benefit plan, a defined contribution plan, or hybrid plans that combine features of traditional defined benefit and defined contribution plans. Defined benefit plans guarantee retirement benefits specified in the plan document. This benefit usually is expressed in terms of a monthly sum equal to a percentage of a participant's preretirement pay multiplied by the number of years he or she has worked for the employer. Defined contribution plans may require that employers and employees make annual contributions to retirement fund accounts established for each participating employee, based on a formula contained in the plan document.

In addition, tax incentives encourage companies to offer pension programs. Some of the Employee Retirement Income Security Act of 1974 (ERISA) Title I and Title II provisions set the minimum standards required to "qualify" pension plans for favorable tax treatment. Failure to meet any of the minimum standard provisions "disqualifies" pension plans for favorable tax treatment. Pension plans that meet these minimum standards are known as **qualified plans. Nonqualified plans** refer to pension plans that do not meet at least one of the minimum standard provisions; typically, highly paid employees benefit from participation in nonqualified plans. We will discuss qualified plans in this chapter and touch upon nonqualified plans in Chapter 12 on executive compensation.

From here, we will explore the minimum standards that distinguish qualified plans from nonqualified plans. Afterward, we will examine the features of alternative company-sponsored pension plans, including defined benefit plans, defined contribution plans, and hybrid plans.

Origins of Employer-Sponsored Retirement Benefits

Until World War II, pension plans were adopted primarily in the railroad, banking, and public utility industries. The most significant growth occurred since the favorable tax treatment of pensions was established through the passage of the Revenue Act of 1921 and government-imposed wage increase controls during World War II in the early 1940s. This led companies to adopt discretionary employee benefits plans such as pensions that were excluded from those wage increase restrictions.

The current tax treatment of qualified plans continues to provide incentives both for employers to establish plans and for employees to participate in them. In general, a contribution to a qualified plan is deductible in computing the employer's or employee's taxes based on who made the contribution. Employees pay taxes only on the amount they withdraw from the plan each year. As we discussed in Chapter 2, this preferential tax treatment is contingent on the employer's compliance with ERISA.

Trends in Retirement Plan Coverage and Costs

According to the U.S. Bureau of Labor Statistics, nearly 55 percent of workers employed in the private sector participated in at least one company-sponsored retirement plan in 1992–1993.[2] Since then, the participation rate has declined to approximately 48 percent in 2012.[3] However, there has been a noticeable decrease in participation rates for defined benefit plans over the past several years. In 1992–1993, 32 percent of private sector employees participated in defined contribution plans, and slightly fewer participated in defined benefit plans.[4] In 2012, 41 percent participated in defined contribution plans, but only 17 percent participated in defined benefit plans.[5]

There are two important explanations for these trends in retirement plan participation. First, there has been a shift in the labor force toward different occupations and industries. There has specifically been a relative decline in employment among full-time workers, union workers, and workers in goods-producing businesses. The decline in full-time workers and increase in part-time workers has led to fewer opportunities for participation in company-sponsored retirement plans. Employers quite simply often employ part-time workers to save benefits costs. The decline in union affiliation (i.e., union members or just part of the bargaining unit) also contributes to the overall trends described earlier. In 2012, more employees affiliated with unions were eligible to participate in a retirement plan (defined benefit, 66 percent; defined contribution, 45 percent) than nonunion employees (defined benefit, 12 percent; defined contribution, 41 percent).[6] As we discussed in Chapter 2, unions represent workers in negotiations with management over terms of employment. The inclusion of lucrative retirement plans was among the top priorities in negotiations to maintain the support of middle-age and older workers. Finally, among employment trends, the expansion of service industries relative to somewhat stable employment in the goods-producing sector helps to explain retirement plan participation. In 2012, fewer service-oriented workers had access to defined benefit plans (17 percent versus 27 percent), although the percentage of workers with access to defined contribution plans was higher in both industries (57 percent versus 69 percent); however, actual employee participation in defined contribution plans was substantially lower in service employers than in goods-producing companies.[7] Wages in the service-producing companies tend to be lower than they are in goods-producing companies. It is possible that service employees simply do not have enough money to set aside for retirement.

There is a second reason for changes away from participation in defined benefit plans to defined contribution plans. Defined benefit plans are quite costly to employers compared with defined contribution plans: Companies struggle to fund these plans adequately to ensure that retirees receive entitled benefits for the remainder of their lives. In addition, as discussed in Chapter 2, the Pension Benefit Guaranty Corporation (PBGC) serves as the insurer by taking over pension obligations for companies that terminate their defined benefit plans because of severe financial stress. Companies with defined benefit plans pay premiums to the PBGC to insure defined benefit plans in the event of severe financial distress. The Pension Protection Act requires that companies that are at high risk of not meeting their pension obligations pay substantially more to insure defined benefit plans, adding to the substantial cost.

QUALIFIED PLANS

Qualified plans entitle employers and employees to substantial tax benefits. Employers and employees specifically do not pay tax on their contributions within dollar limits that differ for defined benefit and defined contribution plans. In addition, the investment earnings of the trust in which plan assets are held are generally exempt from tax. Finally, participants or beneficiaries do not pay taxes on the value of retirement benefits until they receive distributions.

Minimum Standards for Qualified Plans

Qualified plans possess 13 fundamental characteristics. Table 10-1 lists these characteristics. We will review some of the more fundamental standards in this chapter.

PARTICIPATION REQUIREMENTS   Strict participation requirements apply to pension plans. Employees must specifically be allowed to participate in pension plans after they have reached age 21[8] and have completed 1 year of service (based on 1,000 work hours).[9] These hours include all paid time for performing work and paid time off (e.g., vacation, sick leave, and holidays).

TABLE 10-1   Characteristics of Qualified Pension Plans

- Participation requirements
- Coverage requirements
- Vesting rules
- Accrual rules
- Nondiscrimination rules: Testing
- Key employee and top-heavy provisions
- Minimum funding standards
- Social Security integration
- Contribution and benefit limits
- Plan distribution rules
- Qualified survivor annuities
- Qualified domestic relations orders
- Plan termination rules and procedures

COVERAGE REQUIREMENTS **Coverage requirements** limit the freedom of employers to exclude employees. Qualified plans do not disproportionately favor highly compensated employees.[10]

VESTING RULES **Vesting** refers to an employee's nonforfeitable rights to pension benefits.[11] There are two aspects of vesting. First, employees are always vested in their contributions to pension plans. Second, companies must grant full vesting rights to employer contributions on one of the following two schedules: **cliff vesting** or **6-year graduated schedule**). Cliff vesting schedules must grant employees 100 percent vesting after no more than 3 years of service. That is, after 3 years of participation in the pension plan, an employee has the right to receive all of the contributions plus interest on the contributions made by the employer. This schedule is known as cliff vesting because leaving one's job prior to becoming vested under this schedule is tantamount to falling off a cliff because an employee loses all of the accrued employer contributions. On the other hand, companies may use a gradual vesting schedule. The 6-year graduated schedule allows workers to become 20 percent vested after 2 years and to vest at a rate of 20 percent each year thereafter until they are 100 percent vested after 6 years of service. Table 10-2 shows an example of the 6-year graduated schedule. Plans may have faster gradual schedules to 100 percent vesting in fewer than 6 years. The graduated schedule is preferable to employees who anticipate changing jobs frequently because they will earn the rights to keep part of the employer's contribution sooner. Moreover, employees recognize that layoffs are more common in today's volatile business environment, and they stand to benefit by earning partial vesting rights sooner than earning full vesting rights at a later date. On the other hand, employers prefer the cliff vesting schedule recognizing that many employees tend to change jobs more frequently than ever before, allowing the employers to reclaim nonvested contributions for employees who leave before becoming vested.

ACCRUAL RULES Qualified plans are subject to minimum accrual rules based on the Internal Revenue Code (IRC) and ERISA.[12] **Accrual rules** specify the rate at which participants accumulate (or earn) benefits.

Defined benefit and defined contribution plans use different accrual rules. These will be discussed briefly in subsequent sections of this chapter.

NONDISCRIMINATION RULES: TESTING **Nondiscrimination rules** prohibit employers from discriminating in favor of highly compensated employees in contributions or benefits, availability of benefits, rights, or plan features.[13] In addition, employers may not amend pension plans so that highly compensated employees are favored.

BENEFIT AND CONTRIBUTION LIMITS Benefit limits refer to the maximum annual amount an employee may receive from a qualified defined benefit plan during retirement. Contribution limits apply to defined contribution plans. Employers are limited in the amount they may contribute to an employee's defined contribution plan each year. The Economic Growth and Tax Relief Reconciliation Act of 2001 amended IRC Section 415, mandating increases in these

TABLE 10-2 **Sample of a 6-Year Graduated Vesting Schedule under ERISA**

Years of Vesting Service	Nonforfeitable Percentage (%)
2	20
3	40
4	60
5	80
6	100

limits effective after December 31, 2001, and indexing them each year for inflation to keep retirement savings from falling behind increases in the cost of goods and services, thereby making retirees less dependent on Social Security retirement benefits (Chapter 11). The limits were set to expire after 2009, but the Pension Protection Act of 2006 made the limits permanent. We will review these limits in our respective discussions of defined benefit and defined contribution plans.

ALLOWABLE TAX DEDUCTIONS FOR EMPLOYERS Employers may take tax deductions for contributions to employee retirement plans based on three conditions. First, as you have read, retirement plans must be qualified. Second, an employer must make contributions before the due date for its federal income tax return for that year. For example, an employer received a tax deduction on contributions for 2013 when the contributions were made before April 15, 2014. Third, deductible contributions are based on designated amounts set forth by the IRC (as subsequently amended by the Economic Growth and Tax Relief Reconciliation Act of 2001 and the Pension Protection Act of 2006).

PLAN DISTRIBUTION RULES **Distribution** refers to the payment of vested benefits to participants or beneficiaries. Distributions are payable in a variety of ways. **Lump sum distributions** are single payments of benefits. In defined contribution plans, lump sum distributions equal the vested amount (i.e., the sum of all employee and vested employer contributions and interest on this sum). In defined benefit plans, lump sum distributions equal the equivalent of the vested accrued benefit.

A second form of distribution is the annuity. **Annuities** represent a series of payments for the life of the participant and beneficiary. Annuity contracts are usually purchased from insurance companies, which make payments according to the contract. The inherent risk of defined contribution plans has given rise to income annuities. **Income annuities** distribute income to retirees based on retirement savings paid to insurance companies in exchange for guaranteed monthly checks for life.

PLAN TERMINATION RULES AND PROCEDURES **Plan termination rules** and procedures apply only to defined benefit plans. There are three types of plan terminations: standard termination, distress termination, and involuntary termination. Qualified plans must follow strict guidelines for plan terminations including sufficient notification to plan participants, notification to the PBGC, and distribution of vested benefits to participants and beneficiaries in a reasonable amount of time.

DEFINED BENEFIT PLANS

Defined benefit plans guarantee retirement benefits specified in the plan document. This benefit is usually expressed in terms of a monthly sum equal to a percentage of a participant's preretirement pay multiplied by the number of years he or she has worked for the employer. Although the benefit in these plans is fixed by a formula, the level of required employer contributions fluctuates from year to year. The level depends on the amount necessary to make certain that benefits promised will be available when participants and beneficiaries are eligible to receive them.

Annual benefits are usually based on age, years of service, and final average wages or salary. Retirement plan formulas specify annual retirement benefits as a percentage of final average salary. Table 10-3 illustrates these percentages for one retirement plan based on age and years of service. Looking at this table, let's assume Mary retires at age 59 with 35 years of service. Let's also assume her final average salary is $52,500. Mary multiplies $52,500 by the annual percentage of 68.20 percent. Her annual benefit is $35,805.00 ($52,500 × 68.20 percent).

Minimum Funding Standards

As we discussed in Chapter 2, ERISA imposes strict funding requirements on qualified plans. Under defined benefit plans, employers make an annual contribution that is sufficiently large to ensure that promised benefits will be available to retirees. Actuaries periodically review several

TABLE 10-3 **Annual Retirement Benefits for a Defined Benefit Plan**

Years of Service	Age					
	60	59	58	57	56	55
5	...	...	...	...	...	...
6	...	...	...	...	...	...
7	...	...	...	...	...	...
8	13.36	12.56	11.76	10.96	10.15	9.35
9	15.03	14.13	13.23	12.32	11.42	10.52
10	16.70	15.70	14.70	13.69	12.69	11.69
	.					
	.					
	.					
	.					
35	68.20	68.20	68.20	68.20	68.20	68.20
36	70.50	70.50	70.50	70.50	70.50	70.50
37	72.80	72.80	72.80	72.80	72.80	72.80
38	75.10	75.00	75.00	75.00	75.00	75.00
39	77.40	75.00	75.00	75.00	75.00	75.00
40	79.70	75.00	75.00	75.00	75.00	75.00
+40	80.00	75.00	75.00	75.00	75.00	75.00

kinds of information to determine a sufficient funding level: life expectancies of employees and their designated beneficiaries, projected compensation levels, and the likelihood of employees terminating their employment before they have earned benefits. ERISA imposes the reporting of actuarial information to the Internal Revenue Service (IRS), which in turn submits these data to the U.S. Department of Labor. The Department of Labor reviews the data to ensure compliance with ERISA regulations.

Benefit Limits and Tax Deductions

The IRC sets a maximum annual benefit for defined benefit plans that is equal to the lesser of $205,000 in 2013 or 100 percent of the highest average compensation for 3 consecutive years.[14] The limit is indexed for inflation in $5,000 increments each year beginning after 2006.[15]

DEFINED CONTRIBUTION PLANS

Under **defined contribution plans,** employers and employees make annual contributions to separate accounts established for each participating employee, based on a formula contained in the plan document. Formulas typically call for employers to contribute a given percentage of each participant's compensation annually. Employers invest these funds on behalf of the employee, choosing from a variety of investment vehicles such as company stocks, diversified stock market funds, or federal government bond funds. Employees may be given a choice of investment vehicles based on the guidelines established by the employer. Defined contribution plans specify rules for the amount of annual contributions. Unlike defined benefit plans, these plans do not guarantee particular benefit amounts. Participants bear the risk of possible investment gain or loss. Benefit amounts depend on several factors, including the contribution amounts, the performance of investments, and forfeitures transferred to participant accounts.

Individual Accounts

Defined contribution plans contain accounts for each employee into which contributions are made and losses are debited or gains are credited. Contributions to each employee's account come from four possible sources. The first, employer contributions, is expressed as a percentage of an employee's wage or salary. In the case of profit sharing plans, company profits are usually the basis for employer contributions. The second, employee contributions, is usually expressed as a percentage of the employee's wage or salary. The third, **forfeitures,** comes from the accounts of employees who terminated their employment prior to earning vesting rights. The fourth contribution source is return on investments. In the case of negative returns (or loss), the corresponding amount is debited from employees' accounts.

Investments of Contributions

ERISA requires that a named **fiduciary** manage investments into defined contribution plans. Fiduciaries are individuals who manage employee benefit plans and pension funds. Fiduciaries also possess discretion in managing the assets of the plan, offering investment advice to employee participants and administering the plan. Fiduciaries ultimately are responsible for minimizing the risk of loss of assets.[16]

Employee Participation in Investments

Some companies may allow plan participants to choose the investment of funds in their individual accounts. It is not uncommon for large companies to offer investment alternatives through such companies as Fidelity, Vanguard, and T. Rowe Price.

Minimum Funding Standards

The minimum funding standard for defined contribution plans is less complex than it is for defined benefit plans. This standard is met when contributions to the individual accounts of plan participants meet the minimum amounts as specified by the plan.[17]

Contribution Limits and Tax Deductions

Employer contributions to defined contribution plans represent one factor in annual additions. **Annual addition** refers to the annual maximum allowable contribution to a participant's account in a defined contribution plan. The annual addition includes employer contributions, employee contributions, and forfeitures allocated to the participant's account.[18] In 2013, annual additions were limited to the lesser of $51,000 or 100 percent of the participant's compensation.[19]

The amount of an employer's annual deductible contribution to a participant's account depends on the type of defined contribution plan.[20] The Economic Growth and Tax Reconciliation Act of 2001 raised the allowable contribution amounts in effect before January 1, 2002. In 2013, the maximum contribution to a profit sharing, stock bonus, or employee stock ownership plan was 25 percent of the compensation paid or accrued to participants in the plan. Section 401(k), 403(b), and 457 plans have contribution limits of $17,500 in 2013. The limit is indexed for inflation in $500 increments beginning in 2007.

TYPES OF DEFINED CONTRIBUTION PLANS

There are a variety of defined contribution plans. These include Section 401(k) plans, profit sharing, stock bonus plans, employee stock ownership plans, savings incentive match plans for employees (SIMPLEs), Section 403(b) tax-deferred annuities, and Section 457 plans. We will review each of these plans in turn.

Section 401(k) Plans

Section 401(k) plans are retirement plans named after the section of the IRC that created them. These plans, also known as cash or deferred arrangements (CODAs), permit employees to defer part of their compensation to the trust of a qualified defined contribution plan. Only private sector or tax-exempt employers are eligible to sponsor 401(k) plans.

Section 401(k) plans offer three noteworthy tax benefits. First, employees do not pay income taxes on their contributions to the plan until they withdraw funds. Second, employers deduct their contributions to the plan from taxable income. Third, investment gains are not taxed until participants receive payments.

Profit Sharing Plans

Companies set up **profit sharing plans** to distribute money to employees. Companies start by establishing a **profit sharing pool** (i.e., the money earmarked for distribution to employees). Companies may also choose to fund profit sharing plans based on gross sales revenue or some basis other than profits. Companies may also take a tax deduction for their contributions not to exceed 25 percent of the plan participants' compensation in 2013.[21] As described in the previous section, a qualified profit sharing plan may be the basis for a company's 401(k) plan.

Stock Bonus Plans

A stock bonus plan may be the basis for a company's 401(k) plan. Qualified stock bonus plans and qualified profit sharing plans are similar because both plans invest in company securities. These plans are also similar regarding nondiscrimination testing requirements and the deductibility of employer contributions; however, stock bonus plans reward employees with company stock (i.e., equity shares in the company). Benefits are usually paid in shares of company stock.

Employee Stock Ownership Plans

Employee stock option plans (ESOPs) may be the basis for a company's 401(k) plan, and these plans invest in company securities, making them similar to profit sharing plans and stock bonus plans. ESOPs and profit sharing plans differ because ESOPs usually make distributions in company stock rather than cash. ESOPs are essentially stock bonus plans that use borrowed funds to purchase stock.

Table 10-4 summarizes selected differences between defined benefit and defined contribution plans.

TABLE 10-4 Selected Differences between Defined Benefit and Defined Contribution Plans

Characteristic	Defined Benefit Plan	Defined Contribution Plan
Benefit formula	Determines pension due at normal retirement age.	Determines amount regularly contributed to individual account.
Form of benefit expressed by formula	An annuity—a series of payments beginning at the plan's normal retirement age for the life of the participant.	A single lump sum distribution at any time.
Funding	Annual funding is based on an actuarial formula subject to strict limits set by the IRC and is not equivalent to annual increases in pension benefits.	Annual contributions and investment earnings are held in an individual account.
Investment risk/profit	Employee is guaranteed benefits regardless of investment returns on trust. Employer is responsible for ensuring sufficient funding to pay promised benefit.	Employee bears the investment risk, which can result in higher investment returns or the loss of previously accumulated pension benefits.
Insured benefit	Generally insured by PBGC.	By individual investment vehicle, if any.

Source: U.S. General Accounting Office (2000). *Cash Balance Plans: Implications for Retirement Income*, GAO/HEHS-00-207. Washington, DC: General Accounting Office, pp. 9–10.

HYBRID PLANS: CASH BALANCE PLANS

Hybrid plans combine features of traditional defined benefit and defined contribution plans. We will discuss the cash balance plans, a type of hybrid plan that has stirred tremendous controversy in recent years.

In January 2012, employees had worked for their current employer for a median value of 4.6 years; those ages 45–54 had worked for their current employer a median value of 7.8 years.[22] Younger workers ages 25–34 had worked a median value of 3.2 years. These data suggest workers may be accumulating retirement benefits from several jobs; employers have attempted to deal with these changing needs by seeking alternative approaches to providing retirement income.

The different career plans of the younger generations in particular have led many employers to conclude that their retirement plans were not beneficial to these younger, more mobile workers. This was not conducive to attracting potentially valuable employees that could help increase efficiency.[23]

Internal Revenue Service guidelines define **cash balance plans** as "defined benefit plans that define benefits for each employee by reference to the amount of the employee's hypothetical account balance."[24] Cash balance plans are a relatively new phenomenon compared to traditional defined benefit and defined contribution plans. Many companies have chosen to convert their defined benefit plans to cash balance plans for two key reasons. First, cash balance plans are less costly to employers than defined benefit plans. Second, they pay out benefits in a lump sum instead of a series of payments. This feature increases the portability of pension benefits from company to company. Companies are presumably in a better position to recruit more mobile workers

In sum, we explored the origins of retirement plans and the trends in coverage. We also reviewed the criteria that must be met in order to qualify retirement plans for tax benefits for employers and employees. Finally, we reviewed the major types of retirement plans, including defined benefit plans, defined contribution plans, and hybrid plans.

DEFINING AND EXPLORING HEALTH INSURANCE PROGRAMS

Health insurance covers the costs of a variety of services that promote sound physical and mental health, including physical examinations, diagnostic testing, surgery, hospitalization, psychotherapy, dental treatments, and corrective prescription lenses for vision deficiencies. Employers usually enter into a contractual relationship with one or more insurance companies to provide health-related services for their employees and, if specified, employees' dependents. An **insurance policy** refers to a contractual relationship between the insurance company and the beneficiary. The contractual relationship, or insurance policy, specifies the amount of money the insurance company will pay for such particular services as physical examinations. Employers pay insurance companies a negotiated amount, or **premium,** to establish and maintain insurance policies. The term *insured* refers to employees covered by the insurance policy.

Companies can choose from three broad classes of health insurance programs in the United States, including *fee-for-service plans*, *managed care plans*, and *point-of-service plans. Point-of-service plans* combine features of fee-for-service and managed care plans. An emerging class of health insurance programs is based on *consumer-driven health care*, where employees play a greater role in decisions on their health care, have better access to information to make informed decisions, and share more in the costs. We discuss these types of plans later in this chapter.

Origins of Health Insurance Benefits

The Great Depression of the 1930s gave rise to employer-sponsored health insurance programs. Widespread unemployment made it impossible for most individuals to afford health care. During this period, Congress proposed the Social Security Act of 1935 to address many of the social maladies caused by the adverse economic conditions, incorporating health insurance programs.

President Franklin D. Roosevelt, however, opposed the inclusion of health coverage under the Social Security Act. Health insurance did not become part of the Social Security Act until an amendment to the act in 1965 established the Medicare program.

The government's choice not to offer health care benefits created opportunities for private sector companies to meet the public's need. In the 1930s, hospitals controlled nonprofit companies that inspired today's Blue Cross and Blue Shield plans. At the time, Blue Cross plans allowed individuals to make monthly payments to cover the expense of possible future hospitalization. For-profit companies also formed to provide health care coverage, creating fee-for-service plans.

In the 1940s, local medical associations created nonprofit Blue Shield plans, which were prepayment plans for physician services. The federal government also imposed wage freezes during World War II, which did not extend to employee benefit plans. Many employers began offering health care benefits to help compete for and retain the best employees, particularly during the labor shortage when U.S. troops were overseas fighting in World War II. In addition, employers recognized the possibility that they could promote productivity with healthier workforces. Without the assistance of employer-sponsored health insurance, employees could not afford to pay for medical services on their own. Many companies sought ways to promote productivity and morale through the implementation of welfare practices. We define welfare practices as "anything for the comfort and improvement, intellectual or social, of the employees, over and above wages paid, which is not a necessity of the industry nor required by law."[25] Health insurance programs were among these practices.

Many companies discontinued health insurance benefits soon after the government lifted the wage freeze. The withdrawal of these and other benefits created discontent among employees, who viewed benefits as an entitlement. Legal battles ensued based on the claim that health protection was a fundamental right. In unionized companies, health insurance benefits became a mandatory subject of collective bargaining.

The 1950s were relatively uneventful years regarding employee benefits. In the 1960s, the federal government amended the Social Security Act. Titles XVIII and XIX of the act established the Medicare and Medicaid programs (Chapter 11), respectively. These public programs provided access to health care services for a wide segment of the U.S. population in a relatively short period. The demand for health care services rose quickly relative to the supply of health care providers, prompting inflation in the price of health care services.

Congress enacted ERISA to protect employee interests (Chapter 2). By providing financial incentives to companies, subject to becoming federally qualified, the **Health Maintenance Organization Act of 1973 (HMO Act)** promoted the use of health maintenance organizations.

Since the 1970s, there has been substantial emphasis on managing costs, and consideration has been given to providing coverage to the uninsured (e.g., the failed national health care proposal under President Bill Clinton). Some factors have eroded health insurance practices in companies. Unionized companies set the standards for employee benefits practices. In the 1980s, unions made concessions on wages and benefits in exchange for promises of greater job security. Also, the decline in the manufacturing or goods-producing sector (e.g., automobiles, steel, and mining), which was traditionally highly unionized, gave way to the typically non-union service and information sectors of the economy (e.g., health care industry, retail trade, and high-technology companies such as in software development). Furthermore, foreign competition created pressures, forcing U.S. companies to reduce costs. For example, many U.S. manufacturers moved operations to foreign countries with cheaper labor and fewer legal protections for employees (e.g., People's Republic of China and India). Notwithstanding these pressures, health insurance still is the mainstay of employee benefits programs in companies.

Health Insurance Coverage and Costs

Both employees and employers place a great deal of significance on company-sponsored health insurance benefits. Of course, company-sponsored programs provide employees with the means

TABLE 10-5 **Percentage of Workers with Access to Health Care, by Selected Characteristics, Private Industry**

	Medical Care	Dental Care	Vision Care	Prescription Drug Coverage
All employees	70	45	25	69
Worker characteristics				
Full-time	86	56	30	85
Part-time	24	13	8	23
Union	94	73	56	93
Nonunion	67	42	21	66
Establishment characteristics				
Goods producing	86	56	32	82
Service producing	67	43	23	75
1–99 workers	41	30	12	56
100 workers or more	63	63	27	84

Source: U.S. Department of Labor. (September 2012). *Employee Benefits in the United States, March 2012.* Available: *www.bls.gov,* accessed March 31, 2013.

to afford expensive health care services. As we noted before, companies stand to gain from sponsoring these benefits in at least two ways. First, a healthier workforce should experience a lower incidence of sickness absenteeism. By keeping absenteeism in check, a company can keep overall productivity and product or service quality higher. Second, health insurance offerings should help the recruitment and retention of employees. It is not surprising that a large percentage of companies include health insurance programs as a feature of employee benefits programs, extending coverage to substantial numbers of employees and their dependents. At the same time, the rampant rise in health care prices is putting substantial pressure on cost-conscious companies.

Approximately 70 percent of all private sector employees had access to at least one employer-sponsored health insurance program in 2012.[26] Employees' access to health insurance programs vary by their size, industry group, and union presence. A higher percentage of employees in larger companies had access to employer-sponsored health insurance than employees in smaller companies. This is also the case for employees in goods-producing companies compared with service-producing companies and for union employees compared with nonunion employees. Table 10-5 illustrates these facts in greater detail.

Many private sector companies require employees to contribute a portion of health insurance premiums because of the considerable cost.[27] In 2012, employee contributions represented a relatively small percentage of the health insurance premiums. Employees with single coverage, on average, contributed 21 percent, and those with family coverage contributed 32 percent. **Single coverage** extends benefits only to the covered employee, averaging $356.33 monthly per employee. **Family coverage** offers benefits to the covered employee and his or her family members as defined by the plan (usually, spouse and children). Family coverage is substantially more expensive than single coverage, averaging $857.66 monthly per employee.[28]

We will now turn our attention to long-standing and newer approaches to health insurance coverage.

FEE-FOR-SERVICE PLANS

Three long-standing forms of health insurance programs include fee-for-service plans, managed care plans, and point-of-service plans. Larger employers commonly offer employees one or more types of health insurance programs. We discuss each of these in turn.

Fee-for-service plans provide protection against health care expenses in the form of a cash benefit paid to the insured or directly to the health care provider after the employee has received health care services. These plans pay benefits on a reimbursement basis. Three types of eligible health expenses are hospital expenses, surgical expenses, and physician charges. Under fee-for-service plans, policyholders (employees) may generally select any licensed physician, surgeon, or medical facility for treatment, and the insurer reimburses the policyholders after medical services are rendered.

There are two types of fee-for-service plans. The first type, **indemnity plans,** is based on a contract between the employer and an insurance company. The contract specifies the expenses that are covered and the rate. The second type, **self-funded plans,** operates in the same fashion as indemnity plans.

The main difference between insurance plans offered by insurance companies and self-funded insurance plans centers on how benefits provided to policyholders are financed. When companies elect indemnity plans, they establish a contract with an independent insurance company. Insurance companies pay benefits from their financial reserves, which are based on the premiums companies and employees pay to receive insurance. Companies may instead choose to self-fund employee insurance. Such companies pay benefits directly from their own assets, either current cash flow or funds set aside in advance for potential future claims. The decision to self-fund is based on financial considerations. **Self-funding** makes sense when a company's financial burden of covering employee medical expenses is less than the cost to subscribe to an insurance company for coverage. By not paying premiums in advance to an independent carrier, a company retains these funds for current cash flow.

Fee-for-service plans provide three types of medical benefits under a specified policy: hospital expense benefits, surgical expense benefits, and physician expense benefits. Companies sometimes select major medical plans to provide comprehensive medical coverage instead of limiting coverage to the three specific kinds just noted or to supplement these specific benefits.

Features of Fee-for-Service Plans

Fee-for-service plans contain a variety of stipulations designed to control costs and to limit a covered individual's financial liability. Common fee-for-service stipulations include deductibles, coinsurance, out-of-pocket maximums, preexisting condition clauses, preadmission certification, second surgical opinions, and maximum benefits limits.

DEDUCTIBLE A common feature of fee-for-service plans is the **deductible.** Over a designated period, employees must pay for services (i.e., meet a deductible) that they have to pay before insurance benefits become active. The deductible amount is modest, usually a fixed amount ranging anywhere between $100 and $500 depending on the plan. Deductible amounts may also depend on annual earnings, expressed either as a fixed amount for a range of earnings or as a percentage of income. Table 10-6 illustrates deductibles based on annual salary. The deductible feature applies to a designated period, usually a 1-year period that corresponds with the calendar year or the company's benefit plan year (see Chapter 11).

COINSURANCE Insurance plans feature coinsurance, which becomes relevant after the insured pays the annual deductible. **Coinsurance** refers to the percentage of covered expenses paid by the insured. Most indemnity plans stipulate 20 percent coinsurance. This means that the plan will pay 80 percent of covered expenses, whereas the policyholder is responsible for the difference, in this case 20 percent.

Coinsurance amounts vary according to the type of expense. Insurance plans most commonly apply no coinsurance for diagnostic testing and 20 percent for other medical services. Many insurance plans provide benefits for mental health services. Coinsurance rates for these services tend to be the highest, usually 50 percent.

TABLE 10-6 Plan Year Deductibles

The benefits described in this summary represent the major areas of coverage. The plan year is July 1–June 30 of the following year.

Plan year deductible	The plan year deductible is indexed to salary for employees. See the following table for current plan year information.	
Additional deductibles	Each emergency room visit	$200
	Non-PPO hospital admission	$200
	Transplant deductible	$100

Employee's Annual Salary (Based on each employee's annual salary as of April 1)	Member Plan Year Deductible	Family Plan Year Deductible Cap
$52,700 or less	$250	$300
$52,701–$66,000	$350	$400
$66,001 or more	$450	$550
Retiree/annuitant/survivor	$250	$300
Dependents	$200	NA

OUT-OF-POCKET MAXIMUM As discussed earlier, health care costs are on the rise. Despite generous coinsurance rates, the expense amounts for which individuals are responsible can be staggering. These amounts are often beyond the financial means of most individuals. Thus, most plans specify the maximum amount a policyholder must pay per calendar year or plan year, known as the **out-of-pocket maximum** provision.

The purpose of the out-of-pocket maximum provision is to protect individuals from catastrophic medical expenses or expenses associated with recurring episodes of the same illness. Out-of-pocket maximums are usually stated as a fixed dollar amount and apply to expenses beyond the deductible amount. Unmarried individuals often have an annual out-of-pocket maximum of $1,000, and family out-of-pocket maximums are as high as $3,500. For example, an insurance plan specifies a $200 deductible. An unmarried person is responsible for the first $200 of expenses plus additional expenses up to $800 per year (i.e., the out-of-pocket maximum) for a total of $1,000.

Table 10-7 shows an example of an out-of-pocket maximum as well as coinsurance rates and deductible amounts for specific services.

TABLE 10-7 Deductibles and Out-of-Pocket Maximums

General Deductibles: $1,250 per Individual; $2,500 per Family per Plan Year
Professional and physician coinsurance (20 percent)
Physician network, where available (10 percent)
PPO inpatient coinsurance (10 percent)
Transplant deductible ($100)
Transplant inpatient and outpatient coinsurance (20 percent)
Standard hospital coinsurance (20 percent)
Standard hospital admission deductible ($200)
All emergency room deductibles ($200)
Emergency room coinsurance (20 percent)

PREEXISTING CONDITION CLAUSES A **preexisting condition** is a condition for which medical advice, diagnosis, care, or treatment was received or recommended during a designated period preceding the beginning of coverage. The designated period for preexisting conditions usually spans between 3 months and 1 year. Insurance companies impose preexisting conditions to limit their liabilities for serious medical conditions that predate an individual's coverage. As discussed in Chapter 2, the Patient Protection and Affordable Care Act limits waiting periods to no more than 90 days and has eliminated preexisting condition clauses altogether.

PREADMISSION CERTIFICATION Many insurance plans require **preadmission certification** of medical necessity for hospitalization. Physicians specifically must receive approval from a registered nurse or medical doctor employed by an insurance company before admitting patients to the hospital on a nonemergency basis (i.e., when a patient's life is not in imminent danger). Insurance company doctors and nurses judge whether hospitalization or alternative care is necessary. In addition, they determine the length of stay appropriate for the medical condition. Precertification requirements reserve the right for insurance companies not to pay for unauthorized admissions or hospital stays that extend beyond the approved period.

SECOND SURGICAL OPINIONS **Second surgical opinions** reduce unnecessary surgical procedures (and costs) by encouraging an individual to seek an independent opinion from another doctor. Following a recommendation of surgery from a physician, many individuals are inclined to seek an independent opinion to avoid the risks associated with surgery. With second surgical opinion provisions, insurance companies cover the cost of this consultation. Some insurance companies require second surgical opinions before authorizing surgery, whereas others offer second surgical opinion consultations as an option to each individual.

MAXIMUM BENEFIT LIMITS Insurance companies specify **maximum benefit limits,** expressed as a dollar amount over the course of 1 year or over an insured's lifetime. In many cases, insurance policies specify both annual maximums and lifetime maximums. They may also choose not to set any dollar limit to benefits. Setting annual maximums provides insurance companies with greater control over total cost expenditures. A maximum lifetime benefits provision protects employers from the costs of long-term or catastrophic claims and repeating incidences of illness.

MANAGED CARE PLANS

Managed care plans emphasize cost control by limiting an employee's choice of doctors and hospitals. Three common forms of managed care are *health maintenance organizations* (HMOs), *preferred provider organizations* (PPOs), and *point-of-service* (POS) plans.

Health Maintenance Organizations

HMOs are sometimes described as providing **prepaid medical services** because fixed periodic enrollment fees cover HMO members for all medically necessary services only if the services are delivered or approved by the HMO. HMOs generally provide inpatient and outpatient care as well as services from physicians, surgeons, and other health care professionals. Most medical services are either fully covered or, in the case of some HMOs, participants are required to make nominal **copayments.** Copayments represent nominal payments an individual makes as a condition of receiving services. HMOs express copayments as fixed amounts for different services (e.g., office visits, prescription drugs, and emergency room treatment). Common copayment amounts vary between $15 and $50 for each doctor's office visit and between $10 and $50 per prescription drug. We address the reason for the wide variation in prescription drug copayment amounts later in this chapter.

Features of Health Maintenance Organizations

HMO plans share several features in common with fee-for-service plans, including out-of-pocket maximums, preexisting condition clauses, preadmission certification, second surgical opinions, and maximum benefits limits. HMOs differ from fee-for-service plans in three important ways.

TABLE 10-8 HMO Benefits

	HMO Plan Design
Plan year maximum benefit	Unlimited
Lifetime maximum benefit	Unlimited
	Hospital Services
Inpatient hospitalization	100 percent after $150 copayment per admission
Alcohol and substance abuse* (*maximum number of days determined by the plan*)	100 percent after $150 copayment per admission
Psychiatric admission* (*maximum number of days determined by the plan*)	100 percent after $150 copayment per admission
Outpatient surgery	100 percent
Diagnostic lab and X-ray	100 percent
Emergency room hospital services	100 percent after $200 or 50 percent copayment, whichever is less
	Professional and Other Services
Physician visits (*including physical exams and immunizations*)	100 percent, $15 copayment may apply
Well baby care	100 percent
Psychiatric care* (*maximum number of days determined by the plan*)	100 percent after $20 or 20 percent copayment per visit
Alcohol and substance abuse care* (*maximum number of days determined by the plan*)	100 percent after $20 or 20 percent copayment per visit
Prescription drugs restrictions may apply. Formulary durable medical equipment	$12 copayment, generic incentive, and formulary are subject to change during the plan year; 80 percent

*HMOs determine the maximum number of inpatient days and outpatient visits for psychiatric and alcohol/substance abuse treatment. Each plan must provide for a minimum of 10 inpatient days and 20 outpatient visits per plan year. These are in addition to detoxification benefits that include diagnosis and treatment of medical complications. Some HMOs may provide benefit limitations on a calendar year basis.

First, HMOs offer prepaid services, whereas fee-for-service plans operate on a reimbursement basis. Second, HMOs include the use of primary care physicians as a cost-control measure. Third, coinsurance rates are generally lower in HMO plans than in fee-for-service plans.

Table 10-8 illustrates the features of an HMO.

PRIMARY CARE PHYSICIANS HMOs designate some of their physicians, usually general or family practitioners, as primary care physicians. HMOs assign each member to a primary care physician or require each member to choose one. **Primary care physicians** determine when patients need the care of specialists. HMOs use primary care physicians to control costs by significantly reducing the number of unnecessary visits to specialists. As primary care physicians, doctors perform several duties. The most important duty is perhaps to diagnose the nature and seriousness of an illness promptly and accurately, after which the primary care physician refers the patient to the appropriate specialist.

COPAYMENTS The most common HMO copayments apply to physician office visits, hospital admissions, prescription drugs, and emergency room services. Office visits are nominal amounts, usually $15–$50 per visit. Hospital admissions and emergency room services are higher, ranging between $50 and $150 for each occurrence. Mental health services and substance abuse treatment require copayments as well. Inpatient services require copayments that are similar in amount to those for hospital admissions for medical treatment; however, copayments for outpatient services (e.g., psychotherapy, consultation with a psychiatrist, or treatment at a substance abuse facility) are generally expressed as a fixed percentage of the fee for each visit or treatment. HMOs usually charge a copayment ranging between 15 and 25 percent.

PREFERRED PROVIDER ORGANIZATIONS

Under a **preferred provider organization (PPO),** a select group of health care providers agrees to furnish health care services to a given population at a higher level of reimbursement than under fee-for-service plans. Physicians qualify as preferred providers by meeting quality standards, agreeing to follow cost-containment procedures implemented by the PPO, and accepting the PPO's reimbursement structure. In return, the employer, insurance company, or third-party administrator helps guarantee provider physicians minimum patient loads by furnishing employees with financial incentives to use the preferred providers.

Features of Preferred Provider Organizations

PPO plans include features that resemble fee-for-service plans or HMO plans. Features most similar to fee-for-service plans are out-of-pocket maximums and coinsurance, and those most similar to HMOs include the use of nominal copayments. Preexisting condition clauses, preadmission certification, second surgical opinions, and maximum benefits limits are similar to those in fee-for-service and HMO plans. PPOs contain deductible and coinsurance provisions that differ somewhat from other plans.

Deductibles

PPOs include deductible features. The structure and amount of deductibles under PPO plans most closely resemble practices commonly used in fee-for-service plans. Unlike fee-for-service plans, PPOs often apply different deductible amounts for services rendered within and outside the approved network. Higher deductibles are set for services rendered by non-network providers to discourage participants from using services outside the network.

Coinsurance

Coinsurance is a feature of PPO plans, and its structure is most similar to fee-for-service plans. PPOs calculate coinsurance as a percentage of fees for covered services. PPOs also use two sets of coinsurance payments: The first set applies to services rendered within the network of care providers and the second to services rendered outside the network. Coinsurance rates for network services are substantially lower than they are for non-network services. Coinsurance rates for network services range between 10 and 20 percent. Non-network coinsurance rates run between 60 and 80 percent.

POINT-OF-SERVICE PLANS

A **point-of-service plan (POS)** combines features of fee-for-service systems and HMOs. Employees pay a nominal copayment for each visit to a designated network of physicians. In this regard, POS plans are similar to HMOs. Unlike HMOs, however, employees possess the option to receive care from health care providers outside the designated network of physicians, but they pay somewhat more for this choice. This choice feature is common to fee-for-service plans.

SPECIALIZED INSURANCE BENEFITS

Employers often use separate insurance plans to provide specific kinds of benefits. Benefits professionals refer to these plans as **carve-out plans.** Carve-out plans are set up to cover dental care, vision care, prescription drugs, mental health and substance abuse, and maternity care. Specialty HMOs or PPOs usually manage carve-out plans based on the expectation that single-specialty practices may control costs more effectively than multispecialty medical practices. We will focus on prescription drug plans and mental health and substance abuse plans because of the rampant inflation in prescription drug costs and the increased recognition that mental health disorders may hinder worker productivity.

Prescription Drug Plans

Prescription drug plans cover the costs of drugs. These plans apply exclusively to drugs that state or federal laws require to be dispensed by licensed pharmacists. Prescription drugs dispensed to individuals during hospitalization or treatment in long-term care facilities are not covered by prescription drug plans. Insurers specify which prescription drugs are covered, how much they will pay, and the basis for paying for drugs.

Three kinds of prescription drug programs are currently available to companies that choose to provide these benefits to employees. The first, **medical reimbursement plans** reimburses employees for some or all of the cost of prescription drugs. These programs are usually associated with self-funded or independent indemnity plans. The second kind of plan, often referred to as a **prescription card program,** operates similarly to managed care programs because it offers prepaid benefits with nominal copayments. The name arose from the common practice of pharmacies requiring the presentation of an identification card. Prescription card programs limit benefits to prescriptions filled at participating pharmacies, similar to managed care arrangements for medical treatment.

The third type of plan, a **mail order prescription drug program,** dispenses expensive medications used to treat chronic health conditions such as human immunodeficiency virus (HIV) infection or such neurological disorders as Parkinson's disease. Health insurers specify whether participants must receive prescription drugs through mail order programs or locally approved pharmacies. Cost is the driving factor for this decision. Mail order programs offer a cost advantage because they purchase medications at discounted prices in large volumes.

Mental Health and Substance Abuse

Approximately 20 percent of Americans experience some form of mental illness (e.g., clinical depression) at least once during their lifetimes.[29] Nearly 20 percent develop a substance abuse problem. As a result, insurance plans provide mental health and substance abuse benefits designed to cover treatment of mental illness and chemical dependence on alcohol and legal and illegal drugs. Delivery methods include fee-for-service plans and managed care options. Employee assistance programs (EAPs) represent a portal to taking advantage of employer-sponsored mental health and substance abuse treatment options. EAPs help employees cope with personal problems that may impair their personal lives or job performance, including alcohol or drug abuse, domestic violence, the emotional impact of AIDS and other diseases, clinical depression, and eating disorders. EAPs also assist employers in helping troubled employees identify and solve problems that may be interfering with their job or personal life.

Features of Mental Health and Substance Abuse Plans

Mental health and substance abuse plans cover the costs of a variety of treatments, including prescription psychiatric drugs (e.g., antidepressant medication), psychological testing, inpatient hospital care, and outpatient care (e.g., individual or group therapy).

Mental health benefits amounts vary by the type of disorder. Psychiatrists and psychologists rely on the *Diagnostic and Statistical Manual of Mental Disorders (DSM-5)* to diagnose mental disorders based on symptoms, and both fee-for-service and managed care plans rely on the *DSM-5* to authorize payment of benefits. As discussed earlier, HMOs usually charge a copayment ranging between 15 and 25 percent.

From the employee's perspective, coinsurance and maximum benefits amounts are generally less generous than general health plans in three ways. First, coinsurance amounts for mental health and substance abuse benefits, expressed as a percentage of treatment cost for both indemnity and managed care plans, range between 40 and 50 percent. Second, mental health and substance abuse plans limit the annual number of outpatient visits or days of inpatient care. Third, annual and lifetime maximum benefits are set significantly lower. The **Mental Health Parity Act and Addiction Equity Act of 2008** requires that any group health plan that includes mental health and substance use disorder benefits along with standard medical and surgical coverage must treat them equally in terms of out-of-pocket costs, benefit limits, and practices such as prior authorization and utilization review. These practices must be based on the same level of scientific evidence used by the insurer for medical and surgical benefits. For example, a plan may not apply separate deductibles for treatment related to mental health or substance use disorders and medical or surgical benefits—they must be calculated as one limit.[30]

CONSUMER-DRIVEN HEALTH CARE

Managed care plans became popular alternatives to fee-for-service plans mainly to help employers and insurance companies more effectively manage the costs of health care. As discussed, managed care plans by design imposed substantial restrictions on an employee's ability to make choices about from whom they could receive medical treatment, the gatekeeper role of primary care physicians, and the level of benefits they could receive based on designated in- and non-network providers.

Despite the cost control objectives of managed care, health care costs have continued to rise dramatically over the years while also restricting employee choice. **Consumer-driven health care** refers to the objective of helping companies maintain control over costs while also enabling employees to make greater choices about health care. This approach may enable employers to lower the cost of insurance premiums by selecting plans with higher employee deductibles. The most popular consumer-driven approaches are flexible spending accounts and health reimbursement accounts. These accounts provide employees with resources to pay for medical and related expenses not covered by higher deductible insurance plans at substantially lower costs to employers.

Flexible spending accounts (FSAs) permit employees to pay for specified health care costs that are not covered by an employer's insurance plan. Prior to each plan year, employees elect the amount of pay they wish to allocate to this kind of plan. Employers then use this money to reimburse employees for expenses incurred during the plan year that qualify for repayment.

Qualifying expenses include an individual's out-of-pocket costs for medical treatments, products, or services related to a mental or physical defect or disease, along with certain associated costs (e.g., health insurance deductibles or transportation to get medical care).

A significant advantage to employees is the ability to make contributions to their FSAs on a pretax basis; however, a noteworthy drawback is the "use it or lose it" provision of FSAs. FSAs require employees to estimate the amount of money they think they will need for eligible medical expenses. Of course, it is difficult to predict many medical needs and to estimate the costs of anticipated medical needs. Employees lose contributions to their FSAs when they overestimate the cost of medical needs because employers neither allow employees to carry balances nor do employers reimburse employees for balances remaining at the end of the year.

On the other hand, employers may establish **health reimbursement accounts (HRAs).** The purposes of HRAs and FSAs are similar with three important differences. First, employers make the contributions to each employee's HRA, whereas employees fund FSAs with pretax contributions deducted from their pay. Employees do not contribute to HRAs. HRA arrangements are particularly appealing to employees with relatively low salaries or hourly wage rates because they do not contribute to them. Second, HRAs permit employees to carry over unused account balances from year to year, whereas employees forfeit unused FSA account balances present at the end of the year. Third, employers may offer employees HRAs as well as FSAs, and the use of these accounts is not limited to participation in high-deductible health care plans, which is the case for HSAs (to be discussed shortly).

The idea of consumer-driven health care has most recently received substantially greater attention than before because of the Bush administration (President George W. Bush) and the

Republican-led Congress, who favor greater employee involvement in their medical care and reducing the cost burden for companies to help maintain competitiveness in the global market. The **Medicare Prescription Drug, Improvement and Modernization Act of 2003**[31] added section 223 to the IRC, effective January 1, 2004, to permit eligible individuals to establish **health savings accounts (HSAs)** to help employees pay for medical expenses. In 2013, an employer, an employee, or both may contribute as much as $3,250 annually for unmarried employees without dependent children or as much as $6,450 for married or unmarried employees with dependent children. Employers may require employees to contribute toward these limits. Employee contributions would be withheld from an employee's pay on a pretax basis. Employers offer HSAs along with a high deductible insurance policy, established for employees. **High-deductible health insurance plans** require substantial deductibles and low out-of-pocket maximums. For individual coverage, the minimum annual deductible was $1,250 with maximum out-of-pocket limits at or below $6,250 in 2013. For family coverage, the deductible was $2,500 with maximum out-of-pocket limits at or below $12,500.

HSAs offer four main advantages to employees relative to FSAs and HRAs. First, HSAs are portable, which means that the employee owns the account balance after the employment relationship ends. Second, HSAs are subject to inflation-adjusted funding limits. Third, employees may receive medical services from doctors, hospitals, and other health care providers of their choice, and they may choose the type of medical services they purchase, including such items as long-term care, eye care, and prescription drug coverage. FSAs and HRAs substantially limit employee choice. Fourth, HSA assets must be held in trust and cannot be subject to forfeiture. That is, any unspent balances in the HSA can be rolled over annually and accumulate tax-free until the participant's death. FSAs and HRAs have no legal vesting requirement, which means employees do not possess the right to claim unused balances when they terminate employment.

COMPENSATION IN ACTION

Retirement and health care benefits are critical features of the employment exchange. These benefits will be weighed out and assessed by employees as they make decisions about where they want to work and for how long they will stay with a particular employer. As a manager on the line or in HR, you should be adept at accurately explaining key features so that when questions arise within your employee populations, they have the benefit of a knowledgeable and sensitive resource to help them work through options and concerns. As was mentioned in the Compensation in Action feature in Chapter 9, many companies outsource the benefits management function so employees are directed to a call center or Web site to understand their benefits; however, this function should not exempt HR and line managers from understanding and being able to explain some of the nuances to employees.

Action checklist for line managers and HR—being prepared to assist employees in benefits decisions

HR takes the lead
- Set up a session for HR professionals to meet with the legal team (or outside employment lawyers) to understand amendments to ERISA under the 2006 Pension Protection Act (PPA).

- Educate line managers so they can field basic employee questions regarding the PPA [e.g., although employers can enroll employees in a plan automatically, employees can opt out of 401(k) plans at any time and they can change the percentage of their contributions at any time] and outline investment alternatives (bonds versus stock, high risk versus low risk, and so on).
- Create online portals that walk an employee through various health care plans in an interactive and informative manner. If the company already requires some form of online training, this session could be built in as an additional requirement.

Line managers take the lead
- Initiate "Health Care and Retirement" workshops during work hours where employees have time to sit down with an HR professional or benefits specialist to ask specific questions related to their individual approach to health care and retirement.
- As part of ongoing discussions with employees, ask them explicitly if they have questions or concerns about health care or retirement; answer questions when appropriate, and point employees in the right direction when additional explanation is required.

END OF CHAPTER

MyManagementLab

Go to **mymanagementlab.com** to complete the problems marked with this icon ⭐.

Summary

This chapter reviewed the fundamental concepts of company-sponsored retirement plans and company-sponsored health insurance plans. Companies must follow a set of strict guidelines in designing and implementing pension plans to qualify for favorable tax treatment. We also reviewed the main features of defined benefit, defined contribution, and hybrid plans. Following company-sponsored retirement plans, we started our review of health insurance plans with basic definitions and a perusal of the level of health insurance coverage and costs in the United States. We also studied a variety of health plans (e.g., fee-for-service plans, managed care plans, and consumer-driven health care) and discussed how these plans differ in cost control features.

Key Terms

✪ Discussion Questions

10-1. Are employees more likely to favor defined contribution plans over defined benefit plans? How about employers? Explain your answer.

10-2. Summarize the controversial issues regarding cash balance plans.

10-3. Discuss the basic concept of insurance. How does this concept apply to health care?

10-4. Describe the principles of fee-for-service plans and managed care plans. What are the similarities and differences?

10-5. Discuss some of the choices an employer may make to help control health care costs.

CASE
A Health Savings Account at Frontline PR

✪ *An additional Supplemental Case can be found on MyManagementLab.*

Susan Berry just returned from a national conference on compensation and benefits where she attended a session on health savings accounts (HSAs). Susan is the human resources director at Frontline PR, and the company has been struggling with the cost of health care insurance. After speaking with several experts at the conference, Susan now thinks an HSA might be a viable option for the company.

Frontline PR is a public relations firm located in the Northeast that employs close to 150 people in four different offices. Public relations professionals make up most of the staff, but the company also employs a complete administrative and operations staff. All of Frontline's employees work full-time schedules and are eligible to participate in its health care insurance plan. Frontline currently offers a standard fee-for-services health care insurance option. The plan has a modest deductible of $300 per year and a 20 percent coinsurance requirement. In addition, the company offers a flexible spending account (FSA) that allows employees to set aside pretax earnings to pay for the deductible, coinsurance, and other medical expenses.

Susan is considering offering a HSA along with a high-deductible health insurance plan instead of the current insurance plan and FSA. At the conference, Susan learned that making such a change could result in significant cost savings for a company. The high-deductible health insurance plan would cost a lot less for a company than the standard fee-for-services plan that Frontline currently offers. While Susan suggests that Frontline make contributions to each employee's HSA, the overall costs for the health care benefit would still be less than its current option. Beyond cost savings on premiums, many believe that consumer-driven health care tends to reduce overall health care costs. Some of the experts Susan spoke to at the conference stated that when employees have a greater say in their health care decisions, they make wiser decisions and do not spend as much on health care.

Susan has discussed the HSA option with Frontline's director of finance, Allison Jones. From the financial perspective, Allison agrees that the option would be a good step to start controlling health care costs. However, as an employee who would use the benefit, Allison isn't so sure that an HSA with a high-deductible health insurance plan is the right option for the company. Based on Susan's initial explanation, Allison didn't really understand how the HSA worked. Further, she was concerned that she would have to spend more out of pocket on her own health care.

Susan is convinced that the HSA option would offer a significant cost savings to Frontline. However, after her discussion with Allison, Susan is still unsure if it is the right path to recommend for her company.

Questions:

10-6. What are some advantages of implementing the HSA option?

10-7. What are some potential disadvantages of the HSA option?

10-8. What do you recommend? Why?

MyManagementLab

Go to **mymanagementlab.com** for Auto-graded writing questions as well as the following Assisted-graded writing questions:

 10-9. Compare and contrast defined contribution plans with defined benefit plans.

 10-10. Define health insurance concepts such as insurance policy and premium, and explain the different types of health insurance programs. What are the differences among these programs?

Endnotes

1. ERISA §3(2)(A), 29 U.S.C. §1002(2)(A).
2. Costo, S. L. (2006). Trends in retirement plan coverage over the last decade. *Monthly Labor Review*, February, pp. 58–64.
3. Ibid.; U.S. Department of Labor. (July 2012). *Employee Benefits in the United States, March 2012*. Available: *www.bls.gov*, accessed March 31, 2013.
4. Costo, "Trends in retirement."
5. U.S. Department of Labor. (December 2012). *Retirement costs for defined benefit plans higher than defined contribution plans*, Vol. 1, No. 21. Available: *http://www.bls.gov/opub/btn/volume-1/retirement-costs-for-defined-benefit-plans-higher-than-for-defined-contribution-plans.htm*, accessed March 31, 2013.
6. U.S. Department of Labor. (July 2012). *Employee Benefits in the United States, March 2012*. Available: *http://www.bls.gov,* accessed March 31, 2013.
7. Ibid.
8. I.R.C. §§410(a)(1), 410(a)(4); Treas. Reg. §1.410(a)-3T(b); ERISA §202(a).
9. I.R.C. §410(a)(3), Treas. Reg. §1.410(a)-5, 29 C.F.R. §2530.200b-2(a), ERISA §202(a)(3).
10. I.R.C. §414(q).
11. I.R.C. §§411(a)(2), 411(a)(5); Treas. Reg. §1.411(a)-3T; ERISA §203(a).
12. I.R.C. §§411(a)(7), 411(b); ERISA §§204, 3(23); Treas. Reg. §1.411(b)-1.
13. I.R.C. §401(a)(4).
14. I.R.C. §415(b).
15. I.R.C. §404(a)(1)(A)(i)–(iii).
16. §404(a)(1)(C).
17. Prop. Treas. Reg. §§1.412(b)–1(a).
18. I.R.C. §415(c)(2); Treas. Reg. §1.415–6(b)(1).
19. I.R.C. §415(c).
20. I.R.C. §§404(a)(3), 402(g).
21. I.R.C. §404(a)(3).
22. U.S. Department of Labor, Bureau of Labor Statistics. (September 18, 2012). *Employee Tenure in 2012* (12-1887). Available: *www.bls.gov*, accessed February 16, 2013.
23. Green, L. B. (October 29, 2003). *What Is a Pension Equity Plan? Compensation and Working Conditions Online*. Available: *www.bls.gov/opub/cwc/cm20031016ar01p1.htm*, accessed July 29, 2004.
24. 26 Code of Federal Regulations §§1.401(a)(4)-8(c)(3)(I).
25. U.S. Bureau of Labor Statistics. (1919). Welfare Work for Employees in Industrial Establishments in the United States. *Bulletin #250*, pp. 119–123.
26. U.S. Department of Labor. (July 2012). *Employee Benefits in the United States, March 2012*. Available: *http://www.bls.gov*, accessed March 31, 2013.
27. Ibid.
28. Ibid.
29. U.S. Surgeon General. (2011). *Epidemiology of Mental Illness*. Available: *http://www.surgeongeneral.gov/library/mentalhealth/chapter2/sec2_1.html*, accessed February 22, 2011.
30. U.S. Department of Health & Human Services. (2010). *Obama Administration Issues Rules Requiring Parity in Treatment of Mental, Substance Use Disorders*. Available: *http://www.hhs.gov/news/press/2010pres/01/20100129a.html*, accessed February 22, 2011.
31. Public L. No. 108–173.

11 LEGALLY REQUIRED BENEFITS

LEARNING OBJECTIVES

When you finish studying this chapter, you should be able to:

1. In a historical context, discuss at least two main reasons why the U.S. government required certain employee benefits.
2. Summarize three main components of legally required benefits.
3. Indicate the main benefits and costs of legally required benefits.
4. Summarize the five fundamental objectives of employee benefits program design.

Multiple laws require employer participation in some employee benefits programs. The Social Security programs (e.g., retirement and disability) most notably influence many people, and these are perhaps the most widely publicized legally required benefits in the United States. For years, there have been valid concerns that there will be insufficient funding to meet promised benefits. As time passes, these concerns are growing stronger. There are also ongoing political debates about how to ensure the viability of Social Security programs. President George W. Bush signed an executive order on May 2, 2001 (see Chapter 2 for a definition of executive orders), to create the new Presidential Commission to Strengthen Social Security. Politicians have debated the merits and drawbacks of various solutions to shore up the Social Security system. Under Bush's administration, the focus was to encourage tax credits for individuals who save for retirement and to encourage more savings through employer-sponsored retirement plans. The Democrats have called for increasing the tax under the Federal Income Contributions Act to bolster the trust fund; however, such an increase has been met with strong opposition by business leaders, particularly small businesses, which usually possess smaller profit margins. The Pension Protection Act of 2006 (discussed in Chapter 2) is expected to increase the number of people who participate in their employer-sponsored defined contribution plans by giving employers the authority to enroll new employees in the plan automatically.

AN OVERVIEW OF LEGALLY REQUIRED BENEFITS

The U.S. government established programs to protect individuals from catastrophic events such as disability and unemployment. Legally required benefits are protection programs that attempt to promote worker safety and health, maintain family income streams, and assist families in crisis. The cost of legally required benefits to employers is quite high. As of September 2012, U.S. companies spent an average $4,950 per employee annually to provide legally required benefits.[1] Human resource (HR) staffs and compensation professionals in particular must follow a variety of laws as they develop and implement programs.

Legally required benefits historically provided a form of social insurance. Prompted largely by the rapid growth of industrialization in the United States in the early nineteenth century and the Great Depression of the 1930s, initial social insurance programs were designed to minimize the possibility that individuals who became unemployed or severely injured while working would become destitute. In addition, social insurance programs aimed to stabilize the well-being of dependent family members of injured or unemployed individuals. Furthermore, early social insurance programs were designed to enable retirees to maintain subsistence income levels. These intents of legally required benefits remain intact today.

Legally required benefits currently apply to virtually all U.S. companies, and they "level the playing field," so to speak. These programs are unlikely to directly lead to a competitive advantage for one company over another; however, legally required benefits may indirectly promote competitive advantage for all companies by enabling unemployed individuals, disabled employees, and their dependent family members to participate in the economy as consumers of products and services. The government has a vested interest in promoting a vigorous economy that exhibits regular buying and selling, such that the demand for goods and services does not substantially outpace or fall below the supply of those goods and services. The key to maintaining a vigorous economy is clearly the participation of individuals as consumers of the products and services sold in the marketplace. In this chapter, it will become evident how many elements of employee benefits serve this end.

COMPONENTS OF LEGALLY REQUIRED BENEFITS

The key legally required benefits are mandated by the following laws: the Social Security Act of 1935, various state workers' compensation laws, and the Family and Medical Leave Act of 1993. All provide protection programs to employees and their dependents.

Social Security Act of 1935

HISTORICAL BACKGROUND Income discontinuity caused by the Great Depression led to the Social Security Act as a means to protect families from financial devastation in the event of unemployment. The Great Depression of the 1930s was a time when many businesses failed and masses of people became chronically unemployed. During this period, employers shifted their focus from maximizing profits to simply staying in business. Overall, ensuring the financial solvency of employees during periods of temporary unemployment and following work-related injuries promoted the well-being of the economy and contributed to some companies' ability to remain in business. These subsistence payments specifically contributed to the viability of the economy by providing temporarily unemployed or injured individuals with the means to contribute to economic activity by making purchases that result in demand for products and services.

The Social Security Act of 1935 also addresses retirement income and the health and welfare of employees and their families. Many employees could not meet their financial obligations (e.g., housing expenses and food) on a daily basis, and most employees could not retire because they were unable to save enough money to support themselves in retirement. Furthermore, employees' poor financial situations left them unable to afford medical treatment for themselves and their families.

As a result of these social maladies, three programs within the act aim to relieve some of the consequences of these social problems:

- Unemployment insurance
- Old Age, Survivor, and Disability Insurance (OASDI)
- Medicare

Each of those programs will be reviewed in turn.

TABLE 11-1 Eligibility Criteria for Unemployment Insurance Benefits

To be eligible for unemployment insurance benefits, an individual must:

1. Not have left a job voluntarily
2. Be able and available for work
3. Be actively seeking work
4. Not have refused an offer of suitable employment
5. Not be unemployed because of a labor dispute (exception in a few states)
6. Not have had employment terminated because of gross violations of conduct within the workplace

UNEMPLOYMENT INSURANCE The Social Security Act founded a national federal–state employment insurance program for individuals who become unemployed through no fault of their own. Each state administers its own program and develops guidelines within parameters set by the federal government. States pay into a central unemployment tax fund administered by the federal government. The federal government invests these payments, and it disburses funds to states as needed. The unemployment insurance program applies to virtually all employees in the United States, with the exception of most agricultural and domestic workers (e.g., housekeepers).

Individuals must meet several criteria to qualify for unemployment benefits. Unemployment itself does not necessarily qualify a person, although these criteria vary somewhat by state. Those applying for unemployment insurance benefits must have been employed for a minimum period of time. This **base period** tends to be the first four of the last five completed calendar quarters immediately prior to becoming unemployed. In addition, all states require sufficient previous earnings, typically $1,000 during the last four quarters combined. Other criteria are listed in Table 11-1.

Individuals who meet the eligibility criteria receive weekly benefits. Because the federal government places no limits on a maximum allowable amount, the benefits amount varies widely from state to state. Most states calculate the weekly benefits as a specified fraction of an employee's average wages during the highest calendar quarter of the base period.

Unemployed individuals usually collect unemployment insurance benefits for several weeks. Since 1972, the average duration of benefits has ranged between 12 and 18 weeks. The average duration refers to the mean number of weeks for which unemployment insurance claimants collect benefits under regular state programs. The deep economic recession, which began in late 2007, and the subsequent loss of millions of jobs left most of the millions of newly unemployed unable to secure work within the scope of state unemployment insurance programs. As a result, Congress approved the Emergency Unemployment Insurance (EUC) Program in June 2008 by the Supplemental Appropriations Act of 2008.[2] The EUC program provided 13 additional weeks of federally funded unemployment insurance benefits to the unemployed who had exhausted all state unemployment insurance benefits for which they were eligible. As the economic recession deepened, particularly in several states such as Michigan, it became apparent to the federal government that the EUC program extensions were not sufficient to bridge the lengthening gap between periods of employment. In response, Congress enacted the Unemployment Compensation Act of 2008[3] on November 21, 2008. This law expanded the EUC benefits to 20 weeks nationwide (from 13 weeks), and it provided for 13 more weeks of EUC (for a total of 33 weeks) to individuals who reside in states with high unemployment rates. This temporary program was extended three times, most recently in January 2013 under the American Taxpayers Relief Act of 2012. Under the extension, unemployment insurance benefits were available to individuals for up to 99 weeks of unemployment ending on or before January 1, 2014. The number of weeks an individual is eligible to receive unemployment insurance benefits depends upon the unemployment rate of the state in which unemployed individuals reside.

Unemployment insurance benefits are financed by federal and state taxes levied on employers under the **Federal Unemployment Tax Act (FUTA).** State and local governments, as well as not-for-profit companies (e.g., the United Way), are generally exempt from FUTA. Alaska is currently the only state that requires employee contributions. Employer contributions amount to 6.2 percent of the first $7,000 earned by each employee (i.e., the taxable wage base). FUTA specifies $7,000 as the minimum allowable taxable wage base. Relatively few states' taxable wage base is as low as the FUTA-specified minimum (e.g., Florida, Indiana, and South Carolina). States typically set the taxable wage base according to the average wage level. In 2013, states' taxable wage bases ranged from $7,000 to $39,800.

The federal government deposits 5.4 percent to the Federal Unemployment Trust Fund, which is administered by the Treasury Department. The Treasury Department invests this money in government securities, crediting the principal amount contributed by each state and investment income to an account. The federal government retains 0.8 percent to cover administrative costs and to maintain a reserve to bail out states with very low balances in their accounts.

States also impose taxes on employers to fund their unemployment insurance programs. An employer's actual tax burden varies according to an experience rating system. Every state applies different tax rates to companies, subject to statutory minimum and maximum rates. Each company's tax rate depends on its prior experience with unemployment. Accordingly, a company that lays off a large percentage of employees will have a higher tax rate than a company that lays off relatively few or none of its employees. This **experience rating system** implies that a company can manage its unemployment tax burden.

OLD AGE, SURVIVOR, AND DISABILITY INSURANCE OASDI contains a number of benefits that were amended to the act following its enactment in 1935. Besides providing retirement income, the amendments include survivors' insurance (1939) and disability insurance (1965). The phrase *old age* in the title refers to retirement benefits.

Virtually all U.S. workers are eligible for protections under the OASDI and Medicare programs, except for three exempt classes. First, civilian employees of the federal government and railroad employees with at least 10 years of service are exempt from the retirement program; however, these individuals are not exempt from the Medicare program. Second, employees of state and local governments who are already covered under other retirement plans are exempt from Social Security retirement contributions unless these government organizations choose to participate in this program. Third, children under age 21 who work for a parent are exempt, except children age 18 or older who work in the parent's business.

OLD AGE BENEFITS Individuals may receive various benefit levels upon retirement, or under survivors' and disability programs, based on how much credit they have earned through eligible payroll contributions. They earn credit based on **quarters of coverage,** which each equal three consecutive months during the calendar year. In 2013, a worker earned credit for one quarter of coverage for each quarter in which she made $1,160 of Social Security taxable income. This figure is based on the average total wages of all workers as determined by the Social Security Administration (SSA). Of course, workers may earn up to four quarters of coverage credit each year. Individuals become **fully insured** when they earn credit for 40 quarters of coverage, or 10 years of employment, and remain fully insured during their lifetime.

An individual who has become fully insured must meet additional requirements before receiving benefits under the particular programs. Under the retirement program, fully insured individuals may choose to receive benefits as early as age 62, although their benefit amounts will be permanently reduced if elected prior to age 65. Congress recently instituted changes in the minimum age for receiving full benefits. It increased the full retirement age for people born in 1938 or later because of higher life expectancies of 65-year-old individuals. For example, the U.S. Bureau of the Census estimated that individuals age 65 in 1997 would live an additional 17.7 years. In 2007, this estimate increased significantly to 22.5 years.[4] The age for collecting full Social Security retirement benefits is gradually increasing from 60 to 67 over a

22-year period ending in 2022. The average monthly benefit for all retired workers was $1,261 in 2013.[5]

SURVIVOR BENEFITS The SSA calculates survivors' benefits based on the insureds' employment status and the survivors' relationship to the deceased. Dependent, unmarried children of the deceased and a spouse of the deceased who is caring for a child or children may receive survivors' benefits if the deceased worker was fully insured. A widow or widower at least age 60 or a parent at least age 62 who was dependent on the deceased employee is entitled to survivors' benefits if the deceased worker was fully insured. In 2013, the average monthly benefit was $1,214.[6]

The retirement program contains incentives to encourage individuals to delay their retirement after reaching full retirement age. The Social Security Administration increases retirement benefits by a designated percent for each month worked beyond full retirement until age 70, subject to a maximum percentage increase. The percentage increase depends on the year of birth. For example, let's assume that an individual's full retirement age is 66 years and his monthly benefit at that age is $1,000. If he were to take retirement as early as age 62, his monthly benefit would be $750. If he were to delay his retirement until age 70, his monthly benefit would be substantially larger at $1,320.

DISABILITY BENEFITS The SSA pays benefits to seriously disabled workers and family members. In particular, Social Security pays only for total disability. Disability under Social Security is based on a person's inability to perform work done before becoming disabled and inability to adjust to other work because of the medical condition. The disability must also last or be expected to last for at least 1 year or to result in death.

ELIGIBILITY Disability benefits are available to disabled workers who are unable to work as a result of a serious medical or mental impairment that lasts at least 12 months. Seriously disabled workers are eligible to receive disability benefits as long as they meet two criteria. First, the worker must have accumulated at least 40 credits. Second, the worker must have earned at least 20 credits of the last 40 calendar quarters in the last 10 years ending with the year of disablement.

Younger workers need fewer quarters of coverage because they have fewer years to accumulate quarters of coverage. For example, workers ages 24–31 may qualify with half as many credits between age 21 and becoming disabled. For instance, becoming disabled at age 29 requires credit for 4 years of employment (equivalent to 16 credits based on earning 4 credits per year) since the 8-year period beginning at age 21. The average monthly disability benefit in 2013 was $1,132.

MEDICARE The Medicare program serves nearly all U.S. citizens age 65 or older by providing insurance coverage for hospitalization, convalescent care, and major doctor bills. The Medicare program includes five separate features:

- *Medicare Part A*—Hospital insurance
- *Medicare Part B*—Medical insurance
- *Medigap*—Voluntary supplemental insurance to pay for services not covered in Parts A and B
- *Medicare Part C: Medicare Advantage*—Choices in health care providers, such as through HMOs and PPOs
- *Medicare Part D: Medicare Prescription Drug Benefit*—Prescription drug coverage

Most individuals who are eligible to receive protection under Medicare may choose to receive coverage in one of two ways. A person may receive coverage under the original Medicare Plan or Medicare Advantage Plans as illustrated in Figure 11-1.

In a nutshell, the original Medicare Plan is a fee-for-service plan that is managed by the federal government. As we discussed in Chapter 10, fee-for-service plans include many health care services, medical supplies, and certain prescription drugs. Participants in fee-for-service plans possess the choice to receive care from virtually any licensed health care provider or facility.

Original Medicare Plan		OR	Medicare Advantage Plans like HMOs and PPOs

Part A (Hospital)	Part B (Medical)

Medicare provides this coverage. Part B is optional. You have your choice of doctors. Your costs may be higher than in Medicare Advantage plans.

Called "Part C," this option combines your Part A (Hospital) and Part B (Medical)

Private insurance companies approved by Medicare provide this coverage. Generally, you must see doctors in the plan. Your cost may be lower than in the Original Medicare Plan, and you may get extra benefits.

+

Part D (Prescription Drug Coverage)

You can choose this coverage. Private companies approved by Medicare run these plans. Plans cover different drugs. Medically necessary drugs must be covered.

+

Part D (Prescription Drug Coverage)

Most Part C plans cover prescription drugs. If they don't you may be able to choose this coverage. Plans cover different drugs. Medically necessary drugs must be covered.

+

Medigap (Medicare Supplement Insurance) Policy

You can choose to buy this private coverage (or an employer/union may offer similar coverage) to fill in gaps in Part A and Part B coverage. Costs vary by policy and company.

FIGURE 11-1 Options for Receiving Medicare Benefits

Source: U.S. Department of Health and Human Services. (2011). *Medicare & You.* Available: *www.medicare.gov,* accessed February 14, 2011.

On the other hand, Medicare Advantage Plans include a variety of insurance options, including health maintenance organizations, preferred provider organizations, Medicare special needs plans, and Medicare medical savings account plans (MSA). Medicare Advantage Plans are run by private companies subject to strict regulations specified in the Medicare program. Restrictions pertain to pricing of the different plans.

MEDICARE PART A COVERAGE This compulsory hospitalization insurance covers both inpatient and outpatient hospital care and services. Social Security beneficiaries, retirees, voluntary enrollees, and disabled individuals are all entitled. Both employers and employees finance **Medicare Part A** benefits through payroll taxes of 1.45 percent on all earnings.

Examples of Part A coverage include:

- Inpatient hospital care in a semiprivate room, meals, general nursing, and other hospital supplies and services.
- Home health services limited to reasonable and essential part-time or intermittent skilled nursing care and home health aide services and physical therapy, occupational therapy, and speech-language pathology ordered by a doctor.
- Skilled nursing facility care, including semiprivate room, meals, skilled nursing and rehabilitative services, and supplies for up to 100 days per year. Examples of skilled nursing care include physical therapy after a stroke or serious accident.

In 2013, the monthly Part A premium was $441.

MEDICARE PART B COVERAGE This voluntary supplementary medical insurance covers 80 percent of medical services and supplies after the enrolled individual pays an annual deductible for services furnished under this plan. Part B helps pay for physicians' services and for some medical services and supplies not covered under Part A. **Medicare Part B** pays for medical care such as doctors' services, outpatient care, clinical laboratory services (e.g., blood tests and urinalysis) and some preventive health services (e.g., cardiovascular screenings and bone mass measurement). Part B also provides ambulance services to a hospital or skilled nursing facility when transportation in any other vehicle would endanger a person's health.

Part A coverage automatically qualifies an individual to enroll in Part B coverage for a monthly premium. The monthly premium amount is based on annual income, and the premium amounts will be revised annually. In 2013, monthly Part B premiums ranged from $104.90 to $335.70.

MEDIGAP INSURANCE **Medigap** insurance supplements Part A and Part B coverage and is available to Medicare recipients in most states from private insurance companies for an extra fee. Most Medigap plans help cover the costs of coinsurance, copayments, and deductibles. Federal and state laws limit the sale of these plans to up to 10 different standardized choices that vary in terms of the level of protection. For example, some policies cover costs not covered by the original Medicare plan.

Some insurers offer Medicare Select plans. **Medicare Select plans** are Medigap policies that offer lower premiums in exchange for limiting the choice of health care providers. Three states (Massachusetts, Minnesota, and Wisconsin) do not subscribe to this system for offering Medigap insurance. Separate rules apply in these states.

The Balanced Budget Act of 1997 established Medicare+Choice—renamed to **Medicare Advantage** in 2004 as a third Medicare program—as an alternative to the original program (Parts A and B). The Medicare Advantage program, informally referred to as Part C, provides beneficiaries the opportunity to receive health care from a variety of options, including private fee-for-service plans, managed care plans, or medical savings accounts. **Fee-for-service plans** provide protection against health care expenses in the form of cash benefits paid to the insured or directly to the health care provider after receiving health care services. These plans pay benefits on a reimbursement basis. Medicare Parts A and B are based on fee-for-service arrangements. **Managed care** plans often pay a higher level of benefits if health care is received from approved providers.

MEDICARE PRESCRIPTION DRUG BENEFIT The passage of the Medicare Prescription Drug, Improvement, and Modernization Act of 2003 (also known as the Medicare Modernization Act of 2003 for short) instituted a prescription drug benefit for Medicare program participants. Commonly referred to as Part D, the drug benefit was first offered in 2006. Medicare covers 75 percent of prescription drug costs after a calendar year deductible of $325 in 2013, up to $2,930. After that, expenditures up to $4,750 are not covered by Medicare. All costs are out of pocket. This coverage gap is known as the "donut hole" because Medicare contributes to the payment of approved prescription medications for amounts outside the $2,930–$4,750 range less the annual deductible. Finally, Medicare covers 95 percent of the cost of prescriptions for each dollar spent in excess of $4,750 spent during the calendar year. The dollar amounts were valid in 2013 and are subject to change from year to year.

The Patient Protection and Affordable Care Act of 2010 contains many provisions to make health care more affordable. As an example of the types of improvements under way, this new law will slowly eliminate the "donut hole" coverage gap over several years to make prescription drugs more affordable. In 2011, Medicare participants who reached the coverage gap received a 50 percent discount on brand-name prescription drugs. Additional savings will be provided to Medicare participants each year until the "donut hole" coverage gap is eliminated altogether.

FINANCING OASDI AND MEDICARE PROGRAMS Funding for OASDI and Medicare programs requires equal employer and employee contributions under the **Federal Insurance Contributions**

Act (FICA).[7] FICA requires that employers pay a tax based on their payroll; employees contribute a tax based on earnings, which is withheld from each paycheck. The **Self-Employment Contributions Act (SECA)**[8] requires that self-employed individuals contribute to the OASDI and Medicare programs, but at a different tax rate. In either case, the tax rate is subject to an increase each year in order to fund OASDI programs sufficiently. FICA requires employers and employees to contribute 7.65 percent each. Self-employed individuals generally doubled that amount, or 15.3 percent. As we will discuss next, this tax amount is apportioned between OASDI and Medicare programs.

OASDI PROGRAMS The largest share of the FICA tax funds OASDI programs. In 2013, of the total 7.65 percent FICA tax, 6.20 percent was set aside. Self-employed individuals contributed 12.40 percent. OASDI taxes are subject to a **taxable wage base.** Taxable wage bases limit the amount of annual wages or payroll cost per employee subject to taxation. The taxable wage base may also increase over time to account for increases in the cost of living. In 2013, the taxable wage base was $113,700. Annual wages, payroll costs per employee, and self-employed earnings above this level were not taxed.

MEDICARE PROGRAMS The **Medicare tax,** or **hospital insurance tax (HI),** supports the Medicare Part A program. Employers, employees, and self-employed individuals contribute 1.45 percent. Self-employed individuals contribute double the amount, or 2.9 percent. The Medicare tax is not subject to a taxable wage base. All payroll amounts and wages are taxed. Beginning in 2013, an additional HI tax of 0.9 percent has been assessed on earned income exceeding $200,000 for individuals and $250,000 for married couples filing jointly.

According to the Social Security Administration, many people believe that the Social Security taxes they pay are held in interest-bearing accounts set aside by the federal government to meet their own future retirement income needs. To the contrary, the Social Security system represents a pay-as-you-go retirement system. In other words, Social Security taxes paid by today's workers and their employers are used to pay the benefits for today's retirees and other beneficiaries.

The Social Security Board of Trustees announced in its annual report for fiscal year 2012 that there should be sufficient resources to pay full retirement benefits through 2033.[9] From 2034 through 2086, the OASDI program will be able to pay only 75 percent of recipients' annual benefits. The disability insurance program trust fund is projected to be exhausted in the year 2016. The Medicare program's financial status is expected to be stronger than the other programs because the HI tax has increased for high-income individuals beginning in the year 2013. It is expected that there will be sufficient funding to meet benefits obligations through the year 2024.

For years, the viability of the Social Security programs has been the subject of heated debates between Democrats and Republicans across the country with no satisfactory solution. The Republican George W. Bush administration most recently diverted more than $10 billion from the Social Security trust fund to pay for general government expenses. The Democrats criticized the Republican administration for putting the security of current and prospective Social Security benefits at risk. Debates have arisen about whether the federal government is obligated to guarantee future benefits or simply to promise benefits when economic conditions permit them.

State Compulsory Disability Laws (Workers' Compensation)

HISTORICAL BACKGROUND Workers' compensation insurance came into existence during the early decades of the twentieth century, when industrial accidents were very common and workers suffered from occupational illnesses at alarming rates.[10] The first constitutionally acceptable workers' compensation law was enacted in 1911. By 1920, all but six states had instituted workers' compensation laws.[11] State workers' compensation laws are based on the principle of liability without fault[12] (i.e., an employer is absolutely liable for providing benefits to employees that result from occupational disabilities or injuries, regardless of fault). Another key principle of workers' compensation laws is that employers should assume costs of occupational injuries and accidents. These expenses presumably represent costs of production that employers are able to recoup through setting higher prices.

Workers' compensation insurance programs, run by states individually, are designed to cover expenses incurred in employees' work-related accidents. Maritime workers within U.S. borders and federal civilian employees are covered by their own workers' compensation programs. The maritime workers' compensation program is mandated by the **Longshore and Harborworkers' Compensation Act,** and federal civilian employees receive workers' compensation protection under the **Federal Employees' Compensation Act.** Thus, workers' compensation laws cover virtually all employees in the United States, except for domestic workers, some agricultural workers, and small businesses with fewer than a dozen regular employees.[13]

WORKERS' COMPENSATION OBJECTIVES AND OBLIGATIONS TO THE PUBLIC Six basic objectives underlie workers' compensation laws:[14]

- Provide sure, prompt, and reasonable income and medical benefits to work-accident victims or income benefits to their dependents, regardless of fault.
- Provide a single remedy and reduce court delays, costs, and workloads arising out of personal injury litigation.
- Relieve public and private charities of financial drains.
- Eliminate payment of fees to lawyers and witnesses as well as time-consuming trials and appeals.
- Encourage maximum employer interest in safety and rehabilitation through appropriate experience-rating mechanisms.
- Promote frank study of causes of accidents (rather than concealment of fault), reducing preventable accidents and human suffering.

Employers must fund workers' compensation programs according to state guidelines. Participation in workers' compensation programs is compulsory in all states with the exception of Texas, where employers are not required to provide workers' compensation insurance. Self-insurance, another funding option allowed in the majority of states, requires companies to deposit a surety bond, enabling them to pay their own workers' claims directly.[15] Many companies select self-insurance because it gives employers more discretion in administering their own risks. Nevertheless, self-insured companies must pay their workers the same benefits as those paid by state funds or private insurance carriers.

The National Commission on State Workmen's Compensation Laws specified six primary obligations of state workers' compensation programs. This commission established these obligations to ensure prompt and just remedy for workers injured on the job.[16] Table 11-2 lists these obligations.

HOW WORKERS' COMPENSATION COMPARES TO SOCIAL SECURITY BENEFITS Workers' compensation differs from Social Security disability insurance and Medicare in important ways. Workers' compensation pays for medical care for work-related injuries beginning immediately after the injury occurs; it pays temporary disability benefits after a waiting period of 3–7 days; it pays permanent partial and permanent total disability benefits to workers who have lasting consequences of disabilities caused on the job; in most states, it pays rehabilitation and training benefits for those unable to return to pre-injury careers; and it pays benefits to survivors of workers who die of work-related causes. Social Security, in contrast, pays benefits to workers with long-term disabilities from any cause, but only when the disabilities preclude work. Social Security also pays for rehabilitation services and for survivor benefits to families of deceased workers. Social Security begins after a 5-month waiting period and Medicare begins 29 months after the onset of medically verified inability to work.

RECENT TRENDS IN WORKERS' COMPENSATION In recent years, workers' compensation claims have risen dramatically in terms of both numbers of claims and claims amounts. The increased

TABLE 11-2 Primary Obligations of State Workers' Compensation Programs

1. Take initiative in administering the law.
2. Continually review performance of the program and be willing to change procedures and to request the state legislature to make needed amendments.
3. Advise workers of their rights and obligations and assure that they receive the benefits to which they are entitled.
4. Apprise employers and insurance carriers of their rights and obligations; inform other parties in the delivery system (e.g., health care providers) of their obligations and privileges.
5. Assist in voluntary and informal resolution of disputes that are consistent with law.
6. Adjudicate claims that cannot be resolved voluntarily.

Source: Nackley, J. V. (1989). *Primer on Workers' Compensation,* 2nd ed. Washington, DC: Bureau of National Affairs.

prevalence of repetitive strain injuries resulting from the use of keyboards has contributed to this trend. In September 2012, workers' compensation cost nearly 19 percent of all legally required benefits for all civilian employees.[17]

EMPLOYERS' RIGHTS UNDER WORKERS' COMPENSATION PROGRAMS Participation in workers' compensation programs and compliance with applicable regulations protect employers from **torts*** initiated by injured workers based on the no-fault principles of these programs; however, there are four possible exceptions to immunity from legal action:

1. An employer's intentional acts
2. Lawsuits alleging employer retaliation for filing a workers' compensation claim
3. Lawsuits against noncomplying employers
4. Lawsuits relating to "dual capacity" relationships

AN EMPLOYER'S INTENTIONAL ACTS Most state courts consider intentional actions to harm employees as reasonable cause for holding an employer liable. There are two kinds of lawsuits that allege an employer's intentional acts to harm employees. The first, **deliberate and knowing torts,** entails an employer's deliberate and knowing intent to harm at least one employee. The second, **violations of an affirmative duty,** takes place when an employer fails to reveal the exposure of one or more workers to harmful substances or when the employer does not disclose a medical condition typically caused by exposure. In particular, failure to notify violates an employer's affirmative duty when the illness is either correctable at the point of discovery or its progress may be stopped by removing employees from further exposure.

RETALIATION AGAINST WORKERS WHO FILED WORKERS' COMPENSATION CLAIMS In most states, employees possess the right to sue employers who retaliate against them for either filing a workers' compensation claim or pursuing their rights established in workers' compensation programs. Retaliation usually entails an adverse effect upon a worker's status (e.g., a demotion or pay cut) or termination of a worker's employment. Employees may initiate these lawsuits by claiming retaliatory action. Employers then possess the burden of proof to establish their actions as a legally sanctioned business necessity.

EMPLOYER NONCOMPLIANCE Workers' compensation laws oblige employers to comply with applicable state laws. Employers begin to fulfill their obligations by purchasing insurance from state

*Tort laws offer remedies to individuals harmed by the unreasonable actions of others. Tort claims usually involve state law and are based on the legal premise that individuals are liable for the consequences of their conduct if it results in injury to others. Tort laws involve civil suits, which are actions brought to protect an individual's private rights.

funds, from private insurance carriers, or through self-insurance. Failure to carry workers' compensation insurance may lead to one or more consequences such as monetary and criminal penalties.

DUAL CAPACITY **Dual capacity** is a legal doctrine that applies to the relationship between employers and employees. A company may specifically fulfill a role for an employee that is completely different from its role as employer. Even though an employer meets its obligations under workers' compensation laws, it may be susceptible to common-law actions. An employer's immunity does not protect it from common-law actions by employees when the company also serves a dual capacity that confers duties unrelated to and independent of those imposed upon it as an employer. A Supreme Court of Pennsylvania decision offers a clear illustration of the dual capacity doctrine:

> A hospital employee who became ill while performing his job received injuries during medical treatment of the illness (by the same hospital). The hospital's role as an employer was completely unrelated to its role as a medical services provider. The court ruled that Presbyterian University Hospital fulfilled a dual capacity role as an employer and provider of medical treatment to this employee. Specifically, the court concluded that the employee's injuries were sustained because of its role as medical services provider rather than as employer—(a) the purpose of the emergency room visit was to treat the illness, (b) the immediate purpose of seeking treatment was personal, and (c) the hospital billed the employee's insurance carrier for the treatment as it would have for any patient. As a result, this employee gained the right to sue the hospital for injuries sustained during treatment because an X-ray table harness broke, causing the employee to fall onto the floor and sustain injuries.[18]

Becoming injured while using an employer's product to perform work is another instance of dual capacity. For instance, a door-to-door salesperson for Company X, a manufacturer of vacuum cleaners, becomes injured while demonstrating the use of her employer's products. A defective vacuum cleaner explodes during the demonstration, causing serious burns and the loss of her left eye. The salesperson is eligible to file a workers' compensation claim because she was injured while performing her job. She may also have the right to initiate a products liability lawsuit as the user of her employer's defective product.

FINANCING WORKERS' COMPENSATION PROGRAMS Workers' compensation laws specify the permissible methods of funding. Employers generally subscribe to workers' compensation insurance through private carriers or, in some instances, through state funds. A third funding option, self-insurance, requires companies to deposit a surety bond, enabling them to pay their own workers' claims directly.[19] Many employers select self-insurance when available because it gives them greater discretion in administering their own risks. Nevertheless, self-insured companies must pay their workers the same benefits paid by state funds or private insurance carriers.

In most states, the insurance commissioner sets the maximum allowable workers' compensation insurance premium rates for private insurance carriers. Rates are based on each $100 of payroll. Increasingly, some states permit insurance carriers to set rates on a competitive basis.

EMPLOYER AND EMPLOYEE TAX OBLIGATIONS In general, employees do not pay any income taxes on the amount of workers' compensation benefits.[20] Survivors of deceased workers do not pay any taxes on death benefits; however, three circumstances may require payment of taxes. First, employees pay taxes on their workers' compensation benefits when they return to work for light duty. Second, workers' compensation benefits are taxable when they offset (reduce) Social Security OASDI benefits. Third, employees pay taxes on workers' compensation benefits when they do not directly result from work-related illness or injury.*

---

*Workers' compensation benefits for nonwork-related illnesses or injuries are inconsistent with the objectives of workers' compensation programs; however, an IRS ruling (Rev. Rul. 72–191, 1972–1 CB 45) classifies these benefits as part of state workers' compensation programs.

Employers typically do not pay taxes on workers' compensation benefits, with one main exception: Workers' compensation benefits for nonwork-related illnesses or injuries. For this circumstance, the Federal Insurance Contributions Act (FICA) and the Federal Unemployment Tax Act (FUTA) apply. FICA requires that an employer pay a tax based on its payroll; employees contribute a tax based on earnings, which is withheld from each paycheck. FUTA requires that employers contribute 6.2 percent of the taxable wage base, currently $7,000.

Family and Medical Leave Act of 1993

The Family and Medical Leave Act (FMLA) aims to provide employees with job protection in cases of family or medical emergency. The basic thrust of the act is guaranteed leave, and a key element of that guarantee is the right of the employee to return either to the position he or she left when the leave began or to an equivalent position with the same benefits, pay, and other terms and conditions of employment. The passage of the FMLA reflects a growing recognition that many employees' parents are becoming elderly, rendering them susceptible to a serious illness or medical condition. These elderly parents are likely to require frequent (if not constant) attention for an extended period while ill, which places a burden on their adult children.

The passage of the FMLA also recognizes the increasing prevalence of two-income families and the changing roles of men regarding child care. Both partners in a marriage are now more likely to work full time and share family responsibilities, including child rearing. Much like elderly parents, children can also become seriously ill, requiring parents' attention. The FMLA also enables fathers to take paternity leave to care for their newborn babies. Until the passage of the FMLA, men did not have protection comparable to what women receive under the Pregnancy Discrimination Act.

Title I of the FMLA states:

An eligible employee is entitled to 12 unpaid work weeks of leave during any 12-month period for three reasons: because of the birth or placement for adoption or foster care of a child; because of the serious health condition of a spouse, child, or parent; or because of the employee's own serious health condition. Leave may be taken for birth or placement of a child only within 12 months of that birth or placement.

…family leave provisions apply equally to male and female employees: "A father, as well as a mother, can take family leave because of the birth or serious health condition of his child; a son as well as a daughter is eligible for leave to care for a parent."

The minimum criteria for eligibility under this act include the following: Eligible workers must be employed by a private employer or by a civilian unit of the federal government. Eligible workers must also have been employed for at least 12 months by a given employer. Finally, eligible workers have provided at least 1,250 hours of service during the 12 months prior to making a request for a leave. Employees who do not meet these criteria are excluded, as are those who work for an employer with fewer than 50 employees within a 75-mile radius of the employee's home. The FMLA does not explicitly define "hours of service." As a result, many disgruntled employees have filed lawsuits against employers' definitions of hours of service.

Employers may require employees to use paid personal, sick, or vacation leave first as part of the 12-week period. If an employee's paid leave falls short of the 12-week mandated period, then the employer must provide further leave—unpaid—to total 12 weeks. While on leave, employees retain all previously earned seniority or employment benefits, though employees do not have the right to add such benefits while on leave. Furthermore, while on leave, employees are entitled to receive health insurance benefits. Finally, employees may be entitled to receive health benefits if they do not return from leave because of a serious health condition or some other factor beyond their control.

The first major revisions to the FMLA were instituted in January 2009. The changes create leave opportunities for the military and require employees to adhere to stricter guidelines for taking leave. Relatives of seriously injured members of the military may take up to 26 weeks off to care for their injured military family members. In addition, relatives of members of the National Guard or reserves who are called to activity duty may receive up to 12 weeks of leave to attend military programs (official send-off of the family member's troop), arrange child care, or make financial arrangements. Nonmilitary workers who claim to have chronic health conditions (e.g., ongoing back pain) must see their doctor at least twice per year for documentation. Additional revisions to the FMLA may be on the horizon. For example, President Barack Obama may ask Congress to extend coverage by including companies that employ at least 25 workers. As noted, the current law applies to companies that employ at least 50 workers.

One final comment about family and medical leave warrants mention. As discussed, the FMLA provides *unpaid* leave. On September 23, 2002, the California governor signed legislation that allows employees to take partially paid family leave beginning after July 1, 2004. This paid family leave program allows workers to take up to 6 weeks off to care for a newborn, a newly adopted child, or an ill family member. Under this law, employees are eligible to receive 55 percent of their wages during their absence, up to a maximum of $1,011 per week in 2012.

THE BENEFITS AND COSTS OF LEGALLY REQUIRED BENEFITS

Employee benefits are unlike most bases for monetary compensation (e.g., merit, pay-for-knowledge, and incentives). Under these programs, the amount of compensation employees receive varies with their level of contributions to the company. Instead, benefits tend to emphasize social adequacy. Under the principle of social adequacy, benefits are designed to provide subsistence income to all beneficiaries regardless of their performance in the workplace.[21] Thus, although humanitarian, legally required benefits do not directly meet the imperatives of competitive strategy. Legally required benefits, however, may contribute indirectly to competitive advantage by enabling individuals to remain participants in the economy.

Nevertheless, legally required benefits may be a hindrance to companies in the short term because these offerings require substantial employer expenditures (e.g., contributions mandated by the Social Security Act and various state workers' compensation laws). Without these mandated expenditures on compensation, companies could choose to invest these funds in direct compensation programs designed to boost productivity and product or service quality.

How can HR managers and other business professionals minimize the cost burden associated with legally required benefits? Let's consider this issue for both workers' compensation and unemployment insurance benefits. In the case of workers' compensation, employers can respond in two ways. The first response is to reduce the likelihood of workers' compensation claims. The implementation of workplace safety programs is one strategy for reducing workers' compensation claims. Effective safety programs include teaching safe work procedures and safety awareness to employees and supervisors. Another strategy for reducing workers' compensation claims is health promotion programs that include inspections of the workplace to identify health risks (e.g., high levels of exposure to toxic substances) and then to eliminate those risks.

The second employer response is to integrate workers' compensation benefits into the rest of the benefits program. Because of the rampant cost increases associated with workers' compensation, several state legislatures have considered integrating employer-sponsored medical insurance and workers' compensation programs. This "24-hour" coverage would specifically roll the medical component of workers' compensation into traditional employer-provided health insurance. Some companies have already experimented with 24-hour coverage. For instance, Polaroid Corporation found cost advantages associated with integrating medical insurance and workers' compensation: reduced administrative expense through integration of the coverages, better access to all employee medical records, and a decrease in litigation.[22]

Use of 24-hour coverage is not widespread for a number of reasons.[23] Many insurance companies view this approach as complicated. In addition, some companies are concerned that this coverage would cost them in unanticipated ways.

CHAPTER 11 • LEGALLY REQUIRED BENEFITS

Employers also can contain their costs for unemployment insurance. As discussed earlier, the amount of tax employers contribute to providing unemployment insurance depends partly on their experience rating. Thus, employers can contain costs by systematically monitoring the reasons they terminate workers' employment and avoiding terminations that lead to unemployment insurance claims whenever possible. For example, it is not uncommon for companies to employ workers on a full-time basis when they experience increased demand for their products or services. Adding full-time workers is reasonable when companies expect that the higher demand will last for an extended period (e.g., more than 2 years); however, when demand is lower in the short term, companies usually reduce their workforce through layoffs. Unless the laid-off employees immediately find employment, they will file claims with their local employment security office for unemployment insurance. Their claims contribute to the companies' unemployment experience rating and, thus, their cost expenditures.

DESIGNING AND PLANNING THE BENEFITS PROGRAM

As noted earlier, discretionary benefits can work strategically by offering protection programs, paid time off, and services. As they plan and manage employee benefits programs, HR professionals should keep these functions in mind. There is probably no single company that expects its employee benefits program to meet all these objectives. Company management, along with union representatives as appropriate, must therefore determine which objectives are the most important for a particular workforce.

Many experts argue that employee input is key to developing a "successful" program. Such input helps companies target the limited resources they have available for employee benefits to those areas that best meet employees' needs. For example, if a company's workforce includes mostly married couples who are raising young children, family assistance programs would probably be a priority. By involving employees in program development, they are most likely to accept and appreciate the benefits they receive. Companies can involve employees in the benefits determination process in such ways as surveys, interviews, and focus groups.

As they design benefit programs, HR professionals must address fundamental issues, including:

- Who receives coverage
- Whether to include retirees in the plan
- Whether to deny benefits to employees during their probationary periods
- Financing of benefits
- Degree of employee choice in determining benefits
- Cost containment
- Communication

Employers can ascertain key information from employees that can be useful in designing these programs. The areas of input emphasize employees' beliefs about other employers' benefits offerings and employees' thoughts about the value of the benefits they receive.

Determining Who Receives Coverage

Companies decide whether to extend benefits coverage to full-time and part-time employees or to full-time employees only. The trend is toward offering no benefits to part-time employees.

DECIDING WHETHER TO INCLUDE RETIREES IN THE PLAN This decision centers on whether to extend medical insurance coverage to employees beyond the Consolidated Omnibus Reconciliation Act (COBRA)-mandated coverage period, as discussed earlier. Offering medical coverage to retirees benefits them in obvious ways because employers usually finance these benefits either wholly or partly, enabling many retirees on limited earnings to receive adequate medical protection. Extending medical insurance coverage to retirees also benefited employers: The money they spent to extend coverage to retirees was tax deductible. Since 1997, employers' contributions to extend medical coverage to retirees are no longer tax deductible, which means that such expenses will reduce company earnings in the short term. As a result, fewer employers are expected to finance medical insurance coverage for retirees in the future.

Moreover, the rapidly rising cost of retiree health care benefits has created a tremendous financial strain on companies that choose to offer them. Of course, the various sources of economic uncertainty since 2001 have made it more difficult for companies to support full workforces, as evidenced by sluggish pay increases, reductions in benefits offerings, and layoffs. Many companies have found it more difficult to meet their pension obligations to retirees. There is presently a sobering realization that the soaring costs of retiree health care benefits may be pushing some companies to the limit.

PROBATIONARY PERIOD Another scope issue companies must address is employees' status. In many companies, employees' initial term of employment (usually shorter than 6 months) is deemed a **probationary period,** and companies view such periods as an opportunity to ensure that they have made sound hiring decisions. Many companies choose to withhold discretionary employee benefits for all probationary employees. Companies benefit directly through lower administration-of-benefits costs for these employees during the probationary period; however, probationary employees may experience financial hardships if they require medical attention.

Financing

Human resource managers must consider how to finance benefits. In fact, the available resources and financial goals may influence, to some extent, who will receive coverage. Managers may decide among noncontributory, contributory, and employee-financed programs or some combination thereof. **Noncontributory financing** implies that the company assumes total costs for each discretionary benefit. Under **contributory financing,** the company and its employees share the costs. Under **employee-financed benefits,** employers do not contribute to the financing of discretionary benefits. The majority of benefit plans today are contributory, largely because the costs of benefits have risen so dramatically.

Employee Choice

Human resource professionals must decide on the degree of choice employees should have in determining the set of benefits they will receive. If employees within a company can choose from among a set of benefits, as opposed to all employees receiving the same set of benefits, the company is using a **flexible benefits plan** or **cafeteria plan.** Companies implement cafeteria plans to meet the challenges of diversity, as discussed earlier. Although there is limited evidence regarding employees' reactions to flexible benefits, the existing information indicates benefit satisfaction, overall job satisfaction, pay satisfaction, and understanding of benefits increased after the implementation of a flexible benefits plan.[24] Many of these outcomes are desirable because they are known to lead to reduced absenteeism and turnover.

Cafeteria plans vary,[25] so only the two most common will be discussed here. Flexible spending accounts (FSAs) permit employees to pay for certain benefits expenses (e.g., child care) with pretax dollars. Prior to each plan year, employees elect the amount of salary-reduction dollars they wish to allocate to this kind of plan. Employers then use this money to reimburse employees for expenses incurred during the plan year that qualify for repayment. Table 11-3 illustrates the features of an FSA for Illinois state employees. These features are typical of FSAs used by private- and public-sector employers.

Core plus option plans extend a preestablished set of such benefits as medical insurance as a program core, which is usually mandatory for all employees. Beyond the core, employees may choose from an array of benefits options that suit their personal needs. Companies establish upper limits of benefits values available to each employee. If employees do not choose the

TABLE 11-3 Features of a Flexible Spending Account (FSA)

How the FSA Program Works

The FSA program lets you use tax-free dollars to pay for medical expenses, dependent care expenses, or both, increasing your take-home pay and giving you more spendable income. Through convenient payroll deductions, you may contribute up to $5,000 tax-free to a spending account for either one or both plans.

Spending accounts are like getting a tax rebate every time you pay for eligible health and child (dependent) care expenses. The FSA program is simple to use:

- You sign up during one of the enrollment periods and determine how much pretax earnings you wish to put into your FSA account.
- You put pretax money into your spending accounts. (The amount you choose is taken out of your paycheck through payroll deduction and deposited into your FSA account before taxes are calculated.)
- When you have an eligible expense, you send in a claim form with the required documentation.
- You then get a check back from your account.

When you are reimbursed from your spending accounts, you receive that money tax-free. This amount doesn't appear on your W-2 Form as taxable income—and a lower taxable income means you pay less taxes.

Employees have two types of FSAs available: the Medical Care Assistance Plan (MCAP) for eligible health-related expenses and Dependent Care Assistance Plan (DCAP) for eligible child or other dependent care expenses.

Important Notes

- **Federal Tax Deductions.** Expenses reimbursed through an FSA may not also be used as itemized deductions on your federal tax return.
- **Forfeitures.** Money contributed to your FSA in any plan year can only be used to reimburse eligible expenses incurred during that same plan year. Per IRS regulations, any amounts not claimed by the end of the filing deadlines are forfeited.
- **FSA Accounts Are Separate.** The IRS requires that amounts contributed for reimbursement of health care expenses be accounted for separately from those for day care. In other words, you cannot use amounts deposited in your MCAP account to cover DCAP expenses, or vice versa.
- **Tax Savings.** The employer does not guarantee any specific tax consequence from participation in the FSA program. You are responsible for understanding the effects on your individual situation as a result of directing earnings into tax-free spending accounts. You are also responsible for the validity and eligibility of your claims. You may wish to consult with your personal tax adviser regarding your participation.
- **Changing Your FSA Midyear.** Unless you are newly hired or experience a qualifying change of family status, you may not enroll in, withdraw from, or change your contribution to an FSA account outside of the annual benefit choice period.

Dependent Care Assistance Plan (DCAP)

Who Is Eligible to Participate in DCAP?

Eligible Employees Include:

- Employees who are actively at work and are receiving a paycheck from which deductions can be made.
- If you are married, your spouse must be either gainfully employed or looking for work (but must have earned income for the year); a full-time student for at least 5 months during the year; or disabled and unable to provide for his or her care.

Eligible Dependents for DCAP Are Defined by the IRS and Include:

- Your spouse.
- Children or other individuals you are eligible to claim as dependents on your federal income tax return.
- Individuals who could have been claimed as dependents on your income tax except that the person had income that exceeded the amount allowable to be claimed as a dependent.

What Expenses Are Eligible for Reimbursement under DCAP?

- Nursery schools and preschools.
- Schooling prior to the first grade if the amount you pay for schooling is incidental to and cannot be separated from the cost of care.
- Day care centers that comply with all applicable state and local laws and regulations.
- Work-related babysitters—whether in or out of your home.
- Before- and after-school care.
- Housekeepers in your home if part of their work provides for the well-being and protection of your eligible dependents.
- Adult day care facilities (but not expenses for overnight nursing home facilities).
- Employment taxes you pay on wages for qualifying child and dependent care services.
- Other expenses that meet program and IRS criteria.

(continued)

TABLE 11-3 (Continued)

Medical Care Assistance Plan (MCAP)

Who Is Eligible to Participate in MCAP?

- Employees who are working full-time or not less than half-time, are receiving a paycheck from which deductions can be taken, and are participating in one of the state's health plans are eligible.

What Expenses Are Eligible for Reimbursement under MCAP?

- Health and dental care costs not fully covered by the insurance plans in which you or your family members participate, for example:
  - deductibles
  - copayments
  - amounts in excess of the maximum benefit
  - amounts in excess of the reasonable and customary charge limits of the health or dental plans
  - Health and dental care not considered as covered services by the insurance plans in which you or your family members participate.
  - Other expenses that meet program and IRS criteria.

maximum amount of benefits, employers may offer an option of trading extra benefits credits for cash. Table 11-4 illustrates the choices of a typical core plus plan.

Cost Containment

Overall, HR managers today try to contain costs. As indicated earlier, the rise in health care costs is phenomenal, so employee benefits now account for a substantial percentage of total compensation costs incurred by companies. In March 2011, employee benefits accounted for 30.4 percent.[26] The current amount has risen dramatically over the past few decades. This increase would not necessarily raise concerns if total compensation budgets were increasing commensurably. As we discussed in Chapter 8, the growth in funds available to support all compensation programs has stagnated. As a consequence, employers face difficult trade-offs between employee benefits offerings and increases to core compensation.

Communication

Earlier, we noted that employees often regard employee benefits as an entitlement. Thus, it is reasonable to infer that employees are not aware of their value. In fact, employees often either

TABLE 11-4 Core Plus Option Plan

The core plus option plan contains two sets of benefits: core benefits and optional benefits.

All employees receive a minimum level of core benefits:

- Term life insurance equal to one times annual salary
- Health protection coverage (e.g., indemnity plan, self-funded, HMO, PPO) for the employee and dependents
- Disability insurance

All employees receive credits equal to 4–7 percent of salary, which can be used to purchase optional benefits:

- Dental insurance for employee and dependents
- Vision insurance for employee and dependents
- Additional life insurance coverage
- Paid vacation time up to 10 days per year

If an employee has insufficient credits to purchase the desired optional benefits, he or she can purchase these credits through payroll deduction.

are not aware of or undervalue the employee benefits they receive. Given the significant costs associated with offering employee benefits, companies should try to convey to employees the value they are likely to derive from having such benefits. A benefits communication plan is therefore essential. An effective communication program should have three primary objectives:[27]

- To create an awareness of and appreciation for the way current benefits improve the financial security and the physical and mental well-being of employees
- To provide a high level of understanding about available benefits
- To encourage the wise use of benefits

TABLE 11-5 Sample Personal Statement of Benefits

A PERSONAL BENEFITS STATEMENT FOR:

John Doe

SSN: *xxx-xx-xxxx*

Marital Status: *Single*

Date of Birth:

04/10/61

REVIEW OF YOUR CURRENT BENEFIT CHOICES

As of March 2013 our records indicate you have chosen the following benefits (rates may change July 1, 2013):

MEDICAL

For you:

PERSONAL CARE HMO

For your dependent(s):

NONE

State's monthly contribution:

For you:	*$285.00*
For your dependent(s):	*None*
Your monthly contribution:	*$37.50*

DENTAL

QUALITY CARE DENTAL PLAN

Your monthly contribution:	*$9.50*

State's annual contribution:

For you:	*$110.00*
For your dependent(s):	*None*

LIFE INSURANCE

As a full-time employee, you receive state-paid life insurance equal to your annual salary. If you work part-time, your state-paid amount is less. When you retire at age 60 or older, you still receive $5,000 worth of state-paid life insurance

State's monthly contribution for your state-paid life insurance:

Basic life ($90,000): $32.50

Your monthly contribution for the following optional coverage:

For you	*(None):*	*None*
Spouse life	*(None):*	*None*
Child life	*(None):*	*None*
Accidental Death and Dismemberment:		
	(None):	*None*

FLEXIBLE SPENDING ACCOUNTS

You are enrolled in the following plan(s):

Dependent Care Assistance Plan

Annual deduction	*Not Enrolled*

Medical Care Assistance Plan

Annual deduction	*Not Enrolled*

DEPENDENTS

You have chosen to cover the following dependent(s) under your Health Plan:

No Dependents

Note: Any corrections for either premium paid or insurance coverage may only be applied retroactively for up to 6 months from the month in which the change was reported to the group insurance representative. Be sure to review your paycheck for proper deductions and report any concerns to your group insurance representative immediately.

DOLLAR VALUE OF YOUR BENEFITS

Your total annual compensation is your salary or retirement payment plus the value of state-paid medical, dental, and life insurance coverage.

State-paid medical insurance coverage for you:	*$3,420.00*
State contribution for medical insurance coverage for your dependent(s):	*None*
State-paid dental insurance coverage for you and your dependent(s):	*$110.00*
State-paid life insurance coverage for you:	*$390.00*
Total Value of Your State-Paid Benefits:	*$3,920.00*

Companies have traditionally used printed brochures to summarize the key features of the benefits program and to help potential employees compare benefits offerings with those of other companies they may be considering. When new employees join the company, initial group meetings with benefits administrators or audiovisual presentations can detail the elements of the company's benefits program. Shortly after group meetings or audiovisual presentations (usually within a month), new employees should meet individually with benefits administrators, sometimes known as "counselors," to select benefits options. After employees select benefits, the company should provide them with personal benefits statements that detail the scope of coverage and value of each component. Table 11-5 illustrates a personal statement of benefits. Beyond these particulars, companies may update employees on changes in benefits (i.e., reductions in or additions to benefits choices or coverage) with periodic newsletters.

Contemporary communications methods include a company's intranet. An intranet is a useful way to communicate benefits information to employees on an ongoing basis beyond the legally required written documents. In an era of the paperless office, employees are less likely to have written materials readily available. Employees can review general information about the benefits program whenever they want. For example, Table 11-6 lists general information about the kinds of benefits options available at the University of Illinois. In the online version, each item in the list (e.g., announcements, benefits directory) contains a hyperlink that leads to more detailed information.

TABLE 11-6 Menu of Employee Benefit Options

This section is designed to provide detailed information regarding your benefits as a University of Illinois employee. It will give you a comprehensive explanation of each benefit and the resources you will need to initiate enrollment, make changes, or find answers to questions regarding your benefits.

Please select from the following categories:

- *Announcements*—Provides announcements of upcoming sign-up periods or events and updated information relating to your benefits
- *Benefits Directory*—Provides a listing of staff members, including addresses, phone numbers, and e-mail addresses for the Benefits Service Center and each campus.
- *Benefit Choice*—Benefit Choice is an annual open enrollment period that allows employees to make changes to their state of Illinois health, dental, and life insurance coverages, and enroll or re-enroll in flexible spending accounts.
- *Benefit Forms*—Provides links to printable and online benefit forms.
- *Benefits on Call*—Provides an explanation and step-by-step instructions on how to access your benefits information by calling the Benefits On Call voice response system.
- *Benefits Statement*—Provides a statement outlining your current benefit enrollments and instructions for accessing that information.
- *Benefits Summary*—Provides a detailed, comprehensive description of each benefit plan and its provisions.
- *Change in Illinois State Plan (CMS) Coverages*—Provides guidelines and required documentation on when and how you can make changes to your state insurance plans.
- *Frequently Asked Questions*—Provides a list of commonly asked questions relating to your benefits.
- *Leave Information*—Provides time-off–related information for such benefits as family medical leave, sick leave, and vacation leave.
- *Retirement Planning Seminars*—Provides dates and sign-up information.
- *Shared Benefit*—Provides information on the sharing of sick leave between eligible employees and the process to apply for time or donate time to the shared sick leave pool.
- *SURS Information*—Provides links to information on the State University Retirement System.
- *University Plans*—Provides plan information and enrollment procedures for University-administered benefit plans.

COMPENSATION IN ACTION

To both employees and employers, legally required benefits can, at first glance, appear to be a burden. These costs mean that less capital will be devoted to investments or available for expenditures in other areas. However, by thoroughly understanding the principles behind the establishment of these laws, they will be viewed as less of a burden and more of a benefit. As HR and line managers, you will have the responsibility of educating employees about the broader array of benefits options, as well as protecting the company from liabilities associated with a failure to comply with certain legally mandated benefits.

Action checklist for line managers and HR—protecting the company and educating employees

HR takes the lead

- Benchmark other companies to see how flexible benefit plans are chosen and administered. This flexibility will empower employees and will likely lead to positive work-related outcomes (e.g., reduced absenteeism and low turnover).
- Involve employees in the discussion as the benefits plan is adjusted to better align the cost of the benefits plan and its attractiveness to employees.

- Make recommendations on wellness programs and other benefits that support and enhance legally required benefits (which could also decrease overall cost for the company; e.g., health care). Assess the cost up front and provide justification for the cost by comparing it to potential future costs.

Line managers take the lead

- Ensure that all employees are properly trained on equipment and that the work environment is safe. This will serve as a preventative measure against certain benefits that have a cost to employee and employer (e.g., workers' compensation).
- Seek education on certain legally required benefits that are likely to be encountered (e.g., FMLA). Become comfortable with talking about these issues; dealing sensitively with these issues when they are brought up by employees may mitigate the risk of employees filing a grievance on how their legally granted right was compromised (akin to "bedside manners" with hospitals).
- Work with HR to create a communication plan that clearly demonstrates the benefits of the plan, describes how to take full advantage of its benefits, and increases awareness and appreciation.

END OF CHAPTER

MyManagementLab

Go to **mymanagementlab.com** to complete the problems marked with this icon ⭐.

Summary

This chapter provided a discussion of the legally required benefits concept, the rationale for legally required benefits, varieties of legally required benefits, and the implications of benefits for strategic compensation. Although companies have little choice with regard to the implementation of these benefits, the company management can proactively manage the costs of these legally required benefits to some extent. In the coming years, employees, employers, unions, and the government will pay greater attention to the adequacy of Social Security benefits for the succeeding generations. Likewise, these groups will closely monitor the effectiveness of the FMLA. We also discussed important features for designing benefits programs, particularly with emphasis on explaining the value of benefits to employees and facilitating their access to employee benefits information.

Key Terms

base period   242
Federal Unemployment Tax Act (FUTA)   243
experience rating system   243
quarters of coverage   243
fully insured   243
Medicare Part A   245
Medicare Part B   246
Medigap   246
Medicare Select Plan   246
Medicare Advantage   246
fee-for-service plans   246

managed care   246
Federal Insurance Contributions Act (FICA)   246
Self-Employment Contributions Act (SECA)   247
taxable wage base   247
Medicare tax   247
hospital insurance tax (HI)   247
Longshore and Harborworkers' Compensation Act   248
Federal Employees' Compensation Act   248

torts   249
deliberate and knowing torts   249
violations of an affirmative duty   249
dual capacity   250
probationary period   254
noncontributory financing   254
contributory financing   254
employee-financed benefits   254
flexible benefits plan   254
cafeteria plan   254
core plus option plans   254

Discussion Questions

11-1. Except for the Family and Medical Leave Act, the remaining legally required benefits were conceived decades ago. What changes in the business environment and society might affect the relevance or perhaps the viability of any of these benefits? Discuss your ideas.

11-2. Provide your reaction to the statement, "Employee benefits are seen by employees as an entitlement for their membership in companies." Explain the rationale for your reaction.

11-3. Conduct some research on the future of the Social Security programs (see the Web site *www.ssa .gov*). Based on your research, prepare a statement, not to exceed 250 words, that describes your view of the Social Security programs (e.g., whether they are necessary, their viability, or whether there should be changes in how the programs are funded). Refer to the information obtained from your research efforts, indicating how it influenced your views.

CASE
Benefits for Part-Time Workers

An additional Supplemental Case can be found on MyManagementLab.

With just under 100 employees, Jackson, Smith and Henderson CPA (JSH) is considered one of the fastest-growing certified public accounting (CPA) firms in the area. Alan Jones was recently hired as the director of human resources and has many challenges ahead of him as he works to formalize the human resource practices of the firm.

As the benefit open enrollment period is approaching quickly, his first job is to review the benefit offerings of the firm to ensure that JSH is competitive with other area firms. Beyond the legally required benefits, the firm currently offers a fairly basic benefit package including health care insurance, a 401(k) plan, vacation days, and sick days.

Currently, all employees are full-time, and all employees are eligible for benefits. However, two employees have recently requested part-time schedules. Further, in order to meet future unique staffing needs, the firm is considering hiring part-time workers in several departments, including CPAs. Therefore, Alan must make a recommendation to the company's board of directors on whether they should extend the benefits to part-time workers.

A recent compensation survey of businesses in the local geographic area includes information about benefits. The survey reports that about 90 percent of companies in the area offer time off benefits to part-time employees, but only 40 percent offer health care insurance and 15 percent offer a retirement savings plan. A national survey of CPA firms showed a different picture for part-time workers: 95 percent of firms reported time off offerings, 75 percent offered health care insurance, and 67 percent offered retirement benefits to part-time workers.

The job market for talented CPAs is competitive, and Alan knows that the firm will need to hire both full-time and part-time CPAs in the future. Alan's initial reaction is that the firm needs to offer all benefits to both full-time and part-time workers in order to be competitive with other CPA firms. However, the costs to do so are significant. The current benefits package is approximately 30 percent of the total compensation package for full-time workers. While time off benefits and 401(k) contributions for part-time workers would be pro-rated based on the number of hours each employee works, offering health care insurance is a fixed cost. That is, the firm must pay the same to cover a part-time worker as a full-time worker. As a result, benefit costs could potentially approach nearly 50 percent of the total compensation for part-time employees. Part of this cost could be offset by asking part-time workers to pay a higher percentage of the premium, but the cost would still be significant. Alan must balance recruiting needs against a tight budget, and he is concerned about the right path to take.

Questions:

11-4. What are some factors that Alan should consider when determining whether to offer benefits to part-time workers?

11-5. Do you think the firm should offer benefits to part-time workers? If yes, should it offer paid time off, the 401(k) plan, and health insurance? Or only one or two of the benefits? Explain your recommendation.

MyManagementLab

Go to **mymanagementlab.com** for Auto-graded writing questions as well as the following Assisted-graded writing questions:

⭐ **11-6.** How does a state determine if an individual is eligible for unemployment insurance benefits?

⭐ **11-7.** Explain disability benefits under OASDI. Compare it with workers' compensation.

Endnotes

1. U.S. Department of Labor. (December 11, 2012). Employer costs for employee compensation, September 2012 (USDL: 12-2404). Available: *www.bls.gov,* accessed March 3, 2013.
2. P.L. 110-252.
3. P.L. 110-449.
4. U.S. Bureau of Census. (2001). *Statistical Abstract of the United States: 2001.* Available: *http://www.census.gov /prod/2001pubs/statab/sec02.pdf,* accessed February 17, 2011; U.S. Bureau of Census. (2011). *Statistical Abstract of the United States: 2011.* Available: *http://www.census .gov/compendia/statab/2011/tables/11s0103.pdf,* accessed February 17, 2011.
5. Social Security Administration. (2013). *Fact Sheet.* Available: *www.ssa.gov,* accessed March 10, 2013.
6. Ibid.
7. 26 U.S.C. §§3101–3125.
8. 26 U.S.C. §§1401–1403.
9. U.S. Social Security Commission. (2012). *2012 Annual Report of the Board of Trustees of the Federal Old-Age and Survivors Insurance and Federal Disability Insurance Trust Funds.* Available: *www.socialsecurity.gov,* accessed April 13, 2013.
10. Dulles, F. R., & Dubofsky, M. (1993). *Labor in America: A History.* Arlington Heights, IL: Harlan Davidson.

11. Rejda, G. E. (1994). *Social Insurance and Economic Security.* Upper Saddle River, NJ: Prentice Hall.
12. U.S. Chamber of Commerce. (2011). *2011 Analysis of Workers' Compensation Laws.* Washington, DC: Author.
13. Ibid.
14. Nackley, J. V. (1987). *Primer on Workers' Compensation.* Washington, DC: Bureau of National Affairs.
15. Ibid.
16. Ibid.
17. U.S. Bureau of Labor Statistics, *Employer Costs.*
18. *Tatrai v. Presbyterian University Hospital,* 439 A.2d 1162 (PA 1982).
19. Nackley, *Primer on Workers' Compensation.*
20. I.R.C. §104(a).
21. Martocchio, J. J. (2011). *Employee Benefits: A Primer for Human Resource Professionals* (4th ed.). Burr Ridge, IL: Irwin/McGraw-Hill.
22. Tompkins, N. C. (1992). Around-the-clock medical coverage. *HR Magazine* (June), pp. 66–72.
23. Baker, L. C., & Krueger, A. B. (1993). *Twenty-Four-Hour Coverage and Workers' Compensation Insurance.* Working paper, Princeton University Industrial Relations Section.
24. Barber, A. E., Dunham, R. B., & Formisano, R. (1990). *The Impact of Flexible Benefit Plans on Employee Satisfaction.* Paper presented at the Fiftieth annual meeting of the Academy of Management, San Francisco, CA.
25. Martocchio, *Employee Benefits* (4th ed.).
26. U.S. Bureau of Labor Statistics, *Employer Costs.*
27. Martocchio, *Employee Benefits* (4th ed.).

CONTEMPORARY STRATEGIC COMPENSATION CHALLENGES

Where We Are Now:

PART IV, EMPLOYEE BENEFITS, explained the most widely used employee benefits practices and approaches to planning the employee benefits program. We have studied the context for compensation, concepts for awarding pay increases, tools for structuring core compensation (base pay and pay increases), and employee benefits, rounding out the principles and practices for building strategic total compensation systems. Now we turn to contemporary strategic compensation challenges. Our focus will be on two important strategic employee groups: executives and the flexible workforce. Many principles and practices for compensating these two employee groups differ from what we applied to the vast majority of employee groups.

In **PART V, WE WILL COVER**

12

COMPENSATING EXECUTIVES

MyManagementLab®

⭐ **Improve Your Grade!**

When you see this icon, visit **www.mymanagementlab.com** for activities that are applied, personalized, and offer immediate feedback.

LEARNING OBJECTIVES

When you finish studying this chapter, you should be able to:

1. Explain the difference between executive pay with pay for nonexecutives.
2. List the main components of executive compensation packages.
3. Discuss with examples the principles and processes of setting executive compensation, including the key players and the theoretical explanations for setting executive compensation.
4. Summarize the executive compensation disclosure rules and the reasons why they have been established.
5. Concisely present the "say on pay" practice.
6. Briefly explain the executive compensation controversy as it relates to whether U.S. executives are paid too much.

Executive compensation practices in U.S. companies have received substantial attention in the press. As we will see in this chapter, executive pay practices have raised concerns that many executives receive lucrative compensation and benefits even when company performance falls below shareholder expectations. Many critics have questioned whether such practices may interfere with some executives' motivation to achieve excellent performance. Moreover, applying such practices to executives contradicts the main assumptions of performance-based pay discussed in Chapters 3 and 4 that *successful performance* triggers merit and incentive awards and the *degree of success* determines the amount of award. After all, pay-for-performance applies to most nonexecutive employees in U.S. companies. In some instances that we will discuss, executives are rewarded after they have not performed well, with multimillion dollar awards contingent on their leaving the company. It is not surprising that those instances are often referred to as *pay-for-nonperformance* or, more harshly, *pay-for-failure* and that they have become increasingly common events in the world of executive compensation.

CONTRASTING EXECUTIVE PAY WITH PAY FOR NONEXECUTIVE EMPLOYEES

From an economic standpoint, the chief executive officer (CEO) is the seller of his or her services, and the compensation committee is the buyer of these services. Under classic economic theory, a reasonable price is obtained through negotiations that are at arm's length between an informed seller and an informed buyer. An awkward situation can result when the CEO hires a professional compensation director or compensation consultant. In this case, the compensation consultant who makes the recommendation to the compensation committee works for the CEO. In theory, the CEO hires the consultant to perform an objective analysis of the company's executive pay package and to make whatever recommendations the consultant feels are appropriate. This relationship has the potential to promote a conflict of interest because of the perceived pressure for the consultant to protect the CEO's financial interests. The irony is that the consultant is often viewed as representing the shareholders' interests. In a sense, the buyers of the CEO's services are the shareholders and their representatives, the compensation committee of the board of directors. They tend to act upon the compensation consultant's recommendation.[1]

This passage illustrates just one of the main differences between compensating executives and compensating other employees. There are many other contrasts. The income disparity between executives and other employees is astounding. We take this issue up in greater detail later in this chapter.

PRINCIPLES OF EXECUTIVE COMPENSATION: IMPLICATIONS FOR COMPETITIVE STRATEGY

Executives are the top leaders in their companies. It intuitively seems reasonable that executives should earn substantial compensation packages. After all, their skills and experience enable them to develop and direct the implementation of competitive strategies. Few dispute the key role executives play in promoting competitive advantage; however, public scrutiny of executive compensation packages intensified since the 1990s because of heightened concerns about global competitiveness, rampant corporate downsizing, and the more recent practice of relocating jobs to countries with lower labor costs (i.e., offshoring) that left hundreds of thousands of employees jobless. The number of layoff events initiated by companies and the number of employees who have lost their jobs have risen to unprecedented levels since September 2008, following the start of perhaps the deepest economic recession in the United States. An alarming trend is that extended mass layoffs (periods of unemployment exceeding 30 days) continue to affect more people each year than prior to the start of the most recent recession.[2]

We will take up the executive compensation controversy later in this chapter. We will next review fundamental concepts: defining executive status and the components of executive compensation packages.

DEFINING EXECUTIVE STATUS

Who Are Executives?

Virtually all the components of executive compensation plans provide favorable tax treatment for both the executive and the company. Who are executives? From a tax regulation perspective, the Internal Revenue Service (IRS) recognizes two groups of employees who play a major role in a company's policy decisions: highly compensated employees and key employees. The IRS uses "key employees" to determine the necessity of top-heavy provisions in employer-sponsored qualified retirement plans that cover most nonexecutive employees. It uses "highly compensated employees" for nondiscrimination rules in employer-sponsored health insurance benefits. Although these two designations were created for federal tax rule applications, employees in both groups typically participate in executive compensation and benefits plans.

Key employees and highly compensated employees hold positions of substantial responsibility. Figure 12-1 illustrates the placement of key employees in a typical organizational structure. Although titles vary from company to company and in pay structures, CEOs, presidents, executive vice presidents, vice presidents of functional areas (e.g., human resources), and the directors below them usually meet the criteria for key employees.

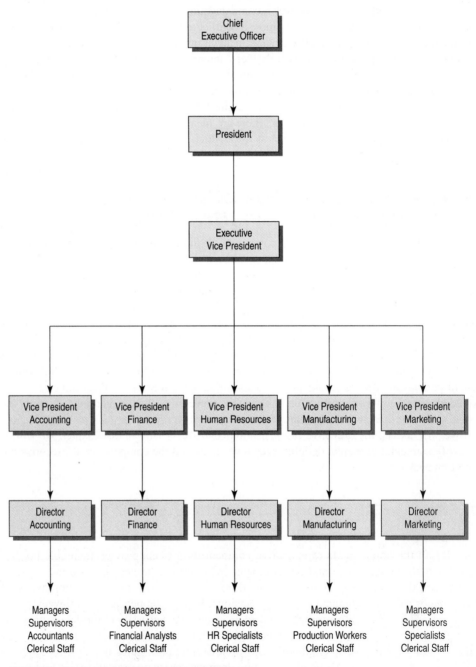

FIGURE 12-1 Examples of Key Employees

Key Employees

The term **key employee** means any employee who at any time during the year is:[3]

- A 5 percent owner of the employer
- A 1 percent owner of the employer having an annual compensation from the employer of more than $165,000
- An officer of the employer having an annual compensation greater than $165,000 in 2013 (indexed for inflation in increments of $5,000 beginning in 2003)

  U.S. Treasury Regulations define the term *officer* used in this definition of key employees:[4]

  Generally, the term officer means an administrative executive who is in regular and continued service. The term officer implies continuity of service and excludes those employed for a special and single transaction. An employee who merely has the title of an officer but not the authority of an officer is not considered an officer for purposes of the key employee test. Similarly, an employee who does not have the title of an officer but has the authority of an officer is an officer for purposes of the key employee test.

Highly Compensated Employees

The IRS defines a **highly compensated employee** as one of the following during the current year or preceding year:[5]

- A 5 percent owner at any time during the year or the preceding year
- For the preceding year had compensation from the employer in excess of $115,000 in 2013
- If the employer elects the application of this clause for a plan year, was in the top-paid group of employees for the preceding year

EXECUTIVE COMPENSATION PACKAGES

Executive compensation has both core and employee benefits elements, much like compensation packages for other employees; however, one noteworthy feature distinguishes executive compensation packages from nonexecutive compensation packages. Executive compensation packages emphasize long-term or deferred rewards over short-term rewards. The main components of executive compensation include:

- Current or annual core compensation
- Deferred core compensation: stock compensation
- Deferred core compensation: golden parachutes and platinum parachutes
- Employee benefits: enhanced protection program benefits and perquisites
- Clawback provisions

Components of Current Core Compensation

Executive current core compensation packages contain two components: annual base pay and bonuses.

BASE PAY Base pay is the fixed element of annual cash compensation. Companies that use formal salary structures may have specific pay grades and pay ranges (Chapter 8) for nonexempt employees and exempt employees, including supervisory, management, professional, and executive jobs, with the exception of the CEO.

As discussed in Chapter 8, compensation professionals generally apply different range spreads across pay grades. They most commonly use progressively higher range spreads for pay grades that contain more valuable jobs in terms of a company's competitive strategies. Higher-level jobs afford employees greater promotion opportunities than do entry-level jobs. Employees also tend to remain in higher pay grades longer, and the specialized skills associated with higher-pay-grade jobs are considered valuable. It therefore makes sense to apply larger range spreads to these pay grades.

Chief executive officer jobs do not fall within formal pay structures for two reasons. First, CEOs' work is highly complex and unpredictable. It is not possible to specify discrete responsibilities and duties. The choice of competitive strategy by CEOs and other executives and the influence of external and internal market factors make it impossible to describe CEOs' jobs. Second, setting CEO compensation differs dramatically from the rational processes compensation professionals use to build market-competitive pay structures (Chapter 7). We will discuss agency theory, tournament theory, and social comparison theory later as explanations for setting CEO compensation.

In most cases, annual base pay represents a relatively small part of a CEO's total compensation for two reasons. First, it typically takes years before the fruits of the CEOs' strategic initiatives are realized. Second, the IRS limits the amount of annual salary a company may exclude as a business expense. Only the first $1 million annually for an executive's pay may be excluded from the company's income tax liability. This ruling was put into place to keep companies from boosting CEO annual pay to astronomical levels for the purposes of tax savings. More recently, the **Emergency Economic Stabilization Act of 2008 (EESA)** authorized the Secretary of the Treasury to establish the **Troubled Assets Relief Program (TARP)** to "purchase, and to make and fund commitments to purchase troubled assets from any financial institution, on terms and conditions as are determined by the Secretary." In other words, banks with financial assistance from the federal government could deduct only the first $500,000 annually for an executive's pay as a business expense.[6]

BONUSES Bonuses represent single pay-for-performance payments companies use to reward employees for achievement of specific, exceptional goals. As discussed in previous chapters, compensation professionals design bonuses for merit pay programs (Chapter 3), gain sharing plans and referral plans (Chapter 4), and sales incentive compensation programs (Chapter 8). Bonuses also represent a key component of executive compensation packages.

Companies' compensation committees recommend bonus awards to boards of directors for their approval (as we will discuss later in this chapter). Four types of bonuses are common in executive compensation:

- Discretionary bonus
- Performance-contingent bonus
- Predetermined allocation bonus
- Target plan bonus

As the term implies, boards of directors award **discretionary bonuses** to executives on an elective basis. They weigh four factors in determining the amount of discretionary bonus: company profits, the financial condition of the company, business conditions, and prospects for the future. For example, boards of directors may award discretionary bonuses to executives when a company's position in the market is strong.

Executives receive **performance-contingent bonuses** based on the attainment of specific performance criteria. The performance appraisal system for determining bonus awards is often the same appraisal system used for determining merit increases or general performance reviews for salary (Chapter 3).

Unlike the previous executive bonuses, the total bonus pool for the **predetermined allocation bonus** is based on a fixed formula. The central factor in determining the size of the total bonus pool and bonus amounts is company profits.

The **target plan bonus** ties bonuses to executives' performance. The bonus amount increases commensurately with performance. Executives do not receive bonuses when their performance falls below minimally acceptable standards. The target plan bonus differs from the predetermined allocation bonus in an important way: Predetermined allocation bonus amounts are fixed, regardless of how well executives perform.

TABLE 12-1 **Short-Term Incentive Compensation: Current Profit Sharing Plans and Gain Sharing Plans**

Current Profit Sharing Plans

As we discussed in Chapter 4, profit sharing plans pay a portion of company profits to employees, separate from base pay, cost-of-living adjustments, or permanent merit pay increases. Two basic kinds of profit sharing plans are used widely today. First, current profit sharing plans award cash to employees, typically on a quarterly or annual basis. Second, deferred profit sharing plans place cash awards in trust accounts for employees. These trusts are set aside on employees' behalf as a source of retirement income. Current profit sharing plans provide cash to employees as part of their regular core compensation; thus, these payments are subject to IRS taxation when they are earned. Deferred profit sharing plans are not taxed until the employee begins to make withdrawals during retirement.

Gain Sharing Plans

As we discussed in Chapter 4, gain sharing describes group incentive systems that provide participating employees with an incentive payment based on improved company performance such as increased productivity, increased customer satisfaction, lower costs, or better safety records. Gain sharing was developed so that all employees could benefit financially from productivity improvements that result from the suggestion system. Along with serving as a compensation tool, most gain sharing reflects a management philosophy that emphasizes employee involvement.

Short-Term Incentives

Companies award short-term incentive compensation to executives to recognize their progress toward fulfilling competitive strategy goals. Executives may participate in current profit sharing plans and gain sharing plans. Table 12-1 describes these plans. Whereas short-term objectives reward nonexempt and lower-level management employees for achieving major milestone work objectives, short-term incentives applied to executives are designed to reward them for meeting intermediate performance criteria. The performance criteria relate to the performance of a company as dictated by competitive strategy. Change in the company's earnings per share over a 1-year period, growth in profits, and annual cost savings are criteria that may be used in executives' short-term incentive plans.

Short-term incentive compensation programs usually apply to a group of select executives within a company. The plan applies to more than one executive because the synergy that results from the efforts and expertise of top executives influences corporate performance. The board of directors distributes short-term incentive awards to each executive based on rank and compensation levels. Thus, the CEO will receive a larger performance award than will the executive vice president, whose position is lower in the company's structure than the CEO's position.

For example, let's assume that the CEO and executive vice president of a chain of general merchandise retail stores have agreed to lead the corporation as the lowest-cost chain of stores in the general merchandise retail industry. The CEO and executive vice president establish a 5-year plan to meet this lowest-cost competitive strategy. The vice president of compensation recommends that the company adopt a gain sharing program to reward top executives for contributing to the cost reduction objective. After 1 year, the complementary decisions made by the CEO and executive vice president have enabled the corporation to save $10,000,000. The board of directors agrees that the executives' collaborative decisions led to noteworthy progress toward meeting the lowest-cost strategy and award the CEO 2 percent of the annual cost savings ($200,000) and the executive vice president 1 percent ($100,000).

Components of Deferred Core Compensation

STOCK COMPENSATION **Deferred compensation** refers to an agreement between an employee and a company to render payments to an employee at a future date. Deferred compensation is a hallmark of executive compensation packages. As an incentive, deferred compensation is supposed to create a sense of ownership, aligning the interests of the executive with those of the

TABLE 12-2 Employee Stock Terminology

Stock option. A right granted by a company to an employee to purchase a number of stocks at a designated price within a specified period of time.

Stock grant. A company's offering of stock to an employee.

Exercise of stock grant. An employee's purchase of stock, using stock options.

Disposition. Sale of stock by the stockholder.

Fair market value. The average value between the highest and lowest reported sales price of a stock on the New York Stock Exchange on any given date. The IRS specifies whether an option has a readily ascertainable fair market value at grant. An option has a readily ascertainable fair market value if the option is actively traded on an established stock exchange at the time it is granted.

owners or shareholders of the company over the long term. The amount of long-term incentive compensation varies tremendously from CEO to CEO. It isn't unusual for CEOs to be awarded $3 million or more each year.

Apart from the incentive value, deferred compensation provides tax advantages to executives. In particular, deferring payment until retirement should lead to lower taxation. Why does deferment create a tax advantage? Executives do not pay taxes on deferred compensation until they receive it. Executives' income tax rates will presumably be substantially lower during retirement, when their total income is lower, than they are while they are employed.

Company stock shares are the main form of executives' deferred compensation. As described in Chapter 4, **company stock** represents total equity of the firm. **Company stock shares** represent equity segments of equal value. Equity interest increases positively with the number of stock shares. Stocks are bought and sold every business day in a public stock exchange. The New York Stock Exchange is among the best-known of the stock exchanges. Table 12-2 lists basic terminology pertaining to stocks.

Companies design executive stock compensation plans to promote an executive's sense of ownership of the company. A sense of ownership should presumably motivate executives to strive for excellent performance. Stock value generally increases with gains in company performance. In particular, a company's stock value rises in response to reports of profit gains; however, factors outside executives' control often influence stock prices despite executives' performance. For example, forecasts of economywide recession, increases in the national unemployment rate, and threats to national security (e.g., the September 11 attacks) often lead to declines in stock value.

Six particular forms of deferred (stock) compensation include:

- Incentive stock options
- Nonstatutory stock options
- Restricted stock
- Phantom stock plans
- Discount stock options
- Stock appreciation rights

INCENTIVE STOCK OPTIONS **Incentive stock options** entitle executives to purchase their companies' stock in the future at a predetermined price. The predetermined price usually equals the stock price at the time an executive receives the stock option. In effect, executives are purchasing the stocks at a discounted price. Executives generally buy after the price has increased dramatically. An executive receives **capital gains** as the difference between the stock price at the time of purchase and the lower stock price at the time an executive receives the stock option. Executives receive income tax benefits by participating in incentive stock option plans. The federal government does not recognize capital gains until the disposition of the stock.

NONSTATUTORY STOCK OPTIONS Much like incentive stock options, companies award stock options to executives at discounted prices. In contrast to incentive stock options, **nonstatutory stock options** do not qualify for favorable tax treatment. Executives pay income taxes on the difference between the discounted price and the stock's fair market value at the time of the stock grant. They do not pay taxes in the future when they choose to exercise their nonstatutory stock options.

Nonstatutory stock options do provide executives an advantage. Executives' tax liability is ultimately lower over the long term: Stock prices generally increase over time. As a result, the capital gains will probably be much greater in the future when executives exercise their options rather than when their companies grant these options.

RESTRICTED STOCK The term **restricted stock** means that executives do not have any ownership control over the disposition of the stock for a predetermined period, often 5–10 years. Executives must sell the stock back to the company for exactly the same discounted price they had at the time of purchase if they terminate their employment before the end of the designated restriction period.[7] In addition, restricted stock grants provide executives tax incentives. They do not pay tax on any income that results from an increase in stock price until after the restriction period ends.[8] Restricted stock is a common type of long-term executive compensation. Boards of directors award restricted stock to executives at considerable discounts.

PHANTOM STOCK A **phantom stock** plan is a compensation arrangement whereby boards of directors promise to pay a bonus in the form of the equivalent of either the value of company shares or the increase in that value over a period of time. For instance, a company could promise Mary, its new employee, that it would pay her a bonus every 5 years equal to the increase in the equity value of the firm times some percentage of total payroll at that point. Or it could promise to pay her an amount equal to the value of a fixed number of shares set at the time the promise is made.[9] Phantom stock plans are similar to restricted stock plans because executives must meet specific conditions before they can convert these phantom shares into real shares of company stock.[10] There are generally two conditions. First, executives must remain employed for a specified period, anywhere between 5 and 20 years. Second, executives must retire from the company. Upon meeting these conditions, executives receive income equal to the increase in the value of company stock from the date the company granted the phantom stock to the conversion date. Phantom stock plans provide executives with tax advantages. Executives pay taxes on the capital gains after they convert their phantom shares to real shares of company stock during retirement. Executives' retirement incomes will probably be significantly less than their incomes prior to retirement. Thus, the retirees' income tax rates will be lower. Employers receive a tax deduction in the same amount when employees pay taxes on the capital gains.

DISCOUNT STOCK OPTION PLANS **Discount stock option plans** are similar to nonstatutory stock option plans with one exception. Companies grant stock options at rates far below the stock's fair market value on the date the option is granted. This means that the participating executive immediately receives a benefit equal to the difference between the exercise price and the fair market value of the employer's stock.

STOCK APPRECIATION RIGHTS **Stock appreciation rights** provide executives income at the end of a designated period, much like restricted stock options; however, executives never have to exercise their stock rights to receive income. The company simply awards payment to executives based on the difference in stock price between the time the company granted the stock rights at fair market value to the end of the designated period, permitting the executives to keep the stock. Executives pay tax on any income from gains in stock value when they exercise their stock rights,[11] presumably after retirement when their tax rates are lower.

GOLDEN PARACHUTES Most executives' employment agreements contain a golden parachute clause. **Golden parachutes** provide pay and benefits to executives after a termination that results from a change in ownership or corporate takeover, that is, the merger or combining of two separate companies. For example, Anheuser-Busch was an independent U.S. corporation known for brewing beer, and InBev was an independent corporation in Belgium also known for brewing beer. InBev purchased or acquired Anheuser-Busch (the target company) in 2008, creating a merged or combined corporation named Anheuser-Bush InBev. Golden parachutes extend pay and benefits from 1 to 5 years, depending on the agreement. Boards of directors include golden parachute clauses for two reasons. First, golden parachutes limit executives' risks in the event of these unforeseen events. Second, golden parachutes promote recruitment and retention of talented executives.

Companies benefit from golden parachute payments because they can treat these payments as business expenses. This means that companies can reduce their tax liability by increasing the parachute amount. The total value of golden parachutes came to exceed executives' annual income levels by far. Public outcry led to government-imposed intervention that limited tax benefits to companies. Companies may generally receive tax deductions on golden parachutes that amount to less than several times an executive's average annual compensation for the preceding 5 years.

PLATINUM PARACHUTES In an ideal world, CEOs will perform on an exemplary basis, making decisions to drive up company profits. As you know, we do not live in a perfect world; sometimes, CEOs do not perform their jobs well and companies lose out on profit opportunities. After a period of unsatisfactory performance as determined by shareholders and other company executives, CEOs may often be terminated even before the expiration of their employment contracts. Many companies reach agreements with CEOs to terminate employment, awarding a platinum parachute as an incentive. **Platinum parachutes** are lucrative awards that compensate departing executives with severance pay, continuation of company benefits, and even stock options. Companies use platinum parachutes to avoid long legal battles or critical reports in the press essentially by paying off a CEO to give up his or her post. For example, Jay S. Sidhu resigned from Sovereign Bancorp amid growing criticism from investors. He left the company with a platinum parachute worth $73.56 million lined with $24.4 million in cash and stock options, 5 years of free health care, and a 3-year, $40,000 per month consulting contract.

CLAWBACK PROVISIONS **Clawback provisions** in CEO employment contracts allow boards of directors to take back performance-based compensation if they were to subsequently learn that performance goals were not actually achieved, regardless of whether the CEO was responsible for performance falling short of target levels. Increasingly, these provisions are becoming more common because of the increasing scrutiny of CEO compensation packages by the public and shareholders, particularly since the recent global financial crisis in the late 2000s. For example, Wilmington Trust Corporation rescinded more than $1.8 million in compensation from Chief Executive Donald Foley. Wilmington Trust participated in the TARP program (described earlier in this chapter), which subjected it to strict limits on executive pay. As it turns out, Wilmington's purchase of another bank at a price below market value lowered the overall value of the combined company.

TIGHTER REGULATION OF DEFERRED COMPENSATION PLANS Well-publicized corporate accounting scandals have recently led to tighter accounting standards. New corporate tax law puts tighter restrictions on deferred compensation payouts to prevent corporate executives from siphoning money out of their corporations. There specifically was a rash of executives withdrawing deferred compensation money before their companies went bankrupt. The most well-known scandal occurred at Enron. In response to corporate accounting scandals, the Securities and Exchange Commission (SEC) administered the Sarbanes-Oxley Act of 2002. The Sarbanes-Oxley Act is perhaps the most significant legislation because it imposes rigorous requirements for companies' financial disclosure to limit the chance that covert misuses of corporate funds will occur. In 2002, President George W. Bush strengthened the oversight of the SEC when he signed the **Sarbanes-Oxley Act of 2002** into law. The act mandated a number of reforms to enhance corporate responsibility, enhance financial disclosures, and combat corporate and accounting fraud in response to corporate accounting scandals in Enron, Tyco, and other large U.S. corporations. The act established **Public Company Accounting Oversight Board (PCAOB)** to oversee the activities of the auditing profession.

Section 103 of the Sarbanes-Oxley Act of 2002 directs the board to establish auditing and related attestation, quality control, ethics, and independence standards and rules to be used by registered public accounting firms in the preparation and issuance of audit reports as required by the act or the rules of the Securities and Exchange Commission. The board's Office of the Chief Auditor advises the board on the establishment of such auditing and related professional practice standards. The board also seeks advice from its Standing Advisory Group and ad hoc task forces and working groups.

Employee Benefits: Enhanced Protection Program Benefits and Perquisites

Executives receive discretionary benefits like other employees (e.g., protection program benefits, paid time off, and employee services); however, executives' discretionary benefits differ in two ways. First, protection programs include supplemental coverage that provides enhanced benefit levels. Second, the services component contains benefits exclusively for executives. These exclusive executive benefits are known as **perquisites** or **perks.** Legally required benefits apply to executives, with the exception of one provision of the Family and Medical Leave Act of 1993.

ENHANCED PROTECTION PROGRAM BENEFITS Supplemental life insurance and supplemental executive retirement plans distinguish protection programs for executive employees from protection programs for other employees. As discussed in Chapter 9, employer-provided life insurance protects employees' families by paying a specified amount to an employee's beneficiaries upon an employee's death. Most policies pay some multiple of the employee's salary (e.g., benefits paid at twice the employee's annual salary). In addition to regular life insurance, executives receive **supplemental life insurance** protection that pays an additional monetary benefit. Companies design executives' supplemental life insurance protection to meet two objectives.[12] First, supplemental life insurance increases the value of executives' estates bequeathed to designated beneficiaries (usually family members) upon their deaths. Life insurance programs may be designed to provide greater benefits than standard plans usually allow. Second, these programs provide executives with favorable tax treatments.

Supplemental retirement plans are designed to restore benefits restricted under qualified plans. As discussed in Chapter 10, qualified plans entitle employers to tax benefits from their contributions to pension plans. In general, this means that employers may take current tax deductions for contributions to fund future retirement income. Employees may also receive some favorable tax treatment (i.e., a lower tax rate). In Chapter 10, we discussed the characteristics of qualified plans. A qualified plan generally entitles employees to favorable tax treatment of the benefits they receive upon their retirement. Any investment income that is generated in the pension program is not taxed until the employee retires.

The IRS limited the annual earnings amount for determining qualified plan benefits to $255,000 in 2013 (indexed for inflation, in increments of $5,000). In general, all annual earnings greater than this level cannot be included in defined benefit plan formulas or the calculation of annual additions to defined contribution plans. In addition, the IRS limits the annual benefit amounts for defined benefit plans to the lesser of $205,000 in 2013, indexed for inflation, or 100 percent of the highest average compensation for 3 consecutive years.[13] Limits on annual additions to defined contribution plans were the lesser of $51,000 in 2013, indexed for inflation, or 100 percent of the participant's compensation.[14] The annual addition includes employer contributions, employee contributions, and forfeitures allocated to the participant's account. For example, an executive's three highest annual salaries are $690,000, $775,000, and $1,100,000. The average of these three highest salaries is $855,000. Of course, $205,000 is less than $855,000; therefore, an executive's retirement income based on the company's qualified pension plan cannot exceed $205,000 adjusted for inflation.

TABLE 12-3 Common Executive Perks

- Company cars
- Supplemental life insurance
- Legal services (e.g., income tax preparation)
- Recreational facilities (e.g., country club and athletic club memberships)
- Travel perks (e.g., use of corporate jet)

A supplemental retirement plan can make up this difference. For illustrative purposes, let's assume that the annual benefit under a qualified pension plan is 60 percent of the final average salary for the past 15 years of service, which is $400,000. Based on this formula, the executive should receive an annual retirement benefit of $240,000 ($400,000 × 60 percent). This annual benefit exceeds $205,000 (the statutory limit for qualified retirement plans). Because of the statutory limit, companies may offer a supplemental executive retirement plan that provides the difference between the value derived from the pension formula ($240,000) and the statutory limit ($205,000). In this example, the executive would receive a supplemental annual retirement benefit of $35,000.

PERQUISITES Executive perquisites are an integral part of executive compensation. Perquisites cover a broad range of benefits, from free lunches to the free use of corporate jets. Table 12-3 lists common executive perks. Perquisites serve two purposes. First, these benefits recognize executives' attained status. Membership in an exclusive country club reinforces executives' attained social status. Second, executives use perks for personal comfort or as a business tool. For example, a company may own a well-appointed cabin in Vail, Colorado. Executives may use the cabin for rest and relaxation or as a place to court new clients or close a lucrative business deal. Arranging relaxing weekends in Vail benefits executives and their families and provides executives opportunities to develop rapport with prospective clients. It is possible that companies will provide cash in lieu of perquisites because of stricter reporting requirements by the Securities and Exchange Commission. Particularly after the corporate scandals at Enron and other corporations, company shareholders expect management to display greater accountability for the nonbusiness use of such company property as corporate jets. Since 2008, companies have had to report perks valued at $10,000 or more apiece.

A survey of executive compensation practices revealed that fewer companies are offering perks to their chief executive officers, down from 89.8 percent in 2009 to 77.6 percent in 2010.[15] The most common perks offered in 2010 were supplemental life insurance (31.7 percent), company cars (30.7 percent), and country club memberships (26.1 percent). The prevalence of fewer perks offerings may be due to greater economic uncertainties and the recent requirement that companies report perks valued at $10,000 or more apiece.

PRINCIPLES AND PROCESSES FOR SETTING EXECUTIVE COMPENSATION

We discussed the processes compensation professionals use to reward performance (e.g., merit pay and alternative incentive pay methods) and acquisition of job-related knowledge and skills (e.g., pay-for-knowledge and skilled-based pay) in previous chapters. Although pay-for-performance is the public rationale for setting executive compensation, reality is often quite different. Three alternative theories explain the principles and processes for setting executive compensation: agency theory, tournament theory, and social comparison theory. We will begin by discussing the key players in setting executive compensation.

The Key Players in Setting Executive Compensation

Different individuals and groups participate in setting executive compensation. They include compensation consultants, compensation committees, and boards of directors. Each plays a different role in setting executive compensation.

EXECUTIVE COMPENSATION CONSULTANTS **Executive compensation consultants** usually propose several recommendations for alternate pay packages. Executive compensation consultants are often employed by large consulting firms that specialize in executive compensation or advise company management on a wide variety of business issues. The regulations involving executive compensation plans are extremely complex. To understand them fully requires expertise often found in leading executive compensation and benefits consulting firms. Some of the leading and most well-respected firms in this area include the following:

- Aon (*www.aon.com*)
- Buck Consultants (*www.buckconsultants.com*)
- Frederic W. Cook & Company (*www.fwcook.com*)
- The Hay Associates (*www.haygroup.com*)
- Pearl Meyer & Partners (*www.pearlmeyer.com*)
- Towers Watson (*www.towerswatson.com*)
- William M. Mercer (*www.mercer.com*)

You will find useful updates about executive compensation and benefits on these firms' Web sites.

Consultants make recommendations about what and how much to include in executive compensation packages based on strategic analyses, which entail an examination of a company's external market context and internal factors. Examples of external market factors include industry profile, information about competitors, and long-term growth prospects. Financial condition is the most pertinent internal factor regarding executive compensation. Strategic analyses permit compensation consultants to see where their client company stands in the market based on external and internal factors. Strong companies should be able to devote more financial resources to fund lucrative executive compensation programs than weaker companies. More often than not, executive compensation consultants find themselves in conflict-of-interest situations:

> Ostensibly, compensation consultants were hired by the CEO to perform an objective analysis of the company's executive pay package and to make whatever recommendations the consultant felt were appropriate. In reality, if those recommendations did not cause the CEO to earn more money than he was earning before the compensation consultant appeared on the scene, the latter was rapidly shown the door.[16]

Executive compensation consultants' professional survival may depend on recommending lucrative compensation packages. Recommending the most lucrative compensation packages will quickly promote a favorable impression of the consultant among CEOs, leading to future consulting engagements.

Since 2008, the Securities and Exhange Commission rulings require companies to include the identity of the consulting firm in public disclosure statements. This ruling has created concerns about possible conflicts of interest for consulting firms that also provide consulting services in other areas (e.g., performance management and change management) for the same client firms. Executive compensation consulting represents just one of many possible areas of management consulting. The conflict potentially arises when a consultant intentionally recommends a more-lucrative-than-warranted executive compensation package in the hope of gaining management favor and additional other management consulting opportunities. Of course, compensation consulting firms are concerned about the public image of possible conflicts of interest and have considered a variety of tactics to ensure the integrity of their recommendations to client firms. For example, there has been some speculation that executive consulting practices will be spun off into independent businesses. Many companies are concerned about their own public image and have instituted policies to prevent compensation consultants from conducting other work for management.

BOARD OF DIRECTORS A **board of directors** represents shareholders' interests by weighing the pros and cons of top executives' decisions. Boards of directors have approximately 15 members. These members include CEOs and top executives of other successful companies, distinguished community leaders, well-regarded professionals (e.g., physicians and attorneys), and possibly a few top-level executives of the company.

Boards of directors give final approval of the compensation committee's recommendation. Some critics of executive compensation have argued that CEOs use compensation to co-opt board independence.[17] CEOs often nominate candidates for board membership, and their nominations usually lead to candidates' placement on the board. Board members receive compensation for their service to the boards. It's not uncommon for a board member to earn more than $50,000 per year plus a fee ($10,000 or more) for each board meeting attended. Along with monetary and stock compensation, companies are using such benefits as medical insurance, life insurance, and retirement programs to attract top-notch individuals to join boards of directors. In general, board members' failure to cooperate with CEOs may lead either to fewer benefits or their removal.

> The board determines the pay of the CEO. But who determines the pay of the outside directors? Here, a sort of formal Japanese Kabuki has developed. The board of directors determines the pay of the CEO, and for all practical purposes, the CEO determines the pay of the board of directors. Is it any accident, then, that there is a statistical relationship between how highly the CEO is paid and how highly his outside directors are paid?[18]

As we will discuss shortly, recent changes in Securities and Exchange Commission rulings and the passage of the Dodd-Frank Act have increased the transparency of how executives are compensated as well as board members' accountability for approving sound executive compensation packages—supportive of shareholders' best interests.

COMPENSATION COMMITTEE Board of directors members within and outside the company make up a company's **compensation committee**. Outside board members serve on compensation committees to minimize conflict of interest. Thus, outside directors usually are the committee's membership majority.

Compensation committees perform three duties. First, compensation committees review consultants' alternate recommendations for compensation packages. Second, compensation committee members discuss the assets and liabilities of the recommendations. The complex tax laws require compensation committees to consult compensation experts, legal counsel, and tax advisors. Third, based on these deliberations, the committee recommends the consultant's best proposal to the board of directors for its consideration.

Theoretical Explanations for Setting Executive Compensation

Three prominent theories describe the processes related to setting executive compensation: agency theory, tournament theory, and social comparison theory. The following discussion provides concrete interpretations of these theories. In addition to the works cited throughout this chapter, several excellent scholarly journal articles provide full explanations of these theoretical frames as applied to executive compensation.[19]

AGENCY THEORY Ownership is distributed among many thousands of shareholders in such large companies as Microsoft, General Electric, General Motors, and IBM. For example, owning at least one share of stock in IBM bestows ownership rights in IBM. Each shareholder's ownership is quite small, amounting to less than 1 percent. Inability to communicate frequently or face to face to address business concerns is a major disadvantage of thousands of shareholders.

Under **agency theory,** shareholders delegate control to top executives to represent their ownership interests; however, top executives usually do not own majority shares of their companies' stocks. As a result, executives usually do not share the same interests as the collective shareholders. These features make it possible for executives to pursue activities that benefit themselves rather than the shareholders. The actions of executives on behalf of their own self-interest are known as the **agency problem.**[20] Executives may specifically emphasize the attainment of short-term gains (e.g., increasing market share through lower costs) at the expense of long-term objectives (e.g., product differentiation). Boards of directors may be willing to provide executives generous annual bonuses for attaining short-term gains.

Shareholders negotiate executive employment contracts with executives to minimize loss of control. Executive employment contracts define terms of employment pertaining to performance standards and compensation, specifically current and deferred compensation and benefits. The main shareholder objective is to protect the company's competitive interests. Shareholders use compensation to align executives' interests with shareholders' interests. As discussed earlier, boards of directors award company stock to align executives' interests with shareholders' interests.

TOURNAMENT THEORY **Tournament theory** casts lucrative executive compensation as the prize in a series of tournaments or contests among middle- and top-level managers who aspire to become CEOs.[21] Winners of the tournament at one level enter the next tournament level. In other words, an employee's promotion to a higher rank signifies a win, and more lucrative compensation (e.g., higher base pay, incentives, enhanced benefits, and perks) represents the prize. The ultimate prize is promotion to CEO and a lucrative executive compensation package. The chance of winning competitions decreases dramatically as employees rise through the ranks: There are fewer positions at higher levels in corporate hierarchical structures. Figure 12-2 depicts a visual representation of CEO compensation as a tournament.

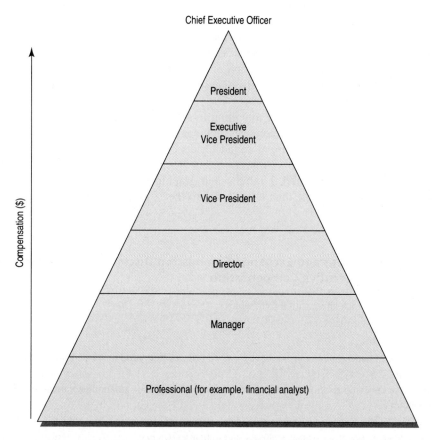

FIGURE 12-2 CEO Compensation as a Tournament

SOCIAL COMPARISON THEORY According to **social comparison theory,** individuals need to evaluate their accomplishments, and they do so by comparing themselves to similar individuals.[22] Demographic characteristics (e.g., age or race) and occupation are common comparative bases. Individuals tend to select social comparisons who are slightly better than themselves.[23] Researchers have applied social comparison theory to explain the processes for setting executive compensation.[24]

As we discussed earlier, compensation committees play an important role in setting executive compensation, and compensation committees often include CEOs from other companies of equal or greater stature. Based on social comparison theory, compensation committee members probably rely on their own compensation packages and the compensation packages of CEOs in companies of equal or greater stature to determine executive compensation.

EXECUTIVE COMPENSATION DISCLOSURE RULES

Companies that sell and exchange securities (e.g., company stocks and bonds) on public stock exchanges are required to file a wide variety of information with the **Securities and Exchange Commission (SEC),** including executive compensation practices. The SEC is a nonpartisan, quasi-judicial federal government agency with responsibility for administering federal securities laws. The **Securities Exchange Act of 1934** applies to the disclosure of executive compensation. In 1992 and 1993, the SEC modified its rules pertaining to the disclosure of executive pay.[25] Table 12-4 lists types of information about executive compensation that companies should disclose. The SEC rulings have two objectives. The first is to clarify the presentation of the compensation paid to the CEO and the four most highly paid executives. The second is to increase the accountability of company boards of directors for executive compensation policies and decisions. Companies' board members may be subject to personal liability for paying excessive compensation. Under securities law, publicly held corporations are required to disclose detailed information on executive compensation to shareholders and the public. Shareholders can bring derivative lawsuits on behalf of a corporation, claiming that executive compensation is excessive.

The courts are thus far generally unwilling to substitute their judgment for the business judgment of a board of directors or compensation committee. Nevertheless, these SEC rulings suggest that directors should exercise more independent judgment in approving executive compensation plans.

The SEC rules are presented in tabular and graphic forms, making information more accessible to the public at large than it was prior to the 1992 and 1993 modifications. These

TABLE 12-4 **Securities and Exchange Commission Disclosure Requirements for Executive Compensation**

- Stock option and stock appreciation right tables
- Long-term incentive plan table
- Pension plan table
- Performance graph comparing the company's stock price performance against a market index and a peer group
- Report from the compensation committee of the board of directors explaining compensation levels and policies
- Description of the directors' compensation, disclosing all amounts paid or payable
- Disclosure of certain employment contracts and golden parachutes

TABLE 12-5 **2008 Summary Compensation Table**

Keith S. Sherin,				
Vice Chairman and CFO	2008	$1,500,000	$2,550,000	$2,987,493
	2007	$1,354,167	$3,000,000	$3,076,095
	2006	$1,225,000	$2,550,000	$2,808,919
Michael A. Neal,				
Vice Chairman	2008	$1,650,000	$2,900,000	$3,512,898
	2007	$1,550,000	$3,880,000	$4,212,201
	2006	$1,400,000	$3,300,000	$3,906,929
John G. Rice,				
Vice Chairman	2008	$1,650,000	$2,700,000	$3,659,090
	2007	$1,550,000	$3,000,000	$4,406,900
	2006	$1,400,000	$2,550,000	$4,122,437
Brackett B. Denniston,				
Senior Vice President, General				
Counsel and Secretary	2008	$1,200,000	$1,850,000	$2,284,110
David R. Nissen,				
Former President & CEO, GE Money	2008	$1,350,000	$1,310,000	$6,777,594
Robert C. Wright,				
Former Vice Chairman	2008	$916,667	$2,783,000	—
	2007	$2,750,000	$7,590,000	$1,943,665
	2006	$2,500,000	$6,900,000	$2,516,712

rules indirectly regulate compensation levels through enhanced public access to information by discouraging corporations from granting potentially embarrassing executive pay, especially when corporate performance is weak. There are several tables, but the most important here is the Summary Compensation Table,[26] which discloses compensation information for the CEO and the four most highly paid executives over a 3-year period. As you can see in Table 12-5, the Summary Compensation Table for General Electric covers the compensation paid to the named executive officers during the past completed fiscal year and the two preceding fiscal years. The table contains two main subheadings: annual compensation and long-term compensation. Annual compensation includes salary (i.e., base pay), bonus, and other annual compensation. Long-term compensation includes restricted stock awards, stock appreciation rights, and long-term incentive payouts. The last column, "All Other Compensation ($)," is a catchall column to record other forms of compensation. Information in this column must be described in a footnote.

In 2008, the SEC unveiled additional rules for disclosing executive compensation. These rules require that companies reveal how much executives are paid, making such previously hard-to-find information as pension and estimated severance package totals transparent. Although the new rules represent a substantial improvement in pay disclosure, the SEC made a revision that resulted in a less-meaningful disclosure of stock options.

In 2009, the SEC chairperson announced further changes in the disclosure of executive compensation in a company's Summary Compensation Table. The change pertains to the reported value for stock options and stock awards. The SEC disclosure rules show components of compensation previously hidden as well as provide clarity into elements of compensation already disclosed. The most significant changes follow:

Total. The Summary Compensation Table of a company's proxy will now have a column that adds up and displays the total compensation an executive received for the previous year. In the SEC pay database this year, this is labeled SEC Total.

Change in Pension Value and Nonqualified Deferred Compensation. This column in the Summary Compensation Table shows the increase in actuarial value to the executive officer of all defined benefit pension plans and earnings on nonqualified deferred compensation plans.

All Other. This column captures compensation that does not fit in any other column of the Summary Compensation Table, including perquisites and other personal items (e.g., aircraft usage, car service, and club memberships). Each item of compensation included in All Other that exceeds $10,000 will now be separately identified and quantified in a footnote.

Pension Benefits. The new rules require companies to disclose the present value of accumulated pension benefits, showing the total lump sum amount of money an executive would receive in retirement.

Severance Benefits. Companies must disclose any termination or change-in-control agreements with executives. They must disclose the specific circumstances that will trigger payment and the estimated total payments and benefits provided for each circumstance.

The following table describes each component of the All Other Compensation column.

2008 All Other Compensation Table

We provide our named executives with additional benefits, reflected in the table below for 2008, that we believe are reasonable, competitive, and consistent with the company's overall executive compensation program. The costs of these benefits constitute only a small percentage of each named executive's total compensation.

Name of Executive	Other Benefits[a] ($)	Tax Payments[b] ($)	Value of Supplemental Life Insurance Premiums[c] ($)	Payments Relating to Employee Savings Plan[d] ($)	Total ($)
Immelt	212,293	0	152,476	8,050	372,819
Sherin	178,522	14,403	87,743	8,050	288,718
Neal	185,253	0	150,741	8,050	344,044
Rice	130,547	12,915	109,561	8,050	261,073
Denniston	74,943	21,000	146,864	8,050	250,857
Nissen	34,695	4,923	142,758	8,050	190,426
Wright	1,274,024	13,195	784,789	8,050	2,080,058

[a] See the 2008 Other Benefits Table below for additional information.

[b] This column reports amounts reimbursed for the payment of taxes with respect to financial counseling, tax preparation services, and the personal use of car service. Starting in 2009, the company will no longer reimburse named executives for the payment of these taxes. See the 2008 Other Benefits Table below for the incremental costs associated with providing these services.

[c] This column reports taxable payments made to the named executives to cover premiums for universal life insurance policies owned by the executives. These policies include: (1) Executive Life, which provides universal life insurance policies for the named executives totaling $3 million in coverage at the time of enrollment, increased 4 percent annually thereafter, and (2) Leadership Life, which provides universal life insurance policies for the named executives with coverage of two times their salary plus 100 percent of their latest bonus payments. The amount for Mr. Wright also includes Supplemental Life, the predecessor plan to Executive Life.

[d] This column reports company matching contributions to the named executives' 401(k) savings accounts of 3.5 percent of pay up to the limitations imposed under IRS rules.

OTHER BENEFITS

The following table describes other benefits and the cost to the company of providing them. The total amount of these other benefits is included in the All Other Compensation Table above for each named executive.

2008 Other Benefits

The following table describes other benefits and the incremental cost to the company of providing them in 2008. The total amount of these other benefits is included in the 2008 All Other Compensation Table above for each named executive.

Name of Executive	Use of Aircraft[a] ($)	Leased Cars[b] ($)	Financial Counseling and Tax Preparation[c] ($)	Other[d] ($)	Total ($)
Immelt	189,449	0	0	22,844	212,293
Sherin	116,673	31,170	20,575	10,104	178,522
Neal	175,060	0	0	10,193	185,253
Rice	69,484	18,534	18,450	24,079	130,547
Denniston	9,713	28,620	30,000	6,610	74,943
Nissen	0	21,040	7,033	6,622	34,695
Wright	244,083	8,832	12,790	1,008,319	1,274,024

[a] The calculation of incremental cost for personal use of company aircraft includes the variable costs incurred as a result of personal flight activity: a portion of ongoing maintenance and repairs, aircraft fuel, satellite communications, and any travel expenses for the flight crew. It excludes nonvariable costs, such as exterior paint, interior refurbishment, and regularly scheduled inspections, which would have been incurred regardless of whether there was any personal use of aircraft.

[b] Includes expenses associated with the leased cars program, such as leasing and management fees, administrative costs, and gas allowance.

[c] Includes expenses associated with the use of advisors for financial, estate, and tax preparation and planning, as well as investment analysis and advice.

[d] This column reports the total amount of other benefits provided, none of which individually exceeded the greater of $25,000 or 10 percent of the total amount of these benefits for the named executive. These other benefits included: (1) car service fees, (2) home alarm and generator installation, maintenance, and monitoring, (3) costs relating to company-sponsored events at board meetings for the executives' spouses, (4) participation in the Executive Products and Lighting Program pursuant to which executives can receive GE appliances or other products with incremental cost calculated based on the fair market value of the products received, and (5) an annual physical examination. For Mr. Wright, the amount includes contributions aggregating $1 million made by the company to charitable organizations upon Mr. Wright's retirement as a director.

SAY ON PAY

President Barack Obama signed the **Wall Street Reform and Consumer Protection Act of 2010** to further enhance the transparency of executive compensation practices. Also commonly referred to as the **Dodd-Frank Act,** the act requires the companies that trade stock on public exchanges to comply with three major provisions. The first provision requires **say on pay.** Say on pay gives company shareholders the right to vote yes or no on executive compensation proposals, including current and deferred components, including golden parachute agreements, at least once every 3 years. Although the say on pay provision guarantees shareholders the right to vote on executive compensation proposals, the vote is nonbinding. That is, the outcome of shareholders' voting does not overrule any compensation decision made by the company's board of directors. The nonbinding vote advises the company's board of directors of possible concerns about the structure of executive compensation packages, including excessive perks and the lack of clarity between compensation and business results.

The second provision details independence requirements for compensation committee members and their advisors such as compensation consultants and legal counsel. Members of compensation committees typically receive compensation for their services, and this practice is considered to be acceptable. However, possible violations of the Dodd-Frank independence requirement may arise when at least one committee member also receives compensation as a company employee. For example, a compensation committee member who also serves as the company's executive vice president may be considered violating the independence requirement. On the other hand, a compensation committee member who does not receive compensation from the company as an employee or external consultant would not violate the independence requirement.

Similarly, the Dodd-Frank Act specifies independence requirements for advisors to the compensation committee such as compensation consultants and legal counsel. A company's compensation committee must consider whether the fees charged by advisors exceed reasonable limits based on the amount of the fees as a percentage of the company's total revenue. Another consideration is whether an advisor has a business or personal relationship with committee members.

The third provision requires that companies disclose the circumstances under which an executive would benefit from a golden parachute arrangement. Specifically, disclosure is required of all agreements and understandings that the acquiring and target companies have with the executive officers of both companies.

EXECUTIVE COMPENSATION: ARE U.S. EXECUTIVES PAID TOO MUCH?

Are U.S. executives paid too much? Popular press and newspaper accounts generally suggest that executives are overpaid. Of course, you should form your own opinion based on the following pertinent information:

- Comparison between executive compensation and other worker groups
- Strategic questions: Is pay for performance?
- Ethical considerations: Is executive compensation fair?
- International competitiveness

Comparison between Executive Compensation and Compensation for Other Worker Groups

The median annual earnings for all civilian workers was $45,790 in May 2012.[27] Among the nonexecutive employees, shampooers earned the least (median annual earnings = $18,600) and anesthesiologists earned the most (median annual earnings = $232,830).[28] The typical annual salary and annual bonus for chief executives in 2011 was about $3.5 million.[29]

Strategic Questions: Is Pay for Performance?

There are several measures of corporate performance (Table 12-6). Are CEOs compensated commensurately with their companies' performance? It is difficult to answer just *yes* or *no* because the evidence is mixed based on decades of academic research and the compensation of executives relative to company performance; therefore, a simple statement cannot be made about the relationship between CEO pay and company performance. Shareholder returns most often describe company performance, but there are complex forces beyond the control of CEOs that may influence shareholder returns. For example, in the pharmaceutical industry, substantial investments in research to identify promising medicines require trial and error before a promising outcome occurs in the laboratory. Then lengthy clinical trials that span multiple years may show that the new medication does not cure an illness for which it was created. Such public failures often result in lower confidence in the company, which often translates into lower shareholder returns. In the intervening time, the company hires a new CEO who was not involved in the decision to pursue the failed initiative, raising the question whether she should receive lower compensation following a decline in shareholder returns.

Ethical Considerations: Is Executive Compensation Fair?

Is executive compensation fair? Three considerations drive this question: companies' abilities to attract and retain top executives, income disparities between executives and other employees, and layoffs of thousands of nonexecutive employees.

ATTRACT AND RETAIN TOP EXECUTIVES Many compensation professionals and board of directors members argue that the trends in executive compensation are absolutely necessary for attracting and retaining top executives.

TABLE 12-6 Corporate Performance Measures

Size
- Sales
- Assets
- Profits
- Market value
- Number of employees

Growth
- Sales
- Assets
- Profits
- Market value
- Number of employees

Profitability
- Profit margin
- Return on assets (ROA)
- Return on equity (ROE)

Capital Markets
- Dividend yield
- Total return to shareholders
- Price–earnings ratio
- Payout

Liquidity
- Current ratio
- Quick ratio
- Working capital from operations
- Cash flow from operations

Leverage
- Debt-to-equity ratio
- Short-term vs. long-term debt
- Cash flow vs. interest payments

INCOME DISPARITIES Table 12-7 illustrates the marked income disparity between annual pay for various nonexecutive jobs and pay for CEOs. The typical annual earnings for the lowest-paid occupation (shampooers) amounted to a mere 0.53 percent (yes, about than one-half of 1 percent) of the average annual CEO salary and bonus. The ratio of highest-paid occupation (anesthesiologiests) to the average annual CEO salary and bonus was not much better (i.e., 6.7 percent). Said differently, the typical CEO's annual salary plus bonus was 178 times greater than the typical shampooer's annual pay and nearly 21 times greater than the typical anesthesiologiest's annual pay!

LAYOFFS BORNE BY WORKERS BUT NOT EXECUTIVES Millions of workers have been laid off since 1990. Between late 2008 and mid-2009 alone, more than 2 million employees lost their jobs.[30] Top management typically advances several reasons that necessitate these layoffs (e.g., global competition, reductions in product demand, technological advances that perform many jobs more efficiently than employees, mergers and acquisitions, establishing production operations in foreign countries with lower labor costs, and the steep economic downturn following the recession). A scant few executives lost their jobs, but millions of workers lost theirs in the years following the attacks of September 11.

TABLE 12-7 Selected Median Annual Nonexecutive Earnings, May 2012

Occupation	Annual Earnings ($)
Anesthesiologists	232,830
Lawyers	130,880
General and operations managers	114,850
Registered nurses	67,930
Construction workers	43,860
Office clerks	29,270
Teacher assistants	25,310
Shampooers	18,600

Source: U.S. Bureau of Labor Statistics. (2013). *Occupational Employment Wages—May 2012.* Available: *www.bls.gov*, accessed April 7, 2013.

International Competitiveness

Increased global competition has forced companies in the United States to become more productive. Excessive expenditures on compensation can threaten competitive advantage. Compensation expenditures are excessive when they outpace the quality and quantity of employees' contributions. In addition, compensation expenditures may be excessive when they are substantially higher than competitors' compensation outlays. Concerns about U.S. companies' competitiveness in global markets are common because of the vast differences in compensation levels between the CEOs of U.S. and foreign companies.

INTERNATIONAL COMPENSATION COMPARISONS The SEC rules require the disclosure of executive compensation in U.S. companies; however, comparable rules do not exist in foreign countries. As a result, it is difficult to make detailed comparisons between U.S. and foreign executive compensation.

UNDERMINING U.S. COMPANIES' ABILITY TO COMPETE At present, there is no evidence showing that U.S. executive compensation pay practices have undermined U.S. companies' ability to compete with other companies in the global marketplace. Might executive compensation practices undermine U.S. companies' competitiveness in the future?

On one hand, it is reasonable to predict that CEO pay will not undermine U.S. companies' ability to compete because CEO pay increased as company profits increased. On the other hand, the current wave of widespread layoffs may hinder U.S. companies' competitiveness. The U.S. companies use layoffs to maintain profits and cut costs, heightening workers' job insecurities. The remaining workers may lose their faith in pay-for-performance systems and their trust in their employers as colleagues lose their jobs and CEOs continue to receive higher compensation. Workers may not feel that working hard will lead to higher pay or job security; therefore, they may choose not to work proficiently. As a result, reduced individual performance and destabilized workforces may make it difficult for U.S. companies to compete against foreign companies.

COMPENSATION IN ACTION

Executive compensation, long under the watchful eye of the public and politicians, has been under a microscopic lens during the recent global economic crisis. Executive compensation decisions are approved in the end by the board of directors (in response to recommendations provided to them by the compensation committee of the board and external executive compensation consultants); however, line managers and HR should seek to understand the principles being applied and the compensation plans being employed. This knowledge will help as employees raise questions about executive compensation, and it will make you more aware of practices that are fair and successful versus practices that are blatantly contrary to law, thus being able to protect the company and its employees. Perhaps if line managers and HR managers had been more vigilant about these processes, the tragedies at Enron and Tyco would never have occurred.

Action checklist for line managers and HR—assessing executive compensation in your company

HR takes the lead
- Conduct an analysis of the company's culture, ideals, values, and history. Does the executive compensation plan align with those factors?
- Is the executive compensation plan balanced with regards to cash versus equity, reward versus risk, short-term versus long-term performance? An overemphasis on any one side could result in behaviors that help executives but hurt the shareholders and the company in the end.
- What severance plans are being offered? Do the platinum parachutes in your company essentially minimize all risks for executives? Will the financial windfall be so large that an executive has little reason to avoid failure?

- If you believe the practices of your organizations are not in accordance with the disclosure regulations of the SEC or the requirements outlined explicitly under the Sarbanes-Oxley Act, it may be necessary for you to bring this to the attention of line managers. Together you can take these concerns to the proper people inside or outside the company.

Line managers take the lead
- What are the objectives by which the executives in your company are being measured? Are these similar to the objectives by which you are measured?
- What are the long-term incentives? Is this completely tied to stock price? Ideally, the long-term plan should include multiyear stock and a cash plan. With the plan too tied to stock price (through stock options), the wrong behaviors are encouraged and shareholders suffer in the long term. (Note: At the start of 2000, 90 percent of long-term incentives were in the form of stock options; now it is closer to 50 percent.)

END OF CHAPTER

MyManagementLab

Go to **mymanagementlab.com** to complete the problems marked with this icon ⭐.

Summary

We reviewed the components and principles of executive compensation. The components include base pay, bonuses, short-term incentives, stock and stock option plans, enhanced benefits, and perquisites. Next, we examined the principles and processes underlying executive compensation. Finally, we addressed whether U.S. executive compensation is excessive. Although popular press accounts suggest that it is, you will have to form your own opinion, particularly as you assume compensation management responsibilities for your employer. As a compensation professional, you are likely to face many difficult questions from employees regarding the rationale for and the fairness of lucrative executive compensation packages.

Key Terms

key employee 267
highly compensated employee 267
Emergency Economic Stabilization
   Act of 2008 (EESA) 268
Troubled Assets Relief Program
   (TARP) 268
discretionary bonuses 268
performance-contingent
   bonuses 268
predetermined allocation
   bonus 268
target plan bonus 268
deferred compensation 269
company stock 270
company stock shares 270
incentive stock options 270

capital gains 270
nonstatutory stock options 271
restricted stock 271
phantom stock 271
discount stock option plans 271
stock appreciation rights 271
golden parachutes 271
platinum parachutes 272
clawback provisions 272
Sarbanes-Oxley Act of 2002 272
Public Company Accounting
    Oversight Board (PCAOB) 273
perquisites 273
perks 273
supplemental life insurance 273
supplemental retirement plans 273

executive compensation
   consultants 275
board of directors 276
compensation committee 276
agency theory 276
agency problem 277
tournament theory 277
social comparison theory 278
Securities and Exchange
   Commission (SEC) 278
Securities Exchange Act of
   1934 278
Wall Street Reform and Consumer
   Protection Act of 2010 281
Dodd-Frank Act 281
say on pay 281

✪ Discussion Questions

12-1. What can be done to make the function of compensation committees consistent with shareholders' interests? Explain your answer.

12-2. Which component of compensation is most essential to motivate executives to lead companies toward competitive advantage? Discuss your rationale.

12-3. Discuss your position on executive compensation. Is executive compensation excessive or appropriate?

12-4. Discuss the differences between enhanced benefits and perquisites.

12-5. Consult three recent articles (from newspapers, Internet news sources, or business magazines) on executive pay. Using these articles, describe the main issues and then your opinion about whether (or how) executive pay practices should change.

CASE
CEO Pay in the News

✪ *An additional Supplemental Case can be found on MyManagementLab.*

A recent campaign by organized labor unions has brought the issue of executive compensation into the public eye. Media coverage of executive compensation concerns has been extensive over the past few weeks with articles in national publications and a featured story on a television special, in addition to stories on local news stations. This extensive coverage has highlighted public concerns of the high level of pay that top executives receive. The union promotes an executive compensation awareness campaign every year as a strategy to build awareness of perceived inequities between the pay of CEOs and frontline employees. Such awareness often prompts employees to consider forming a union, resulting in the growth of national unions.

    The publicity has caused some turmoil at Oakwood Lawns. For the first time, the company's CEO pay is featured as an example of perceived excess in the executive suite. Several field managers have been in touch with Don Henry, the director of human resources, to report that employees are outraged at the rate of pay of the company CEO and other top executives. In addition to the company's desire to remain union-free, Don also knows that such outrage could lead to low morale and other problems at Oakwood.

The union targeted Oakwood because it is a big company that has faced some financial challenges. The landscaping company has more than 15,000 employees in offices throughout the Midwest, and most of its employees are frontline laborers. The media coverage has been extensive in the area, and many company employees who viewed the story were surprised to learn the CEO is among the highest paid in the United States. The news was especially difficult to hear as the company recently announced that employees would not receive an annual pay increase due to the financial challenges the company is facing.

Oakwood CEO's annual salary is $975,000. Add in a bonus, stock awards, retirement benefits, and other benefits, and his total compensation is close to $10 million a year. The average landscaping technician is paid $28,000 annually. The disparity is clear, and Don must now plan a response to address the employees' concerns.

Questions:

12-6. What additional information about the CEO's pay package should Don identify to potentially share with the employees?

12-7. How can Don explain the pay disparity to the employees to ease their concerns about the fairness of the CEO's pay?

MyManagementLab

Go to **mymanagementlab.com** for Auto-graded writing questions as well as the following Assisted-graded writing questions:

⭐ **12-8.** Discuss the six forms of deferred (stock) compensation.

⭐ **12-9.** Briefly discuss the current core compensation and employee benefits of executive compensation.

Endnotes

1. Walters, B., Hardin, T., & Schick, J. (1995). Top executive compensation: Equity or excess? Implications for regaining American competitiveness. *Journal of Business Ethics, 14*, pp. 227–234.

2. U.S. Bureau of Labor Statistics. (2008). *Extended Mass Layoffs in the Fourth Quarter of 2007 and Annual Totals for 2007*. USDL 08-0204. Washington, DC: Government Printing Office. Available: *www.bls.gov*, accessed April 7, 2013. U.S. Bureau of Labor Statistics (2013). *Extended Mass Layoffs—2012*. USDL 13-0236. Washington, DC: Government Printing Office. Available: *www.bls.gov*, accessed April 7, 2013.

3. Internal Revenue Code, §416 (i).

4. Treas. Reg. §1.416–1, Q13.

5. Internal Revenue Code, §414 (q).

6. U.S. Treasury Department. (2009). Emergency Economic Stabilization Act Programs. Available: *www.treas.gov /offices/management/budget/budget-documents/cj/010 /CJ-ESSA.pdf*, accessed June 25, 2009.

7. Internal Revenue Code 83; *Treasury Regulations* 1.83–1(b) (2), 1.83–1(e), 1.83–2(a).

8. Internal Revenue Code 83; *Treasury Regulations* 1.83–1(b) (1), 1.83–1(c).

9. National Center for Employee Ownership. (2011). *Phantom Stock and Stock Appreciation Rights (SARs)*. Available: *www.nceo.org*, accessed February 19, 2011.

10. Internal Revenue Code 61, 83, 162; *Treasury Regulations* 1.83.

11. Internal Revenue Code 61, 83, 162, 451; *Treasury Regulations* 1.83.

12. Martocchio, J. J. (2011). *Employee Benefits: A Primer for Human Resource Professionals*. Burr Ridge, IL: McGraw-Hill.

13. I.R.C. §415 (b)(1)(A).

14. I.R.C. §415 (c)(1)(A).

15. Dolan Technologies. (2010). *Executive Compensation 2010/2011*. Survey results reported by WorldatWork (2010), Fewer companies offer executive perquisites in 2010. Available: *www.worldatwork.org*, accessed February 20, 2011.

16. Crystal, G. S. (1991). Why CEO compensation is so high. *California Management Review, 34*, pp. 9–29.

17. Ibid.

18. Ibid.

19. Eisenhardt, K. M. (1989). Agency theory: An assessment and review. *Academy of Management Review, 14*, pp. 57–74; Jensen, M., & Meckling, W. H. (1976). Theory of the firm: Managerial behavior, agency costs, and owner-ship structure. *Journal of Financial Economics, 3*, pp. 305–360; Tosi, H. L., Jr., & Gomez-Mejia, L. R. (1989). The decoupling of CEO pay and performance: An agency theory perspective. *Administrative Science Quarterly, 34*,

pp. 169–189; Goodman, P. S. (1974). An examination of referents used in the evaluation of pay. *Organizational Behavior and Human Performance*, *12*, pp. 170–195; Lazear, E., & Rosen, S. (1981). Rank-order tournaments as optimum labor contracts. *Journal of Political Economy*, *89*, pp. 841–864; O'Reilly, C. A., III, Main, B. G., & Crystal, G. S. (1988). CEO compensation as tournament and social comparison: A tale of two theories. *Administrative Science Quarterly*, *33*, pp. 257–274.

20. Jensen, M. C., & Meckling, W. H. (1976). Theory of the firm: Managerial behavior, agency costs, and ownership structure. *Journal of Financial Economics*, *3*, pp. 305–360.

21. Lazear, E., & Rosen, S. (1981). Rank-order tournaments as optimum labor contracts. *Journal of Political Economy*, *89*, pp. 841–864.

22. Festinger, L. (1954). A theory of social comparison processes. *Human Relations*, *7*, pp. 117–140.

23. Tversky, A., & Kahneman, D. (1974). Judgment and uncertainty: Heuristics and biases. *Science*, *185*, pp. 1124–1131.

24. O'Reilly, C. A., III, Main, B. G., & Crystal, G. S. (1988). CEO compensation as tournament and social comparison: A tale of two theories. *Administrative Science Quarterly*, *33*, pp. 257–274.

25. SEC Release No. 33–6962 (October 16, 1992); SEC Release No. 33–6940 (July 10, 1992); SEC Release No. 34–33229 (November 29, 1993).

26. Summary Compensation Table: 17 C.F.R 229.402(b), as amended November 29, 1993, effective January 1, 1994.

27. U.S. Bureau of Labor Statistics. (2013). *Occupational Employment Wages—May 2012* (USDL: 13-0543). Available: *www.bls.gov*, accessed April 7, 2013.

28. Ibid.

29. Hay Group. (2012). *The Wall Street Journal/Hay Group CEO compensation study reveals a substantial increase in CEO pay levels in 2011* (news release). Available: *www.haygroup.com*, accessed April 7, 2013.

30. U.S. Bureau of Labor Statistics, *Mass Layoffs*; U.S. Bureau of Labor Statistics, *Extended Mass Layoffs*.

13 COMPENSATING THE FLEXIBLE WORKFORCE
Contingent Employees and Flexible Work Schedules

MyManagementLab®

⭐ **Improve Your Grade!**

When you see this icon, visit **www.mymanagementlab.com** for activities that are applied, personalized, and offer immediate feedback.

LEARNING OBJECTIVES

When you finish studying this chapter, you should be able to:

1. List and define each of the four groups of contingent workers and the reasons for U.S. employers' increased reliance on them.
2. Discuss at least one compensation issue and one employee benefits issue for each of the four groups of contingent workers.
3. List the four categories of flexible work schedules.
4. Summarize one pay and employee benefits issue for flexible work schedules, compressed workweeks, and telecommuting arrangements.
5. Describe at least three reactions unions have about the use of contingent work and flexible work schedule arrangements.
6. Identify two strategic issues and choices companies have regarding the use of contingent workers.

Changing business conditions and personal preferences for flexibility to accommodate non-work demands have led to an increase in contingent workers and the use of flexible work schedules in the United States. Companies employed as many as 5.7 million contingent workers in February 2005, representing about 4 percent of total employment.[1] Likewise, the complexities of employees' personal lives (e.g., dependent children and elderly relatives, dual career couples, and disabilities) make working standard 8-hour days for 5 consecutive days every week difficult. About 27 million employees worked flexible work schedules during May 2004.[2] Altogether, contingent and flexible-schedule employees represent about 27.5 percent of the U.S. civilian labor force. (These statistics represent the most recently available comprehensive data at the time of publication; data on contingent workers and workers on flexible schedules are collected infrequently.)

This chapter looks at compensation issues for contingent workers and demonstrates that compensating contingent workers is a complex proposition. Human resource (HR) and compensation professionals encounter tremendous challenges in managing both the core and contingent workforces. Many companies employ both types of workers, often in the same jobs. To the casual onlooker, including coworkers, there are no visible differences between these workers; however, HR and compensation professionals must take many factors into consideration.

The previous chapters addressed compensation issues for core employees. **Core employees** have full-time jobs (i.e., they work at least 35 hours per week), and they generally plan long-term or indefinite relationships with their employers. In addition, all core employees were assumed to work standard schedules (i.e., fixed 8-hour work shifts, 5 days per week). Compensation practices differ somewhat for the flexible workforce.

THE CONTINGENT WORKFORCE

According to the U.S. Bureau of Labor Statistics, **contingent workers**[3] are those who do not have an implicit or explicit contract for ongoing employment. Persons who do not expect to continue in their jobs for such personal reasons as retirement or returning to school are not considered contingent workers, provided that they would have the option of continuing in the job were it not for these reasons. Figure 13-1 details questions that determine whether workers expect their employment to continue, that is, whether their work arrangement is considered to be contingent.

The duration of their employment varies according to their convenience and employers' business needs. A slightly larger proportion of contingent workers than noncontingent workers were women (49 versus 47 percent). Contingent workers most commonly hold professional (e.g., accountant), clerical (e.g., secretary), or laborer (e.g., construction worker) positions; they perform jobs in the service and retail trade industries. More and more companies favor contingent employment to control staffing levels and costs.

Groups of Contingent Workers

There are four distinct groups of contingent workers:

- Part-time employees
- Temporary and on-call employees
- Leased employee arrangements
- Independent contractors, freelancers, and consultants

Table 13-1 shows the number of contingent workers in categories.

PART-TIME EMPLOYEES   The Bureau of Labor Statistics distinguishes between two kinds of part-time employees: voluntary and involuntary. A **voluntary part-time employee** chooses to work fewer than 35 hours per regularly scheduled workweek. In some cases, individuals supplement full-time employment with part-time employment to meet financial obligations.

Some workers, including a small but growing number of professionals, elect to work part-time as a lifestyle choice. These part-timers sacrifice pay, and possibly career advancement, in exchange for more free time to devote to family, hobbies, and personal interests. They often have working spouses whose benefits, generally including medical and dental insurance, extend coverage to family members.

TABLE 13-1 Number of Contingent Employees, February 2005

Type of Contingent Workers	Number
Part-time employees	2,294,000
On-call employees	2,500,000
Temporary help agency workers	1,200,000
Leased employees	813,000

Source: U.S. Bureau of Labor Statistics. (2005). *Contingent and Alternative Employment Arrangements, February 2005.* USDL: 05-1433. Available: *www.bls .gov/ncs/cps/,* accessed April 6, 2013.

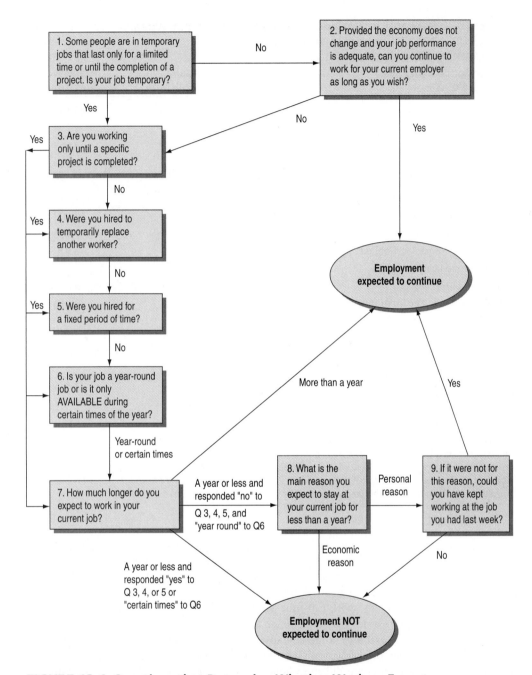

FIGURE 13-1 Questions that Determine Whether Workers Expect Their Employment to Continue

Source: Polivka, A. E. (1996). Contingent and alternative work arrangements, defined. *Monthly Labor Review*, *119(10)*, p. 5.

Involuntary part-time employees work fewer than 35 hours per week because they are unable to find full-time employment. Involuntary part-time work represents the lion's share of all part-time employment. There is a commonly held but inaccurate stereotype of involuntary part-time workers as being low skilled and uninterested in career advancement. To the contrary, many involuntary part-time workers hold entry-level career-track jobs.[4] Although we have discussed

TABLE 13-2 **Reason for Working Less than 35 Hours per Week, 2012 (Numbers in Thousands)**

Reason for Working Less than 35 Hours	Total	Usually Work Full-Time	Usually Work Part-Time
Total, 16 years and over	34,425	9,324	25,101
Economic reasons	8,122	1,828	6,294
Slack work or business conditions	5,255	1,587	3,668
Could only find part-time work	2,541	—	2,541
Seasonal work	212	126	85
Job started or ended during week	114	114	—
Noneconomic reasons	26,303	7,497	18,806
Child-care problems	853	67	786
Other family or personal obligations	4,631	661	3,970
Health or medical limitations	790	—	790
In school or training	5,765	88	5,678
Retired or Social Security limit on earnings	2,313	—	2,313
Vacation or personal day	3,586	3,586	—
Holiday, legal, or religious	530	530	—
Weather-related curtailment	263	263	—
All other reasons	7,571	2,302	5,269
Average hours:			
Economic reasons	22.7	23.9	22.4
Other reasons	21.2	24.7	19.9

Note: Dash indicates no data or data that do not meet publication criteria.
Source: U.S. Bureau of Labor Statistics. (February 5, 2013). *Labor Force Statistics from the Current Population Survey.* Available: *http://www.bls.gov/cps/cpsaat20.htm*, accessed April 6, 2013.

voluntary and involuntary part-time work as part of the contingent workforce, it is important to emphasize that many core workers negotiate part-time schedules with employers.

Table 13-2 lists the specific reasons for part-time work and the number of individuals who work part-time, defined as fewer than 35 hours weekly, for each reason. As previously noted, some individuals who usually work full-time also hold part-time jobs. Others typically work part-time jobs only. Companies may experience advantages and disadvantages from employing part-time workers. Flexibility is the key advantage. Most companies realize a substantial cost savings because they offer few or no discretionary benefits. In addition, companies realize cost savings for benefits that are linked to hours worked (e.g., retirement plan contributions). Table 13-3 shows employers' costs for providing various discretionary benefits and legally required benefits to full-time and part-time employees. Employers save considerable money in the areas of paid leave, insurance, and legally required benefits.

Companies also save on overtime pay expenses. Hiring part-time workers during peak business periods minimizes overtime pay costs. As we discussed in Chapter 2, the Fair Labor Standards Act of 1938 (FLSA) requires that companies pay nonexempt employees at a rate equaling one and one-half times their regular hourly pay rates. Retail businesses save by employing part-time sales associates during the peak holiday shopping season.

Job sharing is a special kind of part-time employment agreement. Two or more part-time employees perform a single full-time job. These employees may perform all job duties or share the responsibility for particular tasks. Some job sharers meet regularly to coordinate their efforts.

TABLE 13-3 Employers' Hourly Costs for Full- and Part-Time Employee Benefits, December 2012

Benefit	Full-Time ($)	Part-Time ($)
Paid leave	2.52	0.42
Supplemental pay	1.03	0.19
Insurance	2.92	0.76
Retirement and savings	1.31	0.25
Legally required benefits	2.62	1.65
Total hourly benefits costs	10.41	3.26

Source: U.S. Bureau of Labor Statistics. (2013). *Employer Costs for Employee Compensation, December 2012*. USDL: 13-0421. Washington, DC: U.S. Government Printing Office.

Job sharing represents a compromise between employees' needs or desires not to work full-time and employers' needs to staff jobs on a full-time basis. Both employers and employees benefit from the use of job sharing. Table 13-4 lists some of the benefits of job sharing to employers and employees.

TEMPORARY AND ON-CALL EMPLOYEES Companies traditionally hire temporary employees for two reasons. First, temporary workers fill in for core employees who are on approved leaves of absence, including sick leave, vacation, bereavement leave, jury duty, and military leave. Second, temporary workers offer extra sets of hands when companies' business activities peak, during such times as the holiday season for retail businesses or summer for amusement parks. Temporary employees perform jobs on a short-term basis usually measured in days, weeks, or months.

Companies have been hiring temporary workers for three additional reasons. First, temporary employment arrangements provide employers the opportunity to evaluate whether legitimate needs exist for creating new positions. Second, temporary employment arrangements give employers the opportunity to decide whether to retain particular workers on an indefinite basis. "The temp job is often what one university placement director calls the '3-month interview'—and

TABLE 13-4 Benefits of Job Sharing

Benefits to Employers

- Maintenance of productivity because of higher morale and maintenance of employee skills
- Retention of skilled workers
- Reduction or elimination of the training costs that result from retraining laid-off employees
- Greater flexibility in deploying workers to keep operations going
- Minimization of postrecession costs of hiring and training new workers to replace those who found other jobs during layoff
- Strengthening employees' loyalty to the company

Benefits to Employees

- Continued employee benefits protection
- Continued employment when the likelihood of unemployment is high
- Maintenance of family income
- Continued participation in qualified retirement programs

a gateway to a full-time job and perhaps a new career."[5] In effect, the temporary arrangement represents a probationary period, when employers observe whether workers are meeting job performance standards. As a corollary, such temporary arrangements provide workers the chance to decide whether to accept employment on a full-time basis after they have had time to "check things out." Third, employing temporary workers is often less costly than employing core workers because temporary workers are less likely to receive costly discretionary benefits (e.g., medical insurance coverage).

Companies hire temporary employees from a variety of sources. The most common source is a **temporary employment agency.** In 2005, companies employed approximately 1.2 million temporary workers (most current data available at time of publication).[6] Most temporary employment agencies traditionally placed clerical and administrative workers. Now, some temporary agencies also place workers with specialized skills (e.g., auditors, computer systems analysts, and lawyers). These agencies are becoming more common.

Companies generally establish relationships with temporary employment agencies based on several factors. First, companies consider agencies' reputations as an important factor, judging reputations by how well agencies' placements work out. Some agencies place a wide range of employees, yet others specialize in one type of placement (e.g., financial services professionals). When companies plan to hire a variety of temporary workers, it is often more convenient to work with agencies that do not specialize. Companies should ultimately judge these agencies' placement records for each type of employee.

Second, companies also should consider agencies' fees. Cost is a paramount consideration for companies that are pursuing lowest-cost competitive strategies. Temporary agencies base fees as a percentage of their placements' pay rates. The percentage varies from agency to agency. The competition among temporary agencies fortunately keeps these rates in check.

Although temporary employees work in a variety of companies, their legal employers are the temporary employment agencies. Temporary employment agencies take full responsibility for selecting temporary employee candidates and determine candidates' qualifications through interviews and testing. Many temporary agencies train candidates to use such office equipment as fax machines, e-mail, and spreadsheet and word processing software programs, particularly for clerical and administrative jobs. Temporary employees receive compensation directly from the agency.

Companies may hire temporary employees through other means. For example, some companies hire individuals directly as temporary workers. Under **direct hire arrangements,** temporary employees typically do not work for more than 1 year. In addition, the hiring companies are the temporary workers' legal employers. Thus, companies take full responsibility for all HR functions that affect temporary employees, including performance evaluation, compensation, and training.

On-call arrangements are another method for employing temporary workers. On-call employees work sporadically throughout the year when companies require their services. Companies can schedule workers for several days or weeks in a row. Some unionized skilled trade workers are available as on-call employees when they are unable to secure permanent, full-time employment. These employees' unions maintain rosters of unemployed members who are available for work. When employed, on-call workers are employees of the hiring companies. Thus, the hiring companies are responsible for managing and implementing HR policies, including compensation.

LEASED EMPLOYEE ARRANGEMENTS **Lease companies** employ qualified individuals and place them in client companies on a long-term basis. Most leasing companies bill the client for the direct costs of employing the workers (e.g., payroll, benefits, and payroll taxes) and then charge a fixed fee. Lease companies base these fees on either a fixed percentage of the client's payroll or a fixed fee per employee.

Leasing arrangements are common in the food service industry. ARAMARK Food Services is an example of a leasing company that provides cafeteria services to client companies.

ARAMARK staffs these companies' in-house cafeterias with cooks, food preparers, and check-out clerks. These cafeteria workers are employees of the leasing company, not the client company. Leasing companies also operate in other industries, including security services, building maintenance, and administrative services. Lease companies and temporary employment agencies are similar because both manage all HR activities. Thus, lease companies provide both wages and benefits to their employees. Lease companies and temporary employment agencies differ in an important respect, however. Lease company placements generally remain in effect for the duration of the lease company's contract with the host company.

INDEPENDENT CONTRACTORS, FREELANCERS, AND CONSULTANTS **Independent contractors, freelancers,** and **consultants** (the term *independent contractor* will be used in this discussion) establish working relationships with companies on their own rather than through temporary employment agencies or lease companies. Independent contractors typically possess specialized skills that are in short supply in the labor market. Companies select independent contractors to complete particular projects of short-term duration (i.e., usually a year or less). Adjunct faculty members represent a specific example of independent contractors. Colleges and universities hire them to cover for permanent faculty members who are on sabbatical leave or until they hire tenure-track replacements. In addition, some companies staff segments of their workforces with independent contractors to contain discretionary benefits costs.

Reasons for U.S. Employers' Increased Reliance on Contingent Workers

Structural changes in the U.S. economy have contributed to the rise of contingent employment:

- Economic recessions
- International competition
- Shift from manufacturing to a service economy
- Rise in female labor force participation
- Runaway costs to provide employer-sponsored health insurance

ECONOMIC RECESSIONS Many companies layoff segments of their workforces during economic recessions as a cost-control measure. Following economic recessions, some companies restore staffing levels with permanent employees. Many companies are increasingly restoring staffing levels with contingent workers. Since the early 1970s, the U.S. economy experienced several economic recessions. These repeated recessions have shaken employers' confidence about future economic prosperity. Staffing segments of workforces with contingent workers represents a form of risk control because employers save on most discretionary benefits costs. In addition, companies can terminate contingent workers' services more easily: These employment relationships are explicitly tentative. Both the host employer and the workers understand that these engagements are of limited duration.

INTERNATIONAL COMPETITION International competition is another pertinent structural change. American companies no longer compete just against each other. Many foreign businesses have demonstrated the ability to manufacture goods at lower costs than their American competitors. As a result, successful American companies have streamlined operations to control costs. These companies are saving costs by reducing the numbers of core employees and using contingent workers as an alternative.

THE SHIFT FROM MANUFACTURING TO A SERVICE ECONOMY The service sector refers to six broad divisions of industries: transportation, communication, and public utilities; wholesale trade; retail trade; finance, insurance, and real estate; services; and government. Manufacturing companies' (e.g., automobile makers and textiles) employment declined substantially during the past several years,[7] and economic forecasts predict a loss of jobs in the manufacturing and mining sectors through 2018.[8] During this period, a steady decrease in employment in manufacturing industries is expected to be offset by a substantial rise in employment in the retail trade and service sectors such as professional and business services as well as health care and social assistance.[9] Service sector employment is expected to add nearly 15 million new jobs to the economy by 2018.[10] In addition, contingent workers typically find employment in service businesses, which are more labor intensive than capital intensive (e.g., heavy manufacturing equipment).

> A number of trends depict a society that is in some ways increasingly dedicated to future investment by means of both capital and increased effort. Business-oriented services—such as upgrading of software and intelligent machinery, services related to construction, and improvement of business processes with the aid of consultants—may all be interpreted as present investments for a wealthier future. The extension of business operating hours may be interpreted in the same way. Even two rapidly increasing social services, daycare and residential care, enable some people to work outside the home instead of caring for relatives, and to contribute to economic expansion.[11]

RISE IN FEMALE LABOR FORCE PARTICIPATION The increase in female participation in the labor force has promoted growth in the use of contingent workers. One-income families were commonplace until the early 1970s, and males headed these households. Since then, several economic recessions in the United States left large numbers of individuals unemployed.

Many wives entered the labor force temporarily to supplement family income during their husbands' unemployment spells.[12] The majority took low-paying jobs as clerical or service workers because they did not have sufficient education to attain high-paying jobs. Even educated women could not find high-paying jobs because the recessions limited such opportunities. As a result, many well-educated women also assumed low-paying clerical or service positions.

A large segment of these women remained in the contingent labor force following the end of these economic recessions because their husbands' salaries did not keep up with inflation. Contingent employment enabled women to balance the demands of home and work. Although men have been taking greater responsibility for child rearing, women still bear the brunt of these duties.[13] Thus, contingent employment, compared with core employment, affords women opportunities to balance the demands of home and work.

The rise in single-parent households also contributed to the rise in contingent employment. Many single female parents possess low levels of education, which limits job opportunities. As a result, single mothers accept such low-paying contingent jobs as domestic work, retail sales, and low-level clerical positions. Apart from low educational attainment, single mothers accept contingent work because it enables them to spend more time with their children. As an aside, these women generally cannot afford to pay for regular day care services.

A large segment of well-educated females enter the contingent workforce because of dual-career pressures. In many areas of the country, employers have the luxury of large pools of educated, skilled workers who have followed as their spouses pursue job opportunities. These areas typically have few large employers such as in Fort Collins, Colorado, and Champaign-Urbana, Illinois, where universities are the main employers. Many spouses with professional credentials take low-paying, part-time jobs because there are few good job opportunities.

RUNAWAY COSTS TO PROVIDE EMPLOYER-SPONSORED HEALTH INSURANCE Both employees and employers place a great deal of significance on company-sponsored health insurance benefits. Of course, company-sponsored programs provide employees with the means to afford expensive health care services. Companies stand to gain from sponsoring these benefits in at least two ways, as we noted in Chapter 10. First, a healthier workforce should experience a lower incidence of sickness absenteeism. By keeping absenteeism in check, a company's overall productivity and product or service quality should be higher. Second, health insurance offerings should help the recruitment and retention of employees. It's not surprising that a large percentage of companies include health insurance programs as a feature of employee benefits programs, extending coverage to substantial numbers of employees and their dependents. At the same time, the rampant rise in health care prices is putting substantial pressure on cost-conscious companies.

The most recent comprehensive national data indicate that just more than approximately 86 percent of all full-time private sector employees had access to employer-sponsored health insurance programs in March 2012.[14] In contrast, only 24 percent of part-time employees had access to such plans. Health insurance premiums are quite high, often amounting to as much as one-third of annual benefits costs. Most companies choose not to offer health care benefits to part-time workers (and other contingent workers for that matter) because the cost of employers' contributions to provide health insurance coverage is about the same for full- and part-time employees. Part-time employees work far fewer hours than full-time employees, in effect making the hourly cost of benefits substantially higher for part-time employees than for full-time employees. For example, in March 2012, employers spent an average $467 per employee per month for life, health, and disability insurance.[15] The employer's hourly cost to provide health care insurance per full-time employee per hour is approximately $2.92 . For part-time employees, the amount is $0.76.

Health insurance premiums are likely to increase based on the trend in prices for medical services, perhaps increasing the likelihood that companies will rely on contingent employment relationships. For example, the prices for medical care services overall have increased nearly 400 percent since 1982 (compared with about a 200 percent increase for all goods and services purchased by consumers during the same period). The substantially higher rate increases for medical services may be explained by several factors, including:

- Longer life expectancies
- Aging baby boom–era individuals who place higher demands on health care
- Advances in medical research that add such diagnostic tests and treatments as substantially more effective (and expensive) treatments to save low-birth-weight babies
- A general tendency for the health profession and family members to treat death as unnatural rather than as a natural ending to life, leading to higher expenditures to prolong the lives of the terminally ill

There is no reason to expect that health care costs will decrease in the foreseeable future. Continuing medical research, more advanced diagnostic tools, and higher demand due to the aging population and for better treatment will contribute to higher costs.

PAY AND EMPLOYEE BENEFITS FOR CONTINGENT WORKERS

Compensation practices for contingent workers vary. We will discuss these practices shortly. Nevertheless, all parties involved in employing contingent workers possess liability under federal and state laws, including:

- Overtime and minimum wages required under the FLSA
- Paying insurance premiums required under state workers' compensation laws
- Nondiscriminatory compensation and employment practices under the Employee Retirement Income Security Act of 1974 (ERISA), National Labor Relations Act (NLRA), Title VII of the Civil Rights Act of 1964, Americans with Disabilities Act of 1990 (ADA), and the Age Discrimination in Employment Act (ADEA)

Temporary employment agencies and leasing companies that place workers in clients' firms are liable under these laws. In addition, the client company may also be liable. "The fact that a worker is somebody else's employee while he or she is on your premises, or performing services for the business, is not necessarily a defense to alleged violations of federal and state labor laws including Title VII of the Civil Rights Act, the Fair Labor Standards Act, and the Americans with Disabilities Act."[16] As we discussed in Chapter 2, each of these laws applies to compensation practice.

Part-Time Employees

Companies that employ part-time workers are the legal employers, as is the case for core employees. Compensating part-time employees poses the following challenges for employers:

- Should companies pay part-time workers on an hourly basis or a salary basis?
- Do equity problems arise between core employees and part-time employees?
- Do companies offer benefits to part-time workers?

PAY Part-time employees earn less, on average, than core employees. In March 2012, part-time workers in private industry earned an average $11.95 per hour, whereas full-time employees earned $23.22 per hour.[17] Full-time management and professional employees earned $37.05 per hour, whereas their part-time counterparts earned $26.70 per hour. Full-time production workers earned substantially more than their part-time counterparts ($17.57 per hour versus $11.09 per hour). Full-time service employees similarly earned more than part-timers ($12.16 per hour versus $9.18 per hour).[18]

Companies often expect salaried part-time employees to do much more than their fair share of the work because the effective hourly pay rate decreases as the number of hours worked increases. An explicit agreement pertaining to work-hour limits can minimize this problem. An agreement similarly may specify explicit work goals. On the other hand, companies may avoid this problem by paying part-time employees on an hourly basis. Part-time and full-time employees may perceive the situation as inequitable under certain circumstances. For example, equity problems may arise when salaried full-time employees and hourly part-time employees work together. It is possible that highly skilled full-time employees might effectively be underpaid relative to less-skilled part-time employees performing the same work (i.e., full-time employees' "hourly" pay rate will be lower when they perform more and better work in a shorter period than less-skilled part-time workers).

EMPLOYEE BENEFITS Companies generally do not provide discretionary benefits to part-time employees; however, benefits practices for part-time workers vary widely according to company size as well as between the private and public sectors. In March 2012, approximately 38 percent of part-time employees had access to retirement benefits compared to 78 percent of full-time employees.[19] As noted earlier, fewer part-time workers had access to medical care benefits.

Employers are not required to offer protective insurance (e.g., medical, dental, vision, or life insurance) to part-time employees; however, part-time employees who do receive health insurance coverage under employer-sponsored plans are entitled to protection under the Consolidated Omnibus Budget Reconciliation Act (COBRA). As discussed in Chapter 2, COBRA provides employees the opportunity to continue receiving employer-sponsored health care insurance coverage temporarily following termination or layoff. Employees who qualify for COBRA protection receive insurance coverage that matches the coverage level during employment.

Employers may be required to provide qualified retirement programs to part-time employees.[20] Part-time employees who meet the following two criteria are eligible to participate in qualified retirement programs:

- Minimum age of 21 years
- Completion of at least 1,000 hours of work in a 12-month period (i.e., "year of service")

Special considerations apply to seasonal employees' eligibilities for qualified retirement benefits because most seasonal employees do not meet the annual service pension eligibility criterion. Maritime industries such as fishing represent seasonal employment, and fishermen are seasonal employees. The Department of Labor defines 125 service days as the "year of service" for maritime workers. Part-time and seasonal employees cannot be excluded from pension plans if they meet the Department of Labor's "year of service" criterion.

Temporary Employees

Temporary employment agencies are the legal employers for temporary employees. Temporary employment agencies are therefore responsible for complying with federal employment legislation with one exception (i.e., workers' compensation), which we will address shortly. Compensating temporary employees poses challenges for companies.

- Do equity problems arise between core employees and temporary employees?
- How do the FLSA overtime provisions affect temporary employees?
- Do companies offer temporary workers benefits?
- Who is responsible for providing workers' compensation protection: the temporary agency or the client company?

PAY Temporary workers who worked full-time typically earned $414 per week in February 2005, and those working on a part-time basis earned $224 per week (again, the most recently available information).[21] Pay rates varied widely by occupation and workers' particular qualifications. Equity problems may (or may not) arise where core and temporary employees work together. On one hand, temporary employees may work diligently because they know that their assignments in client companies are explicitly of limited duration. In addition, frequent moves from one company to the next may limit workers' opportunities or desires to build careers with any of these companies. Furthermore, temporary workers may neither take the time nor have the time to scope out pay differences because their engagements are brief (i.e., anywhere from 1 day to a few weeks). These temporary employees are therefore not likely to perceive inequitable pay situations.

On the other hand, some temporary employees may not work diligently because they did not choose temporary employment arrangements. Individuals who lose their jobs because of a sudden layoff and who have few core job alternatives are most susceptible. Pay differences between these temporary employees and core employees are likely to intensify perceptions of inequity.

It is important to distinguish between temporary employees and seasonal employees for determining eligibility under the FLSA minimum wage and overtime pay provisions. Companies hire temporary employees to fill in as needed. This means that companies may hire temporary employees at any time throughout a calendar year; however, seasonal employees work during set regular periods every year. Lifeguards on New England beaches are seasonal employees because they work only during the summer months when people visit beaches to swim. Summer camp counselors are also seasonal employees.

The FLSA extends coverage to temporary employees. Temporary employment agencies must therefore pay temporary workers at least the federal minimum wage rate. In addition, the FLSA requires employers to provide overtime pay at one and one-half times the normal hourly rate for each hour worked beyond 40 hours per week. Host companies are responsible for FLSA compliance if temporary employment agencies are not involved, as in the case of direct hire or on-call arrangements.

Some seasonal employees are exempt from the FLSA's minimum wage and overtime pay provisions.[22] The FLSA itself as drafted does not explicitly address minimum wage and overtime pay practices for seasonal employees; however, professional legal opinions were added as needed to resolve ambiguities and guide practice. The opinions pertain to specific employers' questions about the act's scope of coverage (e.g., the applicability of FLSA overtime and minimum wage provisions to seasonal amusement park workers). Professional opinions do not automatically generalize to all seasonal employees. For example, all amusement or recreational establishment employees are covered by the FLSA's minimum wage and overtime pay provisions when the establishments operate at least 7 months per year; however, youth counselors employed at summer camps are generally exempt from the FLSA minimum wage and overtime pay provisions.

EMPLOYEE BENEFITS Anecdotal evidence indicates that companies typically do not provide discretionary benefits to temporary employees. This information should not be surprising. As we discussed earlier, many companies employ temporary workers to minimize discretionary benefits costs; however, temporary employees (and seasonal workers) are eligible for qualified pension benefits if they meet ERISA's minimum service requirements for seasonal and part-time employees, as discussed earlier.

The **dual employer common law doctrine** establishes temporary workers' rights to receive workers' compensation.[23] According to this doctrine, temporary workers are employees of both temporary employment agencies and the client companies. The written contract between the employment agency and client company specifies which organization's workers' compensation policy applies in the event of injuries.

Leased Workers

Designating leased employees' legal employers is less clear than it is for part-time and temporary employees. Leasing companies are the legal employers regarding wage issues and legally required benefits; however, leasing companies and client companies are the legal employers regarding particular discretionary benefits. Compensating leased employees is therefore complex.

- Do leased employees receive discretionary benefits?
- Who is responsible for providing discretionary benefits: the leasing company or the client company?

PAY In February 2005, leased employees who worked on a full-time basis typically earned $756 per week; part-time leased workers earned $204.[24] Detailed systematic compensation data for leased employees are currently very limited. It is therefore not possible to compare leased employees' and core employees' wages and salaries.

EMPLOYEE BENEFITS Both pension eligibility and discretionary benefits are key issues. Leased employees are generally entitled to participation in the client companies' qualified retirement programs; however, the leasing company becomes responsible for leased employees' retirement benefits when the **safe harbor rule**[25] requirements are met. Table 13-5 lists the safe harbor rule requirements.

Another section of the Internal Revenue Code (IRC) influences companies' discretionary benefits policies (excluding retirement benefits) for leased employees.[26] Under this rule, client companies are responsible for providing leased employees with group medical insurance, group life insurance, educational assistance programs, and continuation coverage requirements for group health plans under COBRA.

Independent Contractors, Freelancers, and Consultants

The Bureau of Labor Statistics does not monitor pay levels for independent contractors. Companies are not obligated to pay the following on behalf of independent contractors, freelancers, and consultants:

- Federal income tax withholding.

TABLE 13-5 Safe Harbor Rule Requirements

- The leased employee must be covered by the leasing company's pension plan, which must (1) be a money purchase plan with a nonintegrated employer contribution rate for each participant of at least 10 percent of compensation, (2) provide for full and immediate vesting, and (3) allow each employee of the leasing organization to immediately participate in such a plan; and
- Leased employees cannot constitute more than 20 percent of the recipient's "nonhighly compensated workforce." Nonhighly compensated workforce means the total number of (1) nonhighly compensated individuals who are employees of the recipient and who have performed services for the recipient for at least 1 year or (2) individuals who are leased employees of the recipient (determined without regard to the leasing rules).

Source: I.R.C. §414(n)(5).

TABLE 13-6 Economic Reality Test: Six Criteria to Determine Whether Workers Are Financially Dependent on the Employer

1. The extent to which the worker has the right to control the result of the work and the manner in which the work is performed
2. The degree to which the individual is "economically dependent" on the employer's business or, in other words, the amount of control the employer has over the individual's opportunity to realize a profit or sustain a loss
3. The extent to which the services are an integral part of the employer's business operations
4. The amount of initiative or level of skill required for the worker to perform the job
5. The permanency, exclusivity, or duration of the relationship between the employer and the worker
6. The extent of the worker's investment in equipment or materials required for the job

- Overtime and minimum wages required under the FLSA; however, employers are obligated to pay financially dependent workers overtime and minimum wages.
- Insurance premiums required under state workers' compensation laws, except where states explicitly require that companies maintain workers' compensation coverage for all workers regardless of whether they are independent contractors.
- Protection under the Employee Retirement Income Security Act of 1974 (ERISA), the Family and Medical Leave Act, the National Labor Relations Act (NLRA), Title VII of the Civil Rights Act of 1964, and the Americans with Disabilities Act (ADA).

To determine whether employees are financially dependent, employers must first apply the **economic reality test.** Table 13-6 lists the criteria to determine whether workers are financially dependent on the employer. For example, are topless nightclub dancers entitled to minimum wage under FLSA? A nightclub's owners claimed that the dancers were not eligible because they were independent contractors:

- The dancers could perform whenever and wherever they wanted.
- The club had no control over the manner of performance.
- The dancers must furnish their own costumes.

A federal district court ruled that the nightclub's topless dancers were entitled to minimum wage because they were economically dependent on the nightclub.[27] The dancers were economically dependent on the nightclub for the following reasons:

- The club owners set hours in which the dancers could perform.
- The club owners issued guidelines on dancers' behavior at the club.
- The club owners deducted 20 percent from the credit card tips of each dancer to cover administrative costs.

Again, employers' obligations under many federal and state employment laws depend on whether workers are employees or independent contractors. Companies must use the IRC's **right to control test** to determine whether such individuals are employees or independent contractors. Possessing the right to control work activities classifies individuals as employees rather than independent contractors. Table 13-7 lists 20 criteria of the right to control test.

FLEXIBLE WORK SCHEDULES: FLEXTIME, COMPRESSED WORKWEEKS, AND TELECOMMUTING

Many companies now offer employees flexible work schedules to help them balance work and family demands. Flextime and compressed workweek schedules are the most prominent flexible work schedules used in companies. Flexible work schedule practices apply to both core

TABLE 13-7   Right to Control Test: 20 Factors to Determine Whether an Employer Has the Right to Control a Worker

1. ***Instructions.*** Requiring a worker to comply with another person's instructions about when, where, and how he or she is to work ordinarily indicates an employer–employee relationship.

2. ***Training.*** Training a worker indicates that the employer wants the services performed in a particular manner and demonstrates the employer's control over the means by which the result is reached.

3. ***Integration.*** Integration of the worker's services into the business operations and the dependence of success or continuation of the business on the worker's services generally indicate that the worker is subject to a certain amount of direction and control by the employer.

4. ***Services rendered personally.*** If the services must be rendered personally, then the employer is presumably interested in the methods used to accomplish the work as well as the result, and control is indicated.

5. ***Hiring, supervising, and paying assistants.*** The employer's hiring, supervising, and paying the worker's assistants generally indicates control over the worker; however, if it is the worker who hires, supervises, and pays his or her assistants and is ultimately responsible for their work, then the worker has an independent contractor status.

6. ***Continuing relationship.*** A continuing relationship between the worker and the employer indicates that an employer–employee relationship exists.

7. ***Set hours of work.*** The establishment of set hours of work by the employer indicates control.

8. ***Full-time required.*** If the worker must devote full-time to the employer's business, the employer has control over the worker's time. An independent contractor, on the other hand, is free to work when and for whom he or she chooses.

9. ***Doing work on employer's premises.*** If the work is performed on the employer's premises, control is suggested, especially if the work could be performed elsewhere.

10. ***Order or sequence set.*** If a worker must perform services in the order or sequence set by the employer, control is indicated because the worker is unable to follow his or her own pattern of work.

11. ***Oral or written reports.*** Requiring the worker to submit regular or written reports to the employer suggests control.

12. ***Payment by hour, week, or month.*** Payment by the hour, week, or month suggests an employer–employee relationship unless it is just a convenient way of paying a lump sum agreed upon as the cost of a job. Payment by the job or on commission generally indicates an independent contractor status.

13. ***Payment of business or traveling expenses, or both.*** If the employer ordinarily pays the worker's business or traveling expenses, the worker is an employee.

14. ***Furnishing of tools and materials.*** If the employer furnishes significant tools, materials, and other equipment, an employer–employee relationship usually exists.

15. ***Significant investment by worker.*** If a worker invests in facilities that he or she uses to perform services and that are not typically maintained by an employee (e.g., rental of office space), an independent contractor status is usually indicated. Lack of investment in facilities tends to indicate that the worker depends on the employer for such facilities.

16. ***Realization of profit or loss.*** A worker who cannot realize a profit or suffers a loss as a result of his or her services generally is an employee.

17. ***Working for more than one firm at a time.*** If a worker performs more than *de minimis* services for a multiple of unrelated persons or firms at the same time, independent contractor status is generally indicated.

18. ***Making services available to general public.*** If a worker makes his or her services available to the general public on a regular and consistent basis, independent contractor status is indicated.

19. ***Right to discharge.*** The employer's right to discharge a worker indicates employee status.

20. ***Right to terminate.*** If a worker can terminate his or her relationship with the employer at any time without incurring liability, employee status is indicated.

Source: Rev. Rul. 87-41, 1987-1 C.B. 296.

employees and contingent employees. Research shows that employees highly value flexibility as a workplace policy.

Flextime Schedules

Flextime schedules allow employees to modify their work schedules within specified limits set by the employer. Employees adjust when they will start work and when they will leave. Flextime, however, generally does not lead to reduced work hours. For instance, an employee may choose to work between 10 A.M. and 6 P.M., 9 A.M. and 5 P.M., or 8 A.M. and 4 P.M.

All workers must be present during certain workday hours when business activity is regularly high. This period is known as **core hours.** The number of core hours may vary from company to company, by departments within companies, or by season. Although employees are relatively free to choose start and completion times that fall outside core hours, management must carefully coordinate these times to avoid understaffing. Some flextime programs incorporate a **banking hours** feature that enables employees to vary the number of work hours daily as long as they maintain the regular number of work hours on a weekly basis.

Employers can expect three possible benefits from using flextime schedules. First, flextime schedules lead to less tardiness and absenteeism. Flexibly defining the workweek better enables employees to schedule medical and other appointments outside work hours. As a result, workers are less likely to be late or miss work altogether.

Second, flexible work schedules should lead to higher work productivity. Employees have more choice about when to work during the day. Individuals who work best during the morning hours may schedule morning hours, and individuals who work best during the afternoons or evenings can choose these times. In addition, possessing the flexibility to attend to personal matters outside work should help employees focus on doing better jobs.

Third, flexible work schedules benefit employers by creating longer business hours and better service. Staggering employees' schedules should enable businesses to stay open longer hours without incurring overtime pay expenses. In addition, customers should perceive better service because of expanded business hours. Companies that conduct business by telephone on national and international bases are more likely to be open during customers' normal operating hours in other time zones.

Two possible limitations of flexible work schedules are increased overhead costs and coordination problems. Maintaining extended operations leads to higher overhead costs, including support staff and utilities. In addition, flexible work schedules may lead to work coordination problems when some employees are not present at the same time.

Compressed Workweek Schedules

Compressed workweek schedules enable employees to perform their work in fewer days than a regular 5-day workweek. As a result, employees may work four 10-hour days or three 12-hour days. These schedules can promote companies' recruitment and retention successes by:

- Reducing the number of times employees must commute between home and work
- Providing more time together for dual-career couples who live apart

Telecommuting

Telecommuting represents an alternative work arrangement in which employees work at home or at some other location besides the office. Telecommuters generally spend part of their time working in the office and the other part working at home. This alternative work arrangement is appropriate for work that does not require regular direct interpersonal interactions with other workers (e.g., accounting, systems analysis, and telephone sales). Telecommuters stay in touch with coworkers and superiors through e-mail, telephone, and faxes. Table 13-8 summarizes the variety of possible telecommuting arrangements.

TABLE 13-8 Alternative Telecommuting Arrangements

- *Satellite work center.* Employees work from a remote extension of the employer's office that includes a clerical staff and a full-time manager.
- *Neighborhood work center.* Employees work from a satellite office shared by several employers.
- *Nomadic executive office.* Executives who travel extensively maintain control over projects through use of telephone, fax, and e-mail.
- *Employees sometimes work entirely outside the office.* Others might work off-site only once a month or 2–3 days a week.
- *Telecommuters can be full- or part-time employees.*
- *Telecommuting arrangements can be temporary or permanent.* A temporarily disabled employee may work at home until fully recovered. A permanently disabled employee may work at home exclusively.

Source: Adapted from Bureau of National Affairs, Telecommuting. (2005). *Compensation & Benefits.* Available: *www.bna.com*, accessed March 7, 2005.

Potential benefits for employers include increased productivity and lower overhead costs for office space and supplies. Telecommuting also serves as an effective recruiting and retention practice for employees who strongly desire to perform their jobs away from the office. Employers may also increase the retention of valued employees who choose not to move when their companies relocate.

Employees find telecommuting beneficial. Telecommuting enables parents to be near their infants or preschool-age children and to be home when older children finish their school days. In addition, telecommuting arrangements minimize commuting time and expense, which are exceptional in such congested metropolitan areas as Boston, Los Angeles, and New York City. Travel time may increase threefold during peak "rush hour" traffic periods. Parking and toll costs can be hefty. Monthly parking rates alone often exceed thousands of dollars per car. Finally, employees' involvement in office politics will be reduced, which should promote higher job performance.

Telecommuting programs may also lead to disadvantages for employers and employees. Some employers are concerned about not having direct contact with employees, which makes conducting performance appraisals more difficult. Employees sometimes feel that work-at-home arrangements are disruptive to their personal lives. In addition, some employees feel isolated because they do not personally interact as often with coworkers and superiors.

Flexible Work Schedules: Balancing the Demands of Work Life and Home Life

Some U.S. companies use flexible work schedules to help employees balance the demands of work life and home life. Flextime, compressed workweeks, and telecommuting should provide single parents or dual-career parents the opportunity to spend more time with their children. Flextime gives parents the opportunity to schedule work around special events at their children's schools. Compressed workweeks enable parents on limited incomes to save on day care costs by reducing the number of days at the office. Parents can benefit from telecommuting in a similar fashion. Likewise, dual-career couples living apart also benefit from flexible work schedules. Compressed workweeks and telecommuting reduce the time spouses have to spend away from each other.

PAY AND EMPLOYEE BENEFITS FOR FLEXIBLE EMPLOYEES

The key pay issue for flexible work schedules is overtime pay. The main employee benefits issues are paid time off benefits and working condition fringe benefits.

Pay

In many cases, "flexible" employees work more than 40 hours during some weeks and fewer hours during other weeks. The FLSA requires that companies compensate nonexempt employees at an overtime rate equal to one and one-half times the normal hourly rate for each hour worked in excess of 40 hours per week. The overtime provisions are based on employees working set hours during fixed work periods. How do FLSA overtime provisions apply to flexible work schedules?

Let's assume the following flexible work schedule: An employee works 40 hours during the first week, 30 hours during the second week, and 50 hours during the third week. Although this employee worked 40 hours per week, on average, for the 3-week period ([40 + 30 + 50 hours]/ 3 weeks), is that employee entitled to overtime pay for the additional 10 hours worked during the third week?

Some employees' weekly flexible schedules may fluctuate frequently and unpredictably according to such nonwork demands as chronically ill family members. Unpredictable flexible schedules make overtime pay calculations difficult. It is possible that companies may make inadequate or excessive overtime payments. A Supreme Court ruling (*Walling v. A. H. Belo Corp.*)[28] requires employers to guarantee fixed weekly pay for employees whose work hours vary from week to week:

- The employer typically cannot determine the number of hours employees will work each week.
- The workweek period fluctuates both greater and less than 40 hours per week.

This pay provision guarantees employees fixed weekly pay regardless of how many hours they work, and it enables employers to control weekly labor cost expenditures. The use of compressed workweek schedules may lead to differences in overtime practices in some states. Whereas the federal government bases overtime pay on a weekly basis, some states use other time bases to determine overtime pay eligibility. Table 13-9 lists maximum hour provisions for select states. As you can see, there is wide variation in daily overtime practices.

Employee Benefits

Flexible workweek schedules have the greatest impact on paid time off benefits. Many companies determine employees' sick leave benefits and vacation days based on the number of hours they work each month. The determination of paid vacation and sick leave for employees on standard work schedules is relatively straightforward; however, flexible employees work fewer hours some months and more hours during other months. This variability complicates companies' calculations of paid time off benefits.

Another issue is the treatment of paid time off for holidays. Under standard work schedules, the vast majority of employees work five 8-hour days from Monday through Friday. For example, all employees take Thanksgiving Day off (a Thursday) with pay. Under flexible schedules, some employees may not be scheduled to work on Thursdays. As a result, standard-schedule employees receive 1 day off with pay during Thanksgiving week, and some flexible employees work their regular schedules, missing a paid day off from work. Companies must establish policies that provide flexible workers with comparable paid time off benefits or alternative holidays. Such policies are necessary to maintain equity among employees; however, scheduling alternative holidays may lead to coordination problems for small companies: Companies with small staffs may not have enough employees to cover for flexible workers during their alternative holiday time off work.

An employee benefits issue known as **working condition fringe benefits** applies to telecommuters. Employers are likely to provide telecommuters with the necessary equipment to perform their jobs effectively while off-site: computers, modems, printers, photocopy machines, sundry office supplies, and Telex machines. In addition, some employers provide similar equipment to

TABLE 13-9 **Maximum Hours before Overtime for Selected States**

Alaska

Under a voluntary flexible work hour plan approved by the Alaska Department of Labor, a 10 hour day, 40 hour workweek may be instituted with premium pay after 10 hours a day instead of after 8 hours.

California

Any work in excess of 8 hours in one workday and any work in excess of 40 hours in one workweek and the first 8 hours worked on the seventh day of work in any one workweek shall be at the rate of one and one-half times the regular rate of pay. Any work in excess of 12 hours in one day and any work in excess of 8 hours on any seventh day of a workweek shall be paid no less than twice the regular rate of pay. California Labor Code section 310. Exceptions apply to an employee working pursuant to an alternative workweek adopted pursuant to applicable Labor Code sections and for time spent commuting. (See Labor Code sections 510 for exceptions.)

Rhode Island

Time and one-half premium pay for work on Sundays and holidays in retail and certain other businesses is required under two laws that are separate from the Fair Labor Standards Act minimum wage provision.

Oregon

Premium pay required after 10 hours a day in nonfarm canneries, driers, or packing plants and in mills, factories, or manufacturing establishments (excluding sawmills, planning mills, shingle mills, and logging camps).

Washington

Premium pay is not applicable to employees who request compensating time off in lieu of premium pay.

Source: U.S. Department of Labor. (2013). *Minimum Wage Laws in the States.* Available: *http://www.dol .gov/whd/minwage/america.htm*#footnote, accessed June 6, 2013.

employees who wish to work additional hours outside their regular work schedules during the evenings or weekends. This arrangement does not qualify as telecommuting.

The IRS treats the home use of office equipment and supplies as employees' taxable income when the use falls outside established telecommuting relationships; however, employees are not taxed when the home use of employer-provided equipment falls within established telecommuting relationships. Under this condition, the IRS treats the home use of employer-provided equipment as a working condition fringe benefit.

UNIONS' REACTIONS TO CONTINGENT WORKERS AND FLEXIBLE WORK SCHEDULES

Unions generally do not support companies' use of contingent workers and flexible work schedules. Most union leaders believe that alternative work arrangements threaten members' job security and are prone to unfair and inequitable treatment. The most common concerns include:

- Employers exploit contingent workers by paying them lower wages and benefits than core employees.
- Employers' efforts to get cheap labor will lead to a poorly trained and less skilled workforce that will hamper competitiveness.
- Part-time employees are difficult to organize because their interests are centered on activities outside the workplace. Part-time workers are therefore probably not good union members.
- Part-time employment erodes labor standards: Part-time workers are often denied fringe benefits, job security, and promotion opportunities. Increasing part-time employment would promote inequitable treatment.

- Temporary employees generally have little concern about improving the productivity of a company for which they will work for only a brief period.
- Unions' bargaining power becomes weak when companies demonstrate their ability to perform effectively with temporaries.
- The long days of compressed workweeks or flextime could endanger workers' safety and health, even if the workers choose these long days themselves.
- Concerns about employee isolation, uncompensated overtime, and company monitoring in the home are among the reasons unions have been reluctant to permit telecommuting by their members.

Unions' positions against contingent employment are unlikely to change because this practice undermines efforts to secure high wages and job security for members; however, some unions, particularly in the public sector, have begun to accept the use of flexible work schedules. The benefits of these arrangements (e.g., increased productivity, lower absence rates, and tardiness) strengthen unions' bargaining power.

STRATEGIC ISSUES AND CHOICES IN USING CONTINGENT AND FLEXIBLE WORKERS

What role do contingent workers and flexible work schedules play in promoting competitive advantage? These work arrangements, when properly applied, can ultimately contribute to meeting the goals of cost control and product or service innovation; however, the rationale for the appropriateness of contingent employment and flexible work schedules differs according these objectives.

A cost control objective requires firms to reduce output costs per employee. Contingent employment saves companies considerable amounts of money because they do not give these workers most discretionary benefits or provide less generous amounts of such benefits. Discretionary benefits represent a significant fiscal cost to companies.

Employers' use of well-trained contingent workers also contributes through reduced training costs; however, not all contingent workers know company-specific work practices and procedures. Company-specific training represents a significant cost to companies. Companies that do not employ contingent workers long enough to realize the productivity benefits from training undermine cost control objectives. Company-sponsored training may seem to contradict the lowest-cost imperative in the short term.

The following factors can increase short-term costs:

- Costs of training materials and instructors' professional fees
- Downtime while employees are participating in training
- Inefficiencies that may result until employees master new skills

A longer-term perspective, however, may lead to the conclusion that contingent work arrangements support the lowest-cost imperatives. Over time, productivity enhancements and increased flexibility should far outweigh the short-run costs if companies establish track records of high productivity, quality, and exemplary customer service.

Flexible schedules should also contribute to lowest-cost imperatives. Limited evidence suggests that flexible employees demonstrate lower absenteeism than employees with fixed work schedules.

A product and service innovation objective requires creative, open-minded, risk-taking employees. Compared with cost control objectives, companies that pursue differentiation strategies must take a longer-term focus to attain their preestablished objectives. Both arrangements should contribute to innovation; however, systematic studies that demonstrate these relationships are lacking. Contingent employment probably is appropriate because companies will benefit from the influx of "new" employees from time to time who bring fresh ideas with them. Over the long run, contingent employment should minimize problems of **groupthink,** which occurs when all group members agree on mistaken solutions because they share the same mind-set and view issues through the lens of conformity.[29]

Flexible work schedules should also promote differentiation strategies for two reasons. First, flexible work schedules enable employees to work when they are at their physical or mental best. Some individuals are most alert during morning hours, whereas others are most alert during afternoon or evening hours because of differences in biorhythms. Second, flexible work schedules allow employees to work with fewer distractions and worries about personal matters. The inherent flexibility of these schedules allows employees to attend to personal matters as needed.

COMPENSATION IN ACTION

Both companies and people adopt strategies to achieve the professional outcomes they desire. As those desired outcomes shift, so too do the strategies. The use of a flexible workforce (in the form of temporary workers or contractors) is one method for companies to deal with the changing needs of the company. At the individual level, changes in family demands and career priorities may prompt employees to seek flexible work arrangements that allow them to balance various demands. You will likely have the challenge of managing both of these scenarios as a line manager or HR professional. There will be factors that must be assessed to ensure the company continues to operate at a high level, while at the same time providing a work arrangement that meets the needs of the people who are critical to the company's success. By understanding the needs of the employer and the employee, you will be prepared to manage the situation in a way that allows both parties to meet their goals.

Action checklist for line managers and HR—leveraging flexibility to address changing needs

HR takes the lead
- Identify various options (e.g., part-time employees, temporary workers, and contractors) that may be employed to meet the pressing business factors.
- Pulse current employees to gain insight on the value placed on flexible work arrangements. Assess whether these types of desired arrangements might support the needs of the business and what associated costs and cost savings would be with the offering of the arrangement.
- Ensure that compensation and benefits being offered to flexible workers are in accordance with provisions outlined by FLSA and other legally mandated standards.

Line managers take the lead
- Identify business factors that may make the use of flexible workers a necessity (e.g., predictable season of increased customer demand, layoffs to cut headcount, and desire to employ lowest-cost strategy).
- Recognize which jobs may be carried out by some type of flexible work arrangement (e.g., telecommuter and temporary worker) and work with HR to identify which arrangement works best for those jobs.
- After plan is in place and successful arrangements have been realized, work with HR to create a communication plan outlining these successes in order to further promote the feasibility and validity of these types of arrangements. Produce online testimonial videos that speak to the value these arrangements offer to the business and its people.

END OF CHAPTER

MyManagementLab

Go to **mymanagementlab.com** to complete the problems marked with this icon .

Summary

This chapter discussed contingent workers and flexible work arrangements, reasons companies rely on contingent employment arrangements and flexible work schedules, special compensation issues, unions' reactions to contingent employment and flexible work schedules, and their fit for competitive advantage. Companies that choose to employ contingent workers must give serious consideration to the possible long-term benefits and consequences. Flexible work schedules seem to accommodate the changing workers' needs well. Given the possible limitations of contingent employment and flexible work schedules, companies should strike a balance between the use of core employment and contingent employment, as well as a balance between standard work schedules and flexible work schedules.

Key Terms

core employees   290
contingent workers   290
voluntary part-time employees   290
involuntary part-time employees   291
job sharing   292
temporary employment agency   294
direct hire arrangements   294
on-call arrangements   294
lease companies   294

independent contractors   295
freelancers   295
consultants   295
dual employer common law
    doctrine   300
safe harbor rule   300
economic reality test   301
right to control test   301
flextime schedules   303

core hours   303
banking hours   303
compressed workweek
    schedules   303
telecommuting   303
Walling v. A. H. Belo Corp.   305
working condition fringe
    benefits   305
groupthink   308

Discussion Questions

13-1. Discuss some of the problems that companies are likely to face when both contingent workers and core employees work in the same location. Does it matter whether contingent workers and core employees are performing the same jobs? Explain your answer.

13-2. Companies generally pay temporary employees lower wages and offer fewer benefits than they extend to their core counterparts. Nevertheless, what are some of the possible drawbacks for companies that employ temporary workers? Do you believe that these drawbacks outweigh the cost savings? Explain your reasoning.

13-3. What arguments can be made in favor of using compressed workweek schedules for companies that pursue lowest-cost strategies? What are the arguments against using compressed workweek schedules in such situations?

13-4. What impact will flexible work schedules have on employees' commitment to their employers? On employee productivity? On company effectiveness?

13-5. Provide your reactions to the following statement: Contingent workers should be compensated on a pay-for-knowledge system.

CASE
Telecommuting at MedEx

⭐ *An additional Supplemental Case can be found on MyManagementLab.*

Harry Davis just finished interviewing a candidate to fill another medical billing specialist opening. As the human resources manager for MedEx, a medical billing company, Harry is concerned about the high turnover rate for the specialists. Turnover is very costly for the company, and Harry is trying to identify ways to lower the turnover rate. The candidate he just interviewed asked Harry if any of the specialists worked from home. Harry informed him that they do not right now, but telecommuting may be an option in the near future.

MedEx employs more than medical billing specialists in its office located in a busy downtown metropolitan area. Each specialist works on a group of specific accounts, coding medical records and entering them into the computer system. The specialist position requires an intense 3-week training program to learn the coding system, but once they are proficient at their work, the specialists work independently on their assigned accounts.

In an attempt to identify the cause of the high turnover rate, Harry asked the specialists to complete an employee survey that asked about their satisfaction with their pay, benefits, and working conditions. In general, the employees indicated satisfaction with pay levels and benefits, but were not satisfied in some other areas. In the "comments" section of the survey, several employees noted challenges in getting to work each day. Some mentioned heavy traffic that caused long commutes, while others noted the high cost of parking downtown. Further, many employees noted high stress levels due to trying to balance their work and personal responsibilities.

When asked for specific ideas on how to improve the work environment, more than half of the specialists noted the option to telecommute as a desirable benefit. Because the specialists work independently, telecommuting is a feasible option. The specialists would need to work in the office at least 1 or 2 days per week in order to get updates on their accounts, but it would be possible for the employees to work from home the other days. Harry now must carefully consider whether to recommend offering the telecommuting option.

Questions:

13-6. Would offering telecommuting as an option benefit MedEx? How?
13-7. Are there any disadvantages or challenges in offering telecommuting?
13-8. What do you recommend MedEx do? Why?

MyManagementLab

Go to **mymanagementlab.com** for Auto-graded writing questions as well as the following Assisted-graded writing questions:

⭐ **13-9.** Explain leased employee arrangements. Discuss employee benefits for leased workers.

⭐ **13-10.** Discuss flexible work schedules from the perspective of both unions and employees.

Endnotes

1. U.S. Bureau of Labor Statistics. (2005). *Contingent and Alternative Employment Arrangements, February 2005.* USDL: 05-1433. Available: *www.bls.gov/*, accessed January 17, 2011.
2. U.S. Bureau of Labor Statistics. (2005). *Workers on Flexible and Shift Schedules, May 2004.* USDL: 05-1198. Available: *www.bls.gov*, accessed January 17, 2011.
3. U.S. Bureau of Labor Statistics, *Contingent and Alternative.*
4. Fallick, B. B. (1999). Part-time work and industry growth. *Monthly Labor Review, 122*, pp. 22–29.
5. Burgess, P. M. (1994). *Making It in America's New Economy.* Commencement address, University of Toledo, June 11.

6. U.S. Bureau of Labor Statistics, *Contingent and Alternative*.

7. U.S. Bureau of Labor Statistics. (2009). *Employment Projections: 2008–2018*. USDL: 09-1503. Available: *http://www.bls.gov*, accessed January 17, 2011.

8. Ibid.

9. Ibid.

10. Ibid.

11. U.S. Bureau of Labor Statistics. (2007). *Industry at a Glance*. Available: *http://www.bls.gov/iag/iaghome.htm*, accessed June 14, 2007.

12. England, P. (1992). *Comparable Worth: Theories and Evidence*. New York: Aldine DeGruyler.

13. Pierret, C. R. (2006). The "sandwich generation": Women caring for parents and children. *Monthly Labor Review*, *129*, pp. 3–9.

14. U.S. Bureau of Labor Statistics. (2012). *Employee Benefits in the United States—March 2012*. USDL: 12-1380 . Available: *www.bls.gov*, accessed April 6, 2013.

15. U.S. Bureau of Labor Statistics. (2013). *Employer Costs for Employee Compensation, December 2012*. USDL: 13-0421. Available: *www.bls.gov*, accessed April 6, 2013.

16. Cooper, S. F. (1995). The expanding use of contingent workers in the American economy: New opportunities and dangers for employers. *Employee Relations Law Review*, *20*, pp. 525–539.

17. U.S. Bureau of Labor Statistics. *Employer Costs for Employee Compensation*.

18. Ibid.

19. U.S. Bureau of Labor Statistics, *Employee Benefits in the United States—March 2012*.

20. Internal Revenue Code 410(a)(1).

21. U.S. Bureau of Labor Statistics, *Contingent and Alternative*.

22. Internal Revenue Code 411(b)(4)(c).

23. Bureau of National Affairs. (1994). *Employee Relations Weekly*, October 24, 1994. Washington, DC: Author.

24. U.S. Bureau of Labor Statistics, *Contingent and Alternative*.

25. Internal Revenue Code 414(n)(5).

26. Internal Revenue Code 414(n)(1)(2)(3).

27. *Martin v. Priba Corp.*, USDC N. Texas, No. 3:91-CV-278-G (11/6/92).

28. *Walling v. A. H. Belo Corp.*, 316, U.S. 624, 2WH Cases 39 (1942).

29. Sheppard, C. R. (1964). *Small Groups*. San Francisco, CA: Chandler.

Where We Are Now:

PART V, CONTEMPORARY STRATEGIC COMPENSATION CHALLENGES, explained the principles and practices for compensating executives and the flexible workforce. Until now, we studied compensation principles and practices employed by U.S. companies in the United States context. Compensation practices outside the United States require your attention because companies are becoming increasingly global in their reach. Now, we turn to the principles and practices of expatriate compensation and employee benefits in addition to a review of compensation and benefits in a sample of countries around the world.

In **PART VI, WE WILL COVER**

14

COMPENSATING EXPATRIATES

⭐ Improve Your Grade!

When you see this icon, visit **www.mymanagementlab.com** for activities that are applied, personalized, and offer immediate feedback.

LEARNING OBJECTIVES

When you finish studying this chapter, you should be able to:

1. Summarize the four reasons international activities facilitate the attainment of competitive advantage.
2. Describe and explain the four preliminary considerations compensation professionals should take under advisement before designing international compensation programs.
3. List the three main components of international compensation programs, and provide a specific example of each one.
4. Explain the three approaches available to companies for setting expatriate employees' base pay.
5. Summarize the three types of incentive payments that are commonly used in international compensation programs.
6. Give a description of two standard employee benefits and two illustrations of enhanced benefits for U.S. employees.
7. Describe the issue of repatriation.

International compensation programs have strategic value as U.S. businesses continue to establish operations in such foreign locales as Pacific Rim countries, Eastern Europe, and Mexico. The general trend for expanding operations overseas serves as just one indicator of the "globalization" of the economy. U.S. companies place professional and managerial (U.S. citizen) employees overseas to establish and operate satellite plants and offices. Although there are many glamorous aspects about working overseas, the glamour comes at the price of personal and, sometimes, professional sacrifices. Compensation takes on strategic value by providing these employees minimal financial risk associated with working overseas, as well as lifestyles for them and their families comparable to their lifestyles in the United States. Multinational companies (i.e., companies with operations in more than one country) develop special compensation packages to help compensate for the personal sacrifices international assignees and their immediate families make. These sacrifices are associated with cultural variations that affect their lifestyle (e.g., dealing with an unfamiliar culture, enhanced responsibilities, and potentially higher living expenses).

COMPETITIVE ADVANTAGE AND HOW INTERNATIONAL ACTIVITIES FIT IN

The presence of U.S. companies in foreign countries is on the rise. You might forget that you are in China while taking a taxi ride through the streets of Beijing: Billboards and establishments for such U.S. companies as McDonald's, Pizza Hut, Pepsi, and Coca-Cola are common sights. In addition, many large U.S. companies such as Motorola and General Motors have manufacturing establishments there.

Several factors have contributed to the expansion of global markets. These include such free trade agreements as the **North American Free Trade Agreement (NAFTA),** the unification of the European market, and the gradual weakening of Communist influence in Eastern Europe and Asia. Likewise, foreign companies have greater opportunities to invest in the United States.

Lowest-Cost Producers' Relocations to Cheaper Production Areas

Many U.S. businesses have established manufacturing and production facilities in Asian countries and in Mexico because labor is significantly less expensive than it is in the United States. There are two key reasons for the cost difference. First, labor unions generally do not have much bargaining power in developing Asian countries or in Mexico, where the governments possess extensive control over workplace affairs. Second, Asian governments historically have not valued individual employee rights as much as does the U.S. government. As we discussed in Chapter 2, the Fair Labor Standards Act of 1938 (FLSA) provides employees a minimum hourly wage rate, limits exploitation of child labor, and mandates overtime pay. The National Labor Relations Act of 1935 requires management to bargain with labor unions over terms of employment such as wages and some employee benefits.

Differentiation and the Search for New Global Markets

Coca-Cola and Pepsi products are well known worldwide because these companies aggressively introduced their soft drink products throughout numerous countries. Coke and Pepsi products worldwide could distinguish themselves from competing companies by taking on new business initiatives that depart from "business as usual" and meet specific market needs.

For Coke and Pepsi, "business as usual" means marketing soft drink products (i.e., carbonated water with artificial colors and flavors). Marketing bottled spring water would clearly be a departure from business as usual for them. The People's Republic of China (PRC) possesses a definite need for bottled spring water: The Chinese government is unable to provide its citizens and visitors with drinkable water because the country does not maintain adequate water purification plants. Coke and Pepsi could distinguish themselves from other soft drink companies by marketing spring water along with their regular soft drink products. Coke and Pepsi would be known as companies that serve necessary (bottled water) and recreational (soft drinks) beverage needs.

How Globalization Is Affecting HR Departments

The globalization of business requires that companies send employees overseas to establish and operate satellite plants and offices. Companies naturally must invest in the development of appropriate human resource (HR) practices. International business operations are destined to fail without the "right" people. HR professionals must be certain to identify the selection criteria that are most related to successful international work assignments. For example, do candidates possess adequate cultural sensitivity? Do they believe that U.S. customs are the only appropriate way to approach problems? Are candidates' families willing to adjust to foreign lifestyles?

Another key HR function is training. Expatriates must understand the cultural values that predominate in foreign countries; otherwise, they risk hindering business. For example, one of Procter & Gamble's Camay soap commercials was successful in the United States, but the Japanese perceived the very same commercial that aired in Japan to be rude. The commercial depicted a man barging into the bathroom on his wife while she was using Camay soap. Japanese cultural values led Japanese viewers to judge this commercial as offensive. The Japanese deemed the commercial as acceptable after Procter & Gamble modified the commercial to show a woman using Camay soap in privacy.

Companies' investments in cross-cultural training vary. Some companies provide release time from work to take foreign-language courses at local colleges or universities. Highly progressive companies (e.g., Motorola) run corporate universities that offer cross-cultural training courses.

The use of international assignments is an important issue addressed by companies located in countries across the world. A multitude of large consulting firms (e.g., Mercer, www.mercer.com) conduct extensive research for client companies to ensure the most effective deployment of expatriates worldwide. Such consulting firms focus on pay and benefits issues for expatriates, labor law, and useful information to help expatriates select and train local country nationals. For example, "The most sophisticated companies are trying to integrate international programs with talent management programs," said ORC Worldwide executive vice president Geoffrey W. Latta: "These companies understand the importance of integrating international experience with local talent, particularly if the company wants to become a true leader among global organizations."[1]

Complexity of International Compensation Programs

The development and implementation of international compensation programs typically pose four challenges to companies that U.S. compensation programs do not have to consider. First, successful international compensation programs further corporate interests abroad and encourage employees to take foreign assignments. Second, well-designed compensation programs minimize financial risk to employees and make their and their families' experiences as pleasant as possible. Third, international compensation programs promote a smooth transition back to life in the United States upon completion of the international assignment. **Repatriation** is the process of making the transition from an international assignment and living abroad to a domestic assignment and living in the home country. Fourth, sound international compensation programs promote U.S. businesses' lowest-cost and differentiation strategies in foreign markets.

PRELIMINARY CONSIDERATIONS

We must take some basic issues under advisement before examining the elements of international compensation programs. Compensation professionals must distinguish among host country nationals (HCNs), third country nationals (TCNs) (to be discussed next), and expatriates as compensation recipients with their own unique issues. In addition, compensation professionals should consider such matters as terms of the international assignment, staff mobility, and equity because these factors pertain directly to the design elements of international compensation programs.

Host Country Nationals, Third Country Nationals, and Expatriates: Definitions and Relevance for Compensation Issues

There are three kinds of recipients of international compensation:

- Host country nationals (HCNs)
- Third country nationals (TCNs)
- Expatriates

We will define these recipients as employees of U.S. companies doing business in foreign countries; however, these definitions also apply to employees of non-U.S. companies doing business in foreign countries.

Host country nationals (HCN) are foreign national citizens who work in U.S. companies' branch offices or manufacturing plants in their home countries. Japanese citizens working for General Electric in Japan are HCNs.

Third country nationals (TCN) are foreign national citizens who work in U.S. companies' branch offices or manufacturing plants in foreign countries—excluding the United States and their own home countries. Australian citizens working for General Motors in the People's Republic of China are TCNs.

Expatriates are U.S. citizens employed in U.S. companies with work assignments outside the United States. U.S. citizens employed in CitiBank's London, England, office are expatriates.

Our primary focus is on compensation for expatriates. Following an extensive discussion of expatriate compensation, we will consider some of the challenges compensation professionals face when compensating HCNs and TCNs.

As a reminder, our focus is on U.S. companies, and these definitions reflect this focus. Other countries can be the focus as well. For example, let's define HCN, TCN, and expatriate from the Australian perspective. BHP, an Australian company, conducts business worldwide in such countries as the People's Republic of China and the United States. A Chinese citizen who works for BHP in Shanghai is an HCN. A U.S. citizen who works for BHP in Shanghai is a TCN. An Australian citizen who works for BHP in Shanghai is an expatriate.

HR professionals construct international compensation packages on the basis of three main factors:

- Term of international assignment
- Staff mobility
- Equity: pay referent groups

Term of International Assignment

The term of the international assignment is central in determining compensation policy. Short-term assignments (i.e., usually less than 1 year in duration) generally do not require substantial modifications to domestic compensation packages; however, extended assignments necessitate features that promote a sense of stability and comfort overseas. These features include housing allowances, educational expenses for children, and adjustments to protect expatriates from paying "double" income taxes (i.e., U.S. federal and state taxes as well as applicable foreign taxes).

Staff Mobility

Companies must also consider whether foreign assignments necessitate employees' moving from one foreign location to another (e.g., from Beijing, China, to the Special Economic Zone in China or from England to Brazil). Such moves within and across foreign cultures can disrupt expatriates' and their families' lives. Staff mobility comes at a price to companies in the form of monetary incentives and measures to make employees' moves as comfortable as possible.

Equity: Pay Referent Groups

Well-designed U.S. compensation programs promote equity among employees: Employees' pay is commensurate with performance or knowledge attainment. Expatriates are likely to evaluate compensation, in part, according to equity considerations. Many U.S. companies use domestic employees as the pay referent groups when developing international compensation packages because virtually all expatriate employees eventually return to the United States.

Some companies use local employees as the pay referent groups for long-term assignments because they wish to facilitate expatriates' integration into foreign cultures. As we discuss later, Mexican managerial employees' compensation packages include base pay and such cash allowances as Christmas bonuses. On the other hand, the main components of U.S. managerial employees' compensation packages include base pay and long-term incentives. U.S. expatriates working in Mexico on long-term assignments are likely to have compensation packages that are similar to Mexican managerial employees' compensation packages.

COMPONENTS OF INTERNATIONAL COMPENSATION PROGRAMS

The basic structure of international compensation programs is similar to the structure of domestic compensation programs. The main components include base pay and fringe compensation. The inclusion of nonperformance-based incentives and allowances distinguishes international compensation packages from domestic compensation packages. Table 14-1 lists the main components of international compensation programs.

SETTING BASE PAY FOR U.S. EXPATRIATES

U.S. companies must determine the method for setting expatriates' base pay. Final determination should come only after companies carefully weigh the strengths and limitations of alternative methods. In addition, the purchasing power of base pay is an important consideration. Purchasing power affects standard of living. The following quote from a U.S. expatriate stationed in Italy captures the essence of purchasing power for expatriates: "Does the euro in Italy purchase as much macaroni today as it did yesterday?" Two key factors influence purchasing power: the stability of local currency and inflation, both of which we discuss shortly.

Methods for Setting Base Pay

U.S. companies use one of three methods to calculate expatriates' base pay:

- Home country–based method
- Host country–based method
- Headquarters-based method

HOME COUNTRY–BASED METHOD   The **home country–based pay method** compensates expatriates the amount they would receive if they were performing similar work in the United States. Job evaluation procedures enable employers to determine whether jobs at home are equivalent to comparable jobs in foreign locations based on compensable factors. How does location create differences in jobs that are otherwise considered equal? One example may be that foreign-language skills are probably essential outside English-speaking countries. Adjustments to expatriates' pay should reflect additional skills.

TABLE 14-1 U.S. Expatriates' Compensation Package

Core Compensation
    Base pay
    Incentive compensation
    Foreign service premium
    Hardship allowance
    Mobility premium
Employee Benefits
    Standard benefits
    Protection programs
    Paid time off
Enhanced Benefits
    Relocation assistance
    Educational reimbursement for expatriates' children
    Home leave and travel reimbursement
    Rest and relaxation leave allowance

The home country–based pay method is often most appropriate for expatriates. Equity problems are not very likely to arise because expatriates' assignments are too short to establish local national employees as pay referents. Instead, expatriates will base pay comparisons on their home country standards. In general, the home country–based pay method is most suitable when expatriate assignments are short in duration and local nationals performing comparable jobs receive substantially higher pay. As we discussed earlier, expatriates may rely on local cultural norms over extended periods as the standard for judging the equitableness of their compensation.

HOST COUNTRY–BASED METHOD   The **host country–based method** compensates expatriates based on the host countries' pay scales. Companies use various standards for determining base pay, including market pricing, job evaluation techniques, and jobholders' past relevant work experience. Other countries use different standards. For instance, the Japanese emphasize seniority. Expatriates' base pay will be competitive with other employees' base pay in the host countries. The host country–based method is most suitable when assignments are of long duration. As we noted previously, expatriates are then more likely to judge the adequacy of their pay relative to their local coworkers rather than to their counterparts at home.

HEADQUARTERS-BASED METHOD   The **headquarters-based method** compensates all employees according to the pay scales used at the headquarters. Neither the location of the international work assignment nor home country influences base pay. This method makes the most sense for expatriates who move from one foreign assignment to another and rarely, if ever, work in their home countries. This system is administratively simple because it applies the pay standard of one country to all employees regardless of the location of their foreign assignment or their country of citizenship.

Purchasing Power

Decreases in purchasing power lead to lower standards of living. Expatriates quite simply cannot afford to purchase as many goods and services as they could before, or they must settle for lower quality. Diminished purchasing power undermines the strategic value of expatriates' compensation because top-notch employees are probably not willing to settle for lower standards of living while stationed at foreign posts. In addition, changes in the factors that immediately influence standard of living (i.e., the stability of currency and inflation) are somewhat unpredictable. This unpredictability creates a sense of uncertainty and risk. As we will discuss later in this section, most U.S. companies use the balance sheet approach to minimize this risk.

CURRENCY STABILIZATION   Most U.S. companies award expatriates' base pay in U.S. currency, not in the local foreign currency; however, foreign countries as a rule do not recognize U.S. currency as legal tender. Expatriates must therefore exchange U.S. currency for local foreign currency based on daily exchange rates. An **exchange rate** is the price at which one country's currency can be swapped for another.[2] Exchange rates are expressed in terms of foreign currency per U.S. dollar or in terms of U.S. dollars per unit of foreign currency. For example, on April 5, 2013, the exchange rate for the Swedish krona was 6.48 KR for each U.S.$1. It is also possible to receive fewer units of foreign currency for each U.S. dollar exchanged. On April 5, 2013, the exchange rate was 0.77 euro for each U.S. dollar exchanged.

Government policies and complex market forces cause exchange rates to fluctuate daily. Exchange rate fluctuations have direct implications for expatriates' purchasing power. For example, let's start with the previous exchange rate of 6.48 KR per U.S.$1. In addition, the exchange rate was 8.50 KR per U.S.$1 on December 31, 1999. This example illustrates a decline in the exchange rate for Swedish money. U.S. expatriates experience lower purchasing power because they receive less Swedish KR for every U.S.$1 they exchange.

INFLATION   **Inflation** is the increase in prices for consumer goods and services. Inflation erodes the purchasing power of currency. Let's assume that ABC Corporation did not award pay increases to its expatriates stationed in the United Kingdom during 2011 and 2012. Expatriates'

TABLE 14-2 **Annual Inflation Rates (%) for Selected Countries, 2008–2012 (November)**

Period	United States	Canada	Japan	France	Germany	Italy	Sweden	Switzerland	United Kingdom
2008	3.8	2.3	1.4	2.8	2.6	3.3	3.4	2.4	4.0
2009	−0.4	0.3	−1.4	0.1	0.4	0.8	−0.5	−0.5	−0.5
2010	1.6	1.8	−0.7	1.5	1.1	1.5	1.2	0.7	4.6
2011	3.2	2.9	−0.3	2.1	2.3	2.8	3.0	0.3	5.2
2012	2.1	1.5	0.0	2.0	2.0	3.0	0.9	−0.7	3.2

Note: These percent changes are based on national consumer price indexes as published by each country.
Source: U.S. Department of Labor, Bureau of Labor Statistics, Division of International Labor Comparisons. Available: *www.bls.gov*, accessed April 5, 2013.

purchasing power remains unaffected as long as there isn't any inflation (and reduced exchange rate) during the same period. These expatriates, however, had lower purchasing power ever since because inflation averaged between 5.2 percent and 3.2 percent, respectively. Table 14-2 shows the annual inflation rates for various countries between 2008 and 2012.

INCENTIVE COMPENSATION FOR U.S. EXPATRIATES

In the United States, companies offer incentives to promote higher job performance and to minimize dysfunctional turnover, which results when high performers quit their jobs. International compensation plans include a variety of unique incentives to encourage expatriates to accept and remain on international assignments. These incentives also compensate expatriates for their willingness to tolerate less desirable living and working conditions. The main incentives are foreign services premiums, hardship allowance, and mobility premiums.

Foreign Service Premiums

Foreign service premiums are monetary payments above and beyond regular base pay. Companies offer foreign service premiums to encourage employees to accept expatriate assignments. These premiums generally apply to assignments that extend beyond 1 year. The use of foreign service premiums is widespread.

Companies calculate foreign service premiums as a percentage of base pay, and these premiums range between 10 and 30 percent of base pay. The percentage amount increases with the length of the assignment. Larger amounts are sometimes necessary when there is a shortage of available candidates. Companies disburse payment of the foreign service premium over several installments to manage costs and to "remind" expatriates about the incentive throughout their assignments.

Employers that use foreign service premiums should consider the possible drawbacks. First, employees may misconstrue this premium as a regular permanent increase to base pay, and resentment toward the employer may develop following the last installment. Second, foreign service premiums may not have incentive value when employers make several small installments rather than fewer large installments. Third, employees may feel as if their standard of living has declined when they return to the United States because they no longer receive this extra money.

Hardship Allowances

The **hardship allowance** compensates expatriates for their sacrifices while on assignment. Specifically, these allowances are designed to recognize exceptionally hard living and working conditions at foreign locations. Employers disburse hardship allowances in small amounts throughout the duration of expatriates' assignments. It is easy for expatriates to lose sight of the foreign service premiums and hardship allowances because they appear as relatively small increments to their paychecks. Companies should take care to communicate the role of these payments.

TABLE 14-3 **Hardship Locations, Differentials, and Danger Pay, Effective March 24, 2013**

Country Name	Post Name	Rate (%)
AFGHANISTAN	Kabul	35
CHINA	Guangzhou	20
INDIA	Mumbai	20
IRAQ	Baghdad	25
KENYA	Wangige	30
MEXICO	Mexico City, D.F.	15
PHILIPPINES	Manila	20
RUSSIA	Saint Petersburg	15
TAIWAN	Taipei	0
VENEZUELA	Caracas	20

Source: A complete listing of current locations with hardship differential for federal civilian employees can be found in Section 920 of the Department of State *Standardized Regulations* (*Government Civilians, Foreign Areas*), available from the Superintendent of Documents, U.S. Government Printing Office, Washington, DC 20402. Available: *http://aoprals.state.gov/Web920/hardship.asp*, accessed April 5, 2013.

Companies offer hardship allowances at exceptionally severe locations only. The U.S. Department of State has established a list of hardship posts where the living conditions are considered unusually harsh. Most multinational companies award hardship allowances to executive, managerial, and supervisory employees. Hardship allowances range from 5 percent to 35 percent of base pay (i.e., the greater the hardship, the higher the premium). The U.S. Department of State uses three criteria to identify hardship locations:

- Extraordinarily difficult living conditions (e.g., inadequate housing, lack of recreational facilities, isolation, inadequate transportation facilities, and lack of food or consumer services)
- Excessive physical hardship, including severe climates or high altitudes and the presence of dangerous conditions affecting physical and mental well-being
- Notably unhealthy conditions (e.g., diseases and epidemics, lack of public sanitation, and inadequate health facilities)

The U.S. Department of State has deemed more than 150 places as hardship locations. Table 14-3 lists examples of hardship locations and recommended hardship differentials.

Mobility Premiums

Mobility premiums reward employees for moving from one assignment to another. Companies use these premiums to encourage employees to accept, leave, or change assignments—usually between foreign posts or between domestic positions to ones in a foreign country. Expatriates typically receive mobility premiums as single lump sum payments.

ESTABLISHING EMPLOYEE BENEFITS FOR U.S. EXPATRIATES

Benefits represent an important component of expatriates' compensation packages. Companies design benefits programs to attract and retain the best expatriates. In addition, companies design these programs to promote a sense of security for expatriates and their families. Furthermore, well-designed programs should help expatriates and their families maintain regular contact with other family members and friends in the United States.

Benefits fall into three broad categories: protection programs, paid time off, and services. Protection programs provide family benefits, promote health, and guard against income loss caused by such catastrophic factors as unemployment, disability, or serious illnesses. Paid time off provides employees such paid time off as vacation. Service practices vary widely. Services provide such enhancements as tuition reimbursement and day care assistance to employees and their families.

Just like domestic employee benefits packages, international employee benefits plans include such protection programs as medical insurance and retirement programs.[3] In most cases, U.S. citizens working overseas continue to receive medical insurance and participate in their retirement programs.

International and domestic plans are also similar in that they offer paid time off; however, international packages tend to incorporate more extensive benefits of this kind, which we will discuss later. Moreover, international employee benefits differ from domestic compensation with regard to the types of allowances and reimbursements. For international assignees, these payments are designed to compensate for higher costs of living and housing, relocation allowances, and education allowances for expatriates' children.

Employers should take several considerations into account when designing international benefits programs, including:[4]

- Total remuneration: What is included in the total employee pay structure (e.g., cash wages, benefits, mandated social programs, and other perquisites)? How much can the business afford?
- Benefit adequacy: To what extent must the employer enhance mandated programs to achieve desired staffing levels? Programs already in place and employees' utilization of them should be critically examined before determining what supplementary programs are needed and desirable.
- Tax effectiveness: What is the tax deductibility of these programs for the employer and employee in each country, and how does U.S. tax law treat expenditures in this area?
- Recognition of local customs and practices: Companies often provide benefits and services to employees based on those extended by other businesses in the locality, independent of their own attitude toward these same benefits and services.

International employee benefits packages contain the same components as domestic fringe compensation packages and enhancements. U.S. expatriates receive many of the same standard benefits as their counterparts working in the United States. Expatriates also receive enhanced benefits for taking overseas assignments.

Standard Benefits for U.S. Expatriates

Protection programs and paid time off are the most pertinent standard benefits.

PROTECTION PROGRAMS We previously discussed legally required protection programs (Chapter 11) and discretionary protection programs (Chapters 9 and 10). Let's consider the application of each kind to the international context.

The key legally required protection programs are mandated by the following laws: the Social Security Act of 1935, various state workers' compensation laws, and the Family and Medical Leave Act of 1993. All provide protection programs to employees and their dependents. Expatriates continue to participate in the main Social Security programs (i.e., retirement insurance, benefits for dependents, and Medicare). The Family and Medical Leave Act also applies to expatriates; however, state workers' compensation laws generally do not. Instead, U.S. companies can elect to purchase private insurance that provides equivalent protection.

Discretionary protection programs provide family benefits, promote health, and guard against income loss caused by such catastrophic factors as unemployment, disability, or serious illnesses. U.S. companies provide these protection programs to expatriates for the same reasons they do in the United States (i.e., as a strategic response to workforce diversity and to retain the best-performing employees). Withholding these benefits from expatriates would create a disincentive for employees to take international assignments.

PAID TIME OFF Standard paid time off benefits include annual vacation, holidays, and emergency leave.

Expatriates typically receive the same annual vacation benefits as do their domestic counterparts. These benefits are particularly common among expatriates with relatively short-term assignments. Companies do not provide expatriates extended regular vacation leave because expatriates are likely to perceive the removal of these benefits on their return to domestic assignments as punitive; however, U.S. companies must comply with foreign laws that govern the amount of vacation awarded.

Expatriates generally receive paid time off for foreign national or local holidays that apply to their foreign locations. Foreign holiday schedules may provide fewer or more holidays than the United States. In addition, some countries require employers to provide all employees paid time off for recognized holidays. In the United States, companies offer paid holidays as a discretionary benefit or as set in collective bargaining agreements.

Paid leave for personal or family emergencies is also a component of most expatriate compensation packages. Such emergencies may include critically ill family members or their deaths in the United States or in the foreign posts. Most companies provide paid emergency leave, but some companies provide unpaid leaves of absence. In either case, companies cover travel expenses between the foreign post and the United States.

Enhanced Benefits for U.S. Expatriates

Enhanced benefits for U.S. expatriates include:

- Relocation assistance
- Education reimbursements for expatriates' children
- Home leave benefits and travel reimbursements
- Rest and relaxation leave and allowance

RELOCATION ASSISTANCE **Relocation assistance payments** cover expatriates' expenses to relocate to foreign posts. Table 14-4 lists the items most commonly covered under relocation assistance programs. Relocation assistance is generally large enough to pay for major expenses. Companies usually base these payment amounts on three main factors: distance, length of assignment, and rank in the company.

EDUCATION REIMBURSEMENTS FOR EXPATRIATES' CHILDREN Expatriates typically place their children in private schools designed for English-speaking students. Tuition in foreign countries is often more expensive than tuition for private U.S. schools. These companies choose to

TABLE 14-4 **Relocation Assistance Payments**

The relocation allowance or reimbursement provides employees with money for:

- Temporary quarters prior to departure because the expatriate's house has been sold or rented
- Transportation to the foreign post for employees and their families
- Reasonable expenses incurred by the family during travel
- Temporary quarters while waiting for delivery of household goods or while looking for suitable housing
- Moving household goods to the foreign post
- Storing household goods in the United States

reimburse expatriate children's education for two reasons. First, some foreign public schools are generally not comparable to U.S. public schools. Some are better, and others are below the U.S. standard. Companies make generous educational reimbursements where public school quality is low. Second, most U.S. children do not speak foreign languages fluently. Thus, they cannot enroll in foreign public schools.

HOME LEAVE BENEFITS AND TRAVEL REIMBURSEMENTS Companies offer home leave benefits to help expatriates manage the adjustment to foreign cultures and to maintain direct personal contact with family and friends. As the name implies, **home leave benefits** enable expatriates to take paid time off in the United States. Home leave benefits vary considerably from company to company. The length and frequency of these leaves usually depend on the expected duration of expatriates' assignments (i.e., longer assignments justify longer home leaves). In addition, expatriates must serve a minimum period at the foreign post before they are eligible for home leave benefits (i.e., anywhere from 6 to 12 months). Companies offer these extended benefits along with the standard paid time off benefits.

Companies compensate expatriates while they are away on home leave. In addition, most companies reimburse expatriates for expenses associated with travel between the foreign post and the United States. These reimbursements apply to expatriates and to family members who live with expatriates at foreign posts. Companies typically reimburse the cost of round-trip airfare, ground transportation, and accommodations while traveling to and from the foreign post.

REST AND RELAXATION LEAVE AND ALLOWANCE Expatriates who work in designated hardship foreign locations receive rest and relaxation leave benefits. Rest and relaxation leave represents additional paid time off. Progressive employers recognize that expatriates working in hardship locations may need extra time away from the unpleasant conditions to "recharge their batteries." Rest and relaxation leave benefits differ from standard vacation benefits because companies designate where expatriates may spend their time. For example, many U.S. companies with operations in China's Special Economic Zone designate Hong Kong as an acceptable retreat because it is relatively close by and has many amenities not present in the Special Economic Zone (e.g., diverse ethnic restaurants and Western-style entertainment).

Rest and relaxation leave programs include allowances to cover travel expenses between the foreign post and the retreat location. Companies determine allowance amounts based on such factors as the cost of round-trip transportation, food, and lodging associated with the designated locations. Allowances usually cover the majority of the costs. The U.S. Department of State publishes per diem schedules for various cities. Location and family size determine per diem amounts.

BALANCE SHEET APPROACH FOR U.S. EXPATRIATES' COMPENSATION PACKAGES

Most U.S. multinational companies use the balance sheet approach to determine expatriates' compensation packages. The **balance sheet approach** provides expatriates the standard of living they normally enjoy in the United States. Thus, the United States is the standard for all payments.

The balance sheet approach has strategic value to companies for two important reasons. First, this approach protects expatriates' standards of living. Without it, companies would have a difficult time placing qualified employees in international assignments. Second, the balance sheet approach enables companies to control costs because it relies on objective indexes that measure cost differences between the U.S. and foreign countries. We will discuss these indexes shortly.

The use of the balance sheet approach is most appropriate when:

- The home country is an appropriate reference point for economic comparisons.
- Expatriates are likely to maintain psychological and cultural ties with the home or base country.

- Expatriates prefer not to assimilate into the local foreign culture.
- The assignment is of limited duration.
- The assignment following the international assignment will be in the home country.
- The company promises employees that they will not lose financially while on foreign assignment.

Companies that use the balance sheet approach compare the costs of four major expenditures in the United States and the foreign post:

- Housing and utilities
- Goods and services
- Discretionary income
- Taxes

Employees receive allowances whenever the costs in the foreign country exceed the costs in the United States. Allowance amounts vary according to the lifestyle enjoyed in the United States. In general, individuals with higher incomes tend to live in more expensive homes, and they are in better positions to enjoy more expensive goods and services (e.g., designer labels versus off-brand labels). Higher income also means higher taxes.

Where do U.S. companies obtain pertinent information about costs for foreign countries? U.S. companies may rely on three information sources. First, they can rely on expatriates who have spent considerable time on assignment or foreign government contacts. Second, private consulting companies (e.g., Towers Watson) or research companies (e.g., Bureau of National Affairs) can conduct custom surveys. Third, most U.S. companies consult the *U.S. Department of State Indexes of Living Costs Abroad, Quarters Allowances, and Hardship Differentials*, which is published quarterly. It is the most cost-effective source because it is available at no charge in libraries with government depositories as well as at www.state.gov.

Housing and Utilities

Employers provide expatriate employees with **housing and utilities allowances** to cover the difference between housing and utilities costs in the United States and in the foreign post. The U.S. Department of State uses the term **quarters allowances.** Table 14-5 displays pertinent information from the U.S. Department of State's quarters allowances.

TABLE 14-5 Quarters Allowances, 2011

Country and City	Family Status	Rate ($93,177 and Above)	Rate ($54,028 to $93,176)	Rate (Less than $54,028)
BELGIUM:	*Family*	*46,400*	*43,200*	*38,900*
Brussels	*Single*	*43,200*	*40,700*	*34,100*
CANADA:	Family	58,200	49,600	44,600
Montreal	Single	51,400	44,600	39,600
CHINA:	*Family*	*71,200*	*65,600*	*58,200*
Beijing	*Single*	*65,600*	*58,200*	*51,700*
MEXICO:	Family	47,900	45,000	41,400
Mexico City	Single	47,900	45,000	41,400
TAIWAN:	*Family*	*23,100*	*23,100*	*19,100*
Taipei	*Single*	*23,100*	*23,100*	*19,100*

Source: U.S. Department of State. (2013). *Annual Living Quarters Allowance in U.S. Dollars* (*Rates Effective: 03/24/2013*). Washington, DC: U.S. Government Printing Office. Available: *www.state.gov*, accessed April 5, 2013.

The quarters allowances table contains three main sections: the survey date, exchange rate, and annual allowance by family status and salary range. The survey date is the month when the Office of Allowances received housing expenditure reports.

The exchange rate section includes three pieces of information: effective date, foreign unit, and number per U.S. dollar. We reviewed the concept of exchange rate earlier. It is expressed as the number of foreign currency units given in exchange for U.S.$1. The U.S. Department of State uses the exchange rate to compute the quarters allowances. In Montreal, Canada, expatriates receive 6.2 Chinese yuan for every U.S.$1 exchanged (April 5, 2013).

Table 14-5 contains information on family status and salary range. The term *single* is self-explanatory. In Beijing, the quarters allowance is $65,600 for single expatriates with annual incomes of $93,177 and higher. In Taipei, the allowance is $23,100!

The term *family* refers to two-or-more-person families. Employees with larger families living with them at the foreign posts receive supplements. Families of two to three persons receive a 10 percent supplement, families of four or five persons receive a 20 percent supplement, and families of six or more persons receive a 30 percent supplement.

Goods and Services

Expatriates receive **goods and services allowances** when the cost of living is higher in that country than it is in the United States. Employers base these allowances on **indexes of living costs abroad,** which compare the costs (U.S. dollars) of representative goods and services (excluding education) expatriates purchase at the foreign location with the cost of comparable goods and services purchased in the Washington, DC, area. The indexes are place-to-place cost comparisons at specific times and currency exchange rates.

Discretionary Income

Discretionary income covers a variety of financial obligations in the United States for which expatriates remain responsible. These expenditures are usually of a long-term nature. Companies typically do not provide allowances because expatriates remain responsible for them despite international assignments. Table 14-6 lists examples of discretionary income expenditures.

Tax Considerations

All U.S. citizens working overseas for U.S. corporations are subject to the Federal Unemployment Tax Act (FUTA).[5] Expatriates continue to pay U.S. income taxes and Social Security taxes while on assignment. The Internal Revenue Service (IRS) taxes U.S. citizens' income regardless of whether they earn income in the United States or while on foreign assignment.[6] Expatriates must also pay income taxes to local foreign governments based on the applicable income tax laws. Paying taxes to both the U.S. government and foreign governments is known as "double" taxation.[7] The Internal Revenue Code (IRC) includes regulations that address taxation issues.

TABLE 14-6 Discretionary Income Expenditures

- Pension contributions
- Savings and investments
- Insurance payments
- Equity portion of mortgage payments
- Alimony payments
- Child support
- Student loan payments
- Car payments

EMPLOYER CONSIDERATIONS: TAX PROTECTION AND TAX EQUALIZATION Under the balance sheet approach, companies choose between two approaches to help address concerns of double taxation:

- Tax protection
- Tax equalization

A key element of both tax protection and tax equalization methods is the **hypothetical tax.** Employers calculate the hypothetical tax as the U.S. income tax based on the same salary level, excluding all foreign allowances. Under **tax protection,** employers reimburse expatriates for the difference between the actual income tax amount and the hypothetical tax when the actual income tax amount—based on tax returns filed with the IRS—is greater. Expatriates simply pay the entire income tax bill when the taxes are less than or equal to the hypothetical tax. Expatriates realize a tax benefit whenever actual taxes amount to less than the hypothetical tax because they will have paid lower income taxes on their overseas assignments than on assignments in the United States.

Under **tax equalization,** employers take the responsibility for paying income taxes to the U.S. and foreign governments on behalf of the expatriates. Tax equalization is a process that ensures that the tax costs incurred by an expatriate approximate the cost of taxes had he or she remained at home. The intent of tax equalization is that the expatriate neither suffers significant financial hardship nor realizes a financial windfall from the tax consequences of an international assignment. Tax equalization starts with the calculation of the hypothetical tax. Based on this hypothetical tax amount, employers deduct income from expatriates' paychecks that total the hypothetical tax amounts at year end. Employers reimburse expatriates for the difference between the hypothetical tax and actual income tax whenever the actual income tax amount is less. Expatriates reimburse their employers whenever the actual income tax amount exceeds the hypothetical income tax amounts.

Tax equalization offers employers two important advantages over tax protection. Expatriates receive equitable treatment regardless of their location and do not keep the unexpected tax gain from being posted in countries with income tax rates lower than in the United States. As a result, employers should have an easier time motivating expatriates to move from one foreign post to another. In addition, companies save money by not allowing expatriates to keep tax windfalls.

REPATRIATION PAY ISSUES

Special compensation considerations should not end with the completion of international assignments. Effective expatriate compensation programs promote employees' integration into their companies' domestic workforces. Returnees may initially view their domestic assignments as punishment because their total compensation decreases. Upon return, former expatriates forfeit special pay incentives and extended leave allowances. Although most former expatriates understand the purpose of these incentives and allowances, it often takes time for them to adjust to "normal" compensation practices. Many expatriates may not adjust very well to compensation-as-usual because they feel their international experiences have made them substantially more valuable to their employers. Their heightened sense of value may intensify when former expatriates compare themselves with colleagues who have never taken international assignments. Two consequences are likely. First, former expatriates may find it difficult to work collaboratively with colleagues, which can undermine differentiation objectives. Second, strong resentments may lead former expatriates to find employment with competitors. Adding insult to injury, competitors stand to benefit from former expatriates' international experiences.

Companies can actively prevent many of these problems by the following two measures. First, companies should invest in former expatriates' career development. Career development programs signal that companies value returnees. In addition, former expatriates may view their employers' investments in career development as a form of compensation, reducing the equity problems described earlier. Second, companies should capitalize on expatriates' experiences to gain a better understanding of foreign business environments. In addition, former expatriates can contribute to the quality of international assignments by conveying what did and did not work well during their assignments.

COMPENSATION IN ACTION

International assignments can be one of the most rewarding experiences during an employee's career. However, along with the excitement and novelty of living in a different part of the world comes the reality of dealing with new customs, living in different communities, and arranging lifestyle in a way that makes the experience logistically enjoyable. As an HR manager or line manager, you will likely deal with expatriate employees on a number of occasions. By asking the right questions, establishing sound and consistent policy, and working to meet the requests and needs of the individual employee (within established guidelines), you can take steps to maximize the employee experience that in the long run could prove to have significant value to the company.

Action checklist for line managers and HR—maximizing the experience of expatriate employees

HR takes the lead
- Identify what type of training or other areas of preparation are necessary prior to the employee beginning the expatriate assignment.
- Sit down with employee to discuss particulars that may need to be considered prior to the employee beginning the assignment (e.g., family needs, pets, and expectations of employee).
- With compensation specialists, align the individual needs of the employee with the policies already in place in the company. For example, if the expatriate will be compensated on a home country–based pay method, are foreign

service premiums necessary to "sweeten the deal"? Is the host country an area where hardship allowance will be awarded? Will the employee have a spouse or children who will need special benefits (e.g., private schooling and language lessons)?

Line managers take the lead
- Establish a pipeline of talented employees who are ready for an international assignment. As these opportunities arise, work with HR to identify which of those employees match up best with the specific opportunities.
- Partner with other line managers who have had experience working with expats to understand the ideal length of time for the assignment, and what issues should be considered to guarantee successful transition into the assignment (this should include discussions with domestic line managers and host country managers).
- Work with HR to keep the expatriate employee connected to operations in the United States; prior to repatriation establish a plan to keep the employee engaged through experiences wherein he or she can use the critical skills acquired during the assignment (e.g., mentoring an employee preparing for a similar experience). Accurately communicate changes in compensation and other areas which could be of concern to the employee so that appropriate expectations are established.

END OF CHAPTER

MyManagementLab

Go to **mymanagementlab.com** to complete the problems marked with this icon ⭐.

Summary

This chapter provided a discussion of international compensation and its strategic role. The globalization of the economy necessitates U.S. companies' investments overseas. Well-designed expatriate compensation programs support strategic initiatives by attracting and maintaining the best performers. Effective expatriate compensation programs reduce risk and promote expatriate families' comfort while they are stationed at foreign posts. The balance sheet approach minimizes financial risk to expatriates, and various incentives and allowances promote comfort. We also discussed that successful expatriate compensation programs facilitate returnees' transition to domestic assignments.

Key Terms

North American Free Trade
   Agreement (NAFTA)   315
repatriation   316
host country nationals (HCN)   316
third country nationals (TCN)   317
expatriates   317
home country–based pay
   method   318
host country–based method   319

headquarters-based method   319
exchange rate   319
inflation   319
foreign service premiums   320
hardship allowance   320
mobility premiums   321
relocation assistance
   payments   323
home leave benefits   324

balance sheet approach   324
housing and utilities allowances   325
quarters allowances   325
goods and services allowances   326
indexes of living costs abroad   326
discretionary income   326
hypothetical tax   327
tax protection   327
tax equalization   327

⭐ Discussion Questions

14-1. Discuss the strengths and weaknesses of the following methods for establishing base pay in international contexts: home country–based pay, headquarters-based pay, and host country–based pay.

14-2. For a country of your choice, conduct research into the cultural characteristics that you believe should be important considerations in establishing a core compensation program for a U.S. company that plans to locate there. Discuss these characteristics. Discuss as well whether you feel that pay-for-performance programs are compatible. If compatible in any way, what course of action would you take to promote this compatibility?

14-3. Discuss your reaction to the following statement: "U.S. companies should increase base pay (beyond the level that would be paid in the United States) to motivate employees to accept foreign assignments."

14-4. Allowances and reimbursements for international assignments are costly. Should companies avoid international business activities? Explain your answer. If you answer *no*, what can companies do to minimize costs?

14-5. Of the many reimbursements and allowances that U.S. companies make for employees who take foreign assignments, which one is the most essential? Discuss your reasons.

CASE
Jenkins Goes Abroad

⭐ *An additional Supplemental Case can be found on MyManagementLab.*

Jenkins Consulting is a national firm that helps companies improve their performance and effectiveness by advising on all aspects of business management and operations. Companies hire consultants from Jenkins Consulting for a variety of projects such as assisting with companywide cost reduction initiatives or revenue growth initiatives, improving supply-chain management, and/or improving individual departments such as information technology. Jenkins employs consultants in 200 offices across the United States and will soon expand its operations internationally.

A company located in the United Kingdom has hired Jenkins for a major project that will be based at the company's headquarters in London. Jenkins will assist the company with an organization-wide effort to restructure and reposition the company to succeed in a more competitive market. To complete this project, Jenkins will assign five full-time consultants for a period of approximately 2 years. Because of the significant time commitment, Jenkins has decided to relocate the selected consultants to the United Kingdom for the duration of the project.

Dale Kugar, the human resource director at Jenkins, must prepare to transition the consultants to the new assignment. This is the company's first exposure to expatriate management, and Dale needs to ensure that the consultants who move to the United Kingdom for the project are compensated appropriately. His intention is to have the consultants maintain their current benefits, including health care insurance, retirement savings, and paid time off. However, he must make a recommendation on any changes to each consultant's salary.

Dale has a few concerns as he prepares his recommendation. First, the United Kingdom is currently experiencing a high level of inflation. The value of the American dollar compared to the British pound is fairly low. That is, the consultant's U.S. salary will not have the same purchasing power in the United Kingdom as it does at home. He is also concerned about the consultants' interest in taking on the international assignment. Some of the consultants he spoke to about the assignment are concerned about the impact the assignment will have on their career. Because this is Jenkins' first international experience, the consultants are concerned that being out of the country for 2 years may affect their future career opportunities because they will not have regular interactions with the firm partners who make decisions on promotions. These concerns weigh heavily on Dale's mind as he starts to draft his recommendation.

Questions:

14-6. How should Dale approach the determination of the consultant's salaries as expatriates?

14-7. Should Jenkins offer any incentive compensation or additional benefits to the expatriates? Why or why not?

MyManagementLab

Go to **mymanagementlab.com** for Auto-graded writing questions as well as the following Assisted-graded writing questions:

⭐ **14-8.** Describe the four challenges that companies face in the development and the implementation of international compensation programs. How can a company prevent problems that are driven by repatriation?

⭐ **14-9.** Explain the headquarters-based method to calculate expatriates' base pay. Which incentive might work better for this method?

Endnotes

1. Quotation excerpted from WorldatWork Web site, *Companies Are Leveraging International Assignments to Better Compete Globally*. Available: *www.worldatwork.org*, accessed July 7, 2007.
2. Munn, G. G., Garcia, F. L., & Woelfel, C. J. (1991). *Encyclopedia of Banking and Finance*. Chicago, IL: St. James Press.
3. Bureau of National Affairs. (2009). Expatriate pay. *Compensation and Benefits* (CD-ROM). Washington, DC: Author.
4. Horn, M. E. (1992). *International Employee Benefits: An Overview*. Brookfield, WI: International Foundation of Employee Benefit Plans.
5. *Internal Revenue Code*, Section 306(c), paragraph 3306(j).
6. ORC Worldwide. (February 18, 2009). *Savings Initiatives in Expatriate Programs Underway*. Available: *www.orcworldwide.com,* accessed June 14, 2009.
7. Ibid.

15 PAY AND BENEFITS OUTSIDE THE UNITED STATES

MyManagementLab®

⭐ **Improve Your Grade!**

When you see this icon, visit **www.mymanagementlab.com** for activities that are applied, personalized, and offer immediate feedback.

LEARNING OBJECTIVES

When you finish studying this chapter, you should be able to:

1. Explain the differences between pay and benefits in the United States and in countries around the world (included in this chapter).
2. State the total costs of hourly compensation in manufacturing settings around the world.
3. List the countries that impose minimum wage rates.
4. Summarize the paid time off benefits in at least two countries.
5. Briefly summarize the protection benefits such as retirement, health care, and social security in at least two countries.

The current state of globalization has resulted in a high level of interconnections between the economies of various parts of the world. U.S. employers will increasingly conduct business with entities in a variety of other countries as former underdeveloped parts of the world experience tremendous economic, trade, and standard of living growth. In addition, the move from traditional manufacturing to knowledge- and service-based employment also means that jobs as well as markets are more likely to be dispersed geographically. As the need for employers to interact globally increases, HR management professionals are going to have increased opportunities to develop compensation and benefits programs for U.S. employees in foreign assignments, as well as for indigenous employees in foreign offices of the parent company.

It is essential that compensation professionals know the basic legal employment context and the minimum statutory employment standards of the country where they propose to do business, just as we've discussed throughout this book for U.S. employment (e.g., recall the Fair Labor Standards Act of 1938). After that, compensation professionals may consider the norms for competitive pay and benefits needed to attract the desired talent.

In this chapter, we will provide a glimpse of the wide variation in compensation and benefits practices across several regions of the world.

We will start off each review with a brief treatment of governmental structure, norms, and historical events that helps shed light on pay and benefits. For each country, we will peruse statutory minimum wage rates. Next, we will consider such basic benefits issues as paid time off, protection programs (including retirement and health care), and stand-out benefits in particular regions. We will note where such protection programs as retirement and health care are required by the government or offered at the discretion of the employer.

It is important to note that many other governments do not regularly assess pay levels in their economies, which stands in stark contrast to the wealth of data provided regularly on U.S. markets by the U.S. Bureau of Labor Statistics (Chapter 7). The U.S. Bureau of Labor Statistics, however, regularly compares the hourly compensation costs in several countries. Table 15-1 shows the costs expressed in U.S. dollars. For example, in 2011, the hourly cost to pay a manufacturing worker employed in the United States, expressed in U.S. dollars, was $35.33. In Mexico, the hourly cost per employee was $6.48, and it was $2.01 in the Philippines. The hourly cost per employee was significantly higher elsewhere than in the United States. For example, the cost was $47.38 in Germany and $64.15 in Norway.

NORTH AMERICA

This section takes a brief glance at the employment relationship and employee benefits in Mexico and Canada. Both countries and the United States are part of a trade bloc known as NAFTA— the North American Free Trade Agreement. According to the Office of the United States Trade Representative, formed on January 1, 1994, NAFTA called for the elimination of duties and the phasing out of tariffs over a period of 14 years.[1] Trade restrictions were removed under NAFTA from such industries as motor vehicles and automotive parts, computers, textiles, and agriculture. In addition, the treaty also delineated the removal of investment restrictions between the three countries. As a result of supplemental agreements signed in 1993, worker and environmental protection provisions were added.

The labor side of NAFTA is the North American Agreement on Labor Cooperation (NAALC). This was created in order to promote cooperation between trade unions and social organizations in order to champion improved labor conditions.[2] Although there has definitely been a convergence of labor standards in North America as a result of NAALC, there has not been a convergence in employment, productivity, or salary trends.[3] Overall, NAFTA is reported as having been good for Mexico, which saw a fall in poverty rates and a rise in real income as a result of the trade agreement.[4] This section will present a brief overview of the employment relationship in Canada and Mexico and some basic employee benefits required by law in these countries.

Canada

According to the Central Intelligence Agency's *CIA World Factbook*, Canada is a constitutional monarchy that is also a parliamentary democracy and a federation consisting of 10 provinces and 3 territories.[5] With a per capita gross domestic product (GDP) of $41,500 and 18.85 million people in the labor force, the Canadian economy is very similar to that of the United States' market-based economy. Even though Canada has enjoyed a trade surplus and balanced budgets for many years, concern and debate have recently grown over the increasing cost of the publicly funded health care system.

As an important aside, the gross domestic product (GDP) describes the size of a country's economy. Size is expressed as the market value of all final goods and services produced within the country over a specified period. The GDP is typically calculated by the country's national statistical agency. GDP per capita generally indicates the standard of living within a country: The larger the per capita GDP, presumably the better the standard of living. Table 15-2 lists per capita GDP for the countries reviewed in this chapter. These figures are reported at each nation's GDP at purchasing power parity (PPP) exchange rates. That is, these figures indicate the sum value of all goods and services produced in the country valued at prices prevailing in the United States. This is the measure most economists prefer when looking at per capita welfare and when comparing living conditions or use of resources across countries.

TABLE 15-1 **Components of Hourly Compensation Costs in Manufacturing, U.S. Dollars, 2011**

	Hourly Compensation Costs		
	Direct Pay		
	Total	Social Insurance[1]	Directly Paid Benefits[2]	Pay for Time Worked[3]
Norway	64.15	10.98	53.18[4]	
Switzerland	60.40	9.25	11.24	39.92
Belgium	54.77	17.64	11.05	26.07
Denmark	51.67	4.97	7.54	39.15
Sweden	49.12	16.18	5.13	27.82
Germany	47.38	10.24	9.44	27.70
Australia	46.29	9.25	4.41	32.63
Finland	44.14	9.20	8.51	26.43
Austria	43.16	11.07	9.26	22.82
Netherlands	42.26	8.97	9.01	24.29
France	42.12	12.61	7.80	21.70
Ireland	39.83	6.39	6.00	27.43
Canada	36.56	7.49	3.59	25.48
Italy	36.17	10.47	5.27	20.43
Japan	35.71	6.46	9.02	20.23
United States	**35.53**	**8.65**	**3.17**	**23.70**
United Kingdom	30.77	4.73	4.05	21.98
Spain	28.44	7.22	5.57	15.65
New Zealand	23.38	0.99	2.69	19.70
Singapore	22.60	3.64	3.95	15.00
Greece	21.78	5.03	4.08	12.66
Israel	21.42	3.49	1.50	16.42
Korea, Republic of	18.91	3.70	15.21[4]	
Argentina	15.91	2.77	2.23	10.92
Czech Republic	13.13	3.59	1.77	7.77
Portugal	12.91	2.54	2.49	7.88
Slovakia	11.77	3.19	2.20	6.38
Brazil	11.65	3.72	1.66	6.27
Estonia	10.39	2.69	0.98	6.73
Taiwan	9.34	1.35	8.00[4]	
Hungary	9.17	2.16	1.81	5.20
Poland	8.83	1.25	2.23	5.35
Mexico	6.48	1.95	4.53[4]	
Philippines	2.01	0.17	0.35	1.49

(1) Social insurance expenditures are legally required, private, and contractual social benefit costs and labor-related taxes minus subsidies.

(2) Directly paid benefits are primarily pay for leave time, bonuses, and pay in kind.

(3) Pay for time worked is wages and salaries for time actually worked.

(4) Separate measures of directly paid benefits and pay for time worked are not available. Data relate to total direct pay.

Source: U.S. Department of Labor, Bureau of Labor Statistics. (2012, USDL 12-2460). International Comparisons of Hourly Compensation Costs in Manufacturing, 2011. Available: *http://www.bls.gov*, accessed August 31, 2013.

TABLE 15-2 **Per Capita Expenditures by Country, 2012 (estimates)**

Country	Per Capita GDP ($)	Labor Force Size (millions)
United States of America	49,800	154.90
Canada	41,500	18.85
Mexico	15,300	50.01
Brazil	12,000	107.10
Germany	39,100	44.01
People's Republic of China	9,100	795.40
India	3,900	498.40

Source: Central Intelligence Agency. (2013). *World Factbook.* Available: *http://www.cia.gov /library/publications/the-world-factbook/index.html,* accessed March 17, 2013.

The United States clearly shows the largest per capita GDP whereas India reports the lowest amount. These differences are evident in the extent of government-sponsored benefits offered in those countries.

Employment law researchers report that the basic rule of Canadian law holds that labor and employment law fall within the exclusive jurisdiction of the provinces.[6] Thus, both individual and collective employment relationships are controlled at the province level. Federal legislation cannot override provincial laws, even when the industry or employer primarily conducts business overseas (except in the cases where the industries are expressly assigned to federal jurisdiction). The origins of the common law governing individual employment contracts are in the English Statute of Labourers of 1562, which established working hours and wages. This statute was eventually repealed in the early nineteenth century, but it became part of the English common law and later became part of the common law governing all the provinces other than Quebec. Quebec has the Civil Code of Quebec, which came into effect in 1866. A modernized version of the Civil Code came into effect on January 1, 1994.

WAGE AND SALARY[7] Canada does possess a statutory minimum wage law. At the federal level, there is an obligation placed upon provincial governments to establish minimum rates of pay by or under an act of the legislature. The jurisdiction defined by province determines the minimum hourly rate. In 2012, Alberta currently had the lowest minimum wage rate (i.e., $9.75). The highest rate (i.e., $11.00) can be found in Nunavut.

PAID TIME OFF BENEFITS Canadian employment law holds that employees are entitled to between 8 and 9 annual paid holidays as well as 2 weeks' paid vacation time along with a sum of money as vacation pay (increasing to 3 weeks after 6 years of employment).[8] The amount of vacation pay is equal to 2 percent of an employee's pay for the preceding year per week of vacation. There are slight variations from province to province. Maternity and paternity leave provisions are coordinated under the Federal Employment Insurance Act. Employees are eligible for a total of 17 weeks' benefits during pregnancy and after childbirth. The Canadian government most recently introduced compassionate care leave, which provides 8 weeks of unpaid leave to care for a seriously ill family member. For the purposes of this leave, family members include spouse, common law partner, children, and parents.[9] No laws require the granting of time off for military service.

PROTECTION BENEFITS

Pensions and Retirement Benefits Canada has two state pension plans: one for Quebec residents only and one for the rest of Canada. Both plans are funded by matching contributions from employers and employees, and both are fully portable upon employment changes, much like 401(k) plans in the United States.[10] In addition to the public plans, many employers provide supplementary pension plans that are regulated by provincial or federal legislation that establishes minimum funding standards; specifies the types of investments that the plans may make; and deals with such matters as portability, benefit vesting, and locking-in contributions. Employers frequently have different plans for executive, managerial, and other employees.

Health and Disability Benefits Medical and basic hospital care in Canada is paid for by provincial medical insurance plans with compulsory coverage for all residents and funding revenue derived from both general federal taxation and from provincial taxes.[11] Even though public health plans normally do not provide employed persons with prescription drugs except while they are hospitalized, additional benefits are provided by private supplementary insurance through employers, including dental and vision care. Employers also provide long- and short-term disability benefits for sickness or injury as part of a benefits package.[12] Canada's per capita expenditure on health (the sum of Public Health Expenditure and Private Expenditure on Health) at the international dollar rates was $4,404 in 2010.[13]

Mexico

Mexico is a federal republic,[14] and Mexican labor law is based on the Constitution of the United States of Mexico, adopted in January 1917.[15] The *CIA World Factbook* reports that Mexico's labor force is nearly 19 million people and its per capita GDP is $15,300.[16] Its free-market economy is composed of a mix of new and old industry as well as agriculture, which are both increasingly becoming dominated by the private sector. The "Labor and Social Security" article of the constitution is still in effect.[17] Employment relationships in Mexico fall under the Federal Labor Law, which was last revised in January 1997 and clearly defines the terms *worker* and *employer* for the purpose of individual employment. Some of the employee benefits ensured under federal jurisdiction in Mexico will be discussed shortly.

WAGE AND SALARY The Mexican government requires that two minimum wage rates be applied. The first, general minimum wage, applies to all workers, and the amount depends on the region of the country. For instance, the minimum wage in Geographic Area C was 56.70 pesos per day in 2011. The rate was only slightly higher in Geographic Areas A and B at 59.80 and 58.13 pesos per day, respectively.

The second is the occupational minimum wages that are higher than the general minimum wages. Similar to the U.S. General Schedule (Chapter 3), occupations that require greater skill, knowledge, and experience are compensated at higher rates.

PAID TIME OFF BENEFITS Mexican employment laws stipulate certain paid time off benefits for all employees, as reported in publications on international employment laws.[18] Workers are entitled to paid time off during public holidays, and workers required to work during a mandatory holiday are entitled to double pay. Female employees are entitled to maternity leave (i.e., 6 weeks' leave prior to giving birth and 6 weeks' leave after birth on full salary). Maternity leave can also be extended with half pay for as long as necessary and does not affect seniority rights. Employees are entitled to 6 vacation days after being employed for 1 year and to 2 more days for each subsequent year, up to a maximum of 12 days. As of the 5th year, the worker is entitled to 14 days' vacation and for each additional group of 5 years 2 more vacation days are added. Employers must pay workers a vacation premium equivalent to 25 percent of the salary earned during scheduled vacation days; vacations must be taken on the date indicated by the employer, within the 6 months following the end of the work year.

PROTECTION BENEFITS
Social Security Social security programs in Mexico are administered by the Mexican Social Security Institute, which protects employees in the matters of occupational accidents and illnesses, maternity, sicknesses, incapacitation, old age, retirement, survivor pensions, day care for children of insured workers, and social services.[19] The system is financed by contributions from workers, employers, and the government, with contributions based on salary levels, and with workers

earning minimum salary exempt from making contributions, whereas employers bear the bulk of the contributions to the different insurance funds.[20]

The benefits for employees are laid out as follows.[21] Workers with at least 52 weeks' worth of payments into the system who withdraw are entitled to continue making voluntary payments. Should they return to salaried employment again, they may return to the system and maintain all benefits, which may be in cash or in kind. Cash benefits take the form of transfer payments in the early stages of illness or incapacitation, depending on the medical condition and its effects on work and pensions. In-kind benefits take the form of medical attention, including surgery and medicines, hospitalization services, and so forth.

Pensions and Retirement Benefits The U.S. Social Security Administration (SSA) Office of Policy reports that effective July 1, 1997, all workers must join the mandatory individual account system, slowly replacing the former social insurance system.[22] At retirement, employees covered by the social insurance system before 1997 can choose to receive benefits from either the social insurance system or from the mandatory individual account system.

Health Benefits Medical services are normally provided directly to patients (including old-age pensioners covered by the 1997 law) through the health facilities of the Mexican Social Security Institute.[23] Benefits include general and specialist care, surgery, maternity care, hospitalization or care in a convalescent home, medicines, laboratory services, dental care, and appliances; they are payable for 52 weeks but may in some cases be extended to 104 weeks.[24] In addition, the wife of an insured man also receives postnatal benefits in kind, and medical services are provided for dependent children up to age 16 (age 25 if a student, no limit if disabled).[25] Mexico's per capita expenditure on health (sum of Public Health Expenditure and Private Expenditure on Health) at the international dollar rate was $959 in 2010.[26]

Other Benefits[27] A national system of worker housing exists paid for by employer contributions in the form of payroll tax fixed at 5 percent and helps workers obtain sufficient credit for the acquisition of houses. Workers not employed after age 50 are entitled to receive the full balance of contributions made in their name to the housing fund.

SOUTH AMERICA

According to the International Monetary Fund's World Economic Outlook Database, Brazil, Argentina, Colombia, and Chile are the largest economies in South America.[28] Venezuela and Peru are experiencing economic development as well. On the other hand, Argentina, Chile, and Uruguay have the best human development index (HDI—a comparative measure of life expectancy, literacy, and standard of living measured by the United Nations),[29] and Venezuela has large oil reserves that have turned the nation into an important player in world trade. The biggest trade bloc in South America used to be Mercosur, or the Southern Common Market, which was composed of Argentina, Brazil, Paraguay, Uruguay, and Venezuela as the main members and Bolivia, Chile, Colombia, Ecuador, and Peru as associate states.[30] The second-biggest trade bloc was the Andean Community of Nations, made up of Bolivia, Colombia, Ecuador, Peru, Venezuela, and Chile.[31] These two trade blocs merged as of a declaration signed on December 8, 2004, at the Third South American Summit, and they formed one large trade bloc known as the South American Community of Nations, which plans to model itself on the European Union.[32] This section will take a brief look at one of the largest economies in South America, Brazil.

Brazil

The *CIA World Factbook* reports that Brazil is a federal republic with a workforce of 107.10 million and a per capita GDP of $12,000 and that Brazil's economy is by far the strongest in South America.[33] This country has a well-developed mining, manufacturing, agricultural, and services sector and is increasingly taking on a larger share of global trade and work.[34] The *Consolidation of Labor Laws (Consolidacao das Leis do Trabalho)* accords many employee benefits the status of fundamental constitutional rights, and in general the employment relationship in Brazil is highly regulated by statute. For example, Brazilian law states that any and all benefits habitually granted by the employer, whether expressly or tacitly, are considered part of the employee's salary for all legal purposes and cannot be abolished. The status of employment contracts is based on the country's legal principle of continuity. This principle applies to all employment contracts, written and oral; however, in practice, employers discharge employees arbitrarily because there is a substantial supply of readily available workers who are willing to accept lower pay.[35] There simply is not enough incentive provided for employers to engage in good faith labor relations. Job security is also often lacking for most employees.[36]

WAGE AND SALARY Brazil does impose a minimum wage. In accordance with the Federal Constitution, the minimum wage rate is nationally uniform and set by law. The minimum wage is fixed by a provisional measure, namely an act of the executive having the force of law, in accordance with Article 62 of the Federal Constitution and placed before Congress for conversion into law. In 2011, this monthly minimum wage was 545 R$ (Reais).

PROTECTION BENEFITS

Social Security The social security system that went into effect in 1991 details various benefits for workers in Brazil.[37] Comprehensive social security benefits are provided by law to all workers regarding retirement for illness, old age, or length of service; death benefit pensions; assistance during imprisonment of worker; savings fund; social services; professional rehabilitation assistance; work accident payments; maternity leave payments; family salary support; accident insurance; and sick leave benefits.

Pensions The U.S. SSA Office of Policy reports that social insurance in Brazil is provided to persons employed in industry, commerce, agriculture, domestic servants, some categories of casual workers, elected civil servants, and the self-employed.[38] There is also voluntary coverage for students, housewives, the unemployed, and other categories, as well as a special system for public-sector employees and military personnel. The monthly benefit is equal to 70 percent of average earnings plus 1 percent of average earnings for each year of contributions, up to a maximum of 100 percent. Employees contribute 8.5 percent of gross earnings, and voluntary contributors and members of cooperatives contribute 20 percent of declared earnings. These contributions also finance sickness and maternity benefits and family allowances.

Employers are required to contribute 20 percent of payroll (22.5 percent of payroll for employers in the financial sector), 15 percent of earnings for work cooperatives, 12 percent of payroll on behalf of domestic workers, and 2.7 percent of earnings for rural employers. There are no maximum monthly earnings for contribution purposes. Small-enterprise employers may contribute from 1.2 to 4.3 percent of monthly declared earnings, depending on annual earnings declared in the last year.

Health Benefits In Brazil, medical services are provided directly to patients in rural and urban areas through the Unified Health System, and they include such benefits as general, specialist, maternity, and dental care; hospitalization; medicines (some cost sharing is required); and necessary transportation.[39] Brazil's per capita expenditure on health (sum of Public Health Expenditure and Private Expenditure on Health) in 2010 at the international dollar rate was $1,028.[40]

EUROPE

The European Union (EU) is a unique international organization that aims at becoming an economic superpower, while still retaining such quintessential European practices as high levels of employment, social welfare protection, and strong trade unions.[41] Even though the EU has its own legal powers and performs executive, legislative, and judicial functions like any other governing body, it has limited authority in the area of labor and employment laws. Although the EU does not attempt to harmonize the employment laws of member states, under the laws of all member states employers must provide employees with a written document about the terms of the employment contract. The concept of "employment at will" does not exist in the EU as it does in the United States. The EU makes use of Directives and Community Legislations to ensure that some minimum standards are adopted by member states. All member states either have specific legislation or unfair dismissal or general civil code provisions that apply to termination of employment contracts. They all provide employers with a substantive basis for challenging employment dismissal and procedural mechanisms for adjudicating claims.[42]

The EU Web site reports that community labor law was designed with the aim of ensuring that the creation of the single market did not result in a lowering of labor standards or distortions in competition.[43] It has also been increasingly called upon, however, to play a key role in making it easier for the EU to adapt to evolving forms of work organization. On the basis of article 137 of the treaty, the Community shall support and complement the activities of the member states in the area of social policy. In particular, it defines minimum requirements at the EU level in the fields of working and employment conditions and with regard to the information and consultation of workers. Improving living and working conditions in member states depends on national legislation, but also to a large extent on agreements concluded by the social partners at all levels (i.e., country, sector, and company). This section will briefly present some of the basic employee benefits practices in the EU member state of Germany.

Germany

Germany is a federal republic with the fifth largest economy in the world as indicated by a per capita GDP of $39,100, according to the *CIA World Factbook*.[44] The German labor force has about 44.01 million workers. The integration of the former East German economy is a strain on the overall economy of unified Germany, and unemployment rates have been very high. Germany has recently been pushing such labor market reforms as increasing the retirement age and increasing female workforce participation. There have been increasing concerns about the aging workforce and high unemployment bankrupting the social security system, but for now Germany has managed to bring the deficit to within the EU debt limit. Germany's employment laws provide considerable voice to labor and job security to employees, and the German Civil Code provides numerous statutes that deal with individual employment as well as collective agreements.[45]

WAGE AND SALARY Minimum wage in Germany is established through the collective bargaining process. In Germany, there are two types of collective agreements. First, association agreements are made between trade unions and employers' associations. Second, company agreements are made between trade unions and individual employers. An extension of either type of agreement to other sectors or employers may be granted upon request of at least one party to the collective agreement.

As an example, the agreement for the metalworking industry in Baden-Württemberg has been selected because it concluded a new pay framework agreement (ERA-Eckentgelt) in 2003 and in February 2004 concluded a collective agreement fixing the projected percentage increases in the minimum wage for the next 26 months. The German government does not mandate a minimum wage, except for construction workers, electrical workers, janitors, roofers, painters, and letter carriers, set by collective bargaining agreements in other sectors of the economy and enforceable by law.

PAID TIME OFF BENEFITS[46] Employees cannot be required to work on official holidays, which range from 10 holidays per year in northern Germany to 13 in southern Germany. The statutory minimum vacation has been set at 24 working days (or 4 weeks because Saturdays are counted). Younger workers have a right to a vacation of 25–30 working days; disabled workers have an additional 5 days of vacation. There is minimum 6-month employment eligibility for vacation.

Under the terms of the Maternity Leave Law, time away from work as a result of maternity leave or other limits on work by pregnant women and mothers must be counted as time worked for the purpose of determining entitlement to vacation time. Employees may take 5 days annually or 10 days every 2 years (under individual state level statutes) as paid holidays for continuing education purposes at only state-approved institutions. The employee retains a job if he is drafted for military or called for military exercises with a suspended employment relationship. The employee should receive regular pay during illness for a period of 6 weeks.

Expectant mothers can take 6 weeks' leave before the due date and 8 weeks after giving birth. During this time the employee must be paid at least average salary or wages calculated on the basis of the last 13 weeks before commencement of leave. An employee can request up to 3 years of child-rearing leave. Employers must guarantee return to the same job following completion of this leave. Any payments for child-rearing leave are made solely by the national health authority.

PROTECTION BENEFITS

Pensions[47] Germany has a statutory pension system analogous to the Social Security system in the United States. In addition, employers offer the company pension plan and a tax-favored investment plan. Employees have three different sources for their pension benefits: statutory pension insurance, company pension plans, and private life insurance.

Health Insurance German laws stipulate guidelines for minimal health welfare of worker.[48] For blue-collar workers (and some white-collar workers), mandatory state health insurance premiums are borne 50 percent by the insured and 50 percent by the employer. The employer is required to collect the employees' contributions and to pay the entire amount to the appropriate collector. Employees whose income exceeds a certain amount can opt out of the state plan and purchase private health insurance. In such cases, employees may request that the employer's health insurance contribution be included in their salary. Germany's per capita expenditure on health (sum of Public Health Expenditure and Private Expenditure on Health) in 2010 at the international dollar rate was $4,332.[49]

ASIA

In 2013, China was the largest economy in Asia, followed by India and Japan.[50] Asia has several trade blocs, including Asia-Pacific Economic Cooperation, Asia-Europe Economic Meeting, Association of Southeast Asian Nations, and South Asian Association for Regional Cooperation. Given the wide variation and diversity in the world's largest and most populous continent, however, there is no unifying economic body like the EU or NAFTA that represents all the countries of Asia. This section will examine a representative sample of the relatively more developed and developing economies in Asia: India and China. A bloc of countries that is not examined here, but that nonetheless deserves mention because considerable jobs are being outsourced there, are those in southeast Asia: Thailand, Vietnam, Singapore, Malaysia, Philippines, Cambodia, and Laos. These economies are seeing a current influx of foreign investment, although they are not close to the countries discussed here in terms of annual growth rates.

India

According to the *CIA World Factbook*, India is a democratic federal republic with a diverse economy ranging from traditional farming to high-technology industries.[51] India's labor force is quite large with 498.40 million individuals with a per capita GDP of only $3,900. The Indian economy, though steadily growing at a close to 2.2 percent annual rate, is plagued with income disparity and developmental challenges similar to China. More than half of India's output is created with less than one-quarter of its labor force, and services are the major source of economic growth. Strong economic growth combined with easy consumer credit and a real estate boom is fueling inflation concerns, and the huge and growing population poses fundamental social, economic, and environmental problems. Basic constitutional legislation governs the employment relationship for all employees, ensuring equality of opportunity to public employment and prohibition of child labor.

The Directive Principle of State Policy has statutes that affect various aspects of the employment relationship (e.g., working conditions and participation in management).[52] Some of the key employee benefits provided by employers in India are provident fund, gratuity (bonus), pension (i.e., either defined benefit or defined contribution), housing, car, loans, life insurance protection for dependents, health and disability benefits, medical benefits for employees and their families, and leave encashment.[53] The Employees' Provident Fund Organization is one of the world's largest Social Security programs with more than 35 million members. Gratuities apply to most employees in India, and these are funded through employer contributions totaling 4.5 percent of payroll.

There are wide variations between the public and private sectors, with the Ministry of Labour and labor laws governing employment relationships in the public sector and with more employer discretion allowed in the private sector. In addition, all blue-collar employees and factory workers are governed under existing labor laws.

WAGE AND SALARY. Minimum wage is fixed by an authority dual system. Minimum wage rates are determined by the government for certain sectors, and a collective agreement determines others. Minimum wage rates for occupations that are largely nonunionized or have little bargaining power may be set in accordance with the Minimum Wages Act, 1948. This act applies throughout India, including the provinces of Jammu and Kashmir. Schedules 1 and 2 of the act set forth the occupations for which applicable central and regional governments may set minimum wage rates. The central government sets minimum wages for 45 different occupations, including agricultural work, construction, road maintenance work, work in mines, railway work, and stone breaking or crushing work. In addition, states have set minimum wages for 1,232 different occupations in their respective regions. Minimum wage rates set apply only to those scheduled occupations that have more than 1,000 employees working in the applicable state. For example, in Delhi, the minimum wage rate ranged between 279 and 339 rupees per day in 2013.[54] The wage rate varies by the level of job skill and industry.

PAID TIME OFF BENEFITS[55] Leave is usually calculated for each year based on the number of days worked in the previous year. If a worker does not take all of the accumulated leave, she or he is allowed to roll over to the succeeding calendar year up to a maximum of 30 days. There is no statutory provision of paternity leave, but maternity leave is allowed in the form of paid time off and possible medical bonus. All employees get paid time off for various public and national holidays.

PROTECTION BENEFITS
Pensions[56] First and current laws regarding pensions were passed in 1952 (i.e., employees' provident funds), with amendments in 1972 (i.e., payment of gratuity), 1976 (i.e., employees' deposit-linked insurance), 1995 (i.e., employees' pension scheme), and 1995 (i.e., national social assistance program). Pension benefits include provident fund with survivor (i.e., deposit-linked) insurance and a pension fund, a gratuity scheme for industrial workers, and a social assistance system. In 2004, a voluntary old-age, disability, and survivors' benefits scheme was enacted. This program is part of the Unorganized Sector Social Security Scheme for employees and self-employed persons ages 36–50 with monthly earnings of 6,500 rupees or less but without mandatory coverage and was introduced as a pilot program in 50 districts. Contributions are income related and flat rate. Coverage includes employees, including casual, part-time, and daily wage workers and those employed through contractors, with monthly earnings of 6,500 rupees or less working in establishments with a minimum of 20 employees in one of the

182 categories of covered industry (the establishment remains covered even if the number of employees falls below 20).

Employees covered by equivalent occupational private plans may contract out. Voluntary coverage exists for employees of covered establishments with monthly earnings of more than 6,500 rupees, with the agreement of the employer and for establishments with less than 20 employees if the employer and a majority of the employees agree to contribute. Provident fund contributions include 12 percent of basic wages (10 percent of basic wages in five specified categories of industry) in covered establishments with less than 20 employees and some other specific cases. The maximum monthly earnings for contribution purposes are 6,500 rupees (1 USD = 50.80 rupees).

Health Benefits SSA reports that state governments arrange for the provision of medical care on behalf of the Employees' State Insurance Corporation.[57] Services are provided in different states through social insurance dispensaries and hospitals, state government services, or private doctors under contract. Benefits include outpatient treatment, specialist consultations, hospitalization, surgery and obstetric care, imaging and laboratory services, transportation, and the free supply of medications, dressings, artificial limbs, aids, and appliances. The duration of benefits is from 3 months to 1 year, according to the insured's contribution record. India's per capita expenditure on health (sum of Public Health Expenditure and Private Expenditure on Health) at the international dollar rate was $132 in 2010.[58]

People's Republic of China

The People's Republic of China (PRC), as reported by the *CIA World Factbook*, is a communist state characterized by a fast-growing economy that has shifted over the past couple of decades from a centrally planned system to a more market-oriented one.[59] With a labor force of 795.40 million people and a per capita GDP of $9,100, PRC has been experiencing continuously high annual GDP growth at around 10 percent. Even though the purchasing power parity of PRC has become one of the top in the world, the lower per capita GDP is an indication of income disparity within various strata of society. One of the key challenges for the government has been to sustain adequate job growth for tens of millions of workers laid off from state-owned enterprises, migrants, and new entrants to the workforce.

The PRC Labor Law was established in 1995, resulting in a break from the traditional "iron rice bowl" system of employment, with a shift from state-owned enterprises to private ones, a move that has given rise to new employment relationship issues.[60] Under the older welfare system, the workforce was considered the property of the state, and such benefits as housing, medical, and retirement schemes were payable directly by the state-owned enterprises to the employees. Since the introduction of the PRC Labor Law, the employment relationship is now defined by individual contracts.[61]

WAGE AND SALARY According to China's Labor Act, 1994, the state possesses the responsibility to implement a system of guaranteed minimum wages. There is no national minimum wage rate in China; instead, minimum wage rates are set by region. Separate standards are stipulated by provincial, regional, and municipal peoples' governments for their respective region and reported to the State Council for consent. The provisions concerning minimum wages apply to enterprises, private nonenterprise entities, individual industrial and commercial households with employees (the employing entities), and the laborers who have formed a labor relationship with them. The minimum wage rate varies by region. In 2011, the monthly minimum wage was 1,300 yuan in Gaunghzho (the highest in China) and 1,120 yuan in Shanghai, and it was lowest in Anhui Province and Jiangxi Province at 500 yuan.

PAID TIME OFF BENEFITS[62] The length of an employer-approved medical treatment period generally depends on employee age and period of service and can range from 3 to 24 months. During this period the salary paid to the employee may not be less than 80 percent of the local minimum wage. Employees who have worked for 1 to 10 years are entitled to paid annual leave of 5 days. Employees who have worked 10 to 20 years are entitled to paid annual leave of 10 days, and those with more than 20 years experience are entitled to 15 days. Employees who have worked for more than 1 year are entitled to "home leave" if they do not live in the same place as their spouse or parents. Employees earn normal wages during this period, and employers are obligated to pay all travel expenses for employees visiting their spouse and for unmarried employees visiting their parents. Women are entitled to no less than 90 days of maternity leave starting 15 days prior to birth.

PROTECTION BENEFITS

Pensions The Office of Policy of the SSA reports that there has been a new law to decouple the employment relationship from the social insurance system, setting up a unified basic pension system.[63] The system now has social insurance and mandatory individual accounts, and provincial and city or county social insurance agencies and employers do adapt central government guidelines to local conditions. Coverage includes employees in urban enterprises and urban institutions managed as enterprises and the urban self-employed. In some provinces, coverage for the urban self-employed is voluntary. (Urban enterprises comprise all state-owned enterprises, regardless of their location.) Old-age provision in rural areas is based mainly on family support and through community and state financial support. Pilot schemes in the form of individual accounts, supported at the town and village level and subject to preferential support by the state, operate in some rural areas. Employees of government and communist party organizations, and of cultural, educational, and scientific institutions (except for institutions financed off-budget), are covered under a government-funded, employer-administered system. Enterprise-based pension systems cover some employees (including the self-employed) in cities.

An employee contribution to mandatory individual accounts is 8 percent of gross insured earnings. (The contribution rate is higher in some provinces.) The minimum earnings for employee contribution and benefit purposes are equal to 60 percent of the local average wage for the previous year. The maximum earnings for employee contribution and benefit purposes vary, but they may be as much as 300 percent of the local average wage for the previous year. Employer contribution to mandatory individual accounts is up to 20 percent of insured payroll based on local regulations The contribution is taken from the total contribution made to basic pension insurance. Central and local government subsidies are provided to city and council retirement pension pools as needed.

Health Insurance[64] There is a unified medical insurance system with all employers and workers participating in this system. Employers contribute 6 percent of payroll to the system, whereas employees contribute 2 percent of their salary. Health insurance is based on Basic Medical Insurance Fund consisting of a Pooled Fund and Personal Accounts. Employees' contributions go directly to their personal accounts and 30 percent of employer contributions are paid into this account. Covered workers receive medical benefits at a chosen accredited hospital or clinic on a fee-for-service basis. The individual account is used to finance medical benefits only, up to a maximum equal to 10 percent of the local average annual wage. The social insurance fund reimburses the cost of the medical benefit from 10 up to 400 percent of the local average annual wage, according to the schedule. Medical treatment in high-grade hospitals results in lower percentage reimbursements, and vice versa. Reimbursement for payments beyond 400 percent of the local average annual wage must be covered by private insurance or public supplementary schemes. Contract workers receive the same benefits as permanent workers. Per capita expenditure on health (per capita amount of the sum of Public Health Expenditure and Private Expenditure on Health) at the international dollar rate was $379 in 2010.[65]

COMPENSATION IN ACTION

With companies operating seamlessly across borders, employees will come to expect you (their line managers and HR managers) to respond to their compensation and benefits needs accordingly. You will need to carefully educate managers who have supervisory responsibility for employees in other parts of the world. Because these two parties operate under different laws and norms, the expectations of the employment exchange can be radically different. While it isn't the expectation that managers know the details of employment law in every country around the world, it will be your responsibility to equip them with the resources necessary to provide educated answers to questions the employees may raise, and to do so with sensitivity to the perspective and expectations of those employees who are many time zones away.

Action checklist for line managers and HR—seamless and sensitive strategies for a global workforce

HR takes the lead
- Be familiar with the laws and norms of all countries wherein there are client group operations; read reports on these countries, deal with employment experts specializing in these areas, and talk with other HR professionals who are native to the location. Educate line managers about the pertinent high-level particulars of these laws.

- As the company seeks to expand into emerging markets wherein minimal business has been conducted in the past, proactively seek out information on employment laws, events of historical significance, societal values, and general employee expectations.
- Identify areas of difference that could potentially cause conflict between line mangers in the United States and their employees who are natives of the locales in which they work (e.g., paid leave in France).

Line managers take the lead
- Be a visible presence in areas of the world where there are direct reports (set a predictable schedule that allows you to travel to these locations consistently). This presence will ensure better awareness of—and exposure to—compensation and benefits laws that may be radically different from those in the United States.
- Work with HR to provide a packet of information that can be shared with other managers. This packet would include specifics that should be taken into serious consideration as other line managers work with employees in certain countries. HR could elaborate on this packet by turning it into various training sessions for managing employees across the globe.

END OF CHAPTER

MyManagementLab

Go to **mymanagementlab.com** to complete the problems marked with this icon ⭐.

Summary

We reviewed minimum wage and benefits offerings mandated by the governments of several countries across the world. There is extensive variation in minimum standards.

A striking difference between the United States and other countries is the less generous family leave benefits in the United States and the relatively fewer paid days off. The governments in other countries mandate paid time off, reflecting the importance of family and religion. Most countries offer social security pensions, and, in many cases, these benefits are not lucrative. We also noticed that health care costs are a concern in all countries. Various health care delivery systems—single-payer and multiple-payer—struggle with rising health care costs and adequate coverage.

✪ Discussion Questions

15-1. Discuss the main differences between the minimum pay regulations in the United States (Chapter 2) and one other country's practices discussed in this chapter. How do these differences affect companies' ability to compete with other companies worldwide?

15-2. Discuss the main differences between retirement systems in the United States (taking into account legally required and discretionary programs) and one other country discussed in this chapter. Does it appear that the costs of retirement programs are creating burdens for competitive advantage?

CASE
North American Expansion for Threads Apparel

✪ *An additional Supplemental Case can be found on MyManagementLab.*

As Heather Johnson, CEO of Threads Apparel, prepares for the next board of directors meeting, the company's expansion plans weigh heavily on her mind. Threads Apparel manufactures women's ready-to-wear clothing for several large chain department stores. The company has experienced tremendous growth over the past 15 years and is now positioned to grow even more as it has just secured a contract with a major department store that has locations throughout North America.

Threads's reputation for producing high-quality clothing is based, in part, on its human resource management practices. It has a talented staff that is committed to consistently meeting its quality standards. In addition to effective management practices, Threads provides competitive compensation and benefits to its nearly 1,500 employees, and, as a result, the company experiences a relatively low turnover rate.

In order to meet the increased production requirements of the new contract, Threads will need to open a new manufacturing facility. The company currently operates ten manufacturing facilities in seven different states. As it considers a location for the new facility, Heather plans to recommend moving beyond the borders of the United States to ease the distribution of its products throughout North America. In addition to its new contract, NAFTA has allowed it to expand the distribution of its products into Mexico and Canada through several smaller stores. Therefore, opening its new facility in Mexico or Canada makes sense due to its expanding markets in these countries. It has located property options in both Mexico and Canada and must now begin discussions on which country it should select for its first international facility.

The board of directors will be making a decision on where to locate the new plant based on Heather's recommendation. The board is in agreement with Heather on opening its next plant outside of the United States. At this point, it is looking for a recommendation from Heather on whether it should expand to Mexico or Canada, and it is also looking for data to support her recommendation. In addition to many location considerations such as the availability of transportation and local tax laws, Heather must also understand the labor markets within Canada and Mexico in order to make her decision. Heather has set up a meeting with the director of human resources at Threads to gather information on labor-related considerations for the new facility.

Questions:
15-3. What are some labor-related factors that Threads should consider when comparing Mexico and Canada?

15-4. What are some labor-related factors that would favor Canada as the location of the new facility? Or Mexico, for that matter?

MyManagementLab

Go to **mymanagementlab.com** for Auto-graded writing questions as well as the following Assisted-graded writing questions:

⭐ **15-5.** Why is it important for HR and compensation professionals to learn about compensation practices in other parts of the world? Discuss.

⭐ **15-6.** Briefly compare minimum wage rates and paid time off policies in Canada and Mexico.

Endnotes

1. Office of the U.S. Trade Representative (2013). *North American Free Trade Agreement (NAFTA)*. www.ustr.gov /Trade_Agreements/Regional/NAFTA/Section_Index.html, accessed June 6, 2013.
2. *Worldtradelaw.net* (2013). NAFTA and Related Legal Instruments. *www.worldtradelaw.net/nafta/*, accessed March 17, 2013.
3. Floudas, D. A., & Rojas, L. F. (2000). *Some Thoughts on NAFTA and Trade Integration in the American Continent, International Problems*, Vol. 4. Available: *http://www.diplomacy.bg.ac.rs/mpro_sa00_4.htm*, accessed March 17, 2013.
4. Ibid.
5. Central Intelligence Agency (2013). *The World Factbook. https://www.cia.gov/library/publications/the-world-factbook/index.html*, accessed March 17, 2013.
6. Heenan, R. L., & Brady, T. E. F. (2003). In Keller, W. L. & Darby. T. J. (Eds.), *International Labor and Employment Laws*, 2nd ed., Vol. I, pp. 21-2–21-6.
7. Information in this chapter about minimum wage policy was found on the International Labour Organization Web site. (2013). ILO Database on Conditions of Work and Employment Laws. ILO, Geneva. *Wages and Income.* Available: *http://www.ilo.org/dyn/travail*, accessed March 17, 2013.
8. Heenan and Brady, *International Labor and Employment Laws*, pp. 21-54–21-56.
9. Ibid., p. 21-9.
10. Ibid., pp. 21-66–21-67.
11. Ibid., p. 21-67.
12. Ibid., p. 21-68.
13. World Health Organization (2013). *Canada.* Available: *www.who.int/countries/can/en/*, accessed March 17, 2013.
14. Central Intelligence Agency (2013). *The World Factbook. https://www.cia.gov/library/publications/the-world-factbook/index.html*, accessed March 17, 2013.
15. de Buen Lozano, N., & de Buen Unna, C. (2003). In Keller, W. L. & Darby, T. J. (Eds.), *International Labor and Employment Laws*, 2nd ed., Vol. I, p. 22-1.
16. U.S. Department of Labor, Bureau of Labor Statistics. (2010, USDL 10-1173). Available: *http://www.bls.gov*, accessed February 21, 2011.
17. de Buen Lozano & de Buen Unna, *International Labor*, p. 22-1.
18. Ibid., p. 22-60.
19. Ibid., p. 22-67.
20. Ibid., p. 22-68.
21. Ibid.
22. U.S. Social Security Administration (2010). *Mexico.* Available: *http://www.socialsecurity.gov/policy/docs /progdesc/ssptw/2008-2009/americas/mexico.html*, accessed June 6, 2013.
23. de Buen Lozano and de Buen Unna, *International Labor*, p. 22-1.
24. Ibid.
25. Ibid.
26. World Health Organization (2013). *Mexico.* Available: *www.who.int/countries/mex/en/*, accessed June 6, 2013.
27. de Buen Lozano & de Buen Unna, *International Labor*, pp. 22-69–22-70.
28. International Monetary Fund (2013) *World Economic Outlook Database.* Available: *http://www.imf.org/external /pubs/ft/weo/2010/02/weodata/index.aspx*, accessed March 17, 2013.
29. Human Development Reports (2010). *The Real Wealth of Nations: Pathways to Human Development.* Available: *http://hdr.undp.org/en/reports/global/hdr2010/chapters/en/*, accessed June 6, 2013.
30. Bilaterals.org (2013). *North & South America.* Available: *http://www.bilaterals.org/spip.php?rubrique7*, accessed June 6, 2013.
31. Communidad Andina (2013). *www.comunidadandina.org /endex.htm*, accessed February 21, 2011.
32. BBC News (2004). *S American Launches Trading Bloc.* Available: *news.bbc.co.uk/2/hi/business/4079505.stm*, accessed August 31, 2013.
33. Pires, P. R. F., & Gomes, L. C. M. (2003). In Keller, W. L., & Darby, T. J. (Eds.), *International Labor and Employment Laws*, 2nd ed., Vol. I, pp. 30-2–30-19.

34. Central Intelligence Agency (2013). *The World Factbook.* *https://www.cia.gov/library/publications/the-world-factbook/index.html*, accessed March 17, 2013.

35. Ibid., p. 30-3.

36. Ibid., p. 30-3.

37. Ibid., p. 30-57.

38. U.S. Social Security Administration (2013). *International Update, Brazil:* Available: *http://www.socialsecurity.gov/policy/docs/progdesc/intl_update/2012-06/index.html#brazil*, accessed March 17, 2013.

39. Ibid.

40. World Health Organization (2013). *Brazil.* Available: *www.who.int/countries/bra/en/*, accessed June 6, 2013.

41. Kenner, J. (2003). In Keller, W. L., & Darby, T. J. (Eds.), *International Labor and Employment Laws*, 2nd ed., Vol. I, pp. 1-1–1-2.

42. Ibid., p. 1-68.

43. Europa (2013). *The Renewed Social Agenda.* Available: *http://europa.eu/legislation_summaries/employment_and_social_policy/social_agenda/em0010_en.htm*, accessed March 13, 2013.

44. Central Intelligence Agency (2013). *The World Factbook.* *https://www.cia.gov/library/publications/the-world-factbook/index.html*, accessed March 17, 2013.

45. Lutringer, R., & Dichter, M. S. (2003). In Keller, W. L., & Darby, T. J. (Eds.), *International Labor and Employment Laws*, 2nd ed., Vol. I, pp. 4-4–4-5.

46. Ibid., pp. 4-86–4-91.

47. Ibid., p. 4-99.

48. Ibid., p. 4-103.

49. World Health Organization (2013). *Germany.* Available: *www.who.int/countries/deu/en/*, accessed February 21, 2011.

50. Central Intelligence Agency (2013). *The World Factbook.* *https://www.cia.gov/library/publications/the-world-factbook/index.html*, accessed March 17, 2013.

51. Central Intelligence Agency (2013). *The World Factbook.* *https://www.cia.gov/library/publications/the-world-factbook/index.html*, accessed March 17, 2013.

52. Singhania, R. (2003). In Keller, W. L., & Darby, T. J. (Eds.), *International Labor and Employment Laws*, 2nd ed., Vol. II, pp. 24-10–24-13.

53. The Associated Chambers of Commerce and Industry of India (2013). *Recent Events.* Available: *http://www.assocham.org/events/recent/event*, accessed March 17, 2013.

54. Paycheck.in (2013). *Minimum Wages in India.* Available: *www.paycheck.in/main/officialminimumwages/delhi*, accessed March 17, 2013.

55. Singhania, R., *International Labor and Employment Laws*, pp. 24-56–24-57.

56. U.S. Social Security Administration (2010). *India.* Available: *www.socialsecurity.gov/policy/docs/progdesc/ssptw/2008-2009/asia/india.html*, accessed June 6, 2013.

57. Ibid.

58. World Health Organization (2013). *India.* Available: *www.who.int/countries/ind/en/*, accessed March 17, 2013.

59. Central Intelligence Agency (2013). *The World Factbook.* *https://www.cia.gov/library/publications/the-world-factbook/index.html*, accessed March 17, 2013.

60. Lauffs, A. W., et al. (2003). In Keller, W. L., & Darby, T. J. (Eds.), *International Labor and Employment Laws*, 2nd ed., Vol. I, p. 31-5.

61. Ibid.

62. Lauffs, et al., *International Labor and Employment Laws*, pp. 31-38–31-39.

63. U.S. Social Security Administration (2013). *International Update, China.* Available: *http://www.socialsecurity.gov/policy/docs/progdesc/intl_update/2010-11/index.html#china*, accessed March 17, 2013.

64. Ibid.

65. World Health Organization (2013). *China.* Available: *www.who.int/countries/chn/en/*, accessed March 17, 2013.

EPILOGUE

Chapter **16** CHALLENGES FACING COMPENSATION PROFESSIONALS

CHALLENGES FACING COMPENSATION PROFESSIONALS

MyManagementLab®

⭐ **Improve Your Grade!**

When you see this icon, visit **www.mymanagementlab.com** for activities that are applied, personalized, and offer immediate feedback.

LEARNING OBJECTIVES

When you finish studying this chapter, you should be able to:

1. Explain the impact of economic recession and underemployment on compensation practice.
2. Point to the reasons for rising wages in China.
3. Describe the challenges associated with executive compensation.
4. Summarize the challenges associated with health care reform.
5. Describe the influence of changing workforce demographics on employee benefits practice.
6. Summarize the issue of marriage between same-sex individuals and the U.S. Supreme Court ruling on the Defense of Marriage Act.

Thus far in *Strategic Compensation*, we have studied the fundamentals of employee compensation and benefits programs. This approach to studying compensation arms compensation professionals with the knowledge to more effectively make compensation decisions that fit with companies' competitive advantages. There is much more to consider besides the fundamentals. In this chapter, we will examine seven key issues among many that will shape the work of compensation and benefits professionals in the future:

- Fallout from the "Great Recession"
- Underemployment: Implications for compensation
- Executive compensation
- Rising wages in China
- Challenges in health care reform
- Workforce demographic shifts
- Marriage between same-sex individuals and the U.S. Supreme Court ruling on the Defense of Marriage Act

FALLOUT FROM THE "GREAT RECESSION"

The U.S. economy experienced an economic recession from December 2007 through June 2009. The term "Great Recession" is widely used to describe the significance of this recession. It was the longest recession since World War II, lasting 19 months. Although the recession ended a few years ago, its effects still remain evident. In this section, we will review the definition of an economic recession and its relevance to employee compensation through two important issues: underemployment and the compensation–productivity gap.

What Is an Economic Recession?

The term **economic recession** refers to a general slowdown in economic activity. As we will see shortly, evidence of economic recessions includes reduced gross domestic product (GDP) and increased unemployment rates. Multiple complex factors lead to recessions. Reduced consumer spending is among the primary causes of economic recessions. Consumers' demand for products and services such as automobiles declines. For example, automobile manufacturers, among them General Motors and Chrysler, respond to lower consumer demand for their products by cutting production levels in order to avoid excess inventory. Oftentimes, companies respond to lower demand through significant layoffs of employees. Among the economic reasons for extended mass layoffs, events related to seasonal factors accounted for 44 percent of events and 39 percent of related separations during the fourth quarter of the year 2012.[1] Over the year, the largest decrease in separations occurred in layoffs due to business demand reasons such as in this example. Table 16-1 shows layoff activity between 2005 and 2012. The number of layoff events along with separations and initial claimants rose dramatically during the recession and began decreasing following the recession, although the numbers following the recession remain substantially higher than prior to the recession. The preliminary 2013 data show a continuation of this trend.[2]

Reduced production adversely affects other companies' operations. Automobile manufacturing companies do not produce every component of vehicles. In fact, these companies rely on specialty companies to produce vehicle components such as windshields and bumpers. Reduced consumer demand for automobiles leads to reduced automobile manufacturers' need for components from suppliers. Hundreds of companies alone supply components to automobile makers. Layoffs occur in these companies as well as in the automobile manufacturing companies.

TABLE 16-1 **Selected Measures of Layoff Activity, 2005–2012**

Period	Layoff Events	Separations	Initial Claimants
2005	4,881	884,661	834,533
2006	4,885	935,969	951,155
2007	5,363	965,935	978,712
2008	8,259	1,516,978	1,670,042
2009	11,824	2,108,202	2,442,000
2010	7,158	1,213,638	1,288,750
2011	6,596	1,112,710	1,289,273
2012	6,051	1,152,258	1,177,143

Note: Layoff events refer to the number of company decisions to lay off employees. Separations refer to the number of employees who lost their jobs as a result of the number of layoff events. Initial claimants refer to the number of unemployed persons from the layoff events who applied for unemployment insurance benefits.

Source: U.S. Bureau of Labor Statistics. (2013). *Extended Mass Layoffs—Fourth Quarter 2012 (USDL 13-0236)*. Available: *www.bls.gov*, accessed April 21, 2013.

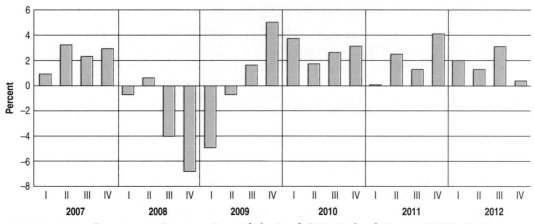

FIGURE 16-1 Quarter-to-Quarter Growth in Real GDP, United States, 2007–2012

Source: U.S. Department of Commerce, Bureau of Economic Analysis. Available: *http://www.bea.gov*, accessed April 22, 2013.

Companies in other industries similarly experience adverse effects. Reduced demand for products and services across industries contributes to economic recessions. The Federal Reserve Bank revealed that approximately 86 percent of industries have cut back production since the beginning of the Great Recession; this reduction is the most widespread since 1969 when the Federal Reserve Bank began tracking this information.

The impact of widespread cutbacks on various industries' output becomes evident in a declining GDP. As discussed in Chapter 15, GDP describes the size of a country's economy. GDP size is expressed as the market value of all final goods and services produced within the country over a specified period. Figure 16-1 shows the change in GDP growth rates for each quarterly period between 2007 and 2012. Clearly, GDP fell virtually each quarter during the Great Recession. Although GDP began rising following the end of the recession, it will take quite some time before its size surpasses prerecession levels.

UNDEREMPLOYMENT: IMPLICATIONS FOR COMPENSATION

Underemployment refers to employees who wish to work full-time, but are forced to work part-time for economic reasons, such as poor business conditions or inability to find a job. During October–November 2007, the 2-month period preceding the onset of this recession, the number of underemployed workers in the United States was estimated to be slightly more than 4.2 million.[3] Following the onset of the recession, the number of underemployed individuals rose dramatically. Table 16-2 displays the number of underemployed individuals just prior to the beginning of the recession through the end of 2012. Since then, the number of underemployed continued to rise; however, the number is slowly declining. Nevertheless, the number remains high. Compared to prerecession levels, the rise in the number of employed through the end of 2012 equals 93 percent.

Underemployment poses implications for employees' earnings. According to the U.S. Bureau of Labor Statistics, the mean hourly earnings of the underemployed were low compared to those who were not underemployed.[4] The mean hourly wages for all underemployed workers was $12.80. Mean hourly wages were as follows based on educational attainment, clearly showing an increase for higher educational attainment:

- High school dropouts: $11.23
- High school graduates: $11.78

TABLE 16-2 Underemployment in the United States, 2007–2012

Period	Number Underemployed
October–November 2007	4,201,000
October–December 2008	7,217,333
October–December 2009	8,907,333
October–December 2010	8,902,666
October–December 2011	8,443,333
October–December 2012	8,114,000
Absolute change, 2007–2012	3,913,000
Percent change, 2007–2012	93

Sources: Sum, A., & Khatiwada, I. (2010). The Nation's Underemployed in the "Great Recession" of 2007–09. *Monthly Labor Review, 133(11)*, pp. 3–15. Available: *http://www.bls.gov*, accessed April 1, 2011; U.S. Bureau of Labor Statistics. *2013 Data Retrieval: Labor Force Statistics, Employed Persons by Class of Worker and Part-time Status.* Available: *http://www.bls.gov*, accessed April 21, 2013.

- Bachelor's degree holders: $14.35
- Master's or higher degree: $21.46

In addition, the mean hourly earnings of the underemployed were considerably below those of full-time workers, both overall and in each educational group, as shown in Table 16-3. The mean hourly earnings for full-time wage and salary workers were $20.96, exceeding those of the underemployed by $8.16, or 64 percent. In each of the five education groups whose members were not enrolled in school, mean hourly earnings of the underemployed were anywhere from 88 cents to $11.82 below those of their full-time employed peers. Many of the underemployed, particularly those with higher educational attainment, were considered to be malemployed. **Malemployment** occurs when job holders possess greater education, skills, or knowledge than is required to perform their jobs.[5] In sum, underemployment leads to earning losses because the underemployed work fewer hours and take jobs within lower-paying occupations. For example, a person holding a bachelor's degree in psychology whose job is a part-time grocery store clerk is considered to be underemployed and malemployed.

TABLE 16-3 Mean Hourly Wages of Underemployed Persons and Full-Time Wage and Salary Workers, 16 Years and Older, by Educational Attainment, October–December 2009

Education group	Underemployed	Full-time Workers	Difference
All workers	$12.80	$20.96	$8.16
High school students	7.07	8.20	1.13
College students	13.04	12.67	0.37
High school dropouts	11.23	12.11	−0.88
High school graduates[a]	11.78	16.67	4.89
1–3 years of college[b]	13.83	18.96	5.13
Bachelor's degree	14.35	26.17	11.82
Master's or higher degree	21.46	32.07	10.61

[a] Including those who received a General Education Development (GED) certificate.
[b] Including those who received an associate's degree.
Source: U.S. Bureau of Labor Statistics.

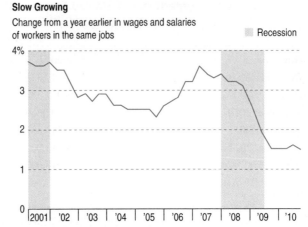

FIGURE 16-2 Annual Changes in Wages and Salaries of Workers in the Same Jobs

Source: U.S. Bureau of Labor Statistics.

Finally, there are longer-term implications of underemployment besides current lower pay. Underemployed workers are likely to have lower future earnings partly because employers provide less or no training to part-time workers. Figure 16-2 shows the rate of increase in pay levels during and following the Great Recession, which is lower than these rates prior to this recession. Also, this figure indicates that the rate of increase during the Great Recession was much lower than the rate during the recession that occurred in 2001. Data for 2011 and 2012 (not shown in Figure 16-2) show a continuation of the trend. As a result, underemployment may slow down the economic recovery from recession. Lower current pay and anticipated lower future earnings will likely reduce the consumption of goods and services, thus holding back increases in spending, business production, and employment levels.

The previous figures chronicle pay information for the underemployed. The pay situation for those becoming employed full-time following periods of unemployment is less encouraging. According to the U.S. Bureau of Labor Statistics, approximately 55 percent are earning less, of which nearly 36 percent are earning at least 20 percent less than they were prior to becoming unemployed. In comparison, approximately 45 percent are earning more, of which only 25 percent are earning at least 20 percent more than they were prior to becoming unemployed.

The Compensation–Productivity Gap

The gap between real hourly compensation and labor productivity indicates whether workers' pay is keeping up with productivity. **Real hourly compensation** measures the purchasing power of a dollar while **nominal hourly compensation** is the face value of a dollar. Increases in the costs of goods and services cause nominal pay to be less than real pay. For example, let's assume that an employee accepted a job at $10 per hour. This figure—$10 per hour—represents nominal pay. At the same time, $10 also represents real pay. However, over 1 year, let's assume that the price of goods and services increased, on average, 5 percent. At the end of the year, nominal hourly pay remains at $10. Hourly real pay, on the other hand, declined by 5 percent, or $0.50. In other words, $10 purchases only $9.50 worth of goods and services. In this example, $9.50 represents hourly real pay.

Productivity growth promotes rising living standards in the following manner. Increases in productivity growth indicate companies' investments in capital equipment and information technology. Examples of capital equipment include new manufacturing facilities, research and development labs, and sales distribution centers. Examples of information technology include structured databases containing expert information to help end users make informed decisions in complex situations. For instance, physicians may access databases to help them diagnose health

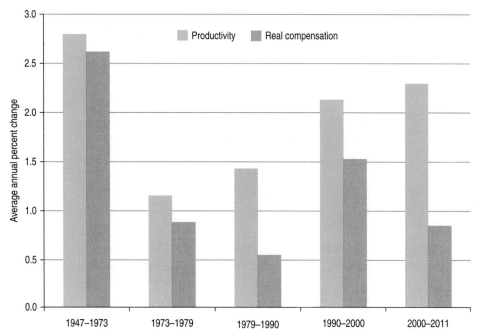

FIGURE 16-3 **Productivity Growth and Real Hourly Compensation Growth, Selected Years, 1947–2011**

Source: U.S. Bureau of Labor Statistics.

conditions based on patients' symptoms and health histories. Another example occurs in the marketing field where information systems enable companies to identify customers for new products and services based on a variety of factors including household income and purchasing history.

Since the 1970s, real hourly compensation has lagged behind labor productivity growth as shown in Figure 16-3.[6] The growth of productivity and real hourly compensation in the nonfarm business sector (which accounts for three-fourths of output and employment in the total U.S. economy) was comparable until 1973. The annual change in productivity averaged 2.8 percent and real hourly compensation growth averaged 2.6 percent during the 1947–1973 period. In 1973–1979, the annual averages were at 1.1 and 0.9 percent, respectively. Real hourly compensation growth failed to keep pace with accelerating productivity growth over the past three decades, and the gap between productivity growth and compensation growth widened. Hence, during 2000–2011, average annual growth in productivity and real compensation equaled 2.3 percent and 0.9 percent, respectively.

Figure 16-4 shows the gains or losses in hourly wages relative to the increases in productivity for the 18-month period following each recession after World War II. Companies experienced increases in productivity each time, but the gain in real compensation has been substantially less. Most noteworthy is the difference between increases in real compensation relative to increases in productivity since the end of the Great Recession, which is much more substantial than in any of the prior recessions.

There are two reasons that may explain the compensation–productivity gap. First, high unemployment following recessions leaves employees with relatively lower power to bargain for higher pay because the supply of individuals seeking work is greater than the company's demand for new workers. Second, most companies experience profit losses during economic recessions, and, then, profits generally increase following recessions. Companies promote profits, in part, by holding down employees' pay.

In sum, we considered the impact of the Great Recession on compensation. We described an economic recession. Then we examined the underemployment phenomenon. Finally, we reviewed problems stemming from the compensation–productivity gap.

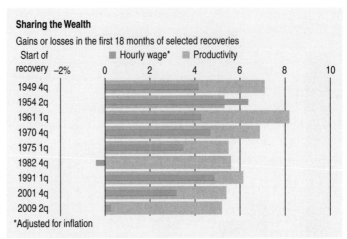

FIGURE 16-4 Gains or Losses in Real Hourly Pay Compared to Productivity Increases, 18 Months Following Economic Recessions

Source: U.S. Bureau of Labor Statistics.

EXECUTIVE COMPENSATION

As we learned in Chapter 12 about compensating executives, company boards of directors possess the authority to set executive pay in U.S. companies. For at least three decades, executive pay has come under scrutiny of many from among the public at large, labor unions, the federal government, and even company shareholders because of the extraordinary differences between their pay and that of non-executive employees. In addition, criticisms were levied because the executive pay setting process lacked transparency and even some of the components of the pay package were not disclosed.

Most recently in the United States, the Dodd-Frank Act requires greater transparency and an opportunity for shareholders to cast a vote on their support for proposed executive compensation packages through a practice commonly known to as "say on pay." As we've also learned, however, the vote is simply advisory to its company's board of directors. Should the result of the shareholder voting process become binding?

Already, in the European Union, at least four countries enacted laws that establish the practice of shareholders casting a binding vote to approve or disapprove proposed executive compensation. Most recently, voters in Switzerland passed a law that follows suit.

Within the scope of this book, it is difficult to give full treatment to the question of whether shareholders should play a formal role in determining executive compensation. Nevertheless, it is within the scope to pose some questions for consideration to help inform your perspective:

Do shareholders have sufficient knowledge about the qualifications of the executive and whether the proposed compensation package is fitting?

Do shareholders have sufficient knowledge about the availability of appropriately qualified individuals for the executive position?

Should all shareholders have an equal say on pay? That is, would it be appropriate to count votes in proportion to the number of shares?

Should we assume that individuals will factor in executive compensation practices as part of their decision to invest in a company or to divest from it?

RISING WAGES IN CHINA

In recent decades, many U.S. companies relocated manufacturing facilities from the United States to other countries such as the People's Republic of China because the cost of labor was substantially lower there than in the United States. These companies' goal was to lower the cost of production ultimately to maintain competitive prices and to preserve profits. As we will discuss shortly, the costs of labor in China have been increasing rapidly. Rising costs are quickly reducing the competitive advantage gained from moving manufacturing operations to China.

Among developing Asian economies, China's average pay rate is highest (versus Indonesia, Philippines, Vietnam, and Bangladesh). In recent years, the Chinese central government has been substantially raising minimum wage rates, creating pressure throughout the wage structure. Minimum wage rates increased an average of 24 percent across the country's 31 provinces, and the government is planning an annual increase in minimum wages through 2015. Average monthly income for migrant workers increased 13 percent (approximately $257).

Chinese policy makers are supportive of increased wages for the following reason. In recent history, the growth in the Chinese economy was based in large part on its trade surplus. A trade surplus occurs when the value of goods and services being shipped for sale outside the country, in this case, China, exceeds the value of goods and services shipped from other countries to China. Encouraging higher wages promotes domestic consumption, that is, the purchase and use of goods and services within its national borders. Increased domestic consumption will decrease the country's reliance on exports to sustain growth. Reduced reliance on exports is particularly necessary as labor costs within China increase rapidly. As China's labor costs rise, so would the cost of its exports, making the country less competitive in the global economy.

Labor shortages have also contributed to wage increases in China. These shortages are due, in part, to the rapidly aging Chinese population after 30 years of its one-child policy. This policy, still in effect, limits most couples to having one child only. The Chinese government implemented the policy to curb population growth in large cities.

Economic growth is creating the need for new jobs; however, the one-child policy has slowed population growth as intended, vastly reducing the number of young workforce entrants. As a result, this policy has inadvertently contributed to an aging population. The largest segment of the Chinese population is currently in the 35–44 age range.

CHALLENGES IN HEALTH CARE REFORM

On March 23, 2010, President Barack Obama signed into law the Patient Protection and Affordable Care Act (PPACA). Shortly thereafter, on March, 30, 2010, PPACA was amended by the passage of the Health Care and Education Reconciliation Act of 2010. Together, these laws provide the basis for health care reform in the United States.

The goal of health care reform is to reduce the number of uninsured U.S. residents by 32 million in 2016.[7] The U.S. Congressional Budget Office estimates that the cost of health care reform over the next 10 years will cost approximately $971 billion through the year 2019,[8] which will be paid by individual taxpayers and companies.

The Health Care and Education Reconciliation Act adds several requirements that may be broken down into two categories. First, there are a multitude of revisions to PPACA such as limiting the penalty, to be discussed shortly, to companies that choose not to offer health insurance. Second, this act adds a variety of provisions that will enable more students and families to qualify for financial aid. For example, this act terminates the process of the federal government giving subsidies to private banks that offer federally insured loans. Instead, loans will be administered directly by the U.S. Department of Education, which will lower the fees students will pay to get such loans.

Health care reform will substantially influence the way employers provide health care benefits to employees. Prior to the passage of PPACA, companies generally chose whether to offer health care insurance to employees. The new legislation will require most employers to provide health care insurance to employees; otherwise, they will incur significant financial penalties. Beginning in 2015, if the employers with 50 or more full-time employees fail to offer health insurance coverage, they must pay a penalty to the government that equals $2,000 per employee. These terms represent the general rule, but there are higher fines for employers that offer unaffordable health insurance. It is possible that employers may lower wages to offset the costs of health insurance, decrease the size of their workforce, or, most unfavorably, go out of business.

It is expected that the cost of health care insurance will become more expensive to employers because of certain new requirements. These changes will include the elimination of the lifetime benefits cap. (We discussed maximum benefits caps in Chapter 10.) Until this health care reform, employers could choose to control costs by imposing lifetime benefit caps, say, at $1 million. Also previously, employers chose longer waiting periods to limit the rising costs of offering health care coverage. But now, PPACA will also limit waiting periods before new employees may receive health care coverage to a maximum of 90 days.

The expected increased costs associated with PPACA have led many companies to consider whether to offer health insurance at all in spite of the $2,000 per employee penalty for not offering health insurance coverage. Moreover, under the act, companies will be required to pay a 40 percent excise tax, referred to as the "Cadillac" tax, on overly generous benefit plans beginning in 2018. The term comes from the Cadillac car brand, which has signified American luxury since its introduction in the early twentieth century. Most noteworthy, generous plans contain low deductible amounts and generous medical coverage. Employers that offer overly generous plans will be taxed under the premise that such plans encourage participants to overuse and ultimately burden the U.S. health care system. (As a you may recall, high-deductible plans are often characteristic of consumer-driven health care, which we reviewed in Chapter 10, and those plans are not subject to the excise tax noted here.)

WORKFORCE DEMOGRAPHIC SHIFTS

Labor force diversity is on the rise. We expect that demographic diversity will influence employee benefits, a key component of total compensation.

Labor Force Diversity

According to the U.S. Bureau of Labor Statistics,[9] labor force diversity will continue to increase based on age, gender, race, and ethnicity. This increase is the result of changes both in the composition of the population and in labor force participation rates across demographic groups.

The projected growth of the labor force will be affected by the aging of the baby boom generation—persons born between 1946 and 1964. In 2018, baby boomers will be 54 to 72 years old. The number of workers in this age group is expected to increase significantly during the 2008–2018 decade. The labor force will continue to age, with the number of workers in the 55-and-older group projected to grow substantially. The labor force participation rate for younger workers (ages 16–24) is expected to decline during the period 2008–2018 from 58.8 to 54.5 percent. The participation rate for older workers (ages 55 and older) is expected to rise from 39.4 to 43.5 percent.

The labor force participation rates of women in nearly all age groups are projected to increase slightly. The number of women in the labor force is projected to grow by nearly 9 percent, slightly faster than the 7.5 percent growth projected for men. Women's share of the labor force is expected to increase by less than 1 percent, from 46.5 percent in 2006 to 46.9 percent by 2018. In contrast, men's share is projected to decline by less than 1 percent—from 53.5 in 2008 to 53.1 percent in 2018.

By 2018, the Hispanic labor force is expected to reach nearly 30 million, due to faster population growth resulting from a younger population, higher fertility rates, and increased immigration from Mexico to the United States. Despite relatively slow growth for other ethnic groups, white non-Hispanics will far outnumber the Hispanic count (approximately 107 million versus approximately 30 million).

Relevance for Employee Benefits

An employer-sponsored benefits program is most effective when the workforce is relatively similar in terms of needs and preferences. For example, let's assume a company's workforce is entirely female. *On the surface*, one could say that this workforce is not very diverse. *Below the surface,* however, it is possible that there will be substantial differences in the needs and preferences for benefits among these employees. For example, what if half of the workforce has young children under the age of six while the other half does not have young children? In this scenario, only half of the workforce (i.e., those with young children under the age of six) would value extensive employer-sponsored day care benefits. As a rule, employees are more likely to endorse employer-sponsored benefits as long as these benefits fulfill their needs and preferences. Differences in employee preferences and needs based on life stage and life circumstances call for flexible benefits offerings.

Benefits professionals may use surveys once every year or two to collect information about employee demographics, needs, preferences, recent or anticipated life changes, and the extent to which they find particular benefits useful. Statistical analyses will show whether there is an association among these factors. Benefits professionals may compare current offerings with survey results. Over time, they can check whether changes in age, family status, needs, and preferences influence employees' views of benefits. Offering relevant employee benefits is important to companies' attainment of a positive return on investment in benefits programs. As we discussed previously in this book (Chapters 9, 10, and 11), the cost of employee benefits is high, and rapid increases in the costs make them substantially more expensive every year.

Considerations for Employee Motivation

Companies expect that employee benefit offerings will motivate employees to perform their jobs as well as possible. This expectation is based on a scientific assumption that employees have similar attitudes toward, and will be motivated similarly by, employee benefits systems.[10] However, given changing demographics of the U.S. workforce, the context has changed, and many of the assumptions underlying our reward and motivation theories may not be applicable in all company contexts.[11] For instance, due in part to variation across generational and regional norms regarding the appropriate age of marriage,[12] the age at which an employee becomes concerned with life insurance has likely increased over time for some (older employees with dependents), but not for others (younger employees without dependents). As a consequence, it is possible that employee benefits systems do not effectively motivate all employees equally well.

MARRIAGE BETWEEN SAME-SEX INDIVIDUALS AND THE U.S. SUPREME COURT RULING ON THE DEFENSE OF MARRIAGE ACT

Over the past several decades, more companies have offered domestic partner benefits for unmarried employees that are similar to benefits for married employees. Domestic partner benefits may entail as little as extending employee discounts to their partners or as much as having domestic partners and children covered under company-sponsored health insurance. Offering domestic partner benefits is largely done on a discretionary basis to recruit and retain highly qualified applicants and employees, but some states do require that companies offer these benefits. In 2011, only 7 percent of private sector employees with same-sex partners were eligible to receive defined benefit retirement survivor benefits. In the public sector, 50 percent were eligible. In addition, 29 percent of private sector workers with same-sex partners were eligible to receive health care benefits. Thirty-three percent were eligible in the public sector.[13]

For example, California mandates under state law that companies grant registered domestic partners of employees the same rights and benefits extended to married spouses. New Jersey requires all health insurers to offer domestic partner coverage and prohibits employers from discriminating based on domestic partnership status. However, New Jersey does not require employers to provide domestic partner coverage under employee health plans. If such coverage is offered, employers can have employees pay part or all of the premium. In 2007, the New Jersey attorney general issued an opinion concluding that same-sex marriages and civil unions from out-of-state jurisdictions will be afforded "all of the rights and benefits of marriage" under New Jersey's civil union law. Same-sex civil unions recognized by Vermont and Connecticut as well as same-sex partnerships under California law will be treated as equivalents of civil unions in New Jersey.

Not all companies and states define domestic partners similarly. In some cases, employers offer domestic partner benefits to unmarried partners (in heterosexual relationships) and children of all employees, while others limit this coverage to same-sex couples. In any event, employers require endorsement of the domestic partnership through proof of shared residence, signed statements attesting to a long-term relationship, or other information to show that the domestic partnership is not a short-term relationship (e.g., joint bank accounts and being the beneficiary of a partner's life insurance policy can establish that a long-term relationship is in place).

Limiting domestic partner benefits to same-sex partners has raised substantial criticism from unmarried heterosexual couples. This criticism has led to legal challenges that allege discrimination against unmarried heterosexual couples. Thus far, the courts have disagreed with these claims of discrimination because unmarried heterosexual partners would have the same benefits if they were to become married—currently not much of an option for same-sex partners.

The issue of same-sex benefits has become (and will continue to be) more complex as the debate continues in the United States about whether same-sex partners may become legally married. As we will discuss, the Defense of Marriage Act, passed in 1996, does not recognize marriage between same-sex individuals; however, some states have legalized such marriages. As of June 2013, the District of Columbia and 13 states—Connecticut, Delware, Iowa, Maine, Maryland, Massachusetts, Minnesota, New Hampshire, New York, Vermont, Maryland, Rhode Island, and Washington—had laws permitting same-sex marriage.

For example, in 2003, the Massachusetts Supreme Judicial Court determined that denying same-sex couples the right to marry violated the state constitution.[14] Then, in 2006, the same court ruled that a proposed state constitutional amendment that would ban same-sex marriage can be placed on the ballot for voter approval if the amendment is approved by the state legislature.[15] In 2007, the Washington State House of Representatives approved a domestic partnership bill (SB 5336) that grants same-sex couples hospital visitation rights, inheritance rights when there is no will, and the power to authorize medical procedures, such as organ donation and autopsies. Then, in 2012, the Washington legislature passed legislation making same-sex marriage legal.

Also, in 2007, the Michigan Court of Appeals ruled that an amendment to the state constitution defining marriage as between a man and a woman also prohibits Michigan public employers from offering benefits, such as health insurance, to same-sex partners of gay or lesbian employees.[16] The appeals court overturned a lower court decision finding no conflict between the 2004 amendment and providing the benefits. Employers and employee benefits professionals will be faced with many questions regarding employers' obligations under employee benefit plans, many of which cannot yet be anticipated.

In 2008, same-sex marriage became legal in California only to be struck down by a voter referendum known as Proposition 8 in November of that year. In 2012, additional developments regarding California's referendum occurred. A federal appeals court decided that California's 2008 voter-mandated ban on gay marriages was unconstitutional. Specifically, the court concluded that California's ban violated the U.S. Constitution's 14th Amendment's Equal Protection clause. In addition, the court maintained that California voters used the referendum to remove from gay people constitutional rights they previously held under a 2008 California Supreme Court ruling that the state's equal-protection clauses did not permit the state's marriage laws to discriminate on the basis of sexual orientation. Supporters of Proposition 8 requested that the U.S. Supreme Court overturn the California Supreme Court's decision; thus, prohibiting marriage between same-sex couples in California. In June 2013, the U.S. Supreme Court rejected the appeal. The Court reasoned that supporters of this California law did not have the right to appeal the court decision that ruled against it. As a result, the ban on Proposition 8 remains in effect, and marriage between two men or two women remains legal in California.

While some companies may choose to extend benefits such as health insurance coverage to same-sex spouses, Employee Retirement Income Security Act (ERISA) does not address this issue. In fact, until June 2012, the Defense of Marriage Act prohibited same-sex spouses from being recognized as beneficiaries for federal benefits. That is, for example, federally mandated legally required benefits such as Social Security or leave under the Family and Medical Leave Act of 1993 did not recognize same-sex spouses. However, in June 2012, the 1st U.S. Circuit Court of Appeals in Boston said the 1996 law deprives gay couples of the rights and privileges granted to heterosexual couples, paving the way for same-sex spouses to be recognized as beneficiaries for federal benefits. There are other provisions of the Defense of Marriage Act that were not addressed by the court. Specifically, the court didn't rule on the law's more political provision that states without same-sex marriage cannot be forced to recognize gay unions performed in states where it's legal. For example, Nevada, which doesn't have a same-sex marriage law, is not required to recognize gay unions from states where same-sex marriage is legal such as Connecticut or Iowa. The court also did not address whether gay couples have a constitutional right to marry.

In June 2013, the U.S. Supreme Court ruled that Section 3 of the Defense of Marriage Act is unconstitutional. Specifically, the Court's ruling applies to the part of the law, which had previously denied federal benefits to gay and lesbian couples in states where such unions are permitted. The ruling means that same-sex couples lawfully married in their state can receive the same federal benefits as heterosexual couples, such as possible tax advantages by filing jointly, benefits for veterans' spouses and inheritance-tax exemptions. The U.S. Supreme Court maintained that Section 3 violates the U.S. Constitution's guarantee of equal protection under the law, and treated marriage between same-sex individuals as less worthy than marriage between heterosexual couples.

END OF CHAPTER

MyManagementLab

Go to **mymanagementlab.com** to complete the problems marked with this icon ⭐.

Summary

This chapter provided an epilogue for compensation professionals. Building on our knowledge of compensation system design, we reviewed seven key factors that will influence the work compensation professionals conduct in the coming years. These factors are the fallout from the Great Recession, underemployment, executive compensation, rising wages in China, challenges in health care reform, workforce demographic shifts, and issues surrounding same-sex marriage. There is uncertainty about how these factors will influence compensation and benefits practice, making for great challenges for aspiring professionals in the field!

Key Terms

economic recession   351
underemployment   352

malemployment   353
real hourly compensation   354

nominal hourly
  compensation   354

⭐ Discussion Questions

16-1. This chapter discusses seven important issues that will shape compensation professionals' work for years to come. Which one of these issues stands to create the greatest uncertainty for compensation professionals? Explain your answer.

16-2. Describe the most recent developments in health care reform. How do these developments compare to what is discussed in this chapter?

To help answer this question, conduct a search on the Internet using terms such as "health care reform" or "Patient Protection and Affordable Care Act."

16-3. Please identify one or more issues besides the ones discussed in this chapter that you feel will help define the future of compensation professionals' work.

MyManagementLab

Go to **mymanagementlab.com** for Auto-graded writing questions as well as the following Assisted-graded writing questions.

⭐ **16-4.** List the four challenges for compensation professionals. Among these, describe the challenges brought by wage issues in China.

⭐ **16-5.** Briefly discuss the uncertainties brought by health care reform and changing workforce demographics.

Endnotes

1. U.S. Bureau of Labor Statistics. (2013). *Extended Mass Layoffs—Fourth Quarter 2012 (USDL 13-0236)*. Available: *www.bls.gov*, accessed April 21, 2013.

2. U.S. Bureau of Labor Statistics. (2013). *Mass Layoffs—February 2013 (USDL 13-0479)*. Available: *www.bls.gov*, accessed April 21, 2013.

3. Sum, A., & Khatiwada, I. (2010). The Nation's Underemployed in the "Great Recession" of 2007–09. *Monthly Labor Review, 133(11)*: 3-15. Available: *www.bls.gov*, accessed April 21, 2013.

4. Ibid.

5. Ibid.

6. U.S. Bureau of Labor Statistics. (February 24, 2011). *TED: The Editor's Desk. The Compensation-Productivity Gap*. Available: *www.bls.gov*, accessed April 9, 2011; Fleck, S., Glaser, J., & Sprague, S. (2011). The Compensation-Productivity Gap: A Visual Essay. *Monthly Labor Review*, January, pp. 57–69.

7. U.S. Congressional Budget Office. (March 2011). Estimate of the Effects of the Insurance Coverage Provisions Contained in the Patient Protection and Affordable Care Act (Public Law 111-148) and the Health Care and Education Reconciliation Act of 2010 (P.L. 111-152). Available: *www.cbo.gov*, accessed April 4, 2011.

8. U.S. Congressional Budget Office. (March 2011). *CBO's Analysis of the Major Health Care Legislation Enacted in March 2010*. Available: *www.cbo.gov*, accessed April 4, 2011.

9. Toossi, M. (2009). Labor Force Projections to 2018: Older workers staying more active. *Monthly Labor Review*, pp. 30–51.

10. Martocchio, J. J. (2011). *Employee Benefits: A Human Resource Management Approach* (4th ed.). Burr Ridge, IL: McGraw-Hill.

11. Irvine, D. (2010). How to Reward a Multigenerational and Culturally Diverse Workforce. *Workspan*, April, pp. 63–68.

12. PBS NEWSHOUR (June 19, 2006). Young Women Challenge the Marriage Norms. Available: *http://www.pbs.org/newshour/generation-next/demographic/marriage_06-19.html*, accessed April 12, 2011.

13. U.S. Department of Labor. (2011). *Employee Benefits in the United States—March 2011* (USDL 11-1112). Available: *http://www.bls.gov*, accessed May 10, 2012.

14. *Goodridge v. Mass. Department of Public Health*, 440 Mass. 309, 798 NE2d 941 (November 18, 2003).

15. *Schulman v. Attorney General*, 447 Mass. 189, 850 NE2d 505 (July 10, 2006).

16. *National Pride at Work, Inc. v. Governor of Michigan and City of Kalamazoo*, 265 Mich. 870 (February 1, 2007) lc no. 05-000368-CZ.

Glossary

360-degree performance appraisals incorporate several sources of pertinent information to give a more complete (and presumably) less biased assessment of job performance. Examples of pertinent sources include supervisor, coworkers, and clients.

Aaron v. City of Wichita, Kansas, a court ruling, offered several criteria to determine whether City of Wichita fire chiefs are exempt employees, including the relative importance of management as opposed to other duties, frequency with which they exercise discretionary powers, relative freedom from supervision, and the relationship between their salaries and wages paid to other employees for similar nonexempt work.

Abilities are enduring attributes of the individual that influence performance.

Ability, based on Equal Employment Opportunity Commission guidelines, refers to a present competence to perform an observable behavior or a behavior that results in an observable product.

Accrual rules specify the rate at which participants accumulate (or earn) retirement benefits.

Affirmative action refers to a written document that states a company's goals to recruit and hire underrepresented minorities.

Age Discrimination in Employment Act of 1967 (ADEA) protects older workers age 40 and over from illegal discrimination.

Agency problem describes an executive's behavior that promotes his or her self-interests rather than the interests of the company owners or shareholders.

Agency theory provides an explanation of executive compensation determination based on the relationship between company owners (shareholders) and agents (executives).

Alternation ranking, a variation of simple ranking job evaluation plans, orders all jobs from lowest to highest, based on alternately identifying the jobs of lowest and highest worth.

Americans with Disabilities Act of 1990 (ADA) prohibits discrimination against individuals with mental or physical disabilities within and outside employment settings, including public services and transportation, public accommodations, and employment.

Annual addition is the annual maximum allowable contribution to a participant's account in a defined contribution plan, including employer contributions allocated to the participant's account, employee contributions, and forfeitures allocated to the participant's account.

Annuities are a series of payments for the life of the participant and beneficiary. Annuity contracts are usually purchased from insurance companies, which make payments according to the contract.

Atonio v. Wards Cove Packing Co., a Supreme Court case, ruled that plaintiffs (i.e., employees) in employment discrimination suits must indicate which employment practice created disparate impact and demonstrate how the employment practice created disparate impact (intentional discrimination).

Baby boom generation refers to the generation of people born between 1946 and 1964.

Balance sheet approach provides expatriates the standard of living they normally enjoy in the United States.

Banking hours refers to a feature of flextime scheduling that allows employees to vary the number of hours they work each day as long as they work a set number of hours each week.

Base pay represents the monetary compensation employees earn on a regular basis for performing their jobs. Hourly pay and salary are the main forms of base pay.

Base period is the minimum period of time an individual must be employed before becoming eligible to receive unemployment insurance under the Social Security Act of 1935.

Basic skills information describes developed capacities that facilitate learning or the more rapid acquisition of knowledge.

Behavioral encouragement plans are individual incentive pay plans that reward employees for specific such behavioral accomplishments as good attendance or safety records.

Behavioral observation scale (BOS), a specific kind of behavioral system, displays illustrations of positive incidents (or behaviors) of job performance for various job dimensions. The evaluator rates the employee on each behavior according to the extent to which the employee performs in a manner consistent with each behavioral description.

Behavioral systems, a type of performance appraisal method, require that raters (e.g., supervisors) judge the extent to which employees display successful job performance behaviors.

Behaviorally anchored rating scales (BARS), a specific kind of behavioral system, are based on the critical incident technique (CIT), and these scales are developed in the same fashion with one exception. For the CIT, a critical incident would be written as "the incumbent completed the task in a timely fashion." For the BARS format, this incident would be written as "the incumbent is expected to complete the task in a timely fashion."

Benchmark jobs, found outside the company, provide reference points against which the values of jobs within the company are judged.

Bennett Amendment allows employees to charge employers with Title VII violations regarding pay only when the employer has violated the Equal Pay Act of 1963.

Bias errors happen in the performance evaluation process when the rater evaluates the employee based on the rater's negative or positive opinion of the employee rather than on the employee's actual performance.

Board of directors represents shareholders' interests by weighing the pros and cons of top executives' decisions. Members include chief executive officers and top executives of other successful companies, distinguished community leaders, well-regarded professionals (e.g., physicians and attorneys), and a few of the company's top-level executives.

Boureslan v. Aramco, a Supreme Court case in which the Supreme Court ruled that federal job discrimination laws do not apply to U.S. citizens working for U.S. companies in foreign countries.

Brito v. Zia Company, a Supreme Court ruling, deemed that the Zia Company violated Title VII of the Civil Rights Act of 1964 when a disproportionate number of protected-class individuals were laid off on the basis of low performance-appraisal scores. Zia Company's action was a violation of Title VII because the use of the performance-appraisal system in determining layoffs was indeed an employment test. In addition, the court ruled that the Zia Company had not demonstrated that its performance appraisal instrument was valid.

Broadbanding is a pay structure form that leads to the consolidation of existing pay grades and pay ranges into fewer wider pay grades.

Buy-back provision in Improshare plans sets a maximum productivity improvement payout level on productivity gains. Any bonus money that is generated because of improvements above the maximum is placed in a reserve. If productivity improves to the point where the maximum is repeatedly exceeded, the firm buys back the amount of the productivity improvement over the maximum with a one-time payment to employees.

Cafeteria plan See *flexible benefits plan.*

Capital gains are the difference between the company stock price at the time of purchase and the lower stock price at the time an executive receives the stock options.

Carve-out plans are insurance plans that offer specific kinds of benefits such as dental care, vision care, prescription drugs, mental health and substance abuse, and maternity care.

Cash balance plans represent a cross between traditional defined benefits and defined contributions retirement plans. The rate of monetary accumulation slows as the employee's years of service increase.

Central tendency represents the fact that a set of data clusters around or centers on a central point. Central tendency is a number that represents the typical numerical value in a data set.

Certification ensures that employees possess at least a minimally acceptable level of skill proficiency upon completion of a training unit. Certification methods can include work samples, oral questioning, and written tests.

Civil Rights Act of 1964 is a major piece of federal legislation designed to protect the rights of underrepresented minorities.

Civil Rights Act of 1991 shifted the burden of proof of disparate impact from employees to employers, overturning several 1989 Supreme Court rulings.

Classification plans, particular methods of job evaluation, place jobs into categories based on compensable factors.

Clawback provisions are provisions in CEO employment contracts that allow boards of directors to take back performance-based compensation if they were to subsequently learn that performance goals were not actually achieved, regardless of whether the CEO was responsible for performance falling short of target levels.

Cliff vesting enables employees to earn 100 percent vesting rights after no more than 3 years of service.

Coinsurance refers to the percentage of covered expenses paid by the insured. Most commercial plans stipulate 20 percent coinsurance. This means that the insured will pay 20 percent of covered expenses, whereas the insurance company pays the remaining 80 percent.

Commission is a form of incentive compensation, based on a percentage of the product or service selling price and the number of units sold.

Commission-only plans are specific kinds of sales compensation plans. Some salespeople derive their entire income through commissions.

Commission-plus-draw plans award sales professionals commissions and draws.

Common review date is the designated date when all employees receive performance appraisals.

Common review period is the designated period (e.g., the month of June) when all employees receive performance appraisals.

Company stock represents the total equity or worth of the company.

Company stock shares represent equity segments of equal value. Equity interest increases with the number of stock shares held.

Compa-ratios index the relative competitiveness of internal pay rates based on pay range midpoints.

Comparison systems, a type of performance-appraisal method, require that raters (e.g., supervisors) evaluate a given employee's performance against other employees' performance attainments. Employees are ranked from the best performer to the poorest performer.

Compensable factors are job attributes (e.g., skill, effort, responsibility, and working conditions) that compensation professionals use to determine the value of jobs.

Compensation budgets are blueprints that describe the allocation of monetary resources to fund pay structures.

Compensation committees contain board of directors members within and outside a company. Compensation committees review executive compensation consultants' alternate recommendations for compensation packages, discuss the assets and liabilities of the recommendations, and recommend the consultant's best proposal to the board of directors for its consideration.

Compensation strategies describe the use of compensation practices that support HR and competitive strategies.

Compensation surveys involve the collection and subsequent analysis of competitors' compensation data.

Competency-based pay refers to two specific types of pay programs: pay-for-knowledge and skill-based pay.

Competitive advantage describes a company's success based on employees' efforts to maintain market share and profitability over several years.

Competitive strategy refers to the planned use of company resources—technology, capital, and human resources—to promote and sustain competitive advantage.

Compressed workweek schedules enable employees to perform their full-time weekly work obligations in fewer days than a regular 5-day workweek.

Concessionary bargaining focuses on unions promoting job security over large wage increases in negotiations with management.

Consolidated Omnibus Budget Reconciliation Act of 1985 (COBRA) was enacted to provide employees with the opportunity to continue receiving their employer-sponsored medical care insurance temporarily under their employer's plan if their coverage would otherwise cease due to termination, layoff, or other change in employment status.

Consultants See *independent contractors*.

Consumer-driven health care refers to employer-sponsored programs that shift a greater amount of the responsibility to employees for selecting health care providers.

Consumer Price Index (CPI) indexes monthly price changes of goods and services that people buy for day-to-day living.

Content Model of O*NET lists six categories of job and worker information. Job information contains the components that relate to the actual work activities of a job (i.e., information that HR professionals should include in the summary and duties sections of job descriptions). Worker information represents characteristics of employees that contribute to successful job performance.

Contingent workers engage in explicitly tentative employment relationships with companies.

Contrast errors occur when a rater (e.g., a supervisor) compares an employee to other employees rather than to specific explicit performance standards.

Contributory financing implies that the company and its employees share the costs for discretionary benefits.

Copayments represent nominal payments individuals make for office visits to their doctors or for prescription drugs.

Core compensation describes the monetary rewards employees receive. There are seven types of core compensation: two forms of base pay hourly pay (or wage) and salary, seniority pay, merit pay, incentive pay, cost-of-living adjustments (COLAs), and pay-for-knowledge and skill-based pay.

Core employees possess full-time jobs, and they generally plan long-term or indefinite relationships with their employers.

Core hours, as applied to flextime schedule, are the hours when all workers must be present.

Core plus option plans establish a set of benefits (e.g., medical insurance) as mandatory for all employees who participate in flexible benefits plans.

Cost-of-living adjustments (COLAs) represent periodic base pay increases that are based on changes in prices, as indexed by the consumer price index (CPI). COLAs enable workers to maintain their purchasing power and standard of living by adjusting base pay for inflation.

Coverage requirements limit an employer's freedom to exclude employees from qualified plans. Tests to determine whether coverage requirements are met include the ratio percentage test and the average benefit tests.

Critical incident technique (CIT), a specific kind of behavioral system, requires job incumbents and their supervisors to identify performance incidents—on-the-job behaviors and behavioral outcomes—that distinguish successful performance from unsuccessful performance. The supervisor then observes the employees and records their performance on these critical job aspects.

Cross-departmental models, a kind of pay-for-knowledge program, promote staffing flexibility by training employees in one department with some of the critical skills they would need to perform effectively in other departments.

Cross-functional skills information indicates developed capacities that facilitate performance of activities that occur across jobs.

Current profit sharing plans award cash to employees, typically on a quarterly or annual basis.

Davis–Bacon Act of 1931 established employment standards for construction contractors holding federal government contracts valued at more than $2,000. Such contractors must pay laborers and mechanics at least the prevailing wage in their local area.

Day care refers to programs that supervise and care for young children and elderly relatives when their regular caretakers are at work.

Deductible is the out-of-pocket expense that employees must pay before dental, medical, or vision insurance benefits become active.

Deferred compensation refers to an agreement between an employee and a company to render payments to an employee at a future date. Deferred compensation is a hallmark of executive compensation packages.

Deferred profit sharing plans place cash awards in trust accounts for employees. These trusts are set aside on employees' behalf as a source of retirement income.

Defined benefit plans guarantee retirement benefits specified in the plan document. This benefit usually is expressed in terms of a monthly sum equal to a percentage of a participant's preretirement pay multiplied by the number of years he or she has worked for the employer.

Defined contribution plans require that employers and employees make annual contributions to separate retirement fund accounts established for each participating employee, based on a formula contained in the plan document.

Deliberate and knowing torts are a type of tort that entails an employer's deliberate and knowing intent to harm at least one employee. See also *torts.*

Dental insurance provides reimbursement for routine dental checkups and particular corrective procedures.

Depth of knowledge refers to the level of specialization, based on job-related knowledge, an employee brings to a particular job.

Depth of skills refers to the level of specialization, based on skills, an employee brings to a particular job.

Differentiation strategies focus on product or service development that is unique from those of its competitors. Differentiation can take many forms, including

design or brand image, technology, features, customer service, and price.

Direct hire arrangements refer to companies' recruitment and selection of temporary workers without assistance from employment agencies.

Discount stock options plans, a kind of executive deferred compensation, entitle executives to purchase their companies' stock in the future at a predetermined price. Discount stock options are similar to nonstatutory stock options with one exception. Companies grant stock options at rates far below the stock's fair market value on the date the option is granted.

Discretionary benefits are benefits that employers offer at their own choice. These benefits fall into three broad categories: protection programs, pay for time not worked, and services.

Discretionary bonuses are awarded to executives on an elective basis by boards of directors. Boards of directors weigh four factors in determining discretionary bonus amounts: company profits, the financial condition of the company, business conditions, and prospects for the future.

Discretionary income covers a variety of financial obligations in the United States for which expatriates remain responsible.

Disparate impact represents unintentional employment discrimination. It occurs whenever an employer applies an employment practice to all employees, but the practice leads to unequal treatment of protected employee groups.

Disparate treatment represents intentional employment discrimination, occurring whenever employers intentionally treat some workers less favorably than others because of their race, color, sex, national origin, or religion.

Distribution refers to the payment of vested retirement benefits to participants or beneficiaries.

Dodd-Frank Act See *Wall Street Reform and Consumer Protection Act of 2010.*

Draw is a subsistence pay component (i.e., to cover basic living expenses) in sales compensation plans. Companies usually charge draws against commissions that sales professionals are expected to earn.

Dual capacity is a legal doctrine that applies to the relationship between employers and employees. Specifically, a company may fulfill a role for employees that is completely different from its role as employer.

Dual employer common law doctrine establishes temporary workers' rights to receive workers' compensation. According to this doctrine, temporary workers are employees of both temporary employment agencies and the client companies. The written contract between the employment agency and the client company specifies which organization's workers' compensation policy applies in the event of injuries.

Early retirement programs contain incentives designed to encourage highly paid employees with substantial seniority to retire earlier than they planned. These incentives expedite senior employees' retirement eligibility and increase retirement income. In addition, many companies include continuation of medical benefits.

Economic Growth and Tax Relief Reconciliation Act of 2001 created tax benefits to individuals and companies in various ways (e.g., increasing the amount companies and employees can contribute to qualified retirement plans on a pretax basis).

Economic reality test helps companies determine whether employees are financially dependent on them.

Economic recession refers to a general slowdown in economic activity. Evidences of economic recessions include reduced gross domestic product (GDP) and increased unemployment rates.

Education, based on Equal Employment Opportunity Commission guidelines, refers to formal training.

EEOC v. Chrysler, a district court ruling, deemed that early retirement programs are permissible when companies offer them to employees on a voluntary basis. Forcing early retirement upon older workers represents age discrimination.

EEOC v. Madison Community Unit School District No. 12, a circuit court ruling, sheds light on judging whether jobs are equal based on four compensable factors: skill, effort, responsibility, and working conditions.

Elimination period refers to the minimum amount of time an employee must wait after becoming disabled before disability insurance payments begin. Elimination periods follow the completion of the preeligibility period.

Emergency Economic Stabilization Act of 2008 (EESA) authorized the secretary of the Treasury to establish the **Troubled Assets Relief Program (TARP)** to "purchase, and to make and fund commitments to purchase troubled assets from any financial institution, on terms and conditions as are determined by the Secretary." In other words, banks with financial assistance from the federal government could deduct only the first $500,000 annually for an executive's pay as a business expense.

Employee assistance programs (EAPs) help employees cope with personal problems that may impair their job performance (e.g., alcohol or drug abuse, domestic violence, the emotional impact of AIDS and other diseases, clinical depression, and eating disorders).

Employee benefits include any variety of programs that provide paid time off (e.g., vacation), employee services (e.g., transportation services), and protection programs (e.g., life insurance).

Employee-financed benefits do not require the employer to finance discretionary benefits because employees bear the entire cost.

Employee Retirement Income Security Act of 1974 (ERISA) was established to regulate the establishment and implementation of various fringe compensation programs. These include medical, life, and disability insurance programs, as well as pension programs. The essence of ERISA is the protection of employee benefits rights.

Employee stock option plans represent one type of companywide incentives. Companies grant employees the right to purchase shares of company stock.

Employee stock ownership plans (ESOPs) may be the basis for a company's Section 401(k) plan, and these plans invest in company securities, making them similar to profit sharing plans and stock bonus plans, presumably when the value of stock has increased.

Employee's anniversary date represents the date an employee began working for his or her present employer. Employees often receive performance appraisals on their anniversary dates.

Equal benefit or equal cost principle contained within the Older Workers Benefit Protection Act (OWBPA) requires employers to offer benefits to older workers of equal to or of greater value than the benefits offered to younger workers.

Equal Employment Opportunity Commission, a federal government agency, oversees and enforces various employment laws that guard against illegal discrimination including Title VII of the Civil Rights Act of 1964.

Equal Pay Act of 1963 requires that men and women should receive equal pay for performing equal work.

Equity theory suggests that an employee must regard his or her own ratio of merit increase pay to performance as similar to the ratio for other comparably performing people in the company.

Errors of central tendency occur when raters (e.g., supervisors) judge all employees as average or close to average.

Exchange rate is the price at which one country's currency can be swapped for another.

Exclusion provisions are the particular conditions that are ineligible for coverage. For example, most disability insurance plans do not provide coverage for disabilities that result from self-inflicted injuries.

Executive branch enforces the laws of various quasi-legislative and judicial agencies and executive orders.

Executive compensation consultants propose recommendations to chief executive officers and board of director members for alternate executive compensation packages.

Executive Order 11246 requires companies holding contracts (worth more than $50,000 per year and employing 50 or more employees) with the federal government to develop written affirmative action plans each year.

Executive Order 11478 prohibits employment discrimination on the basis of race, color, religion, sex, national origin, handicap, and age (401 *FEP Manual* 4061).

Executive Order 11935 prohibits employment of nonresidents in U.S. civil service jobs (401 *FEP Manual* 4121).

Executive orders influence the operation of the federal government and companies that are engaged in business relationships with the federal government.

Exempt refers to an employee's status regarding the overtime pay provision of the Fair Labor Standards Act of 1938 (FLSA). Administrative, professional, and executive employees are generally exempt from the FLSA overtime and minimum wage provisions.

Expatriates are U.S. citizens employed in U.S. companies with work assignments outside the United States.

Experience and training information describes specific preparation required for entry into a job plus past work experience contributing to qualifications for an occupation.

Experience rating system establishes higher contributions to fund unemployment insurance programs for employers with higher incidences of unemployment.

Extrinsic compensation includes both monetary and nonmonetary rewards.

Fair Labor Standards Act of 1938 (FLSA) addresses major abuses that intensified during the Great Depression and the transition from agricultural to industrial enterprises. These include substandard pay, excessive work hours, and the employment of children in oppressive working conditions.

Fairpay Rules specify the criteria for distinguishing between work that is not exempt from the overtime pay provision of the Fair Labor Standards Act.

Family and Medical Leave Act of 1993 (FMLA) requires employers to provide employees 12 weeks of unpaid leave per year in cases of family or medical emergency.

Family assistance programs help employees provide elder care and child care. Elder care provides physical, emotional, or financial assistance for aging parents, spouses, or other relatives who are not fully self-sufficient because they are too frail or disabled. Child care programs focus on supervising preschool-age dependent children whose parents work outside the home.

Family coverage offers health insurance benefits to the covered employee and his or her family members as defined by the plan (usually, spouse and children).

Federal constitution forms the basis for employment laws.

Federal Employees' Compensation Act mandates workers' compensation insurance protection for federal civilian employees.

Federal government oversees the entire United States and its territories. The vast majority of laws that influence compensation were established at the federal level.

Federal Insurance Contributions Act (FICA) taxes employees and employers to finance the Social Security Old-Age, Survivor, and Disability Insurance Program (OASDI).

Federal Unemployment Tax Act (FUTA) mandates employer contributions to fund state unemployment insurance programs. FUTA also specifies two criteria used to determine whether employers must participate in state unemployment insurance programs: the 1-in-20 test and the wage test.

Fee-for-service plans provide protection for three types of medical expenses: hospital expenses, surgical expenses, and physician's charges.

Fiduciaries are individuals who manage employee benefits plans and pension plan funds.

First-impression effect occurs when a rater (e.g., a supervisor) makes an initial favorable or unfavorable judgment about an employee and then ignores or distorts the employee's actual performance based on this impression.

Flexible benefits plan allows employees to choose a portion of their discretionary benefits based on a company's discretionary benefits options.

Flexible scheduling and leave allows employees to take time off during work hours to care for relatives or react to emergencies.

Flexible spending accounts (FSAs) permit employees to pay for certain benefits expenses (e.g., child care) with pretax dollars.

Flextime schedules allow employees to modify work schedules within specified limits set by the employer.

Forced distribution is a specific kind of comparison performance appraisal system in which raters (e.g., supervisors) assign employees to groups that represent the entire range of performance.

Foreign service premium is a monetary payment awarded to expatriates above their regular base pay.

Forfeitures are amounts from the accounts of employees who terminated their employment prior to earning vesting rights.

Freelancers See *independent contractors.*

Free-rider effect occurs when employees of lower ability, skill, and effort benefit equally as employees of higher ability, skill, and effort in group incentive plans. The free-rider effect can lead to resentment and turnover of stronger contributors because weaker contributors are getting a "free ride."

Fully insured refers to an employee's status in the retirement income program under the Social Security Act of 1935. Forty quarters of coverage lead to fully insured status.

Gain sharing describes group incentive systems that provide participating employees an incentive payment based on improved company performance, whether for increased productivity, increased customer satisfaction, lower costs, or better safety records.

General Schedule (GS) classifies federal government jobs into 15 classifications (GS-1 through GS-15), based on such factors as skill, education, and experience levels. In addition, jobs that require high levels of specialized education (e.g., a physicist), significantly influence public policy (e.g., law judges), or require executive decision making are classified in three additional categories: Senior Level (SL), Scientific & Professional (SP) positions, and the Senior Executive Service (SES).

Generalized work activities information describes general types of job behaviors occurring on multiple jobs.

Golden parachutes, a kind of executive deferred compensation, provide pay and benefits to executives following their termination resulting from a change in ownership or corporate takeover.

Goods and services allowances compensate expatriates for the difference between goods and services costs in the United States and in the foreign post.

Government Employee Rights Act of 1991 protects U.S. Senate employees from employment discrimination on the basis of race, color, religion, sex, national origin, age, and disability (401 *FEP Manual* 851).

Graduated commissions increase percentage pay rates for progressively higher sales volume in a given period.

Great Depression refers to the period during the 1930s when many businesses failed and many workers became chronically unemployed.

Green circle rates represent pay rates for jobs that fall below the designated pay minimums.

Group incentive programs reward employees for their collective performance, rather than for each employee's individual performance.

Groupthink occurs when all group members agree on mistaken solutions because they share the same mindset and view issues through the lens of conformity.

Hardship allowance compensates expatriates for their sacrifices while on assignment.

Headquarters-based method compensates all employees according to the pay scales used at the headquarters.

Health insurance covers the costs of a variety of services that promote sound physical and mental health, including physical examinations, diagnostic testing (X-rays), surgery, and hospitalization. Companies can choose from two broad classes of health insurance programs including fee-for-service plans and managed care plans.

Health Maintenance Organization Act of 1973 (HMO Act) encouraged the use of HMOs as an alternative approach to delivering health care services.

Health maintenance organizations (HMOs) are sometimes described as providing "prepaid medical services" because fixed periodic enrollment fees cover HMO members for all medically necessary services, as long as the services are delivered or approved by the HMO. HMOs represent an alternative to commercial and self-funded insurance plans.

Health reimbursement accounts (HRAs) are established and funded by employers for employees as a source to cover eligible health care costs.

Health savings accounts (HSAs) are established by employers for employees as a source to cover eligible health care costs. Employees, employers, or both may make contributions to fund these accounts.

High-deductible health insurance plans require substantial deductibles and low out-of-pocket maximums.

Highly compensated employees are defined by the Internal Revenue Service as an officer, a shareholder owning more than 5 percent of the voting power or value of all classes of stock, an employee who is highly compensated based on all facts and circumstances, and a spouse or dependent of one of the preceding.

Highly compensated individuals are defined by the Internal Revenue Service as an officer, a shareholder owning more than 5 percent of the voting power or value of all classes of stock, an employee who is highly compensated based on all facts and circumstances, and a spouse or dependent of one of the above.

Home country–based pay method compensates expatriates the amount they would receive if they were performing similar work in the United States.

Home leave benefits enable expatriates to take paid time off in the United States.

Horizontal knowledge refers to similar knowledge (e.g., record keeping applied to payroll applications and record keeping applied to employee benefits).

Horizontal skills refer to similar skills (e.g., assembly skills applied to lawn mowers and assembly skills applied to snow blowers).

Hospital insurance tax (HI) supports the Medicare Part A program. Also known as *Medicare tax.*

Host country–based methods compensate expatriates based on the host countries' pay scales.

Host country nationals (HCNs) are foreign national citizens who work in U.S. companies' branch offices or manufacturing plants in their home countries.

Hourly pay is one type of base pay. Employees earn hourly pay for each hour worked.

Housing and utilities allowances compensate expatriates for the difference between housing and utilities costs in the United States and in the foreign post.

Human capital refers to employees' knowledge and skills, enabling them to be productive. See also *human capital theory.*

Human capital theory states that employees' knowledge and skills generate productive capital known as human capital. Employees can develop knowledge and skills from formal education or on-the-job experiences.

Human resource strategies specify the particular use of HR practices to be consistent with competitive strategy.

Hybrid plans are retirement plans that combine features of defined benefit and defined contribution plans.

Hypothetical tax is the U.S. income tax based on the same salary level, excluding all foreign allowances.

Illegal discriminatory bias occurs when a supervisor rates members of his or her race, gender, nationality, or religion more favorably than members of other classes.

Improshare is a specific kind of gain sharing program that rewards employees based on a labor hour ratio formula. A standard is determined by analyzing historical accounting data to find the number of labor hours needed to complete a product. Productivity is then measured as a ratio of standard labor hours and actual labor hours.

Incentive effect refers to a worker's willingness to work diligently to produce more quality output than simply attending work without putting in the effort.

Incentive pay or variable pay is defined as compensation, other than base wages or salaries, that fluctuates according to employees' attainment of some standard (e.g., a preestablished formula, individual or group goals, or company earnings).

Incentive stock options entitle executives to purchase their companies' stock in the future at a predetermined price. The predetermined price usually equals the stock price at the time an executive receives the stock options. Incentive stock options entitle executives to favorable tax treatment.

Income annuities distribute income to retirees based on retirement savings paid to insurance companies in exchange for guaranteed monthly checks for life.

Indemnity plans refer to traditional health insurance plans in which the insurance company agrees to pay a designated percentage of the costs for health insurance procedures and the insured (i.e., recipient of the insurance benefit) agrees to pay a designated percentage.

Independent contractors are contingent workers who typically possess specialized skills that are in short supply in the labor market. Companies select independent contractors to complete particular projects of short-term duration—usually a year or less.

Indexes of living costs abroad compare the costs (U.S. dollars) of representative goods and services (excluding education) expatriates purchase at the foreign location and the cost of comparable goods and services purchased in the Washington, DC, area. Companies use these indexes to determine appropriate goods and service allowances.

Individual incentive plans reward employees for meeting work-related performance standards (e.g., quality, productivity, customer satisfaction, safety, and attendance). Any one or a combination of these standards may be used.

Inflation is the increase in prices for consumer goods and services. Inflation erodes the purchasing power of currency.

Insurance policy refers to a contractual relationship between the insurance company and beneficiary. It specifies the amount of money that the insurance company will pay for such particular services as physical examinations.

Integrated paid time off policies enable employees to schedule time off without justifying the reasons.

Interests represent individuals' liking or preference for performing specific jobs.

Interindustry wage or compensation differentials represent the pattern of pay and benefits associated with characteristics of industries. Interindustry wage differentials can be attributed to a number of factors, including the industry's product market, the degree of capital intensity, and the profitability of the industry.

Internal Revenue Code (IRC) is the set of federal government regulations pertaining to taxation in the United States (e.g., sales tax, individual income tax, corporate income tax).

Internally consistent compensation systems clearly define the relative value of each job among all jobs within a company. This ordered set of jobs represents the job structure or hierarchy. Companies rely on a simple, yet fundamental, principle for building internally consistent compensation systems: Jobs that require greater qualifications, more responsibilities, and more complex duties should be paid more highly than jobs that require lesser qualifications, fewer responsibilities, and less complex job duties.

Intrinsic compensation reflects employees' psychological mind-sets that result from performing their jobs.

Involuntary part-time employees work fewer than 35 hours per week because they are unable to find full-time employment.

Job analysis is a systematic process for gathering, documenting, and analyzing information in order to describe jobs.

Job-based pay compensates employees for jobs they currently perform.

Job content refers to the actual activities that employees must perform in the job. Job content descriptions may be broad, general statements of job activities or detailed descriptions of duties and tasks performed in the job.

Job-content evaluation, an approach to evaluating job worth, takes skill, effort, responsibility, and working conditions into account.

Job control unionism refers to a union's success in negotiating formal contracts with employees and establishing quasi-judicial grievance procedures to adjudicate disputes between union members and employers.

Job descriptions summarize a job's purpose and list its tasks, duties, and responsibilities, as well as the skills, knowledge, and abilities necessary to perform the job at a minimum level.

Job duties, a section in job descriptions, describe the major work activities and, if pertinent, supervisory responsibilities.

Job evaluation systematically recognizes differences in the relative worth among a set of jobs and establishes pay differentials accordingly.

Job-point accrual model, a type of pay-for-knowledge program, provides employees opportunities to develop skills and learn to perform jobs from different job families.

Job sharing is a special kind of part-time employment agreement. Two or more part-time employees perform a single full-time job.

Job summary, a statement contained in job descriptions, summarizes the job based on two to four descriptive statements.

Job titles, listed in job descriptions, indicate job designations.

Judicial branch refers to the organization of the federal government that interprets laws.

Just-meaningful pay increase refers to the minimum pay increase that employees will see as making a substantial change in compensation.

Key employees, as defined by the Internal Revenue Service, include any employee who during the current year is an officer of the employer having an annual compensation greater than $160,000 in 2011 (indexed for inflation in increments of $5,000 beginning in 2003), a 5 percent owner of the employer, or a 1 percent owner of the employer having an annual compensation from the employer of more than $160,000.

Knowledge, based on Equal Employment Opportunity Commission guidelines, refers to a body of information applied directly to the performance of a function.

Labor hour ratio formula, used in determining the payouts in Improshare plans, refers to a standard determined by analyzing historical accounting data to find the number of labor hours needed to complete a product. Productivity is then measured as a ratio of standard labor hours and actual labor hours.

Lease companies employ qualified individuals and place them in client companies on a long-term, presumably "permanent" basis. Lease companies place employees within client companies in exchange for fees.

Ledbetter v. Goodyear Tire & Rubber Co. a court case in which a female employee named Ledbetter sued Goodyear Tire & Rubber Co. after she learned that some male employees with the same job had been paid substantially more than her over a period of several years. Ledbetter claimed that the statute of limitation period began when each discriminatory pay decision was made and communicated to her. She argued that multiple pay decisions were made over the years each time Goodyear endorsed each paycheck, making each paycheck a separate act of illegal pay discrimination.

Legally required benefits are protection programs that attempt to promote worker safety and health, maintain family income streams, and assist families in crisis. The key legally required benefits are mandated by the following laws: the Social Security Act of 1935, various state workers' compensation laws, and the Family and Medical Leave Act of 1993.

Legislative branch refers to the organization of the federal government in which Congress passes and enacts laws.

Leniency errors occur when raters (e.g., supervisors) appraise an employee's performance more highly than it really rates, compared with objective criteria.

Licensing information describes licenses, certificates, or registrations that are used to identify levels of skill or performance relevant to occupations.

Life insurance protects employees' families by paying a specified amount to employees' beneficiaries upon employees' deaths. Most policies pay some multiple of the employees' salaries.

Lilly Ledbetter Fair Pay Act enables a female employee to file of charge of illegal pay discrimination within 180 days following receipt of a paycheck in which she feels that she may be discriminated against.

Line employees are directly involved in producing companies' goods or service delivery. Assembler, production worker, and sales employee are examples of line jobs.

Local governments refer to municipal or county-level organizations that provide public services and ensure that the rights of citizens and employees are upheld in accordance with pertinent laws and regulations.

Longevity pay systems reward with permanent additions to base pay those employees who have reached pay grade maximums and who are not likely to move into higher pay grades.

Longshore and Harborworkers' Compensation Act mandates workers' compensation insurance protection for maritime workers.

Long-term disability initially refers to illnesses or accidents that prevent an employee from performing his or her "own occupation" over a designated period. The term *own occupation* applies to employees based on education, training, or experience. After the designated period elapses, the definition becomes more inclusive by adding the phrase "inability to perform any occupation or to engage in any paid employment." The second-stage definition is consistent with the concept of total disability in workers' compensation programs.

Long-term disability insurance provides benefits for extended periods of time anywhere between 6 months and life.

Lorance v. AT&T Technologies, a Supreme Court case, limited employees' rights to challenge the use of seniority systems to only 180 days from the system's implementation date.

Lowest-cost strategy focuses on gaining competitive advantage by being the lowest-cost producer of a good or service within the marketplace, while selling the good or service at a price advantage relative to the industry average.

Lump sum distributions refer to single payments of benefits. In defined contribution plans, lump sum distributions equal the sum of the vested amount of all employee and vested employer contributions and interest on this sum.

Mail order prescription drug programs dispense expensive medications used to treat chronic health conditions.

Major occupational groups refer to the 23 broad classifications of similar jobs in the Standard Occupational Classification system.

Malemployment occurs when job holders possess greater education, skills, or knowledge than is required to perform their jobs.

Managed care plans emphasize cost control by limiting an employee's choice of doctors and hospitals. These plans also provide protection against health care expenses in the form of prepayment to health care providers.

Management by objectives (MBO), a goal-oriented performance-appraisal method, requires that supervisors and employees determine objectives for employees to meet during the rating period, and then employees appraise how well they have achieved their objectives.

Management incentive plans award bonuses to managers who meet or exceed objectives based on sales, profit, production, or other measures for their division, department, or unit.

Market-based evaluation, an approach to job evaluation, uses market data to determine differences in job worth.

Market-competitive pay systems represent companies' compensation policies that fit the imperatives of competitive advantage.

Market lag policy distinguishes companies from the competition by compensating employees less than most competitors. Lagging the market indicates that pay levels fall below the market pay line.

Market lead policy distinguishes companies from the competition by compensating employees more highly than most competitors. Leading the market denotes pay levels above the market pay line.

Market match policy most closely follows the typical market pay rates because companies pay according to the market pay line. Thus, pay rates fall along the market pay line.

Market pay line is representative of typical market pay rates relative to a company's job structure.

Maximum benefit limits refer to the maximum amount of money an insurance company expressed on a per–health care procedure basis for a benefits plan year or for the lifetime of the insured employee.

Mean is a measure of central tendency calculated as the sum of numbers (e.g., annual salaries in the marketing department) divided by the number of salaries.

Median is the middle value in an ordered sequence of numerical data.

Medical reimbursement plans reimburse employees for some or all of the cost of prescription drugs. These plans pay benefits after an employee has met an annual deductible for the plan.

Medicare Advantage refers to a variety of health insurance coverage options for individuals eligible for Medicare protection who choose not to participate in Parts A and B. It is informally referred to as Medicare Part C.

Medicare Part A refers to compulsory hospitalization insurance that covers both inpatient and outpatient hospital care and services.

Medicare Part B is voluntary supplementary medical insurance that covers 80 percent of medical services and supplies (for example, outpatient care, laboratory tests).

Part B also provides ambulance services when other modes of transportation may endanger the patient's life.

Medicare Prescription Drug, Improvement and Modernization Act of 2003 led to changes in the Medicare program by adding prescription drug coverage and recognizing health savings accounts (HSAs).

Medicare Select plans are Medigap policies that offer lower premiums in exchange for limiting the choice of health care providers.

Medicare tax See *hospital insurance tax (HI).*

Medigap insurance supplements Medicare Part A and Part B coverage and is available to Medicare recipients in most states from private insurance companies for an extra fee.

Mental Health Parity Act and Addiction Equity Act of 2008 is a law that requires that any group health plan that includes mental health and substance use disorder benefits along with standard medical and surgical coverage must treat them equally in terms of out-of-pocket costs, benefit limits, and practices such as prior authorization and utilization review.

Merit pay increase budget limits the amount of pay raises that can be awarded to employees for a specified time period. A merit pay increase budget is expressed as a percentage of the sum of employees' current base pay.

Merit pay programs reward employees with permanent increases to base pay according to differences in job performance.

Midpoint pay value is the halfway mark between the range minimum and maximum rates. Midpoints represent the competitive market rate determined by the analysis of compensation survey data.

Mobility premiums reward employees for moving from one assignment to another.

Multiple-tiered commissions increase percentage pay rates for progressively higher sales volume in a given period only if sales exceed a predetermined level.

National Compensation Survey (NCS) is a U.S. Bureau of Labor Statistics program that comprehensively describes pay and benefits information in U.S. companies.

National Labor Relations Act of 1935 (NLRA) establishes employees' rights to bargain collectively with employers on such issues as wages, work hours, and working conditions.

Negative halo effect occurs when a rater (e.g., a supervisor) generalizes an employee's negative behavior on one aspect of the job to all aspects of the job.

Nominal hourly compensation is the face value of a dollar.

Noncontributory financing implies that the company assumes total costs for discretionary benefits.

Nondiscrimination rules prohibit employers from discriminating in favor of highly compensated employees in contributions or benefits, availability of benefits, rights, or plan features. Also, employers may not amend pension plans to favor highly compensated employees.

Nonexempt refers to an employee's status regarding the overtime pay provision of the Fair Labor Standards Act of 1938 (FLSA). Employees whose jobs do not fall into particular categories (e.g., administrative, professional, and executive employees) are generally covered by overtime and minimum wage provisions.

Nonqualified plans are welfare and pension plans that do not meet various requirements set forth by the Employee Retirement Income Security Act of 1974 (ERISA), disallowing favorable tax treatment for employee and employer contributions.

Nonrecoverable draws act as salary because sales employees are not obligated to repay the loans if they do not sell enough.

Nonrecurring merit increases or merit bonuses are lump sum monetary awards based on employees' past job performances. Employees do not continue to receive nonrecurring merit increases every year. Employees must instead earn them each time.

Nonstatutory stock options, a kind of executive deferred compensation, entitle executives to purchase their companies' stock in the future at a predetermined price. The predetermined price usually equals the stock price at the time an executive receives the stock options. Nonstatutory stock options do not entitle executives to favorable tax treatment.

North American Free Trade Agreement (NAFTA) became effective on January 1, 1994. NAFTA has two main goals. First, NAFTA was designed to reduce trade barriers among Mexico, Canada, and the United States. Second, NAFTA also set out to remove barriers to investment among these three countries.

Occupation requirements in O*NET include information about typical activities required across occupations. Identifying generalized work activities and detailed work activities summarizes the broad and more specific types of job behaviors and tasks that may be performed within multiple occupations.

Occupational Information Network (O*NET) is a database designed to describe jobs in the relatively new service sector of the economy and to more accurately describe jobs that evolved as the result of technological advances. O*NET replaces the **Revised Handbook for Analyzing Jobs.**

Occupational Safety and Health Act of 1970 ensures safe and healthful working conditions for working men and women by authorizing enforcement of the standards under the act.

Occupation-specific requirements information describes the characteristics of a particular occupation. These particular requirements are occupational skills, knowledge, tasks, duties, machines, tools, and equipment.

Older Workers Benefit Protection Act (OWBPA), the 1990 amendment to the ADEA, indicates that employers can require older employees to pay more than younger employees for health care insurance coverage. This practice is permissible when older workers collectively do not make proportionately larger contributions than the younger workers.

On-call arrangements are a method for employing temporary workers.

O*NET database See *Occupational Information Network (O*NET).*

O*NET User's Guide provides detailed information about the O*NET job content model, its applications, and how to use it the system.

Organizational context information indicates the characteristics of the organization that influence how people do their work.

Out-of-pocket maximum provisions in medical insurance plans limit the total dollar expenditure a beneficiary must pay during any plan year. These provisions are most common in commercial medical insurance plans.

Outplacement assistance refers to company-sponsored technical and emotional support to employees who are being laid off or terminated.

Paid time off represents discretionary employee benefits (e.g., vacation time) that provide employees time off with pay.

Paid time off banks are policies that compensate employees when they are not performing their primary work duties. Companies offer most paid time off as a matter of custom, particularly paid holidays, vacations, and sick leave.

Paired comparison, a variation of simple ranking job evaluation plans, orders all jobs from lowest to highest based on comparing the worth of each job in all possible job pairs. Paired comparison also refers to a specific kind of comparison method for appraising job performance. Supervisors compare each employee to every other employee, identifying the better performer in each pair.

Partial disabilities inclusion refers to a provision of many company-sponsored long-term disability plans. Specifically, this provision offers supplemental benefits to cover a portion of income loss associated with part-time employment.

Patient Protection and Affordable Care Act of 2010 (PPACA) enacted on March 23, 2010, is a comprehensive law that has been in the implementation phase since its passage. The implementation of all provisions will be complete by 2018.

Pay compression occurs whenever a company's pay spread between newly hired or less qualified employees and more qualified job incumbents is small.

Pay grades group jobs for pay policy application. Human resource professionals typically group jobs into pay grades based on similar compensable factors and value.

Pay ranges represent the span of possible pay rates for each pay grade. Pay ranges include midpoint, minimum, and maximum pay rates. The minimum and maximum values denote the acceptable lower and upper bounds of pay for the jobs within particular pay grades.

Pay structures represent pay rate differences for jobs of unequal worth and the framework for recognizing differences in employee contributions.

Paycheck Fairness Act is a second key initiative in closing the pay gap between men and women. This bill strengthens the Equal Pay Act of 1963 by strengthening the remedies available to put sex-based pay discrimination on par with race-based pay discrimination. That is, employers are now required to justify unequal pay by showing that the pay disparity is not sex based, but, rather, job related. This act also prohibits employers from retaliating against employees who share salary information with their coworkers.

Pay-for-knowledge plans reward managerial, service, or professional workers for successfully learning specific curricula.

Pension plans provide income to individuals and beneficiaries throughout their retirement. Also called *retirement programs.*

Pension programs provide income to individuals throughout their retirement.

Pension Protection Act of 2006 is supposed to help shore up the financial solvency of defined benefit plans in private sector companies and to automatically enroll employees in defined contribution plans (e.g., 401(k) plans).

Percentiles describe dispersion by indicating the percentage of figures that fall below certain points. There are 100 percentiles ranging from the first percentile to the 100th percentile.

Performance-contingent bonuses, awarded to executives, are based on the attainment of such specific performance criteria as market share.

Perks See *perquisites.*

Perquisites are benefits offered exclusively to executives (e.g., country club memberships).

Person-focused pay plans generally reward employees for acquiring job-related competencies, knowledge, or skills rather than for demonstrating successful job performances.

Phantom stock, a type of executive deferred compensation, is an arrangement whereby boards of directors compensate executives with hypothetical company stock rather than actual shares of company stock. Phantom stock plans are similar to restricted stock plans because executives must meet specific conditions before they can convert these phantom shares into real shares of company stock.

Piecework plan, an individual incentive pay program, rewards employees based on their individual hourly production against an objective output standard, determined by the pace at which manufacturing equipment operates. For each hour, workers receive piecework incentives for every item produced over the designated production standard. Workers also receive a guaranteed hourly pay rate regardless of whether they meet the designated production standard.

Plan termination rules are specifications set forth by the Pension Benefit & Guaranty Corporation regarding the discontinuation of an employer's defined benefit pension plan.

Platinum parachutes are lucrative awards that compensate departing executives with severance pay, continuation of company benefits, and even stock options.

Point method represents a job-content evaluation technique that uses quantitative methodology. Quantitative methods assign numerical values to compensable factors that describe jobs, and these values are summed as an indicator of the overall value for the job.

Point-of-service plans (POSs) combine features of fee-for-service systems and health maintenance organizations. Employees pay a nominal copayment for each visit to a designated network of physicians; alternatively, they may receive treatment from providers outside the network, but they pay more for this choice.

Portal-to-Portal Act of 1947 defines the term hours worked that appears in the FLSA.

Positive halo effect occurs when a rater (e.g., a supervisor) generalizes employees' positive behavior on one aspect of the job to all aspects of the job.

Preadmission certification is a certification by a medical professional of a health insurance company that may be necessary before a doctor can authorize hospitalization of a policyholder. Failure to ascertain preadmission certification may lead to denial of hospitalization benefits.

Predetermined allocation bonuses, awarded to executives, are based on a fixed formula. Company profits are often the main determinant of the bonus amounts.

Preeligibility period spans from the initial date of hire to eligibility for coverage in a disability insurance program.

Preexisting condition is a mental or physical disability for which medical advice, diagnosis, care, or treatment was received during a designated period preceding the beginning of disability or health insurance coverage.

Preferred provider organizations (PPOs) are select groups of health care providers that provide health care services to a given population at a higher level of reimbursement than under commercial insurance plans.

Pregnancy Discrimination Act of 1978 (PDA) is an amendment to Title VII of the Civil Rights Act of 1964. The PDA prohibits disparate impact discrimination against pregnant women for all employment practices.

Premium is the amount of money an individual or company pays to maintain insurance coverage.

Prepaid medical services refer to most benefits offered by HMOs because fixed periodic enrollment fees cover HMO members for all medically necessary services only if the services are delivered or approved by the HMO. Also, alternative name for HMOs.

Prescription card programs operate like HMOs by providing prepaid benefits with nominal copayments for prescription drugs.

Prescription drug plans cover the costs of drugs that state or federal laws require be dispensed by licensed pharmacists.

Primary care physicians are designated by HMOs to determine whether patients require the care of a medical specialist. This functions to control costs by reducing the number of medically unnecessary visits to expensive specialists.

Probationary period is the initial term of employment (usually less than 6 months) during which companies attempt to ensure that they have made sound hiring decisions. Employees are often not entitled to participate in discretionary benefits programs during their probationary periods.

Profit sharing plans pay a portion of company profits to employees, separate from base pay, cost-of-living adjustments, or permanent merit pay increases. Two kinds of profit sharing plans are used widely today: current profit sharing and deferred profit sharing.

Profit sharing pool is money earmarked for distribution to employees who participate in profit sharing plans. Companies may choose to fund profit sharing plans based on gross sales revenue or some basis other than profits.

Protection programs are either legally required or discretionary employee benefits that provide family benefits, promote health, and guard against income loss caused by such catastrophic factors as unemployment, disability, or serious illnesses.

Public Company Accounting Oversight Board (PCAOB) See *Sarbanes-Oxley Act of 2002*.

Qualified plans are welfare and pension plans that meet various requirements set forth by the Employee Retirement Income Security Act of 1974; these plans entitle employees and employers to favorable tax treatment by deducting the contributions from taxable income. Qualified plans do not disproportionately favor highly compensated employees.

Quarters allowance is the U.S. Department of State term for housing and utilities allowances.

Quarters of coverage refers to each 3-month period of employment during which an employee contributes to the retirement income program under the Social Security Act of 1935.

Quartiles allow compensation professionals to describe the distribution of data, usually annual base pay amount, based on four groupings.

Range spread is the difference between the maximum and the minimum pay rates of a given pay grade.

Rating errors in performance appraisals reflect differences between human judgment processes versus objective, accurate assessments uncolored by bias, prejudice, or other subjective, extraneous influences.

Real hourly compensation measures the purchasing power of a dollar.

Recertification ensures that employees periodically demonstrate mastery of all the jobs they have learned.

Recoverable draws act as company loans to employees that are carried forward indefinitely until employees sell enough (i.e., earn a sufficient amount in commissions) to repay their draws.

Red circle rates represent pay rates that are higher than the designated pay range maximums.

Referral plans are individual incentive pay plans that reward employees for referring new customers or recruiting successful job applicants.

Regression analysis describes the linear relationship between two variables (i.e., simple regression) or between the linear composite of multiple variables and one other variable (i.e., multiple regression).

Rehabilitation Act mandates that federal government agencies take affirmative action in providing jobs for individuals with disabilities (401 *FEP Manual* 325).

Relevant labor markets represent the fields of potentially qualified candidates for particular jobs.

Reliable job analysis yields consistent results under similar conditions.

Relocation assistance payments cover expatriates' expenses to relocate to foreign posts.

Repatriation is the process of making the transition from an international assignment and living abroad to a domestic assignment and living in the home country.

Restricted stock, a type of executive deferred compensation, requires that executives do not have any ownership control over the disposition of the stock for a predetermined period, often 5 to 10 years.

Retirement programs provide income to individuals and beneficiaries throughout their retirement. Also called *pension plans*.

Right to control test helps companies determine whether their workers are employees or independent contractors.

Rucker plan is a particular type of gain sharing program that emphasizes employee involvement. Gain sharing awards are based on the ratio between value added (less the costs of materials, supplies, and services rendered) and the total cost of employment.

Sabbatical leaves are paid time off for professional development activities such as professional certification, conducting research, and curriculum development.

Safe harbors refer to compliance guidelines in a law or regulation.

Salary is one type of base pay. Employees earn salaries for performing their jobs, regardless of the actual number of hours worked. Companies generally measure salary on an annual basis.

Salary-only plans are specific types of sales compensation plans. Sales professionals receive fixed-base compensation, which does not vary with the level of units sold, increase in market share, or any other indicator of sales performance.

Salary-plus-bonus plans are specific types of sales compensation plans. Sales professionals receive fixed base compensation, coupled with a bonus. Bonuses are usually single payments that reward employees for achievement of specific, exceptional goals.

Salary-plus-commission plans are particular types of sales compensation plans. Sales professionals receive fixed base compensation and commission.

Sales value of production (SVOP) is the sum of sales revenue plus the value of goods in inventory. This is part of the equation to determine payout amounts in Scanlon gain sharing plans.

Sarbanes-Oxley Act of 2002 mandated a number of reforms to enhance corporate responsibility, enhance financial disclosures, and combat corporate and accounting fraud in response to corporate accounting scandals in Enron, Tyco, and other large U.S. corporations. The act established **Public Company Accounting Oversight Board (PCAOB)** to oversee the activities of the auditing profession.

Say on pay gives company shareholders the right to vote yes or no on executive compensation proposals, including current and deferred components, including golden parachute agreements, at least once every 3 years. Although the say on pay provision guarantees shareholders the right to vote on executive compensation proposals, the vote is nonbinding.

Scanlon plan is a specific type of gain sharing program that emphasizes employee involvement. Gain sharing awards are based on the ratio between labor costs and sales value of production.

Scientific management practices promote labor cost control by replacing inefficient production methods with efficient production methods.

Second surgical opinion is a feature of many health insurance plans, reducing unnecessary surgical procedures and costs by encouraging an individual to seek an independent opinion from another doctor.

Section 401(k) plans are qualified retirement plans named after the section of the IRC that created them. These plans permit employees to defer part of their compensation to the trust of a qualified defined contribution plan. Only private sector or tax-exempt employers are eligible to sponsor 401(k) plans.

Securities and Exchange Commission (SEC) is a nonpartisan, quasi-judicial federal government agency with responsibility for administering federal securities laws.

Securities Exchange Act of 1934 applies to the disclosure of executive compensation.

Self-Employment Contributions Act (SECA) requires self-employed individuals to contribute to the OASDI and Medicare programs but at a higher tax rate than required for non-self-employed individuals.

Self-funded plans are similar to commercial insurance plans with one key difference: Companies typically draw from their own assets to fund claims when self-funded.

Self-funding refers to health insurance plans that pay benefits directly from an employer's assets.

Seniority pay systems reward employees with permanent additions to base pay periodically, according to employees' length of service performing their jobs.

Services represent discretionary employee benefits that provide enhancements to employees and their families (e.g., tuition reimbursement and day care assistance).

Severance pay usually includes several months of pay following involuntary termination and, in some cases, continued coverage under the employer's medical insurance plan. Employees often rely on severance pay to meet financial obligations while searching for employment.

Short-term disability refers to an inability to perform the duties of one's regular job usually for fewer than 6 months.

Short-term disability insurance provides income benefits for limited periods of time, usually less than 6 months.

Similar-to-me effect refers to the tendency on the part of raters (e.g., supervisors) to judge employees favorably who they perceive as similar to themselves.

Simple ranking plan, a specific method of job evaluation, orders all jobs from lowest to highest according to a single criterion (e.g., job complexity or the centrality of the job to the company's competitive strategy).

Single coverage extends health insurance benefits only to the covered employee.

Six-year graduated schedule allows workers to become 20 percent vested after 2 years and to vest at a rate of 20 percent each year thereafter until they are 100 percent vested after 6 years of service.

Skill, based on Equal Employment Opportunity Commission guidelines, refers to an observable competence to perform a learned psychomotor act.

Skill-based pay, used mostly for employees who do physical work, increases these workers' pay as they master new skills.

Skill blocks model, a kind of pay-for-knowledge program, applies to jobs from within the same job family. Just as in the stair-step model, employees progress to increasingly complex jobs; however, skills do not necessarily build on each other in a skill blocks program.

Skill (knowledge) blocks are sets of skills (knowledge) necessary to perform a specific job (e.g., typing skills versus analytical reasoning) or group of similar jobs (e.g., junior accounting clerk, intermediate accounting clerk, and senior accounting clerk).

Smoking cessation plans are particular types of wellness programs that stress the negative aspects of smoking and can include intensive programs directed at helping individuals to stop smoking.

Social comparison theory provides an explanation for executive compensation determination based on the tendency for the board of directors to offer executive compensation packages that are similar to those in peer companies.

Social Security Act of 1935 (Title IX) established three main types of legally required benefits: unemployment insurance, retirement income and benefits for dependents, and medical insurance (Medicare).

Sorting effect addresses an employee's choice to stay versus leave his or her employer for another job, presumably one without an incentive pay contingency.

Spillover effect refers to nonunion companies' offer of similar compensation as offered by union companies to their employees. The goal is to reduce the likelihood that nonunion workforces will seek union representation.

Staff employees support the functions performed by line employees. Human resources and accounting are examples of staff functions.

Stair-step model, a type of pay-for-knowledge program, resembles a flight of stairs. The steps represent jobs from a particular job family that differ in terms of complexity. Skills at higher levels build upon previous lower-level skills.

Standard deviation refers to the mean distance of each salary figure from the mean (i.e., how larger observations fluctuate above the mean and how small observations fluctuate below the mean).

State governments enact and enforce laws that pertain exclusively to their respective regions (e.g., Illinois and Michigan).

Stock appreciation rights, a type of executive deferred compensation, provide executives income at the end of a designated period, much like restricted stock options; however, executives never have to exercise their stock rights to receive income. The company simply awards payment to executives based on the difference in stock price between the time the company granted the stock rights at fair market value to the end of the designated period, permitting the executives to keep the stock.

Stock compensation plans are companywide incentive plans that grant employees the right to purchase shares of company stock.

Stock options describe an employee's right to purchase company stock.

Straight commission is based on a fixed percentage of the sales price of the produce or service.

Strategic analysis entails an examination of a company's external market context and internal factors. Examples of external market factors include industry profile, information about competitors, and long-term growth prospects. Internal factors encompass financial condition and functional capabilities (e.g., marketing and human resources).

Strategic decisions support business objectives.

Strategic management entails a series of judgments, under uncertainty, that companies direct toward achieving specific goals.

Stress management is a specific kind of wellness program designed to help employees cope with many factors inside and outside their work that contribute to stress.

Strictness errors occur when raters (e.g., supervisors) judge employee performance to be less than what it is when compared against objective criteria.

Supplemental life insurance protection represents additional life insurance offered exclusively to executives. Companies design executives' supplemental life insurance protection to increase the value of executives' estates, bequeathed to designated beneficiaries (usually family members) upon their death, and to provide greater benefits than standard plans usually allow.

Supplemental retirement plans, offered to executives, are designed to restore benefits restricted under qualified plans.

Tactical decisions support competitive strategy.

Target plan bonuses, awarded to executives, are based on executives' performance. Executives do not receive bonuses unless their performance exceeds minimally acceptable standards.

Tax equalization is one of two approaches (the other is tax protection) to provide expatriates tax allowances. Employers take the responsibility for paying income taxes to the U.S. and foreign governments on behalf of the expatriates.

Tax protection is one of two approaches (the other is tax equalization) to provide expatriates tax allowances. Employers reimburse expatriates for the difference between the actual income tax amount and the hypothetical tax when the actual income tax amount—based on tax returns filed with the Internal Revenue Service—is greater.

Taxable wage base limits the amount of annual wages or payroll cost per employee subject to taxation to fund OASDI programs.

Team-based or *small-group incentive plans* a small group of employees shares a financial reward when a specific objective is met.

Telecommuting represents alternative work arrangements in which employees perform work at home or some other location besides the office.

Temporary employment agencies place individuals in client companies as employees on a temporary basis.

Term life insurance is the most common type of life insurance offered by companies; provides protection to an employee's beneficiaries only during a limited period based on a specified number of years or maximum age. After that, insurance automatically expires.

Third country nationals (TCNs) are foreign national citizens who work in U.S. companies' branch offices or manufacturing plants in foreign countries—excluding the United States and their home countries.

Time-and-motion studies analyzed the time it took employees to complete their jobs. Factory owners used time-and-motion studies and job analysis to meet this objective.

Title I of the Americans with Disabilities Act of 1990 (ADA) requires that employers provide "reasonable accommodation" to disabled employees. Reasonable accommodation may include such efforts as making existing facilities readily accessible, job restructuring, and modifying work schedules.

Title VII of the Civil Rights Act of 1964 indicates that it shall be an unlawful employment practice for an employer to discriminate against any individual with respect to compensation, terms, conditions, or privileges of employment because of such individual's race, color, religion, sex, or national origin.

Torts are laws offering remedies to individuals harmed by the unreasonable actions of others. Tort claims usually involve state law and are based on the legal premise that individuals are liable for the consequences of their conduct if it results in injury to others. Tort laws involve civil suits, which are actions brought to protect an individual's private rights.

Tournament theory provides an explanation for executive compensation determination based on substantially greater competition for high-ranking jobs. Lucrative chief executive compensation packages represent the prize to those who win the competition by becoming chief executives.

Trait system, a type of performance-appraisal method, requires raters (e.g., supervisors or customers) to evaluate each employee's traits or characteristics (e.g., quality of work, quantity of work, appearance, dependability, cooperation, initiative, judgment, leadership responsibility, decision-making ability, and creativity).

Transportation services represent energy-efficient ways to transport employees to and from the workplace. Employers cover part or all of the transportation costs.

Troubled Assets Relief Program (TARP) See *Emergency Economic Stabilization Act of 2008 (EESA)*

Tuition reimbursement programs promote employees' education. Under a tuition reimbursement program, an employer fully or partially reimburses an employee for expenses incurred for education or training.

Two-tier pay structures reward newly hired employees less than established employees on either a temporary or permanent basis.

Underemployment refers to employees who wish to work full-time but are forced to work part-time for economic reasons, such as poor business conditions or inability to find a job, both of which are common problems during economic recessions.

Universal compensable factors, based on the Equal Pay Act of 1963, include skill, effort, responsibility, and working conditions.

Universal life insurance provides protection to employees' beneficiaries based on the insurance feature of term life insurance and a more flexible savings or cash accumulation plan than is found in whole life insurance plans.

Value-added formula is the difference between the value of the sales price of a product and the value of materials purchased to make the product. This is part of the equation to determine payout amounts in Rucker gain sharing plans.

Variable pay See *incentive pay*.

Variation represents the amount of spread or dispersion in a set of data.

Vertical knowledge refers to knowledge traditionally associated with supervisory activities (e.g., performance appraisal and grievance review procedures).

Vertical skills are those skills traditionally considered supervisory skills (e.g., scheduling, coordinating, training, and leading others).

Vesting refers to employees' acquisition of nonforfeitable rights to pension benefits.

Vietnam Era Veterans Readjustment Assistance Act applies the principles of the Rehabilitation Act to veterans with disabilities and veterans of the Vietnam War (401 *FEP Manual* 379).

Violations of an affirmative duty are violations taking place when an employer fails to reveal the exposure of one or more workers to harmful substances or when the employer does not disclose a medical condition typically caused by exposure.

Voluntary part-time employees choose to work fewer than 35 hours per regularly scheduled workweek.

Volunteerism refers to giving of one's time to support a meaningful cause. More and more companies are providing employees with paid time off to contribute to causes of their choice.

Wage See *hourly pay*.

Wall Street Reform and Consumer Protection Act of 2010 enhances the transparency of executive compensation practices. Also commonly referred to as the **Dodd-Frank Act**.

Walling v. A. H. Belo Corp requires employers to guarantee fixed weekly pay for employees whose work hours vary from week to week when certain conditions are met.

Walsh–Healey Public Contracts Act of 1936 mandates that contractors with federal contracts meet guidelines regarding wages and hours, child labor, convict labor, and hazardous working conditions. Contractors must observe the minimum wage and overtime provisions of the FLSA. In addition, this act prohibits the employment of individuals younger than 16 and convicted criminals. Furthermore, it prohibits contractors from exposing workers to any conditions that violate the Occupational Safety and Health Act.

Weight control and nutrition programs, a particular type of wellness program, are designed to educate employees about proper nutrition and weight loss, both of which are critical to good health.

Welfare practices were generous endeavors undertaken by some employers, motivated to minimize employees' desire to seek union representation, to promote good management, and to enhance worker productivity.

Wellness programs promote employees' physical and psychological health.

Whole life insurance is a type of life insurance that provides protection to employees' beneficiaries during employees' employment and into the retirement years.

Work context information describes physical and social factors that influence the nature of work.

Work styles are personal characteristics that describe important interpersonal and work style requirements in jobs and occupations.

Worker characteristics refer to ability, interests, and work styles.

Worker requirements represent the minimum qualifications and skills that people must have to perform a particular job. Such requirements usually include education, experience, licenses, permits, and specific abilities such as typing, drafting, or editing.

Worker specifications, a section in job descriptions, lists the education, skills, abilities, knowledge, and other qualifications individuals must possess to perform the job adequately.

Workers' compensation refers to state-run insurance programs that are designed to cover medical, rehabilitation, and disability income expenses resulting from employees' work-related accidents.

Workforce characteristics refer to variables that define and describe the general characteristics of occupations that may influence occupational requirements.

Working condition fringe benefits refer to the work equipment (e.g., computer) and services (e.g., an additional telephone line) employers purchase for telecommuters' use at home.

Working conditions are the social context or physical environment where work will be performed.

Author Index

Note: The letters "f" and "t" following the locators refers to figure and table cited in the text.

Subject Index

Note: The letters "f" and "t" following the locators refers to figure and table cited in the text.